TO
THE MEMORY
OF
W. G. POGSON-SMITH

TABLE OF CONTENTS

PREFACE

IN this book I have endeavoured to tell the story of the ancient history of the Near East within the limits of a single volume. Those who know the great works of Maspero and of Meyer will realize that in order to effect this great compression has been necessary, and will guess that many matters of great interest have had to be treated more cursorily than I would have wished. But, while writing as succinctly as possible, I have of set purpose refused to sacrifice too much on the altar of brevity, and have aspired to make the book readable as well as moderate in size.

Of all regions of the earth probably the Near East has had and will have the greatest interest for us Europeans, for from it sprang our civilization and our religion.

There took place the mingling of the Indo-European from the North with the Mediterranean of the South, which produced the culture, art, and law of the Greeks and Romans; and there, on the Semitic verge of Asia, the home of religious enthusiasms from the beginning, arose the Christian Faith. And if the Near East has from the first seen the mingling of the ideas of the East and West, it has also seen their secular struggle for mastery, the first phase of which ended at Salamis, when the Aryan invader made good his footing in the Mediterranean world, and threw back the Asiatics from Greece, now become the most eastern of western lands instead of the most westerly of the eastern. The second phase ended with Arbela and the complete triumph of the West. At the end of the third, Kossovopolje and Constantinople registered the return of the pendulum, which swung its weight from east to west as far as Vienna. Then it swung back, and the end of the fourth phase seems to be approaching as I write, when Bulgars and Greeks are hammering at the gates of Constantinople.

It is with the history of the first phase of the great drama that this book deals, from the beginning of things to the grand climacteric of Salamis. The story begins with prehistoric Greece. Of the Bronze Age civilization of Greece which has been revealed to us by the discoveries of Schliemann, Halbherr, and Evans we cannot yet write the history: we can only guess at the probable course of events from the relics of antiquity which archaeology has revealed to us. It is otherwise with Egypt, with Babylonia, and Assyria. Of them we have intelligible records upon which we can base history. Therefore it seems best to treat the "pre-history" of Greece separately, and before we pass to real history with Egypt and Babylonia. We pass then from Greece to the Nilotic and Mesopotamian communities, treating them separately till in the second millennium B.C. they came into connexion with each other and with the Anatolian culture of Asia Minor. It then becomes impossible to treat them separately any longer. At different periods one or the other more or less dominated the rest and took the most prominent part in the history of the time. I have therefore told the story of each period more or less from the standpoint of the chief actor in it. During the First Egyptian Empire, from about 1550 to 1350 B.C., one regards the world from the standpoint of imperial Thebes; during the ensuing period, till about 1100, one looks down upon it from the bleak heights of Asia Minor; till about 850 the rise of the Israelitish kingdom centres our attention upon Palestine; from 850 to 650 we watch from Nineveh the marching forth of the hosts of Ashur and the smoke of their holocausts spreading over all the lands. Then, with dramatic swiftness of overthrow, comes the Destruction of Nineveh. The destroyers, the Scyths of the Northern Steppes and the Medes and Persians of Iran, found their kingdoms on the ruins of the Semitic empires, while Egypt and even Babylonia spring once more into life. And the great event was contemporaneous with the expansion of the young Greece of the Iron Age, young with the new Indo-European blood from the north which had begun to invade the Aegean lands towards the end of the Egyptian imperial period. Persia took the place of Assyria in the world, and all the lands of the Near East but Greece coalesced in her Empire. Greece alone, possessed of a stronger spirit and with a brain many times more intelligent than those of the Easterns, resisted successfully. The barbarian recoiled: Greece had saved the West, and with it the future civilization of the world.

I have intended the book mainly for the use of students in the school of Litter ae Humaniores at Oxford, whose work necessitates a competent general knowledge of the early history of the west-oriental world, without which the history of Greece cannot be understood fully. Greece was never, as the older historians seemed to think, a land by itself, fully Western in spirit, supremely civilized in a world of foolish Scythians and gibbering black men. Originally she seems to have been as much or as little oriental as originally was Egypt, with whose culture hers may have had, at the beginning, direct affinity. Later she was westernized, but in the fifth century she was not more distinct from the more oriental nations of the Near East than she is now. She called them "barbarian": that only meant that they did not talk Greek. Greece respected Persia while she fought her, Aeschylos knew better than to make Darius a savage. In fact, the Greeks hardly realized as yet how much more intelligent they were than the other nations. Herodotus has no feeling of great superiority to his Median and Egyptian friends. And when he set himself to write the history of the great struggle which the preceding generation had seen, it was in no spirit of contempt and aloofness that he gathered his information as to the early history of the peoples of the Near East who had marched against Greece under the Persian banner. He did not separate Greece absolutely from the rest of mankind, though no doubt he felt that she was better than the rest.

I hope, therefore, that this book may serve as a very general "companion" to Herodotus for university students. But at the same time I have endeavoured to make it no less useful to the general reader whose interest is keen on the history of these ancient civilizations, the relics of which have been and are being discovered day by day by the archaeologists. In the case of Egypt and prehistoric Greece, new material of the utmost importance may turn up at any moment. I have tried to make the book as up-to-date as possible, and in order to do so, during the work of writing it, which has occupied several years, several chapters have been re-cast, even wholly re-written, as the work of discovery necessitated. Owing to the indulgence of the publishers I have had unlimited time in which to complete the work, and I hope that the present moment, when there seems to be a lull in the work of discovery, may be a favourable one for its publication, and that I shall not have to wish that I had delayed a little longer in order to register this or that new fact of importance. I have recounted the facts of the history so far as they are known without, I hope, undue generalization or theorizing, except, of course, in the case of prehistoric Greece, where the whole is theory, based however upon the evidence of material things. For an acute generalization of the history of the early peoples of the world I may refer the reader to Prof. J. L. Myres's little book, The Dawn of History, published last year, and for a suggestive study on certain natural causes which have influenced the history of the East to Mr. Ellsworth Huntington's most interesting Pulse of Asia.

In dealing with the early history of "classical" Greece I have simply endeavoured to present an impression or sketch of the development of Greek culture and its relations with the Eastern nations. I have not considered it necessary or desirable to treat the history in any detail. So much more is known of it than of the early history of the other lands concerned that to do so would be to make the latter part of the book (and the Greek section especially) totally disproportionate in size. This part too is written rather from the Persian-Egyptian than from the Greek standpoint. And Greece when she became Hellenic ceased to belong wholly to the Near East. It is only her "foreign relations," her connexions with the East, that interest us now. Her internal affairs we leave to the historians of Greece. They call for our attention only in so far as they bear directly upon the general progress of Hellenic culture, especially towards the east and south, or affect directly the approach of the conflict with Persia.

I have myself specially translated for this book all the Egyptian inscriptions from which I quote at length, with the exception of that containing the hymn of King Akhenaten to the sun-disk (p. 306), which is quoted, with his very kind permission, from Prof. Breasted's translation in his History of Egypt.

I have tried not to weary the reader by too rigid an insistence on the use of diacritical marks on my transliterations of Egyptian and Semitic names, giving the fully-marked forms usually only on the first appearance of a name in the book, and dispensing with them afterwards unless it would seem better to retain them in order to mark the pronunciation.

I have to thank various friends who have assisted me in the reading of portions of my proofs. To them I owe many corrections and suggestions. Chapters I., V., IX. and X., in which Babylonian and Assyrian matters are chiefly dealt with, have been read by my colleague Mr. L. W. King, author of The History of Sumer and Akkad. Chapters IX. and X. have also been read by the Rev. C. F. Burney, D.D., of St. John's College, Oxford, to whom I am specially indebted for my preservation from the many pitfalls that beset the path of a general historian in dealing with early Jewish history. My friend Prof. M. A. Canney, of Manchester University, has also read Chapter IX., and has made several very useful suggestions. Chapter II. has been read by Mr. E. J. Forsdyke, of the Greek and Roman Department of the British Museum; and Mr. G. F, Hill, the Keeper of Coins and Medals, and Mr. F. J. Marshall, of Emmanuel College, Cambridge, have most kindly read Chapters XI. and XII., with results valuable both to myself and to the reader. Only in those chapters of the book which are written more or less from the Egyptian point of view, namely. Chapters III., IV., VI., VII. and VIII., have I not submitted my work to the judgment and criticism of another. But in those chapters which any friends have read I alone am responsible for the opinions ultimately expressed. Dr. Burney, for instance, must not be taken to agree with everything I have said in Chapter IX.; as, for example, with my revival, for which I only am responsible, of Josephus's idea that the Biblical account of the Exodus is possibly a reminiscence of the Expulsion of the Hyksos. I have recorded divergences of view when necessary; and have also, when I am indebted to one of my friends for a new view, indicated the fact in a footnote.

H. R. HALL
November 1912

CHAPTER I: PROLEGOMENA

1. Herodotus and Modern Knowledge

SOME thirty years after the defeat of Xerxes, Herodotus of Halicarnassus, who had travelled much in the lands of the barbarians as well as in Greece, set himself to write down for the men of his own time and for posterity the events of the great struggle and also to describe, as completely as he could, the long series of events, cause upon cause, effect after effect, which had led up to the final catastrophe. And he began from the beginning of ancient story, from the Trojan War and before that from the rape of Io. For he rightly saw that the Great Event had indeed had its ultimate origin in the furthest recesses of time, when the ancient civilizations of the Eastern Mediterranean first evolved themselves out of chaos, and the peoples of the Nile-land, of Western Asia, and of the Aegean first came into contact with each other. So he told first all he knew of the peoples of Egypt, Babylonia, Persia, and also Scythia, and of their history, and intended, we know, to tell the story of Assyria also. Everywhere he tried to trace back the first contact of his own people with these barbarians, and to identify this or that element of culture which his Greeks, whom he knew to be far younger as a nation than the Orientals, owed to the East which they had defeated. And then he gathered all the threads of his various tales together, as Xerxes gathered the peoples themselves together, for the final story of the collision of East and West, and his history marches straight without digression now, to Salamis, Plataeae, and Mykale.

In dealing with the early history of Greece he groped darkly, because, though he had all the varied store of Hellenic legend to his hand, he had no knowledge of what we know now in some degree, the real story of the first development of Greek civilization. We know that Egyptian priests could tell him the history of Cheops and of Rhampsinitos, but that no Greek could tell him that of the strong men who lived before Agamemnon. Nor do we know the true facts of their history as we do that of Cheops or Rhampsinitos, but we may do so one day, when we read the Minoan writing as we can that of ancient Egypt. Till then, we also must grope, but not so darkly as Herodotus, for modern archaeological discovery has told us the development of the heroic culture of Greece, which we can now trace back to its origins, contemporary with those of Egypt itself. So much further beyond the Trojan War and the Phoenician rape of Io can the modern Xoyioi trace the causes of the quarrel of East and West. But until eighty years ago we were as ignorant as Herodotus, and he, with the Biblical history of the Jews beside him, was our sole good authority for the ancient history of the Near East: the Sacred Record and the "profane" told us all that mattered of what we knew.

2. The Increased Modern Knowledge of Ancient History

But now our knowledge of the early history of mankind is increasing apace. Nowhere is this vast accession of knowledge more noticeable than in the domain of the historian of the ancient peoples of the Nearer East, the portion of the world of which Greece marks the western and Persia the eastern boundary, of which the southern border marches with the lands of the Blacks and the northern is formed by the steppes and deserts of the Scythians and Cimmerians. Now, within the short space of eighty years, the whole history, as distinct from untrustworthy legends of Greek or Jewish origin, of the mighty monarchies of Egypt and of Mesopotamia, of Media and of Persia, has been recovered from oblivion for us, and, what is still more interesting, we are now just beginning to realize that Greece itself was, long before the classical culture of the Hellenes was ever heard or thought of, the seat of a civilization at least the equal of that of Egypt or Chaldaea and possibly as ancient. Nor is it in Mesopotamia, in the Nile Valley, and in Greece alone that man's knowledge of the earliest history of his race has been so vastly increased during the last eighty years: yet another system of culture, exhibiting in different points resemblances to the three foregoing, while in others perfectly distinct from them, has been shown to have existed at least as early as 1500 B.C. in Central Asia Minor; this extended its sway on the west to Sipylus, on the east to the borders of the Canaanites and to Carchemish on the Euphrates.

Furthermore, on the northern and eastern confines of the Babylonian culture-system, new nations pass within our ken; Vannic men of Armenia, ruled by powerful kings; Kassites of the Zagros, whose language seems to contain elements which if really Aryan are probably the oldest-known monuments of Indo-European speech (c. 1600 B.C.); strange-tongued Elamites, also, akin neither to Iranian nor Semite. Nor does it seem to us remarkable that we should read the trilingual proclamations of Darius

Hystaspis to his peoples in their original tongues, although an eighteenth-century philosopher would have regarded the prospect of our ever being able to do so as the wildest of chimeras!

And when we read the story of Egypt, of Babylon, and Persia as it really happened, and not through the mouths of Greek or Jewish interpreters, we wonder not so much at the misinterpretations and mistakes of our former guides, but at the fact that they were able to get so close to the truth as they actually did.

In the cases of Egypt and Greece the new knowledge has taken us back to the beginning of things, to the days before history, but this is not the case with Babylonia. Even as far back as we can go, to about the middle of the fourth millennium B.C., we are still within the age of knowable history, and the inscriptions still contain the names of kings and temples which we can decipher. So far are we from reaching any "prehistoric" period that instead of attaining the beginning of Chaldaean civilization we have apparently dug only as far as the latter end of its early period; we have reached and passed the beginnings of Semitic rule in Mesopotamia only to find ourselves witnessing in this, the most ancient stratum of the known history of the world, the latter end of the pre-Semitic culture to which the civilization of Babylonia owed its inspiration. These evidences of human barbarism which elsewhere in the world precede the traces of civilization are in Babylonia absent; hardly a single weapon of flint or chert testifies to the existence there of a Stone Age; when we first meet with them the Babylonians were already metal-users and already wrote inscriptions which we can read.

In dealing with Mesopotamia, therefore, we never get beyond the domain of true history; we are from the beginning arranging and sifting written contemporary records in order to collect from them the history of the country. In the case of Egypt, however, we go right back to the period before writing began, and have to reconstitute the story of the earliest ages from the evidence which archaeological discovery has recovered as to the earliest development of civilization. And in Greece and Anatolia we depend largely upon the evidence of archaeology alone, for there, though we possess the inscriptions of Greeks and Anatolians who lived in a high state of civilization contemporaneously with Egyptians and Babylonians whose records we read almost as well as our own, they remain a sealed book to us. We cannot yet read a word of them, and so have to guess at the probable course of the history of their authors, with the help of archaeological discovery and the few hints which the Egyptian and Mesopotamian records afford us.

Yet archaeological discovery alone suffices to give us the main outlines of the history of early Greek civilization, though we know nothing of the actual events which moulded its development, and have never heard the names of the authors of these events. Archaeology alone has revealed to us in Greece the monuments of a civilization, "prehistoric" because we cannot yet read its history, which was as highly developed and as important in the annals of the world as those of Egypt and Mesopotamia. And from the study of these monuments and remains we have been enabled to arrive at a knowledge of the cultural relations of early Greece which are nothing less than revolutionary. We see that, instead of belonging originally to the central and North-European "Aryan" race, the group of peoples speaking Indo-European languages to which we ourselves belong, and being in its origins radically distinct from the civilization of Egypt and of Asia, the oldest culture of Greece really belongs to the Mediterranean basin, where it originated, and so is from the beginning part of the culture of the other Mediterranean peoples, to which the civilization of Egypt also attaches itself to some extent. We know now that the Mediterranean peoples have always been and are to this day more or less allied to each other racially. In reality the brunet Italian and Greek of to-day are racially far more closely related to the Palestinian and the Egyptian than to the Celt, the Slav, or the Teuton, although now they speak, and for three thousand years past they have spoken, languages akin to those of their northern neighbours. These languages were imposed upon them by Aryan conquerors, and the period at which this conquest took place is approximately fixed, in Greece at least, by the dark age which intervened between the "prehistoric" and the classical civilizations of Hellas. The Greek civilization which we have always known is the product of the mingling of the invading northern culture of the Aryan-speakers, with the remains of the ancient "Mediterranean" civilization not distantly related to that of Egypt, which had grown up from its earliest beginnings in the Aegean basin, as that of Egypt had grown up in the Nile Valley. That the Aegean "Mediterraneans" were from the first Aryan-speakers is not in the slightest degree probable. We can trace their culture from its Neolithic beginnings, and can even discern a possibility that these beginnings may have been derived from Neolithic Egypt: nobody has yet supposed that the Mediterranean, far less the Nile Valley, was the original home of the Aryans. Yet that seems the necessary corollary of a supposition that the prehistoric Greeks were Indo-Europeans. And we know that almost to the last there survived on the north Mediterranean shores isolated patches of non-Aryan speech (the Basque still survives) which are naturally to be regarded as the survivors of a general pre-Aryan language-stratum.

Archaeology alone has thus assigned the early culture of Greece rather to the Near East, or at any rate to the Mediterranean, than to Europe, to the non-Aryan races than to the Aryan.

The entry of Greece into the ranks of the ancient civilizations of the Near East as the fellow of Egypt and Babylon is one of the most striking results of modern archaeological discovery.

It cannot be denied that the increase of knowledge thus roughly sketched is very considerable, nor can it be doubted that the names of the first discoverers of the New World of ancient history, Champollion and his peers, are full worthy to rank with those of Columbus, of Galileo, of Newton, or of any other discoverer of new worlds of human science.

3. Archaeology and History

There is no need now to recapitulate the steps by which these discoverers arrived at their knowledge, which is now accepted science. The languages of ancient Egypt, of Assyria, of Elam, even of pre-Semitic Babylonia, are now sufficiently known to enable us to translate their ancient inscriptions with an accuracy sufficient for all practical purposes, and from these, the ancient records, combined with the critical analysis of such traditions as have been handed down to us by classical authors, we derive our knowledge of the actual events of the ancient history of Egypt, Mesopotamia, and Persia. Although the hieroglyphic inscriptions of Anatolia are not yet translated with certainty, the use by the ancient Anatolians of the cuneiform (Babylonian) script side by side with their own hieroglyphs has enabled us lately to obtain glimpses of their history. Only in the case of prehistoric Greece are we denied first-hand knowledge of events, and are forced to content ourselves with a knowledge of the development of culture, derived solely from archaeological discoveries and comparisons. Greek legends no doubt would tell us much, had we any firm standpoint of known history from which to criticize them. As it is, they can but give us doubtful and uncertain hints of the events which they shadow forth. In the case of Egypt, Mesopotamia, and Persia, more especially in the case of Egypt, the archaeologist is the chief auxiliary of the historian, for he makes it possible, by means of his excavation of the actual remains of ancient civilization, to supplement the record of events with the story of the development of culture. In the case of early Greece we have this story, though it is as yet far from complete, without any framework, any skeleton of known events which it would clothe; with the exception of a few facts supplied us by the Egyptian records. In Greece and in Anatolia the archaeologists go on discovering, besides the actual remains of the culture and art of the "Minoans" and "Hittites," tablet after tablet, inscription after inscription, which we cannot read. But in Egypt and in Mesopotamia they are every day bringing to light new documents which we can read, and from which we are every day learning new facts of history. If most of the larger monuments of Egypt have always been above ground, and needed but the skill of the copyist and the knowledge of the decipherer to make them yield up their secrets, this was by no means the case with Assyria, where the famous excavations of Layard resulted in the discovery of Assyrian history. And during the last thirty years excavation throughout the Nearer East has resulted in the discovery not only of new inscriptions to be read, but also (and this more especially in Egypt and Greece) of the actual remains of ancient art and civilized life which enable the archaeologist, properly so-called, to reconstruct the story of the development of human culture without the aid either from classical historian or ancient inscription. The work of the Egypt Exploration Fund, with which the names of Naville and Petrie will always be associated, and that of Maciver, Reisner, Garstang, and Legrain in Egypt, that of the French expeditions of M. de Sarzec at Telloh in Babylonia, and of M. de Morgan in Persia, of the Palestine Exploration Fund, of the Austrian Dr. Sellin and the German Dr. Schumacher, and now of the American Reisner in Palestine, that of Dr. Winckler at Boghaz Kyoi in Anatolia, and, last but not least, that of Schliemann in Greece, and of the Italians Halbherr and Pernier, and the Britons Evans and Mackenzie (besides others, Italian, British, and American) in Crete, — all this work of actual excavation during the last three decades has resulted in the production of historical material of the first importance. And the historians await each new season's work of the excavators with impatience, knowing that something new is sure to be found which will add to their knowledge and modify their previous ideas. Our knowledge of the early history of the Near East is still in the making, and the progress effected after the lapse of some years may well be noted by a comparison of the original and the modern editions of the two great rival histories of Professors Maspero and Eduard Meyer, besides the successive landmarks provided by the Egyptian histories of Brugsch (1879), Wiedemann (1884), Petrie (1894-1905), Budge (1901), and Breasted (1906), and the histories of Assyria and Babylonia by Rogers (1901) Goodspeed (1903), and King (1910).

4. Classical Sources

The work of the modern historians is based almost entirely upon our modern knowledge of the ancient records. The accounts of the Greek writers, while of the highest interest as giving the impressions of men in whose time the ancient civilizations still survived, are of little value to the historian. Though they lived when Egyptian was still spoken and the Egyptian culture and religion were still vigorous, they could neither read nor understand Egyptian, while we can. The monuments were a sealed book to them and, indeed, to most of their Egyptian informants. Their material was chiefly folk-tradition, which, in Egypt at least, passed current for history. With our full knowledge we can see how sometimes they are giving us a very fair version of the truth, while at other times they are wandering in realms of fable. Herodotus, while his story of Egypt is curiously jumbled and unequal in value, has in the case of Media provided us with material of first-rate importance which must have been communicated to him by an unusually accurate authority. The work of Ktesias the Knidian, the physician of Artaxerxes Mnemon, is, on the contrary, though he had first-hand knowledge of Persia absolutely valueless for history, and appears to be little more than a mere tissue of fables, at least as far as the pre-Persian period is concerned. Diodorus' sketch of Assyrian history is of little value, and seems to be chiefly based upon Ktesias. His history of Egypt, however, is of much greater value; it is not so accurate on the whole as that of Herodotus, and there is much of the purely legendary and even of the fantastic interwoven with his narrative, but it is interesting as giving us an account written by a visitor to Egypt, independent of either Herodotus or Manetho. That this account is partly derived from Ephoros seems extremely probable. In one matter Herodotus seems to be followed: the mis-dating of the kings who built the Pyramids of Giza. Herodotus placed them entirely wrongly, and Diodorus repeats his mistake. But the latter makes some estimates as to the length of the Pharaonic period which, we now know, may have been curiously near the truth. Herodotus gives, on the whole, a very good account for his time of the different salient periods and characteristic kings, but he has got them in a curiously mixed-up order; he puts the great Pyramid-builders of the IVth Dynasty (c. 3500 B.C.) after Rhampsinitos (Rameses III) of the XXth (c. 1200 B.C.), and is followed in this mistake by Diodorus. An explanation may be given of this curious blunder. It may be of Egyptian origin, and we may be blaming the Father of History unjustly for what is not his fault at all. When we come to deal with the Saite period of Egyptian history, the period of the Psammetichi and Amasis, shortly after the close of which Herodotus visited Egypt, we shall see that one of the most curious and characteristic phenomena of the time is the curious archaism which had set in, and not only in the domain of art. The period selected for imitation was that of the Pyramid-builders, whose gigantic monuments, surrounded by the necropoles of their faithful subjects, still towered above Memphis, and insistently compelled the regard and curiosity of all men, as they do to this day. Not only did the artists and architects of the Saite renascence turn away from the caricatures of the work of the XVIIIth and XIXth Dynasties which had been the pride of their immediate predecessors, and seek new models in the ancient triumphs which were constantly before their eyes: the officialdom of Egypt also reverted to ancient and forgotten titles and dignities, with the result that the Saite period was a kind of parody of the IVth and Vth Dynasties, which had flourished three thousand years before. The idea might then well have grown up among the people generally that the period of the Pyramid-builders was not so very many years before their own time, in any case much nearer to them than the age of Rhampsinitos, the period of the great Theban kings. Herodotus's blunder may then be based upon some such popular mistake as this.

5. Native Sources

It remains to speak of the work of ancient Egyptian and Babylonian historians. Besides the contemporary monuments of various periods, we have at our disposal ancient annals, often fragmentary, and usually telling us nothing more than the succession of the kings and sometimes the length of the dynasties. The most ancient official archive that we possess is Egyptian: part of a stele which when complete contained a regular history of the events of the reigns of the early Egyptian kings up to the time of the Vth Dynasty, when it was compiled. Only a fragment of it is now preserved (in the Museum of Palermo): so far as it goes it is the most complete ancient "history" known, and is probably very accurate; its fragmentary condition is the more tantalizing on this account. The later official lists of kings which we find inscribed on the walls of temples and tombs of the XVIIIth and XIXth Dynasties are complete enough, but give us nothing but a bare string of names. Nevertheless, these have been of the greatest use to us, and in conjunction with the work of the priest Manetho, of which we shall shortly speak, have formed the framework upon which our knowledge of the history of the reigns from the contemporary monuments has been built up. At the same time we have been able to see that one of these lists, that of Karnak, compiled in the reign of Thothmes III, is very inaccurate and of little use; while those of Abydos and Sakkara, of the reigns of Seti I and Rameses ii, are of remarkable accuracy, and have rarely been contradicted by the monuments. The compiler of the Karnak list had included simply prominent traditional names in a guessed order. But Seti's historian, and the priest Tunrei who made the list at Sakkara, were accurate annalists. It seems probable that shortly before the time of Seti the monuments of the most ancient kings at Abydos had been identified, and this may have caused some careful study of the antique archives. We have a written list of kings on papyrus, now preserved at Turin , which is of the same date as the king-lists of Abydos and Sakkara, and, were it in better condition, would be almost as valuable. It should have been more valuable, since it adds the regnal years of each king, and gives the sum-totals of the years of the several dynasties; but, unluckily, these statements of years do not always agree with the evidence of the monuments. Its mutilated fragments have been studied with care, notably of recent years by Professor Eduard Meyer, and though opinions may differ as to its general value, there is no doubt that it may be used with discretion to supplement the other lists. With these our native sources for Egyptian history before the Greek period close. No real historian is known to us in Pharaonic Egypt, nor is it likely that one will ever be discovered. The Egyptian had very little historical sense, and to him, as to his modern descendant, a popular legend was as worthy of credence as the most veracious chronicle.

The Babylonian scribe was, however, of a more critical and careful turn of mind, and collected what he could of genuine history with great industry. To him we owe several fragmentary chronicles, and a list of kings compiled in the time of the second Babylonian kingdom (sixth century B.C.); and to the official scribes of King Ashurbanipal of Assyria (seventh century) we owe an interesting document, a diplomatic memorandum on the ancient relations between Babylon and Assyria, which is known as "The Synchronous History." These Mesopotamian sources are far more historical in character than anything Egyptian save the "Palermo Stone": when they gave more than the bare names of kings they give obvious facts, not mere old wives' tales, like the Egyptians.

We now turn to native historiographers who wrote in Greek and under Greek influence. When Greek kings sat on the throne of the Pharaohs and it became fashionable to inquire into the past history of the extraordinary country which had been brought willy-nilly within the pale of Hellenism, a learned priest named Manetho, "The Gift of Thoth" (Manethoth), or possibly "The Gift of Buto" (Manutjo), of Sebennytos in the Delta, was commissioned by Ptolemy Philadelphos to collect all that was known of the Egyptian annals and translate them into Greek. This was done, and until the discoveries of Champollion Manetho's work, half destroyed as it now is, imitated and garbled by generations of ignorant copyists, was, with the exception of the sketches by Herodotus and Diodorus, the sole Egyptian authority on the history of Egypt. A similar role with regard to the history of Mesopotamia was played by the work of a Babylonian priest named Berossos, who is said to have been a contemporary of Antiochus II (250 B.C.). Like that of Manetho, his work is only known to us through the labours of copyists and compilers. The value of Manetho's work has been differently estimated by different writers. It is quite true that the mistakes of his copyists have caused considerable divergences in many cases as to length of individual reigns and sum-totals of dynasties, but in general it must be said that his work has proved remarkably useful. His arrangement in dynasties, which has been preserved in almost identical form by Julius Africanus, Eusebius, and George the Synkellos, formed the basis of the arrangement by Champollion and Lepsius of the names of the actual kings which had been recovered by the new science of Egyptology from the monuments, and it is worthy of note that these names have fitted on the whole extremely well into the Manethonian dynasties. The number of the kings in each dynasty is usually correct, even if the years of their reigns vary in the different versions, and even if the sum-totals are often added up wrong; and the number of dynasties has been found to be practically correct also, the only apparent mistake being in the intermediate period between the XIIIth and XVIIIth Dynastie; here we seem to have too long a period assigned to the intervening four dynasties. This jumble is, no doubt, primarily due to confusion in the native records from which Manetho drew his materials; the period was one of foreign invasion and conquest. Further, the more important the period is, the more flourishing the dynasty, the more accurately it is given by Manetho; his lists of the XIIth, XVIIIth, and XIXth Dynasties, for instance, the most flourishing periods of Egyptian history, are by no means very widely removed from the truth. In fact, Manetho did what he could: where the native annals were good and complete, his abstract is good; where they were broken and incomplete, his record is incomplete also and confused; and when we take the mistakes of copyists and annal-mongers into account, it will be seen that, as is also the case with Herodotus, so far from stigmatizing Manetho's work as absolutely useless, we may well be surprised at its accuracy, and be grateful for the fact that it agrees with the testimony of the monuments so much as it does! The work of Berossos as it has come down to us is of a slighter character than that of Manetho, and contains much that we should be inclined to assign to the realm of mythology rather than history, but what there is that is historical agrees very well with what has since been discovered. It could never, however, have served as a skeleton whereon to build up the flesh and blood of Mesopotamian history, whereas the scheme of Manetho, fragmentary and disjointed as it is, has actually formed the skeleton which modern discovery has clothed with tangible flesh. The dynasties of Manetho are the dynasties of history.

Other chronographers there were who dealt with Egypt and Assyria, such as Eratosthenes with the one and Abydenus with the other, but their work has not proved very important. With them our survey of the ancient authorities closes.

6. Chronology

Neither the Egyptians nor the Babylonians ever devised a continuous chronological scheme based upon a fixed era. The Sothic cycle of 1461 years, though it was used to regulate the calendar, was never used by the Egyptians as an era. The early Egyptians and the Babylonians spoke of individual years as "the year in which (such-and-such an event) took place", later on the Egyptians reckoned by the regnal years of each individual king. Such a reckoning is singularly useless for the purposes of continuous history, when we have no certain information as to how long a king reigned. In Egypt the only list of regnal years we possess, the fragmentary "Turin Papyrus," often disagrees with the evidence of contemporary monuments, while the Ptolemaic chronicler Manetho's figures have, as we shall see, been so garbled by later copyists that they are of little value. In Assyria it is otherwise. There, the years of the king's reign were currently noted by the yearly appointment of an official, who gave his name to the year. The office of this official was called limmu. Of these officials of the limmu we have long lists, dating from the reign of Adad-nirari II (911-890 B.C.) to that of Ashurbanipal (669-625 B.C.), some of which give an account of events which happened during their years of office. At the same time, on the cylinders and other clay records of Assyrian history, after the account of the events of a particular year, the name of the limmu-official is usually given. It is then evident that, with the lists of the limmi in our hands, if one of these eponymies can be fixed, we can accurately date the events dated by their means in the records. Now we are told that in the eponymy of Pur-shagali (?), in the month Sivan (May-June), there was an eclipse of the moon. This eclipse has been astronomically reckoned to have taken place in 763 B.C. The correctness of the identification is confirmed by the fact that the "Canon of Ptolemy" (a list used by the geographer Ptolemy, giving the names and regnal years of the kings of Babylon from Nabonassar to Alexander the Great, with the eclipses observed during their reigns) assigns to the thirtieth year of the era of Nabonassar (= 709 B.C.) the accession of "Arkeanos." Now Sargon of Assyria, who must be "Arkeanos," ascended the Babylonian throne about this time, and the year of his accession is that of the thirteenth of his rule in Assyria, and of the eponymy of Mannu-ki-Ashur-li. Therefore this eponymy must fall in 709 B.C. And if we trace back the lists of eponymies from Mannu-ki-Ashur-li to Pur-shagali, we find that the year of the latter falls in 763. The dates of the limmu are then absolutely certain.

Therefore, as far back as the tenth century B.C., Assyrian dates are certain, and the value of this certainty when we are dealing with the confused chronologies of the Biblical writers may easily be understood. Thus, when we find that Ahab was one of the allies defeated by Shalmaneser II at Karkar in 854 B.C. (an event not mentioned in the Old Testament record) we know that Ahab was reigning over Israel in 854 B.C., and any chronological theorizing as to Old Testament dates which takes no account of this fact is utterly worthless. Then when we find that the same King Shalmaneser received in 842 tribute from Jehu (an event recorded on the famous "Black Obelisk," now in the British Museum), we know that Jehu was reigning in 842. So that the current Biblical chronology which makes Ahab reign from 899 to 877 and Jehu from 863 to 835 is obviously confused. But with the help of the infallible Assyrian eponym-list we can restore the real dates with some success, with the result that Ahaziah seems to have in reality succeeded Ahab in 851, and was succeeded by Jehoram about 844, while Jehu attained the throne in 843-2, the year of his embassy to Shalmaneser. Reckoning back, we find that the division of the Hebrew kingdom after the death of Solomon must be assigned to somewhere between 950 and 930 B.C. And this fact gives us a very important Egyptian date, that of the beginning of the XXIInd Dynasty, when Sheshenk I invaded Southern Palestine. That this prince is the Shishak of the Biblical record there is no doubt. If Shishak's date is nearer 930 than 950 B.C., we have approximately settled an important landmark in Egyptian chronology; and know that the last Theban dynasty, that of the "Priest-Kings," came to an end +/- 940 B.C.

The regnal years assigned to Solomon, David, and Saul are too obviously traditional for us to place much reliance upon them, but their reigns were evidently long, so that we can reasonably assign to them the duration of a century: we thus find that the earliest possible date for the election of Saul the son of Kish is 1050 B.C., about the time of the division of Egypt between the dynasties of the priest-kings at Thebes and their lay rivals at Tanis, Palestine, as we know, had always been Egyptian territory since the conquests of Thothmes I, and it was not until the Pharaonic kingdom had fallen into utter weakness under the rois faineants of the XXth Dynasty, and their kingdom had been divided between their ecclesiastical Mayors of the Palace at Thebes and the practically independent viceroy of the Delta, that the last remnant of Egyptian empire in Asia fell away, and the Hebrews were enabled, in default of a legitimate overlord in Egypt, to elect a king of their own. The date of 1050 B.C. is then indicated by both Egyptian and Jewish records for the end of the XXth Dynasty, the decease of the last legitimate Ramesside, and the constitution of an independent kingdom in Palestine.

Egyptian sources do not give us much information which will carry us farther back with much certainty: we must again have recourse to Assyrian help to enable us to reconstitute the chronology not only of Assyrian but of Egyptian history also. As has been said, the Egyptians possessed no continuous era of any kind. They did not even proceed as far as the Babylonians and Assyrians in this direction. It is true that on a stele from Tanis mention is made of the year 400 of King Nubti, which corresponded to an undetermined year of Rameses II. No other instance of an era is known in Egypt, and this era, which is dated from the reign of an almost unknown Hyksos king, Set-aa-pehti Nubti, whose only contemporary monument is a scarab in the British Museum, is never found repeated. The only date ordinarily used is that of the year of the king, and when, as was often the case, the heir-apparent was associated with the reigning monarch on the throne, complications ensue: the year 5 of one king may be the same as the year 25 of another, and so on. All we can do is simply to reckon back the known number of years of each king, taking into account known co-regencies and collateral reigns as we come to them, and checking the result by the years of kings and dynasties as given by Manetho, and by the known synchronisms with the more definitely fixed dates of Babylonian and Assyrian history. Attempts have been made to find a heroic remedy for these difficulties with the help of astronomical data. Unluckily the Egyptians seem to have attached no particular importance to eclipses, and never chronicled them. Another, and regular, astronomical event was, however, often recorded. This was the heliacal rising of the star Sothis or Sirius. Properly speaking the heliacal rising of a star means its rising contemporaneously with the sun, but it is obvious that such a rising could not be seen or observed: in practice the "heliacal rising" means the latest visible rising of the star before the sunrise, about an hour before sunrise. Sirius rises heliacally about the time of the beginning of the inundation, which was from the earliest times regarded as a convenient time from which to date the beginning of the year. The Egyptian year, which had originally consisted, like the Babylonian year, of lunar months, had, at a very early period, been re-arranged in an artificial scheme of three seasons, each of four months of thirty days each, with five epagomenal days to make up 365 days, A leap year, to make up the loss of a day in four years, owing to the real length of the year being 365 ¼ days, was never introduced. The first season was that of the Inundation, the second that of the Sowing, the third that of the Harvest, The first month of the first season, originally the month of Mesore, was in later times the month Thoth, and the 1st Thoth was, after the time of the XIIth Dynasty, nominally the beginning of the year. But the actual feast of the New Year was always celebrated on the day of the heliacal rising of Sirius at the beginning of the inundation. When the calendar was introduced this day must have been the 1st day of the 1st month. But eight years later it was the 29th of the preceding month (the 4th of the Harvest Season), because in eight years the calendar, being unprovided with an extra day every fourth year, had lost two days. And so on; and it was not till 1461 years had passed that the heliacal rising of Sirius and the real opening of the year once more fell upon the 1st day of the 1st month, a whole year having been lost out of the 1461. In the meantime the official names of the seasons had of course gradually come to bear no relation to the real periods of Inundation, and Sowing, and Harvest, and then had gradually come into line again.

We are informed by a Latin writer of the third century A.D. named Censorinus that the rising of Sirius coincided with the 1st Thoth in the year 139 A.D., so that a new Sothic cycle of 1461 years began in that year. In the Decree of Canopus (238 B.C.) the rising of Sirius appears as occurring on the 1st of Epiphi, the tenth month: if this were so, the rising would happen on the 1st Thoth in 143 A.D. Thus 143 A.D. seems a more probable date for the beginning of a new cycle than 139; but in any case we see that this event must have taken place about 140 A.D.

The fact that the months came round full circle again after a period of 1461 years had no doubt been noted by the Egyptians, as we find that Theon of Alexandria, who evidently computes from the date 139 A.D, makes the preceding cycle begin in 1322 B.C., and calls it the "Era of Menophres." And the name Menophres is extremely like the "throne-name" of Rameses I, Men-peh-ra, whom on other grounds we should be inclined to place very near this date.

But this does not mean that the Egyptians ever used the Sothic cycle as an era: they never computed by its years. This, however, in no way affects the fact that the cycle of the risings of Sirius may be of considerable use to us in reconstructing Egyptian chronology. Thus, were it unknown that the Decree of Canopus was inscribed in 238 B.C., we should have been able, taking Censorinus' date for the end of the cycle, to have arrived very near the correct date by calculating when the star rose heliacally on the last day of Epiphi.

Now, leaving out of account the date of Menophres (since, though he is probably Men-peh-ra, we do not certainly know this), we find that in a certain year of the reign of Thothmes III the New Year feast fell upon the 28th day of the eleventh month (Epiphi). This can only have been between the years 1474 and 1470, which must therefore have fallen in his reign.

Going farther back, we find that in the ninth year of Amenhetep I, the feast fell upon the 9th Epiphi, which means that his ninth year falls between 1550 and 1546 B.C. Now this period of eighty years between

24

Amenhetep I and Thothmes III is very much what we should have expected from our knowledge of the history of the time.

The date for Thothmes III is confirmed by the identification of two New-Moon festivals in his twenty-third and twenty-fourth years (on the 21st Pachon and 30th Mekheir) with those of May 15, 1479, and Feb. 23, 1477, according to Meyer.

These two very important dates for Thothmes III and Amenhetep I are amply confirmed by evidence from the Babylonian side, which makes it impossible for us to place Thothmes later than the earlier half of the fifteenth century. We know from the great collection of cuneiform tablets containing the official correspondence of the Egyptian kings Amenhetep III and Akhenaten, of the XVIIIth Dynasty, with the kings and governors of Western Asia, which was discovered at Tell el-Amarna in Egypt in 1888, that King Ashur-uballit of Assyria communicated with Akhenaten. Assyrian chronological evidence assigns to Ashur-uballit the date of circa 1400 B.C.

Ashur-uballit was the great-great-great-grandfather of the Assyrian king Tukulti-Ninib. Now, Sennacherib made a copy upon clay of an inscription of Tukulti-Ninib which had been cut upon a lapis-lazuli seal; this seal had been carried off to Babylon by some successful conqueror of Assyria, and Sennacherib found it there after he had vanquished the Babylonians and had captured their city. We know that Sennacherib reigned from about 705 to 681 B.C., and he tells us in a few lines added to his copy of the writing on Tukulti-Ninib's seal that the lapis-lazuli seal was carried off to Babylon 600 years before his own time. This "600 years" is obviously a round number, but it shews that Tukulti-Ninib must have reigned about the middle of the thirteenth century B.C. Further, in an inscription recently found at Kala' Sherkat, the ancient Ashur, Esarhaddon says that King Shalmaneser I renewed the temple of the god Ashur 580 years before his time, i.e. about 1260 B.C. And Tukulti-Ninib was the successor of Shalmaneser, which gives the same date, about 1250 B.C., for him as Sennacherib's statement.

Ashur-uballit can hardly have lived less than 100 years before Tukulti-Ninib; thus it is clear that the date which we must assign to the reign of Ashur-uballit, and therefore to that of Amenhetep III, cannot be much later than 1400 B.C. And between Thothmes III and Amenhetep III about half a century had elapsed. Incidentally, Esarhaddon's date for Shalmaneser (confirmed by Sennacherib's for Ashur-uballit) gives us the correct date of the Egyptian king Rameses II. For we know that Shalmaneser was a contemporary of Kadashman-turgu and Kadashman-buriash of Babylonia, and that these were contemporaries of the Hittite king Khattusil, a well-known contemporary of Rameses II, who therefore was reigning in 1260 B.C.

Before these synchronisms and astronomical dates were known, Heinrich Brugsch, the greatest master of Egyptological science of his time, had devised for his epoch-making book, Egypt under the Pharaohs, a chronological system which, starting from the synchronism of Sheshenk with Rehoboam (which he placed too early, at 975 B.C.), proceeded by simple computation of the known generations of the kings, and with the allowance of probable generations to those whose exact position was unknown, to the round date of 1460 B.C. for Amenhetep in and 1400 for Horemheb, who restored the orthodox religion after the heresy of Akhenaten. This was a remarkable approximation to the true date, which is evidently to be placed only half a century later.

These astronomically ascertained dates therefore agree both with each other and with the other evidence, a fact which makes it difficult to discredit them upon grounds of possible mistakes of observation or calculation on the part of the ancients or of possible deliberate alterations in the calendar. We are therefore justified in accepting them as a sound foundation for the chronology of Egypt as far back as the beginning of the XVIIIth Dynasty, which will thus be placed about 1580 B.C. The end of the dynasty, and reign of Menpehra Rameses I, will then coincide with the "Era of Menophres" (1322 or 1318 B.C.). To this time is to be assigned the apogee of the Hittite kingdom, whose great princes, Shubbibiliuma, Mursil, and the rest were contemporaries of Rameses I and his successors.

The settlement of the date of the XVIIIth Dynasty means the fixing of the age of the prehistoric antiquities of Greece. The apogee of the prehistoric culture of Crete, the Second Late Minoan period, when the great palace of Knossos was built as we now see it, was contemporary with the XVIIIth Dynasty, and the Third Late Minoan period, the age of decline, began before the end of that dynasty. This we know from archaeological evidence which admits of one interpretation only, and from contemporary representations of Cretan envoys, bearing vases of Late Minoan form as gifts, to the courts of Hatshepsut and Thothmes in. We can pretty accurately date the destruction and abandonment of Knossos, which ended the Second Late Minoan period and marked the beginning of the Third, to about 1400 B.C.

With the beginning of the XVIIIth Dynasty we have reached the limits of comparative certainty in Egyptian chronology. We may place the Hyksos king Set-aa-pehti about 1650 B.C., on the authority of the "Stele of Four Hundred Years," which puts him four centuries before Rameses II, and this date agrees entirely with the evidence sketched above, which puts the end of the Hyksos period about 1580, and with that of his sole contemporary monument, a scarab (already referred to) s which from its style cannot be much older than the time of Aahmes, the expeller of Hyksos. This date of 1650 seems to be the most ancient Egyptian date of which we can be sure with a small possible margin of error.

But the astronomical calculation, based upon a mention of a rising of Sothis, appears to come to our aid again and to provide us with a certain date between 1882 and 1879 B.C. for the seventh year of Senusert III, of the XIIth Dynasty, and therefore, since the length of the reigns of that dynasty are certainly known, with the very definite date of 2000-1788 B.C. for the XIIth Dynasty. Could it be accepted entirely without cavil, this date would be of enormous importance to our knowledge of Egyptian history. There are facts that speak in its favour. There is no doubt that the art of the early XVIIIth Dynasty differs very little from that of the XIIIth: the fact is very well shewn on a small scale in the evolution of the scarab-seal. And the evidence from Crete shews that no very long period of time elapsed between the "Second Middle Minoan" period of the Aegean culture, which was contemporary with the XIIth Dynasty, and the "First Late Minoan" period, which was contemporary with the beginning of the XVIIIth. On the other hand, as will be seen when we come to discuss the history of the "Intermediate" period (Ch. VI.), there are also facts that speak against it. It seems almost impossible to force all the kings of the XIIIth-XVIIth Dynasties into so small a space as 250 years, cut down their reigns as we may. The XIIIth Dynasty gives us the impression of having reigned for a considerable period ; and the new kings, probably to be placed at the beginning of the XVIIth Dynasty, whose statues have lately been found at Karnak, cannot have been purely ephemeral monarchs if they reigned long enough for their colossi to be erected at Thebes. The difficulties in the way of the acceptance of this Sothic date are therefore great. Prof. Petrie cuts the knot by boldly assuming that the calculation is right, but that the date must be pushed back a whole Sothic period of 1460 years earlier, so that

Senusert III reigned about 3300 B.C.! It is curious that the distinguished professor should have committed himself so definitely to so difficult a proposition. We cannot make the period between the XIIth and the XVIIIth Dynasties last sixteen hundred years. One must pause to think that sixteen hundred years is an immense period of time, reckoned by human standards. Sixteen hundred years separated Julius Caesar from Queen Elizabeth, Diocletian from Queen Victoria. What changes of civilization and language, what abolitions and creations of peoples, has the world not seen in sixteen hundred years And the civilization and art of the beginning of the XVIIIth Dynasty hardly differs from that of the end of the XIIth: is in no way so different from it as is that of the IVth. Also the compilers of the king-lists made the XVIIIth Dynasty follow immediately the XIIth, ignoring the intermediate period as that of the rule of pretenders, usurpers, and foreigners.

We cannot suppose that any very long period really elapsed, yet the narrow two centuries and a half which are demanded by the usual interpretation of the new Sothic date seem an impossibly short period. Another century only, and our allegiance to it might have been conceded willingly. Our knowledge of the facts of the history of the time seems to forbid our acceptance of a much less or a much greater period of time than three and a half centuries between the end of the XIIth Dynasty and the beginning of the XVIIIth. It does not seem impossible that our interpretation of the date given by the Kahun temple-book has been in some way faulty. Another calculator has computed the year as 1945 B.C., which is seventy years earlier than the date given by Drs. Borchardt and Meyer. Or some deliberate alteration of the calendar may have taken place in ancient times before the time of the XVIIIth Dynasty: such an alteration, which is not impossible, as we see by Mr. Gardiner's discovery that Mesore, later the twelfth, was till the time of the XVIIIth Dynasty the first month of the year, might throw all our calculations into confusion. It would therefore seem wise to refrain from a complete acceptance of the new Sothic date till further information confirms it. We may rest content for the time with the round date of circa 2000 B.C. for the mid-point of the XIIth Dynasty. This gives us a vaguely approximate date for the Cretan "Middle Minoan" period, when the palace of Phaistos was built. The interesting piece of evidence quoted by Prof. Meyer, the fact that under the XIIth Dynasty an officer sent to Sinai to seek for turquoise notes in his inscription that in the months of Phamenoth-Pachon, when he was there, it was high summer, and the heat "like fire," would suit Prof. Meyer's date or one a century or two earlier equally well, while it would not suit so well the earlier dates adopted years ago by Brugsch. Brugsch's dates for the Middle Kingdom are too high, as they are based upon an exaggerated estimate of the length of the period between the XIIth and the XVIIIth Dynasty, due to a too conservative treatment of the statements of Manetho's copyists, who attribute to the Hyksos 510 years and to the XIIIth Dynasty 453, making an absolutely impossibly long period of 963 years between the two dynasties. Brugsch did not go to this length, but archaeology as well as historical probability shew us that he overestimated the length of the second Intermediate period.

The Manethonian year-numbers for the first Intermediate period, between the VIth and the XIth Dynasties, are again exaggerated. But Brugsch accepted them, with the result that his date for Mena goes back to the figure of 4400 B.C., only four centuries later than that to which Prof. Petrie pins his faith.

Babylonian history gives us no help now. We have reached the time when the two kingdoms had little or no connexion with one another, so that synchronisms of kings no longer present themselves, nor are likely to do so. For the dates of the old Egyptian kingdom we must simply employ a dead reckoning, supplementing our knowledge derived from the monuments by the lists of Manetho and the Turin papyrus, back from the beginning of the XIIth Dynasty. The XIth Dynasty lasted less than 150 years; the period of civil war that preceded it can hardly have endured more than a similar period, as the style of tomb-construction and tomb-furniture in vogue under the XIth Dynasty is little different from that usual under the VIth. So that we can hardly seek earlier than 2500 B.C. for the end of the VIth Dynasty. And this date agrees very well with that indicated for the beginning of the IVth by the dates scribbled in red paint on the casing-blocks of the pyramids of the kings Sneferu and Khufu at Meidum and Gizah: the months given must have fallen at that time in the summer, as it was only in the summer, when the peasantry were not engaged in agricultural work and the Nile was high for transport across the plain, that quarrying could be carried on and great stones transported by river to the desert-marge. The date thus indicated is about 3200-3000 B.C. And a dead reckoning would attribute about 500 years to the IVth-VIth Dynasties.

The first three dynasties seem, by dead reckoning, to have lasted over 400 years. We therefore reach circa 3600-3500 B.C. for the beginning of the 1st Dynasty and the foundation of the kingdom. This is of course somewhat of a guess; but it is unlikely that the 1st Dynasty is to be put very much earlier. Prof. Meyer's date, based upon the Sothic date of the reign of Senusert III, is 3315 B.C., which, if one doubts the validity of this date as computed by him, seems too low and also too definite. He is a bold man who would reckon the date of Menes in anything more closely defined than round centuries.

But it must be remembered that, if we do not accept the placing of the Sothic date of the Kahun book so late as 1945 or 1876-72 B.C., we have no really firm ground for any Egyptian chronology at all before the beginning of the XVIIIth Dynasty. We can only guess, and it is guesswork founded upon what we know of the history of art and civilization as well as of the history of kings' reigns, that brings us to a date for the 1st Dynasty not so very much earlier than that adopted by Prof. Meyer. And it claims to be nothing more than a guess. This being so, those who consider they have no right to reject Manetho's statements as to the length of the two intermediate periods on the strength of purely archaeological evidence, may continue, if they prefer so to do, to use the chronological system of Brugsch. But it must be remembered that this system is a very arbitrary one, that the thirty-year generations on which it is computed are too long, and that its results for the period before the XVIIIth Dynasty are only in the widest sense approximate. It can only be used as a sort of chronologimeter, giving a general idea of time : its dates were never intended by its author to be accepted too strictly. This being so, we can also resort to guesswork, based when possible upon historical and archaeological evidence, otherwise upon probability.

We guess then that the two primitive kingdoms of Northern and Southern Egypt, which preceded the foundation of the monarchy, are to be dated before 3600 B.C., and, seeing that the development of culture was swift in those early days, we may suppose that in 4000 B.C. the inhabitants of Upper Egypt were Neolithic barbarians, and those of Lower Egypt and the Delta little better. Prof. Meyer thinks that in the year 4241 B.C., when a Sothic period began, the calendar was first established by the New Year feast being fixed on the occasion of the heliacal rising of Sothis, that the day was called "the 1st Thoth," and the very arbitrary system of the Egyptian months and seasons was then instituted. Such an arrangement need not have been beyond the mental powers of people in the Neolithic stage of culture, but it would seem more probable that the calendar was really put into its regular shape on the occasion of the Sothic "aeon" of 2781 B.C., about the time of the Vth Dynasty.

To guess the age of the Cretan civilization before the time of the Middle Minoan period and the XIIth Dynasty is impossible. We can only vaguely place the "Early Minoan" period and the beginnings of Cretan culture in the fourth millennium B.C.

We have to guess the age of Babylonian history in much the same way. Since the reign of Khammurabi the great law-giver has been fixed by Mr. L. W. King to somewhere between 1950 and 1900 B.C. (to the confusion of Nabonidus' Babylonian scribe, who said that Khammurabi lived 700 years before Burraburiash, whereas in reality he lived but 500 years before him), 2050 B.C., for the beginning of the 1st Dynasty of Babylon, Khammurabi's dynasty, is the earliest Mesopotamian date of which we have any real certainty. The well-known date of Nabonidus for Sargon of Agade and Naram-Sin, which is 3750 B.C., has no authority whatever to support it. All the other known evidence on the subject goes against it, and indubitably it is grossly exaggerated. We cannot extend the known history of Babylonia before 2050 B.C. by means of a probable dead reckoning further than about 3000. The patesis of Lagash who played the leading role in Babylonia in the period which immediately followed the epoch of Sargon and Naram-Sin cannot on the basis of our present knowledge be placed earlier than 2500; Gudea, the best known of them, must be dated about 2450. How can we, on the authority of Nabonidus' simple statement, admit a gaping void, a hiatus without content of any kind, of thirteen hundred years between Gudea and Naram-Sin? An important testimony against this supposition (which in itself is so improbable) is the fact that the clay tablets of the two epochs hardly differ in shape, and that the forms of the characters with which they are inscribed are almost identical in both periods. Palaeographic evidence makes it impossible to accept any gap between the first Sargonids and the patesis of Lagash, much less a gap of 1300 years! The thing is as unlikely as Prof. Petrie's 1600 years' interval between the XIIth and XVIIIth Egyptian dynasties. Nabonidus must be wrong, nor is it unlikely that he was wrong. The sixth century was far remote from the time of Sargon and Naram-Sin, and in the late Assyro-Babylonian period mistakes were made as to early dates. Thus we find that an inscription of Esarhaddon (seventh century), describing the rebuilding of the temple of Ashur by Shalmaneser I (fourteenth century), states that 560 years had elapsed since its first rebuilding by a chief named Irishum.

But a contemporary inscription of Shalmaneser's states that 739 years had elapsed since the same event. We cannot doubt that Shalmaneser is more likely to be right than Esarhaddon, since he lived seven centuries nearer to the time of Irishum. But when we are confronted with such discrepancies we may well wonder whether the statements of kings of the later period as to early dates are of much value, and may decide to accept them only when they agree with the archaeological evidence. We reject, then, Nabonidus' date of 3800 3750 B C for Sargon and Naram-Sin on archaeological grounds, and place them, following Mr. L. W. King, about 2600 B.C., or, emending Nabonidus' figures by altering his "3200 years before my time" to "2200 years," as Prof. Lehmann-Haupt proposed to do, make him reign about 2750 B.C. We are dealing with a piece of false and exaggerated history, which was no doubt quite to the taste of the late Babylonian literati, chief of whom was the king, Nabonidus. The earlier kings of Sumer, from Ur-Nina to Urukagina of Lagash, and his contemporary the conqueror Lugal-zaggisi of Erech, will then be placed between 3000 and 2800 B.C., and the oldest Babylonian rulers of whom we have any knowledge will fall not long before 3000 B.C. at the earliest.

Apparently, Babylonian history is not so ancient as that of Egypt by some five hundred years. This is, however, an uncertain point, as we do not know how long before 3000 B.C. the ancient Babylonian Sumerian culture first began to develop. We have no traces of a Neolithic age in Babylonia, while the Egyptians of 3500 B.C. had not long emerged from the neolithic stage. The Egyptian writing of 3500 B.C. is still an extremely primitive pictorial script; the Babylonian writing of 3000 B.C. had already developed into a conventionalized and formal system which bore little resemblance to the original pictures from which it was derived. The Babylonians may well have passed into the age of metal at an earlier period than did the Egyptians, and have evolved their "cuneiform" writing before the Egyptians, at the beginning of the 1st Dynasty, began to codify and stereotype their script.

We might therefore begin our survey with Babylonia but that a more convenient arrangement is afforded by the reverse order, in which prehistoric Greece first claims attention. The whole of the "history" of the Greek Bronze Age being "pre-history," without records, we take it first from its beginning to its end, returning to the known history of Egypt and Babylonia in the order named.

CHAPTER II: THE OLDER CIVILIZATION OF GREECE

I. Aegean Civilization

THE great Aegean civilization of the Bronze Age in no way owed its origin to the West, and cannot have been, till near its end, more than but slightly influenced by any possible independent Indo-European culture m the North. Civilization must have come to the Northern land of barren steppes and impenetrable forests by way of the Vardar and Danube-valleys from the Aegean, not in the reverse direction. That the seeds of the Minoan culture of Crete could have been brought from the North would be of itself inconceivable, and as a matter of fact we know that the Minoan culture developed out of its Neolithic origins in the Aegean itself. That the older civilization of Greece was a single culture, which developed out of Neolithic beginnings into the full civilization of the Bronze Age without a break in the same place, is now certain. No cataclysm marks the passage from the Age of Stone to that of Metal. The Bronze Age culture develops directly from the Neolithic, and the Bronze Age people of Greece may naturally be presumed to be the same as the Neolithic people. The later transition from the Age of Bronze to that of Iron was certainly accompanied by and due to the invasion of the Indo-Europeans from the North. But we have no reason to suppose that there, was any racial difference between the Neolithic and the Bronze Age Greeks.

The Neolithic Aegeans were then the ancestors of the Minoans and Mycenaeans, whose dress of a simple waistcloth (sometimes with additions, and developed strangely in the case of the women) is very good evidence that they were Southerners from Africa rather than Northerners from Europe. This simple waistcloth, the natural dress of men in a hotter country than Greece, can be traced as far back in time as we can go, and there is no doubt that it was worn by the Neolithic Greeks and came from Northern Africa with them. The earlier Greeks came then from Africa while they were still stone-users.

There is, however, as we shall see later, a possibility that there existed from the beginning in Northern Greece a second ethnic element, a people which still used stone when the Aegeans had long passed into the Bronze Age. This element, if it is of Northern origin, we can hardly refuse to recognize as of Indo-European stock, and to call, if we wish to coin a word, proto-Achaian.

The Neolithic stage of the southern Greeks is known to us chiefly from Crete, where, at Knossos, the low hill which was afterwards crowned by the palace of Minos was inhabited for many centuries by a Neolithic population before the knowledge of metal came to Greece. In Asia Minor pottery which must be Neolithic has been found, and on the Asiatic shore of the Aegean, at Troy, evidences of Neolithic culture are visible in the lowest strata of human habitation. In Euboea and in the Peloponnese stone weapons have been found. But in the Cyclades no trace of Neolithic inhabitants has come to light, and in Cyprus only one or two isolated stone weapons have been noted.

This last fact may possibly be due to the easy accessibility of copper in the eastern island. It may well be that Cyprus was the original home of copper-working in the Eastern Mediterranean, and that the knowledge of metal came thence both to the predynastic Northern Egyptians and to the Aegeans. But there is a difference between the cases of Egypt and Greece, in that while the Egyptians used copper alone, and did not become acquainted with bronze till the time of the Middle Kingdom, the Aegeans from the first seem to have been acquainted with bronze as well as copper, and among them the use of the alloy soon superseded that of the pure metal. Probably the knowledge of the art of alloying copper with tin or antimony came from the Middle East, where tin is found, to Greece as well as to Babylonia and, eventually, Egypt.

To the introduction of metal the whole development of the prehistoric Greek culture was due. Its appearance is marked by the stirring of an artistic impulse which, swiftly changing and improving, carried the southern Aegeans in a few centuries from the rude hand-made pottery of the Neolithic period to artistic triumphs which have hardly been equalled since. Similarly, in the first few centuries after the introduction of metal, the Egyptians, whose art had early been fixed by religious convention, had progressed in the science of engineering and architecture, where their energies were untrammelled, from the absolute ignorance of the savage to the knowledge of the Pyramid-builders.

2. Minoan Chronology

In the absence of intelligible records, the history of this artistic development is practically the only history of early Greek civilization that we possess, and we are now able to follow its course with some accuracy, thanks to the acumen of Sir Arthur Evans, who has constructed a chronological scheme of three successive periods of development, each of which again is divided into three sub-periods. To these periods he gives the name of "Minoan," after the great Cretan lawgiver and thalassocrat. The name may be fanciful, but the scheme itself is by no means so; it rests upon careful observation and tabulation of ascertained archaeological facts, upon the results of the excavations at Knossos and elsewhere in Crete, and has for the first time given us a solidly based framework upon which we can arrange our facts. The whole of our knowledge of the prehistoric civilization not only of Crete but of Greece generally can with its aid be classified and arranged in chronological sequence. A corresponding scheme of the successive periods of the development of art in the Cyclades, contemporaneously with that of Crete, has been devised; even in the earliest period of the Bronze Age we can bring the culture of Troy into chronological relation with that of the South, while in the latest the Cretan culture has conquered the Greek mainland, and the "Late Minoan" age is as well represented at Mycenae as at Knossos. The scheme agrees very well with the evidence.

The chronological bases of the scheme are given by the various synchronisms with Egyptian history that are known, and have already briefly been mentioned. It is possible that intermittent connexion was maintained by sea between the primitive Northern Egyptians and the primitive Aegeans even in Neolithic times; although the curious resemblances which have been traced between certain religious cults peculiar to the Delta and those of Crete, and the similarities of the funeral rites in both countries, may perhaps be referred rather to an original connexion than to commercial relations. We cannot find a proof of these relations in the supposed vessels which are depicted on the vases of the predynastic Southern Egyptians, as these (if they are boats at all) are obviously mere Nile boats, and the people who depicted them were Nilotes of the south, not seagoing inhabitants of the Delta and the coast. It was not these African ancestors of the dynastic Southern Egyptians that can have been connected with the Aegeans, but a "Mediterranean" folk in the Delta who perhaps lived there side by side with the Semito-Libyan population which we shall see reason to believe existed in Northern Egypt. Whatever communication there may have been in Neolithic times is not likely to have been increased after the conquest of Northern Egypt by the

Southerners, and the foundation of the Egyptian kingdom. The coast population of the Delta, the Haau or swamp-men, as the Egyptians called them, probably maintained a fitful communication with the Aegeans, and to them as intermediaries we may ascribe the presence in Crete of fragments of Egyptian diorite bowls of the period of the Third Dynasty (if we set on one side temporarily the counter-instance of supposed Cretan vases in the royal tombs of the First Dynasty at Abydos as still doubtful). Direct communication with the true Egyptian nation which had now developed there was probably none. That nation had been unified under the hegemony of the kings and people of Upper Egypt, who had conquered the North by force, and had given a Southern complexion to the new state. The Southerners knew nothing of the sea, and the "Fenmen," who still preserved, on account of their proximity to the sea and occasional communication with the Northerners, many peculiarities differing from the orthodox Southern traits of official Egypt, were abhorrent to them. They were foreigners, and the Egypt of the Old Kingdom would have nothing to do with foreigners: she was a world in herself, governed by the gods in human form.

Towards the end of the Old Kingdom, however, this attitude of exclusiveness towards the Northerners began to break down: Egyptian stone vases were copied by the Cretans of the Early Minoan period, whose nascent art began in return to attract the attention of the Egyptians, and the spiral design, already characteristic of Aegean art, was adopted from the "seal-stones" of the Northerners to decorate the Egyptian seal-scarab. During the Middle Kingdom the beautiful Cretan polychrome pottery of the Middle Minoan period was exported to Egypt, and from its occurrence with objects of the Twelfth Dynasty in Egypt we see that the Second Middle Minoan period was contemporary with that dynasty. The succeeding Third Middle Minoan period must have been contemporary with the end of the Middle Kingdom, as the First and Second Late Minoan periods were certainly contemporary with the Eighteenth Dynasty, To the Third Middle Minoan period must be assigned the statuette of the Egyptian Abnub, son of Minuser (a name eminently characteristic of the Thirteenth Dynasty), and the alabaster-lid of King Khian, found at Knossos. The evidence of the contemporaneity of the first two "Late Minoan" periods with the Eighteenth Dynasty is very definite. A possible late "First Late Minoan" vase was found in a burial of the time of Thothmes III by Petrie at Gurob, and the vases carried by Keftian ambassadors to the courts of

Hatshepsut and Thothmes in are of First Late Minoan style. The Third Late Minoan period certainly began before the end of the Eighteenth Dynasty, as the Aegean sherds found in the ruins of Akhenaten's palace at Tell el-Amarna are exclusively of this style. Therefore the Second Late Minoan period must be placed, so far as Knossos is concerned, in the short space between the reigns of Thothmes III and Akhenaten. The Third Late Minoan period, the age which we formerly regarded as the "Mycenaean" age par excellence the period when, as it would seem, the hegemony of Aegean civilization passed from Knossos and Crete to Mycenae and the mainland, was much longer. It lasted in Greece certainly till the time of the Twentieth Dynasty, in Cyprus probably longer. In a tomb at Enkomi in Cyprus has been found a scarab of Rameses III (c. 1200 B.C.), and Mycenaean vases are depicted on the walls of that monarch's tomb. Later traces are doubtful.

Thus Sir Arthur Evans's scheme of the historical development of Aegean culture possesses a solid chronological basis. Using it as our guide, we can now essay to trace the course of Greek "pre-history" in some detail. The story is, as has been said, that of the development of culture as shewn in the evolution of art, and this evolution is traced mainly by means of the careful observation of the development of the ceramic art. The age of metal objects can be told by the style of pottery with which they are found or, in the case of metal vases, with which they can be compared. Similarly the date of a building can be shewn to be not later than the kind of ware which is found in it, and the character of the pottery can sometimes give us clues as to the ethnic character of the people who made it. Invasions and occupations can tentatively be traced, and the indications thus provided by archaeological science can be combined with the information derived from Egyptian and other Oriental records and the vague hints supplied by the Greek legends to form a probable theory of the course of events.

3. The Early and Middle Minoan Periods

The most ancient remains of the Bronze Age yet discovered in Greece are perhaps those of the First Cycladic period in the smaller islands of the Aegean, but it is obvious that the knowledge of bronze must have reached the island of Crete before it was passed on to the Cyclades. From the Cycladic cist-graves and the "Copper Age" necropolis in Cyprus we see how the metal celt was soon supplemented by the short copper or bronze dagger, which was eventually to become a long sword. The spearhead soon followed, and the primitive Aegean was as well armed as the Babylonian, and better than the Egyptian, of his time. The vases of earthenware were now supplemented by vases of the new material and of other and more precious metals, silver, electrum, and gold. Eventually the characteristic forms of the metal vases were imitated in pottery, so that the style of the metal-worker exercised great influence over that of the potter. The development of ceramic art was remarkable. The first Aegean painted ware arose in Crete: in Cyprus an incised red and a similar black ware still carried on during the early Bronze Age the tradition of a Neolithic pottery, akin to that of Crete, of which we have no actual relics. Painted ware came to Cyprus from the Aegean: it was a Cretan invention. The inventors first painted a black ware with dull white pigment in imitation of the incised designs, filled in with white, of the later Neolithic period. The black ground was now produced artificially by means of a "slip" of black glaze-colour, imitating the hand-burnished black surface of the Neolithic ware. This was a notable invention. The converse use of a white "slip" with black decoration was not long in coming. A wide field of artistic possibilities was now thrown open to the Cretan potter, and he was not slow to enter it. The vases of the next period, the Second "Early Minoan" age of Evans, shew great developments of the potter's art. Strange new forms of vases, such as the "Schnabelkannen" or beaked jugs appear, and curved lines, soon to develop into regular spirals, are seen in their simple decoration. In the Third Early Minoan period, which succeeds, the spiral decoration has been evolved, and the foundation of all the wonderful designs of the later Minoan pottery has been laid.

In this period we are able to establish a synchronism between the culture of Crete and that of Troy. There is no doubt that "Early Minoan III" is roughly contemporaneous with the Second "City" of Troy: they mark the same stage of culture. The discoveries of Mr. R. B. Seager in the tombs of the little island of Mochlos, off the north coast of Crete, have shewn that the superfluity of the precious metals which is so characteristic of "Troy II" is equally characteristic of "Early Minoan III." The riches of "Priam's Treasure" with its golden pins and chains and its gold and silver vases is paralleled by the golden bands, flowers, and pins found in the chieftains' graves at Mochlos. In the Second City of Troy we see the sudden development of civilization under the influence of the "Early Minoan" culture of Crete. But the Trojans retained their own style of black pottery, with its peculiar "owl-headed" vases and incised decoration.

Between Troy and Crete lay the Cyclades, where Cretan influence had developed a culture and an art closely akin to that of Crete, especially in respect of ceramic development. But the painted ware of the Cyclades from the first evolved local styles of its own, and, while the processes are the same as the Cretan, the vase-forms and decoration are by no means the same. We know the Cycladic pottery best from the finds in the tombs of Amorgos, Paros, and Syra (Chalandriane), which are of the type known as "cist-graves," being composed of flat slabs of stone in the form of a long box. The same type of grave is found in Early Minoan Crete, as, for instance, atMochlos. In Crete another type of tomb is found, in the Second Early Minoan age, the circular grave or "tholos," which later on developed into the "beehive" tomb, which we know in the "Treasuries" of Mycenae and Orchomenos. In the cist-graves of the Cyclades the dead were buried in the cramped form equally characteristic of the predynastic Egyptians or Babylonians, and the primitive Mediterraneans generally.

We have already mentioned the small idols in human form which were found in these Cretan tholoi as resembling those found in the predynastic Egyptian graves. Similar idols, but of more developed form, are characteristic of the Cycladic cist-graves. In Amorgos and Paros they are sometimes of large size, and are usually made of the local marble.

Characteristic again of the last Early Minoan and Cycladic periods is the development of stone-working. Fine stone vases are now made, of simple yet often beautiful forms, sometimes, in Crete, imitating a flower, sometimes, in the Cyclades, the shape of the sea-urchin. Most of these vases are made of the easily worked steatite found in Crete, but many of those from the Cyclades are of white marble. On some of them a fully developed system of connected spiral decoration appears. The system of spiral decoration now makes its appearance in Greece, and is seen in the goldwork of Troy and the stonework of the Cyclades perhaps before it appears as a decorative motive on pottery. The origin of the Aegean spiral patterns is probably to be sought in metal-working. The "Early Minoan" goldsmith invented it, and we see the first-fruits of his invention in the spiral coils of the gold wire pins of the "Treasure of Priam." From metal the new pattern passed to stonework in relief and then to pottery, painted on the flat. The Egyptians adopted it and incised it on their seals, an example afterwards followed by the makers of the Cretan "seal-stones." From the Aegean the beautiful pattern spread northwards to Central Europe, to Scandinavia, and eventually to Celtic Britain.

On Cretan pottery the spiral design does not properly appear till the beginning of the next period of artistic development, the "Middle Minoan." At the same time that a pattern derived from the coils of metal wire was used to ornament pottery, the forms of earthenware vases became for the first time directly modelled upon those of vases of metal. The pottery of the Middle Minoan period is constantly made in forms which are obviously imitated from those of metal originals. The potter had now obtained such mastery of his material that he could mould his clay in any form he chose. This mastery had been obtained as the result of two inventions of first-rate importance in the history of art: the baking-furnace and the potter's wheel. It is probable that both were originally invented in Egypt somewhere between the time of the First and the Fourth Dynasties. In the age of the Pyramid-builders we find well-baked wheel-made pottery universal, whereas the pre-dynastic ware had all been built up by hand and baked in an open fire, like the Neolithic and First "Early" Minoan or Cycladic pottery of Greece. Both inventions must have reached Greece during the Third Early Minoan (Cycladic) period (= Troy II), During the Second period pottery made in the old manner was still used in Greece, as we see from the black and red ware of Vasiliki, and from the primitive pottery of the Cyclades. But in the Third period the new inventions have definitely established themselves, and the result is the remarkable ceramic development of the Middle Minoan age in Crete.

Not only were metal shapes imitated by the Middle Minoan potter, armed with his new mastery of furnace and wheel. For the first time pottery was made of thin and delicate, often of "egg-shell," ware, and plant forms appear in relief, clustering on the sides and over the lips of his vases. And, above all, the painter aided him to beautify the vases he made by introducing polychrome decoration. The pottery of the Middle Minoan period is characterized by a profuse use of colour — red, blue, and white, usually on a black ground. Spiral coils of red and white combine with the black ground to produce a hitherto unknown richness of decoration. Combined with the metallic forms of the vases the result is often extraordinarily striking.

Characteristic also of this period are the "seal-stones" on which are cut the remarkable signs which Sir Arthur Evans has shown to belong to a hieroglyphic system, which was now giving rise to the regular system of writing which we find, impressed on clay tablets by means of a stilus (much in the Babylonian manner), in the remains of the next age. Of the origin of this system of writing we know nothing, but it is significant that some of the signs on the seal-stones are closely paralleled by, a few even identical with, certain Egyptian hieroglyphics. We can at least assume a considerable Egyptian influence on the development of the script.

The Middle Minoan period saw a great advance not only in the arts of the potter, metal-worker, and seal-cutter, but also in that of the architect. The roughly built stone houses of the earlier age had now developed into splendid buildings of hewn and squared stone. The earlier palaces at Knossos and Phaistos were now built. Of the former we can only identify fragments here and there in the great palace of the Late Minoan age, but at Phaistos much of the earlier building still remains.

4. The Kingdom of Knossos and Phaistos

We know nothing of the political constitution of prehistoric Crete, and cannot tell whether in the days when Knossos and Phaistos were first built the whole island was under one dominance or was divided into several independent kingdoms. Later on, in the heyday of Minoan civilization, we feel that political unity is probable, and that Knossos was the metropolis of a Cretan state. The legend of the thalassocracy of Minos also indicates that Crete was a state united under the rule of the kings of Knossos, and possessed of wide-reaching power over the neighbouring seas and islands. It may be that at least the central portion of Crete, between Ida and Dikte, was already unified from sea to sea under the rule of Knossos as early as the Middle Minoan period, and that Phaistos and the neighbouring palace of Agia Triada were originally built by a Knossian king. Legend makes Phaistos a colony of Knossos.

With the building of the first palace of Knossos above the heaped-up strata of the Neolithic age the kingdom of Minos first takes form and substance. The Neolithic settlement occupied the sides of a hill that slopes down to the valley of a little river, the Kairatos, which enters the sea four miles away, a short distance to the east of the modern city of Candia, on the north coast of the island. Candia owes its modern importance to its central position. Politically, Canea, at the western extremity of the island, is now the capital, owing partly to its greater proximity to Europe, and partly to its possession of some sort of a harbour, while Candia has, for modern purposes, none. But the central portion of the island, of which Candia is the capital, is the richest and most important part of Crete, and must always have been so. In Roman days the capital was Gortyna, in the

Messara, a city which evidently succeeded to the inheritance of the neighbouring Phaistos. In Early Minoan days the central portion of the land must always have been in advance of the mountainous eastern and western portions in civilization, and it is here that the first unified political power must have been formed. All tradition points to Knossos as the original seat of this power, and we cannot doubt that the traditions are correct, and that Knossos owed its pre-eminence to its central position. And its situation on the northern coast contributed largely to make it the centre of an over-sea dominion. So the Neolithic settlement at Knossos developed into the seat of a powerful dynasty and the centre of the culture which has been revealed to us by the excavations of Sir Arthur Evans and Dr. Mackenzie. These excavations are gradually exposing to view the extensive remains of the palace of the kings, built above the Neolithic settlement. The remains of the town which surround it have hitherto not been investigated to any great extent, though some houses have been excavated by Mr. Hogarth. The cemetery, on a neighbouring hillside called Zafer Papoura, has been explored by Dr. Evans; but all the tombs found contained objects which are much later in date than the time of the first founding of the palace. A great tomb has, however, been found on the hill of Isopata, a mile or so nearer the sea, which was probably originally constructed at the close of the Middle Minoan age.

Like the potters, the architects of the Middle Minoan age had new and great ideas. The sudden development of civilization which differentiates this age from that which preceded it produced men with splendid conceptions, just as the similar but earlier development in Egypt had produced the designs of the Pyramids. The Minoan architects did not design mighty masses like these, but in the grand western entrance and "Stepped Theatral Area" of Phaistos they translated into stone a fine and spacious architectural conception such as hitherto only Egypt could have produced.

In both cases when the palaces were designed, a flat platform was prepared for them by the levelling of a portion of the hill on which each stands. This shews that the architects worked at the bidding of powerful rulers with large ideas, as the levelling must have involved the destruction of a large portion of the old town of the Early Minoan period in which the original king's house stood. To this designed destruction we owe the fact that our knowledge of the Early Minoan age is derived in small measure from Knossos and Phaistos, but rather from other excavations.

The similarity of the process in both cases points to a practical contemporaneity of execution. At the same time that the king of Knossos built his new palace in his capital, or not long after, he also built himself a southern palace in the Messara. There was probably an earlier town here also. As at Knossos, a low hill, such as was the usual position of a primitive town, was utilized. As from the near neighbourhood of Knossos a fine view of the sea, the haven, and the ships of the thalassocrats could be obtained, with Dia beyond and perhaps Melos far away on the horizon, so from Phaistos itself an equally fine, but different, prospect greeted the royal eyes; from this hill top he could contemplate on one-side the snowy tops of Ida and on the other the rich lands of the Messara; the southern mountain-range shut out the Libyan sea from his view. Later, some king desired to see the southern sea, and built himself a palace, but little inferior to Phaistos in splendour, and not far off, from which the bay of the Messara, with the island now known as Paximadhi ("Cake"), and the splendid mountain group of Kentros and Ida together, were visible. This newer palace is now known as Agia Triada, from a little church of the Holy Trinity that stands upon it. Like Phaistos, it has been excavated by the Italian archaeologists, Halbherr, Pernier, and their colleagues.

Here again the site of an older settlement was utilized and levelled for the new royal house: Agia Triada was inhabited in very early days, as we know from the tribal tholos-burial of the Early Minoan period, already mentioned, which has been discovered there.

Agia Triada is wholly a work of the Late Minoan period, to which we now come. Still tracing the development of Cretan civilization by means of the evolution of its pottery, we find that in the Third Middle Minoan period much of the inspiration of the "Kamaraes" potters was evaporating, and the polychrome decoration was becoming poor in execution and weak in effect. The first stage of the Late Minoan period, which followed, was ushered in by a new course in ceramic decoration. The polychrome principle was abandoned, and a system of plain dark colour upon a light ground was introduced, or rather revived. Contemporaneously with the polychrome ware, the older style of vase-painting had continued to exist, and now came to the front in a perfected form. The Cretan invention of lustrous glaze-paint now finally ousted the older style of matt colour, and with the use of brown colour on the buff-slip of the vase the principle of dark-upon-light decoration finally defeated that of light-upon-dark which had been inherited from Neolithic days. The designs of the vases of the

First and Second Late Minoan periods (the "Great Palace style" of Knossos), whether the motives are developments of the spiral, or are derived from plants, and from the rocks and seaweed and marine creatures, cuttle-fish, nautili, and the rest, which were so well known to a seafaring people, or from the wall-paintings of the palace itself, are always good, and fully worthy of the civilization that could produce the architecture of Knossos and Phaistos and the splendid metal-work which the Keftiu bore as "tribute" to Egypt.

The Knossian palace was wholly remodelled at the end of the Middle Minoan period, and apparently largely altered and enlarged in the Late Minoan period. As it stands to-day, with its extraordinary complex of halls, staircases, and chambers descending the slope towards the Kairatos, and its outlying buildings such as the "Royal Villa" below it to the north and the "Western House" higher up the hill to the west, it is a monument of the phenomenal growth of Cretan civilization during the few centuries that had elapsed since the beginning of the Middle Minoan period, when the Cretans first emerged from barbarism. This palace is, one would say a modern building. It is far more "modern" than any Greek building of the Classical period, or than anything in Italy before the Augustan age. One of its most modern features is the elaborate system of sanitary drainage with which it is provided, a thing unparalleled till Roman days, and since then till the nineteenth century. In comparison with this wonderful building the palaces of Egyptian.Pharaohs were but elaborate hovels of painted mud. Only the sculptured corridors of Ashurbanipal's Nineveh probably surpassed it in splendour; but Assyrian splendour was after all as old, cold, and lifeless as that of Egyptian temples, while Knossos seems to be eloquent of the teeming life and energy of a young and beauty-loving people for the first time feeling its creative power and exulting with the pure joie de vivre.

No Byzantine emperor and his consort dwelt here alone within the royal palace fenced off even from the nobles by armed guards. No Assyrian monarch paced, followed by eunuchs, solitary here those corridors ornamented with bas-reliefs depicting nothing but his own triumphs in war and the chase and the meaningless, staring visages of his gods. No inhuman Egyptian Pharaoh or Japanese Mikado received here the worship due to a god from prostrate ministers and retainers. The halls of Knossos were inhabited by a crowd of courtiers and retainers, men and women both, who surrounded the king, and lived with him to enjoy the beauties and good things of life. The Minoan Court must have resembled the joyous surroundings of an European prince of the thirteenth and fourteenth centuries, with a touch here and there of the Tuileries under the Second Empire. From the fragments of the paintings, often bizarre and crude in execution, often weirdly powerful in design and framed in decorative borders of every conceivable form and colour, which covered the walls of the palace-corridors, we see what these people looked like. We see the women depicted as often as, if not more often than, the men, whereas in Assyria they never appear at all. Probably in Minoan Crete women played a greater part than they did even in Egypt, and it may eventually appear that religious matters, perhaps even the government of the State itself as well, were largely controlled by women. It is certain that they must have lived on a footing of greater equality with the men than in any other ancient civilization, and we see in the frescoes of Knossos conclusive indications of an open and easy association of men and women, corresponding to our idea of "Society," at the Minoan Court unparalleled till our own day.

The Minoan artists represented the women as white, the men as red in colour, thus following the same convention as the Egyptians. True to their bizarre summary ways, a crowd of men and women is sometimes shewn by the crude method of outlining merely the heads of a number of men on a red background, and those of a number of women on a white one. But for this distinction in the background it would be impossible to say whether the heads are those of men or women, since the Minoan courtiers were clean-shaved and wore their hair as long and as elaborately dressed as did the women. In the scenes of bull-fighting which often occur, and in which women are represented as taking part, one can only distinguish the girls from the boys by their colour: the same flying hair, of the same length, is common to both sexes.

In some frescoes we see the ladies of Minos' Court depicted sitting at the windows of the palace, openly and unveiled. Their dress is extraordinarily modern in appearance: it is decollete, with bare necks and arms, the breasts covered apparently with gold or silver guards reproducing their outline, their waists pinched in, and, below, ample skirts with parallel rows of flounces, resembling nothing so much as the crinolines of the mid-nineteenth century. Anything more unlike our usual conception of "Greek dress" it is impossible to conceive. At an earlier period (Middle Minoan I) we find the women in similar skirts, but with high ruff-like collars and horned headdresses which may or may not be their hair. The coiffure of the Late Minoan ladies of Knossos, with its knots and sidecurls, closely resembles that of the ladies of the Court of Charles II. On their heads they wear tiaras or head-bands: a goddess is represented with an extraordinary high hat.

The dress of the men was simple, consisting merely of a waist-cloth over which was worn a short kilt, often arranged so as to give the appearance of a pair of bathing-drawers or boating "shorts." This simple costume was ornamented in the usual way with spiral and other designs in bright colour, thus differing from the related Egyptian waist-cloth, which was always pure white: bright colours in costume were regarded by the Egyptians as barbaric. The significance of this costume as indicating the Southern and specifically African origin of the Minoans has already been pointed out: even the women's dress is nothing but a developed kilt. As in Egypt, the upper part of the men's bodies was nude but for a necklace, except when, on occasions of ceremony, and doubtless often by older men, a gala-robe was donned.

Even in war, no body-panoply was put on. This was an invention of the Northerners, in all probability. For the Minoan, his great 8-shaped shield was sufficient protection for his body. A helmet, probably of leather, was, however, often worn in gladiatorial combats as well as in war. This helmet has cheek-pieces and is very Roman in appearance. Sometimes it had a crest, and one appears in a scene of combat on a gold ring found at Mycenae. The most usual weapon was a straight thin sword meant for thrusting: often ornamented with designs in inlaid metals.

Ordinarily, no headgear was worn by the men, but a conical cap is sometimes represented, and a prince or god at Knossos wears a mighty head-dress of feathers.

The characteristic long hair of the men, which has already been mentioned, was apparently sometimes coiled up on the top of the head, but, even when the wearer was engaged or about to engage in active work, it was ordinarily worn hanging down the back to the waist or below it, usually loose, sometimes in plaits or curls. On the head fantastic knots or curls, like those of the women, were often worn — the "horns" of which Paris was so proud. This coiffure was as characteristic of the Bronze Age Cretans as was the waist-cloth, and is represented accurately even to the small detail of the curls on the top of the head by the Egyptian artists of the tomb of Rekhmara.

Characteristic also of the Minoan men's dress were the high boots which were worn in Crete then as now, and were also faithfully represented by the Egyptian as well as by the Minoan artists. Practically the same boot was worn by the Hittites.

Such was the remarkable outward appearance of the men and women of Knossos, which in the case of the men was accurately reproduced by the Egyptian painters of the Keftiu of the reign of Thothmes III; an appearance as distinctive and as characteristic of racial custom as the shaven heads, wigs, and white garments of the Egyptians, or the oiled locks, beards, and parti-coloured robes of the Semites, their contemporaries.

From the pictures we see that the Minoans were a brunet race resembling the modern Italians more than any other people, with ruddy skins, dark brown to black hair, and "Caucasian" features. One of the first representations of them that we have is the famous wall-painting of the "Cupbearer", one of the first Knossian discoveries of Mr. Evans, and one which did more than aught else to direct general attention to the new finds in Crete.

Frescoes of this kind were the regular decoration of the Cretan palace-walls. Relief sculpture in stone, like sculpture of the round, on a large scale was rarely used by the Cretan decorators, though its place was taken to some extent by coloured reliefs in hard stucco.

Inscriptions were not used to decorate the walls in the Egyptian and Assyrian manner. No signs appear by the side of the pictures, and this gives us the idea that the Minoans dissociated their script from their art as the Egyptians never did. It is sometimes difficult in Egypt to know where inscription ends and pure picture begins: the inscriptions are themselves pictures, the pictures have meanings. But by the Cretans of the Late Minoan period the cursive writing that had developed out of the older signary of the seal-stones was confined to the clay tablets, of which great stores have been found at Knossos, and some at Phaistos and elsewhere. These were, apparently, but lists and accounts of objects preserved in the palace-magazines, with perhaps a letter or two among them: but we cannot read them. Their picture-signs and those on the seals have, however, told us much concerning the culture of the Minoans that we might not otherwise have known. Thus we know that they possessed chariots at this time (the sixteenth and fifteenth centuries B.C.) and also horses: on a seal-impression we have a picture of a great war-horse, with proudly arched neck, being carried in a ship (which is, by the way, much smaller, proportionally, than the horse). This may represent a scene of actual importation of a horse, probably from Egypt. The shapes of weapons and vases sketched on the tablets, though rough, are useful as an aid to archaeology.

In material civilization the Minoan Cretans were at least as highly developed as the Egyptians or Mesopotamians, in some ways more highly developed, at any rate as regards the amenities of life. Their sense of beauty and mental freedom seem to have been untrammelled by Semitic asceticism or Egyptian religious conventionality. They lived, cruelly perhaps, and possibly (according to our ideas) wickedly, but certainly beautifully.

Of their religious ideas we know but little. In later Greek religion there seems to be a stratum, underlying the Indo-European mythology which the Aryan Greeks brought with them, and more especially represented in Crete, which probably is the remnant of the old Aegean religion: a stratum of minor deities of woods and streams and stones and of the ocean, of huntress-goddesses and sun-warriors, Dryads, Satyrs, and Fauns, Naiads and Nereids and Old Men of the Sea, whom we find on many a Minoan seal-intaglio. The water-demon with the head of an animal is a familiar appearance there, and Artemis often occurs. It is to the seals that we must look for representations of the deities, as the Minoans seem to have made no large figures of them. In official religion a pillar with a horned altar before it represented the devotion of the State: individuals pictured the gods on their seals or venerated small and rude household images of them. From the seals we gather a universal worship of a supreme female goddess, the Rhea of later religion, who is accompanied sometimes by a youthful male deity. The parallel with the Anatolian religion of Kybele and Attis is obvious, and argues a not distant ethnic connexion with Asia Minor and the "Hittites." The goddess appears in many forms; in one of the most peculiar she brandishes serpents. The god was no doubt in later days identified with Zeus; his symbol was the Double Axe which is so constantly found as a votive object.

Of their funerary religion we know least, but have evidence that the ceremonies at the grave were, if not connected in their origin with certain Nilotic beliefs, certainly influenced by Egyptian rites. In the internal arrangements of the tombs we find, on the other hand, remarkable resemblance to Etruscan funerary customs, a fact that is of great interest in view of a possible racial connexion between the Aegeans and the

Etruscans. Various forms of tomb were used in the Late Minoan Age, and the dead were usually placed in pottery coffins ox larnakes, sometimes in baths. The tombs are without mural decoration of any kind.

Of the frescoes with which, on the contrary, the houses of the living were adorned, and of the art of the seal-engravers, we have already spoken. The magazines and chambers of the palaces and towns at Knossos, Phaistos, Agia Triada, Gournia, Pseira, Palaikastro, and Zakro, have yielded to us the vases and other objects of metal, stone, and pottery which are to be seen in the Museum of Candia, and give us our knowledge of the art of this age. The "small art" is often much finer than the "great art" of the frescoes and stucco-reliefs: stone sculpture in relief or in the round we can hardly mention, as it was never developed to any extent. This draws our attention to the limitations of Minoan art. Probably among the finest pieces of small sculpture in the world are the two steatite vases (of the First Late Minoan period) from Agia Triada, on one of which we see a procession of drunken roistering peasants with agricultural implements, and on the other the reception or dismissal of a warrior with his followers by a king or prince. The first is a masterpiece of relief, resembling nothing so much as the best Egyptian reliefs of the reigns of Amenhetep III and Akhenaten, while the second is full of Greek reticence and sense of proportion. But the figures of gladiators on the larger "Boxer" vase of the same period, also from Agia Triada, are clumsy, as also, in comparison, are the famous reliefs on the gold cups of Vaphio, also of the same date. The steatite cups are imitations of gold repousse work, and herein we see why the Cretan sculptors never became sculptors on the great scale. They were the disciples and imitators of the toreutic artists, and never became independent of them. The example of Egypt never moved them to great sculpture, and it is probable that they would have seen no beauty in the cold lifelessness of Egyptian colossi, magnificent though they might have deemed them. To them the little ivory leapers from Knossos were the highest expression of the art of sculpture in the round; size had no charm for them The love of life and beauty dominated the Cretan artists; they were bound by no trammels of convention, and to this was due the inequality of their work. Side by side, more especially in the domain of wall and vase painting, we see the most childish and the most perfect art. Such inconsistency would have been impossible in rigidly formal Egypt; and even when Akhenaten allowed his artists to break the chain of convention and imitate the freedom of their Cretan brethren, he would never have allowed them to produce such crude works as the Cretan princes often accepted without demur from their subjects. And, indeed, the highly trained hands of the Egyptian craftsman, an artist rather from education than in spirit, would have been incapable of such unequal work. The Cretan, however. a true artist, did what pleased him.

The wall-paintings exercised considerable influence on the decoration of pottery in the Second Minoan Period, the "Great Palace" period, to which we have now come. Architectonic motives, copied from the representations of buildings in frescoes, are characteristic of the ceramic art of this time. This fact betrays a certain degeneration in the ideas of the vase-painter, and in other ways we see that the art of the "Great Palace" period was somewhat vulgarized, and even rococo. And indeed degeneracy was fast coming. The rococo period, which seems to have been a local peculiarity of Knossos, lasted but a century, the period which in Egypt elapsed between the reigns of Thothmes III and Amenhetep in (about 1500-1400 B.C.). In the reign of Akhenaten (about 1380) the Aegean vase-fragments found at Tell el-Amarna are already exclusively of the Third Late Minoan style, which in Crete, elsewhere than at Knossos, and on the mainland, had developed out of the First. The long age of decadence now begins, in which the great art and culture of Crete slowly declined to their fall.

5. Crete and Greece

The reason for this decline is probably to be found in the results of the northward expansion of the Cretan culture which, at first slow, had, during the great age of Minoan power, developed greatly, and was probably accompanied by an assertion of temporal as well as spiritual control, which in the end brought about its own inevitable defeat and the wreck of Cretan civilization. Similar results are not always due to similar causes, but there is enough similarity between the contemporary decadence of both Egypt and Crete for us to predicate much the same cause in Crete as in Egypt, the empire-making spirit, which, in its inception and triumph a sign of national energy, brings with it inevitable national exhaustion. That in the end Egypt survived when Crete died is due to the fact that Egypt, though she was temporarily conquered by the Assyrians, was never overrun in her exhaustion by the virile tribes of the North, who in Greece could settle and survive, while in Egypt, had they ever reached her (as the Cimmerians and Scythians nearly did), they would soon have died out and left even a less lasting mark than did the Hyksos.

Contemporary written evidence of the existence of a Cretan empire in Greece we have none, of course; but the tradition of the thalassocracy of Minos is well borne out by archaeological results.

We have seen that in its earliest days the Aegean culture (reckoning the Cycladic and Cretan civilizations as one) reached the northern ends of the Aegean, and may have penetrated to the Danube valley. By way, too, of the Black Sea its influence may have reached Bessarabia and Southern Russia, and here, in the North, arose a beautiful ceramic art, owing its inspiration to early Aegean models, belonging to a people which never reached the age of metal at all, but seems to have perished out of the land while still stone-using, leaving no heirs. These Mediterraneans, as we believe them to be, had spread too far from their base. They perished of pure inappropriateness to their environment, assisted, perhaps, by the more virile Indo-European tribes, who by this time must have made their way into Europe from Siberia.

In Asia Minor Aegean culture could not make much headway. The coast-land had its own primitive civilization, akin, no doubt, to that of the Aegean, but distinct from it, with a very different idea of ceramic art, and one which remained uninfluenced by Aegean ideas till near the end of the Bronze Age. The Peloponnese, however, lay open to Aegean influence, and it was here and in Northern Greece that this influence first translated itself, probably, into actual Aegean domination, through the energy of the Cretan thalassocrats. In the Middle Minoan period, the first great age of Knossos and Phaistos, the art of the Cyclades, at first ahead of that of Crete, gradually approximates more and more to Cretan styles, and actual Cretan works of art begin to be imported. There is no difference, also, between the script of Crete and that of Melos. Cretan domination at this period of the obsidian and marble-yielding islands is probable enough. And thence it spread to the mainland, probably in the Middle Minoan period, when the Cretan civilization suddenly expanded to its full efflorescence.

The antiquities found on the mainland of Greece which, before the Cretan discoveries, we called "Mycenaean," are the products of the same culture as the "Minoan" antiquities of Crete. Many of them are evidently actual importations from Crete or the Cyclades; most, if they were made in Greece, were made in the Cretan style, while some perhaps shew evidence of Cycladic rather than Cretan influence. The most ancient of these objects of Aegean art found in Greece itself are no older than the Third Middle Minoan period. These are sherds found in considerable quantity at Tiryns during the recent German excavations. To "Late Minoan I" belong the contents of the shaft-graves on the Acropolis of Mycenae and of the tholoi or "beehive-tombs" at Kakovatos (Old Pylos) in Messenia; the famous cups of Vaphio also evidently belong to this period. The objects from Kakovatos are of the later period of the First Late Minoan period, when the peculiarly Knossian style which we call the "Second Late Minoan" was just beginning to appear. The newly discovered frescoes of a boar-hunt, from Tiryns, are, again, of the First Late period. It is evident that the foundations of the "Mycenaean" culture which we find in the Peloponnese in the First Late Minoan period must have been laid during the preceding age, and it is to that time, the later Middle Minoan period, that we must ascribe the first Cretan colonies in Greece.

It is probable that at that time the Aegeans had not confined their colonies to the Peloponnese, but had also advanced from the Saronic Gulf and the Euripus into Boeotia, since we find at Orchomenos the famous and splendid "beehive-tomb" called the "Treasury of Minyas," which is of the same type as the "Treasuries of Atreus and Klytaimnestra" at Mycenae, and the tholoi of Kakovatos. The last are of the First Late Minoan period, and it is to the same age that the Orchomenos tholos may also be assigned, and perhaps those of Mycenae as well. As one goes backwards in the study of Cretan civilization and its beginnings, one finds that architecture, decadent in the "Second Late Minoan" period, improves fast till it reaches its apogee in the Second Middle Minoan period: the better the style of architecture of a building the more it may be held to be older than the Second Late Minoan period, much more may it be held to be older than the Third, the decadent period of Aegean art. So this criterion, as well as the definite antiquities found at Kakovatos, dates the great beehive-tombs to the First Late Minoan period. And this brings Cretans to Boeotia, as well as to the Peloponnese, in the preceding age; for such a tomb as the "Treasury of Minyas" would not have been built for a prince whose family had not been firmly established in its possession of the land for a considerable period. So splendid a building implies secure possession. Further, ordinary tombs of the I-II Later Minoan period have lately been discovered at Boeotian Thebes.

It may be asked: why should these Cretan monuments and relics not argue, not Cretan invaders and colonizers at all, but merely the peaceful adoption of the creations of the more civilized Cretans by the native Greek princes? Here legend speaks, and tells us with no uncertain voice that the bringers of civilization to Greece came from across the sea. It must be remembered that we know little of any civilization in the Peloponnese before the Aegean culture appeared there in its "First Late Minoan" stage, while in the North, though a native culture existed, it was of low type, and had hardly emerged from the Stone Age. The coming of the Aegeans was in truth the first bringing of civilization to Greece.

Now the chief centres in which the oldest Cretan or Aegean antiquities in Greece have been discovered — Mycenae, Orchomenos, Lakonia, and Pylos — are all connected in legend with the heroic houses who ruled Greece in the days before the Trojan War. And these houses are either descended from foreign immigrants, or owe much of their power to the help of foreigners. These foreigners in one case reach Greece by the Gulf of Nauplia, the most obvious haven for Aegean ships and most obvious place for the earliest landing of Cretan conquerors coming from the Cyclades. Tiryns, the fortress at the head of the Gulf, was built for Proitos by the Kyklopes from Lycia; in them we see the doubles of the wondrous artificers, the Daedalids and Telchines of Crete. To the valley of the Inachos came Io and Epaphos, in whose story we should perhaps, for Egypt, read Crete. On the Saronic Gulf we have a definite tradition of Cretan overlordship, which demanded a yearly tribute of youths and maidens for the bull-demon of Knossos, an overlordship overthrown by the great folk-hero of Athens, Theseus. And when we come to Boeotia, is it not probable that the builders of the great tomb at Orchomenos were the legendary Minyae, who brought civilization to Boeotia, and were the first to drain Lake Kopais by means of the tunnels through the northern hill-wall to the Euripus? The similarity of the name of Minyas, "son of Chryses" the Golden, to the Cretan royal name Minos may, in spite of the difference in quantity, mean a real connexion. Athamas, Phlegyas, and Minyas, the first kings of Orchomenos, may represent the first Cretan princes who settled among the Neolithic Boeotians, and brought Minoan culture into the land. And then the "Phoenician" Cadmeans of Thebes, whose Phoenician origin seems so inexplicable and improbable, may, in spite of the fact that in legend they are often the foes of the Minyae, be in reality Cretans.

In Thessaly we find Minyae at Iolkos, at the head of the Gulf of Volo, another gulf that points southwards towards the Cyclades, and is a probable point for a Minoan landing. The Nelidae of Pylos (Kakovatos) in the Peloponnese, which, as we have seen, was an early centre of Minoan colonization, were said to be Minyae from Iolkos, though they may just as well have come direct from Crete. For in Thessaly the extant Minoan remains are later than at Thebes or Orchomenos. The tholoi of Volo and Dimini seem to be of the Third Late Minoan period, and we have no proof of Minoan connexion before then.

In the Peloponnese, besides Pylos, we find traces of the Minoans in the Eurotas valley in the splendid golden cups from the tomb at Vaphio, which are probably of the First Late Minoan period, judging from their style. And here Leleges (Carians) were said to have lived in early times. The shore of the Gulf of Lakonia is again a probable place for Cretan occupation.

In the Peloponnese the Minoans must have established themselves during the Middle Minoan age; possibly they reached Boeotia a little later, but as to this we have no evidence. But while in the Peloponnese they probably found an Aegean population akin to themselves, this was by no means the case in Northern Greece. There we have to explain a phenomenon, recently discovered, which to a great extent bears out the view, lately published by Prof. Dorpfeld, that there were from the first two races in Greece, a Southern (the Aegeans or "Karians," as he calls them), and a Northern, who were the Aryan Achaians of history. Excavations recently carried on in Boeotia and in Thessaly have shewn us that there existed there a race of primitive Neolithic culture, which remained stone-using down to the Third Late Minoan period. Their pottery was peculiar, and in its scheme of ornament quite different from that of the Aegeans. The characteristic curved lines, spirals, and natural forms of the Aegean ceramic decoration are replaced by purely geometric designs unknown at any period to the Aegeans. But at the same time some evidence of Aegean influence is to be seen in them in the shape of clumsy attempts to reproduce spirals, which appear quite out of place and exotic amid their geometric surroundings; and the polychromy which characterises them may be due to imitation of the Cretan polychromy of the Middle Minoan period. In Boeotia there is evidence in a single Cycladic vase, found in a Neolithic grave at Chaironeia, of trade with the Aegeans at the end of the preceding age.

That the Boeotians continued stone-users down to the Third Late Minoan period, as the Thessalians certainly did, seems improbable, in view of the fact that among them the Cretan art and architecture of the grand period had been established during the First Late Minoan age. In this fact we see evidence of Cretan princes (Minyae and Cadmeans?), or at least native chiefs, employing Cretan architects and artists, ruling for a space over more barbarous subjects of a different race. And we see the same thing in Thessaly later on. It was only when in the period of its decadence Cretan art had become generally diffused over the Aegean area, and even at Troy temporarily dispossessed the native Trojan art, that Thessaly became Aegeanized. And this was probably also only for a time. For it seems by no means impossible that the Northern geometric art of the "Dipylon" period, which is usually associated with the invading Achaians or Dorians (more generally with the latter), is the descendant of the earlier geometric art of the Neolithic Thessalians, Phocians, and Boeotians. There is no doubt that the "Geometric" art of Greece is the art of the oldest Aryan Greeks, from the tenth to the eighth centuries, or at any rate as late as the middle of the eighth century. And it seems reasonable to suppose that it was a renascence of the older native art of Northern Greece in the midst of which Cretan art made but a temporary stay, leaving as its chief bequest the technical methods of the Minoan ceramic artists, which were taken on by the "Geometric" potters, while they kept to their own non-Aegean style of ornament.

This view is confirmed by a further discovery in Thessaly. Characteristic of the later period of the Third Late Minoan age is the building of palaces in a style quite different from that which had been in vogue during the great Minoan age in Crete. We find them at Mycenae, at Tiryns, and perhaps in Crete, at Agia Triada. These buildings were much simpler in plan than the older Cretan palaces, and in their main arrangements are identical with the typical Achaian chief's house as described in the Homeric poems. They mark a set of ideas in architecture as distinct from those of the Minoan Cretans as do the earlier and later Geometric ceramics of Northern Greece. They are obviously an introduction from the North, to whose colder climate they are suited, while the Cretan palaces are more appropriate to the South. Now, in Thessaly have been found in the chiefs' houses of the Neolithic people the prototypes of these "Achaian" palaces. The arrangements of these Neolithic Northern houses are the same, on a smaller scale, as those of the "Achaian" palaces of Mycenae, Tiryns, and Crete. In these last the architectural skill handed down from the Minoan culture has been used with effect; that is the sole difference.

We see, then, that in later times, first the North-Greek type of house found among the Neolithic Thessalians, then later the North-Greek style of pottery found among the Neolithic people of the North, was adopted in the South. And this change was contemporary with the partial substitution of burning for inhumation in the disposal of the dead, with the first adoption of iron to replace bronze for weapons and tools, and finally with the coming of the Aryan Greeks into the Aegean and the Peloponnese.

To the introduction of iron (from the Danube-valley) and of cremation we shall return later. At present, we are only concerned to shew that the Aryan Greeks who introduced them, and the "geometric" pottery into the South, were probably the descendants of the Neolithic Northern tribes among whom the Minoan culture had been introduced during the Late Minoan age. And this conclusion seems not impossible from the facts adduced above.

The Neolithic Northerners may then have been the ancestors of some of the Hellenes, whom all tradition brings from Thessaly. They were probably Indo-Europeans, with their own undeveloped culture, which the non-Aryan culture of Crete and the Aegean was only able to displace temporarily after many centuries of contact, when it was itself decadent.

The Cretan domination was unable to affect the native culture, at any rate in Thessaly, more than temporarily. It brought the Northerners the knowledge of bronze, and taught them how to build, but the peculiar artistic ideas of the conquered held true, and when the civilization of their conquerors declined, and the conquered in their turn became the conquerors, the Hellenic (Achaian) house came South with the Hellenes or Achaians even to Crete itself, and later on, the Northern Geometric pottery followed.

The end of the Second Late Minoan period is marked by a catastrophe, the destruction of Knossos. The royal palace-city had been destroyed before, and we see from the small provincial towns of Gournia and Pseira, excavated by American explorers, that fire and sword were not uncommonly the fate of Aegean settlements in the Minoan age. But the destruction of Knossos was complete, its site was deserted, and its great art disappeared, to be succeeded by the far inferior productions of the Third Late Minoan age, which were not specifically Cretan, but rather the common property of Greece. This marks the difference between the ceramic styles of the First and Second and the Third Late Minoan periods. That of the earlier period is Cretan, that of the later may be only indirectly of Cretan origin. It appears suddenly when the "Great Palace" ceramic style as suddenly disappears, about 1400 B.C. Its motives of decoration are derived from those of the Cretan potters, but its direct continuity with the Cretan wares is not obvious. There is a gap, though not one of time, between them, and this may be accounted for by supposing that the Third Late Minoan style of pottery is in reality "Mycenaean," as it used to be called, that it is, in fact, a style that arose in the Peloponnese and the islands, developed on Cretan models by the Minoan conquerors of Continental Greece and the Aegean.

And the coming of this pottery to Crete may tell us who the conquerors were who destroyed Knossos and brought the Minoan empire to an end. They were, it may be, the descendants of those Cretans who had gone forth to colonize Pylos, Mycenae, and Orchomenos, and had sent the yearly tribute of Athenian youth to be sacrificed to the deity of Knossos, And with them marched their subjects, the Achaeans or Danaoi of the North.

Did the Minoans simply submit to their conquerors, or did they seek refuge in another land? The coming of the Cadmeans to Boeotia ought, we think, to be assigned to an earlier period, and the descendants of the Cadmeans probably took part in the destruction of Knossos. The legends of the expedition of Minos to Sicily against Kokalos, King of Kamikos, and his death, of the second expedition to avenge his death, and of the Cretan colonization of Hyria in Italy, may have arisen from a confusion of an actual attempt of the Knossian thalassocrats to wage war in Sicily, and an actual colonization in Italy of dispossessed Minoans after the fall of Knossos, A more definite answer to our question may perhaps be found in the history of the civilization of Cyprus. The Bronze Age culture of Cyprus pursued a path of its own, producing a peculiar style of art, as exemplified in its pottery, related rather to that of Asia Minor than that of the Aegean, till, suddenly, the Cretan culture appears in its midst. And the earliest Cretan art found in Cyprus, as we see it in certain of the remains discovered at Enkomi, Curium, and Hala Sultan Tekke, are of the Second and Third Late Minoan periods, or at any rate of the beginning of the Third. Of the First style (only a century older) but a few examples have been found; of the Middle Minoan a single sherd. With these remains were found Egyptian objects which are of one period only, the end of the XVIIIth Dynasty, that is to say the very time of the destruction of Knossos. Is it too rash to suppose that the Cretan colony in Cyprus, which appears so suddenly at this time, with no previous history behind it, was a colony of fugitives from Crete, who, by virtue of their superior culture, easily and soon won for themselves a dominant position amid the lethargic eastern islanders? These seem to have submitted at once to the conquerors, as we find their pottery placed side by side with that of the new-comers in the same sepulchres.

Henceforward a peculiar form of decadent Minoan culture, a Cyprian version of "Late Minoan III," lived on in Cyprus, and of it we have splendid relics in the later remains from Enkomi, now, with those of the period of the conquest, in the British Museum. The later vases shew an important modification of Minoan traditions in that the human form is constantly depicted on them (in Crete it had never occurred), and their forms shew the strong Northern influence of the later "Third Late Minoan" style in Greece.

The "Third Late Minoan" period must be the period of the political hegemony of the kings of Mycenae and the Argolid in Greece, to which the Homeric poets ascribed the ancient glories of the heroic civilization of Greece. It was they who destroyed Knossos and to whom the sceptre of Minos passed. Whether the poets were right in calling them "Achaians" and "Danaoi" we do not know. Legend brought Pelops, the founder of the house of Agamemnon, from Asia Minor, and it is by no means impossible that some Anatolian invasion may not have established rulers of Anatolian (Hittite) origin in Greece. There is nothing Achaian about the Pelopids. The Homeric poets were themselves Achaians, and may well have made their heroes Achaians. And, as we shall see, it is by no means impossible that the whole poetical description of the Peloponnesian princes as Achaians was a mistake, due to a confusion of the Thessalian Argos, where Achaians certainly lived, with the Peloponnesian Argos. There may never have been any Achaians in the Peloponnese till, much later, the great invasion of the Thesprotian tribes from beyond Pindus, of which Herodotus speaks, drove the Achaians and the later Boeotians and Dorians out of Thessaly, and resulted in the expulsion of the Minyae from Boeotia and the settlement of the Pelasgi in Attica. It was only then that the Achaians possessed themselves of the Peloponnese, and succeeded to the heritage of the older Mycenaean chiefs, to lose it after a short time to the Dorians. The use of the word "Achaians" to describe the Mycenaeans of the Pelopid dynasty is therefore to be deprecated; they may more probably have been Ionians, for the Achaians took the north coast of the Peloponnese from its inhabitants, who were Ionians. And the Ionians were certainly less purely Hellenic in race than the other Greeks, and were probably just such a mixture of Indo-European (Greek) and Aegean elements as the "Mycenaeans" of the Third Late Minoan period probably were, a mixture of Achaians (if one likes) with Aegeans, but not pure Achaians.

6. The Period of the Invasions

The great Thessalian or Thesprotian invasion, which probably took place in the thirteenth century B.C., and followed that of the Boeotians, had far-reaching effects. By it an overwhelming Aryan and iron-using population was first brought into Greece. The earlier Achaian (?) tribes of Aryans in Thessaly, who had perhaps lived there from time immemorial, and had probably already infiltrated southwards to form the mixed Ionian population about the Isthmus, were scattered, only a small portion of the nation remaining in its original home, while of the rest part conquered the South and another part emigrated across the sea to the Phrygian coast. Of this emigration to Asia the first event must have been the war of Troy, originally, as we shall see, perhaps an expedition of Thessalian Achaians and Thessalian Argives, not of Peloponnesians at all. The Boeotian and Achaian invasion of the South scattered the Minyae, Pelasgians, and Ionians. The remnant of the Minyae emigrated to Lemnos, the Pelasgi and Ionians were concentrated in Attica and another body of Ionians in the later Achaia, while the Southern Achaeans pressed forward into the Peloponnese. A mixed body of Peloponnesians, Ionians, Kythnians, Arcadians, Ionians, and Laconians took ship across the sea and appeared in the midst of the probably non-Greek Minoan colonists of Cyprus, who had established themselves there some two centuries before. These second colonists from Greece brought with them a Peloponnesian dialect of Greek, which henceforth became the language of the island. With the same movement must be associated the immigration into Pisidia of the Pamphylians, a similar "mixed multitude," and the colonization of the Aleian plain in Cilicia by Mopsos and his men, who occupied the cities of Mallos and Tarsus. Further, with the same migration must be associated the great wandering of the Philistines and their allies from Crete, driven out probably by Achaians, who overran Palestine and were finally brought to a stop by Rameses III on the borders of Egypt. The traditional date of the Trojan War, as given by the Parian Chronicle, 1194-1184 B.C., accords remarkably with the known date of the war of Rameses III with the Philistines, about 1190 B.C.

The indications of archaeology and of legend agree marvellously well with those of the Egyptian records in making the Third Late Minoan period one of incessant disturbance, very different from the comparative peace of the great Minoan days. The whole basin of the Eastern Mediterranean seems to have been a seething turmoil of migrations, expulsions, wars, and piracies, started first by the Mycenaean (Achaian) conquest of Crete, and then intensified by the constant impulse of the Northern iron-users into Greece. "The Isles were restless: disturbed among themselves," say the Egyptian chroniclers, who, as we shall see, record at least two distinct attacks upon Egypt by the "Peoples of the Sea" in the thirteenth and twelfth centuries. Some of these tribes, Lukki or Luka (Lycians), the Danuna, who were Greeks, while others, the Shardina and Shakalsha, may have been Italians or from Asia Minor, are already found hovering on the Asiatic coasts and taking service in the wars of Palestine as early as the time of the Tell el-Amarna letters (c. 1370 B.C.), very shortly after the destruction of Knossos and the Keftian power.

Already the first wave of disturbance had reached the coast of Asia, and the sea-tribes were endeavouring to possess themselves of strongholds on the Palestinian coast from which to carry on their piracies. The Danuna had apparently already succeeded in doing this, and others soon followed. For three centuries these outposts of Greek pirates maintained themselves, and at the end of the XXth Dynasty we find the town of Dor still occupied by the Aegean Tjakarai, whom we shall soon mention.

None of the tribes who made war on Rameses II (c. 1295 B.C.) as subject-allies of the Hittites were Aegeans, all being natives of Asia Minor. The westernmost of them, the Dardenui or Dardanians and the Masa or Mysians, were (if correctly so identified), though dwellers by the Aegean, probably not included within the circle of Aegean civilization, as, owing to the domination of the Hittites as far as the Aegean, the Minoan culture had never been able to effect any foothold on the coast of Asia Minor. The Luka or Lycians, who had already appeared a century before as sea-rovers, and had then attacked Alashiya and the coast of the Egyptian Delta, were the only seafaring tribe among them, and the only one which was probably affected at all by Aegean influence. But the Akaiwasha who directly attacked Egypt from, the sea, in company with Shardina and Shakalsha and another tribe, the Tursha, together with a horde of the restless Libyans, in the reign of Meneptah, were probably Greeks. If we regard the termination of their name as a "Mediterranean" ethnic suffix akin to the Lycian -azi or -aza, we can fairly regard these Akaiwasha as the first representatives in history of the Achaians. The date of their expedition is about 1230 B.C.

This date agrees very well with the probable time of their wanderings after the conquest of Thessaly by the Thesprotians, and we can regard the Akaiwasha ravagers of the Egyptians as a body of Achaian warriors of the same kind as those who laid siege to Troy and founded the colonies of Aeolis at this same period. The Tursha may very well be Tyrsenians, Turs(c)i, whose sea-migration from Asia Minor to Italy is probably to be placed about this time.

The main body of the horde which passed through Asia Minor and Palestine to the borders of Egypt in the reign of Rameses III (c. 1196 B.C.) seems to have come from Greece. "Their main strength," says the inscription recording this great event, "was Pulesatha (Pulesti), Tjakarai, Danauna, and Uashksha." All these tribes were probably Aegeans, and one was certainly, two were probably, of Cretan origin. For the Pulesti were the Philistines, whom both Hebrew and Greek traditions bring from Caphtor (Keftiu) or Crete to Palestine, and, this being certain, the identity of the Uashasha with the Cretan Axians is rendered highly probable, while the possibility that the Tjakarai came from the eastern end of Crete, where the place-name Zakro still exists, is by no means to be dismissed lightly. There are evidently dispossessed Cretans, who migrated both by land and sea from Lycia, probably in alliance with a horde of western Anatolians, perhaps displaced by the Phrygian invasion, which must have taken place about this time, along the Asiatic coast, "no land standing before them, beginning from Kheta and Alashiya." The western dominion of the Hittites of Khatti bowed before this irresistible storm, while Alashiya, the coast-land of Cilicia (and N. Phoenicia?), fell an easy prey. The aim of the Pulesti and their allies was no doubt to reach the rich land of Palestine, with the coast of which they had been familiar for centuries; and they passed on thither. Rameses III prevented them from going farther, and raiding the Egyptian Delta, which they no doubt also intended to do, though they could never have hoped to settle there permanently. A permanent occupation of Palestine was, however, evidently intended, as they came with women, children, and all their belongings. And they succeeded in effecting their aim: the Egyptians, though they defeated them, could do no more than bring the great migratory mass to a standstill, and left them in occupation of the Shephelah, exacting, perhaps, some sort of recognition of Egyptian overlordship, to which it is not probable that the Philistines paid very much attention. The transplanted Aegeans imposed a powerful yoke on Canaan, which lasted till, nearly two centuries later, they had become weakened by all the unfavourable conditions of their existence as a foreign garrison in a strange land, and had begun to be absorbed by the conquered Semites. Then the Israelitish tribes, whom at first they had driven into the hills, and whose budding civilization they had destroyed, gathered themselves together into a national kingdom, which forced the foreigners back towards the sea-coast and finally destroyed their separate existence. Three centuries after their first coming the separate nationality of the Philistines had entirely disappeared, and of their language nothing but a few personal names survived in use in Philistia. The parallel to the extinction of the Danish language and nationality of the Northmen in Normandy two hundred years after Rollo's conquest is curiously exact. So history always repeats itself when conditions are similar.

Of their presence many traces have been found in the shape of Aegean pottery of debased "Late Minoan III" style, such as we should expect to find Cretans using in the twelfth century, chiefly at Tell es-Safi, the ancient Gath, the town of Goliath; and in buildings at Gath and at Gezer. This fact is a conclusive confirmation of the truth of the legend that brings the Philistines from Crete. And with them they brought iron.

7. The Iron Age

It is to the Thesprotian invasion, which displaced the Achaians, that, in all probability, the general introduction of iron into Greece is to be assigned. The invaders came ultimately from the Danube region, where iron was probably first used in Europe, whereas their kindred, the Achaians, had possibly already lived in Thessaly in the Stone Age, and derived the knowledge of metal from the Aegeans. The speedy victory of the new-comers over the older Aryan inhabitants of Northern Greece may be ascribed to their possession of iron weapons. But the defeated must soon have acquired the knowledge of the new metal from the conquerors, and it is to the dispersion of the defeated Achaians throughout the Greek world that we must assign the spreading of the use of iron. Even to Crete Northerners, probably Achaians, brought their iron weapons, with the practice of cremation and the "Geometrical" pottery of the North, which we find in Crete (at Mouliana) in graves side by side with bodies buried in pottery coffins (larnakes) and Mycenaean ware of the latest and most debased type. Whether the Achaeans had always burnt their dead we do not know, but whereas they had probably learnt the use of iron from the Illyrian invaders, the "Geometrical" pottery must, if it is the descendant of the older geometric styles of North Greece developed under Late Mycenaean influence, be Achaian, and have, originally, nothing to do with the Illyrian iron-bringers. However this may be, we know that now the Aryan practice of cremation first appears in Southern Greece, with geometric pottery and iron weapons. And that these new features of national civilization are to be associated with the final conquest of Greece by the Aryan Greeks there is no doubt. And that this conquest was largely effected by the southern and eastern movement of the Achaians, driven out of Thessaly by the Illyrian invaders, seems very probable.

The Cretan discovery at Mouliana shews us how for a time bronze and iron were used side by side, while the old Aegean culture was dying. Other explorations in Crete shew us that the terrible wars and confusion of this period had almost destroyed the ancient culture of the island. The old Minoan cities, unfenced from the attacks of the destroyers, were abandoned, and the population, terribly reduced by strife and emigration, fled to fortresses in the hills. The shore was abandoned to the pirates, Achaians, Italians, and probably Carians and Lycians (Philistines), who infested the seas, while the Phoenician traders, who now for the first time entered the Greek seas, trafficked, as we know from the Homeric poems, with the barbarized Aegeans and stole them to be sold as slaves in the markets of Sidon and Tyre.

So the Iron Age began, amid the ruins of the old Aegean civilization. Only in Cyprus did the bronze-using Minoan culture still persist a little while longer; the copper of that island would favour the continuance of the Bronze Age there, as in Egypt.

We know something of this time, when iron had not yet displaced the use of bronze, but both were used together, from the older lays of the Iliad. A Chian poet, who bore the name Homeros, seems in the ninth century B.C. (this is the traditional date for him) to have welded into a magnificent whole poems which had themselves been put together by earlier poets from lays which described a great event in the story of the Achaian colonization of Aeolis, namely the siege of the Phrygian city of Troy or Ilios, by Agamemnon, King of Argos, and the great quarrel between him and his ally Achilleus, King of the Thessalian Myrmidones. We all know the form which the poem took in the hands of the Chian, but it is improbable that the conception that a huge host, drawn from all parts of Hellas, under the leadership of the king of Peloponnesian Argos and Mycenae, marched against Priam, in any way corresponds to the facts or to the statements of the oldest lays. In them the war was doubtless waged only by the Thessalian Achaians against the Phrygians, who lived on the coast of the Aegean over against them. We have a hint of this in the fact that Argos is called "horse-feeding." This epithet can only refer to the Thessalian Argos. It was this Argos which Agamemnon really ruled, but in the later days when the poems were put together, the chief centre of Achaian power was, or had but lately been, Peloponnesian Argos, which they had taken from the Ionian (?) Mycenaeans when, driven from Thessaly by the Thesprotians, they entered the Peloponnese. To Asiatic Achaian poets of the ninth century Argos could only mean the great neo-Achaian Argos in the plain of the Inachos, and so the Thessalian Achaian chiefs who warred against Troy in the twelfth century were identified with the neo-Achaian lords who ruled the Peloponnesian Argos and Mycenae from the twelfth to the eleventh, and then the whole traditional dominion of the ancient Cretan-Ionian princes of Mycenae in the fourteenth and thirteenth centuries, with their allies from Lakonia, Pylos, and Crete, was brought up in warlike array against Troy beside her original and probably historical enemies, the Thessalian Argeioi. So the ancient glories of Mycenae were appropriated by the Achaians, and the Achaian poets of Asia made the ancient Thessalian heroes of their race lords and kings of all Greece.

The poems probably give us a general idea of Greece as it was from the thirteenth to the tenth centuries: here we see a trait that must belong to the earlier rather than the later time, here is something that bears the impress of later date. In many things the latest poet of all no doubt introduces ideas which belonged to his own time, as in the appearance of Thersites, the first Greek demagogue, meet to be held up to the derision of an aristocratic audience of Achaian chiefs. But in the main the poem which he welded together describes a society older than that which must have existed in the ninth century. Perhaps we cannot say that he consciously archaized: the older songs which he used and put together, and had been put together by his predecessors, described the manners and customs of the old days when they were first sung, the oldest of them probably not very long after the migration. Homer did not translate them into the manners and customs of his own day, though he allows traces of the later ideas of his own time here and there to appear.

We can then say that the Homeric culture is rather that of the Achaians of the twelfth or eleventh than of the ninth century. Bronze is still the usual metal for weapons, but iron is known, and occasionally appears. It is the period when both metals were in use, but bronze was still commoner than iron, and less valuable. The dead are usually burnt in the new fashion, but are also buried (and indeed the older custom always persisted in Greece alongside the newer). The polity of the tribes is entirely of the new age, but is still of the simple Aryan type which has so often been described. Only a few traits, like that of Thersites, shew the influence of the period of final redaction, when the political problems of the new Greece were beginning to make themselves felt. The island of Lesbos is described as still in the possession of a Phrygian population: by the ninth century it must long have been hellenized. Thrace is the land of a rich and civilized prince; we may doubt if this was still the case in the ninth century. The Phoenician traders were no doubt still in evidence then; but it is noticeable that they are called Sidonians, not Tyrians: by the ninth century Tyre had long supplanted Sidon as the chief city of Phoenicia.

The Iliad, and those older parts of the Odyssey that are directly influenced by the more ancient poem, shew us then a Greece that is not yet the Greece of classical days, though this later Greece was already beginning its history when the last Homer sang. A final event had then happened which was to bring about the birth of the new Greece, but of it we find no trace in the poems, the stuff of which belonged to the older day. This was the Dorian invasion, the Return of the Heraklids. That the later legends give the main story of this event more or less correctly we need not doubt. Its result was the bringing into Southern Greece of a population that was the most Aryan of all the Greek tribes, the most free from Aegean admixture. The Dorians, like the Boeotians, were a tribe that had originally lived in Illyria, and had advanced into the Achaian land before the pressure of the Thesprotians behind them. We can hardly doubt that the impulse to their final southward movement was given by the Thesprotians who had taken Thessaly from the Achaians, and that under the name of Dorians were included many tribes of the vigorous Illyrian new-comers. The Dorians properly speaking can only have been a small clan, and were possibly but the leaders of a host of the new inhabitants of the North. That their kings were of Achaian blood is probable enough. That they were at first defeated, in trying to pass the Isthmus, by the Achaian princes of Argolis, and that eventually they gained their purpose by crossing the Gulf of Corinth at Naupaktos ("the place where they made ships"), is no doubt a historical fact. The result we know. The Peloponnese was dorized. Messenia and Argolis exchanged Achaian for Dorian princes, the dispossessed Achaians were driven into the Ionian territory which became the historical Achaia, while in Laconia was established the most definitely Dorian state of all, which enslaved the older population, Achaian as well as Aegean (as the Thessalians had reduced their predecessors to the status of Penestae), and ruled with a rod of iron from the village which they built by the older Achaian capital, Lacedaemon. The peculiar Spartan institution of the double kingship may conceivably represent the dual character of the new nation, Illyrian as well as Dorian-Achaian.

In Northern Greece Boeotia was also dorized, and the Megarid was torn from Attica, from which land the great Ionian migration now carried a crowd of the dispossessed, Achaians no doubt as well as Ionians, to the shores of Asia, where Achaians from Thessaly and Cretans from Crete had already gone a century or more before. The Dorian invasion and Ionian migration may safely be placed in the eleventh century, though it may be doubted whether the conquest of the Peloponnese and establishment of the new Spartan and Argive kingdoms was finally effected till the tenth, and the occupation of Aigina may have taken place still later. The Dorian sea-migration, which took Dorians to Crete, and the Southern Cyclades, and eventually to the new Doris in Asia, can hardly have begun till the ninth century, only a hundred years or less before the beginning of the great colonizing movement from Ionia that proclaimed the dawn of the Greek renascence.

With the Dorian migration the prehistoric and legendary period of Greek history ends. The dawn of the historic period, though not yet the dawn of history, may be seen in the time of the Homeric poets of Asia, who lived at the courts of Aeolis and Ionia, where the remnants of the old Aegean culture which had been brought by the Aeolian and Ionian emigrants were now working with the ruder elements of Aryan Greek culture to form the second civilization of Greece. It was in Aegean Ionia that the torch of Greek civilization was kept alight while the home-land was in a mediaeval condition of comparative barbarism: Cyprus too, helped, though she was too far off for her purer Minoan culture to affect the Aegean peoples very greatly. It was in Ionia that the new Greek civilization arose: Ionia, in whom the old Aegean blood and spirit most survived, taught the new Greece, gave her coined money and letters, art and poesy, and her shipmen, forcing the Phoenicians from before them, carried her new culture to what were then deemed the ends of the earth.

CHAPTER III: ARCHAIC EGYPT

1. The Stone Age

THAT Upper Egypt was already inhabited during the earlier Stone Age we know from various discoveries of implements of palaeolithic type which have been discovered upon the crests of the limestone and sandstone walls which bound the Nile valley on either side. The valley must at that time, before fertilizing mud left by the yearly inundation had been turned to account for the production of cereals, and a system of irrigation introduced for the purpose of conveying water to the boundaries of the cultivated land when the flood had subsided, have been mere jungle and swamp, the home of great herds of hippopotami and of innumerable crocodiles. Man was confined to the arid waste on either hand, and there, even if the oryx and the gazelle afforded him occasional food, he was still in the midst of deadly enemies: the desert is the abiding-place of scorpion and deadly snake, the horned cerastes and the death-dealing cobra. Nevertheless, mankind continued to increase and multiply, and slowly and painfully Man raised himself from the position of a mere beast among other beasts to that of lord of the other animals: the Man that stood erect sharpened flints, made fire, and cooked. Slowly his flint-knapping improved, he descended into the side wadys, he ventured into the swamp which the waters left when each year they retired from off the face of the earth, he began to plant and to irrigate. Villages of mud and reeds arose upon the small palm-crowned mounds which stood up here and there above the plain, and were never overflowed even by the highest inundation; reed canoes carried men from one to the other in flood-time and across the swift main stream itself; eventually artificial dykes began to be made to connect village with village in flood-time; these are still there as one of the most characteristic features of Egypt, the gisrs or causeways, and will always be necessary. So the Egyptian gradually learnt the arts of ditch-digging and embanking, and came to understand the amount of work that can be done by gangs of men acting together. It was by means of the inclined plane of earth and the hauling power of gangs of men that in later days he erected his mightiest temples and even raised the Pyramids themselves.

Then the first beginnings of art and handicraft arose: reed mats were plaited and cloth was woven; pottery, made of the Nile mud without the aid of the wheel, but often of the most beautiful form, was rudely decorated in colour; the flint implements reached a pitch of accuracy in their chipping that was never attained elsewhere in the world: the Neolithic Egyptian was already passing out of barbarism into civilization.

All this we know from the necropoles of the primitive inhabitants of Upper Egypt which have been of late years discovered in many places. These primitive Egyptians belonged to the Late Neolithic period; in a few of the later cemeteries copper already appears; towards the end of the prehistoric age, therefore, the Egyptians had already passed into the "Chalcolithic" stage of development, in which, to all intents and purposes, they remained till the end of the "Old Kingdom." Their implements of chert and flint are often of types unknown to Europe, and are always beautifully chipped and finished.

Towards the end of the prehistoric period the art of making stone vases arose. These were often made of the hardest stones, and the art of making them continued under the earliest dynasties. Some of the latest prehistoric pottery is evidently imitated from these stone vases. But a much earlier type of the same ware, buff in colour with decoration in red, is more characteristic of the prehistoric pottery. Its decorations represent men, women, antelopes, ostriches, palm trees, boats, etc. The same style of decoration is found on the walls of a tomb near Hierakonpolis, which are the earliest known Egyptian paintings. An earlier type, also well known to us now, is a plain polished ware, usually without decoration, of polished red with black tops; another and later type is of white or pale buff ware, and for its shapes greatly affects the simple cylinder, thus producing a sort of tall jam-pot, usually decorated merely with a wavy lug or bracket-handle just below the lip. This type continued in use into the historical period: the black and red style belongs mainly to the Neolithic age, though it may have survived in the hands of more backward sections of the population even as late as the VIth Dynasty, and in Nubia continued to be made always. Queer ivory and bone figures of men and women, the men often represented as fully bearded, a fashion unknown in later days, are also characteristic of this period, and peculiar flat objects of slate, usually rudely fashioned to represent an antelope, or a tortoise, or a bat, were used as palettes upon which to grind the green malachite which the prehistoric Egyptians used to paint their faces.

The Neolithic Egyptian was buried, usually in a curled-up position with his head resting upon his knees, lying upon his left side, in a very shallow grave, usually oval in shape. With him were buried his pots, his flint knives, his kohl palette, and his reed mat, so that he might pass fully equipped into the next world. These graves are not found isolated, but are always grouped together in necropoles, often consisting of many hundred graves. Between one grave and its neighbour sometimes not more than a few inches of desert sand intervenes. This close packing often led to disturbance in Neolithic times, and it is possible that the many cases of dismemberment of the bodies, usually considered to indicate a regular practice of piecemeal burial, is really to a great extent due to ancient disturbance. Until further evidence is available on this point, it would be as well to hold in abeyance the conclusion that the Neolithic Egyptian constantly separated the limbs of the deceased before burial.

The contracted method of burial survived in Egypt among the poorer classes of the settled population as late as the time of the VIth Dynasty, when even the primitive and half-named tribes of the desert-fringe, corresponding to the Beduins and ʿAbabdeh of to-day, though still, perhaps, making pottery of the Neolithic fashion, had already adopted the new fashion of burying at length, which after the VIth Dynasty became universal. This custom is first seen at the end of the IIIrd Dynasty in the case of the higher classes only; and with it had come into fashion the practice of mummification: the Neolithic bodies had merely been dried or smoked. The contracted bodies of the VIth Dynasty were to some extent mummified. Here we have an interesting alteration of primitive custom, almost corresponding to the substitution of cremation for inhumation in prehistoric Europe. That we are to assign it to a change of race is more than doubtful. We have, as we shall see, evidence that an ethnic element, distinct from that of Upper Egypt, existed in Lower Egypt before the beginning of the 1st Dynasty. But there is no doubt that while this foreign element in Northern Egypt contributed not a little to the common culture of dynastic times, the main fabric of archaic Egyptian civilization was developed straight out of the Upper Egyptian culture of the Neolithic period. This fact has been proved beyond dispute by the work of Maciver at Al-ʾAmrah, followed by that of Reisner and Mace at Nag' ed-Der, and in nothing is the continuity of the archaic culture with the neolithic of Upper Egypt shewn more clearly than in the development of the graves, which progress uniformly from the oldest shallow oval pit to the characteristic chambers of the 1st Dynasty, and through the staircased graves of the IIIrd to the Vth, to the deep pits with chambers of the VIth and the XIth. The gradual change in the form of the tomb was evidently merely a change in fashion, a natural development, and thus also we must regard the gradual change in the mode of treating and laying out the body. Ideas were altering at the time; civilization was advancing, and religious views were by no means yet fixed.

All that is most characteristically Egyptian, especially in the religion and in the writing, is to be found in germ in the Upper Egyptian predynastic period. The gods and their emblems were known to the Neolithic Egyptian, and he used their sacred animals as the symbols of his village and name. The standards of the gods already appear, and in these primitive representations of the divine emblems we see the beginnings of writing. They are the first Egyptian hieroglyphs. Under the 1st Dynasty the writing developed swiftly, answering to the needs of a swiftly developing civilization. But in the hieroglyphs of the 1st Dynasty we cannot see any exotic element that we recognize: the signs are all Egyptian and represent Egyptian objects, and their descent from the simple predynastic ideographs is evident.

2. The Races of Egypt and the Introduction of Metal

Yet in the religion there was a foreign element, though it does not assert itself vigorously till the time of the IVth and Vth Dynasties. This was the worship of the Sun, and his sacred stones, the forerunners of the obelisks; a cult that is apparently of Semitic, and at any rate of Palestinian, origin. As we find it under the IVth and Vth Dynasties, this worship centred in the important town of Annu, On, or Heliopolis, on the eastern edge of the Delta, next to the lands of the Semites. We can find no trace of Sun-worship in what we can see of the religious beliefs of the Neolithic Egyptians. It is the old veneration of the sacred animals and the weird visions of the Lower World that are so characteristically Egyptian, and undoubtedly go back to the beginning of things in the Nile valley: the Sun-god was an invader from the East. He bore, too, a Semitic name. Further, another god of the North, Ptah, the "opener," bears from the first a purely Semitic name.

And with this possible Semitic invasion must be connected a most important fact. The language which was written with these characteristically native and Egyptian hieroglyphs was, even as we know it as early as the time of the IVth Dynasty or earlier, strongly affected by Semitic influence. That it is entirely "proto-Semitic" in character may be doubted, but that it contained Semitic elements is certain. The personal pronouns are Semitic in character, and it has been supposed by philologists, though the supposition is not yet universally accepted, that the verbs follow Semitic rules of conjugation. This original Semitic element in the language must be dissociated from later Semitic "contaminations" due to later connexion with the Semites.

We thus see that while archaeology knows of no definite foreign invasion of the Nile valley, and can with justification regard the whole of Egyptian culture as of indigenous growth, a study of Egyptian religion does seem to shew a very early Semitic element, and the philologists claim Ancient Egyptian as a more or less Semitic language. Craniological study contributes the important fact that during the early dynastic period the physical type of the Egyptians altered from that of predynastic days, and it seems most natural to suppose that this alteration was due to infiltration of a different population from the North, which would naturally ensue when the two parts of the country were united under one crown. This postulates a separate population in the North.

Now the early representations of Northern Egyptians on the monuments of the Southern king Narmer at Hierakonpolis shew them as decidedly Semitic or Semito-Libyan in type. And we find this Semitic type in a 1st-Dynasty representation of a Beduin from the First Cataract. This type is not the same as that of the predynastic Egyptian of the South, who, as we know from skulls and from contemporary representations, was smaller-headed and smaller-featured than the Beduin and the North Egyptian "Semite," though racially he may have been distantly connected with him. We have then in the South the delicate, small-bearded Upper Egyptian prehistoric race, the makers of the pots and flints we have described, who greatly resembled the Gallas and Somali of farther South, and probably belonged to that "Hamitic" race, which may be akin to the Southern Arabians. Evidently they came from the South. Then we have in Northern Egypt the Semito-Libyans, bridging the gap between the Berbers of North Africa, whose languages are akin both to Semitic and to Ancient Egyptian, and the true Semites. Evidently they came from the East, They brought Sun-worship and the more definitely Semitic elements in the Egyptian language.

Finally, craniological research has shewn that there was a third racial element in early Egypt, large-skulled, round-faced, and short-nosed. This element is not apparent, however, in prehistoric times in Upper Egypt: it only gradually spread southwards under the early dynasties. And we have interesting confirmation of the Northern origin of this type in the portrait-statues of the Pharaohs and great men of Memphis from the IVth to the VIth Dynasties, which shew the type of the ruling classes in the North as that of the large skulled people. Now these people were almost European in features, and not in the slightest degree "Semitic," whether of the strong-nosed Syrian or slight-nosed Arab type. They were not Semites, nor again were they Anatolians, as their noses were not of the Armenian or "Hittite" style or their skulls of the strongly brachycephalic type of Asia Minor. I regard them as Mediterraneans, akin to the early Cretans, who had been settled in Northern Egypt from time immemorial, and belonged to the North African stock from which perhaps the early Aegeans sprang. This stock will have been at an early period overrun by the Semite-Libyans, but when the Southern or true Nilotic Egyptians conquered the latter and founded the kingdom, the Mediterraneans, naturally more gifted and more civilized than the Semite-Libyans, reasserted themselves in the North, and gradually, owing to their superior intelligence, became more and more dominant in the nation, and their blood naturally diffused itself southward as they amalgamated with the Southern race. If this was so, there can be little doubt that many of the resemblances both in religious cults and in art between early Egyptians and Cretans are due to this North Egyptian race.

The above is a theory which may or may not be correct, but at least endeavours to give some explanation of the facts. We see at any rate that we have to deal with a second element in Northern Egypt by the side of the Semite-Libyans, and that it is this element, and not the Semite-Libyan, that modified the Egyptian race so materially under the early dynasties.

We have still to reconcile the archaeological with the philological and other facts mentioned. It might be urged that archaeology does not altogether reject the possibility of an early Semitic element even in Upper Egypt, so long as the similarities between certain early objects of Egyptian and Babylonian culture remain otherwise unexplained. These objects are the seal-cylinder, the mace-head, and the method of building crenellated brick walls, which were alike in both countries. It has been supposed that the invention of brick itself came to Egypt from Babylonia.

In the first place, these resemblances might be considered to prove, properly speaking, not a Semitic invasion or even connexion at all, but an invasion by or connexion with the Sumerian Babylonians, who were not Semites. Nevertheless, as there were probably Semites in Babylonia before the invasion of the Sumerians, this objection may be waived. The similarity of the crenellated walls of Egypt and Babylonia might be dismissed at once as proving, if anything, Babylonian indebtedness to Egypt rather than the reverse, as the crenellated walls of Telloh, which are compared with Egyptian fortress and mastaba-walls of the first three dynasties, are perhaps a thousand years later in date than these. But it is probable that this custom was in Babylonia as old as in Egypt, where we find crenellated walls represented as characteristic of the cities of the Northerners or Anu, who were probably of proto-Semitic blood. The cylinder cannot be dismissed at all. The fact that from the beginning both Egyptians and Babylonians used the same peculiar method of impressing seals on clay by means of a rolling cylinder, instead of, like other nations, stamping directly upon the clay, was a powerful argument in favour of early connexion. The conclusion that Egypt owed the cylinder to Babylonia derived support from the fact that in Egypt, after about a thousand years of use, the cylinder was practically given up in favour of the direct-stamping scarab or signet-ring, while in Babylonia it remained always in general use: this looked as if the cylinder-seal were in Egypt a foreign importation, an exotic which did not survive on a strange soil. But we have in Egypt more primitive cylinders than those of Babylonia: wooden seal-cylinders of the late predynastic period which are not far removed from the original notched piece of reed, which, according to a most plausible theory, was the original cylinder-seal. The cylinder-seal and the mace-head are the most difficult objects which the antagonists of an early connexion with Babylonia have to deal with. It is difficult to explain their absolute identity in form in both countries by anything but a cultural connexion of some kind. And it is significant that from the first the Egyptians called the seal by the Semitic name of khetm. The invention of brick was probably made independently in Babylonia and in Egypt, as the oldest Babylonian bricks are of a completely different form (plano-convex) from the Egyptian, which are rectangular.

It has been supposed that the knowledge of corn came to Egypt from Babylonia, because wheat grows wild in the province of Irak. But wild wheat has also been found in Palestine, and it seems more probable that it was from Palestine that the knowledge of corn passed on the one side to Babylonia, on the other to Egypt. The knowledge of the grape and of wine-making very probably came in the same way to both countries from Palestine, which may well be the Nysa whence, according to Diodorus, Osiris brought the knowledge of corn and wine to Egypt.

The resemblances of the mace-head, the cylinder-seal, and possibly the crenellated walls may point to some connexion between early Egypt and Babylonia through the medium of the Northern Semito-Libyans, but no more. To these Semites the nation that was to arise after the union of North and South owed elements in its language and its religion, and possibly the introduction of corn, as well as the knowledge of agriculture and viticulture, and probably that of metal, if, as seems likely, Sinai, Syria, and Cyprus were the original focus of the distribution of copper over Europe and the Near East. Copper came gradually into use among the prehistoric Southern Egyptians towards the end of the predynastic age. And they must have obtained their knowledge of it from the Northerners.

We now turn to the question of the origin of the Southern Egyptian race, the predynastic Nilotes whose remains we have described. They can only have come from the South, if they were not absolutely indigenous. Egypt is a tube, which can only be entered at top and bottom. If the "Semitic" Northerners entered at the top, as they obviously did, the non-Semitic Southerners must have entered at the bottom, from Africa. And it must be admitted that their primitive culture has a decidedly African appearance. Yet they were not negroes or even negroid: their skull-form shews this conclusively. We can only call them Karaites, and class them under this head with the Gallas and other related races of the North-Eastern "Horn" of Africa and Southern Arabia, to whom they undoubtedly bore a considerable resemblance. If they were not indigenous Nilotes, it is from this quarter that they must have come. And the evidence of their legends indicates that they actually did migrate thence to the Nile valley.

When, a few years ago, it still seemed probable that the impulse of the great development of civilization that produced the Pharaonic kingdom was due to an invasion of Semites from Arabia who were influenced by Babylonian culture, these legends were used to prove that the predynastic people of Upper Egypt were conquered by a Semitic or proto-Semitic people which came from Somaliland and Southern Arabia by way of the Red Sea coast and the Wadi Hammamat, a great depression in the Eastern Desert which leads directly from Kuser on the Red Sea to Koptos on the

Nile. Now, however, that it seems more probable that the (undoubted) proto-Semitic element in early Egypt belongs to the conquered North, rather than to the conquering South, and must have entered the Nile valley by way of the isthmus of Suez, and that the early Pharaonic culture was directly descended from that of the predynastic people of the South, who were not conquered by any Semites, either from South or North, but conquered them, these legends may be explained in a different way.

Tradition brings Hathor and the great gods from the "Holy Land," Ta-neter, which lay south of Egypt. This land appears to be in the neighbourhood of, if not identical with, the country which the Egyptians called Punt, the modern coast of Eritrea and Somaliland, with which the Egyptians of historical times had relations of a somewhat peculiar nature. The Punites are represented on the monuments as almost identical with the Egyptians in features and dress, with a significant exception: they wear the curious plaited beard, turned up at the ends, which is characteristic of the Egyptian representations of their gods, and is never depicted as worn by mortal men, even by kings. But this beard had been worn by the Egyptians at one time; as we see from the archaic monuments, it was worn by them in the period immediately preceding and following the beginning of the 1st Dynasty. Only when dead and become a god could the later Egyptian, whether prince or peasant, be represented as wearing his beard in the peculiar fashion characteristic of his gods, his remote ancestors of the time of the followers of Horus, and his contemporaries in the land of Punt. Now this is a very curious piece of evidence directly connecting the Punites with the invaders of Egypt, and confirming the testimony of the tradition which brought some of the Egyptian gods from this part of the world. It is evident from several facts, notably the circumstance that the name of the land of Punt was usually written without the sign "determinative" of a foreign people, that the Egyptians regarded themselves as racially connected with the Punites. M. Naville, the distinguished excavator of the great temple of Queen Hatshepsut at Der el-Bahri which contains the representations of her great expedition to Punt, and at the same time the editor of the legends of Horus of Edfu and his followers, — the chief authority, therefore, on this particular subject, which he has made peculiarly his own, — thinks that there was among the Egyptians a "vague and ancient tradition that they originally came from the land of Punt, and that it had been their home before they invaded and conquered the lower valley of the Nile."

It is then very probable that an invading race originally came from Somaliland to the Nile valley. Ordinarily, one would suppose that they came by way of Abyssinia and the Upper Nile, and another legend points to the same route. This is the story of the followers of the Sky-god Horus, the Mesniu or "Smiths." According to this legend, as we have it in a Ptolemaic version, at the beginning of history the god Horus of the Two Horizons (Harmachis or Horakhti) was ruling in Nubia, and in the 363rd year of his reign his son Horus of Edfu (Hor-Behudet, the winged sun) led a conquering expedition into Egypt against the aboriginal inhabitants or Anu, who were adherents of his enemy and rival the god Set. The "followers of Horus" (Shemsu-Hor) who formed the army of the Southern Sun-god, were also called Mesniu ("Smiths" or "Metal-workers"), and their spears were tipped with metal. The conquest of Egypt was completed after a terrible struggle. We may doubt the accuracy with which battles are chronicled as having taken place at Tjedmet near Thebes, at Khade-neter near Dendera, at the modern Minieh, Behnesa, and Ahnas in Middle Egypt, and finally on the Asiatic borders of the Delta. The influence of the later sagas of the Expulsion of the Hyksos is evidently at work here, especially in the case of the last item; but the fight at Khade-neter may be held to be genuine enough, on account of the ancient name, which means "The God's Slaughter," i.e. the place where Horus slaughtered the Anu. And the general direction of the conquest, from south to north, is a detail which is sure to be original and correct. Further, it agrees with the legend which brings the company of the Great Gods, led by Hathor, from the south-east into Egypt.

Now the leader of the invaders was the Elder Horus, the Sky-god, whose emblem and sacred animal was the hawk. He was the prototype of all Egyptian Pharaohs: kings did not exist before his time in Egypt: i.e. the supreme kingly dignity was an introduction of the invaders. So he was the especial patron and protector of the King of Egypt, one of whose titles was the "Golden Horus," and above whose ka-name the hawk, crowned with the kingly crown of Upper and Lower Egypt, is always represented. The hawk then is the emblem of the king as heir and representative of the deity who was fabled to have led the conquerors who founded the kingdom into the land. The head-centre of the worship of this god was Behdet, in Upper Egypt, the modern Edfu, where the magnificent pylons of his temple, as restored in Ptolemaic days, still stand up in the midst of the town on the western bank of the Nile, a landmark for miles around. Here it was that the worship of the Sky-god, which the invaders brought with them, was first established. Now recent discoveries shew us that at El-Kab and Kom al-Ahmar, which face each other across the Nile somewhat north of Edfu, the ancient cities of Nekheb and Nekhen formed the most ancient political centre of Upper Egypt, where the capital of the oldest kingdom of Upper Egypt was first fixed, and this kingdom was, historically, the nucleus of the later Pharaonic realm.

The Horus-legend as we have it is very late in date. The question is, leaving out of account the possible contamination by legends of the expulsion of the Hyksos, how far the older stuff of the story relates to the original immigration of the Southern Egyptians from the South, and how far to the historical conquest of the North and the Semites by the early kings of Hierakonpolis, who founded the united kingdom of Egypt. I think that we can see in the story as we have it a mingled reminiscence of both events, the first invasion from the South and the far later conquest of the North by "Mena" and his predecessors and successors. The predynastic Egyptians came from the South by way of the Upper Nile and Nubia, where, according to the legend, Horus originally reigned. This is at least more probable than that they came by way of the Red Sea coast at the Wadi Hammamat. The easy way from Punt through Ethiopia and Nubia, which legend assigns to them, was open. This, and not the Hammamat route, was the way by which Egyptian caravans and ambassadors passed in the reverse direction to Punt throughout the period of the Old Kingdom, until negro enmity seems to have closed it; when the Hammamat route and a sea-voyage along the coast necessarily replaced it. Finally, in favour of this view is the new discovery that certain Nubian tribes remained in a state of culture closely resembling that of the Neolithic men of Upper Egypt, and clearly of the same origin, even as late as the time of the XVIIIth Dynasty; nay, even to this day pottery of the Neolithic Egyptian type is made in Nubia. The conclusion is that the Nubians were the descendants (in later times much mixed with negroes) of these Southern tribes which remained in Nubia after the greater part of the race had passed into Egypt, where, by contact with the proto-Semitic Northerners, they developed Egyptian civilization, leaving Nubia as a backwater of barbarism.

The later element in the story is, I think, that which describes the campaign of Horus against the "Anu" with the aid of his Mesniu or "Smiths." Horus Set-worshipping here represents the King of Hierakonpolis, the living "Horus," as Pharaoh was always called, the king being identified with his protecting deity. The Mesniu are his Shemsu or "followers," his soldiers and retainers, now armed with the metal weapons, the use of which was only learnt by the predynastic Egyptians, presumably from the Northerners, shortly before the time of the Hierakonpolite kings and the conquest of the North: their ancestors of the original immigration from the South were stone-users. The "Anu" are the Semite-Libyans or "proto-Semites" of the North, whom we see on the Hierakonpolite king Narmer striking down on his monuments. A festival of "Striking down the Anu" was regularly celebrated by the Egyptian kings in memory of the conquest.

We thus see that legend agrees with archaeological discovery in bringing the Southern Egyptians from Nubia. In the Nile valley as far north probably as the apex of the Delta, they lived for many centuries till the adoption of metal from their neighbours the Semite-Libyans and Mediterraneans of the Delta gave them, as it did to other peoples, an impulse to culture development which resulted in the formation of a strong civilized central government in the district of Edfu and Hierakonpolis, the "home" territory of the national sky-god Horus, whose symbol was the hawk, and of the king, the living "hawk" and representative of Horus, Under the leadership of the Hierakonpolite kings, the Southerners now attacked and conquered the Semite-Libyans of the Delta, whose national gods were the Sun, Ra, and the Memphite Ptah, and possibly the Osiris of Dedu, and whose political centre was probably the city of Buto. The conquest was probably effected by the kings Narmer and Aha, the historical originals of the legendary "Mena," to whom later legend ascribed the union of the two lands and the founding of the 1st Egyptian Dynasty.

3. The Kingdoms of the South and North

It is noticeable that in later official and priestly legend the Northern kingdom of Buto seems a mere reduplication of that of the South. Buto, its centre, appears as another twin-city, Pe-Dep, analogous to the southern Nekheb-Nekhen; and as Nekheb was ruled by the southern goddess Nekhebet, so Buto was ruled by the northern snake-goddess Utjoit (Uto). But we may well surmise that all this is a fiction devised out of love of symmetry, and that the original Buto-kingdom was different enough from that of Hierakonpolis, as we see its Semite-Libyan inhabitants were different from the other Egyptians. The Delta king was not the nsnit, the word that always meant "king" in Egyptian, but bore a title meaningless in

Egyptian, bit, the ideograph of which was the bee, because in Egyptian the bee was called bit. Prof. Petrie has surmised that this royal name was in reality not Egyptian, but was a native word of the presumably half-Libyan half-Semitic original inhabitants of the Delta, taken over by the conquerors, and that it is in reality nothing more or less than the Battos of the Cyrenaeans.

The typical Egyptian nome-system did not exist in the Delta before the conquest. This system of hsapiit or nomes was indigenous to the south. The ideographic symbols of the nomes, their crests or cognizances, in fact, are always represented, from the beginning to the end of Egyptian history, as erected upon standards, just as the sacred animals are also represented acting in their case as the totem-symbols of the gods. These totem-standards of gods, tribes, and probably (at that day) of individuals also, already existed, as we have seen, in the prehistoric period in Upper Egypt, so that the nome-system no doubt was southern. The Delta nome-names all have an artificial character, which stamps them as introductions from the south: they are the sort of names that immigrants would give in a conquered land. Here we have another indication of the foreign character of the Delta-kingdom.

The fact that the Northern kingdom never entirely lost its separate identity points in the same direction. Though conquered, the North was never absorbed by the South. It was gradually Egyptianized: the ideographic system of the South became its official script, and in this script the names of its gods were written; the gods themselves were absorbed into a common official pantheon with the deities of the South. But still the Northerners preserved their individuality, and this separate individuality was recognized officially from the first. From the beginning the king of South and North (Insibya) was not only the nsuit (insi), but also the biti (bia), the Southern title, as the conqueror, taking precedence of the conquered. The king was the "Snake-Lord" of Buto, as well as the "Hawk-Lord of Hierakonpolis.

Another archaic title of the same import is "Two Hawks." And the conservatism which retained this memory of the two ancient kingdoms was justified by facts: the Delta has always been distinct from the Upper Country. We are told in a papyrus of the XIXth Dynasty that it was very difficult for a man of the Delta to understand the dialect of a man from Upper Egypt, and at this day the man of Bohera is a very different being from a man of the Sa'id. After the loss of the Asiatic Empire at the end of the rule of the Ramessides of the XXth Dynasty, Egypt returned for a time to the days of the Followers of Horus, for a king ruled in Tanis and a king ruled at Thebes, each independent of the other. A stray centrifugal and particularist force always balanced the centripetal in Egypt, and was sure to triumph in time of weakness and discord. But in days of prosperity and union no prouder title was borne by the Pharaoh than that of "Lord of the Two Lands."

Of the actual monarchs of the two kingdoms we know little. The Palermo stele, already mentioned, gives us a list of predynastic kings of Lower Egypt, of which seven are legible: Tiu, Thesh, Nehab, Uatjnar, Ska, Hsekiu, and Mekhat. These are names of a curiously primitive cast, which would have seemed as odd to a XIXth Dynasty Egyptian as our Hengest and Horsa, Cissa and AElla, do to us. Of the contemporary kings of Upper Egypt we have no knowledge, since the supposed royal names Tjeser, De(?), Ro, and Ka, discovered at Abydos, and assigned to the time of the Followers of Horus, are probably not royal names at all. The first Southern monuments which are certainly to be assigned to historical kings, belong to the beginning of the First Dynasty. There are the remarkable monuments, found at Hierakonpolis (Nekhen), of the earliest known king of both South and North, Narmer, also called "the Scorpion." They are ceremonial palettes of slate, probably used for the priest to adorn images of the gods at high festivals. On them we see carved in relief representations of the king's triumph over his enemies of the North, who are represented lying headless in rows before him, while, accompanied by a page bearing his sandals and a vase of drink, he inspects them at his leisure. Other representations on this and other similar "palettes" of the time shew highly symbolical representations of the animals typifying the Upper Egyptian nomes making captive the towns and tribes of Lower Egypt.

Of Aha ("the Fighter"), we have an important monument in the shape of his tomb at Nakada in the Thebaid; and farther north again, near the holy city of Abydos, a smaller second tomb, or rather funerary chapel, was built for him as a monument on the sacred soil of Abydos. Narmer also perhaps had a similar "tomb" here, and all the succeeding kings of his dynasty were either actually buried close by, or, as seems more probable, had great cenotaphs erected for them on the holy ground. It is the discovery of these tombs or cenotaphs by M. Amelineau, followed by the work upon them carried out by Messrs, Petrie and Mace, that has given us of late years our remarkable accession of knowledge of the earliest history of Egypt.

4. The Tombs of Abydos

According to the legend preserved by Manetho, the kings of the first three dynasties were Thinites: the centre of their power was the town of Thinis, in the valley not far from Abydos. From this it would seem that the capital had been moved northward by the earliest kings from Hierakonpolis to Thinis, although, as we have seen, Nekhen (Hierakonpolis) continued under them to be a centre of religious devotion, as the centre of the Horus-cult, The God of Thinis was Anhur or Onouris, a warrior-deity who is depicted as a king armed with a lance like that of the Mesniu. He was evidently a patron of the ceaseless war against the Anu. On the eastern bank of the Nile, at Nag' ed-Der, opposite the modern Girga, was a great necropolis containing tombs dating from the predynastic period to the IVth Dynasty, which shews us what an important centre of population the Thinite nome was in the earliest period of Egyptian history: it was the metropolitan nome of Upper Egypt, and no doubt, as Manetho implies, the seat of the earliest dynasties. This necropolis has been excavated by Messrs. Reisner, Mace, and Lythgoe for the University of California, and their discoveries, now being published, have shed a flood of light on the development of early Egyptian civilization. At the place called Abdu, not far from Thinis, on the edge of the western desert, was another necropolis of the new capital, guarded by the jackal or dog-deity Anubis, called Khent-amentiu, "the Head of the Westerners," the chief, that is to say, of the dead who were buried on the western desert.

The necropolis of the capital naturally became a great centre of the cult of the dead, and the earliest kings, though some of them may, like Aha, have been actually buried elsewhere, naturally erected here what may be the cenotaphy of some of them, the actual tombs of others. Their tombs were placed upon an eminence in the great bay of the desert cliffs west of Abydos, and here they were discovered fifteen years ago.

The chief historical results of the discovery were the recovery of the actual names of the oldest Egyptian kings, which had been forgotten by the later Egyptians themselves. When, under the IIIrd Dynasty, the royal court was moved to Memphis in the far north, Thinis and Abydos were forgotten, and veneration was no longer paid at the tomb-shrines of the kings of the 1st Dynasty. The later kings were buried in the Memphite necropolis at Sakkara, the domain of Sokari, the Memphite god of the dead, who now claimed the allegiance of court and capital. It was not till the time of the Middle Kingdom, and the supersession of a Memphite by a Theban dynasty, that Abydos came once more into prominence. And now the (perhaps originally un-Egyptian) dead-god of Busiris in the Delta, Osiris, became identified with Khentamentiu of Abydos, now dissociated from Anubis, who became in the popular theogony the son and minister of Osiris-Khentamentiu. During the time of the Hyksos domination in lower Egypt, Abydos, as the chief necropolis of the national kingdom in the upper country, and Osiris as its god, began to take upon themselves a peculiar atmosphere of holiness, and by the time of the XVIIIth Dynasty the form of Khentamentiu took its final position as the Egyptian metropolis of the dead. Even if an Egyptian could not be himself interred here, he might at least have some memorial of himself set up upon the holy soil. Kings who by patriotic custom and loyalty to Amen, the great god of Thebes, were buried near the capital, could erect cenotaphs for themselves in the "holy land." So Senusert III had a cenotaph and temple here; Aahmes followed his example, and the Queen Tetashera. Then Seti I, of the XIXth Dynasty, erected his great funerary temple here, which still stands, one of the most interesting remains of Ancient Egypt. His son Rameses II followed his example, and had already been associated with his father on the walls of the latter's temple in a relief shewing the king and prince offering incense to the names of their predecessors upon the throne. This is the famous "Tablet of Abydos." We may well surmise that, not long before, the ancient tombs of the 1st Dynasty kings had been discovered, and that the cult of the early monarchs had recommenced, in association with that of Osiris. For it is evident that the tomb of one of these kings was now regarded as the sepulchre of Osiris himself The explanation of this is that the name of this early monarch was read as it appeared upon the stelae marking his grave, as "Khent," and so was identified with that of Khentamentiu-Osiris. This belief was fixed, the mound of Umm el-Ga'ab became covered with the myriad votive pots left by pious pilgrims in honour of Osiris, from which it takes its name ("The Mother of Pots"); and, later on, a figure of Osiris laid out upon a granite lion-headed bier, with protecting hawks at head and feet, was solemnly placed in the tomb of the ancient king, where it was discovered by M. Amelineau.

This misunderstanding, with its interesting sequel, is characteristic of the incapacity of the Egyptians of the XIXth Dynasty fully to understand the ancient relics which they had brought to light. The archaic writing of the

1st Dynasty could no longer be read properly, and so is to be explained the divergence of the royal names in the Tablet of Abydos from the actual archaic forms of the personal names from which those of the list were derived. Also, no doubt, the existence of popular traditions (which the Egyptians, like modern Orientals, accepted uncritically as true history), giving legendary forms of names, served to mislead Seti's historiography.

5. Menes and the 1st Dynasty

Both they and the writers of the almost contemporary official list on a papyrus, now preserved on fragment at Turin, began their line of kings with Mena, the traditional founder of the kingdom, whom we find in Herodotus, in Manetho, and in Diodorus. This is a legendary name. We have not found it at Hierakonpolis, and not certainly at Nakada, where it has been supposed to occur on a tablet as the personal name of Aha. On a newly discovered fragment of the "Palermo Stone" Ateti seems to be given as the personal name of Aha. On account of its nearness in time to the reigns of these kings, the authority of the Palermo Stone is great; but if it disagrees with contemporary monuments it must of course yield place as evidence to the latter, as even so early as the time of the Vth Dynasty the events of the beginning of the 1st may have become legendary, and the names of its kings have been confused. It is therefore uncertain whether the personal name of Aha was Men or Ateti. The name Ateti occurs third on the lists of Abydos and Turin, second in Manetho, as Athothis. The second and fourth names in the Abydos list, Teta and Ata (the Turin list is in these cases illegible), very probably correspond to the kings Khent or Shesti (read Zer by Prof. Petrie), and Tja (Petrie's "Zet"), whose personal names may have been Ta and Ati. But if so, the Abydos list is wrong in placing "Teta" after Mena, and before Ateti, since, whether Aha be Ateti or Mena, there is no doubt that he preceded Khent. The style of his monuments shews this conclusively. Manetho, then, is right in making Athothis the immediate successor of "Menes," and the predecessor of his "Kenkenes" and "Ouenephes." If Ati or Tja is "Ata," he follows in the correct order. But here Manetho has got wrong. This "Ouenephes" must be Khent (the "Teta" of the Abydos list); for "Ouenephes" is simply a Greek form of Unnefer ("Good Being"), a common appellation of the god Osiris, and we have seen that the antiquarians of the XIXth Dynasty had identified the tomb of Khent as that of the god Osiris. "Kenkenes" must then be Tja Ati or "Ata" (we cannot trace the origin of the peculiar Manethonian equivalent of his name), placed erroneously before Ouenephes (Khent) For that Tja succeeded Khent is again deduced from the obvious steady development of the art of the period, which from a more primitive stage under Narmer and Aha suddenly developed under Khent and Tja, till we reach the line of the kings Den Semti and 'Antjab Merpeba, whose works are obviously of far more developed style and therefore of later date than those of Aha and Narmer. With Semti the list (and Manetho, who more or less follows it) first agrees entirely, both in names and order, with the facts Still, the name of Semti was not properly understood: it was misread as "Hesepti," the original of Manetho's "Ousaphais." That of Merpeba was, however, quite well given as "Merbap" or "Merbapen," and with this king the list of Tunrei at Sakkara begins: he does not mention "Mena." The following names of Semerkhat and Ka Sen have been also misunderstood both by the lists and by Manetho, but the identity of "Shemsu" and "Kebhu" with these two kings is certain, and their order is correct.

Narmer is left unidentified. And who was the original of the legendary Mena? It would seem that "Mena" in reality represents the early conquering monarchs of this dynasty: he is a complete personage of tradition, a sort of Egyptian King Arthur who represents the deeds of the Southern Icings who conquered Buto and founded the dual kingdom. Perhaps he represents more especially Narmer, who was the first, as far as we know, to wear the Crown of Lower as well as that of Upper Egypt, and shows us on his monuments at Hierakonpolis how he overthrew the Northerners. Aha, if his personal name was really Men, and not Ateti, may have given his name to the traditional Mena, and contributed to his glory, since he ruled over North and South and called himself the "Fighter" (Aha); but he was not the actual conqueror of the North. And unknown kings of the South who preceded Narmer and warred against the North before him, also have been included in the composite personage who for the Egyptians of later days was the founder of their kingdom. It is a tempting theory to suppose that a king existed named Suia ("Uniter"), who came between Narmer and Aha, and was the actual uniter of both kingdoms: but it is by no means certain that this supposed royal name, discovered by Prof Petrie at Abydos, is (any more than these of "De," "Ro," "Ka," and "Tjeser," also found there) a name at all.

With Narmer we reach the beginnings of Egyptian history. Since he conquered the North, and therefore more or less corresponds to Menes, we must assign him to the 1st Dynasty, and not to the "Followers of Horus," the Hierakonpolite kings, who appear in the Turin Papyrus and Manetho as midway between the rule of the gods on earth and that of Menes, and are called by Manetho "the semi-divine ghosts". They were indeed ghosts of faraway tradition, while Narmer was a very real man, as we see from his monuments. At Hierakonpolis were also found relics of an uncertain king, who is supposed to have borne the appellation of "the Scorpion," but there is no proof that this was his name at all, and in view of the identity of style between his work and that of Narmer, we may assume that he is the same as the latter, and that "Scorpion" was considered an appropriate epithet of royalty.

Aha, the successor of Narmer, while also a "fighter," a conquerer of the Nubians (probably north of the First Cataract), and an upholder of Southern rule in the North, seems to have been a more peaceful ruler than Narmer, and the tablets of his reign seem to chronicle the erection of temples, notably one of the northern goddess Neith, whose name is also borne by women of the royal house at this period. This seems to indicate some attempt at conciliating the Northerners.

Of the reigns of Khent and Tja we have interesting artistic remains, which shew, as has been said, that in their time art progressed with a sudden bound; a fact which makes it possible for us to assign with certainty the works of Aha and Narmer to the period preceding.

Den Semti (called Udimu Khaskheti by Prof. Sethe) seems to have been an energetic and long-lived monarch. He was the first to call himself by the title of nsuit biti (insibya) "king of Upper and Lower Egypt," and built himself a large tomb at Abydos, with the novel addition of two staircases descending into it, and a floor of granite blocks which must have been brought from Aswan; a result probably of the southern victories of Aha. Besides jar-sealings, many of which commemorate a great official named Hemaka or Hekama, a large number of annalistic tablets, chiefly recording religious acts, were found in his tomb; and in later tradition he was celebrated as a pious and learned king, chapters of the Book of the Dead as well as medical treatises being said to have been "found" (i.e. written) in his time, a statement not unlikely in itself. We see him on one tablet performing a solemn religious dance before the god Osiris. And in his reign we see the earliest known mention of a celebration of the Festival of Sed, or "the End" (lit. "Tail"). It would appear that, like many other primitive peoples, the early Egyptians put a period to the reigns of their kings. When they had reigned for thirty years they either were killed or were deposed, amid solemn festival, in which the king, at least officially dead, was carried in procession in the death-robes and with the crook and flail of Osiris, the Busirite god of the dead. In historical times the king had refused any longer to be either immolated or deposed, and merely celebrated the festival pro forma. It became later a jubilee, the distinction of a long reign; while, in the end, any or every king liked to celebrate it, whether he had reigned thirty years or not, sometimes several times in his reign. We do not know whether the ancient custom still so far survived in Den's time that he had to vacate his throne at the end of his thirty years' reign.

The contemporary monuments of his successor, Antjab Merpeba, are comparatively insignificant; but he is noteworthy from the fact that in all probability he was the founder of the city of Memphis. Later tradition, as Herodotus tells us, assigned this great work to "Menes." But it is significant that the royal list of Tunrei at Sakkara, the necropolis of Memphis, places Merpeba at the head of the kings, and knows nothing of "Mena" or of any king before Merpeba. The conclusion that Memphite tradition in the time of the XIXth Dynasty knew of no king before Merpeba, and that he was the "Menes" who founded Memphis, seems a very probable one. Merpeba was sufficiently near in time to the original conquerors of the North, Narmer and Aha, to be easily confounded with "Mena" by the Egyptians of Herodotus' day.

Probably Merpeba merely re-founded Memphis as the official capital of the North in place of Sais or Buto. The god of Memphis, Ptah, bears a Semitic name, "The Opener"; and, as we have seen, he may well, like the sun god R'a (= 'Or, "light") of Heliopolis, have been a pre-Egyptian deity of the proto-Semitic Northerners (or Anu?) who was worshipped in a town called "The White Wall," which was afterwards re-founded by Merpeba and in the time of the VIth Dynasty took the name of Men-nefer, the "Memphis" of the Greeks. The building of the great dike of Kosheish, south of Memphis, also ascribed by Herodotus to Menes, may also have been the work of Merpeba, Memphis speedily increased in importance, and under the IIIrd Dynasty, if not already under the IInd, the king's seat and capital of the whole country was transferred thither from Thinis.

The chief monument of Semerkha Hui (or Nekht?), the next king (who was also buried at Abydos), is also the most ancient monument of Egyptian activity outside the Nile-valley. It is a stele of this king, sculptured on the rocks of the Wadi Magharah, in the Sinaitic peninsula, and shows two figures of the king wearing the crowns of Upper and Lower Egypt respectively, followed by a scene of him striking down with a mace a Semitic inhabitant of the peninsula, whom he seizes by the hair: in front of the royal figures comes his "chief and commander of the soldiers," carrying a bow and arrows. It is thus evident that even so early as the time of the 1st Dynasty the Egyptian kings sent expeditions to Sinai to procure the turquoise or mafkat which was always prized so highly.

Semerkha Nekht is Manetho's Semempses, a name which probably gives the pronunciation which in his time was attributed to the peculiar ideograph of a man with a stick with which the king's name is written, probably an early form of the sign usually read "Nekht."

His successor, Ka Sen, has been supposed to be Manetho's Bieneches or Ubienthis, but it is more probable that the Manethonian name really belongs to the prince who succeeded Ka according to the Tablet of Sakkara, Biuneter. Ka, however, is undoubtedly the Kebhu who on that tablet comes between Nekht and Biuneter, and appears as the successor of Nekht, also that of Abydos. The alteration of his name from its true form Sen to "Kebh" has been well explained by Prof. Petrie. We possess fine relics from Ka's tomb at Abydos in the diorite stelae which were set up above it, and an ivory object with a representation of a prisoner from the Cataract-country (Satet), which shows the Semitic type of the eastern desert tribes clearly.

With Biuneter or Bieneches, who is a mere name, Manetho brings the 1st Dynasty to an end, and we have no reason to reject his arrangement Our knowledge of the IInd Dynasty is fragmentary and confused. The outstanding fact of the period is the assertion of the equality of the North and its god Set with the hitherto dominant South.

7. The IInd and IIIrd Dynasties

The re-founding of Memphis by Merpeba marked the beginning of the shifting of the royal power northwards Hetep-sekhemui, Raneb, and Neneter (who are probably the Betju, Kakau, and Baneneter of the lists; the Boethos, Kaiechos, and Binothris of Manetho) probably reigned at Memphis, and Kaiechos is said by Manetho to have instituted the worship of the Apis-bull there. Sekhemab, probably the next king (he cannot be identified in the lists), emphasized his connexion with the North by adopting, in addition to his Horus-name, a Set-name, Perenmaat preceded by a figure of the sacred animal of Set, the god of the North and enemy of

Horus. Perabsen, who probably succeeded him, bore the Set-name only, but was buried (or more probably, had a cenotaph made for him) at Abydos. Later on he was venerated at Sakkara in conjunction with another king of the dynasty, Send or Senedi ("Terror"), who was sufficiently important for his name to be preserved accurately in the later lists and even by Manetho (as "Sethenes"). He, however, is unknown in the South, and it is probable that he ruled at Memphis. We know nothing of him except that he was venerated there. Several long reigns followed, according to Manetho: then came the founding of a new dynasty by the great Southern conqueror Khasekhem or Khasekhemui, whose known relationship to Tjeser, the great king of the IIIrd Dynasty, makes certain his position at the head of that Dynasty, and probable his identification with the "Tjatjai" or "Bebi" of the lists.

His is an important historical figure. He was a Southerner, and held his court in a great fortress-palace of royal burgh on the edge of the desert at Abydos, now known as the Shunet-ez-Zebib. There also, near the sepulchres or cenotaphs of the 1st Dynasty, he built his tomb, which has yielded antiquities much resembling those of the older kings. Like Narmer, whose career he emulated, he regarded Nekhebet, the vulture-goddess of Hierakonpolis, as his special protectress, and in every way revived the traditions of the Southern kingdom, which had become dimmed under the long Northern rule of the IInd Dynasty. He was not, strictly speaking, an usurper, but ostensibly inherited the throne in right of his wife, who bore the name Ne-maat-Hap, "Possessing the Right of Apis," the tutelary deity of Sakkara. Evidently Ne-maat-Hap was the last of the long line of the IInd Dynasty, and married the energetic Southern chief, whose personal name was Besh, though he ascended the throne as Kha-sekhem "Appearance of the Power."

We may doubt, however, that his wooing of Ne-maat-Hap was peaceful. Probably he took her and her right by conquest. On his monuments he tells us of his victories: he claims on a votive statue dedicated at Hierakonpolis to have slain 47,209 of them. This massacre secured his power over the North as well as South; and on a vase also dedicated at Hierakonpolis, in imitation of Narmer, he claims to be a second unifier of the kingdoms, a second Menes. On it we see the vulture of Nekebet offering with her left claw the symbol of the Union of the Two Lands to the king's Horus-name Kha-sekhem, while in her right she holds the royal signet with his personal name Besh: above and behind is inscribed: "In the temple of Nekheb

(Hierakonpolis): year of fighting the Northern Enemy." The victory gained, the savage warrior shewed political talent of a high order. Apparently he altered his Horus-name to Kha-sekhemui ("Appearance of the Two Powers"), added to his titulary the significant phrase, "He hath opened peace to Horus and Set," thus typifying the renewed union and peace between South and North, and legitimized his position by marrying the Memphite princess, Ne-maat-Hap.

There is no doubt that Khasekhemui was a man of great energy and power. His tomb at Abydos is enormous, and is remarkable as containing the oldest known complete chamber of hewn granite. That he was a clever ruler is shewn by his reconciliation of the two lands, although this had the perhaps unexpected effect of transferring the royal power finally from the victorious South to the conquered North, His fierce and politic reign is a contrast to those of the preceding kings of the dynasty, who seem to have been peaceful monarchs wholly given over to good works. Of the sixteen yearly entries of events preserved to us on the Palermo Stone out of the long reign (at least 35 years) of Neneter, not one refers to war, and only one to a civil act, and this of little importance, the founding of two palaces; the rest record nothing but the institution and celebration of religious festivals. Yet by an irony of fate the name of the undistinguished Neneter was preserved in the official lists till the time of Manetho, while that of Khasekhemui, although his birth-year was solemnly commemorated under the Vth Dynasty, was afterwards wholly forgotten. It is not impossible that his deeds were confused with those of Narmer and "Mena." Certainly none of the five names that follow that of Send or Sethenes in the lists and in Manetho can be identified with his. On the other hand, the name of his son Tjeser survived and was recognized as important till the last. It was correctly preserved in the later lists, and is the Tosorthros of Manetho.

Tjeser, who bore the Horus-name Khetneter, was, like his father, a powerful king. He cut a stele on the rocks of Sinai, and from a late inscription we know that he presented the Nubian territory known in later times as the "Dodekaschoinos," between Aswan and Maharraka, which he had probably conquered, to the gods of the Cataracts, In the necropolis of Memphis he signalized his power, and shews us the speed at which civilization was developing in his day by the erection of, as his tomb, the first pyramid of stone. This is the Step-Pyramid of Sakkara. He also built himself a brick mastaba-tomb in the old style, but of unprecedented size, in the desert at Bet-Khallaf, north of Abydos. One of these tombs must have been built as a concession to the local sentiment of either Lower or Upper Egypt, for we do not know in which he was buried. Sa-nekht, his brother, who probably succeeded him, also built a similar brick tomb at Bet-Khallaf, in which he seems to have been buried. Sa-nekht set up stelae in the Wadi Magharah, but we know no more of him. Manetho follows him with four kings of whom neither the monuments nor the XIXth Dynasty lists know anything: one of them, "Soyphis," is certainly a double of Khufu (Souphis) misplaced. Then comes Manetho's Kerpheres, the historical Neferka or Neferkara, who has got misplaced before Sephouris (Snefru), who, as we see from the lists, followed him. Of this king we have a mighty unachieved monument: the huge rock-cut excavation at Zawiyet el-Aryan, south of Gizah, which has been excavated lately by the Service des Antiquites. It is probably, as M. Maspero thinks, the foundation of a pyramid, which, had it been built, would have marked the transition between the "stone house" of Tjeser and the great pyramids of Snefru and Khufu. On the walls of this excavation occurs besides the name of Neferka, that of Ra-neb-[ka], who is perhaps identical with Sa-nekht. The redundant names of the lists and Manetho we may dismiss with probability as either mythical or due to some confusion: we have only five historical kings of the dynasty, which was probably short, concluding with Snefru (Sephouris), with whom the age of the great Pyramid-builders begins, and the archaic period of Egyptian civilization ends.

The period of time covered by the first three dynasties probably did not much exceed four hundred years. There were several long reigns in the first two dynasties, notably those of Den and Neneter: the latter is said to have died at the age of ninety-five, while others of these primitive rulers were very long-lived. But on the other hand the IIIrd Dynasty probably lasted less than a century, of which Tjeser reigned thirteen years, according to the Turin Papyrus.

8. The Development of Archaic Egyptian Civilization

These four centuries witnessed the development of Egyptian civilization out of comparative barbarism. Under the Pyramid-builders of the IVth and Vth Dynasties we find that the free and unrestrained development of art, culture, and religion comes to a stop, when further progress might have anticipated the triumphs of Greek civilization.

But there had been no halt and no falling back under the early dynasties. Development was steady, sometimes quicker, sometimes slower. We can easily see two periods of greatly accelerated progress, periods in which new ideas appear at every turn, and energetic brains were evidently working freely. The first of these periods may be placed between the reigns of Narmer and Den, and the second in those of Khasekhemui and Tjeser. Probably the first period of acceleration might be extended farther back into the age of the Shemsu-Hor. In the representation of men and animals the art of the first period marks a great advance upon the crude Bushman-like productions of the prehistoric period. This advance we see vigorously pressed during the reigns of the kings of the dynasty. During the reigns of Aha and Narmer the hawk above the "Proclaimer" containing the name of the king's ghost is very oddly fashioned; but in Tja's time an artist arose who could draw a

hawk correctly, and the hieroglyph as fixed by him remained the standard throughout Egyptian history. So also it is with the reign of Semerkhat that we first find animals in general well drawn in the regular Egyptian fashion; in the time of Khent, a century before, lions, for instance, were represented in the round in a way which strikes us as strangely un-Egyptian.

It is to this period of transition between Neolithic barbarism and the later culture of the 1st Dynasty that the first great progress of the art of writing must also be assigned. The Egyptians never made any strict distinction between painting or drawing and writing, and the development of their script must be regarded as part of the development of their art.

The isolated pictographic signs by which the primitive Nilote had learnt to denote the names of his tribe or his god, perhaps of himself and of the animals he kept and hunted, had developed by the time of the kingdoms of Hierakonpolis and Buto into an ideographic system of writing, in which it was not possible to express the sound of the word, only the idea. This purely ideographic system is, as we see in the case of the monuments of Narmer, very difficult for us to interpret. To the reign of Den belongs the first inscription which is sufficiently like those of later days for us to be able to translate it in the proper sense of the word. It reads literally: "Big Heads Come Tomb: He Give Reward." Neither article nor prepositions are yet expressed: the ideographic writing is not developed much further than the paintings of a Red Indian wigwam. But already the syllabic system had been invented during the early reigns of the 1st Dynasty; when we find it used to express proper names, for which purpose indeed it was probably devised. In the reign of Den the progress of the writing is marked, and under the later kings of the dynasty we find its character fixed as a partly ideographic, partly alphabeto-syllabic script. Of course it is still archaic in character, many signs being used which soon afterwards were abandoned, and so is difficult to read.

The second period of swift development began at the end of the IInd Dynasty and came to a stop only when under the Vth Egyptian art reached its first apogee, and the first decline set in. It is chiefly marked by the development of architecture and of sculpture, in relief and in the round. Already at the end of the 1st Dynasty a "king's carpenter" had so far progressed beyond the carving of ivory memorial tablets and slate reliefs as to be able to execute in the round the wonderful little ivory figure of a king found by Petrie at Abydos, which is one of the greatest treasures of the British Museum. His head is bent forward (which has caused him to be taken for an old man), and he clasps his variegated robe about him; on his face there is a curious smile, almost a sneer. This was indeed an extraordinary result of the first development: perhaps no Egyptian figure so good of its kind was ever made in later days. But the maker of this could not yet create good larger figures in stone; he was still a carver, not yet a sculptor. This he became in the time of Khasekhemui, when such clumsy figures as the Statue No. 1 at Cairo (probably made under Neneter), developed into such extremely good representations of the human figure as the sitting statuettes of the conqueror which he dedicated at Hierakonpolis, and are now at Cairo and Oxford. Now the conventional representation of a king is already fixed; he no longer wears such an extraordinary robe as that of the ivory figure of the 1st Dynasty, but might be any later Pharaoh, did we not know who he was. But, as we have said, upon the pedestals of these statuettes we find the bodies of his slain enemies sculptured in a remarkable attempt to represent every conceivable attitude of the dead upon a battlefield, which, though crude and often ill-drawn, is nevertheless extremely realistic, and would undoubtedly have horrified an Egyptian sculptor of a few hundred years later, when the conventions of art had become sternly fixed. No doubt the picturesque attitudes of the slain had been greatly admired by the king or his artists, and so they were sketched and afterwards transferred to the immortal stone. It was an age of cheerful savage energy, like all ages when peoples and kingdoms are in the making.

The sister art of Architecture naturally found little scope in the early days; we can only chronicle the fact that Den was the first to use hewn stone at all, and that only for a floor. The architectural development also, like that of sculpture, began in the age of Khasekhemui and Tjeser, who, as we have seen, built the first pyramid.

The "small art" of the beginning of Egyptian craftsmanship is often wonderfully fine. Gold, perhaps the oldest of metals to be known to man, was commonly employed, and was first used by the Egyptians to ornament necklaces, as its ideograph, a necklace or collar, shews. We possess the ivory lid of a box, inscribed "Golden Seal of Judgment of King Den"; this must have been a cylinder of gold. Silver was unknown. Copper was used ordinarily for tools and weapons, though the Egyptians were still in the "chalcolithic" stage of culture, and used stone side by side with copper. But the stone weapons of the early dynastic period shew a notable falling off from the exquisite workmanship of the purely Neolithic period. Nor is the reason far to seek. The adoption of metal turned all the best skill in the new direction of metal-working. The same phenomenon is noticeable in the case of pottery, which suddenly becomes poor and weak. This was because metal tools had given a new power over hard stones, which were now used for the manufacture of splendid vessels, often of gigantic size, which are among the finest relics of the early dynastic age. Stone vessels of small size now largely took the place of pottery, until the invention of the potter's wheel, somewhere about the time of the IIIrd Dynasty, restored to the potter his rightful place in the hierarchy of artists. But the ceramic artists had already discovered the art of glazing pottery, which, though rarely applied to vases as yet, resulted in the production of beautiful small figures and emblems of glazed clay. The colour was a light blue. True glass was to remain unknown for many centuries yet, but the glazed faience of the 1st Dynasty is equal to any of later times. We find it already well developed in the reign of Aha. Ivory and wood were, as we have seen, well known to the craftsman of this early period; great balks of timber were used for the flooring and roofing of the tombs at Abydos which can hardly have come from anywhere else than Palestine. So that commerce, probably overland across the desert of Suez, with the Semitic world was by no means unknown. By this route was lapis-lazuli imported from the East; turquoise, as we have seen, was already mined in Sinai.

The early Egyptian artists made figures of their gods which hardly differ from those of the time of the Vth Dynasty, when the conventions of religious art were fixed for all time. We have seen the holy animals of Horus, Set, Anubis, Upuaut, and Sebek represented; and the figures and signs of Osiris, Taueret, Hathor, and Neith show that these deities were all worshipped from the beginning. The more human gods of the Libyan and Semitic Northerners had amalgamated with the theriomorphic deities of the Nubian Southerners; perhaps the "appointment" of the sacred animals of Memphis, Heliopolis, and Mendes "to be gods" in the reign of Kaiechos, refers to a formal amalgamation of this kind.

CHAPTER IV: EGYPT UNDER THE OLD AND MIDDLE KINGDOMS—c. 3200-1800 B.C. (?)

I. The IVth Dynasty

WITH Senefru we begin the second era of Egyptian history: the Age of the Pyramid-builders. This king has sometimes been assigned to the beginning of the IVth Dynasty, but if he is Sephouris, not Soris, and Sharu is Soris as seems most probable, he must be regarded as the last king of the IIIrd Dynasy, Sharu as the first of the IVth. Nevertheless Senefru must be grouped with the kings of the IVth Dynasty rather than with those of the IIIrd. The great kings of the first part of this period are, then, Senefru, and Khufu, Khafra, and Menkaura, the Cheops, Chephren, and Mykerinos of Herodotus, the Chemmis, Kephren-Chabryes, and Mencheres of Diodorus, the Souphis I, Souphis II, and Mencheres of Manetho.

The age of these earliest kings, who with the legendary founder of the kingdom were always remembered in Egypt, has been called the Age of the Pyramid-builders. And the great Pyramids of Giza will remain as their monuments till the end. They are the mark which the kings Khufu, Khafra, and Menkaura have for ever placed upon the land which they ruled nearly six thousand years ago. They are, as is universally known, the tombs of these kings, placed among the necropoles of their subjects on the low ridge of the desert which juts up at the edge of the cultivated land north-west of ancient Memphis and south-west of modern Cairo. Already in their time the desert-border in the immediate neighbourhood of the centre of Memphis was too crowded with the sepulchres of kings and commoners to allow of the great structures planned being erected any nearer the city, Tjeser had built the Step Pyramid, the most ancient in the necropolis, some two or three centuries before in the part nearest the city. Senefru had gone farther south, to Dahshur and Medum, to build his two pyramids. Khufu went farther north; his successor Radadf, the Ratoises of Manetho, farther north still, to Abu Roash, northwest of Cairo; Khafra and Menkaura came back to the spot chosen by Khufu. The pyramid of Sharu is as yet unidentified. Of his reign, as of that of Radadf, we know nothing, and both were kings too ephemeral to build much.

In front of the royal tombs stood their funerary temples, already important buildings of hewn stone, with pillared courts forming an outer or public temple and an inner fane, and with numerous magazines for the storing of the goods of the king's temple and the offerings made to his spirit. The temples of Khafra and Menkaura have both been excavated recently. The latter has yielded remarkable treasures of art, for the halls of a royal temple were filled with figures of the king whose memory was venerated in it.

As the retainers of the Thinite monarchs were buried in, or at any rate in annexes of, the tombs of their masters, so the courtiers of the Memphite kings were interred in the neighbourhood of the pyramids of their lords; but the milder manners of a more civilized age probably no longer demanded their enforced departure to the next world in the company of their deceased patrons; when death came to them they were buried as befitted their position in tombs surrounding the tombs of those whom they had faithfully served in life. But while the tombs of the kings were lofty pyramids, those of their nobles were humbler structures, now called, on account of their resemblance to a low bench or seat, mastabas, from the Arabic word mastaba, "bench." These mastabas are on the model of the brick tombs of the earlier period in Upper Egypt, but are built of stone, like the pyramids. Each royal pyramid is surrounded by regular streets of these mastabas, reproducing in death the dwellings of the courtiers round the palace of the king in life.

The pyramids of Seneferu mark a considerable advance in structure on that of Tjeser, but that of Khufu, the "Great Pyramid" of Giza, marks a greater advance still; in size and mass it is the culminating point of the series. That of Radadf is tiny in comparison; Khafra's rivals Khufu's; Menkaura's is far smaller again. But in art of construction and carefulness of work, Khafra's is superior to Khufu's, and Menkaura's would probably have been the most beautiful of all, only it was never quite completed.

Our wonder at the absolute command of men and material to which the building of the pyramids bears witness, is as nothing to that which is inspired by a contemplation of the grandeur of their design, and, still more, the mathematical accuracy with which not only the design generally, but its details, down to the almost imperceptible junction of the stones in the inner passages and chambers, could be carried out in the fourth millennium B.C. The brain-power which is evinced by the building of the pyramids is in no way inferior to that of the great engineers of the present day. The

Egyptians had attained all the essentials of a civilization as fully developed as our own as early as 3000 B.C.

In art, while relief sculpture had not yet attained the excellence of the next dynasty, and we see crude experiments like the coloured inlay of the tombs of Nefermaat and Atet at Medum, yet the sculptors of the IVth Dynasty had attained the mastery of sculpture in the round, a mastery which was not reached by the Greeks until after the re-birth of their civilization and the sixth century B.C. It was to be a limited mastery, and we shall see that the limits that were soon to be set to it were destined never to be passed. But it was the first great art of the world. The enthroned diorite statues of Khafra from Giza, the small standing groups of Menkaura and his queen (Frontispiece), and of Menkaura with the goddesses of the nomes, discovered by Reisner in the king's tomb-temple, and now at Boston and Cairo, the Rahetep and Nefert at Cairo, the "Scribe Accroupi" of the Louvre, the Nenkheftka of the British Museum, to name only the works of the very first rank, are (with the exception of that little ivory king of the 1st Dynasty that we have already mentioned), the most ancient masterpieces of all art. We do not notice coarsely carved legs or wooden arms, when we see those wonderful faces which are the men themselves. The rest of the body is, whether avowedly so or not, a sketch, an impression: it was perhaps not intended to be a faithful transcript as the face was intended to be, and evidently was. Under the next dynasty we find splendid work, and the art of relief-sculpture has now been much developed; but the figures of this time somehow do not please us so well as the freely natural kings and princes of the IVth Dynasty. Statues of this kind were found in most of the chief mastabas of the IVth and VIth Dynasties: they were sealed up in a recess of the tomb, known by the Arabic term serdab, and were apparently intended as secondary residences for the ka or "double," in case the actual body was destroyed.

The tombs of the members of their courts at Medum and Giza give us a great deal of information as to the names of the great nobles of the days of the pyramid-builders, and with regard to the various civil offices and priesthoods which they held. The perusal of a list of these various civil and religious offices shews how far formalism had advanced in Egypt even as early as the days of the IVth Dynasty.

From the inscriptions of these courtiers we gain some hints as to the succession of the kings and their relationship to each other. These hints entirely confirm the testimony of the king-lists; Manetho's names are correct, but his order and dates seem wrong. Mertitfes, the chief wife of Seneferu, survived him and married his successor, Khufu, who was therefore not nearly related to his predecessor. In fact, he does not seem to have been a native of Memphis, and was probably a prince of Middle Egypt, since an important town near the modern Benihasan, the capital of the nome of the Oryx, was named under the Middle Empire Menat-Khufu, "Nurse of King Khufu": it is probable that he came thence. Queen Mertitfes survived Khufu also, and was "honoured in the presence of King Khafra," as she says in her tomb-inscription. She passes over Sharu and Radadf, whose reigns seem to have been very short. Her life was evidently prolonged, but it is quite evident from the fact that she was chief wife of both Seneferu and Khufu, and was an honoured figure at the court of Khafra, that the reigns of these kings can hardly have been as long as the historians pretend, Diodorus, following Herodotus, makes Khufu reign fifty years and Khafra fifty-six; Manetho assigns them sixty-three and sixty-six years respectively. To Sharu and Radadf can hardly be assigned less than about ten years, so that if we assume that she was far younger than Seneferu, and was perhaps only twenty-five at his death, she must, if Manetho's figures are correct, have been nearly ninety at Khafra's accession, which is a great age for Egypt, and she lived on after that. Khufu's reign need not have been longer than the twenty-three years of the Turin papyrus, and Herodotus' fifty years for Khufu is probably "contaminated" by the (very probable) fifty-six of Khafra.

Khafra is said by Herodotus to have been Khufu's brother, which is manifestly impossible; Diodorus is in doubt between the authority of the great, which he is afraid to reject, and that of tradition, which told him that Khufu was succeeded by his son Chabryes. Accordingly he doubles Khafra, and speaks of both "Kephren," the brother, and "Chabryes," the son, of Khufu. Chabryes is evidently another Greek form of the name Khafra, and the fact that Khafra was Khufu's son is confirmed by a papyrus. The succession of Menkaura to Khafra is confirmed by the contemporary monument; Diodorus makes him his brother, but this is improbable, if Khafra's reign was as long as the annalists make it. His pyramid was never finished, so that we may credit Diodorus' information that he died before its completion, and Herodotus' implication that his reign was no long one Manetho's sixty-three years for him is, then, evidently a mere copyist's repetition of the same number of years assigned to Khufu.

Menkaura was succeeded by Shepseskaf, "Noble is his Double," the Sebercheres (i.e. Shepseskara, "Noble is the Double (Ghost) of Ra,") of Manetho, the Sasychis of Diodorus, and Asychis of Herodotus. We know nothing of any king corresponding to Bicheris or Thamphthis, who in Manetho's list respectively precede and succeed him. His immediate succession to Menkaura is made certain by the testimony of his contemporary Shepsesptah, who was admitted among the royal children by Menkaura, married Shepseskaf's daughter Khamaat ("the Goddess of Law appears"), and was raised to fill every office he possibly could fill. It is evident that no man could possibly do all the work which these colossal pluralists were officially credited with doing: the work of most of their offices must have been done by subordinates, but we may be sure that their emoluments went to the noble office-holder.

It is quite evident that the king was, even more than under the 1st Dynasty, the fountain of honour: a despotic monarch surrounded by a servile court to whom he dispensed dignities at his will: the government of the country could be carried out well enough by the stewards and factors of the absentee governors and princes, who were retained in the king's presence-chamber in life and were buried at his feet when they died. The common people could be used to build pyramids with. Yet there is a little doubt that the popular stories of the cruelty and impiety of the Pyramid-builders which are related by Herodotus and Diodorus are grossly exaggerated, if not wholly baseless. They seem to have been pious monarchs enough: Khufu and Khafra both contributed to the building of the Temple of Bubastis, and Hordedef, son of Khufu, was, according to old legends, a most pious person, and "discovered" chapters of the Ritual, like King Semti of old.

Khufu, Khafra, and Menkaura must have left a tremendous impression on the minds of the Egyptians, which was always kept alive by the everlasting presence of the three great pyramids on the Libyan hills: when even the meanest Egyptian looked at the mighty Khuit, the lofty Ueret, and the beautiful Hra, he thought of the three great kings of old whose names his father had told him and which he would repeat to his son, and his son to his son, throughout the generations. The pyramids kept their names fresh in the minds of the people, and folk tales innumerable would naturally gather round them. The archaistic revival of the XXVIth Dynasty, which looked for its inspiration to the models which the tombs of the courtiers of the Pyramid-builders provided, and resuscitated the cults of the kings themselves, must have given a considerable impulse to these popular tales, which Herodotus and Diodorus after him found current in the land in their day, and utilized for their histories.

2. The Vth Dynasty

Though we pass out of the presence of the great Pyramid-builders, we are still in the age of pyramid-building. The civilization of the Vth Dynasty is practically the same as that of the IVth; the face of things is the same. But there is one difference noticeable. Whereas under the older kings Horus had been the supreme deity of Egypt, if supreme deity there was, with the accession of Userkaf, the first king of the Vth Dynasty, the Sun-god Ra of Annu or Heliopolis, the Biblical On, advances to the first place, which, in conjunction later with the Theban deity Amen, he held ever afterwards, Horus becoming in some aspects identified with him. We find the beginnings of this special devotion to Ra already under the IVth Dynasty, when the names of Khafra, Menkaura, and Shepseskaf are compounded with that of Ra, "Shepses-ka-f" meaning "Noble is his (the Sun's) Ghost," as "User-ka-f" means "strong is his Ghost." Names confounded in this way now become common. And in Userkaf's time the royal title "Son of the Sun," which has already appeared under the IVth Dynasty, becomes a regular addition to the royal style. A curious legend current under the Empire relates that a magician named Dedi prophesied to King Khufu that three children should be born to Rud-dedet, the wife of Rauser, a priest of Ra, by Ra, and that the eldest of these, who was to be high-priest of Ra, would succeed to the throne after the reign of Khufu's son. And when the three divinely-begotten children were born, Ra sent the goddesses Isis, Nephthys, Meskhenit who presided over births, and Heket the goddess of sorcery (the original of the Greek Hekate), with the god Khnum who forms the bodies and the kas of kings, to Rud-dedet, and they named the children Useref, Sahra, and Kakau. Now the first three kings of the Vth Dynasty, which, as we have seen, was especially devoted to the cult of Ra of Heliopolis, were Userkaf, Sahura, and Kakaa. We can hardly doubt that this legend points to the fact that the kings of the Vth Dynasty belonged to a new family, descended from a priest of the Sun-god: and in all probability Userkaf himself was, as the legend says, originally high-priest of Ra under the last king of the IVth Dynasty, and succeeded him as king. Each king of the dynasty built for himself a special sanctuary of the sun-god, the central feature of which was a great single obelisk rising out of a mastaba-like erection, and the priesthoods of these Sun-temples were given to specially honoured nobles. The best preserved of these Sun-temples is that at Abu Gurab, between Giza and Abusir, which was built by Ne-user-Ra. On a great mound was erected the truncated obelisk, the stone emblem of the Sun-god. Before it was a great court in which still stands a huge circular altar of alabaster, several feet across, on which slain oxen were offered to the Sun, and behind this are six great basins, also of alabaster, over which the beasts were slain; drains run out of them to carry away the blood.

The great development of art and architecture under the IVth Dynasty was carried to its apogee under the kings of the Vth, who were also Pyramid-builders. Their tombs at Abusir, south of Giza, are neither so large nor so well-built as those of Khufu and Khafra, but the architecture and decoration of the great temples which were attached to them shews a more highly developed art than that of the earlier funerary temples. The Abusir pyramids are also arranged in a great group of three, the graves of the kings Sahura, Neferarikara, and Ne-User-Ra. The three funerary temples, which have been excavated by German archaeologists, have provided us with new material which may be said to have in some sort revolutionized our conceptions of the development of art under the Old Kingdom. The sculptures on their walls are the earliest temple-reliefs known, and it is probable that the custom of decorating the walls of temples, like those of tombs, with sculptured representations of gods and kings and their doings now first began. Important events in the lifetime of the king are now represented on the stone walls of his funerary temple: thus in that of Sahura we have reliefs picturing a naval expedition on the Red Sea, probably sent by him to fetch turquoise from Sinai, where he erected a monumental tablet in the Wadi Magharah. Allegorical representations shew the king, as a hawk-headed sphinx, trampling on his enemies. And as we see them on these ancient monuments the gods appear in their regular hieratic forms and attitudes, and wearing the same costume as in the days of the Ptolemies. This costume of the short waistcloth was that usually worn by the kings and great men of the Old Kingdom. The Vth Dynasty artists depicted the gods dressed like their own contemporary rulers. The proper attire of the gods and of the king when depicted performing religious rites was thus fixed at the time of the Vth Dynasty, and never varied henceforth, though on secular monuments of later times we see the king shewn wearing the actual costume of his period.

In the Abusir pyramids we as yet find no inscription, but in the pyramid of UNAS, the last king of the dynasty, which was built at Sakkara, south of Abusir, the new custom of inscribing the interior chambers of the tomb itself first appears. These inscriptions, which were copied in the pyramids of the succeeding kings of the VIth Dynasty, consist of a series of invocations and incantations intended to ensure the safety and happiness of the king's spirit in the next world, and, though often savage and absurd enough, are of the highest possible interest to the student of anthropology.

We are yet far from the time when higher minds could supplement the barbarous gibberish of the "Pyramid Texts" by splendid hymns to the gods; the probability is that the primitive beliefs still held unmodified sway. Philosophers had not yet progressed beyond the consideration of the vicissitudes of the daily life around them, and the elaboration of wise saws thereon, they had not yet begun to think about the gods: these were still left without question to the stupid interpretation of the priestly sorcerers. The schools of On had not yet arisen, though it was at this time and under this particular dynasty that the foundations were probably laid at On of that specially Heliopolitan tradition of religious interpretation which was later to develop that "wisdom of the Egyptians" which Moses learnt, and the culminating, the beautiful monotheism of Akhenaten the heretic.From this temple-reliefs at Abusir, and other monuments of this period, as well as from the Pyramid Texts, we see that all the gods of the later pantheon were already worshipped, with the exception of the foreign importations of later days, such as Bes, and of course the Theban Triad, Amen, Mut, and Khensu. The last-named is once mentioned as some sort of inferior djinn in the Pyramid Texts, but Amen is unknown. No doubt he was already worshipped at Thebes, a local form of Min, the presiding deity of the Thebaid, and not to be distinguished from him by the Memphite and Heliopolitan priests. Yet after a few centuries he was to be identified with the great Ra of Heliopolis himself, and later still to be elevated to the position of "King of the Gods."

According to Manetho, Unas (Onnos) was the last king of the Vth Dynasty, and his successor Teta founded a new dynasty, the VIth, of Memphite origin. Perhaps by his time the Heliopolitan origin of the existing Pharaonic family had become obscured after a long series of reigns in the royal city. From the monuments no change of dynasty can be perceived. Teta's tomb at Sakkara was decorated in the same style as that of Unas with magical texts for the comfort and protection of his soul, and the pyramid itself bears the same style of name as that of his predecessor. The pyramids of his successors are also decorated in the same way.

3. The VIth Dynasty

The central figure of the VIth Dynasty is the great King Merira Pepi I, the Phiops of Manetho, who left an impression on Egypt that was never forgotten. His younger son, Neferkara Pepi II, born to him late in life, was notable for what is probably the longest reign in history, as he ascended the throne at the age of six and died a centenarian.

Traces of the energy of the elder Pepi are seen all over Egypt from the Delta and Sinai to Elephantine and Sahal. The builder of the great stone temples, forerunners of the triumphs of a later age, which had been begun by the Pyramid-builders at Tanis and Bubastis, the first monumental evidences of Egyptian activity farther north than the Memphite territory was pushed on with vigour by Pepi, who also devoted considerable attention to the ancient religious centres of Dendera, Koptos, and Hierakonpolis. At the latter place a magnificent copper group of the king and a small boy, perhaps Mehtimsaf, was found by Mr. Ouibell in the course of the excavations carried on in 1896; the two statues, that of the king being over life-size, that of his son a little more than two feet high, are built up of plates of copper fastened together with copper nails. The faces are marvellously well modelled, and the inlaid eyes give the two figures an almost uncanny appearance of life.

In the far south the district of the First Cataract, which had apparently been conquered by the kings of the First Dynasty seems also to have occupied much of Pepi's attention. In his time It had become purely Egyptian, and was administered by Egyptian chiefs who lived and were buried at Aswan. Though related ethnically to the Southern Egyptians the population south of Elephantine was regarded as barbarian, and the relations between the Egyptians and the Nubians were much the same as those between Europeans and non-Europeans at the present day. We possess records of the travels of great officials of this period, Una, Herkhuf, Pepinekht, and Sabni, in the southern countries, from which we learn the names of the various Nubian tribes of the day; we see that their territories were regarded as being in some sort included in the Egyptian "sphere of influence," the leaders of the Egyptian expeditions, sent to bring back products of the southern countries to Egypt, and probably with the ultimate idea of penetrating overland to the "holy land" on the Somali coast (Punt), were called in to settle tribal disputes as representatives of the higher intelligence of the great civilized empire in the north, much as English travellers of distinction might be called in to advise by an Indian chief to-day. There is even some sort of half-recognition of Egyptian overlordship; but no actual sovereignty is acknowledged.

In the North Egyptian expeditions, which had reached Sinai as early as the time of the 1st Dynasty, are found in Palestine by the time of the Vth, with warlike intent, as in a tomb of that date at Deshashch we see a picture of an attack upon a Semitic town, which can only have been situated in Southern Palestine. Under the VIth Dynasty we find the much-travelled Una leading primitive expeditions against the Heriu-Sha, "the Sand-Dwellers" of the Isthmus of Suez and the Gulf coast.

It was a magnificent kingdom which was bequeathed by the first Pepi to his two sons. But, imposing as it was in appearance, it had within it a serious defect which after the reign of the second Pepi brought about swift decay, and eventual disintegration. The great kings of the IVth Dynasty marked the apogee of the original patriarchal kingdom founded by "Mena" and his successors. This kingdom was centralized round the king, whose nobles were courtiers who lived and were buried around him. The local government of the country was carried on by deputies of the king or of favoured nobles who held their lands at the king's pleasure. These deputies were probably not hereditary. From the very beginning Egypt had been divided into hsaput, called by the Greeks "nomes"; we find these nomes already under the 1st Dynasty, and in the South they were probably older. In such a country as Egypt, where the yearly inundation obliterates all landmarks every year, fixed boundaries were very early established. The nomes were ruled by the overseers of absentee courtiers. But the accession of the new line of the Vth Dynasty seems to have weakened the royal hold over the court. Up to the end of the reign of Ne-user-Ra, who, judging from the magnificence of his works, was a powerful monarch, the centralizing tradition was no doubt more or less kept going, but during the reigns of his weaker successors it must have been given up. We now find a new development. The great nobles, instead of being buried as a dead court around a dead king, are interred in their country estates, which they now rule directly and locally. They are primarily the "Great Men of the Nomes," and their court functions and titles diminish. Under the VIth Dynasty this becomes the settled constitution of the state, which is now a feudal monarchy, resting on the loyalty of the local princes. Under a strong prince like Pepi I, who would make himself obeyed, this condition of affairs was not detrimental to the state, but under weak kings it meant its destruction. This happened: the successors of Pepi II, whose reign was probably a long and a weak one, were nonentities; the chiefs, having no king whom they could respect, fell to fighting among themselves, and Egypt became a chaos. Art and civilization degenerated woefully, and the Theban kings of the XIth Dynasty, who, after perhaps two centuries of confusion, eventually restored order, had to re-create both.

A series of shadowy kings, the VIIth and VIIIth Dynasties of Manetho, reigned but did not rule at Memphis. Two of them, Neferkauhor and Ncferarikara II, more energetic than the rest, made their authority recognized at Abydos and even as far south as Koptos, but only for a moment. The princes levied war upon one another without check; nome fought against nome, until at length some chief more energetic and unscrupulous than the rest should find himself able to impose his yoke upon his neighbours and so give peace, perhaps only an ephemeral peace, to at least a portion of the distracted land. Some such powerful chief fixed the seat of his power, about two centuries and more after the time of the Pepis, in the city of Henen-nsuit or Henen-su, Herakleopolis Magna in Middle Egypt, and either he or one of his descendants found himself powerful enough to usurp the dignity of the legitimate sovereign at Memphis, and to proclaim himself Pharaoh. It is probable that after this impotent kings of the rightful line still reigned at Memphis, but the centre of real power was Herakleopolis.

4. The Herakleopolites (IXth Dynasty)

Only one of the Herakleopolite kings has left any very tangible evidence of his presence, and he was possibly the most active of them; perhaps the very man who first supplanted the Memphites and assumed the royal dignity. This was Khati or Ekhati, who bore the throne name Meriabra, "Beloved of the Heart of the Sun." The name of the king occurs as far south as the First Cataract, so that it is evident that he securely controlled the whole Upper Country, as well as upon smaller objects. There is little doubt that this king or a second Khati with the throne name Uahkara is identical with the Akhthoes of Manetho, who places him at the beginning of the IXth Dynasty, and says that he became more terrible than all those who had gone before him, that he did evil unto the people in all Egypt, and that he finally went mad and was devoured by a crocodile. This story has the same ring as others about other kings who left a powerful impression, whether of good or evil, behind them; Menes was devoured by a crocodile, Cheops and Chephren were impious oppressors.

The Herakleopolite rule was at first peacefully acquiesced in by the more southerly nomes, but later on it was opposed, especially by the princes of the Thebaid, whose original seat seems to have been Erment (Hermonthis), but whose power was early transferred to the more northerly Apet (Thebes). Here was laid the foundation of the future Theban hegemony in Egypt, which was to last undisputed for over fifteen hundred years. Gradually the chiefs of Apet increased in power, the boundary of their territory was gradually pushed northwards beyond Koptos, until it marched with the southern frontier of the land which owed more direct allegiance to Herakleopolis. Then the Herakleopolite allegiance was thrown off, and a series of bloody wars seems to have begun, in the course of which the Theban princes did as the Herakleopolites had done before them, and themselves assumed the Pharaonic dignity. Finally, the Herakleopolite power was overthrown. Memphis had long been a nome, and her kings, the rightful seed of Ra, had disappeared. Egypt, weary of war, accepted the Theban sceptre, and a new period of Egyptian history began, which we know as the "Middle Kingdom," to distinguish it from the "Old Kingdom" of Thinis and Memphis, and from the "New Empire" which commenced after the expulsion of the Hyksos invaders.

We know of the civil war between Herakleopolis and Thebes chiefly from the inscriptions in the tombs of the princes of the important city of Siut, in Middle Egypt, who were adherents of Herakleopolis, and formed the frontier defence of the Herakleopolite kings against the Thebans. They bore the names of Khati and Tefaba alternately from father to son. The first Khati prided himself on not being a rebel: "I," he says, "am one void of rebellion against his lord: Siut is content under my rule, Herakleopolis praiseth God for me, the Nomes of the South and the Lands of the North say, 'Lo! whatsoever the prince commandeth, that is the command of Horus (the king).'" It would seem that in his time the South was submissive, but Tefaba his son was compelled to reconquer the South.

In the time of Khati II, son of Tefaba, the Herakleopolite king Merikara was driven from his capital by a Northern attack from Memphis, and took refuge at Siut with his feudatory, who also fought with the South. The later chiefs of Siut were unable to maintain their resistance to Thebes: the princes of the hated "Town of the South," which is angrily mentioned in one of these inscriptions, eventually broke through the barrier which had so long stopped their way northwards, and it is probable that after the fall of Siut the fate of the Herakleopolite dynasty was not long delayed. We do not know the name of the prince of Thebes who took Siut and finally destroyed the Herakleopolite power. The most ancient Theban chief of whom we have any knowledge is a certain Meri, who apparently lived not long after the time of the Pepis: two statues of him, in different costumes, from his tomb at Dra Abu'l-Nekka, are preserved in the British Museum. In his day Thebes was no doubt under the rule of the Mentu-worshipping princes of Erment, who later on transferred their residence to the more northern city. An hereditary nomarch of Thebes, belonging apparently to the line of Erment, is known to us, named Antefi. He seems to have been regarded as the founder of the Theban race of kings, for Senusert I dedicated a statue of him at Karnak, and it is very probable that he was either the first Theban chief of his line or the first to establish a southern principality independent of Herakleopolis. One of his descendants, possibly his immediate successor, assumed the Pharaonic dignity and became the first king of the XIth Dynasty, but whether this was before or after the capture of Siut and destruction of the Herakleopolite dynasty, it is difficult to say.

5. The XIth Dynasty

After Antefi I the only kings of the XIth Dynasty who were remembered in later days were the powerful monarch Neb-hapet-Ra Mentuhetep and his successor Sankhkara Mentuhetep, who immediately preceded Amenemhat I, the founder of the XIIth Dynasty. An earlier king, Neb-taui-Ra Mentuhetep, also appears in the lists; he must have preceded Neb-hapet-Ra. From contemporary monuments, however, we know of the existence of a group of three still earlier kings, an Antef "the great" who bore the Horus-name of Uah-ankh, another Antef with the Horus-name Nekhtnebtepnefer, and a Mentuhetep with the Horus-name Sankhabtaui, who succeeded in this order. It is probable that the "Horus Ancestor" (tep-'a) Mentuhetep, and another Antef, mentioned in the inaccurate Karnak list, are to be identified with two of these kings. We know nothing of them, or of one or two kings who ruled in Nubia at this time, and may or may not have been members of the Theban dynasty. Nor is Neb-taui-Ra much more than a shadowy figure. Like the later Egyptians, we know more than a little only of the reigns of Neb-hapet-Ra and Sankhkara. Neb-hepet-Ra was in later times regarded as one of the great pharaohs, and he appears almost as the progenitor of the royal line of Thebes. Like Uah-ankh, the real founder of the dynasty, he reigned long, and it is probable that the two kings were confused in later tradition. It is by no means improbable that Neb-hapet-Ra was the first Theban who really ruled over the whole country. It is significant that Uah-ankh and his two successors bore no throne-name, as rightful pharaohs would but seem to have laid stress upon their Horus-names, which were the appropriate designations of kings who ruled the patrimony of Horus of Edfu, Upper Egypt alone, since originally, as we have seen, the Horus-name was the sacred designation of the Upper Egyptian Kings who founded the 1st Dynasty. Neb-taui-Ra was the first to adopt a throne-name, and he included it in his cartouche with his personal name, thus having only one cartouche. Neb-hapet-Ra was the first to bear two cartouches as undisputed king of all Egypt. He may have deposed the last Memphite, as it is probable that the Memphite kings had continued to reign in the North after the end of the Herakleopolite dynasty. He seems to have altered the official spelling of his throne-name and have changed his Horus-name during his reign; appearing first as the Horus "Neter-hetjet" ("Divine White Crown," the crown of Upper Egypt), later as the Horus "Sam-taui" ("Uniting the Two Lands"). It may well be that this change of name is significant, and that the later Horus-name was adopted to mark the re-union of the two lands, just as, in far earlier days, Khasekhem seems to have changed his name to Khasekhemui ("Appearance of the Two Powers") after he had conquered the North.

Of the details of Neb-hapet-Ra's re-organization we know nothing, but it is probable that even towards the end of his reign a subordinate king, who bore the title of "Son of the Sun," was allowed to exist in Upper Egypt above Thebes. His name was Antef, and it is probable that he is one of the kings whose names are found in Nubia.

Of this important reign an important monument has come down to us, the funerary temple of the king at Der el-Bahri, in the western necropolis opposite Thebes. Here, in a circus of huge cliffs of extraordinarily impressive form and splendid desert colour, Neb-hapet-Ra excavated what is either his tomb or his cenotaph, a long gallery extending far beneath the mountain, and ending in a chamber faced with gigantic blocks of granite and containing a naos or shrine of alabaster and granite, which held either his coffin or the statue of his ka. Above the tomb was cut a great trench in which was a temple with its sanctuary, and on a half-artificial platform jutting out towards the cultivated land was, later in his reign, erected a memorial pyramid of brick cased with thin marble slabs, surrounded by a colonnade and approached by a sloping ramp, on either side of which at the lower level was a colonnade marking the face of the platform, which was faced on the other two sides with splendid walls of fine limestone. Everywhere the walls were sculptured with scenes of the king's wars and hunting-expeditions, which, since they are now in a fragmentary condition, have told us less concerning the events of his reign than the development of art in his time: on this they have shed new and valuable light. Between the pyramid and the tomb were erected six small funerary shrines above the tombs of certain priestesses of Hathor, the goddess of the place, who were also concubines of the king, and that of the queen, Aasheit. It seems very probable that these priestesses were all slain at the death of the king, and accompanied him to the tomb to be with him in the next world. In the time of the 1st Dynasty, courtiers and slaves seem to have been killed, as we have seen, and buried with the kings: and the custom was at least occasionally carried out as late as the time of Amenhetep II.

The development of art under the XIth Dynasty, on which the sculptures of this temple have shed considerable light, is perhaps the most interesting characteristic of the dynasty. The fine Memphite art of the Vth and VIth Dynasties had been not unsuccessfully imitated in Upper Egypt, but civil war had caused a woeful degeneration in the arts, and the Theban sculptors' work of the beginning of the XIth Dynasty is extraordinarily crude and barbarous: modelled relief has been forgotten, and both figures and hieroglyphs are badly sized, spaced, and drawn. But an enormous improvement is seen at the beginning of the reign of Neb-hapet-Ra, to which the shrines of the priestesses, which were completed before the temple as a whole, belong. A remarkably high relief, adorned with brilliant colour, is characteristic of these shrines. The figures have still an awkward, archaic appearance, however, and this hardly vanishes in the later style of the reign, seen in the decoration of the temple-corridors, which otherwise again approaches the standard of the Vth Dynasty. The portraits of the king and his queen are splendidly executed, and bear the same impress of truth as do those of the IVth and XIIth Dynasties.

These sculptures have a personal interest usually lacking in the works of Egyptian art, since we probably know the name of the great artist who carried them out. This was very probably a certain Mertisen, who lived in the reign of Neb-hapet-Ra. He tells us on his funerary stela, now in the

Louvre, "I was an artist skilled in my art. I knew my art, how to represent the forms of going forth and returning, so that each limb may be in its proper place. I knew how the figure of a man should walk and the carriage of a woman; the poising of the arm to bring the hippopotamus low, the going of the runner." He also tells us that no man shared this knowledge with him but his eldest son. Now since Mertisen and his son were the chief artists of their day, it is more than probable that they were employed to decorate their king's funerary temple.

When, therefore, the kings of the XIth Dynasty reunited the whole land under one sceptre, and the long reign of Neb-hapet-Ra Mentuhetep enabled the reconsolidation of the realm to be carried out by one hand, art began to revive; and just as to Neb-hapet-Ra must be attributed the renascence of the Egyptian state under the hegemony of Thebes, so must the revival of art under the XIth Dynasty be attributed to the Theban artists of his time, perhaps to Mertisen and his son. They carried out in the realm of art what their king had carried out in the political realm.

Neb-hapet-Ra was a warrior and warred against Libyans, Nubian, and Semites, the latter being called "Aamu" and (possibly) "Rutenreru," later on to become familiar to the Egyptians as the people of Ruten, or Syria. So that he may have invaded Southern Palestine.

Sankhkaia Alentuhetep was no such great figure as his predecessor. His reign was solely distinguished by a great expedition to the Land of Punt, conducted by a military mandarin of the name of Henu. Henu proceeded by the Hammamat road to the Red Sea coast at Kuser, and then, after great sacrifices had been held, proceeded on shipboard and sailed down the coast to Somaliland, returning eventually in safety to Koptos, whence he had set out, laden with the incense, gum, and myrrh which he had been sent to obtain, and with stone which had been quarried for the king in the Hammamat valley. The tradition of connection with Punt is kept up, and we seem to be reading an account of an expedition of the Vth or VIth Dynasty once more: indeed it is improbable that much more than two or three hundred years had elapsed since Baurdad went to Punt, and Una and Herkhuf explored the regions of the Upper Nile. But there is one point which differentiates Henu's expedition from these of the earlier time. The older explorers often seem to have travelled overland from the Nubian Nile valley by way of Abyssinia to Punt; Henu, like Enenkhet before him, went to Kuser, and thence by sea. It looks as if the overland route was no longer safe for Egyptian caravans; and the southern military expedition of

Mentuhetep II indicates that the peaceful relations of Egypt with her southern neighbours in the days of Asesa had given way to a state of war and unrest, which compelled the Egyptian messengers to Punt to voyage thither by sea. Henceforward, even when Nubia was absolutely subject to Egypt, the sea-route remained the regular way to Punt, and Hatshepsut's great expeditions followed in the steps of that of Sankhkara.

6. The XIIth Dynasty

The XIIth Dynasty, "the Kings of the Court of Itht-taui," as the Turin Papyrus calls them, succeeded the XIth without a break. It is very probable that Amenemhat I, the first king of the new dynasty, was the vizier of Sankhkara, and from his name ("Amen at the head") we may suppose that he was a Theban. His descendants, however, specially favoured the district between Memphis and the modern Fayyum, and there they established their court, in the fortress-palace of Itht-taui, the "Controller of the Two Lands." They were, however, nominally Thebans, and they venerated Amen as well as Sebek, the crocodile-god of the Fayyum.

Amenemhat's accession was not accepted without a struggle. We know from a very curious papyrus book, regarded as a classic under the XVIIIth and XIXth Dynasties, which was apparently written by King Amenemhat I, the Sbayut or "Instructions" of the king to his son Senusert, that upon one occasion at least his life was attempted by conspirators within the palace, probably at the beginning of his reign.

The reigns of the kings of the dynasty were hailed by their contemporaries as marking a veritable renascence of the kingdom. The inscriptions of the time are full of references to the time of disunion which preceded them, compared with the present age of plenty and peace within the frontiers of Egypt of restored sanctuaries and widened borders. "Twice joyful are the gods," says a hymn of praise addressed to the third Senusert, "for thou hast established their offerings. Twice joyful are thy princes; thou hast formed their boundaries. . . . Twice joyful is Egypt at thy strong arm; thou hast guarded the ancient order." If the kings of the XIth Dynasty, after reuniting the two lands, "made them to live," and "increased their life," those of the XIIth also marked the renascence of the kingdom out of the slough of despair into which it had fallen during centuries of civil war in their nomes; Amenemhat I is the "Horus who renews the births" of the people (Uhem-mesut), Senusert I is the "life of the births" (Ankh-mesut), Senusert II is the "helmsman of the two lands" (Semu-taui). And from the evidence other than that of official titles we can see the living interest which these energetic monarchs took in their law and people. Amenemhat III added a whole province to Egypt by his reclamations in the Fayyum, and it has been supposed that he regulated the flow of water in and out of Lake Moiris, which served to hold back part of the surplus of the high Nile and to allow it to flow out when the river was low. The regulation of the Nile-flood, the life of Egypt, was their constant care; as their frontiers advanced southwards into Nubia, Nilo-meters were established at which the height of the water was year by year carefully measured, and whence the important intelligence was transmitted to Egypt. The conquest and annexation of Northern Nubia, if it did not add a fertile province to Egypt, at least enabled the kings to carry out this great object, which seems to have been ever present in their minds, the careful watching and regulation of the Nile. Everywhere throughout the land the boundaries which had been thrown down during the period of confusion were renewed, and it is probable that some sort of cadastral survey was at least partially carried out for this end. The frontiers of the Nomes were finally delimited, and the powers and status of the Nomarch princes carefully defined in relation to each other and to the royal authority. While retaining many tokens of the independence which they had gained during the decline of the central power at Memphis, they were now again brought into due subjection to the royal authority.

We gain a sufficient idea of the wealth and state of the local princes from the splendid tombs of the chiefs who are buried at Beni Hasan and el-Bersheh in Middle Egypt. The princes were laid to rest in chambers at the bottom of pits which were sunk in the floors of the splendid halls of offering, the walls of which were covered with paintings depicting the life of their owners on earth, executed in the hope of securing for the dead similar well-being in the underworld. Of the art with which these paintings are executed we shall have occasion to speak later. Below them on the slopes of the tomb-hill were buried the officials and functionaries of their little courts, their stewards, physicians, and retainers of various ranks, each like his lord, with his own funerary state of great rectangular wooden coffins and the models of fellah servants and boatmen which were supposed to turn into ghostly ministrants in the underworld, and are so characteristic a feature of the burial customs of this period.

But this wealth and state was not destined to last. It has been supposed, though the fact is not certain, that the powerful monarchs Senusert III and

Amenemhat III still further modified the position of the local princes, and laid the foundations of the bureaucratic local government which we find in the time of the Empire. It is certain that splendid nobles of the type of the Khnumheteps of Beni Hasan and the Thutiheteps of el-Bersheh are no longer met with during the second half of the XIIth Dynasty, and that then we find purely royal officials much more prominent than before. Gradually the royal power had increased, largely by means of the king's control of the local levies in war. The continuous wars of Senusert III in Nubia served to establish the control of the king over the bodies of his subjects, to the exclusion of that of their local chiefs. And we cannot imagine that so tremendous a despot as Amenemhat III seems to have been would have allowed local despots like the Khnumheteps and Amenis of Beni Hasan to exist.

7. The Works of The XIIth Dynasty

The power and wealth of the kings of the XIIth Dynasty is well exhibited in the magnificent buildings which they set up. To them the temples of Amen at Karnak, of Ra at Heliopolis, of Ubastet at Bubastis, of Min at Koptos, of Hershef at Herakleopolis, not to speak of many others, owe the beginnings of the splendour which we know under the later Empire. Senusert I was a splendid temple-builder; by him were erected the first great obelisks in Egypt, in front of the temple of Heliopolis, and we possess the account of the ceremonies which marked his founding of the temple of Karnak. Colossal statues of the kings adorned the newly erected fanes, and a large number of the colossi which now bear only the names of later monarchs were really erected by the kings of the XIIth Dynasty.

The huge reclamation works carried out by Amenemhat III in the "Lake-Province" of the Fayyum are a testimony to the energy of this dynasty. The interest of the kings was probably first drawn to this oasis-district by its proximity to their royal burgh or fortress-palace of Itht-taui. Possibly with the view of conciliating Herakleopolitan sentiment, or possibly on account of some family alliance with the descendants of the royal house of Herakleopolis, the earlier kings of the XIIth Dynasty not only devoted special attention to the temples of the erstwhile royal city, but actually transferred their residence from Thebes, where the headquarters of the XII Dynasty had been fixed, to a position midway between Memphis and Herakleopolis, and in close proximity to the Fayyum. Thebes and Upper Egypt being thoroughly loyal to the royal house which was of Theban origin, and was doing so much for the Nubian frontier-territory, this position, which, as has been said, was admirably adapted to secure a general oversight of the whole country, could be safely adopted as the royal headquarters. The old Memphite tradition of burying the kings in pyramids in the neighbourhood of the necropolis of Memphis was also revived.

The interest of the kings of the XIIth Dynasty in the neighbouring lake-province began with its founder, Amenemhat I, who seems to have erected a temple at Shedit (Crocodilopolis). Senusert I is commemorated there by his tall boundary-stone or "obelisk" at Begig or Ebgig, not far off. Amenemhat III's great work was, besides the construction of a dyke at Illahun regulating the outflow from the lake, the reclamation by means of a great curved embankment of, according to Prof. Petrie's estimate, about forty square miles of fertile territory to the north and east of Shedit. On the dam, at a point directly north of Shedit, the king placed as a memorial of the work, two colossal statutes of himself, each thirty-nine feet high, and each cut from a single block of white quartzite. These were mounted on a platform, and must have been seen far and wide across the lake; the effect of the sun's rays reflected from the glittering quartzite must have been remarkable.

The famous Labyrinth at Hawara which amazed Herodotus so much, and is described by Diodorus, Strabo, and Pliny, was a great funerary temple erected by Amenemhat III (Lamaris) in front of his pyramid at Hawara. Shining white stone, probably quartzite and alabaster, was largely used in its construction, probably for facing blocks, and this caused Pliny to describe its walls as of Parian marble. This fact, and the great number of its halls and corridors, caused the Greeks to compare it with the famous labyrinth of Minos at Knossos in Crete, and also, led no doubt by the king's name "Lamaris," to transfer to it the Cretan appellation of "labyrinth." Its halls were decorated with representations of the various nomes of Egypt, a fact which has caused the attribution to the building of the character of a sort of state office or clearing-house for the affairs of the nomes, but there is no probability that this view is in any way correct; the nomes were merely represented as ministering to the glory of King Lamaris or Moiris, and his gods.

8. Foreign Relations

For the building of these mighty works and for their decoration and furniture an extensive provision of fine stone, metal, and wood was necessary. Royal expeditions constantly visited the quarries of Syene and the Western Desert for granite, diorite, and amazon-stone, the mines of Sinai for malachite and turquoise, and the forests of Syria for wood; while the unhappy Nubians were compelled by force to furnish the necessary gold. At the same time commercial relations with the surrounding nations were much developed; in exchange for the products of Egypt, Punt, Syria, and Greece sent to the Nile-land their most valuable commodities.

The Hammamat road led still, as of old, to the port of Sauu (Kuser) and the "Holy Land" which was on the way to Punt; under Senusert II we hear that stelae on the figures of the king were set up in Ta-neter, and in the preceding reign an officer named Khentekhtai-uer returned in peace from Punt, his soldiers with him; his ships voyaged prosperously, anchoring at Sauu. Egyptian settlements existed along the coast south of Sauu: at Nehesit, "the Negro-town," Ptolemy's Nechesia; Tep-Nekhebet, "the head" of the tutelary goddess of Southern Egypt, which is Berenike, and elsewhere. The voyage along this coast to Punt was the theme of many wonder-tales of adventure, one of which, the "Story of the Shipwrecked Sailor," which dates to this period, reminds us of the tale of Sindbad. The hero of this romance set forth in a ship 150 cubits long and 40 wide, with a hundred and fifty of the best sailors in the land of Egypt, who had seen heaven and earth and whose hearts were braver than those of lions. But the great ship was wrecked and only the teller of the tale was wafted safely to the shores of a mysterious isle, a sort of Aeaea or Hy-Brasail, whereon dwelt a gigantic serpent, who was 30 cubits long and whose beard exceeded 2 cubits; his body was encrusted with gold and his colour appeared like that of real lapis. "He uprose before me and opened his mouth; and while I prostrated myself before him, he said to me 'What hath brought thee, little one, what hath brought thee?'" Then he carried the sailor in his mouth to his dwelling without hurting him, and commanded him to tell his tale, which he did, and to which the serpent, commiserating him, replied that he need fear nothing, for after four months he would return safely to Egypt, while after his departure the island would be changed into waves.

So the frankincense and myrrh of Punt, as well as the fine granites and beautiful green felspar (amazon-stone) of the Eastern Desert, were brought through half-mythical dangers by the king's officers to the royal court. The turquoise and the copper of Sinai also needed capable caravan-leaders and bold soldiers who would bear great hardships to bear them back to their master.

A new mining-centre was established at the Sarabit-al-Khadim, and the works in the Wadi Maghara were prosecuted with success. An inscription of an official named Hem-uer gives some idea of the trials and disappointments of the mining captains among the arid rocks and deserts of Sinai. Hem-uer was unsuccessful in his search for the turquoise and copper which he was sent to obtain, and his men threatened to desert. In despair he invoked the aid of the goddess of the mines, Hathor-Mafek, and she aided him. "The desert burned like summer," he says, "the mountain seemed on fire, and the vein exhausted; the overseer questioned the miners, and the skilled workers who knew the mine replied: 'There is turquoise to all eternity in the mountain.' And at that moment the vein appeared." Amenemhat III sent many expeditions to Sinai.

The "land flowing with milk and honey" which lay beyond the desert of Suez as yet tempted no Egyptian king to permanent conquest. Already in the time of the Vth and VIth Dynasties warlike expeditions had reached Southern Palestine, sent in reprisal for marauding attacks on the Delta. But they were never followed up: the climatic conditions of Palestine were strange, and the land itself probably seemed uncanny to the Egyptians, nor were its products sufficiently valuable to attract the cupidity of the Egyptian kings. Also, the Rutenu, the settled and civilized Semites who lived north of the Aamu, the pastoral nomads of the Negeb and Southern Judrea, were formidable in war; occasionally their attacks had to be guarded against. In the reign of Senusert III we find that a place named Sekmekem, or Sekmem, probably some South Palestinian land, had allied itself with the "Vile Rutenu," with the result that an expedition was sent against it, in which an officer named Khusebek took part. He tells us of the war and destruction of the treacherous Sekmekem on his tombstone, which was found at Abydos. No further advance is chronicled, nor any more war with the Rutenu, who continued to live their own civilized life in their "fenced" towns, deriving their civilization chiefly from distant Babylon, and owing but little to the neighbouring Egypt, in spite of a regular commercial connexion with her, which is proved by the fairly common discoveries of Egyptian weapons and scarab-seals of the XIIth Dynasty in Palestine. A peaceful commerce was carried on by caravans of nom.ad or half-nomad Beduins, who found it profitable to bring their products and those of the Rutenu into Egypt and to sell them at the courts of the nome princes; the nomarch Khnumhetep in the reign of Senusert II records in his tomb at Beni Hasan the arrival in his nome of thirty-seven men and women of the "Aamu," under a hik-khaskhut or "desert-chief" named Abesha (Abishu'a), who brought him the green-eye paint of antimony (mestjamut, Ar. kohl) which the Egyptians so much loved, and other products of their land. We have here a picture on a small scale of the way in which the forefathers of the Israelites journeyed into the land of Goshen.

A remarkable picture of the life of the Beduin tribes of Southern Palestine is given in the autobiography of Sanehat or Sinuhe, a scion of the Egyptian royal house, in fact probably a younger son of Amenemhat I, who fled alone from Egypt on the announcement of the death of that king, possibly from fear lest he should be maltreated by the new monarch, Senusert I. He fled by sea to Byblos (already an important city), and thence to the land of Kedme in Syria. Here he was well received by a chief named Ammuanshi (the name is characteristic of the time; cf. the probably nearly contemporary Babylonian king Ammizaduga), and, after a victorious single combat, after the manner of David and Goliath, with a hostile champion, he married the chiefs daughter, and eventually succeeded to his possessions. But in his old age he desired to end his days in Egypt, and besought permission to return. King Senusert answered with a gracious rescript, promising him his favour in life and a splendid burial: "then," he writes, "they shall give thee bandages from the hand of Tait on the night of anointing with the oil of embalming. They shall follow thy funeral, and go to the tomb on the day of burial, which shall be in a gilded coffin, the head painted with blue. Thou shalt be placed upon the bier, and oxen shall draw thee along, the singers shall go before thee, and they shall dance thy funeral dance. The women crouching at the false-door of thy stele shall chant loudly the prayers for funeral-offerings; they shall slay victims for thee at the door of thy pit; and thy stela of white limestone shall be set up among those of the royal children. Thou shalt not die in a strange land, nor be buried by the Aamu: thou shalt not be laid in a sheepskin: all people shall smite the earth and lament over thy body as thou goest to the tomb."

On his return the king received him with open arms, and the princesses, placing collars of state about their necks, and each taking a wand of ceremony in one hand and a sistrum in the other, danced the solemn Hathor dance before the king, praising him for his loving-kindness to Sanehat. Then the returned wanderer passed out of the palace hand in hand with the royal children to the house which had been prepared for him. His foreign clothes were taken away from him, and his head was shaved as an Egyptian's should be; he dressed in fine linen, was anointed with the finest oil, and once more slept on a bedstead like a civilized being, instead of on the sand like a barbarian. The king had a magnificent tomb made for him, and he ends his story with the hope that he may ever continue in the royal favour.

Highly interesting in this story is the contrast between the civilization of the Egyptians and the comparative barbarism of the Beduins, which is well brought out in the matter of funeral rites. As a matter of fact, the elaboration and complexity of the Egyptian funeral customs was one of the great points of difference between the culture of Egypt and that of the Semites, and no doubt to the Egyptian seemed conclusive proof of his higher civilization and a mark of his distinction from the surrounding barbarians.

There is little doubt that relations were also already maintained by sea with the Phoenician cities. We do not know when the Semitic migration took place that brought the Phoenicians to the Mediterranean coast, but it is very probable that it is to be placed much farther back in time than it usually has been; and we need not doubt that the chief Phoenician city-states were already in existence at the time of the Egyptian XIIth Dynasty. Byblos was connected in a very curious way with the myths of the Egyptian Delta; part of the dismembered body of Osiris after his murder by Set was said to have been washed up there in a great chest, and Isis journeyed thither to reclaim it. This points to a connection by sea between the Delta and Phoenicia in the very earliest period. Under the VIth Dynasty the city was well known to the Egyptians by the name of Kabun or Kapun, an evidently very ancient modification of its Semitic name Gebal. It is probable that the ships, called Kabuniut or "Byblos-farers," which sailed from the Nile thither, were Phoenician rather than Egyptian.

Of the relations that existed between Egypt and Greece at this time we have already spoken.

The inhabitants of the coast of Libya, then in all probability less arid than now and more able to sustain a large population, were certainly connected somewhat closely with the Aegeans, and such Greek legends as that of Athene Tritogeneia may point to very ancient relations with Libya. To the Egyptians the Libyans had much the same unsavoury reputation as their friends the Hanebu. They were always, throughout history, trying to set their feet within the charmed circle of the Delta, and share in its wealth. We hear of wars with them as early as the days of the IIIrd Dynasty, and the Egyptians seem to have been no more tolerant of these pushing poor relations of theirs in the time of the XIIth Dynasty than they had been then. Senusert I was engaged upon a Libyan expedition at the very time of the death of his father.

9. The Nubian Wars

The warlike energy of the kings of the XIIth Dynasty was chiefly directed towards the prosecution of the feud with the Nubians, which had began under the preceding dynasty. The chief motive which inspired them to this war of conquest seems to have been a higher one than mere desire of revenge or domination, namely, the wish to control the Nile more effectually, and to be able to foresee more accurately the probable height of the yearly inundation on which the prosperity of Egypt depends. The kings of this dynasty seem to have regarded the regulation of the great river as the highest duty of a ruler of Egypt, as in truth it is. Bound up with this, however, there was also a lower motive; the desire to acquire instant prosperity and wealth by the acquisition of the gold with which the Wadi 'Alaki and other Nubian desert valleys were full.

Amenemhat I tells us in his "Instructions" to his son, already referred to, that he overthrew the Wawat and Matjaiu. The Wawat were the most important tribe of Northern Nubia. And on a rock near Korosko we read the laconic record: "In the 29th year of Sehetepabra, living for ever, they came to overthrow Wawat." Senusert I invaded Nubia in the eighteenth and forty-third years of his reign. He was probably the first Egyptian monarch to march south of Wadi Haifa, as in his second expedition (the first he did not accompany in person) he reached the land of Kush (Ethiopia), now first mentioned in history.

Under his two successors we hear only of gold-seeking expeditions. But Senusert III was a fighter. His eighth, sixteenth, and nineteenth years were marked by military expeditions which finally riveted the Egyptian yoke on the necks of the Nubians. The king prepared his way before him by renewing the canal, originally dating from the time of the VIth Dynasty, by which the First Cataract was avoided.

The king finally established the conquest by building, on the hills on each side of the river about thirty miles above the Second Cataract, the two fortresses of Semneh (Eg. Samnin, Gr. Sammina) and Kummeh (Eg.

Kummu), which remained important throughout Egyptian history, and the ruins of which are still remarkable. At Semneh was set up a boundary-stone with the following inscription: "This is the Southern Frontier, fixed in the eighth year of His Majesty King Khakaura, living for ever. No negro is permitted to pass this boundary northward, either on foot or by boat, nor any cattle, oxen, goats, or sheep belonging to negroes, except when a negro comes to trade in the land of Akin, or on any business whatsoever; then let him be well treated. But no boat of the negroes is to be allowed to pass Heli northward for ever." The benevolent feelings of the king seem to have evaporated eight years later, after his second expedition, for a great stela set up then at Semneh contains the following inscription: "Year 16, third month of Peret, His Majesty fixed the frontier of the South at Heh. I made my boundary, for I advanced upstream beyond my forefathers; I added much thereto, (namely) what was ordained by me. For I am king, and I say it and I do it. What lay in my heart was brought to pass by my hand. I am vigorous in seizing, powerful in succeeding, never resting; one in whose heart there is a word which is unknown to the weak, one who arises against mercy; never showing mercy to the enemy who attacks him, but attacking him who attacks him; silent to the silent, but answering a word according to the circumstances. For to take no notice of a violent attack is to strengthen the heart of the enemy. Vigour is valiant, but cowardice is vile. He is a coward who is vanquished on his own frontier, since the negro will fall prostrate at a word: answer him, and he retreats; if one is vigorous with him, he turns his back, retiring even when on the way to attack. Behold! these people have nothing terrible about them; they are feeble and insignificant; they have buttocks for hearts! I have seen it, even I, the Majesty; it is no lie! I have seized their women; I have carried off their folk. I marched to their wells, I took their cattle, I destroyed their seed-corn, I set fire to it. By my life and my father's, I speak truth! There is no possibility of gainsaying what cometh forth from my mouth! And, moreover, every son of mine who shall have preserved this frontier which my Majesty hath made is indeed my son and born of my Majesty, verily a son who avengeth his father and preserveth the boundary of him who begat him. But he who shall have abandoned it, he who shall not have fought for it, behold! he is no son of mine, he is none born of me. Behold me! Behold, moreover, my Majesty hath set up an image of my Majesty upon this frontier which my Majesty makes, not from a desire that ye should worship it, but from a desire that ye should fight for it!"

This really extraordinary inscription is one of the most remarkable monuments of Egyptian literature that have survived. It gives us a good idea of the vigour of the king. In some ways it conveys the impression of being a manifesto directed against the peaceful and probably somewhat weak methods of the two preceding reigns in dealing with the Nubians; and the half-sarcastic manner in which the king exhorts his subjects not to be afraid of barbarians, and to fight for his image, not merely to worship it, is highly curious. And when we remember that it was to this dynasty that the legendary Sesostris was assigned by Manetho, we also remember the stelae which the great conqueror was said to have set up in various parts of the world, the inscriptions of which, as described by Herodotus and Diodorus, remind us oddly of the phraseology of this stele of Senusert III.

Nubian expeditions were not necessary in the reign of Amenemhat III. His predecessor had done his work well. The great king spent his reign in the prosecution of his vast works of public utility and royal splendour.

10. Amenemhat in and the Art of the XIIth Dynasty

Amenemhat III was a monarch of whom we would fain know more than we do. His building was magnificent, and in his time Egyptian art reached for a brief space a degree of naturalism which it was not to know again till the time of the heretic Akhenaten, and of power which it never again attained. The artistic development begun by the sculptors of Neb-hapet-Ra Mentuhetep continued under the kings of the XIIth Dynasty, in whose days Egyptian art may be said to have in most respects reached its apogee. The taste of the artists of the XIIth Dynasty was admirable. They were Japanese in their sense of fitness and their delicacy; Greek in their feeling for balance and proportion. The best work of the XVIIIth Dynasty is vulgar by the side of that of the XIIth. The tomb of Ameni at Beni Hasan is a revelation to those whose knowledge of Egyptian art is derived chiefly from the gigantic abominations of Karnak or Abu Simbel. Nothing so fine as the perfectly-proportioned tomb-hall of Ameni, with its beautiful pillars, was ever excavated in an Egyptian cliff in later days. And the naturalism of the multitudinous groups of wrestling men which are painted on the walls around the entrance to the inner chamber is paralleled only by that of the Greek vase-paintings of the best period: the decoration of this wall, with its contending figures painted, where in later days only stiff and formal rows of hieroglyphics would have been permitted, and with its stately geometric frame-design, reminds us of nothing so much as of the decoration of a

Clazomenian sarcophagus. Nor are other tombs of this period far behind it in beauty. The smaller art of the time shews the same unparalleled excellence. The ivories, the scarabs, and the goldsmith's work are unrivalled. Nothing like the gold pectorals, and other objects, inlaid with fine stones, of the time of Senusert III which were found at Dashur, was ever made in later times in Egypt. And the great reliefs and statues of the kings, though their bodies are formal and represented in accordance with the convention fixed under the Pyramid-builders, shew us portraits of a power which the artists of the IVth Dynasty cannot rival. The fidelity of these portraits we cannot question. The sculptor who depicted King Mentuhetep at Der el-Bahri set the example, and his successors who shew us the faces of Senusert I at Koptos, and of Senusert III in the series of statues from Der el-Bahri, followed and surpassed him. At Der el-Bahri the great Sesostris is shewn in different figures representing him at different periods of his life, from a young to an old man, and two red granite heads from Abydos and Karnak confirm their portraits of the monarch in old age. It is a remarkable face, but not so remarkable as that of Amenemhat III, whose physiognomy was peculiar. We have an extraordinary portrait of this king's time apparently, in a weird figure, hung with extraordinary magical ornaments, which shews a king's head crowned with a massive wig of unique fashion. This was found at Tanis. The strange group of Nile-gods, heavy-haired and bearing offerings of fish, which comes from the same place, also owes its origin to the same school of sculpture. So apparently do the remarkable sphinxes of Tanis, which for long were regarded, from their remarkable faces, as works of the Hyksos. In them the leonine characteristics of the sphinx are emphasized in a very novel way.

Why the king bade himself and his gods to be represented thus strangely we do not know. It was an aberration from the conventional canons only once paralleled in later days, and that by a king who was half mad and wholly a heretic, in religion as well as art, Akhenaten. We cannot assume any religious heresy in Lamaris, but that he was a monarch of original and powerful mind is obvious.

11. The XIIIth Dynasty and the Hyksos Invasion

His reign marks the apogee of the Middle Kingdom. His successors, Amenemhat IV and the queen Sebekneferura (Skemiophris), were of no account, and their successors of the XIIIth Dynasty are little more than a series of names marking a swiftly accelerating path of degeneration. All were devoted worshippers of the crocodile-god Sebek, whose name they bore, usually in the compound Sebekhetep. It would seem that from the first there was a division in the kingdom, Thebes being held by a dynasty of Thebans, of whom some bore the name Mentuhetep, and one that of Senusert (IV); while in the north, no doubt at Itht-taui, ruled the descendants of the XIIth Dynasty, Khu-taui-Ra Ugafa, Sekhem-ka-Ra Amenemhatsenbef, Sankhabra Ameni-Antef-Amenemhat, and twelve others. We only know of the Thebans from recent discoveries by M. Legrain of their statues at Karnak, and evidently they were not recognized as legitimate, since they are not mentioned in the Turin Papyrus, which only gives Khu-taui-Ra and his fourteen ephemeral successors, till we come to Sekhem-khu-taui-Ra Sebekhetep (I), who certainly ruled over the whole country from Bubastis to Semneh in Nubia. Then we meet with two Thebans named Sebekemsaf, also not mentioned in the Turin Papyrus, but important monarchs in their time. They ruled and were buried at Thebes, and probably did not control the north, as contemporary with them must be two or three names in the Turin Papyrus, notably that of Ra-smenkh-ka Mermeshau, who set up statues of himself at Tanis. Then came a group of legitimate monarchs, mentioned in the Turin Papyrus, who ruled the whole land: Sekhem-suatj-taui-Ra Sebekhetep II, and the two brothers Neferhetep and Khaneferra Sebekhetep III. The monuments of the latter are found from Tanis in the north to the island of Arko in Nubia, so he probably advanced the southern boundary beyond the limit fixed by Senusert III. The succession of these princes passed in the female line; the father of Neferhetep and Sebekhetep III was a simple priest named Haankhef, but his mother Kemi was no doubt a daughter of Sebekhetep II; his mother Auhetabu, however, as well as, apparently, his father Mentuhetep, were of non-royal birth, so that he probably owed his throne to adoption.

Sebekhetep III was the last powerful monarch of the Middle Kingdom. His successors were ephemeral kings, only known to us from scarabs and the Turin Papyrus; Thebes was apparently independent again under princes who bore the name of Antef, and the Delta was ruled by chiefs who bore allegiance to foreign conquerors from Palestine, the famous Hyksos, who now first appear in our history. The Antefs are, as usual, not mentioned in the Turin Papyrus, but the Delta chiefs are, and one of them, Nehesi ("the Negro") is also known from a monument on which he worships the god Set or Sutekh, the tutelary deity of the Hyksos, so that he was, apparently, their vassal. These subjects of the Hyksos are apparently the XIVth (Xoite) dynasty of Manetho.

So the kingdom of the Amenemhats and Senuserts came to its end, in degeneration, division, and barbarian conquest. The Asiatic conquest is the central climacteric of Egyptian history. With it direct relations were for the first time established between Egypt and the Asiatic world. Hitherto the civilizations of Babylonia and Egypt had pursued their own ways independently, having hardly ever come into any contact with each other, so far as we know, since history first began in the Nile-valley. It is therefore possible to treat the story of Babylonian culture up to the end of Khammurabi's dynasty and Egyptian history up to the Hyksos conquest entirely independently of each other. But with the beginning of the second millennium B.C. this is no longer possible. Egypt has been brought into forcible contact with the civilized Asiatics, and henceforward she remains in close contact with them, for her weal or her woe, throughout her history.

But, while Egyptian civilization after the expulsion of the Hyksos and the conquest of Western Asia was in many ways very different from that of the preceding age of isolation, the culture of the Middle Empire differed very little from that of the Old Kingdom, as established at the close of the Archaic Period, the end of the IIIrd Dynasty; the mere transference of the centre of gravity from Memphis to Thebes altered Egyptian civilization very little. The modifications which differentiate the Egypt of the XIIth Dynasty from that of the IVth are merely the effects of time, and in the culture of the VIth Dynasty we see the transition in progress; here we find something which we have met with under the IVth Dynasty, but do not find under the XIIth, there something which we have not met with before, but which we shall find usual under the XIIth.

12. The Civilization of the Old and Middle Kingdoms

It is therefore difficult to compare the civilization of the Middle Kingdom as a whole with that of the Old Kingdom. We might compare the art of the two periods, for art always followed royal fortunes. Under powerful kings it grew and flourished, under weak kings and amid the internecine conflict of warring nobles it languished and withered. So the fine art of the Pyramid-builders degenerated at the end of the VIth Dynasty into the grotesque caricatures of the beginning of the XIth, out of which, however, from the time of the great Neb-hapet-Ra Mentuhetep, developed again the splendid artistic triumphs of the XIIth Dynasty.

Religion, like art, followed the fortunes of the monarchy, for the religion of the Middle Kingdom presents us with a new phenomenon which differentiates it from that of the Old Kingdom, and was directly due to the political events of the beginning of the XIth Dynasty. This was the appearance of a new deity, previously hardly known, who, as the patron of the Prince of Thebes, soon aspires to rank as king of the gods, as his servant had become king of men. This was Amen, already identified at the beginning of the XIIth Dynasty with Ra, the ancient patron of the Memphite kings. The Theban monarchs had to be "Sons of the Sun": the phrase had become fixed in the royal titulary, and carried with it the claim to the loyalty of all Egyptians. But they were also sons of Amen, and therefore the two gods were combined, probably by Senusert I, who built great temples for Ra of Heliopolis and Amen of Thebes, thus shewing his devotion to his double protector. The special worship of Sebek, the crocodile-god of the Fayyum, in deference to royal predilections, again distinguishes the religion of the Middle Kingdom from that of the Old. And at this time Osiris, the dead-god of Busiris in the Delta, who had under the Old Kingdom already been identified with Sokari, "the Coffined One," who presided over the Memphite necropolis, gradually advanced to the position of "Universal Lord" (Nebr-tjer) of the world of the dead by attracting to himself the name and attributes of Khentamentiu, the ancient dead-god of Abydos in the South. "Osiris-Khentamentiu, Lord of Busiris, Great God, Lord of Abydos," is henceforth always invoked in the funerary inscriptions, and Anubis, though he is "He who is on the Serpent-Mountain and in the Oasis, Lord of the Holy Land (the Necropolis), Lord of Sepa," is but his inferior rival, and gradually becomes his son and servitor. Funerary customs under the XIIth Dynasty differed, however, but little from those in vogue under the VIth; the only noticeable development being an increase in the number and variety of those characteristic wooden models of servants that accompanied the dead to the tomb, and the first appearance of those little figures, the Ushabtiu, or "Answerers," which later became so typical a feature of Egyptian burials. The function of the ushabti was to arise and "answer" when the dead man was called upon to do work in the Underworld: "Here am I, whensoever thou callest me!" There can be little doubt that these figures of stone or wood (later also of pottery) represented slaves who at a much earlier period were immolated at the grave and buried with their master, to accompany him to the next world.

The actual condition of the living underwent alterations, owing to changes in the actual method of administering the country, which did not coincide with the division into an Old and a Middle Kingdom according to the fortune of the kings. We have a Feudal Period which bridged the gap between the two, lasting from the Vth to the XIIth Dynasty. During this period the royal officials, headed by the Vizier or Tjate ("The Man," as opposed to "the God," i.e. the King), an official who appears already in the time of Narmer, and the Mer-shema or Mertoris, the "Overseer of the South" (for Upper Egypt), had very little authority. Up till the middle of the Vth Dynasty the land and people were, so far as we can see, exclusively the property of the king, who granted to his court-nobles estates which were administered for them in their absence by his officials. Then the nobles began to reside on their estates. Taxes, at first raised every second year for the royal benefit alone, probably became local imposts, as the court grew poor. And so the great local aristocracy of feudal barons grew up, which administered the land from the end of the Vth till the middle of the XIIth Dynasty. Weak kings allowed this aristocracy to grow up, powerless kings saw it plunge the whole land into war. Then powerful kings again first curbed and then strangled it. There is then but little difference between the local magnates of the XIIth Dynasty and their predecessors of the VIth: here we see no difference between the Old and Middle Kingdoms. But the bureaucracy of town-mayors which succeeded the landed aristocracy at the end of the XIIth Dynasty is quite different from anything that had gone before; here the later Middle Kingdom is entirely different from the earlier Middle Kingdom and the Old Kingdom.

CHAPTER V: THE EARLY HISTORY OF BABYLONIA, 3000-1500 B.C.

I. The Sumerians

THE later culture of Semitic Babylonia and Assyria is based almost entirely upon foundations laid by a non-Semitic people, the Sumerians, as we call them, from the fact that the chief seat of their power was the land of Southern Babylonia, which they called "Sumer." To them was due the invention of the cuneiform script, the outward mark and inward bond of Mesopotamian (and so of all early Semitic) culture; and, our knowledge of this has shewn us that the language which it was originally devised to express was not Semitic, but an agglutinative tongue.

There are, however, certain indications visible in the remains and representations of Sumerian culture that point to a pre-Sumerian and specifically Semitic element in it. Thus the Sumerian gods are always represented as Semites, with very full and long hair and beard, while the Sumerians were always clean-shaven, as to the face, and usually (though not always) also as to the head. The garment worn by the gods is also that assigned in later representation, to Semites, namely, a sort of woollen cloth plaid, while the Sumerians wore clocks which look as if made of either rough wool or possibly skins, or even palm-leaves. There were probably inhabitants in Mesopotamia before the Sumerians arrived, and it is hardly probable that they can have been of other than Semitic race, so that this curious fact as regards the representation of their gods may be thus explained. On conquering the country the Sumerians adopted the Semitic deities of the soil, a proceeding not improbable of itself and entirely consonant with ancient religious ideas. Their own gods were at the same time altered in their appearance in order to agree with their new and predominant colleagues.

The Sumerian culture springs into our view ready-made, as it were, which is what we should expect if it was, as seems on other grounds probable, brought into Mesopotamia from abroad. We have no knowledge of the time when the Sumerians were savages: when we first meet with them in the fourth millennium B.C., they are already a civilized, metal-using people living in great and populous cities, possessing a complicated system of writing, and living under the government of firmly established civil and religious dynasties and hierarchies. They had imposed their higher culture on the more primitive inhabitants of the river-valley in which they had settled, and had assimilated the civilization of the conquered, whatever it may have been, to their own. The earliest scenes of their own culture-development had perhaps not been played upon the Babylonian stage at all, but in a different country, away across the Persian mountains to the eastward. The land of Elam, the later Susiana, where till the end a non-Semitic nationality of Sumerian culture maintained itself in usual independence of the dominant Mesopotamian power, was no doubt a stage in their progress. There they left the abiding impress of their civilization, although the Elamites developed their art on a distinct line of their own. Whether the Elamites, whom they probably civilized, were racially related to them we do not know; the languages of both Elamite and Sumerian were agglutinative, but otherwise are not alike. The Elamite tongue may very well have been allied to the modern Georgian, and we may regard it as the southernmost member of a group of non-Aryan and non-Semitic tongues, to which has been given the name "Alarodian," which in ancient times stretched from the Caucasus to the Persian Gulf along the line of the Zagros, but now is confined to the Caucasian region, Sumerian may also belong to this group, or may (and this seems more probable) have come from much farther afield. The ethnic type of the Sumerians, so strongly marked in their statues and reliefs, was as different from those of the races which surrounded them as was their language from those of the Semites, Aryans, or others; they were decidedly Indian in type. The face-type of the average Indian of to-day is no doubt much the same as that of his Dravidian race-ancestors thousands of years ago. Among the modern Indians, as amongst the modern Greeks or Italians, the ancient pre-Aryan type of the land has (as the primitive type of the land always does) survived, while that of the Aryan conqueror died out long ago. And it is to this Dravidian ethnic type of India that the ancient Sumerian bears most resemblance, so far as we can judge from his monuments. He was very like a Southern Hindu of the Dekkan (who still speaks Dravidian languages). And it is by no means improbable that the Sumerians were an Indian race which passed, certainly by land, perhaps also by sea, through Persia to the valley of the Two Rivers. It was in the Indian home (perhaps the Indus valley) that we suppose for them that their culture developed. There their writing may have been invented, and progressed from a purely pictorial to a simplified and abbreviated form, which afterwards in Babylonia took on its peculiar "cuneiform" appearance owing to its being written with a square-ended stilus on soft clay. On the way they left the seeds of their culture in Elam. This seems a plausible theory of Sumerian origins, and it must be clearly understood that it is offered by the present writer merely as a theory, which has little direct evidence to back it, but seems most in accordance with the probabilities of the case. There is little doubt that India must have been one of the earliest centres of human civilization, and it seems natural to suppose that the strange un-Semitic, un-Aryan people who came from the East to civilize the West were of Indian origin, especially when we see with our eyes how very Indian the Sumerians were in type.

We do not know whether the first foundation of the cities of Babylonia was due to the Sumerians or to their predecessors. At the beginning of history we find the cities of Southern Babylonia (Sumer) exclusively inhabited by them, while Northern Babylonia (Akkad) has also civilized Semitic inhabitants dwellers in cities, like the Sumerians. A common Semito-Sumerian civilization has already been evolved, chiefly, no doubt, on purely Sumerian bases. The Sumerian system of writing is already used to write Semitic. It seems probable that the art of city-building and the practice of town-dwelling was brought in by the more highly cultured Sumerians. The primitive Semite of the valley was probably half-nomadic.

Whether it is to the Sumerians that the first drainage and irrigation of the river-swamps is to be assigned is uncertain. Legends, which were put into the shape in which we have them after the unification of Sumer and Akkad under the headship of Babylon, assign to the Babylonian god Marduk the work of reducing the primeval chaos to order by the separation of land from water, and the first founding of the homes of men on the reclaimed earth. Marduk, having, according to another version, vanquished the demon of the primeval watery chaos, Tiamat, laid a reed upon the face of the waters and poured dust upon it, so that the first land was formed: then he made a dyke by the side of the sea to reclaim the land from it, and manufactured bricks; houses and cities followed, "then was Eridu made, and E-Sagil (the temple of Bel Marduk in Babylon) was built. . . . Nippur he made, E-kur he built; Erech he made, E-ana he built." We evidently have here a very vivid recollection of the time when the whole of Southern Babylonia was a swamp: the primitive inhabitants were scattered about on various islands which emerged out of the fens, and on these islands towns arose, just as Ely and Peterborough arose in England under similar circumstances: dykes were heaped up and the shallows were gradually reclaimed, till the demon of the watery chaos, Tiamat, finally vanquished, retreated from the land; Marduk had created the earth and the two great rivers, and, in the words of the legend, "declared their names to be good."

In this legend Marduk no doubt replaces an earlier local god, probably Enki or Ea of Eridu, which appears as the most ancient foundation of all. Ea, the Sumerian Enki, was primarily the God of the Waters. Whether Ea was originally a Sumerian or a Semitic god is uncertain; his Semitic name Ea seems primitive in form. It is not impossible that the first reclamation and settlements in the marshes were those of the pre-Sumerian Semites, who presumably inhabited Sumer as well as Akkad, and that the first foundation of the city settlements was due to the predecessors of the Sumerians, But we can well imagine that the Sumerian conquest brought about a great advance in civilized development, and that the characteristic importance of the cities in Babylonia was due to the apparent Sumerian instinct for concentration and organization. The Sumerians were the real conquerors of Tiamat, although they may not have begun Ea's work.

The most ancient remains that we find in the city-mounds are Sumerian. The site of the ancient Shurippak, at Farah in Southern Babylonia, has lately been excavated. The culture revealed by this excavation is Sumerian, and metal-using, even at the lowest levels. The Sumerians apparently knew the use of copper at the beginning of their occupation of Babylonia, and no doubt brought this knowledge with them.

The most ancient names of Babylonian kings and chiefs known to us are Sumerian in form, and their inscriptions are written in Sumerian, though there is reason to suppose that the early kings of the city of Kish, in Akkad, were Semites. A Semitic revival, so to speak, was beginning; the Sumerized Semites of Northern Babylonia were preparing to gain the upper hand and to absorb their conquerors and civilizers. For we know only the latter end of the story of Sumerian rule in Babylonia. At the beginning of history the Sumerian power is already declining amid a chaos of civil war and Semitic revolt. We do not know whether the warring cities which we see at the dawn of history had ever been united in one compact Sumerian kingdom under a Sumerian dynasty, with its centre either at ancient Eridu or at Nippur, the primate city of primitive Babylonia and seat of Enlil, the chief god of the country. But it is not impossible that they had been so united.

Legend, at any rate, speaks of a very ancient kingdom of "Babylon," with a long line of semi-divine rulers over the whole land, each of whom reigned for an enormous period of time, thus resembling the Egyptian "Ghosts" and "Followers of Horus." Some of their names have been preserved for us in the extant fragments of the history of Berossos. He tells us of the first of the kings, who reigned for even longer periods, Aloros, who reigned 36,000 years, and his successors down to Xisuthros, in whose time the Deluge took place. Aloros came after the first civilizer of Babylonia, Cannes, a monster half-man and half-fish, who issued out of the Persian Gulf, and taught the use of writing and other arts to savage mankind. We possess no Babylonian text referring to Cannes, but there is no doubt that he was in some way connected, if not identical, with Ea, the god of the primeval waters, who was worshipped in the most ancient city of Babylonia, Eridu, which ages ago stood on a lake near the Persian Gulf, now over a hundred miles away. Neither have we as yet met with any legends of Aloros and his successors in the cuneiform texts, but there is no doubt that Berosus is entirely to be trusted in his compilation of the legends of his people. Xisuthros is evidently the same as Khasisadra or Atrakhasis, in whose time Sit-napishtim went into the Ark, to save himself from the Deluge. Berossos' mention of the Deluge is not derived from Hebrew sources, as used, naturally, to be thought, but is a faithful record of the ancient tradition of his own people, on which the Hebrew legend was founded. After the Deluge, according to the traditions preserved by Berossos, eighty-six kings reigned during 34,080 years, two of them for 2400 and 2700 years respectively, but those at the end of the list for the ordinary span of human life only. It is no wonder that Cicero smiles at the vast antiquity that the Babylonians claimed for themselves.

Other legends, which we hear directly from cuneiform sources, know nothing of a primitive united kingdom. They refer, no doubt, to historical events in a distorted form. Thus there is a legend of an early king of the whole land who reigned in Kutha, which has come down to us in an autobiographical shape. The unknown king is made to say that in his days the land was attacked and overrun by a strange people who had the bodies of birds and the faces of ravens, who lived in the mountains to the north of Mesopotamia. Three long years the king contended with the invaders, and finally in the fourth year he routed them. Then we have the voluminous legends concerning a very early king who reigned in Erech, Gilgamesh, who was regarded as a semi-mythical hero, a sort of Herakles, by the

Babylonians, and may very well be the original of the Biblical Nimrod. In his days Erech was besieged for three years and was brought to the uttermost straits: —

"Men cry aloud like beasts,
And maidens mourn like doves;
The gods of strong-walled Erech
Are changed to flies, and buzz about the streets;
The spirits of strong-walled Erech
Are changed to mice, and glide into holes.
For three years the enemy besieged Erech,
And the doors were barred and the bolts were shot,
And Ishtar did not raise her head against the foe."

It is not certain whether Gilgamesh was the besieger or the saviour of Erech: at any rate, he is said to have afterwards ruled the town in a tyrannical fashion, so that the gods made a creature, half-animal, half-beast, named Ea-bani, who was intended to destroy him. Ea-bani was however captured by the wiles of a singing-woman of the temple of Ishtar at Erech, and was brought to Gilgamesh, whose devoted friend and ally he soon became. The two then performed many feats of valour in company, the most notable being an expedition against an Elamite ogre named Khumbaba, whose castle they took, and killed its owner.

It is probable that in the expedition against Khumbaba and the defence of Erech we have echoes of far-away historical events. In the stories both of Gilgamesh and of the king of Kutha the cities are independent of one another. And so we find them at the beginning of history.

Each was ruled by a hereditary governor, who was also high-priest of the local god and bore the title of patesi, which signified that its possessor was the earthly vicegerent of the gods. The Sumerian language possessed a word denoting the ruler of a higher political organization: this was higal, "king" (literally "great man"). This word had no theocratic connotation, and whether it was a survival of a time when a stable and unified Sumerian kingdom had existed or not, in the period of confusion which is the earliest as yet known to us, it seems to have been assumed by any patesi who succeeded by force or fraud in uniting several cities under his government: in this case the patesis of the subdued cities, even if one or more of them had themselves previously aspired to be called lugal, reverted to the position of patesis, and the conqueror took the title of lugal, only in all probability to himself lose it in a few years to some patesi stronger than he.

One of the earliest rulers of whom we have any knowledge seems to be a certain Utug, of Kish, who dedicated in the great temple of the god Enlil at Nippur, the central navel of Sumer and Akkad, a vase which he had taken as spoil from "the land of Khamazi." Thus we find the internecine war at the beginning of things, and also the position of Nippur as chief city of all Babylonia, which we may, if we please, trace back to an ancient unified Sumerian kingdom with its capital at Nippur.

Utug was probably a Sumerian, but later kings of Kish were Semites. Later on, the hegemony of Kish disappeared for a time, and Lagash appears as the chief city of Babylonia under the king Ur-Nina, the founder of a dynasty, and a most pious servant of the gods, who dedicated countless vases, tablets, and statues in the temples of Ningirsu, Bau his wife, Dunshagga his son, and the goddesses Nina, Ninmakh, and Gatumdug, which were already the glory of Lagash. Urnina was also a great digger of canals, and a builder of granaries and storehouses for the grain-tribute paid to himself and to the gods.

Some of the most ancient relics of Sumerian art date from the time of Urnina. They are relief-plaques, on which we see the king represented in somewhat primitive wise, seated in a chair and holding a cup, and standing with a basket on his head, in the guise of a labourer on his own building-operations, while around him stand in respectful attitudes his children, headed by his daughter Lidda, and his eldest son Akurgal, who succeeded him on the throne. Behind him is his cupbearer. The intention of the relief is the same as that of the early Egyptian relief palettes of Narmer from Hierakonpolis, but its execution is much inferior, and reminds us very much of the crude work of the early XIth Dynasty in Egypt. Another relief shews a meeting of chieftains and their followers.

The reign of Akurgal, Urnina's successor, was undistinguished, but that of Eannatum, his son, was marked by a great war between Lagash and Umma. We know of this war from the inscriptions and reliefs of the famous "Stele of the Vultures," the most splendid result of M. de Sarzec's excavations at Telloh, and one of the chief glories of the Museum of the Louvre. On this monument we see Eannatum setting forth to war both on foot and in his ass-drawn chariot, at the head of his troops. The soldiers, who march in serried ranks behind, trampling on the bodies of the slain, wear waistcloths of skins round their loins and metal helmets of exactly the same shape as the mediaeval bassinet upon their heads; their hair, which was not shaven, appears from beneath the helmets behind. Eannatum wears the same helmet, behind which his long hair is bound up in a club. Both he and his men are clean-shaven as to the face. Farther on, we see the burial of the slain warriors of Lagash, but the fallen of Umma are represented as lying a prey to the vultures, which are seen carrying off the heads of the slain in their beaks. On another part of the stela we see the god Ningirsu, heavily bearded in Semitic fashion, holding in his hand the strange heraldic emblem of his city of Lagash, and clubbing with his mace the men of Umma who he has caught in a great net.

The style of this monument is remarkable. It is conspicuous for great vigour of composition and of execution, which accurately reflect the temper of the ruler who caused it to be sculptured. Eannatum was a most vigorous ruler, as we see from the inscriptions of the Vulture-stele, in which he tells us of the genesis of the quarrel between his city and the neighbouring Umma, and of the way in which he brought the enemy to his knees, and finally secured the disputed territory Gu-edin to Lagash.

The loss of life on both sides seems to have been great, and we can well imagine that two armies battling in the formidable array of the Sumerian soldiery would inflict considerable damage upon one another. No shooting with the bow was used, the fighting being based on shock-tactics only, and the victory inclining to the heavier and more thrusting force. The soldiers, protected by efficient body-armour, fought in solid phalanges, six men in a row. The men of the front rank who were armed with battle-axes, carried huge rectangular bucklers which reached their feet, and formed an impenetrable board-wall behind which the men in rear, who carried no shields, could use their long spears with effect. So phalanx moved slowly against phalanx, the shock and thrusting came, and the better men won. Then the buckler-bearers of the victorious side threw away their cumbrous protection, and joined the pursuit with their axes. This was a highly developed military machine, which had clearly been evolved by long years of constant civil war. The loose order, comparatively feeble armour, and bow-and-arrow and hatchet fighting of the contemporary Egyptians was by no means so efficient. We do not know whether the chariots in which the Sumerian kings drove to war were ever actually used for charging and fighting in battle: most probably they were not, serving merely as conveyances to the field. They were drawn by asses, the horse being still unknown.

Elam also experienced the weight of Eannatum's arm. "By Eannatum," says the king of Lagash himself, "was Elam broken in the head: Elam was driven back to his own land." Then, as ever afterwards, the hardy mountain-tribes of Elam were always ready for a descent upon the fruitful and wealthy Babylonian plain. In this case also, as after the defeat of Umma, Eannatum says that he "heaped up burial mounds," thus indicating the slaughter he had made.

Whereas Eannatum had been primarily a soldier, and had devoted little time to the service of the gods, Entemena, his second successor, was not only a warrior but also a patron of religion and the arts. One of the finest relics of his reign is a magnificent votive vase of silver, found, mounted on its original copper stand, to which it has become united by oxydization, in the ruins of Telloh. On this beautiful object we see a row of representations of Imgig, the lion-headed eagle of Ningirsu, grasping either lions or antelopes by their tails, a representation which served as the heraldic cognizance of Lagash. We have already seen this remarkable emblem accompanying Ningirsu on the Stele of the Vultures.

Entemena was succeeded by four short-lived and undistinguished patesis, to whom succeeded the remarkable usurper and reformer Urukagina, the last king of Lagash. The prosperity of Lagash, due to the huge amount of taxes and tribute in corn, wood, and other things which she had exacted for years from the whole of Sumer and the greater part of Akkad, had demoralized the ruling officials and priests of Ningirsu's state. They had divided the plunder of the other cities among themselves, and had combined to rob and oppress the common people.

The usurper Urukagina stood forth as a champion of reform, in the interests of the ordinary taxpayer. He cut down the perquisites of the priests and restrained the exactions of the lay officials of the palace, abolishing various extortionate fees and dues to which not only the vizier, but even the patesi or king himself had a right. He enacted new laws respecting divorce, and in his reign he says: "To the widow and the orphan the strong man did no harm." He stands out as the anticipator and predecessor of the lawgiver Khammurabi, who obviously modelled himself upon his Sumerian predecessor.

But his reforms endeared him to none but the poor and the powerless. And the enemy at the gate, Umma, was again independent and strong. Lugalzaggisi, son of Ukush, patesi of Umma, determined to take advantage of the weakness of the old foe of his city, and attacked her suddenly, with complete success, ending the reign of Urukagina and the dominion of Lagash at one blow. We know of this event only from a remarkable historical composition written by a priest in Lagash shortly afterwards, and discovered at Telloh: in it the writer recounts the sacrilege of the invaders and heaps curses on the name of Lugalzaggisi, the conqueror.

After overthrowing Lagash Lugalzaggisi became naturally the chief power in Babylonia. Leaving Umma, he established his capital at Erech, and took the title of king of that city, and of the land of Sumer. Then he carried his arms beyond Babylonia into Syria or Amurru, the Land of the West, which he subdued, reaching the Mediterranean at the end of his march. "When the god Enlil, king of the lands," says the conqueror, "had bestowed upon Lugalzaggisi the kingdom of the land, and had granted him success in the eyes of the land, and when his might had cast the lands down, and he had conquered them from the rising of the sun unto the setting of the same, at that time he made straight his path from the Lower Sea, from Euphrates and Tigris, unto the Upper Sea. From the rising of the sun unto the setting of the same has Enlil granted him dominion."

By this march to the Mediterranean the foundations were laid of the actual dominion over Syria exercised by the Semitic kings of Akkad some two centuries later.

We have very little knowledge of the state of Syria and Palestine at this period, when they first appear in history. It is possible that the influence of Sumerian civilization had been perceptible in the West at an even earlier period, but we have no direct proof of this. The recent excavations of the Palestine Exploration Fund at Gezer and of the Germans at Megiddo have shewn that Palestine was originally inhabited by a neolithic population that lived in caves, and was probably related to the troglodytic people of the desert between the Nile and the Red Sea, who are mentioned by Strabo. We may identify them with the pre-Canaanite Horites or Avvim of Biblical tradition. They developed into or were succeeded by the Anakim or Rephaim, the "Giants" of tradition, who built the megalithic monuments, the dolmens and menhirs, of Moab and eastern Palestine. To them may be due the earliest stone walls of the Canaanite cities. Whether they were Semites or not we do not know. It is probable that in Palestine a pre-Semitic "Mediterranean" population existed, which mingled with the Semitic-speakers who came from Arabia(?). By Lugalzaggisi's time the Palestinians had long been semitized, and the Rephaim and the sons of Anak had already given place to the civilized Canaanites, who were perhaps already adopting the script of Sumer for their writing and incorporating the deities of Babylon into their religion.

2. Sumerians and Semites

The inscriptions of Lugalzaggisi have been discovered at Nippur, in the shrine of Enlil, the chief god of the Babylonian pantheon, to whom the King of Erech ascribed his success. He was succeeded in his dominion by three kings of whom we know simply the names. War broke out with Kish, of old the ally of Umma, but now her enemy. Semitic kings now ruled Kish.

To Semitic rulers in Akkad the hegemony of Babylonia now passed, and they, like their predecessors, dedicated their gifts in the central shrine of Enlil at Nippur. Sharru-Gi (or Shar-Rukin), the first Semitic king who has left monuments of any importance, was in later days confused with Shargani-sharri, King of Akkad, whom we shall presently discuss, and the two together formed a kind of "conflate "personage, the hero "Sargon," who inaugurated Semitic rule in Babylonia. Sharru-gi is known to us directly from a monolithic stone, sculptured in relief with battle scenes, which was found by the French excavators at Susa, whither it had been carried by the Elamites; and indirectly from other monuments. Manishtusu, who came after him, was a powerful monarch. Of him again we possess an important monument which was found at Susa, having been removed thither by the Elamites: this is a great obelisk inscribed in Semitic Babylonian with a list of his lands, in which the patesi of Lagash (Urukagina II, son of Engilsa) and men from Umma appear as his humble vassals. Part of an alabaster portrait-statuette of Manishtusu was also found at Susa, which shews him fully-bearded in the Semitic style. The art is not so good as that of the work of Sharru-gi, but the face is unmistakably a portrait.

Whether Mesalim, son of Manishtusu, succeeded him or not, we do not knowr Rimush, or Urumush, who followed Manishtusu at no long interval, and preceded Shargani-sharri of Akkad, conquered Elam and evidently greatly increased the Babylonian power. He was said in a later tradition to have lost his life in a palace-revolution. At any rate, his successor is unknown, and it is highly probable that the helm of Babylonia was now taken by two other Semitic chiefs, Shargani-Sharri and Naram-Sin of Akkad.

Few monarchs of the ancient world are so well known to us moderns as "Sargon of Agade," and we may say that to the Babylonians he was their hero of heroes, their Menes, Charlemagne, or Alfred the Great. A foundling brought up by a water-carrier, according to tradition, he ended as ruler of all Western Asia. His doings were taken as an ensample of life for later kings, and if the omens had been such-and-such when Sargon went forth to battle, under similar omens the later King of Babylonia or Assyria would also march to victory. He, confused naturally enough with the earlier Sharru-gi, typified the first triumphant establishment of the Semites as the dominant race in Babylonia.

Historically, Shargani-sharri was the son of a certain Dati-Enlil, probably the ruler of the town of Agade under the king of Kish. He lived, according to the evidence which has already been discussed, probably about 2750-2700 B.C. That Shargani extended his rule over the whole of Babylonia is clear. Lugal-ushumgal, patesi of Lagash, owed him allegiance; at Nippur he built the great temple of Enlil, E-kur; at Babylon he erected a palace; and he founded a new city, Dur-Shargani, "Sharganiburgh," with inhabitants drawn from Kish and Babylon. In Agade itself he built the temple E-ulbar in honour of Anunitum, the Semitic goddess of the morning-star. As a conqueror beyond the bounds of Babylonia we know from his own contemporary record that he extended his dominions northward and eastward over the land of Guti, in the Zagros mountains, on the modern frontier of Persia and Turkey. Here, and in the neighbouring district of Lulubu, Semitic chiefs ruled, of whom Anu-banini of Guti and Lasirab of Lulubu are known to us in the age before Shargani-sharri, who reduced the Guti king of his day, Sharlak, to obedience.

Naram-Sin, whose position with regard to Shargani-sharri is uncertain, conquered Satuni of Lulubu, and commemorated the exploit on a magnificent monument which will shortly be described. He also carried his arms to the far north of Mesopotamia, where a relief-stele of himself, set up in an ancient town near the modern Diarbekr, commemorates his deeds. He brought stone from Magan (Eastern Arabia), a stone vase inscribed by him with the words "Vase from the booty of Magan" has been discovered, and at Susa has been found a statue with an inscription directly recording the conquest and submission of Mannudannu, King of Magan. He calls himself "King of the Four Quarters of the World"; he erected a temple at Sippar, where Nabonidus discovered his inscription, and ruled as king in Nippur: a cylinder of Nabonidus describes him also as "King of Babylon," but this is probably an error of that blundering royal antiquarian.

Thus far we have derived our information as to these two great kings from their own contemporary monuments and from the archaeological researches of Nabonidus: we have now to turn to a further source of information regarding them, Babylonian legend.

On one of the omen-tablets (of the seventh century B.C.) discovered at Kuyunjik (Nineveh) we read respecting Sargon that "he traversed the Sea of the West, and for three years his hand prevailed in the West. He established his undisputed rule, and in the West his statues [he set up]: he caused the booty of the Sea-lands to be brought." Another version substitutes "Sea of the East" (i.e. the Persian Gulf) for "Sea of the West," and we also read that under certain omens the great king had carried his arms to the Persian Gulf, where the island of Dilmun came under his sway: he also is said, no doubt with truth, to have invaded Elam. An unsuccessful rebellion, in the course of which he was besieged in Agade, is also said to have taken place during his reign. With respect to Naram-Sin, the astrological tablets say that he attacked the city of Apirak, on the borders of Elam, killed its king, Rishramman, and led its people away into slavery. We are led to repose some confidence in the historical accuracy of these traditional accounts because they also mention Naram-Sin's expedition against Magan, which, as we know from his own inscription, did actually take place. If Naram-Sin could go to Magan, so could his father, and the legends of the expedition to Dilmun and the "Sea of the East" state nothing incredible. The variant version which implies an expedition to the Mediterranean may also state a fact, since, if Lugalzaggisi speaks of his own dominion as reaching to the Upper Sea, it is in no way impossible that Sargon also actually waged war and ruled in Syria and Palestine for the space of three years, and set up his statues on the shores of the Mediterranean.

The greatness of these two reigns is worthily commemorated in the splendid stela found by M. de Morgan at Susa (whither it had been carried off, probably by the Elamite king, Shutruk-Nakhkhunte), which records the subjection of Satuni, King of Lulubu, in his mountain-fastness. This is one of the triumphs of ancient art: in it ancient Babylonian art reached its apogee. King Naram-Sin is shewn in high relief, ascending the slopes of a great mountain, bow and arrow in hand. Before him falls Satuni, stricken by an arrow which he strives to pull out of his neck; behind, a retreating figure turns to beg for mercy. Behind and below, on the lower tree-clad slopes of the mountain, climb the king's officers, bearing bows, spears, and standards with heraldic emblems; all in the same attitude of resolute advance, step by step, into the heart of the mountains. Above, shine the sun and stars. The king is bearded, and wears no body-armour, but has a conical horned helmet. His officers are shaven, but wear the helmet without horns. Satuni and his follower have beards and either long hair or hoods with long liripipes like those worn by the Scythians in later times. The use of archery by Naram-Sin and his men is significant: the bow, which was unknown to the Sumerians, had been introduced by the Semites, and was now acclimatized in Babylonia.

Naram-Sin evidently extended the empire bequeathed to him by his father, and assumed the resounding title of "King of the Four Quarters of the World," which henceforth became a regular appellation of the Babylonian kings, often with little reason.

Of the immediate successors of Shargani and Naram-Sin we know little. A period of some two hundred years now elapses, during which an as yet unpenetrated veil of obscurity lies over Babylonia, and when it is lifted we find that the sceptre has departed from Agade and has passed again to Lagash, where about 2500 B.C. a line of princes reigned who called themselves simply patesis, after the old custom of Lagash. Like their ancestors, they were Sumerians, not Semites.

The greatest of these later patesis of Lagash was Gudea (c. 2450 B.C.), statues of whom are now in the Museum of the Louvre. This king conquered the district of Anshan in Elam, and, being commanded to do so in a dream, erected a great temple in honour of the goddess Nina, stone for which was brought from Syria, gold and precious stones from Arabia (?), great beams of cedar-wood from the forests of Mount Amanus and Lebanon, and asphalt from the Dead Sea region. With him the glory of his dynasty ended, however: his son, Ur-Ningirsu, was compelled to submit to the power of a new dynasty, also Sumerian, which had arisen at Ur. Dungi, the second king of this dynasty, who reigned for fifty-eight years (c. 2386-2328 B.C.), adopted a new and unprecedented style in order to signify his dominion over the whole of Babylonia: besides "King of Ur" and "King of the Four Quarters," he called himself "King of Sumer and Akkad," which no king before him had done, and arrogated to himself the divine title. He also erected or restored temples, — at Ur, Erech, Lagash, and Kutha, — and even at Susa, the capital of Elam, which seems to have been completely subdued by his arms. Throughout his long reign he was constantly campaigning in Elam and along the Zagros, and it seems to have been his endeavour to outdo the Semite Naram-Sin.

The dynasty of Ur represents a very definite Sumerian reaction against the Semites. Dungi specially favours the ancient Sumerian city of Eridu, and reduces Babylon, sacking E-sagila, the holy shrine of Marduk, and carrying off the temple-treasures. So strong was the force of reaction against the empire of Sargon. Orthodox Babylonian scribes in later times could not forgive him for the insult offered to the shrine of Bel-Marduk, even though it were offered in the name of Enlil of Nippur, most revered deity of Babylonia. So the annalist who tells us of these events says: "Dungi, the son of Ur-Engur, cared greatly for the city of Eridu, which was on the shore of the sea. But he sought after evil, and the treasure of E-sagila and of Babylon he brought out as spoil. And Bel was [wroth?] and [smote?] his body and so made an end of him." Certainly his dynasty did not last. As it had from Lagash, so after three more reigns, lasting forty-three years, the sceptre departed from Ur, The cause of the collapse was a disaster: Ibi-Sin, the third successor of Dungi, was carried off a captive to Elam. The Elamite conqueror who took Ur and carried away the High-King of Babylonia captive was probably Kudur-nankhundi, who, we are told in an inscription of Ashurbanipal of Assyria, had sacked Erech and taken away its goddess Nana to Susa, 1635 years before 650 B.C., when Ashurbanipal took Susa and brought back the image of the goddess in triumph. This would place the end of the dynasty of Ur in 2285 B.C., or thereabouts, as the Assyrian date is probably not literally correct.

The collapse of Uungi's dynasty was followed by the accession to power of an undistinguished series of kings who form the dynasty of Isin, that city being the town of its founder, Isiibi-Ura. We know from a later chronicle the years of the reigns of these kings. With the fifth king, Libit-Ishtar, the family of Ishbi-Ura ended (about 2180 B.C.), probably amid civil war and foreign invasion. At this time, or a little later, the family of Syrian conquerors which founded the dynasty of Khammurabi first established their authority at Babylon, and at the same time comparatively ephemeral dynasties were also set up at Erech and Larsam. The dynasty of Larsam later became Elamite. An Elamite lord named Kudur-Mabug established himself as King of Ur (c. 1950 B.C.), and was succeeded by his sons, Arad-Sin and Rim-Sin, who made themselves kings of Larsam as well. Rim-Sin was a notable figure in the history of Babylonia, as the contemporary and rival of the great Khammurabi. He ended his days in the reign of the successor of Khammurabi, when the final unification of Sumer and Akkad under the leadership of Babylon was accomplished.

3. The First Dynasty of Babylon

The princes who accomplished this work were foreign Semites, South-Syrian Arabs or Palestinians from Amurru, "the West," which had now for a thousand years been influenced by Babylonian civilization. These "Amorites" were then no strangers to the culture of the land which they were invading. Whether their first appearance in Babylonia is to be dated to the end of Libit-Ishtar's reign (about 2200 B.C.) or not is, as we have seen, uncertain, but we can be sure that the troubles of a century later were caused by their irruption with their tribesmen in force. The city of Babylon lay much exposed to attack from the Western Desert, and offered, probably, an easy prey. Hitherto, Babylon had been an insignificant factor in the history of Akkad, and its god, Marduk, had little renown or wealth. The energy of its new conquerors made it the chief city of Babylonia, and transfigured the humble Marduk into a king of gods, identifying him with Enlil or Bel of Nippur, the old chief deity of the land, much as in contemporary Egypt the new-fangled Amen of Thebes was identified with the ancient Ra.

Whether Sumu-abu (c. 2050 B.C.), the first king of the new Babylonian dynasty, was the actual conqueror or his son we do not know.

His successors in order until Khammurabi ascended the throne were Sumula-Ilu, Zabum, Immerum (a short-lived usurper), Apil-Sin, and Sin-Muballit, the latter being the father of Khammurabi. None of these kings seem ever to have acknowledged the overlordship of the kings of Isin or Larsam, and they seem to have themselves gradually increased their authority in an ever widening circle around Babylon. Sippar, Kutha, and Nippur were added to the dominion of Babylon by these kings, and also after the death of its last king, Damik-Ilishu, Isin, taken by Sin-muballit in his seventeenth year (c. 1947 B.C.) from the King of Larsam, who had occupied it. When Khammurabi came to the throne, he found himself ruling over a prosperous state extending from Sippar in the north to Nippur in the south, i.e. the whole extent of the ancient Akkad. Southwards, Sumer was still in the state of confusion caused by the devastating inroads of the Elamite conquerors, Erech and Ur had both been destroyed, and the rightful king of Larsam, Siniddinam, was still contending for his throne with the Elamite usurper Rim-Sin. It seems that Khammurabi soon after his accession attacked Rim-Sin; in his fourth year (about 1940 B.C.) he seems to have carried his arms to the border of Elam, and in his seventh he took

Erech and Isin from Rim-Sin. But after this year his annals are silent as to any successes against the Elamites, until his thirtieth year is reached. During this period he extended his rule over the greater part of Mesopotamia, and the ex-king of Larsam, Siniddinam, became not only his feudatory, but also took command of the Babylonian troops in the war against Rim-Sin. Further, he reduced to a state of willing obedience the country of Shitullum, to the north of Akkad, and also the still more northerly district of Ashur, on the Tigris, whose capital Ashur (Assur; the modern Kala'at Sherkat, more than two hundred miles north-west of Babylon), became in later times the seat of the monarchs who succeeded to the inheritance of Khammurabi and created the empire of Assyria. Ilu-shuma of Ashir (as the later Ashur or Assyria was then called) attacked Sumu-abu, the founder of the new Babylonian dynasty, and in Khammurabi's time the King of Ashir or Ashur (Shamsi-Adad I, the sixth successor of Ilu-shuma) was tributary to the great King of Babylon. We cannot go much farther back than Ilu-shuma in the history of Assyria. Before him we hear (in an inscription of Esarhaddon's) of an early king, Bel-ibni, son of Adasi, "the founder of the kingdom of Assyria," and before him there are two dim figures of tradition, Ushpia and Kikia, of whom the former was a priest, and the founder of E-kharsag-kurkurra, the temple of Ashur in the city of Ashur, and so the holiest and most ancient sanctuary of Assyria. Ushpia is mentioned in an inscription of Shalmaneser I. His name is of the Northern and probably non-Semitic type which is associated with the mountain-tribes of Armenia, and it is not impossible that the inhabitants of Assyria were of this race, semitized.

Shamshi-Adad supported Khammurabi loyally in his wars against his great enemies, the Elamites of Larsam. While Khammurabi controlled an empire reaching to Armenia and Palestine, his capital was within easy attack from the forces of Arad-Sin and Rim-Sin, who ruled Southern Babylonia and the coast-lands north of the Persian Gulf. Rim-Sin was never able to jeopardize his enemy's position seriously, and eventually he was worn down to extinction by Khammurabi's successor. For a time it would seem, judging from a most interesting Hebrew tradition, that the kings of Babylon and Larsam were subjected to the power of a great Elamite conqueror named Chedorla'omer, a name which is good Elamite, and would be, properly written, Kudur-Lagamar, The Hebrews' account of the origin of their nation brings, in one legend, the ancestral hero Abraham into warlike contact with "Amraphel king of Shinar, Arioch king of

Ellasar, Chedorla'omer, king of Elam, and Tid'al king of the Goyyim," who in alliance were engaged in subduing the revolted Arab tribes of Moab and the Hauran. The conjunction of these names makes it probable that Amraphel is Khammurabi, that Arioch of Ellasar represents the dynasty of Kudur-mabug at Larsam, and that Chedorla'omer represents the power of Elam, Tid'al that of the Khatti or Hittites of Anatolia. The "Goyyim" of the Hebrews were the non-Semitic "Gentile" tribes, the "nations" which lived in the North, and Tid'al is a Hittite name; a Hittite king five centuries later was called Dudhalia. The names are altered: Arioch cannot be identified, as it stands, with either Arad-Sin or Rim-Sin; and Tid'al may owe its existence to a scribe of Dudhalia's time who wrote down the best-known royal Hittite name of his day. But our modern knowledge shews that the tradition is based upon historical fact: Amraphel was a historical king of Shinar (Babylonia), in whose days a powerful king of Ellasar (Larsam) existed side by side with him, and in whose time Elamite conquerors with names of the type of Kudur-lagamar existed (such as Kudur-mabug and the earlier Kudur-nakhkhunte), who from time to time imposed their will on Babylonia, while at this time also the Hittite "Goyyim" of Anatolia were beginning to bestir themselves, and were shortly to overrun Babylonia. The collocation of names is impossible at a later period, and we must regard the tradition as, originally, a piece of contemporary history, adapted later to the Abrahamic legend, and possibly first written down by a Hebrew scribe some five or six centuries after the time of Khammurabi. In the account we see the Elamite Chedorla'omer taking the leading position among the kings: and it may be that a conqueror named Kudur-lagamar did at this time issue from Elam, impose his will upon the rival kings of Babylonia, and so enter into short-lived relations with even the outlying tribes of Hittites.

The tables were turned since the days of Dungi, or even Naram-Sin. In those days the native patesis of Susa, the first Elamite rulers of whom we have any knowledge, Basha-shushinak, Khutrun-tepti, Kal-Rukhurasir, and others, were the obedient vassals of the King of Sumer and Akkad, who even replaced them at will by Babylonian officials. Thus in Dungi's reign the patesis and local governors are all either Babylonians or had adopted Babylonian names, both Semitic and Sumerian. Later on, we find native Elamite names again. These chiefs called themselves usually "patesi of Susa and shakkanakku (governor) of Elam." Their inscriptions have been found by the French excavators of Susa, where Dungi built a temple of

Shushinak, the chief Elamite deity. The lands of Anshan, Kimash, Umliash, and other Elamite districts seem to have been administered by them. Kudur-nankhundi, the conqueror of Ur, came from Anshan; Kudur-mabug from Emutbalim, a district nearer the sea. From the time of Kudur-nankhundi to the latter part of Khammurabi's reign the Elamites were independent, and for a time even dominated Babylonia. As we have seen, Khammurabi warred with Larsam at the beginning of his reign; then there is a cessation of war and a silence which may mean a pax elamitica imposed upon both by Chedorla'omer; then comes war again. In his thirty-first year (about 191 3 B.C.) the armies of Khammurabi, directed by the king from Babylon, and under the command of the veteran Siniddinam, who must by this time have been an old man, and a general named Inukhsamar, took Ur and Larsam, and invaded Emutbalim, the hereditary kingdom of Kudur-mabug and Rim-Sin. For two years the war was waged, and we have an interesting glimpse of the religious ideas of the time in connexion with it. Siniddinam had captured the chief city of Emutbalim and with them the images of the goddesses of the country: these he proposed to send as trophies to Babylon. In answer to his report, Khammurabi writes, ordering him to bring them in state. It seems, however, that some time after this the royal troops experienced some severe check at the hands of the Elamites, and it was thought that this was due to the anger of the goddesses at being taken to Babylon, so, in a second letter, Khammurabi writes to Siniddinam to take them back to their own dwellings again.

Khammurabi did not penetrate farther into Elam itself, and was unable to effect the recapture of the goddesses of Erech who had been carried off to Susa by Kudur-nankhundi three centuries before: this restitution was not effected until 1635 years after their removal, by Ashurbanipal. As a more lasting trophy of his victories than the idols of Emutbalim, he retained Larsam, Ur, and Southern Surner, the borderland of Ashnunak, and the adjoining district of Umliash. In peace he was even more conspicuous as an organizer of victory than in war. The testimony of those actual letters, rescripts, and despatches of his which can be seen any day in the galleries of the British Museum, shew us that the later kings of Babylonia were by no means in error when they looked back to him as their exemplar of what a patriarchal ruler should be. In them, "we see the facts of history in the making."

Of his laws, the discovery of which on a stele found at Susa has made the name of Khammurabi so familiar in these modern days, something will be said later. But it must be remembered that though no doubt there is in them an original element due to the king himself, yet in the main his code was but a reissue of ancient Sumerian laws, and he has little claim to be regarded as himself a great lawgiver. His own actual letters which we possess, are far more interesting evidence of the man's personality. So far as we know, he was the first great organizer in history, and the kingdom of Babylonia, with its capital at Babylon, was the lasting result of his work. Babylon remained the capital of the Mesopotamian world henceforth throughout ancient history.

But he could not secure an undisputed empire to his successors. The Elamite danger had no sooner been removed than others even more formidable appeared. Babylonia was too rich and too vulnerable to go free from attack for long.

Khammurabi was succeeded, after a long reign of forty-three years (about B.C. 1944-1901) by his son, Samsu-iluna, at the beginning of whose reign (second year) the indefatigable Rim-Sin again gave trouble. He had apparently taken Isin, which was recaptured by Samsu-iluna, who also subdued Kish, which had revolted. In Samsu-iluna's tenth year Rim-Sin still lived (having reigned by that time certainly not less than fifty-seven years), but shortly afterwards he was finally defeated and slain. Samsu-iluna was then confronted with a new enemy. Iluma-ilu, a chief of the South, made himself master of the coast of the Persian Gulf, the "Land of the Sea," and founded there (about 1875 B.C.) an independent dynasty which neither Samsu-iluna nor his successors were able to destroy. The "Dynasty of the Sea-Land" continued to rule on the sea-coast well on into the Kassite period. Elam, however, was recovered, and in the reign of Ammi-zaduga, the fourth successor of Khammurabi (c. B.C. 1798-1777), we find it once again tributary. Possibly Babylonia and Elam were drawn together by the necessity of common defence against the inroads of the Kashshu or Kassites, an Indo-European nation of the northeast, whose tribes were now pressing from Media through the Zagros towards the fertility and wealth of Babylonia. We hear of their attacks already in the reign of Samsu-iluna. They were, however, not strong enough to attack Babylon. Their work was done for them by another power, whose strokes were sudden, unexpected, and irresistible, the terrible "Goyyim" of Asia Minor. The reign of Samsu-ditana, the eleventh and last monarch of the 1st

Dynasty of Babylon (c. B.C. 1777-1746)., seems to have been brought to a bloody end by a conquering raid of the King of Khatti (his name is not preserved), in which Babylon was stormed and sacked by the fierce Anatolians (c. B.C. 1746). They retreated, probably, as soon as they came, leaving death and ruin behind them; and the Kassites seized their opportunity. Their leader, Gandash, appropriated the city and vacant throne of Babylon (or Kar-Uuniyash, as it was now called in the tongue of the conquerors), and founded the Kassite dynasty, which endured for six hundred years.

4. The Kassites

The new lords of Babylonia did not for a long time interfere with the southern kingdom of the Sea-Land, which pursued its independent existence for nearly three centuries (c. 1875-1600 B.C.) under kings whose names are mostly Sumerian, a fact which seems to shew that the Sumerian nationality, finally deposed from its position of equality with the Semites after the fall of the dynasty of Ur, was eking out the last remnants of its separate existence in the southernmost portions of the country. The kingdom of the Sea-Land was the last expression of the national consciousness of the ancient Sumerian race. When it fell, the Sumerians disappear, and their language becomes a dead speech, known only to priests and scribes, the Latin of Mesopotamia.

The end of the Sumerians came in the reign of Ea-gamil, the tenth successor of Iluma-ilu, probably about 15S0 B.C. Ea-gamil attempted to invade Elam, but was defeated and driven back. A Kassite leader named Ulam-buriash, "son of Burnaburariash, the king," then attacked him and overthrew his kingdom, reigning in the Sea-Land in his stead as a vassal of his father the King of Babylon. The final scene was reached a few years later, when the Kassite king of Babylon, Agum III (a nephew of Ulam-buriash), finally took Dtar-Ea (Ea's Burgh), the last fortified place of the Sea-Landers.

Of the Kassite kings we know very little. Gandash was succeeded by Agum I, who was followed by Kashtiliash I, Ushshi, Adumetash, Urshigurmash, and Agum II; the last waged war with the Hittite land of Khani, and triumphantly brought back to Babylon statues of the city-gods Marduk and Sarpanitum, which had no doubt been carried off by the Hittites in their great raid. Then there is a gap, followed by Burnaburariash, Kashtiliash II, and Agum III. Then comes a darkness of a century and a half till the veil is again lifted, after the Egyptian conquest of Syria, in the reign of Kara-indash, the contemporary of Thothmes IV. The continuous history of Babylonia begins again with him. The Kassite period thus appears as a very uneventful one. The kings, of whom our list is very imperfect, are mere names, and nothing in particular seems to have happened during their reigns. This impression may be due simply to our unusual lack of information with regard to this period. But it may well be that this lack of information reflects a real lack of incident. The conquest, too, by the Kassite barbarians may very well have caused a temporary retrogression in culture, when the arts of the scribe and historiographer were not so much in demand, in royal circles at any rate, as before. And it is the fact that we find very few records of temple-building or restoration at this period. The Kassite kings worshipped their own deities, and probably did not hasten to put themselves under the protection of the gods of Babylon. Obviously they cared very little for the religion and probably less for the literature and arts of their highly civilized subjects.

The racial difference between the new conquerors and their subjects was great. There is little doubt that the Kassites were Indo-Europeans, and spoke an Aryan tongue. Their chief god was Suryash, the sun, their word for "god" was bugash, the Slav bogu and Phrygian Bagaios. The termination -ash which regularly appears at the end of their names is a nominative, corresponding to the Greek -oc. Such a name as Indabugash is clearly Aryan. They were evidently the advance-guard of the Indo-European southern movement which colonized Iran and pushed westward to the borders of Asia Minor. In the north the kingdom of Mitanni was about this time established between the Euphrates and Tigris by Aryans who must have been of the same stock as the Kassites who conquered Babylonia. The names of the kings of Mitanni which are known to us in later times are Aryan, and among the gods of Mitanni we find the Indian Varuna, Indra, and the Nasatya-twins (Acvins). It is possible that the mass of the population in Mitanni was of partly Semitic, partly Hittite blood, and that the Aryans there were merely a ruling caste: the language of Mitanni was of the Caucasic or Alarodian type. Their further westward progress was barred by the Hittites, who were firmly entrenched in the land of Khani (Coele-Syria) and had already swarmed across the Taurus into Northern Syria, founding outpost principalities on the Euphrates, of which Carchemish may already have existed as the most important. At first the Mitannians must have been checked at the Euphrates, but later on they seem to have crossed the river and have made themselves masters of both Semites and Hittites in Northern Syria, which probably remained tributary to them till the Egyptian conquest in the sixteenth century. The young state of Assyria, of which we know nothing at this period, is found tributary to Mitanni later on, and we cannot doubt that its allegiance was very soon forcibly transferred from the Kassite kings of Babylonia to the rulers of Mitanni.

Mesopotamian civilization was unaffected by the Mitannians and Kassites, who seem to have been entirely uncultured. They learnt civilization from the conquered. The process seems to have taken about two centuries: by the time of Kurigalzu and Burnaburiash the Kassite kings have adopted the Babylonian religion, at any rate for official purposes, and differ from their subjects only in the retention of their Kassite names, which they affected to the last, six hundred years after the time of Gandash. It would seem that the racial distinction between the Kassite settlers and the Babylonians was long preserved, in much the same way as in China the Manchu noble families who came with the late Manchu dynasty still keep separate from the Chinese. The tenacity of power by one dynasty for so many centuries points to a health and vigour in the ruling family and race which was unwonted in highly civilized Babylonia.

5. Babylonian Civilization

With the Kassite conquest we have then reached a pause in the current of Babylonian history which well marks the end of its first period. Looking back, the history of the period which has been sketched above is practically the history of the gradual semitizing of Babylonia, which was finally completed when Khammurabi unified the whole of the country into one Semitic state, which remained one and remained Semitic even when ruled by a foreign dynasty.

The Babylonian culture of Khammurabi's day was not very different from that of old-Sumerian times. Only the writing had developed, the bow had been introduced by the Semites and the horse from Media: and a unified state with its centre at Babylon had been created. We cannot suppose that the methods of irrigation in use under the first king of united Babylonia were more highly developed or more time and labour-saving than those in vogue under the earlier patesis of Lagash. The usual conception of the Babylonian is an energetic tradesman and a money-lender, with a turn for astronomy: this is, however, the man of a later age.

The Babylonian of the earlier time was a merchant also, and a keen litigant as well, as hundreds of early tablets testify, and the astronomical tendencies of his later descendant were founded on the observations of remote forefathers, but first and foremost he was an agriculturist. We know how the corn-bearing capacity of Babylonia astounded Herodotus, and we can well imagine that his statements as to the phenomenal yield of the land, the breadth to which the blades of wheat and barley would grow, and the height of the millet and sesamum there would dispose many of his hearers to unbelief. Yet there is nothing improbable in what he says. Important as was Babylonian agriculture in his day, in the earlier period it was far more important, and in the letters and inscriptions of that the care of the land appears as even more important than the maintenance of the temples of the gods. Marduk himself was said to have inaugurated the irrigation-system of Babylonia, and from the earliest period every king of whom we possess more than fragmentary mention prides himself upon having either constructed or renewed canals to bring water from the two rivers to the broad lands lying between them. A very good reason for a watchful eye being kept by the Government upon the proper repair of the canals was the fact that upon properly regulated irrigation depended a good harvest, and upon a good harvest depended a good inflow of taxes into the treasuries of the king and the gods. Taxes were generally paid in kind, and chiefly in corn, though dates, oil, and wine, etc., also contributed to swell the total. Prices also might be reckoned in grain, dates, or oil, and though metal weights, the talent, the maneh, and the shekel, were all in use, no idea of a true currency had as yet arisen in Babylonia any more than in Egypt: in a purchase of land, for example, the purchase price was first settled in shekel-weights of silver, and the various items exchanged against the land (corn, slaves, weapons, or what not), were often separately valued on the same basis till the purchase price was made up. This was the transition stage between pure barter and a regular currency. Much of the land was owned by the great temples, and the royal domains were no doubt much mixed up with those of the gods: in some places, as in Egypt, the two would be identical, since the king, in his capacity of patesi, would often be a high-priest; but there was apparently, also, besides the class of free labourers, a large number of free-holding farmers. The free labourers were in all probability in some ways the worst off of the population, for their pay rarely amounted to more than their daily food, and they were not entitled to the protection which the slave received from his master. Even the slave was protected from his master by the law. The Babylonians had a most modern idea of "law and order," and to this was no doubt due their commercial stability, which survived all wars and conquests unimpaired. The judges were named by the king, and were his deputies, and they seem to have gone on circuit: their decisions were irrevocable.

The laws which they administered were of Sumerian origin. Under Khammurabi the laws of his day, no doubt with improvements initiated in the highest quarter, were specially codified, as they doubtless had been under previous kings of reforming ideas, like Urukagina. They were inscribed upon a magnificent stela of diorite, found by the French at Susa, whither it had been carried off like the stela of Naram-Sin, and now in the Louvre. Above the writing we see Khammurabi, in relief, receiving the code from the sun-god Shamash.

From this monument we have gained a complete knowledge of ancient Babylonian law, and have seen how very equitable most of its enactments were. Those relating to agriculture, to the recovery of debt, and to the conditions of divorce are especially interesting. In the latter improvement had been made since old-Sumerian times, when the wife had no rights of divorce whatever, these being reserved only to the man. In Khammurabi's time, however, the law had been modified in favour of the woman, for if she was divorced her husband had to make proper provision for her maintenance and that of her children, of whom she had the custody, besides returning the marriage-portion. He could only evade these provisions by proving that his wife had been unfaithful or a careless householder; in the latter case he might enslave her. In the ancient Sumerian laws quoted above it will be noticed that the man is more important than the woman, the father than the mother, the husband than the wife. This is in striking contrast to Egypt, where the "Lady of the House" was usually a more important personage than the mere "Male," as the husband was called, and where men often preferably traced their descent in the female line. In Egypt there were always strong traces of Mutterrecht, but none in Babylonia. Still, women were, generally speaking, quite as independent in Babylonia as in Egypt: they could own property, whether in houses or slaves, and could personally plead in the courts. Also, we find there a remarkable class of honoured women, votaresses who in some ways resembled the Roman Vestals, and possessed unusual rights and privileges. These are not to be confused with the religious prostitutes, mentioned by Herodotus, who were certainly a prominent feature of Babylonian religion.

They were women who took vows of celibacy, though usually dwelling together in special convents, could nevertheless live in the world, and were often nominally married. If married (and to possess a votaress-wife was probably regarded as a distinction), a concubine was provided to bear children to the husband, but had no legal wifely rights, which belonged to the votaress.

The accessibility of the law made lawsuits easy, and the Babylonians were highly litigious in consequence, most of these lawsuits were in connexion with the sale or lease of land houses, etc. Such sales and leases, as well as wills, had always to be drawn up in legal form to be valid, as was also the case in Egypt. For a document to be valid, it had to be attested by witnesses, and was usually impressed with the seals of the parties to it: when one of the parties had no seal he might impress the mark of his nail upon the soft clay of the tablet on which the deed was written. The absolute necessity of the seal as part of the array of a Babylonian is duly noted by Herodotus, whose description of the Babylonian dress of his day is entirely applicable to the early period also, for, though fashions in tiaras altered from time to time, the long robes never changed. Many of the cylinder-seals, used to roll over the clay tablets as a blotting-roller is used nowadays, may be seen in our museums. They are made of black haematite or deep red jasper or white chalcedony, sometimes of translucent crystal: on them was sometimes the name of the owner, always some mythological scene, such as Shamash the sun-god rising above the mountain of the world, Eabani and Gilgamesh contending with the bull of Ishtar, etc., and they are usually triumphs of the glyptic art, far superior to any work of the kind from Egypt.

Attempts have been made to distinguish between the religion of the Sumerians and that of the Semitic Babylonians, but without very great success. It is as difficult to say with certainty that this element in Babylonian religion is of Sumerian origin and that of Semitic as to say that this element in Hellenic religion is pre-Aryan or Pelasgic and that Aryan: one cannot disentangle the Sumerian strands from the rest. Not even can it be said with certainty that a particular deity is non-Semitic, because purely Semitic deities seem very often for the sake of uniformity to have been given Sumerian names by the Babylonian archaeologists. We do not know whether the oldest deities of Shumer, such as Ea (Sum. En-ki), Sin or Nannar (Sum. En-zu; the Moon), Ningirsu of Lagash and others, were really pre-Sumerian or not. En-lil ("Great Spirit") of Nippur, who is probably purely Sumerian, was translated into Semitic as Bel (Ba'al, "Lord"); Utu the Sumerian sun-god was identified with a Semitic sun-god, Shamash. Marduk, the god of Babylon, was no doubt originally Sumerian: his name sounds like a Semitic garbling of a Sumerian name. Ramman or Adad, the thunder-god, seems Semitic; he has a purely Semitic name. When we find by the side of a god a goddess as his consort who is but a shadowy female edition of himself and often bears a feminine form of his name, as Belit by the side of Bel, we know that the goddess is of Semitic origin, and very often the god also, but not necessarily, for in later days the goddess Damkina was invented to stand by the side of the Sumerian Ea, who like others of the Sumerian gods, had no consort. So also Sarpanitum was invented for Marduk, Laz for Nergal, and so on. The deities, male or female, who stand alone, appear to be Sumerian, but here again we find that, the independent goddess Ishtar, who on this theory should be of Sumerian origin, bears an apparently Semitic name. It is by no means certain that she is originally the same as the Sumerian goddess Nina, whom she nearly resembles, and a form of her, Anunitum, the goddess of the morning-star, is purely Semitic, though derived from the Sumerian male deity Ana (Sem. Anu), the sky-god, Ishtar seems of Syrian or Canaanite origin, and there is a possibility, if not a probability, that she, like the Syrian war-goddess whom she so closely resembles, was at an early period modified by a confusion with the Anatolian mother-goddess: like her, she was served by eunuch-priests. Tammuz, her favourite (who does not bear the same relation to her as a Semitic double-god would), would then be, in spite of his occurrence in Sumerian religious texts, the Anatolian Attis, and came to Mesopotamia from beyond the Taurus. In Babylonia Ishtar-Nina was a star-goddess, in Syria Ashtoreth-Tanit was a moon-goddess also, and in Anatolia the Great Mother and Attis, in Syria Astarte and Tammuz, seem to be the female Moon attended by the less important male Sun. The Semitic name of the Sun, Shamash, seems to mean the "servant" or "follower" of Mistress Moon, whom the sun was regarded as attending in her wanderings. No doubt the human face of the moon, its changes, and the obvious means of counting time which could be derived from these changes, marked it out from the beginning as the superior of the brighter, but less changing, sun.

Our knowledge of Babylonian mythical and legendary literature is extensive: the stories of Gilgamesh and of the Deluge have already been mentioned: of other such tales one of the most remarkable is the legend of

Etana and the Eagle. On one occasion Etana's friend the Eagle carried him up to heaven mounted on his back, and he saw the thrones of the gods, but when they flew still higher to explore the dwelling of Ishtar, some accident happened, and they fell headlong to earth and were dashed to pieces. The parallel with the Greek story of Ikaros is obvious. Another hero, Adapa, son of Ea, was fishing from a boat in the Persian Gulf, when the South Wind suddenly blew and upset his boat. Adapa, furious at this attack, caught the South Wind by her wings, and broke them. Other legends refer to the great "Tablets of Destiny," upon which the fate of gods and men were inscribed, and which constituted the title-deeds of the gods to rule the earth. These had originally been in the possession of the demon of chaos, Tiamat, but in the great conflict with her and her giant brood, Enlil or Marduk had won them from Kingu, the leader of her hosts. Afterwards they were stolen from Marduk by a demon named Zu, who aspired to rule the universe. The confusion caused among the gods by this audacious theft was great, a council was held, and Adad and two other gods were asked to rescue them, but they refused. Eventually, however, they were recovered by Shamash, the sun-god, who caught Zu in his net.

There is undoubtedly much in Babylonian religion and myth that can be paralleled in the religious literature of the Hebrews, though whether this resemblance is due to the ancient spread of Babylonian culture into Canaan and its continuous influence from the earliest days, to an actual migration of an Abrahamic clan into Canaan from Ur of the Chaldees by way of Harran, or simply to the influence of the Babylonian environment during the Captivity, cannot yet be determined with certainty. Perhaps all three causes combined to bring about the resemblance. But there are other features of Babylonian legend which can only be paralleled in the mythology of the Greeks, and so close are these parallels sometimes that we can hardly doubt that many Greek myths, especially those of a cosmogonic character, came originally to Greece from Babylonia, probably through the medium of Asia Minor.

CHAPTER VI: THE HYKSOS CONQUEST AND THE FIRST EGYPTIAN EMPIRE (Circa 1800-1350 B.C.)

I. The Asiatic Invasion

THE almost contemporary incursion of the Aryans from Iran and of the Anatolians from Asia Minor into Mesopotamia and Northern Syria must have caused at first a considerable displacement of the Semitic population, which was pressed south-westwards into Southern Syria and Palestine. The result was that the Semites burst the ancient barrier of Egypt, which had weakened in strength under the kings of the XIIIth Dynasty, and the Nile-land was overrun and conquered by the hated Retenu and the despised Aamu. The later Egyptians spoke of their conquerors slightingly as mere "Shepherds," Beduins of the desert, but there is little doubt that they were mainly civilized Syrians and Canaanites, and they may have brought with them Anatolian and even Indo-European warriors. They found a ready welcome from their kin already settled in the land of Goshen, and Manetho tells us that the conquest was consummated with little trouble and that the conquerors were savage and cruel.

Very possibly the swiftness and completeness of the conquest was due not only to the weakness and disunion of the Egyptians, but to the possession by the invaders of a new engine of war, previously unknown to the Egyptian military system, the war-chariot and its horses. The chariot, drawn by asses, had been used by the Babylonians in war from time immemorial, and must have been known, at least by hearsay, to the Egyptians for centuries, but they never adopted it for use with their asses. When the horse was introduced, probably not much before 2000 B.C., into Western Asia from Iran, where it was first domesticated, it replaced the ass in the chariot, which now, with fiery steeds yoked to it, became a terrible instrument of war. But the Egyptians still knew nothing of it; neither horse nor chariot are represented on any Egyptian monument or mentioned in any document before the Hyksos invasion. After it, however, they appear in common use, and one of the words for "chariot" is that used by the Semites, markabata, Assyrian narkabat. The conclusion is obvious: disaster taught the Egyptians once and for all not to despise their eastern neighbours; they adopted the weapon of their adversaries, and to such purpose that they themselves used it to conquer Palestine, and henceforth the strength of Egypt lay not only in her bowmen but in the multitudes of her horses and chariots also.

Manetho's account of the conquest is worth quoting in full. He says: "We had once a king whose name was Timaios. In his time it came to pass, I know not how, that God was adverse to us, and there came out of the East in an extraordinary manner men of ignoble race, who had the temerity to invade our country, and easily subdued it by force without a battle. And when they had our rulers in their power they burnt our cities, and demolished the temples of the gods, and used the inhabitants after a most barbarous manner, slaying some, and leading the wives and children of others into captivity. At length they made one of themselves king, whose name was Salatis; he lived at Memphis, and made both the Upper and Lower Countries tributary, and stationed garrisons in the places best adapted for them. He chiefly aimed to secure the eastern frontier, for he regarded with misgiving the great power of the Assyrians, who, he foresaw, would one day invade the kingdom. And, finding in the Saite (?Sethroite) nome to the east of the Bubastite channel a city well adapted for his purpose, which was called from some ancient mythological reference Avaris, he rebuilt it and made it very strong with walls, and garrisoned it with a force of two hundred and forty thousand men completely armed. Thither Salatis repaired in summer, to collect his tribute and pay his troops, and to exercise them so as to strike foreigners with terror. And when this man had reigned nineteen years, after him reigned another, named Bnon, for forty-four years; after him another, called Apakhnas, thirty-six years and seven months; after him Apophis, who reigned sixty-one years, and then Ianias fifty years and one month. After all these reigned Assis forty-nine years and two months. These six were the first rulers among them, and during the whole period of their power they made war upon the Egyptians, being desirous of destroying them utterly."

2. The Hyksos Kings

Naturally we have no contemporary record of the actual invasion, but the king "Timaios" in whose reign it occurred may be a certain Nefer-Temu who comes in the Turin Papyrus shortly before the Nehesi, who, as we know from his own monuments, was a vassal of the Hyksos and their god Set. Of Salatis we know nothing from Egyptian sources. Avaris, the city which he fortified, is certainly Tell el-Yahudiyah, in the Eastern Delta at the mouth of the Wadi Tumilat (the land of Goshen), where Prof Petrie has found conclusive proofs of special Hyksos occupation.

The original forms of the names Beon or Bnon and Apakhnas or Pakhnas have not yet been certainly identified. Prof. Erman compared Apakhnas with the name Aapehti, which is certainly that of a king of this dynasty, though the only Aapehti known to us was one of the last of the Hyksos kings, and only preceded their expulsion by a few years. If he is Apakhnas, Manetho has misplaced him.

For Manetho's Apophis we have several candidates, for there were at least four Hyksos kings known from the monuments named Pepi or Apepi :— (1) Maa-ab-Ra Pepi, (2) Neb-khepesh-Ra Apepi, (3) Aa-user-Ra ('O-user-R'a) Apepi, and (4) Aa-kenen-Ra ('O-kenen-R'a) Apepi. Of these kings Aa-kenen-Ra is evidently, from the form of his name, a contemporary of the later Theban kings of the XVIIth Dynasty who bore the style of Sekenenra Taa: he is therefore Apepi III. Aa-user-Ra is probably for the same reason the predecessor or successor of the king who, as we shall see, was probably the greatest of the Hyksos, Seuserenra Khian. He too ruled the whole of Egypt, for his name is found at Gebelen, south of Thebes, and it was, as we can judge from what we know of the activity of the contemporary Theban kings of the XVIIth Dynasty, not for very long that the Hyksos actually possessed the whole of Egypt. We may with great probability place the apogee of the Hyksos power at about the middle point of their rule, so that this Apepi will be Apepi II. Neb-khepesh-ra is then Apepi I, and either he or Maa-ab-Ra Pepi may well be Manetho's Apophis, the fourth Hyksos king. His name, Neb-khepesh, "Lord of the Sword," would be very appropriate to one of the kings who, as Manetho tells us, occupied themselves with ceaseless war in the first century of their rule. Only two relics of this king are known: a dagger with embossed gold handle on which is represented a warrior stabbing a lion which is pursuing an antelope (now at Cairo), and part of a vase of siliceous stone with the king's cartouche, in the British Museum. Maa-ab-Ra Pepi is known only from scarabs. Staan or Iannas is no doubt the great king Khian, and Assis or Aseth is evidently Uatjed or Uazed, a king whose scarabs are of the same type as those of Khian.

Besides the few names given by Manetho, who has evidently preserved only those of the most notorious of the foreign invaders, we know many other names of Hyksos kings or chiefs from scarabs, which can be fixed to this period by their style. Of much the same style as the scarabs of Uazed are those of a king named Iepek-Hur, or Iekeb-Hur. The element Iepek is also found in the name of a "king's son Apek," which occurs on scarabs of the same period. It has been proposed to identify this name with the Semitic Yakub, Jacobs who is supposed by some to have been a Syrian god. Whether this be so or not, the identification with the name Jacob is probably correct.

The throne-name of this king was Mer-user-Ra. Other royal names, certainly of Hyksos, and probably successors or contemporaries of Iekeb-hur, are Semken and Ant-Har. The initial element of the second name is no doubt the name of the Syrian goddess Anta or Anait. The prenomens of these kings may no doubt be found in several prenomens of this period found, like the names we have mentioned, on scarabs: Sekhanra, Aa-hetep-Ra, Uatjkara II, and Nekara II. Judging from the style of his scarabs, Nekara II was probably the immediate predecessor of the great Khian.

With this king we reach the first of the later Hyksos, who are known to us from monuments of size and importance, and seem to have been pharaohs of the first rank. Khian dedicated statues of himself in the temple of Bubastis; one of these was discovered by Prof. Naville, and is now in the Museum of Cairo. Great attention has been directed to this king because relics bearing his name have been found at places so far distant from Egypt and so far apart as Bagdad in Mesopotamia and Knossos in Crete. The small lion from Bagdad which bears his throne-name Seuserenra is in the British Museum (No. 987); the alabastron-lid with his personal name Khian, which was discovered in 1901 by Mr. Arthur Evans in the course of his excavations in the Minoan palace at Knossos, is now in the Museum of Candia. Now it is remarkable that Khian assumed an unusual title, that of "Embracer of Territories" (ank adebu); is it possible that his rule actually extended further than that of any Egyptian king before him or after him, and that these objects are actual relics of his dominion over Southern Mesopotamia and the Isles of the Great Sea? It is hardly possible, and we need not jump to so far-reaching a conclusion. The lion of Bagdad may merely be an Assyrian trophy brought back by Esarhaddon; the alabastron-lid of Knossos is evidently a mere (contemporary) importation. So we have no reason to suppose that Khian really owned a rood of land beyond the frontiers of Egypt, though, as a Hyksos, he may well have exercised greater authority than any former Egyptian king over the Southern Palestinians and Bedawin. As a Bedawi, and lord of the

Bedu'w, he also bore the title of hik khaskhut, "Prince of the Deserts," which has already been mentioned.

In all probability, judging again from the style of scarabs, the successor of Khian was Aa-User-Ra Apepi II, who, as a mutilated inscription in the British Museum tells us, set up "great pillars, and gates of copper," in the temple of Bubastis, and left his name at Gebelen in token of his rule over South as well as North. An important date in his reign is given in the famous Rhind Mathematical Papyrus; in it the scribe Aahmes states that he wrote it in the 33rd year of the King of the South and North, Aa-user-Ra, from an ancient copy made in the reign of Ne-maa-Ra (Amenemhat III). Our present copy, the Rhind Papyrus, was written at a later period, and its scribe copied the autograph and date of the scribe Aahmes with the rest. The high date agrees with the long reigns ascribed to the former Hyksos kings by Manetho.

Aa-seh-Ra, whose name is only known to us from a fragment of an obelisk at Tanis, possibly comes between Apepi II and Aa-kenen-Ra Apepi III, who added an inscription to a statue of Mermeshau at Tanis and dedicated an altar of black granite, now in the Cairo Museum, in honour of the god Set of Avaris. In his reign the final revolt of the South seems to have begun, which hardly ceased until the Hyksos were expelled. In the Papyrus Sallier is given an account of the genesis of the quarrel between him and his vassal Sekenenra Tau-aa-ken of the Theban XVIIth Dynasty. Apepi seems to have been victorious at first, and the Theban was killed. The name of the last Hyksos king is unknown to us, but it is probable that between Apepi III and him comes the king Set (or Ra)-Aa-Pehti Nubti, who is mentioned as living 400 years before Rameses li on the "Stele of Four Hundred Years," and is also known to us from a scarab in the British Museum, the style of which is identical with that of those of the early XVIIIth Dynasty and differs from those of the other Hyksos. This would place him about 1650 B.C.

The later Hyksos seem to have become entirely egyptianized. They adopted the full pharaonic dignity, and, as good Egyptian kings, built Egyptian temples and venerated Egyptian gods. The god of the deserts, Sutekh or Set, was naturally adopted by them as their especial patron, and identified with their own Baal or "lord." Since their rule was undisputed from first to last in the Delta, Set became specially identified in the minds of the Egyptians with the Delta, and in later times it was only at Tanis, the capital of the Delta, that he could be worshipped openly and the rule of the

Hyksos be referred to with anything but obloquy. At the same time new religious ideas were imported into Egypt by the Hyksos; the naked goddess Ishtar or Anait is now (and never afterwards) seen represented on scarabs, and the Syrian winged sphinx makes its first appearance in Egyptian iconography.

Manetho implies that the first Hyksos conquered the whole country, and it is possible that they did overrun it; but it seems that their successors could not maintain their hold over it in face of the fanatical opposition of the population of Upper Egypt. Later on, however, they succeeded in imposing their rule over the South, and continued to hold it till the war of liberation began in the reign of Apepi III.

3. The Egyptian Kings of the South

In all probability the South had already become independent in the time of the later kings of the XIIIth Dynasty, under princes of Theban origin, several of whom bore the characteristic Middle Empire Theban name of Antef.

Of these kings, Nub-kheper-Ra is the best known. His most important monument is an inscription upon a gateway of Senusert I in the temple of Min at Koptos, which is a decree of excommunication and degradation, and solemn curse directed against the person, descendants, and heirs of a certain Teta, who had apparently received the king's enemies in the temple. The decree, which is a historical document of importance, reads as follows:

—

"Year 3, third month of Peret, 25th day: under the Majesty of the King of Upper and Lower Egypt Nubu-kheper-Ra Son of the Sun Antef, giving life like the Sun for ever! Decree of the King to the Chancellor, the prince of Koptos Minemhat, the King's Son and Governor of Koptos Kanen, to the Chancellor Menkhmin, the Scribe of the Temple Neferhetep the elder, all the soldiers of Koptos, and all the officials of the temple. Now ye, behold! this decree is brought to you to inform you that My Majesty (life, health, and strength!) hath caused to come the God's Scribe and Chancellor of Amen, Siamen, and the Chief Inspector User-'a-Amen to make inquisition in the temple of Min. Now seeing that an official of the temple of my father Min approached My Majesty (life, health, and strength!), and said: 'An evil thing has come to pass in the temple, for Teta (blasted be his name!) son of Minhetep hath received the Enemy there'; behold! let him be cast out upon the ground from the temple of my father Min; behold! let

160

him be expelled from his dignity in the temple; even unto his son's son and the heir of his heir cast forth upon the ground! Take his loaves and sacred food, let not his name be remembered in this temple, as it is done to one who like him hath transgressed with regard to the Enemy of his God. Let his writings in the temple of Min be destroyed and in the treasury on every roll likewise. And any king and any powerful ruler who shall give him peace, may he not receive the White Crown, may he not support the Red Crown, may he not sit upon the Horus' throne of the living gods, may Nekhebet and Uatjit not give him peace as one who loves them! And any official and any prince who shall approach the Master (life, strength, and health!) to give him peace, let his people and his possessions and his lands be given as a god's offering to my father Min of Koptos, also let not any man of his kinsfolk or of the relations of his father or his mother be raised to this office! Also let this office be given to the Chancellor and Controller in the Palace Minemhat; give to him its loaves and sacred food, established unto him in writing in the temple of my father Min of Koptos unto his son's son and the heir of his heir!"

This is one of the most important Egyptian inscriptions that has come down to us: from it we not only learn the way in which was exercised the royal prerogative of summarily and utterly degrading and excommunicating a high official, but obtain a priceless reference to the relations of Nub-kheper-Ra with the Hyksos. We can have little doubt as to the nature of Teta's offence: "the Enemy of the God" can hardly be other than the abhorred Hyksos. From the mention of a garrison at Koptos we may conclude that this town, the modern Kuft, which even now is the most important strategical point of Upper Egypt, was the northern bulwark of Nub-kheper-Ra's kingdom, and that the traitorous temple-official Teta had either received a Hyksos emissary in its temple or had even treacherously surrendered it to the Hyksos in a siege, and that it was recovered by Minemhat and Kanen. There was evidently no truce with the "Enemy." Of all the Southern kings Nub-kheper-Ra was probably their most energetic and successful antagonist, but it is evident that even he was unable to conquer the North, or even to advance his power much beyond Koptos. But he, like the other kings of his dynasty, never thought for a moment of abandoning his legitimate claims to the rule of the whole of Egypt, and even carried the war into the enemy's camp by assuming the title of "Sopd, lord of the Deserts." Sopd, a form of Horus, was the god of the eastern frontier of the Delta and of the "Red Land," the deserts between the Nile and the Red Sea north of the Wadi Hammamat, and by assuming his appellation as a title Nub-kheper-Ra emphasized his right to rule the very deserts from which the Hyksos came. He was buried at Thebes, his capital, like the other Antefs, and his tomb was examined by the royal commission in the reign of Rameses IX. His portrait at Koptos is that of a keen and energetic man of early middle age.

The connexion of the Sebekemsafs and Antefs with the Sekenenra Taas of the latter part of the XVIIth Dynasty is not clear, but it is probable that the Sekenenras were descended from them, for Aahhetep, the queen of Sekenenra III, repaired the tomb of a queen Sebekemsas (the wife of one of the Antefs) at Edfu, and evinced an interest in her which argues relationship. Probably the throne passed by marriage again. It seems very probable that the reigns of Nubkheperra and his immediate predecessors and successors were contemporary with a period of Hyksos weakness, to which the reigns of Maa-ab-Ra, Sekha-n-Ra are to be assigned. With them the first Hyksos dynasty (the XVth) no doubt came to an end, and a new and more energetic dynasty (the XVIth) followed, the first kings of which were Nekara, Khian, and Apepi II, who attacked the successors of Nub-kheper-ra and overthrew them, reducing the South to a position of vassalage in which it continued for two or three reigns, until the revolt of Sekenenra Taa-ken and the War of Liberation.

The period of the Sekenenras shews no great alteration from that of the Antefs: the royal tombs were in the same cemetery at Dra' Abu 'l-Nekka and the style of the coffin of Sekenenra Taa-aa-ken is much the same as that of those of the Antefs. It is improbable that a period of even as much as a century of Hyksos rule intervened between the two families. During this period, however, the subjection of the South was complete, and Apepi II controlled the whole country as far as Elephantine, as is shewn by his use of the red granite of Aswan in his works in the Delta.

4. The War of Liberation (c. 1620-1573 B.C.)

The rule of the Sekenenras was marked by the final revolt of the Southerners against the Hyksos. A fragment of a historical composition, the "Sallier Papyrus," written under the XIXth Dynasty, gives us the legend of the final cause of quarrel, the beginning of the end, which was current three centuries later.

The Ra-Apepi of the story is doubtless Apepi III, Aa-kenen-ra, whose name shews him to have been a contemporary of the Sekenenras. The ruler of the South Sekenenra has usually been supposed to be Sekenenra III, Taa-aa-ken, but this is not absolutely certain. Manetho says that the kings of the Thebaid and of the rest of Egypt revolted against the Shepherds, and a long and mighty war was carried on until Misphragmouthosis (Aahmes) finally expelled them. But if the war began under Sekenenra III it would not be very long, for this Sekenenra was comparatively young when he was killed in battle, as we can see from his mummy, and the reigns of Kames and Senekhtenra, who intervened between him and Aahmes, were both very short, that of the latter being apparently quite ephemeral. Probably not more than ten or twelve years elapsed between the death of Sekenenra and the accession of Aahmes, and this does not give enough time for a long war according to ancient ideas. Further, the queen of Sekenenra bore the name of Aahhetep, "Offered to the Moon-god," Karnes calls himself "begotten of Aah and born of Thoth," and his brother Aahmase or Aahmes was "born of the Moon"; the name Thutmase or Thothmes ("born of Thoth") became common under the XVIIIth Dynasty. The lunar Thoth was the tutelary deity of the city of Khmenu, Hermopolis, the modern Eshmunen, The choice of these Moon-names argues a special connexion of the later XVIIth and the XVIIIth Dynasties with Hermopolis, and the chronicle of Castor says that the XVIIIth Dynasty was of Hermopolite origin, obviously on account of the names of its founder Aahmes and his descendants the Thothmes. But Hermopolis lay far to the north of the northern frontier of the southern kingdom under the Antefs and within easy striking-distance of the Delta. It cannot have belonged to the Sekenenra of the Sallier Papyrus, and can hardly have been taken from the Hyksos by the Southerners until the War of Liberation had already continued for some time. Therefore the war must have begun before the birth of the wife of Sekenenra III, in the reign of one or the other of the earlier Sekenenras.

We have several relics of Sekenenra I, Tau-aa, and his tomb, as well as that of his successor Sekenenra II, Tau-aa-aa ("Tau the Twice-Great," who was a short-lived monarch in spite of his name), was examined and found intact by the inspectors under the XXth Dynasty. All three Sekenenras bore the full titles of a king of Egypt. It would seem hardly likely that the Apepi of the Sallier Papyrus would have permitted his southern vassal to bear the title of king, and so it seems probable the Sekenenra of the story is really Sekenenra I, who assumed the full royal style as a gage of defiance to the Hyksos after the rupture with his suzerain had taken place. He and his successors thenceforth pursued the long war as the rightful kings of Egypt fighting to expel a dynasty of usurpers. Hermopolis may well have been wrested by him from the Northerners, and in commemoration of this victory, which would call forth a great outburst of royal and national devotion to the liberated Moon-god, the Aah and Thoth-names were probably adopted by the royal family, and the future queen of Sekenenra III, probably a daughter of Sekenenra I, received the name Aahhetep. These Hermopolite names were afterwards retained in the royal family in memory of the War of Liberation.

Sekenenra III was killed in battle, as we know from the appearance of his mummy, found with the other royal bodies at Thebes in 1881, and now in the Cairo Museum.

From the arrangement of the reigns of this dynasty which will be given later, it would seem probable that he had reigned about fourteen years, and was succeeded by his son Kames, a boy of twelve. Since the capture of Memphis is not mentioned in the inscriptions of the reign of Aahmes, the son of Kames, that city was probably recovered by his father. But before this event took place the Egyptian cause had received a serious set-back, for in a newly discovered hieratic inscription (a literary composition on a writing-board) we see that in the seventh year of Kames the territory in his possession only extended as far north as Cusae in Middle Egypt. Probably after the death of Sekenenra III and defeat of his troops the Hyksos pushed the Egyptians back from Hermopolis to Cusae. During the first seven years of the boy-king's reign some sort of truce probably existed, but then in the twentieth year of his age Kames took up the family struggle, and probably marched victoriously to Memphis. He then died or was killed after a reign of not more than ten years, and was succeeded by his younger brother Senekhtnra, whose position is only known from a later inscription in which his name has been garbled as "Sekhentnebra." He either died or was killed very shortly afterwards, and was succeeded by the third brother, Aahmes Nebpehtira, the liberator of Egypt and founder of the XVIIIth Dynasty, who was then, if we consider him to have been about forty-five at the time of his death (which from the appearance of his mummy at Cairo seems very probable), a young man of nineteen or twenty.

The capture of Memphis had sounded the death-knell of the foreign power. The Hyksos king, whoever he was, Set'aapehti Nubti or an ephemeral successor, was driven north and east to Tanis and the great entrenched camp at Avaris in the Wadi Tumilat, whither the young king followed him in hot pursuit. We possess in an inscription an actual account of the final scene of the long war by one who in his youth was one of the actors in it, the admiral Aahmes, son of Baba and Abana. "He says: I speak unto you, all men, in order that I may inform you of the honours which have fallen to my lot." After describing the taking of the fortress of Avaris, he proceeds: "We sat down before Sherohan for three years," and His Majesty took it. I carried off thence two women and one hand, and the gold for valour was given me. The captives were given to me as slaves.

"And when His Majesty had made an end of slaughtering the Asiatics, he went south to Khent-hen-nefer (Nubia), to destroy the Nubians, and His Majesty made a great slaughter of them. I carried into captivity two live men and three hands; I was presented once more with the gold, and behold the two slaves were given to me. Then came His Majesty down the river, his heart swelled with valour and victory, for he had conquered the people of the South as well as of the North.

"Then came Aata southwards, bringing on his fate, namely, his destruction, for the Gods of the South seized upon him. His Majesty found him at Thent-ta-a, and took him prisoner alive, and all his men, with swiftness of capture. And I brought away two slaves whom I had taken on Aata's ship, and there were given to me five heads as my booty and five sta of land at my own city. All the sailors were treated in like manner.

"Then came that enemy Teta-'an, who had raised rebellion. But His Majesty slaughtered him and his retainers even to extinction. And there were given to me three heads and five sta of land at my own city."

Thus the long War of Liberation ended, having lasted about forty-five years, off and on.

5. The Restoration and the Empire

With the liberation and reunification of the kingdom by Aahmes closes one of the most interesting episodes of the ancient history of the Near East. But if the period of the Hyksos conquest of Egypt is interesting on account of its very obscurity and difficulty, that of the new epoch of energy and prosperity which now dawned upon the Nile-land is also of surpassing interest for the opposite reason; for no period of Egyptian history are the contemporary public and private records so full, of none have we so many actual remains, as of that of the XVIIIth Dynasty, which Aahmes founded; at no period of the early history of Western Asia have we such detailed information of events as in the fifteenth century B.C., when the famous cuneiform letters and despatches found at Tell el-Amarna were written. Egypt now enters upon her epoch of imperial greatness, the period of the "First Empire" begins. Having rendered their military power equal to that of the Semites by the acquisition of the chariot, schooled to war by the long struggle against the Hyksos, and inspired to enthusiasm by the restoration of their ancient monarchy to the full extent of its ancestral dominion, the Egyptians were eager to wreak vengeance upon the Semites for the oppression which they and their gods had suffered at foreign hands. Half a century of quiet watching after the expulsion of the Hyksos showed the kings of the XVIIIth Dynasty that the Semites, though formidable to those weaker than themselves, had no real cohesion, and were only dangerous when united from time to time in short-lived confederacies under the military leadership of some momentarily powerful king or dynasty, such as a Kudur-Nankhundi, a Khammurabi, or a Salatis, No such military hegemony existed now; the Babylonians were weakened under the foreign rule of the Kassites; the Hittites had not yet penetrated far to the south, except in an occasional raid; the Hyksos were broken and flying, bringing war and confusion into Palestine in their train; Western Asia lay open to an Egyptian attack. The opportunity was seized, and Thothmes I, the second successor of Aahmes, invaded and overran Palestine and Syria.

Egyptian kings had raided Palestine before, and in the time of the XIIth Dynasty, or even in that of the VIth, may have reached the slopes of Hermon. But the land north of Lebanon and east of the Hauran was now traversed by Egyptian warriors for the first time. From Galilee and the territory of Damascus (already a city of note), the descent of the Orontes valley led into a wide, wealthy, and well-inhabited land, studded with cities, stretching away to the great river Euphrates and the mountain-wall of Amanus. This land the Egyptians called Naharin, "Two River-Land" (using a Semitic appellation derived from the two limiting features of the region, the Orontes and the Euphrates). The native Syrians called their land Nukhashshi. Across the Euphrates lay the more barren North Mesopotamia, the modern districts of Urfa, Diarbekr, and Mardin, then dominated by the Aryan aristocracy of Mitanni: between it and Amanus the way lay into a land more fertile yet than Syria, the Cilicia of the two rivers, Sihon and Gihon, between Amanus and Taurus. Here the great northern wall of mountain seemed to bar all further progress from the south, and beyond it lay the Anatolian uplands and the strange European world of the north, which neither Babylonian nor Egyptian desired to enter.

The cis-Taurus land was, however, well worth raiding, and the successors of Thothmes I rightly deemed it well worth holding and keeping. The whole country between Taurus and Euphrates and farther south is covered with the tells, the mounds which mark the sites of the ancient cities. Northern Syria was from early days a great focus of human life and activity, and did we know more of its history we should see, probably, that this land played from early days a great part in the development of Mediterranean civilization. Its inhabitants were primarily Semites, no doubt of the same Canaanite stock as those of Palestine. But in Cilicia there must from the beginning have been a considerable Anatolian admixture, and, as we have seen, a large part of Northern Syria had been overrun and conquered by the Hittites of Anatolia. As the Hittite population never crossed to the left bank of the Euphrates, and Mitanni appears later as in political control of Nukhashshi, the probabilities are that the Mitannians established a political ascendancy over both the Anatolian invaders and the Syrians. Aryan chiefs from Mitanni now migrated into Syria, and later on we find Aryan names even in Palestine. Mitannian overlordship probably stopped at the Lebanon, and the Phoenician cities preserved each its own independence, owning no overlord, but in constant relations with Egypt on the one side and with Cilicia and the lands farther west on the other. Palestine and no doubt Damascus owned Babylonian hegemony, but the Kassite king of Karduniyash was too far away to give any protection to the Canaanites against an attack from Egypt.

6. The Conquest of Thothmes I and the Truce under Hatshepsut

From the fact that Thothmes I claims the Euphrates as his northern boundary at his succession, and certainly seems to have met with but little resistance in his Asiatic campaign, which carried him to the Euphrates, it has been concluded that the way was perhaps paved for him by some unrecorded conquests of the preceding king Amenhetep I, son of Aahmes. Still, the captains Aahmes son of Abana and Aahmes-Pennekheb, who accompanied Amenhetep in his Nubian and Libyan expeditions, and his son in his Asiatic campaign, can hardly have been left behind if Amenhetep invaded Asia, and would certainly, if they had accompanied him, not omitted to chronicle the fact in their inscriptions. The coronation inscription of Thothmes may well have been emended afterwards to include an assertion of his Syrian sovereignty, and the ease with which he reached the Euphrates may have been due simply to the suddenness and unexpectedness of his attack. Unluckily we have nothing but the accounts of the two generals to tell us of the events of this, the first Egyptian conquest. Conquest indeed it hardly was: it was little more than a razzia like those which every king conducted in Nubia. In the land of Naharin the more organized and formidable tribes of the North collected themselves together to oppose the Egyptian advance, but were overthrown, chariots and horses falling to the booty of the two Aahmes, who were decorated as usual for their valour. Then the king set up a stone tablet by the side of Euphrates to mark the farthest limit of his advance and of his dominion, and returned to Thebes to boast to the priests that he had "made the boundary of Egypt as far as the circuit of the sun," to "that inverted Nile which runs downstream in going upstream," the Euphrates.

For centuries before him Egyptian kings had set up similar tablets in Nubia, and there, among barbarians, the monuments of raids might well be also the monuments of consecutive dominion. In Asia, however, it was otherwise. The Asiatics were not savages like the Nubians, though it is probable that the Egyptians had not quite realized the fact yet, and there is little doubt that the mere setting up of an Egyptian tablet in their midst by no means immediately disposed them to consider themselves the vassals of Egypt. We can be sure that the tablet of Thothmes was thrown down by the Syrians as soon as he had departed, and that tribute to Egypt was only paid so long as there were Egyptian soldiers near to enforce it. If Syria was to be an Egyptian possession some sort of permanent organization binding the various tribes to the Egyptian state was necessary, and this could not be enforced without complete conquest and permanent occupation. This lesson was learnt by Thothmes III during the course of his long wars, and the result was the organized Asiatic empire of Egypt under his successors.

The sudden attack of the Egyptians must have driven the Asiatic princes into some sort of alliance, so far as their mutual jealousies made this possible, in preparation for its renewal. Mitanni dominated North Syria, and the Southern Syrian and Palestinian chiefs seem to have acknowledged some sort of primate in the Prince of Kadesh on the Orontes, probably an immigrant Hittite from Anatolia. It is under this prince that we find the Canaanites arrayed at Megiddo against Thothmes III. During the reign of Hatshepsut the Asiatics gained a breathing-space in which to organize their forces. While the peaceful queen controlled affairs no campaigns were waged either in Nubia or in Asia. The personal presence of a warrior-king, able to march at the head of his troops, was lacking. The young king

Thothmes III, her half-brother or nephew, who was associated with her on the throne after the death of her husband, was evidently not permitted by the peaceful queen to follow the example of his male predecessors and satisfy his love of fighting on the vile bodies of Kush and Rutenu. The queen thought more of sending peaceful expeditions to Somaliland to bring back "marvels of Punt" for the embellishment of her temple at Der el-Bahri than of warlike razzias and pyramids of hands: and certainly she would never have allowed her male colleague to obtain an opportunity to reap warlike prestige which might enable him to throw off her yoke and depose her. And she herself, man-like though she was, arrogating to herself the dignities of a king and causing herself to be depicted on the walls of the temples in male attire, never went so far as to imitate the goddess of her Syrian tributaries, and take the field herself, armed with battleaxe and shield. So the young Thothmes was compelled to fret in silence while the Syrians, gradually losing their fear of an armed raid from Egypt, dared again to raise their heads in independence. Though the queen speaks of herself grandiloquently as ruling such of the Asiatics as remained after the conquests of her father, and though the lands of Roshau and Iu, which may be supposed to represent Asia, may poetically be said to be subject to her, it is probable that she exercised very little control over Palestine. Cedar for her temples she could obtain from the Lebanon by sea, but we know from the opening words of the annals of her successor's campaigns in Syria that at the time of his accession all Palestine had fallen away. Even Sherohan, the old conquest of Aahmes, and Yeraza, not far north of it, had revolted, when the peaceful queen at last died, and Thothmes, freed at last from her control, immediately took the field to restore his father's dominion to Egypt.

7. The "Annals" of Thothmes III

Of his campaigns, which lasted for the greater part of his reign, we have a full description in the annals set up on the walls of the corridor enclosing the sanctuary of the great temple of Amen in Karnak. This is the largest and most important historical inscription in Egypt, and it is at the same time one of the most graphic, often rising to the highest level of descriptive writing, and shewing considerable literary power, especially when dealing with the events of the first campaign. This, the oldest official record of a war that we possess, was probably prepared by Thununi (who was charged with the oversight of the tribute and booty collected during the various campaigns) no doubt under the supervision of the king himself, whose energetic personality seems to live in every line of it.

It was on the twenty-fifth day of the month Pharmuthi in the twenty-second year of his reign (counted from the date of his association with Hatshepsut) that King Thothmes broke up from the frontier town of Tjaru and crossed the desert to Gaza, where he arrived on the anniversary of his coronation-feast, ten days later. One night only did he halt: the next day saw the army march out with all pomp and circumstance, and a few days later, on the sixteenth Pakhon, in his twenty-third year, the town of Yehem was reached, and with it the vicinity of the enemy. Here a council of war was held, and the king explained the actual situation to the captains of his host. "That wretched enemy," said he, "the chief of Kadesh, has come and has entered Megiddo: he is there at this moment. He has gathered to himself the chiefs of all the lands which are linked with Egypt, even as far as Naharin, and including both Kharu and Kedu, with their horses and their soldiers. Says he: I have arisen to fight against the king in Megiddo. Now tell ye me [your plans]." From this it is evident that the revolt of the Southern Palestinians "from Yeraza to the marshes of Egypt" was but the last phase of a general revolt which had spread from the north southwards under the leadership of the King of Kadesh on the Orontes, a city which, not yet a frontier fortress of the Hittites, was in Thothmes' day the focus of all the Syrian national spirit that might be said to have existed. It was not till Kadesh was finally taken that the Egyptian king could regard his conquests as secure. But at present, when the council of war was held at Yehem, there was no possibility of any direct advance on the stronghold of the ringleader of the rebellion. Kadesh lay far away beyond the Lebanon in the direction of Hamath. All Palestine between was in active revolt.

No inconsiderable knowledge of the art of war was shewn by the Prince of Kadesh and his allies when in order to stop the Egyptian advance they took up their position along the ridge, called the "Ruhah," which connects Carmel with the hill-mass of Samaria and Judaea, and separates the Plain of Sharon from that of Esdraelon. An army with chariots and horsemen would naturally cross this comparatively low ridge in order to reach Northern Syria, and it offered the greatest possibility of a successful defence. When, therefore, Thothmes reached Yehem (probably in the present Wadi Yahmur), at the foot of the southern slope of the ridge, he found that the Syrians were preparing to bar his further northward way here, with their headquarters in the town of Megiddo, and their left wing at

Taanach, between four and five English miles away to the southeast. Both Megiddo and Taanach were ancient and important towns, the seats of local chiefs, and were fortified. The name of Taanach still survives in the modern Tell Ta'annek, where an Austrian expedition under Prof. Sellin has been engaged on successful excavations. Megiddo is Tell el-Mutesellim, where the German expedition of Schumacher has also excavated. Both towns stand back behind the ridge half-way down to the plain. They were the natural bases for an army defending the ridge, across which three main roads passed then, as now, from the Plain of Sharon to that of Esdraelon. The southernmost was the easiest for the passage of armies, as it passed over the lowest portion of the ridge through the broad "plain" of Uothan: here had always passed the main road from Egypt and the Shephelah to Damascus, and through it the armies of the first Thothmes had doubtless marched. Just where the Dothan pass spreads out into the Plain of Esdraelon lay to the north-west, but four miles distant, Taanach, where the Prince of Kadesh had posted his left wing. This was in order that he might be able to defend easily either the Dothan road or another, which passed directly between the fronts of the opposing armies, from Yehem to Megiddo, by way of Aruna, the modern Wadi Arab, a long and winding, narrow and stony, glen which reaches the watershed at the spring of 'Ain-Ibrahim, from which the path descends swiftly along the sides of the Ruhah to the site of Megiddo. It is not probable that the Syrians expected Thothmes to use this difficult mountain-way, but their position at Megiddo enabled them to be ready for a possible advance by the third road, that by which the modern telegraph-wire now passes across the moor of the Ruhah at the foot of Carmel to Haifa: this road lay some seven miles north of Megiddo. Thus the Syrians were ready to move either to the south or to the north according as they heard that the Egyptians were advancing by the regular road of Dothan or were intending first of all to reach Phoenicia by the "Zefti road," as the Egyptians called it.

The Egyptian king determined to do neither, but to strike direct at the enemy's central position at Megiddo through the narrow Wadi Arah, and thus surprise him. At the council of war he communicated his decision to his captains, who were much troubled at the rashness of the royal plan of battle. "They spoke in the presence of His Majesty," says the official account, "saying, How are we to advance on this narrow path? The enemy will await us there and (a small force) can hold the way against a multitude. Will not horse come behind horse and man behind man likewise? Shall our van be fighting while our rear is still standing there in Aruna, unable to fight? There are yet two other roads: there is that one which is [best] for us, for it comes out at Taanach, and the other, behold! it will bring us upon the way north of Zefti, so that we shall come out to the north of Megiddo. Let our victorious lord proceed upon the road he desires: but cause us not to go by this difficult path!" But the king would not be turned from his purpose in spite of the very excellent arguments advanced by his captains against the engagement of a large army of chariots and horses in a narrow ravine: he vowed that he himself would lead the van so that if the head of the advancing host were successfully cut off by the defenders of the pass, he himself would fall. Doubtless he saw the danger of his plan, but sought to neutralize it by concentrating all the loyalty and valour of his warriors to fight with him in the van, so that they could carry all before them. "I swear," said he at the council, "that as Ra loveth me and Amen favoureth me, my Majesty will proceed upon this path by Aruna. Let him who will among you go upon those roads ye have mentioned, and let him who will among you come in the following of my Majesty." This, of course, was impossible: submissively replied the captains, "May thy father Amen grant thee life! Behold, we follow thy Majesty everywhere thy Majesty proceedeth; as the servant is behind his master." "Then," says Thununi's account, "His Majesty ordered the whole army to march upon the narrow road. His Majesty swore: 'None shall go forth in the way before my Majesty,' He went forth at the head of his army himself, shewing the way by his own footsteps; horse behind horse. His Majesty being at the head of the army."

So the host threaded the glen of Arah, in Indian file ("horse behind horse"), the king leading, perhaps himself on foot. The passage was not made without opposition. The people of the village of Aruna, where on the night of the 19th Pakhon the royal headquarters had been placed, attacked the troops on the next day, and caused considerable annoyance to the rearguard, which was fighting near Aruna while the king with the van had crossed the head of the pass without resistance and was descending the slope of the Ruhah towards Megiddo. As, however, the main body of the army issued from the hills, it became possible to bring up the rearguard more quickly, so that the whole army debouched into the plain on a broad front under the eye of the king himself, who waited at the mouth of the pass till the rear had come up from Aruna. The official account attributes to the advance of the captains this manoeuvre, which would correspond in the phraseology of a modern drill-book to a change from column of route perhaps merely two deep to a general advance in line of battle.

By the time the whole army had carried out this manoeuvre the day was far spent, "and when His Majesty arrived at the south of Megiddo on the bank of the brook Kina, the seventh hour was turning, measured by the sun." If by the seventh hour is to be understood one or two o'clock p.m., the army had successfully traversed the dreaded ravine in a single morning; and if Aruna itself is the modern Ararah, the rate of advance had been swift, as Ararah is at least eight miles from the brook Kina, and six of the miles are uphill. No modern army could march so fast, and though it is evident that the Egyptian force consisted largely of chariotry, there were, we know, foot soldiers as well.

Evidently the afternoon was considered to provide insufficient time for a regular battle, so the army bivouacked where it stood on the slope reaching down to the southern bank of the brook Kina, opposite Megiddo. The orders for the morrow's fight were given out and all weapons and equipment were overhauled and got ready for the fray. The adjutants or chiefs-of-staff then presented their reports: "All is well." The king rested in his tent, and during the night the guards and sentries went their rounds crying the watchwords: "Firm-heart! firm-heart! be vigilant! be vigilant! watch for life at the royal tent!"

On the morning of the 21st Pakhon the host was arrayed against the Syrians, who though no doubt surprised by the swift advance of the Egyptians, do not seem to have wished to decline the battle. Whether they had been able to bring up their left wing from Taanach during the preceding afternoon and night is not evident; but if they did they were not helped thereby. The result of the fight was a complete victory for the Egyptians, who advanced in line, pivoting on their right wing, which remained upon the spur of hill above el-Lejja and south of the brook Kina, until the left wing had swung round to the north-west of Megiddo (Tell el-Mutesellim) itself. The Egyptian line must have been fully a mile long. In the centre, which must have advanced north of the brook Kina, fought the king himself, "in a chariot of electron, arrayed with his weapons of war, like Horus, the Smiter, lord of power; like Ment of Thebes, while his father Amen strengthened his arms. . . . Then His Majesty prevailed against them at the head of his army, and when they saw His Majesty prevailing against them, they fled headlong to Megiddo in fear, abandoning their horses and their chariots of gold and silver."

The routed army of the Syrians seems to have attempted to take refuge within the walled town of Megiddo, and most picturesque details are given of how the fugitives were hauled up the walls by ropes made of robes knotted together, since the gates had been closed to prevent the entrance of the Egyptians pell-mell with the defeated.

This might have occurred, or at any rate Megiddo might have been taken by storm in the moment of defeat and confusion, so the official chronicler relates: "had not His Majesty's soldiers given their hearts to plundering the enemy's possessions," says he regretfully, "they would have taken Megiddo at this moment, when the wretched foe of Kadesh and the wretched foe of this town were being hauled up in haste in order to bring them into this city." This is a curiously outspoken piece of military criticism on the part of the official historian of the war.

The king was heavily displeased at the failure to take Megiddo, in spite of the rejoicings of the army itself at its victory: "it is as the capture of a thousand cities, this capture of Megiddo, for every chief of every country that has revolted is within it." However, all that could be done now was to invest the town, and a palisade was constructed round it under the inspection of the king, to which the name "Menkheperra-is-the-Surrounder-of-the-Asiatics" was given. Eventually the place surrendered, and a rich booty was captured in it and sent to Egypt, the inventory being recorded on a leather roll in the temple of Amen in Thebes. The list gives a good idea of the civilization of the Canaanites, which was evidently as luxurious as that of Egypt or Mesopotamia. It included so many as 924 chariots, some of which were wrought with gold, 200 suits of armour, and a large number of flocks and herds. The tent and family of the King of Kadesh had been captured and most of the allied chiefs surrendered in the city. The harvests of the people of Megiddo were reaped by the army. It is evident that the prisoners and the people of the city were treated with clemency, as usual with the Egyptians, who never put whole populations to the sword in the barbarous manner of the Semites.

From Megiddo Thothmes seems to have marched northwards into Phoenicia, and probably took Tyre. Eastwards, in the Lebanon, the towns of Yenoam, Anaugasa, and Hurenkaru, which formed a kind of Tripolis under the dominion of the King of Kadesh, were taken, with a rich booty of slaves and of gold and silver vases of Phoenician workmanship and work in ebony and ivory.

Farther into the mountains the king did not penetrate: he returned to Egypt, but the next year saw him again in the field. No resistance was offered to his triumphal march either in this or in the succeeding campaigns. The chiefs vied with each other in heaping up tribute at the feet of the conqueror, and so far had the impression of the victory of Megiddo penetrated that for the first time we read of ambassadors from Assyria coming to greet the King of Egypt with presents from their master, probably Ashir-rabi or Ashir-nirari.

The "tribute," as it is called, of the Assyrian king, is thus specified: "genuine lapis-lazuli, a large block, weighing 20 deben 9 kedet; genuine lapis-lazuli, two blocks (total three), weighing 30 deben: total 50 deben 8 kedet; fine lapis-lazuli from Babylon; vessels of Assur of variegated kherti-stone, . . . very many." Later on, further presents of rare woods and a leopard-skin for the sides of a chariot were dispatched by the propitiatory Assyrian.

The lists of the booty of the third campaign are remarkable for a catalogue of the rare plants and trees which Thothmes caused to be collected in Palestine and removed to Thebes, where he decorated a chamber of his new buildings at Karnak with sculptured representations of them in relief "as a memorial before my father Amen for ever."

Of the fourth campaign we have no record. It was perhaps marked by temporary ill-success; apparently a revolt was brought about by the Prince of Kadesh in Phoenicia, for the fifth campaign was waged there. In this, his twenty-ninth year, we find the king "in Phoenicia (Tjahi), subduing the countries revolting against him." The rebellion seems to have been largely instigated by the Prince of Tunip (a town lying northward of Aleppo), whose army was defeated at a place the name of which is destroyed, but which was on the sea, as many ships were captured in its harbour. The far northern maritime city of Arvad was now taken for the first time, with so much booty that regrettable results followed: "Behold!" says the official account naively, "His Majesty's army was drunk and anointed with oil every day as at a feast in Egypt." Prof. Breasted supposes that after this the king returned to Egypt by sea in the captured ships, but no absolute indication of this can be found in the inscriptions, though it is possible enough, since next year we find him striking out a new line of his own in strategical combinations by sailing with his army to Phoenicia and marching to an attack upon Kadesh from a maritime base, Simyra, at the mouth of the Nahr el-Kebir, the seaport nearest to the threatened city. The successful voyage from Arvad to Egypt may well have given him the idea of this new move, the importance of which in the history of the development of the art of war is very great. We may indeed see in it the first instance of the importance of sea-power to an invading army.

The campaign was entirely successful. So surprised was the enemy at the new move that he seems to have allowed the Egyptians to cross the mountains unscathed, and Kadesh was taken. In this campaign fought a distinguished captain named Amenemheb, whom we shall meet again in later wars.

The king then returned to his base at Simyra, and after again chastising Arvad, sailed back to Egypt, taking with him "the children of the chiefs and their brothers," who were to be kept as hostages, and sent to Syria to take the place of any reigning chief who died. Meanwhile they were educated "in all the wisdom of the Egyptians," impressed with the power of their suzerain, and as far as possible egyptianized. This new act of policy, devised in order to bind the families of the Syrian chiefs to Egypt as much as possible, is a strong testimony to the statesmanship of Thothmes.

During the next year Phoenicia still needed vigorous punishment to bring the cities entirely to their knees, as the Prince of Tunip was still inciting them to resistance. Ullaza was taken, and in it the son of Tunip, with chariots and horses. The king coasted in his ships from harbour to harbour, where the tribute of the mountain-chiefs and their supplies of food were collected to await him. By the end of the campaign the whole of Phoenicia was sufficiently pacified and organized for him to carry out systematically the real conquest of Northern Syria and the Euphrates-land, which his predecessors had merely raided. Phoenicia was his base. Landing again at Simyra, he advanced rapidly across the mountains and down the valley of the Orontes, probably taking Tunip on the way, past Senzar (Kala'at Seidjar?), where a victorious battle was fought, Hamath, and Homs to Aleppo, in the neighbourhood of which he gained the victory of "the Heights of Wan" (Gebel Sim'an?), in which Amenemheb distinguished himself. His opponents were now the tribes of the land of Naharin, the "Two Rivers," probably under the leadership of the king of Mitanni, as well as the chief of Tunip, whose city was now in imminent danger. Pursuing them to the north-eastward, the Egyptians took Tunip and soon reached the Euphrates at Carchemish, where a decisive victory was gained, the enemy being driven into the river, followed by the victors, who crossed hot-foot in pursuit, led by the valiant Amenemheb.

And now the king was enabled to set up a tablet on the eastern bank of the Euphrates, "beside the tablet of his father. King Aakheperkara" (Thothmes I). He made no attempt to extend his dominion into Mesopotamia, but was satisfied with the frontier of the Euphrates, that "inverted Nile" which seemed to be placed athwart the path of the Egyptian kings as their natural boundary. Mitanni no doubt sent tribute, and Ashur also, while the Lord of the mountains of Sinjar (Sengard), sent large quantities of both real and artificial lapis-lazuli of Babylon. And now for the first time the chiefs of the Great Kheta, the Hittites of Cappadocia, thought it advisable to send presents, consisting of eight silver rings, weighing 401 deben, a great block of crystal (?), and much tigu-wood. This is the first recorded political meeting of the Egyptians with the Hittites.

On the return to Egypt the king took part in a great elephant-hunt on the plain of Nii (Kefr-Naya), west of Aleppo, and Amenemheb distinguished himself by cutting off the trunk of the largest "which fought against his Majesty; I cut off his hand (i.e. trunk) while he was alive in his Majesty's presence, while I stood in the water between two rocks." The elephant evidently having pursued him into a rocky streambed, he had taken refuge between two rocks, where the great beast could not well reach him except with his trunk, which the hunter cut off with his small war-axe.

Of the ninth campaign few warlike operations are recorded. Tribute was received by the king in Phoenicia from the more northerly coast-land, here mentioned for the first time under the name of A'seya, a mistake for its real name of Alashiya, which was shortly to become very familiar in Egypt. The Alashiyan king sent 108 blocks of pure copper, weighing 2040 deben; together with blocks and pegs of lead, lapis-lazuli, and a single tusk of ivory, which must have come from inner Syria.

But though they abode still for a year, the chiefs of Naharin were not yet disposed to accept the Egyptian yoke. In spite of the lesson of the complete subjugation of first Canaan and then Phoenicia, they once more tried conclusions with Thothmes, under the headship of a prince called "that foe of Naharin," probably the chief of Tunip or his son. At Arayna, an unidentified place, probably in the neighbourhood of Aleppo, the confederates were defeated, and the usual booty taken.

Of the eleventh and twelfth campaigns no records are preserved: the thirteenth was occupied with a chastisement of Anaugasa in the southern

Lebanon. Alashiya sent tribute of copper in this year for the second time and the chief of distant Arrapachitis (Ararpakli) on the Upper Zab, north-east of Nineveh, for the first time.

The fourteenth yearly campaign was not conducted from Phoenicia. The king was compelled by a revolt of the Beduins of Southern Palestine to advance by land, and defeated the rebels in the Negeb of Judaea. The records of the fifteenth and sixteenth years of war chronicle the reception of tribute only, notably that of the Hittites, who sent gold.

In the forty-second year of his reign, however, after sixteen campaigns, the old king was compelled to take the field in force by a general revolt of Naharin in combination with the original and irreconcilable rebel at Kadesh on the Orontes. Landing at Simyra, Thothmes marched northwards to the towns of Irkata and Kana, and thence struck inland to Tunip, which was taken by storm. Then he turned south and marched up the Orontes-valley to Kadesh, which was stormed also, the valiant Amenemheb being the first to enter the breach in the enemy's wall of defence. Before the battle, so Amenemheb tells us, the prince of Kadesh tried a curious stratagem. He sent forth a mare among the Egyptian stallions, in order to confuse their array, but Amenemheb pursued her on foot, caught her, killed her, and presented her tail as a trophy to the king.

In this year a very interesting event is recorded, the reception of tribute from the prince of Yantinai (Yatnan) or Cyprus, which included a "shuibti-vase of the work of Keftiu," together with other vessels of metal. This vase, "the work of Keftiu," may have come from Minoan Crete, whose ambassadors, as we shall see later, had already appeared at Thebes itself in the reign of Hatshepsut.

Here the record ends. For the remaining twelve years of his life, so far as we know, the veteran warrior was never again called upon to take the field. The fear of his name had sunk into the souls of the Asiatics, and none dared to rebel while he lived. Still less were the foreign powers of the Hittites, Mitanni, Ashur, and Babel inclined to challenge his lordship of the lands west of the Euphrates. Babylon under the Kassite kings was eminently peaceful, and at the same time not inclined to open up relations with Egypt which might eventually prove but a prelude to war. No presents from Babel are recorded in the tribute-lists, though objects of Babylonian origin were presented by the princes of Ashur, Arrapachitis, and the Sinjar, who were too near the Euphrates to ignore the Egyptian king's existence. Mitanni was defeated and sulky, and so sent nothing: the king might come and take it if he willed, but he had no intention of venturing beyond the Euphrates. The Kheta sent presents, as the Cretans did, as a polite recognition of the existence of a great Power which had done them no harm. Cyprus was too near Phoenicia to avoid actual tribute: the king's ships could reach her too easily.

The Asiatic empire of Egypt had in fact been extended to its natural frontiers, the Amanus range and the Euphrates. All within this boundary was Egyptian territory, bound by rightful allegiance to the Egyptian king. Kode, "the land Kue" of the Assyrians, the Cilician coast-region between Amanus and Taurus, was no doubt also subject to Egypt as a frontier-territory, Alashiya was a subject ally. More than this Egypt could not hold. The organization of the vast territory thus annexed — vast in comparison with the actual area of Egypt itself — demanded all the resources of the Nile-land. In the superintendence of this work of organization the king no doubt spent most of the rest of his reign, and in it he shewed the same power that he had displayed upon the field of battle.

8. The Organization of the Empire

When, in the days of the idealist Akhenaten, the King of Egypt thought more of religious theories and artistic whims than of defending his empire, the people of the far northern dependency of Tunip, harassed by the Hittites, looked back regretfully to the days of their great conqueror and defender, Thothmes III. "Who," they cried, "could have plundered Tunip in the old days without being plundered by Manakhbiria?" Even to the Euphrates the organization was complete. We gain an insight into the method of this organization by the passage in the Annals, already quoted, which tells us how the king removed the sons and brethren of the different chiefs to Egypt and there brought them up as Egyptians, sending them back more or less devoted to Egypt to take up their posts as chiefs when their reigning relatives died. We do almost the same thing now in India, though the existence of such seminaries of native princes as the college at Aligarh does not necessitate the deportation of young Indian chiefs to far England. The Romans did the same thing also with Germans and Thracians. And side by side with the Egyptianized chiefs stood Egyptian officials, not so much residents as travelling inspectors, with regular circuits, who collected the tribute, advised, and controlled, with the power of falling back upon the help of Egyptian garrisons when necessary. These garrisons were established in the chief cities and in fortresses specially constructed to overawe specially recalcitrant regions, such as the Lebanon, where, for instance, Fort "Thothmes-Binder-of-the-Barbarians" controlled the upper valleys of the Orontes and Leontes. From the "Tell el-Amarna Letters" we see this organization at work under the most unfavourable auspices: Egyptianized princes at Berut or Jerusalem strive to keep the dominions of the king in spite of the idiocy of the ruler himself, which paralysed the movements of his Egyptian inspectors and commanders, who were utterly unable to obtain proper support even when they were capable of dealing with a threatening situation at all, which does not seem to have been by any means the case with most of them. Far otherwise had it been in the glorious days of Manakhbiria. Then even if the princes were recalcitrant and sullen instead of, as they were in Akhenaten's day, almost pathetically loyal, there had been no possibility of an incapable being appointed to civil or military command, and the pax aegyptiaca was sternly kept. We have a momentary peep into the working of the governmental machine in the cuneiform letters discovered not long ago in the Canaanite citadel of Taanach by Dr. Sellin. Here, at some time between the epoch-making victory gained by Thothmes in its vicinity and the degenerate days of Akhenaten, lived a chief named Ishtar-washur, who left behind him in his castle-keep a box full of clay tablets inscribed in cuneiform, some of which are despatches from the Egyptian travelling inspector Amankhashir, whose headquarters were at Gaza. From these we see what kind of orders were issued by the Egyptian officials to the subject chiefs, and how they were expected to obey. "To Ishtar-washur, Amankhashir: may Adad protect thy life! Send thy brothers with their chariots, and send a horse, thy tribute, and presents and all captives that thou hast: send them to-morrow to Megiddo!" Another interesting point in this correspondence to be noted is the fact that the daughters of the chiefs were sent to Egypt to be added to the royal harim: one of Ishtar-washur's daughters was destined to be given to "the lord." And the Egyptian god Amen is mentioned: no doubt the Theban priests took their tribute, even from the Canaanite baron of Taanach.

9. Thothmes and his Companions

Of the great king's offices we know the names of the highest only. Chief among them was Tahutia or Thutii, the "Administrator of the Lands of the Northerners," who must have governed Naharin and Phoenicia. He probably looked after Cyprus as well, in the important matter of the tribute which the island paid, and doubtless carried on diplomatic relations with the peoples of Southern Asia and Crete, since he is called "the prince and priest who satisfies the king in every country and in the Isles in the midst of the Sea, filling the treasury with lapis-lazuli, silver, and gold, the governor of foreign countries, general of the army, favourite of the king, the royal scribe, Thutii." The term "Isles" no doubt included the southern coast of Asia Minor, which to the Egyptians appeared to consist of a series of islands, much as the Antarctic continent has until lately appeared to us. "Keftiu" was, as its name implies, the "Back-land" the "Back-of-Beyond" to the Egyptians. So that we need not insist on a personal visit of Thutii to Crete: no doubt in his capacity of "Governor of the North-lands" and expeditor of the tribute and gifts of Asia Minor and Cyprus, he acted as "Introducer of Ambassadors" from the Isles to the Court of Thebes.

As organizer of the tribute of the North his office was important. The flow of valuables into Egypt as a result of the conquest of Western Asia was enormous, and we see its speedy effect in the greatly increased wealth and luxury characteristic of Egypt in the reigns of Thothmes' successors.

Of the other "companions" of the king the warrior Amenemheb, whose deeds we have already mentioned, is one of the most interesting. As a paladin he succeeded to the place of the two Aahmes, the younger of whom, Aahmes-Pennekhebet, had died in the preceding reign. Like them he tells us of his deeds on the walls of his tomb, which was at Thebes, for he was a man of the capital, like all the new leaders of the empire, not provincials as the antagonists of the Hyksos had been.

From the sixth campaign to the seventeenth Amenemheb fought with his lord, and when, in the fullness of time, "the king completed his lifetime of many years, splendid in valour, in might, and in triumph, from year 1 to year 54, ... he mounted to heaven, he joined the sun, the divine limbs mingling with him who begat him," the veteran captain was addressed with courteous words by the new king: "I know thy worth: lo, while I was in the nest, thou wert in the following of my father: I commission thee to be commander of the army as I have said; inspect thou the chosen troops of the king!" And when the aged marshal laid down his staff and followed his master to the tomb, we cannot doubt that it was Amenhetep II who provided for him his sumptuous burial in Western Thebes, where the young king stands in veneration before the figure of Thothmes, enthroned as Osiris, on the walls of the tomb of Amenemheb.

Another important personage connected with the king's expeditions to Asia was a certain Sennefer, who was sent to get cedar from Lebanon, and in his inscription he tells us that he pitched his tents on the mountains "above the clouds," an experience which no Egyptian could obtain in his own country.

Nearer to the person of the conqueror than Amenemheb or Thutii stood Antef, the herald, court-marshal, and grand chamberlain, who also acted as chief-of-staff. We do not doubt that he was a doughty warrior like the others: Thothmes left his civilian ministers, such as Rekhmara the vizier, at home. Antef, whose hereditary position in the nobility was that of Count of Thinis and of the Oases (of el-Kharga and Dakhla), tells us on a stela, now in the Louvre, how he acted as intermediary between the king and his army and ministers; how he superintended the movements of the royal headquarters, preparing the king's tents each day and making them "better than the palaces of Egypt"; how he numbered the personal body-guard of the king, and so forth.

Of the conqueror himself we know, after all, but little, though we can gaze upon his face, as it was when he died, while he lies in the Cairo Museum. The face is very much that of an old soldier. To call it brutal is merely to shew the prejudice of the man of books against the man of war. So intelligent a man as Thothmes was not brutal. The mouth is large and, if we can discount the deformity caused by the embalming, not ill-humoured: the chin is vast and strong, as becomes the man. The nose is of course erased by the bandages, but we know that it was prominent, with a pronounced bridge; a "Roman nose," in fact, such as is uncommon among Egyptians, but certainly befits a conqueror. This we know from the beautiful portrait statue of him as a very young man discovered by M. Legrain lately at Karnak, probably one of the finest Egyptian portraits extant. His face here is intelligent and handsome. That he was of short stature, like many other great soldiers, we know from his mummy.

10. The Renown of Thothmes the Great

We can well understand how his name became one to conjure with even to the end of Egyptian history, and how at all periods scarabs bearing his name were regarded as the most potent of talismans to protect their wearers against the attacks of men or devils. To the later Egyptian he was what Alexander the Great, Iskender of the two Horns, is to the modern Oriental, a name of reverence and fear. And in his own day we can well understand how the patriotic pride of an unknown poet among the confraternity of Amen could compose the splendid Hymn of Victory, inscribed on a stela discovered in the temple of Karnak, in which Amen is represented as addressing his glorious son in strophes which are in some ways the finest example of Egyptian poetry, and form the most fitting epodos to our account of the deeds of the great king: —

"Saith Amen-Ra, lord of Karnak:
Thou comest to me, thou rejoicest, seeing my beauty,
My son, my avenger, Menkheperra, living for ever.
I shine because of thy love;
My heart expandeth at thy beautiful comings to my temple;
My two hands make thy limbs to have protection and life.
Doubly sweet is thy might to my bodily form.
I have established thee in my dwelling-place
I have done wondrous things for thee;
I have given to thee might and victory over all lands;
I have set thy will and the fear of thee in all countries,
Thy terror as far as the four pillars of heaven.
I have magnified the dread of thee in all creatures,
I have caused the roaring of thy Majesty to go among the Nine Bows.
The chiefs of all lands are gathered in thy grasp;
I myself have stretched forth my two hands and bound them for thee.
I have bound together the Anit of Satet by myriads,
And the Northerners by hundreds of thousands as captives;
I have struck down thine enemies beneath thy sandals,
Thou hast smitten the hosts of rebels according to my command.
The Earth in its length and breadth, Westerners and Easterners are subject to thee.
Thou treadest down all lands, thy heart is glad ....
Thou hast crossed the Stream of the Great Circle of Naharin with victory and with might.

I have come: I have caused thee to smite the princes of Tjahi,
I have hurled them beneath thy feet among their mountains.
I have caused them to see thy Majesty as a lord of radiance;
Thou hast shone in their faces like my image.

I have come: I have caused thee to smite the Imiu-setit,
Thou hast made captive the chiefs of the Aamu of Retnu,
I have caused them to see thy Majesty equipped in thy panoply,

When thou takest weapons and fightest in the chariot.

I have come: I have caused thee to smite the land of the East,
Thou hast trodden down those who are in the regions of God's Land:
I have caused them to see thy Majesty like a circling star,
When it scattereth its flame and shooteth forth its fire.

I have come: I have caused thee to smite the lands of the West,
Keftiu and Asi are in fear.
I have caused them to see thy Majesty as a young bull,
Firm of heart, sharp-horned, unapproachable.

I have come, I have caused thee to smite those who are in their fens,
The lands of Mitan tremble from fear of thee:
I have caused them to see thy Majesty as a crocodile,
Lord of terror in the water, unassailable.

I have come: I have caused thee to smite the Dwellers in the Isles:
They who are in the midst of the Sea cower beneath thy roarings:
I have caused them to see thy Majesty as the Slayer,
Who riseth above the back of his victim.

I have come: I have caused thee to smite the Tehenu;
The isles of the Utentiu are subject to thy will.
I have caused them to see thy Majesty as a lion,
As thou makest them corpses in their wadis,

I have come: I have caused thee to smite the Hinder-lands:
That which the Great Ring encircleth is enclosed in thy grasp.
I have caused them to see thy Majesty as a soaring hawk,
Who seizeth upon that which he spieth, whatever he may desire.

I have come: I have caused thee to smite the people of the Fore-lands:
Thou hast smitten the Sand-dwellers as living captives.
I have caused them to see thy Majesty as a jackal of the south,
Master of running, stealthy-going, roving the two lands."

11. The Empire under Amenhetep II, Thothmes IV, and Amenhetep III

As was fitting, the son of Thothmes was a soldier also, but one of a different and more ordinary type. Personally, as we can see from his mummy, which still lies in state in its original resting-place, the royal tomb at Thebes, Aakheperura (Okhprur'a) Amenhetep II was a tall man, of imposing presence, and with an intelligent, stern face. He was proud of his physical strength: one of his inscriptions says: "He is a king weighty of arm: neither among his soldiers, nor among the Canaanite chiefs, nor among the princes of Syria is there one who can draw his bow." The identical weapon was found in his tomb, and is now in the Cairo Museum. That he was intelligent is shewn by the fact that after a revolt at the beginning of his reign had been quelled, he made no wars unnecessarily, and never harried the Asiatics with merely cruel raids. That he could be stern enough is shewn by his treatment of the captive princes of Takhisa, which was almost Assyrian in its ferocity. Though the reign of Amenhetep II was long, having lasted twenty-six years, we possess but few monuments of it. Though he was evidently a keen soldier, we hear nothing of further war after his first campaign.

The immediate cause of Amenhetep's campaign, which took place, then, in the second year after the death of Thothmes III, seems to have been a revolt of the ever-intransigeant tribes of the Lebanon, At Shamshu-etume (= Shemesh-edom) in Northern Palestine, the new king met the enemy and overthrew them, capturing eighteen prisoners and sixteen chariot-horses with his own hand. He then entered the Orontes-valley, and took Kadesh and Senzar: then, crossing the river at a ford, he defeated a small force of desert horsemen in a skirmish, again distinguishing himself personally, spearing one of the leaders, who drove a chariot, and capturing his two horses, his chariot, and his armour, in Homeric style, Aleppo was then taken, with the territory of Keden and the town of Takhisa, which seems to have been the centre of the revolt in Naharin. Then "turning southward towards Egypt," he drove his chariot to Nii, which surrendered without resistance. A plot to expel his garrison from the town of Ikathi recalled him to that place, where he succeeded in stamping out the revolt. Then a further northward advances seem to have been made into the land of Khatithana, which was defeated, and its people enslaved. Either now or after the taking of Takhisa the king crossed the Euphrates and advanced some distance into the territory of Mitanni, which immediately purchased peace by submissions which it had never done to his father, whose farthest marches he had thus surpassed north and east. "A great event," says an inscription at Karnak, "was this, and unheard of since the times of the gods, when this country (Mitanni), which knew not Egypt, besought the good god (Amenhetep)." A result of this submission seems to have been the establishment in Mitanni of a new royal family, devoted to Egyptian interests, and shortly to be allied with the pharaonic household by marriage. The king Saushshatar, the father of Artatama, who may have been the father-in-law of Amenhetep's successor, Thothmes IV, and ancestor of Dushratta, the friend and correspondent of Amenhetep III, Tii, and Akhenaten, was the first of his line. It is reasonable to suppose that he owed his throne to Egypt at the time of Amenhetep's conquest. Henceforth Mitanni was a subject-ally of Egypt."

A memorial inscription was later on set up by Minhetep the quarry-master of Turra, near Memphis, in Naharina, no doubt by the side of those of his father and grandfather of the conqueror. They had doubtless used convenient rocks for their stelae, but Amenhetep had a tablet of Egyptian limestone cut at Turra, and transported by the quarry-master to the banks of the Euphrates. A similar tablet was set up at the far southern border of the empire, on the Nubian land of Karei, south of Gebel Barkal.

The young king returned to Egypt in triumph, bringing with him seven chiefs captured at Takhisa, and sailed up the river with them hanging head downwards from the prow of his boat. And when they finally reached Thebes, more dead than alive, the wretched victims were personally sacrificed by the king before Amen at Karnak. Six of the bodies were then hung up on the walls of Thebes, with their hands likewise, while the seventh "was taken up the river to Nubia and hung up on the wall of Napata (at Gebel Barkal), in order to make manifest the victories of his majesty for ever in the lands of the Blacks." It was a gruesome object-lesson in the imperial idea.

Thothmes IV went on a campaign in Naharin soon after the beginning of his reign, but we may well doubt whether it was a serious one. So far as we know, since his father had crossed the Euphrates, no serious challenge to the Egyptian dominion had been given by any Asiatic prince. His master of the horse, Amenhetep, says he went "from Naharin to Karei (upper Nubia) behind His Majesty, while he was upon the battlefield," but it is most probable that these expeditions were but military parades, designed to impress the foreigners with the fact that though a new king reigned, no alteration would be made in the status quo. And we see how in the course of time matters had altered when Thothmes IV (as has been supposed) marries the daughter of Artatama, King of Mitanni, the first Pharaoh, if this supposition is correct, to marry the daughter of a foreign ruling house. Apparently the daughter of Mitanni took the Egyptian name of Mutemua, "Mother-in-the-Boat" (sc. of the sun) on her marriage. Foreign names were not yet possible for the "king's chief wife." She was the mother of the third Amenhetep, whose reign marked the culminating point of the First Empire.

When his father died at the early age of thirty, an united empire was left to his son Neb-maat-Ra (Nimmuria) Amenhetep III, extending from the Euphrates to the Third Cataract of the Nile. Tii, his queen, was indeed, as the inscriptions on the great memorial scarabs commemorating their marriage say, "the wife of a mighty king, whose northern boundary is set in Naharin, and his southern extendeth to Karei (upper Nubia)." In marrying Tii, the new Amenhetep had not followed the example of his father. She was not a foreigner, though not, strictly speaking, an Egyptian of pure blood. Her mother, Tuiu, a lady of the court of Queen Mutemua, was probably an Egyptian, but her father, Iuaa, may have belonged to the Abadeh or Beja race of desert-dwellers, which, then as now, inhabited the Eastern Desert, but was more probably a Semite. So much we can tell from the appearance of the mummies of Iuaa and Tuiu as they lie in their glass cases in the Cairo Museum, surrounded by the gorgeous funeral state in which they were found when their tomb was discovered by Mr. Theodore Davis and Mr, Quibell in 1904. Judging, too, from the portraits of Queen Tii herself which have been found in her tomb, discovered by Mr. Davis and Mr. Ayrton in 1907, at Sarabit el-Khadim, and in the Fayyum, of late years, she herself was facially of pronounced or foreign type.

But though Amenhetep did not imitate his father in taking to wife an entirely foreign princess, yet he admitted a daughter of Mitanni to his harem as an inferior wife. This was Gilukhipa, daughter of the king, Shutarna, who was probably Amenhetep's maternal uncle. Later on another princess from Mitanni, Tadukhipa, daughter of Dushratta, succeeded her aunt Gilukhipa. Amenhetep signalized his marriage with Gilukhipa to the people by an issue of gigantic scarabs, just as he had previously commemorated his marriage with Tii; but there was no possibility of the Mitannian obtaining any real power at the Egyptian court. Tii ruled not only the court but the king also, and we do not wonder at it, when we see the energy of her face as shown in her portraits.

We may, if we please, see in the union of Amenhetep III with Tii, evidence of a romantic element in the king's character which would not be unlikely in the father of the artist-philosopher, Akhenaten. But the marriage had a political effect also. It enabled Amenhetep to keep the foreign princes at a more respectful distance than if he had taken the Mitannian princess Gilukhipa as his chief wife.

12. The Empire of Amenhetep III. Foreign Relations: with Mitanni and Assyria

We now know much of the relations of Amenhetep III and IV with these outer kingdoms, as well as much of the story of the loss of the Asiatic dominion of Egypt under the latter king, from the huge store of letters and despatches, written in cuneiform on clay tablets in the Babylonian manner, which were found in 1887 in the ruins of the city of Amenhetep IV (Akhenaten) at Tell el-Amarna in Middle Egypt. These priceless documents are now divided, chiefly between the museums of London, Berlin, and Cairo, They have been fully published and annotated. In all, no less than 173 despatches and letters from Tell el-Amarna have been published. Quite lately the great find of tablets at Boghaz Kyoi in Asia Minor, the site of Pterion, the ancient capital of the Khatti, has given us still further information as to international relations at this period. It is with the most profound interest that we read these, the actual letters of the kings and princes of the fifteenth century before Christ; the dry bones of history derived from their monuments are indeed vivified by such documents as these. Those of the Tell el-Amarna letters that refer to Mitanni were all sent to Egypt by the king Dushratta to his brother-in-law Amenhetep III (Nimmuria = Neb-maat-Ra), to Tii, and to Amenhetep IV (Napkhururia = Nefer-kheperu-Ra). To them, as his relatives, Dushratta writes in a confidential, almost affectionate, tone. His first letter is to Amenhetep III after his own accession, when, as he says, he had to wage war against a certain Pirkhi, who had murdered Artashumara, his brother. When he had slain Pirkhi and his accomplices, he had to face an invasion of the Hittites, whose army he surrounded and exterminated. Then he wrote to the king of Egypt, greeting him and Gilukhipa, and announcing the despatch of a chariot and horses of the booty of the Hittites as a present to the king, with a pair of breast ornaments for his sister, the king's wife. In later letters Tadukhipa is greeted. When Amenhetep III died, Dushratta writes profuse condolences both to his successor, with greetings to the queen-mother Tii, and also to Tadukhipa, whom he mentions as Amenhetep IV's wife. It is evident that Amenhetep had succeeded to his father's young Mitannian wife, nominally at present, for he was but a boy of eight or nine at his accession.

From an interesting letter to Amenhetep III, sent shortly before the latter's death, we gather that the neighbouring kingdom of Assyria was then in some respects under the control of Dushratta. He says that he is sending to Egypt the holy goddess Ishtar of Nineveh, since she has expressed a wish to visit Egypt, the land which she loves"; just as many years before she had paid a previous visit to Egypt, had been greatly honoured there, and had returned. If he could send the image of the Ninevite goddess from Nineveh to Egypt, Dushratta must have exercised political control over Assyria. This may account for some expressions in a letter sent to Amenhetep IV somewhat later, by the king of Assyria, Ashur-uballit, son of Erba-Adad. This king writes to Akhenaten in a friendly, perhaps rather impertinent, tone, evidently in some surprise at having received a communication from Egypt at all, and expressing considerable pleasure at the unwonted event. In his letter he says that if the king of Khanigalbat (Mitanni) has received twenty talents of gold from Egypt, so ought he. Evidently Ashur-uballit wished to be regarded as the equal of Dushratta, although the latter had not so very long before dominated his country. At the same time Babylonia also laid claim to the allegiance of Ashur. Writing to Akhenaten, Burraburiash of Babylonia says: "Now the Assyrians, my subjects, have I not written to thee concerning them? Why, then, have they come to thy land? If thou lovest me, they shall have no success: let them accomplish nothing at all. As a present for thee, 3 minas of lapis, and 5 span of horses for 5 chariots, have I sent thee." Here we find the Babylonian king laying claim to the overlordship of Ashur, jealous of the direct relations which had been established between Akhenaten and Ashur-uballit, and endeavouring to upset them. As far as we know, the Kassite kings of Babylonia had never succeeded in imposing any real control on Assyria: in this respect they had not retained the heritage of Khammurabi's dynasty. No doubt the union of Elam with Babylonia under their rule had tended to throw the weight of the Babylonian kingdom more over to the south-east and away from the north. Treaties had been concluded by Kara-indash I of Babylonia with Ashur-bel-nisheshu of Assyria and by Burraburiash with Puzur-Ashur II, who must have been the immediate predecessor of Ashur-uballit. The treaties referred to the settlement of the boundaries of the two kingdoms. In reality they implied the independence of Assyria, but evidently it was a point of pride with a Babylonian king to recognize the fact as little as possible, and to prevent others from doing so. During the reigns of Puzur-Ashur and of Ashur-nadin-akhi (the probable predecessor of Erba-Adad, the father of Ashur-uballit), possibly even before, Ashur had evidently been really controlled by Mitanni. In all probability it was Ashur-uballit who threw off the Mitannian yoke.

The Egyptians evidently considered it politic to recognize this independence and enter into communication with the new power, a step which was resented by the Babylonians, who protested, while we do not know that Dushratta made any objection to this first symptom of Egypt's desertion of him.

13. Relations with Babylonia

The kings of Karduniyash no doubt laid claim to a dignity more imperial than that of the young rulers of Ashur, and certainly deemed themselves the full equals of the king of Egypt. Hence, perhaps, a certain asperity which is noticeable in the official communications of the Babylonian king Kadashman-Enlil with Amenhetep III. The Habsburg and the Bourbon met, and neither would cede the pas to the other. It was a new experience for a king of Babylon to meet with a monarch who considered it beneath his dignity to give him his daughter to wife, and for a king of Egypt to meet with one who considered himself worthy of so unprecedented an honour. "From of old," wrote Amenhetep to Kadashman-Enlil, "a daughter of the King of Egypt has not been given to anybody": to which the Kassite retorted: "Why? Thou art a king, and canst do according to thy heart's wish: if thou givest her, who shall say anything? ... if however thou sendest nobody, then hast thou no regard whatever for brotherhood and friendship. . . . Why has not my brother sent me a wife? If thou sendest none, then I, like thee, will withhold from thee a wife." The course of this correspondence is often distinctly amusing to the modern reader.

Kadashman-Enlil (whose name was formerly read in error Kalimma-Sin) is a king who is not mentioned in the Babylonian lists, though it is not probable that he was a usurper. He mentions his father, probably Kara-indash, as also contemporary with Amenhetep III. His successor seems to have been Kurigalzu II, who, like Dushratta of Mitanni, was contemporary with both Amenhetep III and IV, and friendly with both. From the letters of Burraburiash, son of Kurigalzu, to Amenhetep IV, we learn that in Kurigalzu's time the Canaanites plotted revolt against Amenhetep III, and attempted to enlist the Babylonian king on their side. He, however, not only refused, but, as an ally of Amenhetep, threatened them with reprisals from his side should they go up against Egypt. Burraburiash contrasts his father's action in this case with the conduct of Amenhetep IV in receiving the envoys of Ashur-uballit of Assyria. We also learn from this correspondence that Kurigalzu was on friendly terms with Amenhetep IV, and to this amity Burraburiash succeeded on the death of Kurigalzu. His letters to "Napkhuraria" (Amenhetep IV: Akhenaten) are very friendly, and in reference to the episode of the dealings of Egypt with Ashur-uballit, which certainly savoured of treachery both to Mitanni and to Babylon, he writes more in sorrow than in anger. Later on his son was nominally betrothed to one of Akhenaten's daughters.

One piece of politic wisdom communicated to Akhenaten by Burraburiash is amusing enough: "If gold is given to kings, then brotherhood, goodness, and peace rule, and there are friendly relations." So the Egyptian king was to keep the dependent princes quiet by bribing them — for that was, in fact, what under his rule the Egyptian control had come down to. And even when the king dispensed his gifts with imperial lavishness, it was not always that even the half of what he had intended to give ever reached the recipients. All through these letters we read complaints of the dishonesty of the Egyptian officials, who send plated statues for golden to Mitanni, and much-diminished minas to Babylon. And, lastly, we find Burraburiash sharply calling the attention of the Egyptian king to his international obligations. The second revolt of Canaan had spread to the south, and the Babylonian caravans had been plundered. "Since," writes the Babylonian king, "they have plundered him (Salmu, a messenger) in thy land, which is a land of vassalage, let therefore my brother adjust this strife. When my messenger comes into my brother's presence, let Salmu also come before my brother, that they may refund him his ransom, and make good his loss." The Egyptian king is thus expected to compensate the Babylonians for their losses at the hands of his Canaanite subjects. Again, Burraburiash writes more sharply, giving details of the murder of Babylonian merchants in the city of Khinatuni (Khut-aten, "Glory of the Disk"), which Akhenaten had founded in Canaan. "Now," he says, "Canaan is thy land, and thou art the king. I have been violently dealt with in thy land: subdue these people. Make good the money they have stolen, and as for the people who killed my servants, kill them, and avenge their blood. If thou dost not kill these people, they will come again, and they will kill my caravans, or even thy messengers, and the trade between us will be destroyed, and the people (of Canaan) will became alienated from thee." This counsel, in which we read the irritation and contempt which Akhenaten's inactivity was already beginning to arouse, was not followed, as we shall see in the sequel. As Burraburiash had prophesied, the revolt cut off communication between Babylon and Egypt: this letter is the last of the series. We have an interesting document of the time in a passport issued probably by the Babylonian king: "To the Kings of Canaan, Vassals of my brother, the Great King. Verily, Akia, my messenger, to the King of Egypt, my brother, in order to condole with him, have I sent. Let none detain him. In safety to Egypt bring him, and as far as the city of Zukhli in Egypt you shall bring him in haste. And let no violence be done him." This was at the time of the death of Amenhetep III.

14. The Assyrian and Babylonian Succession

Burraburiash lived to see the power of his rival Ashur-uballit gradually increase, and either he or his son Kara-indash II, more probably the latter, consented to wed Muballitat-Erua, the daughter of Ashur-uballit. The question as to the succession of the kings following the Burraburiash who was contemporary with Akhenaten is not yet settled, but from the evidence of the Tell el-Amarna letters it would seem most probable that there was only a single king named Burraburiash (instead of two, as has often been supposed), and that he was the son and the father of a Kurigalzu. The first fact he states himself in a letter already mentioned; the second rests upon the statement of a later chronicler that the king Kurigalzu "Sikhru" (the Little), who was raised to the throne by Ashur-uballit after the defeat of the usurper Nazibugash or Shuzigash, was the son of Burraburiash and, presumably, Muballitat-Erua. It is perhaps more probable that he was a grandson of Burraburiash, who was the contemporary or possibly the senior of Ashur-uballit, and that he was really the son of Kara-indash II, who was probably the immediate successor of Burraburiash and the real husband of Muballitat-Erua. The reign of Kara-indash II was short, and his son Kadashman-kharbe, who must have been a mere boy, was murdered by Nazibugash, who is called "a son of nobody" and seems to have been the leader of a popular revolt against the Assyrian control which Ashur-uballit had brought about by the marriage of his daughter to the Babylonian king.

It was not long, however, before Ashur-uballit appeared in Babylonia to avenge his murdered grandson. Nazibugash was slain, and the young Kurigalzu III, who was a younger son of Burraburiash, possibly by Muballitat-Erua, was placed upon the throne. He was the founder of a stable race of Kassite sovereigns who by no means unsuccessfully maintained their independence of Assyrian tutelage.

This seems to be the most probable explanation of a confused set of events of which uncertain and often mutually contradictory accounts are preserved in the later chronicles: we have to square these accounts as best we can with the contemporary information given us by the Tell el-Amarna tablets.

15. Khatti and Alashiya

No direct connexion between the royal houses of Egypt and Khatti existed as yet. Possibly the Hittites were too barbaric and probably too hostile for marriage-relations with them. The few letters from Shubbiluliuma to Akhenaten (which mention previous relations with Amenhetep III) found at Tell el-Amarna are less courtly than are those of the other kings, and in fact, though professedly friendly, are rough in tone. Probably Egypt's friendship for his enemy Dushratta did not dispose Shubbiluliuma to be over polite. And as a matter of fact it was difficult for him to be so. Already at the end of Amenhetep III's reign he had invaded Naharin, which he regarded as belonging to Dushratta, and had taken the city of Katna, whose king, Akizzi, sent fruitless appeals for help to Egypt. The Hittite king's letters to Akhenaten were a mere blind, intended to deceive the Egyptian Court into a belief in his friendliness.

A subsidiary Hittite kingdom, however, that of Arzawa, in Cilicia, whose southern march probably ran with that of Alashiya, a subject-ally of Egypt, had considerable dealings with Egypt, and Amenhetep III sent one of his daughters (no doubt borne to him by a subordinate wife) to Tarkhundaraush or Tarkhundaraba, its king.

From Alashiya, which, as we have seen, is more probably Northern Phoenicia than Cyprus, several letters are preserved, which evidently date from the time of Amenhetep III. The subjects of the letters, with the exception of an enigmatical request that an "Eagle-Conjurer" or "Eagle-Charmer" (possibly merely a falconer) may be sent, are usually commercial relations and tribute, the sending of wood and copper to Egypt in exchange for gold and oil, and so forth. Alashiyan ships and merchants are often mentioned, and there is an interesting request for the return to Alashiya of the goods of a merchant who had died in Egypt. Such references as this give a good idea of the high organization of international relations at this period. So far as Egypt was concerned, this organization had grown up since the expulsion of the Hyksos, when Egypt first entered the world as one nation among others. The organization of political matters is also exemplified in the case of Alashiya by a letter from the prime minister, the rabisu, of that state to his brother-official in Egypt, whom he addresses as "the rabisu of Egypt, my brother," and to whom he sends a present for himself of eight talents of copper and a tusk of ivory from Mesopotamia, as well as wood, which was always and is now valuable in Egypt. There is a reference to Lycian pirates in another letter.

Such were the relations of Egypt with the states of Western Asia from the time of the epoch-making marriage of Thothmes IV with Mutemua to the immediate imminence of the Hittite invasion of Northern Syria, and the consequent revolt of Canaan, which, unrepressed by the religious reformer Akhenaten, caused the temporary loss of the whole, and the permanent loss of the greater part, of the empire of the Thothmosids.

We now turn from the Asiatic to the African empire, from the boundary in Naharin to that in Karei.

16. The Nubian Empire

No doubt the long final struggle with the Hyksos had caused a weakening of the Theban power, not merely in Kush, but also in the long subdued lands of Amam and Wawat, the "Lower Nubia" of the present day. Here Egyptian authority was soon restored by the earlier kings of the XVIIIth Dynasty, Turi, the viceroy under Amenhetep I and Thothmes I, being specially active in this regard. In the time of Amenhetep I Egyptian authority had already been extended to the land of Karei, the region of the Third Cataract. Hitherto the island of Arko, in the Dongola province, had been one of the southern-most outposts of Egyptian rule, but Amenhetep I or his Viceroy Turi passed round the bend of the Nile where it turns north-eastward towards Abu Hamed, and reached the "Pure Mountain," the isolated Gebel Barkal in whose shadow lay the Nubian town of Napata.

It is by no means impossible that the people whose centre was at Napata were not pure negroes, but belonged to the Abyssinian or Punite race, and had entered the Nile valley not long before to occupy the valley depopulated of its original negro inhabitants by the constant razzias of the

XIIth Dynasty kings. But of this we cannot be certain. All we know is that the Kushites of the XIIth Dynasty were negroes but that the "blameless Ethiopians" of later days were not, although they had a large admixture of both negro and Egyptian blood. They must therefore have reached the Nile somewhere between the time of the XIIth and that of the XVIIIth Dynasty, as from the latter period Kush was in the full and peaceful occupation of the Egyptians, whose culture gradually made great progress among the Ethiopians. There is no period for the irruption of the Ethiopians into the Nile valley more probable than that when the contest with the Hyksos left the Theban kings too weak to hold any of their ancient possessions south of Wadi Haifa. Napata, too, the Ethiopian chief town, seems to have been before the conquest more important a place than a mere negro chiefs kraal. Its Nubian name was retained by the Egyptians, whereas a negro kraal would have had none. So that it must have been the centre of a culture and of a race more highly developed than the negro's.

The capture of Napata therefore marked a new epoch in the development of the southern empire of Egypt. Napata was a town, a more or less civilized centre, to which Egyptian civilization could be transplanted and find a home, and whence it could exercise an influence more appreciated than it had been by the harried and raided barbarians of Wawat, who were incapable of receiving it. It was not long before a flourishing Egyptian colony grew up beneath Mount Barkal, which, as we shall see, exercised in the fullness of time a most important influence on the history of the mother-land. It is probable that the organization of the new territory was the work of Thothmes III, who seems to have done much for the civilization and organization of Lower Nubia, which lay at Egypt's doors, and may be supposed to have extended his work to Upper Nubia also. Then, as now, the land of Lower Nubia was a mere nothing, a strip of palm-land with a village here and there along the inhospitable desert banks of the Nile. It was then capable of no greater development than it is now. All that Thothmes could do was to extend Egyptian civilization among its inhabitants. He built and endowed temples, where the Nubians could worship Egyptian gods and their own in Egyptian fashion and with Egyptian ceremonies, while the Egyptians shared their worship with them. This was a great step towards the incorporation of the Nubians with Egypt, which no previous king had thought of taking: in former days the wretched Wawat and Kush had been regarded merely as outcasts.

Already in his second year, before, apparently, his masterful co-regent Hatshepsut had succeeded in relegating him entirely to the background, he carried out on his own account a renovation of the temple which Senusert III had erected in the fortress of Semneh, rededicating it not only to Khnum the god of the cataracts and to the local Ethiopian god Didun (the Tithonos of the Greeks), but also to the deified Senusert, who thus became tutelary deity of the reconquered land. Here the young hero-worshipper already shewed by his veneration for the great conqueror of the XIIth Dynasty in what direction his ideals tended. He venerated Senusert as the genius of the empire, as he himself was afterwards venerated throughout the centuries, being indeed in popular story more or less identified with the great "Sesostris," and adding to the Nubian renown of his predecessor his own Asiatic glory. Then, after offering to Didun "The water of Wawat," the Nile-water of the Second Cataract, and enjoining the due care of the shrine on the local chiefs and governors of the fortresses of the new "Southern Elephantine," as he not inaptly called the shores and isles of the Second Cataract, he returned to his slavery in the court of the peaceful queen at Thebes.

The peace was unbroken in Nubia till near the end of his long reign, and his viceroy Nehi, the successor of Turi, seems, so far as we can tell, to have ruled peaceably and benignly over the Nubians. But nearly fifty years after he had endowed the temple of Semneh, the king gave the word for the advance of his armies to the south, probably in consequence of some rebellion. Whether the king accompanied the army or not we do not know, nor do we know many details of the war.

Amenhetep II succeeded to the possession of an organized Nubia, whose southern border reached to Karei, where Minhetep the quarrier set up frontier-tablets as he had beyond Euphrates. Napata was a town with a wall, on which rebel chiefs from Naharin could be hung as a warning against similar behaviour among the newly conquered Ethiopians. In the next reign (of Thothmes IV), however, a revolt occurred "above Wawat," which was suppressed without much difficulty, and a colony of Kushite prisoners was established on the domain of the royal mortuary chapel at Thebes.

Amenhetep III, who warred on Nubia at the beginning of his reign, penetrated farther south than any previous Egyptian king. "He made his boundary as far as he desired, as far as the four pillars which bear the heaven." He set up a tablet of victory as far as the "Springs of Horus" (the

Sixth Cataract?); no king of Egypt had done the like. The farthest point reached seems to have been a month's sailing from Napata, "until the mountain of Hua (Jebel Rawiyan or Tyem?) came in sight": south of this a camp was made in the land of Wenshek. The mountain of Hua is described as "behind western Kheskhet," another unknown land.

Later on the viceroy Merimes had to quell a revolt in the land of Abhet (the Dongola province?), but the peace was not again disturbed during the long reign of Amenhetep III, who extended on a large scale to Upper Nubia the civilizing work that had been begun by Thothmes III. Following the example of the latter, Amenhetep II and Thothmes IV had built and endowed temples in Lower Nubia: Amenhetep III now erected south of the Second Cataract sanctuaries on a scale of imperial magnificence which was worthy of him. At Sulb or Soleb, 163 miles south of Buhen or Wadi Halia, he raised a splendid temple, much resembling in style the Colonnades which he added to the Temple of Luxor at Thebes. The traveller Hoskins describes it as being "very imposing, standing proudly at the extremity of the desert, the only beacon of civilisation in this sea of barrenness." And it was as a beacon of civilization that Amenhetep intended it. The god to be worshipped within it by the Nubians was none other than himself, the tutelary genius of the Empire. As, long after, the Roman provincial was expected to worship the Emperor and Roma, so the conquered Nubian was to be bound to the Egyptian Empire by a worship of his Emperor. Thothmes III had, more modestly, enjoined him to venerate the spirit of his ancient conqueror, Senusert III: Thothmes himself after his death was associated in this worship. But Amenhetep developed this idea into a contemporary worship of himself as the impersonification of the Empire, and called his temple after himself, Kha-m-maat, "He who appears as Maat (the goddess of Right and Law)." This sanctuary was built in the most magnificent style of the most magnificent reign in Egyptian history, and was embellished with works of art which were never afterwards rivalled. The famous "Prudhoe Lions," now in the British Museum, which Ruskin declared to be the finest works of sculpture of their kind existing, were dedicated in Kha-m-maat, though afterwards removed to Napata; and so were the great rams, one of which is now at Berlin.

At Sedeinga, a few miles to the north, Amenhetep also built a fine temple in honour of his consort. Queen Tii. In that of his successor the neighbourhood of Soleb was considered one of the chief places of the empire, and worthy to receive the honour of a temple of the Sun-Disk, a

"Gem-Aten" or "place where the Aten is found," like Thebes, Memphis, Tell el-Amarna, and probably Napata. This was at Sesebi, a little south of Soleb.

Thus the Nubian province of Egypt was gradually recovered by the earlier kings of the XVIIIth Dynasty, enlarged and reorganized by the genius of Thothmes III, and magnified into a truly imperial dominion by the splendid Amenhetep III.

Probably the religious revolution of Akhenaten was not sufficiently prolonged to bring this to ruin, as the northern empire had been. The viceroys were, apparently, strong, and there was no rebellion. In Ai's reign, Paser the viceroy set up inscriptions at Gebel Adda, north of Wadi Haifa. He or his predecessor had no doubt already abolished the Aten-temples at Sesebi and Napata; but, oddly enough, the name of that at Napata persisted, and is found still existing in the days of the Nubian king Nastasenen, a thousand years later.

We now turn to the internal history of Egypt under the First Empire.

CHAPTER VII: EGYPT UNDER THE EMPIRE (1600-1100 B.C.)

I. The Reorganization

OF the general reorganization of the whole kingdom which was carried out during the two first reigns of the XVIIIth Dynasty we have an example in the restoration of temples which had fallen into ruin during the Hyksos domination in Lower and Middle Egypt, as we know from Hatshepsut's inscription, already mentioned, at Beni Hasan. The great temples were no doubt restored as soon as possible after their liberation. Memphis, which had probably been retaken shortly before the beginning of his reign, was the especial care of Aahmes; to later monarchs like Hatshepsut were left the smaller and less important fanes, such as that of Hermopolis and this of Cusae. For the necessary works in the temple of Ptah at Memphis, Aahmes reopened the quarries of Turra, and employed Hyksos captives, described as Fenkhu to cut the stone. Amenhetep I also restored temples on the extreme south, which had possibly been damaged by Nubian raids. But of all the sanctuaries of Egypt that of the god of Thebes, the especial patron of the royal house which had led the Egyptians to victory and restored to Egypt the full extent of her patrimony, was most honoured. Aahmes seems to have restored the sanctuary of the XIIth Dynasty in "the Seats of Apet" (Apet-esut; Karnak), and Amenhetep I continued his work on a magnificent scale. Amenhetep seems also to have thoroughly reorganized the whole confraternity of the priests of Amen, and probably added greatly to their possessions: on the coffins of the priests of a later period he is constantly depicted as receiving the offerings of a deceased as a god in company with Osiris Unnefer, Ptah-Tanen, and Anubis, and it would seem that he was the greatest of the benefactors for whom the priests of Thebes were more especially bound to pray.

With this pious monarch and his mother the old Egypt came to an end. His successor, the first Thothmes, inaugurated the new imperial era.

Thebes now finally became the undisputed capital of Egypt and residence of the kings. For we can now speak of a common centre of royal and national strength in Egypt. The kings no longer lived apart and divinely aloof in a royal burgh like Itht-taui, from which they "controlled the two lands," inhabited merely by their ministers, their feudatories, and their people, who were all more or less their slaves. A god no longer ruled the heaven of Egypt, beyond which was nothing in the world but an indefinite hell of foreign "ghosts," who could not penetrate into the heaven unless its god-ruler so willed. Overthrow of their heaven by the forces of devildom had brought king and people together, and henceforth they lived and fought together as far as was compatible with the ideas of the time: a combined royal and national warlike spirit had come into being. And the king lived with his people in his faithful City of Thebes. This alteration in the position of the monarch is one of the most striking characteristics of the imperial period. He was still nominally as divine as before, but one sees the difference between an Amenhetep and a Khufu, or even a Senusert. He was only called a god by his own people. There were other peoples in the world now, and they did not regard the Egyptian King as a god any more than the Egyptians looked upon the King of Babylon or of the Hittites as divine, Babylon or Mitanni wrote to Egypt as his brother, as "Monsieur mon frere," just as a modern monarch might, and Egypt returned the same compliment. And the growing intercommunication between their peoples naturally tended to lower the ancient divine prestige of Pharaoh even in his own land. But instead of the old theocratic relation, a new one grew up now between Pharaoh and his people. They obeyed him now as the leader, their prince and war-lord, the imperator of their armies, who had led them to victory in war and would lead them on to victory still. And in peace-time the king dwelt in his capital like a modern king, and was little more removed from the ken of his subjects than is the latter.

2. The Imperial Administration in Egypt

It is, then, natural that in civil administration, no less than in military and religious matters, we find under the Empire the new phenomenon of centralization in the one capital city. The civil wars and the struggle against the foreigner during the Hyksos period had much the same effect in Egypt as the Wars of the Roses had in England. We have seen that the local authority of the ancient feudal nobility of the land, which was so powerful at the beginning of the XIIth Dynasty, had been curtailed by the later kings of that dynasty, and the foundations laid of a bureaucratic system of local government. When peace was restored the few great families that remained found all their influence and power gone. The definite leadership of the king in the war of liberation, with no committee of nobles around him, but merely captains trained to war and the faithful officials and priests of Thebes, resulted in the establishment of a strongly centralized royal power, which governed the whole country by means of an official bureaucracy.

At the beginning of the XVIIIth Dynasty the details of government were left by the kings to the city-governer of Thebes, who united with his police-control the ancient dignity of the Tjate, or "Man" par excellence, as the vizier was called, as opposed to the Neter, the "God," i.e. the king. This arrangement worked well as long as the king was usually himself at Thebes, or at any rate in Egypt. But when Thothmes III for a long series of years came to spend half the year in Asia, the burden of the home government became too much for one man, and the functions of the Theban governor were restricted to the south, a "Vizier of the North" being created with his seat at Memphis. The first holder of this office seems to have been himself a Mernphite, named Ptahmes. The boundary between the provinces of the two viziers was fixed north of Siut. In the south the authority of the Southern Vizier was extended over the valley south of El-Kab, which had hitherto been, and was afterwards, considered to belong to the domain of the viceroy of Nubia, "the king's son of Kush." Here the boundary was fixed south of the Island of Senemet, the modern Bigeh, close to Philae.

We know much of the office of the Southern Vizier from an inscription in the tomb of Rekhmara, who held the post from the thirty-second year of Thothmes III till after the accession of Amenhetep II, at latest about 1450 B.C. Rekhmara was a Theban, and was buried in the tomb-hill of Shekh 'Abd el-Kurna at Thebes. It is in his tomb that one of the most important paintings of the reception of the Keftians of Crete and other foreign tribute-bearers, already mentioned, is to be seen. As was often the case with the viziers, his great office had been hereditary in his family for many years, and his great-grandfather Aahmes had held it, probably under Amenhetep I and Thothmes I. Under Thothmes II and Hatshepsut a certain Hapuseneb, who was a partisan of the queen, occupied the vizier's chair for a short time, but he was probably dispossessed by Thothmes in, and the dignity restored to the family of Aahmes. After the death of Rekhmara, who succeeded his father User, Amenhetep III gave it to Amenemapet, a scion of another family. Similarly, Ptahmes in the north was succeeded by his son Thothmes. The dignity of vizier, then, though by royal favour it could be continued from father to son, was never so continued indefinitely. No doubt this was politic: the kings had no desire to concentrate too much power in the hands of a single family. As it was, the Southern Tjate was very near the throne. We cannot doubt that his office, combined as it was with that of governor of the capital, was far more important than that of the Northern Vizier, and that when the king was absent in Asia or Kush he became automatically Regent of the whole land. In this case his power could only be checked by a masterful queen, like Tii. He is no doubt the first minister, or rabisu, of Egypt mentioned in the Tell el-Amarna letters.

In his tomb inscription Rekhmara tells us much of his duties and powers. He was formally installed by the king, and lectured on the duties of his office: charged to hold the scales of justice evenly between rich and poor, and to do unright to no man. The whole business of the administration was handed over to him, with the significant exception of the power of the purse. The king's treasurer was responsible only to the king, and to him the vizier had to go for gold. This was a politic check on his power. He, however, superintended the collection and incoming of the taxes, which were received by him from the local authorities, in whom the powers of police, magistrates, and tax-gatherers were concentrated. Rekhmara gives us much information as to this organization in his time, including the statistics of the different provinces of his government from Siut to Bigeh, We see from this list that the local authorities differed in name and powers in different places. In some towns of strategic importance, such as Bigeh on the Nubian border, or Koptos at the mouth of the great Wadi Hamamat, the government seems to have been military in character: in others we find the descendants of the local princes still nominally ruling, but really controlled by a sheriff or royal officer, called the uhem ("herald"). He had his reeve and subordinate officials. At Thebes the king was the chief, and the vizier was his assessor. A Theban herald probably existed, but was attached to the king personally, as comptroller of the household of his chief. We have seen that a certain Antef performed this function for Thothmes III.

The amount of taxes received from the local officials is stated by Rekhmara. It always consisted primarily of so many deben weight of gold, with oxen, pigeons, honey, grain, cloth, beads, and other tribute in kind according to the local circumstances in each case.

These were the king's dues, which Rekhmara collected as vizier: as he held also the office of Steward of the Estates of Amen, he also received the local Theban dues of the god and the proportion of foreign tribute assigned to him.

Of old the office of Ta, or "Chief Justice," had been inseparable from that of the Tjate. So that Rekhmara was Chief Justice as well as Minister of the Interior, as well as, incidentally. Chancellor and Steward of Amen. As Ta, the vizier controlled the higher judges, who were attached to the royal court, and so had their seat in the capital.

Of the "Great Tribunal" (Kenbet aat) which assisted the vizier under the Ramessides, we hear nothing from Rekhmara's inscription. This formal assembly of councillors was probably developed from the Vizier's Hall, as Rekhmara describes it, at the time of the legal reforms of Horemheb, who put things straight after the confusion of Akhenaten's mad reign. We learn from the inscription of a certain Mose or Mes, who lived under Rameses II, and was buried at Sakkara, much of the legal arrangements of his time, and can draw a good idea of how a lawsuit was conducted in the vizier's court. The procedure must have been much the same in Rekhmara's time, but for the fact that the "Great Council" did not then exist. The usual petitions are made, the plaintiff and defendant plead their causes in person (the recorded speeches of Mes and his opponent Khai in this case are the oldest specimens of forensic oratory known), the Vizier sends his apparitor to take the cause back to the local Kenbet of Memphis (the Kenbet aat of the North sat at Heliopolis) that the circumstances might be examined more fully, and so forth: finally, the Vizier himself pronounces judgment.

To the state-organization the Pharaoh bore much the same relation as a Russian Tsar, or other modern autocratic monarch, bears to his state to-day. The army and foreign relations were his real sphere of action. With them the viziers had nothing to do. He was at once the War-Lord, Foreign Minister, and Colonial Administrator of the nation. He represented it in dealings with the gods as well as with other earthly sovereigns. For his people he offered sacrifices and presided over festivals. Thothmes III was for many years absent during the hot Egyptian spring and summer on campaign; the winter he spent in Egypt, returning every year punctually in order to be present at the great metropolitan festival of the goddess Apet.

The king's immediate officers, the chamberlains and comptrollers, accompanied him to Asia and attended him in Egypt, with the exception of the stewards of his estates, who were probably subordinate, not to the viziers, but to their colleague, the Chief Treasurer. Another officer who probably also remained behind was probably responsible to the king only, and watched both the viziers and the treasurer. This was "The two Eyes of the King in the North, the two Ears of the King in the South," as his significant title runs, with variations.

Such was the Egyptian civil state under the Empire. The ecclesiastical state, previously unknown as such, had not yet so far differentiated itself from the civil state as it did a few centuries later. The power of the king was too great. In his ecclesiastical capacity (he was himself always a priest of Amen, though necessarily of subordinate rank), he formed a link between priests and laymen, and so long as he continued to be, while devout enough, in his soul a warrior and a ruler, he was a link that controlled both. Subordinate links which checked priestly ambitions were created by the appointment of the lay vizier to the stewardship of the domains of Amen, and of other lay officials and royal princes to the chief priesthoods. The priests had already begun to be a caste apart, as they never had been before, when the noble was also naturally the priest; but the time had not yet come when priests were to usurp the natural functions of laymen. This only came about when the strength of the strongest controlling link, the king, was weakened by religious heresy and loss of foreign dominion, and its resultant poverty and loss of royal prestige.

3. Rise of the Priests of Amen

Yet already under the XVIIIth Dynasty the foundations were laid of the future priestly domination by the enormous benefactions which the kings, in gratitude, laid upon the altars of Amen. Thothmes III, undisputed ruler though he was, before whom no priest would have dared to raise his head, did more than all. His gratitude to the god who had guided him to victory was great. To his metropolitan temple in "the Seats of Apet" (Karnak) he added the colonnades and halls at its eastern end, among which is the chamber decorated with representations of the rare plants and animals which he had brought back from his campaigns. The architect Menkheperrasenb here essayed a new variation in architecture: he reversed the papyrus-capitals on the columns, with a peculiar effect which was not imitated in later days. But the king shewed his gratitude to Amen in a more tangible fashion. Amenhetep I had been the first to heap favours upon the priests of Amen: his descendant gave them riches. The larger proportion of the slaves and tribute of Asia was given to them: the three towns of Anaugasa, Yenoam, and Hurenkaru in the Lebanon, were bestowed upon them as domains of the god, besides countless lands and serfs in Egypt itself: and so the dominant position of the priesthood of Amen, "King of the Gods," was assured, and with it their favour and support to the kings. Amen became the tutelary deity of the empire abroad, as he was of the metropolis. His name and fame in Asia bid fair to rival that of the native deities, and he was venerated by the Canaanites as the equal of Baal and Ashtoreth. His temples arose in the towns of Canaan and in the sea-cities of Phoenicia. Semitic chiefs and officials, like Amankhashir, bore his name like any Egyptian Amenheteps or Amenemhebs.

In the empire of the South also, so far as it was newly conquered by the kings of the XVIIIth Dynasty, Amen was tutelary deity. His subsidiary shrine at Napata, a sort of filiale of Thebes, became a centre of his worship and focus of anti-Assyrian patriotism under the Ethiopians, much as the temples at Thebes had been the focus of resistance against the Hyksos. The other Egyptian gods do not appear outside Egypt. He was the imperial deity, they remained in their own land: with the new domains of Amen they had nothing to do. The kings naturally conferred favours upon the older local gods also; there was no possibility of Amen-Ra overshadowing the other gods so far as to create even a semblance of monotheism. But Amen-Ra was their king.

Naturally this predominance soon caused the jealousy of the older and rival deities to spring into life. Of all, the priests of Ra at Heliopolis must have been most outraged by the annexation of their god, the most ancient of all, to the comparatively new-fangled Amen. And we can with great probability trace to their influence, as well as to the growing royal displeasure at the power of Amen's priests, the religious revolution of Akhenaten, which amid the collapse of the First Empire momentarily dethroned Amen, and made a transformed idea of Ra the One God of Egypt. This revolution failed, as, being an artificial creation of the king and a few heretical priests, it was bound to do: and the only result of the failure was to rivet the yoke of the priests of Amen on the necks of the kings in a fashion previously undreamt of.

4. The Reign of Hatshepsut

The history of Egypt at this time is the history of her external empire. At home the fellah tilled his lands and worshipped his gods in peace. Nothing happened to disturb the internal tranquillity of the country. There is one mention of some abortive rebellion against Hatshepsut, which seems to have been quelled by Neb-uaui, the High Priest of Abydos, who was high in favour with Thothmes III at the beginning of his reign. We have no other evidence of internal disorder from the repression of the rebellions against Aahmes to the religious revolution of Akhenaten, a period of nearly two centuries. Disorder in the royal house there certainly was at the beginning of this period, if we are to credit Prof. Sethe's theory of the "Thronwirren," or confused succession of Thothmes I and II, Hatshepsut, and Thothmes III. This theory has been not only accepted, but stated to be historical fact, by Prof. Breasted, but has been rejected in toto by Prof. Naville.

The precise relationship of Thothmes I to Amenhetep I is uncertain, and it is supposed by Prof. Sethe that he was not his son, but only ascended the throne in right of his wife, Queen Aahmes. Prof. Sethe is then of opinion that on the death of Aahmes, his wife, Thothmes I was compelled to resign the throne, and Thothmes III, his elder son, ascended it by right of his half-sister and wife, Hatshepsut, who was the eldest surviving descendant of Thothmes I. He himself, being the son of a subsidiary wife, Aset, had no immediate right to it. Thothmes III then ruled for a time alone, Hatshepsut being merely his "Great Wife," as Aahmes had been merely the "Great Wife" of Thothmes I. About the fifth year of his reign, the "legitimists" compelled him to accept his wife as his co-regent and fellow-king. Thothmes after some years got rid of her for a short time, and erased her name on the monuments. Then came a new revolution. Thothmes II took the sceptre from the hands of Thothmes III, and by his side reappeared the ex-king Thothmes I, as co-regent. Thothmes II obliterated the name of Hatshepsut, like Thothmes III. Thothmes I died at last, and Thothmes II ruled alone for a short time after his death, probably from the seventh to the ninth year of Thothmes III. Then Thothmes II also died, and Thothmes III and Hatshepsut returned to power together, having apparently made peace after their quarrel. Hatshepsut finally died, and Thothmes III reigned in peace for the rest of his life.

This (it would really seem improbably) complicated hypothesis is chiefly based on the facts of obliteration and restoration of royal names in Hatshepsut's temple at Der el-Bahri, and other arguments which seem somewhat weak, though we are hardly justified in rejecting them absolutely, as Prof. Naville has done. Until decisive confirmation of Prof. Sethe's theory is discovered, it would seem best to hold (with Prof. Naville to a great extent) that Thothmes I, after having associated his son Thothmes II in the normal way before his death, was succeeded by the latter. Whether Thothmes II married Hatshepsut or not is doubtful: Prof.

Naville believes that he did, while Prof. Sethe denies it. In this matter perhaps Prof. Sethe is right. Thothmes II died after a very short reign, at about the age of thirty, leaving behind him a young son Thothmes, by a lady named Aset. It is evident from his mummy (now at Cairo) that Thothmes II was a man of feeble physique, and was probably diseased: his wife Aset was a person of no account. During his reign it is probable that his half-sister Hatshepsut exercised great influence over the government. If with Prof. Sethe we hold that Thothmes I was not the son of Amenhetep I, she was the eldest, perhaps now the only, member of the royal house directly descended from Aahmes the Liberator, whereas the king Thothmes II was not descended from him at all. Further, she was a woman endowed with no small amount of the energetic spirit of her father, as well as her mother's pride of race; and no doubt, as she says in an inscription at Der el-Bahri, and in this we need not disbelieve her, she was the favourite child of Thothmes I, and intended by him to share the throne of the ruler who should succeed him. If she had been a weak woman, the loyalty of the people to her as the true representative of the descendants of Ra would have amounted to nothing more than mere affection: as it was, it was she, rather than Thothmes II, who was regarded as the real ruler. She may have married him. Whether she did so or not, and it is possible that she refused to do so on account of his sickness, at his death it was natural that she should at least act as regent for his young son. But her blood and her natural energy could not brook this subordinate position perhaps without the title even of queen. Assisted by a great body of influential partisans, whose names we know, and acclaimed by the loyalty of the people, she took the first step by marrying her child-nephew. Then, justifying the act by her pure descent and appealing to the wishes of her father, she took the final step, and, a woman, assumed the king's crown herself, relegating her husband and nephew to the position of associate kings. Thothmes II soon died, but Thothmes III continued to reign as a shadow-king: he was "His Majesty," Menkheper-Ra, always; but of real power he had none till her death. This we see from the fact that his natural inclination towards militarism and conquest had to be suppressed while she lived. That he hated her profoundly, that afterwards he should strive to obliterate her memory from the monuments of their joint rule, was natural. But it may well be that the long years of necessary self-repression in reality exercised a good effect upon his character, and that when he came to his full power he was the better and the wiser king for the discipline and schooling which he had received from Hatshepsut. Few other kings of Egypt had had so severe a training; few other kings of Egypt shewed the same real power of governing and organization as Thothmes the Great.

The result of the extraordinary appearance of a woman as king we see upon her monuments, the peculiarities of which are well known. That she actually wore the male royal costume, as she is represented on them as doing, cannot be doubted. But she did not go forth to war, nor would she allow her young consort to obtain prestige by doing so. The great acts of her reign were the enlargement of Karnak, her great expedition to Punt (which took place in the ninth year of Thothmes III), and the building of Der el-Bahri, the magnificent temple which she erected by the side of the ancient funerary fane of Mentuhetep, in the necropolis of Western Thebes. This building, by which her name is best known to us, was dedicated to Amen, and, as we should say, "to the memory" of her father Thothmes I; Hathor also, as the tutelary deity of the place, was honoured within it, and Anubis as protector of the western necropoles. It also served to commemorate the glory of her own reign, and more especially the expedition to Punt. In its design it was remarkable and unprecedented, except in so far as its architect had borrowed some ideas from the neighbouring temple of Mentuhetep. Like this, it had to be reared up against the face of a great cliff, and Mentuhetep's plan of a terrace, approached by a ramp between two colonnades, was followed; but instead of one, two terraces were built, one behind the other, to lead up to the rock-cut sanctuary. The boldness of the conception, the splendour of the architecture, and the beauty of its sculptured and painted decoration, were the worthy firstfruits of the new imperial grandeur of Egypt, and mark the first progress beyond the ideas of the XIIth Dynasty. Magnificent conceptions were in the air. The great queen, glorying in her "years of peace," sends an expedition of great ships to Punt, which brings back to her treasures of gold, ivory, precious woods, myrrh-trees in pots for transplantation to Egypt, sacks of myrrh and frankincense, apes and all rare denizens of the earth, the air, and the waters, "the like of which was not brought for other kings, being marvels of Punt, because of the greatness of the fame of this revered god, Amen-Ra, lord of Thebes." These the queen presented in solemn state to Amen, and on the walls of Der el-Bahri she employed her artists to represent the events and fruits of her great expedition. The triumph of both artists and architects in the new temple, in which they engrafted the new spirit on to the old, is now evident to our eyes since its complete excavation and publication by Prof. Edouard Naville at the expense of the Egypt Exploration Fund.

Hatshepsut was buried in a rather extraordinary rock-tomb, with a gallery of immense length, but of unfinished appearance, in the Valley of the Tombs of the Kings, the winding wadi at the back of the hill of Dra Abu 'l-Negga. In this valley her father had been buried, and here all the great pharaohs of the empire were laid to rest after her in the splendid subterranean sepulchres which from Greek times till now have been reckoned among the wonders of the world. The latest date of her reign known is apparently that of her 22nd year, and as it was in his 22nd year that Thothmes III set forth to war, we cannot doubt that their reigns began together, and that she died in the 22nd year of their joint reign. On the lowest chronological scheme both then ascended the throne about 1501 B.C.

Thothmes III's persecution of her name after her death extended also to the names of her chief supporters, and no doubt to the persons of those of them who survived her. Chief among these was the architect Senmut, the designer of the temple of Der el-Bahri, and the vizier Hapuseneb.

5. Thothmes in to Amenhetep III

Rid of Hatshepsut and her supporters, the thirty-two years' sole reign of Thothmes III passed in Egypt quietly enough. The family of Rekhmara governed well in his absence from the kingdom, the booty of Asia conciliated the priests of Amen, who, under Hapuseneb, had previously been the foremost supporters of Hatshepsut, the land grew rich by leaps and bounds, and all went well. Nothing happened but the building of temples till the reign of Amenhetep III. Under Thothmes III the imperial destiny of Egypt was consummated, and she became for two centuries the most powerful, the wealthiest, and, all things considered, the most civilized, country in the world. The connexion with the "Minoan" civilization in the Aegean which had already existed under the Hyksos, was greatly developed by the approach of the Egyptian arms to Asia Minor and the submission of Cyprus. Cretan embassies brought the triumphs of the Minoan metal-worker and embosser to Thebes, and specimens of the beautiful faience of Egypt were prized at Mycenae and in Cyprus. We have already spoken of the influence of Egyptian and Aegean art upon each other. It is chiefly in the domain of metal-work that we see the clearest trace of the Minoan influence in Egypt, where magnificent embossed bowls of silver and bronze with scenes of lions hunting deer amid trees, fish amid lilies, and processions of gods, first came into vogue in the reign of Thothmes III. One of the finest known of these was significantly presented by the king to his officer Thutii, the Governor of the Northern Lands and representative of the king among the islanders of the great Green Sea. The designs on these bowls are Egyptian, but the spirit of their execution and their workmanship must be inspired by Minoan originals. In return the Cretan artists borrowed the Egyptian designs of lions and cats hunting deer and wild-fowl for the adornment of their own swords, daggers, and other metal-work. For importation to their own islands they seem to have prized above all the ceramic products of Egypt, which they had themselves imitated with success since the time of the XIIth Dynasty, when, probably, they first became acquainted with the Egyptian art of glazing earthenware. In return, again, the Egyptians strove to imitate in faience, as well as in metal, the bronze one-handled vase-fillers and other vessels, later on the remarkable stirrup-vases, or "Bugelkannen," which were characteristic of the metal-work and pottery of Later Minoan Greece. This welcoming of a foreign influence is characteristic of a period of foreign empire and contact with strange races.

The pride as well as the curiosity of the Egyptians was greatly stirred by the coming and going of the ambassadors and tribute-bearers of the foreigners, who brought these beautiful things to Thebes, and few of the great nobles of the time failed to record upon the walls of their tombs the faces and appearance of the ambassadors of Crete or the tribute-bearers of Syria and the black Sudan who had come in their time. Senmut, the architect of Hatshepsut, and Rekhmara, the chancellor of Thothmes III, thus record the procession of the chiefs of Keftiu (Crete) and the Isles in the midst of the Sea. Confidently the ruddy Minoans or Mycenaeans march along the walls, wearing their high Cretan boots, their typically "Mycenaean" waistcloths, and with their long black hair hanging to their waists, or knotted on their heads, just as we see them on the walls of their own home, Knossos, where the famous fresco of the Cupbearer, discovered by Dr. Arthur Evans, might be a replica of one of these contemporary Egyptian figures. He bears a great vase, just as do the ambassadors to Egypt, who bring their gifts to the court of Hatshepsut or Thothmes III. Confidently they advance to the foot of the throne, in the picture in the tomb of Rekhmara, led by their "Great Chief," a young man with fair face and small European mouth, — markedly small it appeared to the large-mouthed Egyptian who sketched him for the picture, — and followed by a darker and older man whose Roman nose and heavy jowl remind us strongly of an Italian type. Another, a young man, follows, who bears a sword in his hand as well as a great vase on his shoulder; and as he walks he looks back with open mouth to make some loud remark to the next man, much as a young Gothic ambassador might have guffawed in the presence of a Roman Caesar. All is represented to the life. These Minoans were no servile Semites or cowed negroes.

In another tomb we see depicted the arrival of a Phoenician merchant-ship at the Theban quay. She had sailed from Byblos or Tyre along the coast and then up the Nile to the capital, laden with such things as the Sidonian craftsmen could make then as well as in later days, and among them we see Mycenaean vases. Cretan ambassadors might bring treasures to give: Phoenician middlemen brought their commoner goods to sell.

The sepulchre of Thothmes III in the Valley of the Tombs of the Kings is not remarkable, but that of his son Amenhetep II is interesting in many ways. It is the first royal tomb in which the occupant was found lying in his funeral state as he was buried. And some bodies found lying in the tomb-chamber may be those of servants killed at the funeral in order that they might accompany the king to the next world.

The tomb of Thothmes IV was discovered by Mr. Theodore Davis in 1904: in it was found an embossed leather chariot-body, besides beautiful faience vases. This tomb was violated as early as the confusion of Akhenaten's reign, and restored by Horemheb, as we learn from a hieratic inscription on one of its walls.

Amenhetep III chose a different position for his tomb. He was buried not with the other princes of his house, but in the remoter "Western Valley," beneath a magnificent hill which rises as a natural pyramid above it: a fitting resting-place for the most imperial monarch of Egypt. Tii his wife may originally have been buried by Akhenaten at Tell el-Amarna, from which her body was removed to Thebes by Tutankhamen, who wished to place it with Akhenaten's in a small tomb in the Valley of the Tombs of the Kings, which had probably been made for a prince. The operation of removal was, however, effected in such haste and confusion that though Tii's catafalque, dedicated for her by Akhenaten, and her golden diadem were placed in the tomb, her body was either left behind at Tell el-Amarna or buried elsewhere at Thebes: the "canopic jars" and the coffin found with Tii's funeral furniture are apparently that of Akhenaten, and the human remains found are those of a man, apparently Akhenaten himself. The tomb resembles that of Tii's parents Iuaa and Tuiu, also discovered close by a few years ago by Mr. Theodore Davis and Mr. J. E. Quibell. Both are of the simpler type intended for princely personages. But very different in Iuaa and Tuiu's tomb was the scene that greeted the eyes of the discoverers from that which met them in that of Tii. Instead of utter confusion everything was found as it had been left by the undertakers. The father and mother of Tii lay in their gilded coffins surrounded by the state in which they had lived: splendidly upholstered chairs, gilt and silvered ushabti-figures, clothes and wig-boxes of reeds, even a perfectly preserved chariot, were placed with them for their use in the next world. We obtain from this funerary furniture a very complete idea of the magnificence and luxury of the court of Egypt in the time of Amenhetep III. Well might the Mitannian Dushratta say, "Gold is as the dust in thy land, my brother!"

6. The Reign of Amenhetep the Magnificent

It is true, however, that we do not obtain any idea of very great magnificence from the ruins of the Theban palace of Amenhetep III, which were excavated by Messrs. Newberry and Tytus some years ago, and have recently been re-examined by Messrs. Winlock and Evelyn White for the Metropolitan Museum of New York. All we see are the remains of mudbrick walls like those of any fellah's hovel, with a few white limestone column-bases here and there. These walls are however stuccoed, with the peeling remains of fine wall-paintings, including one of a bull galloping among flowers which reminds us of a Mycenaean fresco: and from the floor of one of the rooms a very beautiful painting of ducks and waterfowl has been happily removed to the Cairo Museum. This was a palace of mud, it is true, but it was beautifully decorated, and we must imagine it as a painted summer-house of cool passages and loggias, with light roofs upheld by carved wooden pillars on stone bases, and tent-like awnings of brightly coloured stuffs to keep off the sun, placed by the side of the great artificial lake of Tjarukha, on which Amenhetep and Til were wont to sail with their court in the golden barge Tehen-Aten "The Sun-Disk gleams."

But if Amenhetep had a more permanent palace in the city of Thebes itself, on the eastern bank of the river, it was probably hardly more substantial, and also built of mud-brick, like all the houses of ancient and modern Egypt. Stone was used for the temples of the gods alone. And for them Amenhetep erected houses the like of which Egypt had hardly seen before and was never to see again till the days of the Ptolemies. The great court of Luxor and the temple of Soleb shew how magnificent were the conceptions of Egyptian architects at this period, the apogee of Egyptian civilization and art; and did Amenhetep's funerary temple on the western bank at Thebes survive, we should probably deem it the most splendid temple in Egypt. But the stupid vandal Rameses II destroyed it to build his own "Ramesseum" with its stones, and nothing of it remains but the two huge Colossi which still sit in solitary state amid the waters of the inundation and the waving fields of millet, unchanging throughout the changing years, unchanging as Egypt, and still bearing mute witness to the imperial greatness of the third Amenhetep, "called by the Greeks Memnon."

An imperial magnificence it was, perhaps, rather than true greatness. Thothmes III had been really great: Amenhetep deserves rather the title of "The Magnificent," and he owed his magnificence to the greatness of his ancestor, who had made his empire for him. For, after his first campaign in the Sudan, we hear nothing of any warlike undertakings by the third Amenhetep, who spent his days in peace and in a luxury which, however, was an intelligent and art-loving luxury, in no way symptomatic of decadence in itself. Yet in the golden days of Amenhetep the Magnificent Egypt was beginning to decay. Unchallenged power, unexampled wealth and unbridled luxury worked for decay in an Eastern state whose great men heard no insistent summons to go forth to war. The courtiers of Amenhetep III were lovers of art and of beauty, probably they were men of intelligence and taste in matters literary as well as artistic, but they were not warriors. And an ancient state lacked that activity in scientific discovery and in mechanical invention which in modern states compensates largely for the comparative absence of the mental stimulus of war. The men who surrounded Hatshepsut, Thothmes III, and Amenhetep II had experienced this stimulus; their fathers and grandfathers had fought with Aahmes in the life-and-death struggle against the Hyksos: they themselves or their fathers had marched with Thothmes I in the enthusiasm of the first revenge upon Asia: they themselves were actors in the epopee of Thothmes the Great. We know them all, the aged Aahmes Pen-Nekhebet, Senmut and Hapuseneb the faithful to Hatshepsut, Thutii the taker of Joppa, Amenemheb the elephant-slayer, Rekhmara the great vizier, and Menkheperrasenb his son; and they were men of sterner stuff than their artistic and peaceful descendants who ministered to the luxury of

Amenhetep III or obsequiously acclaimed the mad genius of his son Akhenaten. Of them all only one stands out beyond the others, and he was an old man; the wise minister Amenhetep son of Hapu, who was venerated in later ages as a godlike sage, and whose venerable face still steadfastly regards us in its sculptured presentment, now in the Museum of Cairo. We may hope that the son of Hapu, who was probably born in the reign of Thothmes III, did not live to see the wreck of the empire which his father had perhaps helped to build. When he died, the last of the great men of the XVIIIth Dynasty passed away.

7. The Domination of Queen Tii and the Heresy of Akhenaten

His place was taken by the masterful Queen Tii, and an era of feminine influence ensued, directed from behind the curtains of the harem; a "regiment of women" very different from and far more harmful than the man-like rule of Hatshepsut from Pharaoh's own throne, "monstrous" though that may have been.

The son of Amenhetep III and Tii was no Egyptian warrior like his ancestors. Of mixed race, with, probably, the alien blood of Aryan Mitanni inherited from his father and of the wild desert tribes of the Beja or Ababdeh derived from his mother running in his veins as well as the ichor of the descendants of Ra, the son of a luxurious and art-loving father and of a clever and energetic mother, he was brought up under strong feminine influence. All the requisites for the creation of a striking and abnormal character were present. Amenhetep IV was a man of entirely original brain, untrammelled on account of his position by those salutary checks which the necessity of mixing with and agreeing with other men of lesser mental calibre imposes on those not born in the purple. His genius had full play. And the result was disaster. So insensate, so disastrous, was his obliviousness to everything else but his own "fads" in religion and art that we can well wonder if Amenhetep IV was not really half insane. Certainly his genius was closely akin to madness. Dithyrambs have been penned, especially of late years,! in praise of this philosophic and artistic reformer, "the first individual in ancient history." We might point out that others have an equal right to this characterization, for instance Khammurabi, Hatshepsut, or Thothmes III, or even the shadowy Urukagina. Certainly Akhenaten was the first doctrinaire in history, and, what is much the same thing, the first prig.

His religious heresy, the central fact of his reign, was not altogether his own idea. The veneration of the Aten, the disk of the sun, had been growing in court favour during his father's last years. Both Amenhetep III and Tii venerated the Aten as well as Amen-Ra and the other gods. Amenhetep III, as the son probably of a Mitannian mother, was half an Iranian, and may well have felt drawn towards a cult which resembled not remotely Iranian religion. But at the same time he gives us (also an Iranian trait) the impression of a tolerant and easy-going prince, and even if he believed privately that the Aten was the one real god, he would be the last to make enemies of the priests and plunge his country into civil war by publicly announcing his belief. His son was of a different spirit. The feminine cast of his character shewed itself at once in a reckless doctrinaire proclamation of a belief which could only be anathema to his less clever subjects, of an adhesion to a "principle" which admitted of no compromise even if it brought his kingdom about his ears and plunged the world in war, which it did. His reign lasted in all not more than eighteen years. If the body found in the "tomb of Tii" at Thebes be really his, he was not more than twenty-six or twenty-seven years old at the time of his death. So that he was a boy of eight or nine at his accession, four years before his father's death. Much of the extravagance that followed would probably have been avoided had his father lived longer, and been able to keep him in check. The influence of Tii, which must have been paramount during the first years of his reign, when she apparently acted as regent, can hardly have been wisely exercised.

At first the young Amenhetep IV was represented on the monuments in the conventional style of his forefathers. His real peculiarities of body (which was as strangely constituted as his brain) were ignored. Amen and the other gods are still officially worshipped by him five years after his father's death and his accession. In the thirteenth year of his age, probably, he was married to his sister Nefretiti, who evidently sympathized entirely with his ideas. Then came emancipation. In the sixth year of his reign, when he was presumably fifteen years old, and therefore fully a man in Egypt, he openly proclaimed his heresy, and the religious revolution was begun.

The young reformer proclaimed that the whole pantheon of Egypt, including even the mighty "King of the Gods" at Thebes, was a fiction, and that only one deity in reality existed, an unknown heavenly force which manifested itself to men through the medium of the visible disk of the sun, the Aten of Ra. This heretical doctrine (we do not know how far the king had improved upon the form in which it had been held previously by his father and his teachers) was a monotheism of a very high order. Amenhetep IV (or, as he now preferred to call himself, Akhenaten, "Pleasing to the Sun-Disk") did not, as has usually been supposed, worship merely the sun-disk itself as the giver of life. He venerated the glowing disk merely as the visible emanation of the Deity behind it, who dispersed heat and life to all living things through its medium. The disk was, so to speak, the window in heaven through which the unknown God, the "Lord of the Disk," shed a portion of his radiance upon the world. Given an ignorance of the true astronomical nature of the sun, this was an absolutely rational religion, differing toto mundo from the irrational congeries of irreconcilable superstitions which composed the national faith of Egypt. In effect, the sun is the source of all life upon this earth, and so Akhenaten caused its rays to be depicted each with a hand holding out the sign of life to the earth. But Akhenaten or his teachers went farther than a monotheistic worship of the sun itself. He saw behind the sun a Deity unnamed and unnameable, "the Lord of the Disk." We see in his heresy, therefore, the highest development of religious ideas before the days of the Hebrew prophets.

This, by decree of her ruler, was now to be the official religion of Egypt. Temples were erected to the Attn, to exemplify his character as the new supreme and only deity of the empire, not only in the capital, but also at Sesebi (and possibly Napata) in Nubia and at a place, possibly Jerusalem or Bethshemesh, in Palestine. These buildings bore the name of Gem-Aten, "Found-is-the-Disk"; the Palestinian town was shortly afterwards known as "Khinatuni," the same name as that of Akhenaten's later capital at Tell el-Amarna.

It may well be that the Heliopolitan heresy had been encouraged by Amenhetep in as a protest against the growing imperiousness and domination of the priests of Amen, who, enormously enriched by the donations of the earlier kings of the dynasty, and gorged with the lands, cattle, gold, and precious stones of Egypt, Asia, and Nubia, now bade fair to control the whole state. Akhenaten had the courage of his opinions, and by the founding of the Theban Gem-Aten declared open war upon Amen and his priests in their own city.

The result was curious. The difficulty of governing Thebes must have been enormous, and it may well be that the king was not safe from assassination there. He therefore combined discretion with valour by ostentatiously shaking the dust of Thebes from off his shoes, and proceeding to a new capital which should be free of Amen and his devotees. He would worship his god in his own way, and his court, as was fitting, should worship him too, in his way, in a spot uncontaminated by the previous presence of the absurd superstitions of his unenlightened ancestors. In a desert place, where the unregenerate did not exist, he would found a city called "Akhetaten," "Glory of the Disk," where he could teach his "doctrine" to willing hearers only; and hence the light of the Aten could be dispersed to those without who would listen. The city was founded in a spot north of Siut, where no town had previously been: the spot is the modern Tell el-Amarna. Here, where the desert-cliffs opened out on both sides of the river, the king made his Utopia, or rather Laputa, where he could philosophize, teach, and dally with the arts surrounded by his philosophers and artists, while the rest of his kingdom was left to itself, as far as he personally was concerned. For he marked its boundaries by great stelae carved on the rocks, on which he solemnly recorded his vow never to stir beyond the limits of his Laputa.

We can imagine the effect of these proceedings upon his people: the fury of the priests of Amen; the bitterness of the soldiers and statesmen who saw the work of a dynasty abandoned and thrown aside at the caprice of a boy; the amazement of the Asiatics at the news that the young Napkhurria had gone suddenly mad and had vowed never to stir out of his city for the defence of his empire; the resentment of the mass of the Egyptians, soon to crystallize into active hatred of the "criminal of Akhetaten." Yet no overt resistance was possible. The whole machinery of the state was in the king's hands, and his behests were obeyed by the royal officers, probably many of them convinced adherents of the "doctrine." The king's religion was for the moment the religion of the empire, and Amen was deposed from his imperial throne to make way for the Aten. The whole of the property of Amen was simply transferred to the new god, and the Theban priests were driven out or proscribed. The name of the king of the gods, whom Akhenaten abominated more than all the rest, since he was the arch-enemy of Aten, was ordered to be erased from all the monuments throughout the kingdom. This was done, not even the name of his own father, which contained that of the hated deity, being spared. The names of the other gods soon followed, and even the word "gods" was proscribed as denying the monotheism of the imperial faith.

Yet a king cannot abolish a national religion by decree, although he may obliterate the names of its gods from their temples, and this fact must soon have been learnt by Akhenaten. We do not know the details of the story, but for the last few years of his reign Thebes must have been in more or less open revolt, no doubt under the leadership of Amen's high-priest, whom the king did not recognize as existing. Administrative anarchy must have resulted throughout the South. It was perhaps this revolt of Thebes that in the twelfth year of the reign drove the queen-mother Tii to take up her residence in her son's city, where, probably not long afterwards, she died. In the North, however, less purely Egyptian in feeling, and in no way really bound to the worship of the Theban god, hardly seeing in the Aten-worship much more than a peculiar form of the worship of the Heliopolitan Ra, no revolt probably took place at all. Although the king would not go forth to save Syria for Egypt, his communications with the Asiatic provinces were never severed, as we see from the unbroken series of letters from the Canaanite chiefs and governors preserved in the archives of Tell el-Amarna. The preservation of the royal authority in the North was also in all probability largely due to the energy of its military governor, Horemheb, whom we shall meet with later as king. He was not a monotheistic Aten-worshipper, but served the king well nevertheless.

Foiled by the dispossessed priests of Amen in his attempt to abolish them and their god utterly, the king finally abandoned his empire to go its own way, while he lived his own life with his family and court in the city which he had created. Many of his courtiers no doubt really believed in the new religion, but others, as we see from the readiness with which they abandoned it after his death, never really believed in it, but only conformed to it because it was the king's religion. They were required to worship the Aten with the king, and to accept from him tombs in the cliffs behind Tell el-Amarna, where they, like their king, should be buried when they died. We know the names of many of these courtiers from the inscriptions on their tombs. Chief among them were Rames, the vizier; Merira, the high-priest of the new god, the most favoured of all; Hui, the chief of the harem; Mahu, the chief of police; Tutu, who is mentioned in the Tell el-Amarna letters; and Ai, who eventually for a short time occupied the throne of Egypt. The king's architect and chief sculptor, Bek, "whom the king himself taught," is also mentioned in the tombs. To him was entrusted the execution of the beautiful reliefs which are the chief feature of these tombs, and he carried them out in accordance with the new ideas of freedom and naturalism in art which accompanied the new religion.

It will be noticed that Akhenaten's religion did not demand that the Egyptians should give up their ancient burial-customs. It is somewhat uncertain whether the name of Osiris was or was not actually proscribed as were those of the other gods. Probably the belief in Osiris was restrained to the simple idea that every dead man became an Osiris, while the Aten received the funerary prayer. If it had been deemed necessary to give up the old ideas as to the constitution of the soul, mummification would no longer have been considered necessary. Possibly Akhenaten never clearly formulated his ideas on this subject. As of old, the life of the dead man on earth was represented on the walls of the Tell el-Amarna tombs, and as the life of a courtier at Akhetaten centred in the king and his consort, we find them the central figures of these pictures, represented as they really appeared, with their children, driving in public, or (a favourite scene) appearing on the balcony of the palace, from which they lean to throw necklaces of honour over the heads of favoured officers, while the court bows down before them. The bizarre naturalism of these representations, grafted on to the traditional methods of Egyptian art, reminds us strongly of the same trait in the contemporary Mycenaean art of Greece, by which Bek and his fellow-craftsmen may have been influenced to a considerable extent.

During the reign of Amenhetep III the art of sculpture in relief had developed considerably. In tombs, when the rock was suitable, the place of wall-paintings was taken by reliefs. The outline of many of these was executed en creux in a new and characteristic style, very different from the delicate low relief of Der el-Bahri or the work of Thothmes III at Karnak. Under Amenhetep III we find the delicate low relief used for tombs, as in the sepulchre of Khaemhat at Thebes. At Memphis we find a fine example of the new style of cavo rilievo, in the tomb of a high-priest of Ptah, in which we see the funeral procession admirably represented: the abandon of the two weeping sons who immediately follow the bier contrasts well with the sympathetic dignity and solemnity of the great officials representing the king, who come next. In this relief we have the first sign of the naturalism and fidelity to truth that is characteristic of the work of Akhenaten's sculptors, as we see it in the tombs of Tell el-Amarna. The king always speaks in his inscriptions of his adherence to "truth" with an emphasis worthy of Darius the Persian. He wished everything and everybody, including himself, to be represented as they really were. And Bek and Tuti, the sculptors whom he taught, took him at his word. In the relief of Tell el-Amarna, executed in the new style en creux, we see the king represented in what must be almost a caricature of his facial and bodily peculiarities. Probably he liked these peculiarities to be so exaggerated; his already long nose and chin to be made longer, his belly to be represented as pendulous, his legs as bowed. The contrast to the ancient idealized representations of the kings would thus be accentuated. That in reality he was not (at any rate at first) so ugly as he is represented to have been by Bek seems to be shewn by another representation of him, a remarkable little relief picture in the Berlin Museum, which is the finest known specimen of the art of Tell el-Amarna. Here we see the king, represented as a by no means ungracefully shaped young man, with a not unpleasing face, which is evidently a faithful portrait, standing with his legs crossed and leaning negligently upon a staff, while Nefertiti his wife, with her garments blown about by the wind, offers her lord a bunch of flowers to smell. The streamers of the king's wig and of his dress, like the queen's robe, fly in the wind. From the mere description it will be seen how very different is this sculptured picture from the ordinarily accepted ideas of Egyptian conventions in art. In it we see what the Egyptian artist shewed promise of doing, once these conventions were abandoned. There is some crudity in the figure of the queen, and the whole picture is bizarre: but the king's figure could hardly have been bettered by a Greek: the pose, and especially the treatment of the legs and sandalled feet, is quite Greek, and reminds one of a Hermes. Bek dealt as faithfully with the queen as with her spouse. Both seem to have resembled their mother Tii, who was of much the same Bishari or Abadeh type. The six daughters with whom they were blessed (for Akhenaten had no son to carry on his doctrine) are all represented with the same type of countenance, which is natural, but it is by no means natural that many of the courtiers should, as they do, shew in the reliefs a decided approximation to the same degenerate type. Probably fashion decreed that convinced adherents of the doctrine should be made to ape the countenance and figure, as well as the religion, of their royal teachers, whom the true courtier would vow to be the mirrors of all beauty as well as truth.

It is on the walls of these tombs, too (for they were spared as inviolable houses of the dead when the temples of the Aten were destroyed), that we read the beautiful hymns to the sun-disk that were composed by the poet-king himself. Their phraseology is strangely reminiscent of that of Psalm civ. "When thou," he sings in honour of the Aten, "settest in the horizon of heaven, the world is in darkness like the dead. . . . Every lion cometh forth from his den; all serpents, they sting; Darkness reigns, the world is in silence. He that made them has gone to rest in his horizon.

"Bright is the Earth when thou risest in the horizon.
When thou shinest as Aten by day, the darkness is banished.
When thou sendest forth thy rays, the Two Lands rejoice daily,
Awake and standing upon their feet, for thou hast raised them up.
Their limbs bathed, they take their clothing;
Their arms uplifted in adoration to thy dawning;
Then in all the world, they do their work.

The ships sail upstream and downstream,
Every road is open because thou hast dawned.
The fish in the river leap up before thee,
And thy rays are in the midst of the great sea.
Thou art he who Greatest the man-child in woman,
Who makest seed in man.
Who giveth life to the son in the body of his mother,
Who soothest him that he may not weep,
A nurse even in the womb.
Who giveth breath to animate every one that he maketh.
When he cometh forth from the body.
On the day of his birth,
Thou openest his mouth in speech,
Thou suppliest his needs.

When the fledgeling crieth in the egg,
Thou givest him breath therein, to preserve him alive.
When thou hast perfected him
That he may pierce the egg-shell,
He cometh forth from the egg,
To chirp with all his might;
He runneth about upon his two feet,
When he hath come forth therefrom.

How manifold are all thy works!

They are hidden from us.
O thou only god, whose powers no other possesseth;
Thou didst create the earth according to thy desire.

Thou art in my heart: there is none other that knoweth thee
Save thy son Akhenaten.
Thou hast made him wise in thy designs and in thy might.

The king, living in truth, the lord of the Two Lands Neferkheperura
Uanra,
The son of Ra, living in truth, the crowned lord,
Akhenaten, living for ever;
And for the Great King's Wife whom he loveth, the mistress of the Two
Lands,
Neferneferuaten Nefretiti, who liveth for ever."

Alas for the poet-king! His kingdom had already fallen into anarchy, and the foreign empire which his predecessors had built up had been thrown to the winds in his pursuit of his beautiful ideal. How, we shall see later. The whole story is an example of the confusion and disorganization which, pace Plato, always ensue when a philosopher rules. Not long after the heretic's early death the old religion was fully restored, the cult of the disk was blotted out, and the Egyptians returned joyfully to the worship of their myriad deities. Akhenaten's ideals were too high for them. The debris of the foreign empire was, as usual in such cases, put together again, and customary, conventional law and order restored by the stupid, conservative reactionaries who succeeded him. Henceforward Egyptian civilization ran an uninspired and undeveloping course till the days of the Saites and the Ptolemies.

8. The Successors of Akhenaten (c. 1362-1321 B.C.)
Akhenaten died young, and probably insane, after a reign of some eighteen years (circa 1380-1362 B.C.). His body was buried in a tomb at Tell el-Amarna, whence, as we have seen, it was by some confusion substituted for that of his mother Tii, also buried at Tell el-Amarna, when Tutankhamen wished to transfer her mummy to Thebes. The confusion was probably due to hasty transport, hurried for fear of some fanatical attack upon the bodies of the heretical rulers.

His successor, Smenkhkara, was an ephemeral appearance. In all probability he did not reign more than two or three years, as the highest date we possess of him is year 2, The twelve years assigned to him by Prof Petrie on the supposed authority of Manetho can hardly be accepted without further confirmation. He ascended the throne as the son-in-law and creature of Akhenaten: he had married the princess Meritaten, and was evidently a convinced adherent of the doctrine. On N the faience finger-rings of his time, bearing the names of the monarchs, he is often called "the beloved of Akhenaten," who had associated him in the kingship not long before his death. Smenkhkara was succeeded by a monarch of whom we have greater knowledge, Nebkheperura Tutankhamen. As this king's name shews, it was in his reign that the episode of the Aten-heresy finally died out, and the monarch and court returned to their allegiance to the great god of Thebes. The new king ascended the throne as an Atenite: he called himself Tutankhaten, "the living image of Aten." His wife was Ankhsenpaaten, "Her life belongeth to the Aten," and she was the third daughter of Akhenaten and Nefretiti. Tutankhaten himself was probably a son of Amenhetep III by an inferior wife: when he restored the lions of Soleb (now in the British Museum) he called Amenhetep his father. So that he had a claim to the throne resembling that of Thothmes III. Not long after his accession it became evident that the Aten-heresy was dead, and so both the king and queen formally returned to the national religion, changing their names to Tutankhamen and Ankhsenamen. A proof of the reality of their conversion was an attempt to complete the magnificent colonnade leading out of the halls of Amenhetep III in the temple of Amen at Luxor. The Theban temple of Aten was now demolished, and its materials were used to build walls to enclose the colonnade, which, originally intended by Amenhetep III to be the nave of a great hypostyle hall, had remained unfinished since the death of its founder. Horemheb completed the enclosure of Tutankhamen, and hence the whole building has usually been known as the "Colonnade of Horemheb."

The poverty-stricken nature of the work undertaken, the abandonment of the grandiose plan of Amenhetep III, shews what Akhenaten's revolution had done for the wealth of Egypt. Akhenaten's abandonment of the Asiatic Empire had proved a severe blow to the Amen-priesthood and to Thebes. He could have aimed no more effective blow at Amen than this; and we may indeed see some explanation of his otherwise incredible policy in the fact that the priesthood of Amen was identified with the policy of expansion and conquest on which its wealth largely depended.

However this may be, no sooner had Tutankhamen given his submission to Amen than an attempt was made to reconquer some part of Southern Palestine, with what success we do not know.

The reign of Tutankhamen can hardly have lasted a decade; that of Ai, his successor, probably not more than five years. This Ai had been a priestly official, an iot neter or "god's father," at Akhet-aten, and had married the lady Ti, who was "the great royal nurse, pleasing the good god" Akhenaten. At Tell el-Amarna Ai and Ti were given a splendid tomb, in which they naturally were never buried. Ai was placed upon the throne after the death of Tutankhamen (although he was of no kin to the royal house), and so, when he died, was buried in a royal tomb in the Western Theban valley.

In all probability Ai owed his position to the powerful "mayor of the palace," Horemheb, who succeeded him as king. It has been supposed that Ai made a futile attempt to restore the religion of the Aten; if so, his short reign may have ended in his deposition by Horemheb, who was a fanatical devotee of Amen.

With Horemheb the XVIIIth Dynasty comes to an inglorious end. Prof. Breasted reckons him rather as the first king of the XIXth Dynasty than the last of the XVIIIth, on the ground that he was in no way really related to the kings of the latter dynasty. But we have no right to depart from the tradition of Manetho, who makes him, as Harmais, the last monarch of the XVIIIth Dynasty. We have no knowledge that he was related to Rameses I, who is usually considered as the first king of the XIXth Dynasty, and there is an absolute break in type of name as well as in many other things between him, and his son Seti, and Horemheb. Also Rameses I definitely marks himself as the founder of a new dynasty by imitating in his throne-name or prenomen, Men-peliti-Ra, the form adopted by Aahmes, the founder of the preceding dynasty, Neb-pehti-Ra? So that Manetho's statement is clearly confirmed. Further, Horemheb did ally himself with the preceding dynasty by marrying the princess Mutnetjemet, a sister of Akhenaten and Nefretiti. If we are to begin the XIXth Dynasty with the first king who was in no way connected with the old royal family, we should begin it with Ai.

Horemheb is a dull and uninteresting figure in Egyptian history. He was a soldier, with some organizing ability, but devote and rigidly conservative. He was not a Theban, but a native of the town of Alabastronpolis in Middle Egypt. He rose to high office in Northern Egypt, not at Thebes, and seems to have carried on a military administration of the North under Akhenaten, in succession to the viceroy Yankhamu who is mentioned in the Tell el-Amarna letters. In the necropolis of Sakkara he built a tomb for himself while still simply Commander-in-Chief, in which, while loyally giving thanks to the king for his favours, he resolutely ignores the royal heresy. Probably he was so powerful that it was impossible to interfere with him in religious matters. Under Tutankhamen he seems to have become the real ruler of the country, a sort of Mayor of the Palace, and, as has been said, to him Ai probably owed his elevation to the throne. In the inscription which he afterwards set up at Thebes to commemorate his coronation he states that he was appointed (probably by Tutankhamen) as "Regent of the Land, to administer the laws of the Two Lands as hereditary prince of all this land: he was alone, without a peer. . . . When he was summoned before the king, the court began to fear." This is a somewhat significant statement as to his relations with the court, which was no doubt the sole refuge of Atenism. He represented orthodoxy, and his work was to restore it, with the active aid of the priests of Amen. So that when the reign of Ai had come to an end, and, in the words of his inscription, he had "administered the Two Lands during a period of many years," and had earned (in literal phrase) the title of "Father of his Country," the priests of Amen summoned him to the vacant throne: Horus, his god, lord of Alabastronpolis, led him to Thebes into the presence of Amen, "who assigned to him his office of king, therein to pass his life." The legitimizing marriage with Mutnetjemet followed, and the counter-revolution was consummated.

The new king's mandate from Amen and from the whole people was peaceful regeneration. We have proof of his reconstructive work in the code of revised laws which he promulgated on a stele in the temple of Karnak. These laws are mostly petty regulations of police, shewing that during the carnival of political degeneration under Akhenaten law and order had almost disappeared: the anarchy of Palestine had spread in minor matters to Egypt. Only in the North, where the soldier Horemheb had ruled, probably with extraordinary and, as we should say, "unconstitutional" powers, which he had assumed himself, was there a proper government at all. Then, when, after the death of the "Criminal," the ruler of the North had assumed a virtual regency, and more definitely when he had ascended the throne, was the civil organization of the kingdom restored by "the Father of his Country." The provisions of the new regulations are phrased prosaically enough, as we should expect from their author, and the punishment of evil-doers is for most offences the same simple but no doubt efficacious one of cutting off their noses and exiling them to Tjaru, on the desert-border of Asia.

Horemheb's reign was wholly taken up by this uneventful reorganization. Judging from the date of the 59th year recorded in the Papyrus of Mes, already mentioned, it would seem to have been of extraordinary length. But it is obviously quite impossible that a man who was commander-in-chief under Akhenaten can have reigned for sixty years after the death of Ai. Therefore it is evident that, at any rate in the later years of his life, Horemheb's hatred of the Disk-worshippers, even when they had recanted their heresy, was so great that he ignored their reigns, and counted his own from the death of Amenhetep III. This is confirmed by the fact that Akhenaten and his three successors are ignored in the official lists of Seti I at Abydos, set up little more than half a century after their reigns, and by the reference in the Papyrus of Mes to Akhenaten as no king but as "that Wicked One of Akhetaten." At the beginning of his reign Horemheb did not yet ignore his predecessors, but certainly up to his seventh year, and perhaps longer, counted his years as beginning with his real accession. Later on, the complete victory of orthodoxy resulted in the heretical period being considered officially as never having existed. If we count the reigns of Akhenaten's three successors as having amounted to twenty years in all, we see that Horemheb's real reign was one of considerable length, having lasted about twenty-two years. He is not likely to have reigned beyond his sixtieth nominal year, when, about 1321 B.C., he died, a very old man, and was succeeded by the founder of the XIXth Dynasty, Men-pehti-Ra Rameses I.

9. The XIXth Dynasty

Rameses I was, as Manetho says, the founder of an entirely new dynasty, which had no connexion of any kind with the kings who had gone before. The name of Rameses's son Seti, the devotion of many of his descendants to the worship of Ptah, and the predilection of Rameses II for the Delta, where he preferred to reside, point to a Lower Egyptian origin for the family. Thebes continued to be the national capital on account of the predominance of the priests of Amen and the associations of the city with the imperial idea, revived by Seti I and Rameses II. Therefore Manetho calls the new dynasty Theban, though in all probability it was really of Memphite origin. This being so, it is highly probable that Rameses 1 was not a relation of Horemheb, who came from Alabastronpolis, but one of his old assistants or companions-in-arms, whom he had met while military governor-general of the North at Memphis under Akhenaten. Such a man would naturally have the reversion of the supreme power after the death without issue of his old chief, by whose side he had doubtless served all his life. This probability would make Rameses an elderly, if not an old, man at his accession, and his very short reign of not more than two years confirms this idea. His successor was his son Seti, who was a middle-aged man when his father died. By his time the tangle left by Aknenaten at home had finally been straightened out, and the new king, a man of vigour and military talent, was ready to essay the task of restoring the foreign empire which the philosopher had lost. To do this, Egypt had resolutely to attack and if possible defeat the formidable kingdom of the Hittites, which had engineered the Canaanite revolt against her, and was now exercising dominion over the greater part of the territories that had once been hers. With the march of Seti the First into Palestine to do battle with Mursil the Hittite, the history of the Second Egyptian Empire begins.

The story of the long and exhausting campaigns of Seti's son, Rameses II, with the Hittites will be read in the next chapter. Having achieved the defeat of Mursil, and recovered Palestine for Egypt, Seti desisted from war, and found a worthy expression for his energies in furthering and directing the restoration of the prosperity of his kingdom, now slowly recovering from the effects of the Atenist inferno. Temple-building occupied much of his time and fitly marked the loyalty of the new dynasty to the gods. A new departure was inaugurated in building a great royal funerary temple at Abydos, where the earliest kings had either been buried or had erected cenotaphs. To express veneration for the most ancient kings, and to proclaim the solidarity of the new dynasty with those that had preceded it, the temple was built, and on its walls we see Seti and his son Rameses offering to the name-cartouches of the imperial ancestors back to the legendary Mena, the supposed founder of the monarchy. This is the "List of Abydos," which is so important a document for the historian of Egypt. The temple itself is of very unusual plan, and from the architectural point of view is not of great beauty. In contrast, however, to the architecture, the sculptured reliefs with which the walls are decorated are of the greatest beauty and delicacy, and mark the zenith of Egyptian art in this type of work. It was, so to speak, the swan-song of the splendid art of the XVIIIth Dynasty that was sung by the artists of Abydos. We know their names, Hui and Amenuahsu. The other work of the reign was not good. The funerary temple begun by Seti in memory of his father at Thebes is poor. At Karnak the world-famous Hypostyle Hall, begun by Rameses I, mainly carried out by Seti, and completed by Rameses II, is heavy, majestic, magnificent, but it is not beautiful.

The Theban buildings emphasize the continued devotion of the new rulers to Amen, but since they were of Northern (and probably specifically of Memphite) origin, the worship of Ptah, the ancient god of Memphis, came under them once more into fashion. At the same time Set, the desert-god, who had been associated with Lower Egypt since the time of the Hyksos, who had made him their chief deity, shared with Ptah the devotion of the royal family, at any rate in the Delta. During the XVIIIth Dynasty his worship was unpopular, and except at Ombos, where he had always received special veneration, he seems in Upper Egypt to have been proscribed henceforth for all time. In the Delta, however, this was not the case. There is good reason to suppose that the expulsion of the Hyksos was not as complete as the official accounts of the Thebans would have had us believe. Many of the foreigners doubtless remained behind in the land of Goshen, where the ancient fortress capital of Salatis still stood, and we cannot doubt that in the course of the four centuries which had elapsed since their invasion they had considerably modified the religion as well as the blood of the Delta Egyptians. So we find Set in his Asiatic Sutekh-like aspect, akin on the one side to Resheph of the Canaanites and on the other to Teshub of the Hittites (with whom he was directly identified), as the chief god of the Northern Egyptians and giving his name to the first king of the new Northern dynasty. The Set-worship was abandoned by the kings of the next dynasty, who were Theban in sentiment, which Seti I and Rameses II certainly were not.

The new Northern kings made their chief home in the North — Seti at Memphis, Rameses at Tanis. Thebes was probably in a dismantled condition after the ravages of Akhenaten's reign, and did not fully recover its old prosperity for some time. Both Seti and Rameses built largely at Thebes, it is true, and were buried there like their predecessors, but for most of the time they ruled they never went there except to dedicate spoil to Amen, the official head of the imperial pantheon, in his own city.

For military reasons, also, royal residence in the Delta was preferable. If the Asiatic empire was to be retained even in its diminished extent, and the threatening power of the Hittites warded off from Egypt, it was best that the king should reside near the frontier. From this time dates a new dualism in the Egyptian state, in which Tanite (Bubastite) and Theban elements are to struggle for the mastery just as in the old days Memphis had struggled with Thebes,

The reign of Seti I probably lasted about twenty years (circa 1320-1300 B.C.). This date is rendered necessary if the astronomical date for the birth of Rameses II given by his horoscope (1318 B.C.) is correctly calculated, as Rameses can hardly have been more than eighteen years old when he ascended the throne. And it agrees with that of 1321-13 18 for Rameses II (Menophres).

Rameses II, who ascended the throne under the title of User-ma-Ra Setep-n-Ra Rameses Meri-Amen, was neither the eldest son nor, probably, the destined successor of Seti. The name of the original crown-prince we do not know, as it and his figure seem to have been destroyed carefully or replaced by the jealous Rameses whenever they occurred on the monuments. The actual successor, who thus supplanted his elder brother or half-brother, was destined to enjoy one of the longest reigns in Egyptian history, and partly on that account to hand down to posterity so exaggerated an idea of the importance of that reign that he has until lately been commonly dubbed by the moderns "Rameses the Great," thus usurping an honorific which may fitly be conceded to Thothmes III, but is in no way deserved by Rameses II.

The name of Rameses II bulks largely in Egypt. It is impossible to get away from it for long. Hardly a temple but has been "restored" or otherwise spoilt by him, hardly a statue of a preceding king that has not been partially or wholly usurped by him. Whenever an opportunity offered itself the name of Usermara Setepenra was set up. His most important building was a gigantic usurpation, being erected, apparently, with the stones of the splendid funerary temple of Amenhetep III. This was his own funerary temple, the Ramesseum, which still in Roman days was described by Diodorus Siculus as "the Tomb of Osymandyas" (User-ma-Ra, or "Uashmuariya," as the Semites called him). Strabo named it the "Memnonium," on account of its nearness to the great statues of Amenhetep III, who had long been identified with the Homeric Memnon, owing to a fancied resemblance between his name Men-ma-Ra and that of the Ethiopian hero. Diodorus specially mentions the Osiride figures of one of the courts (though he errs in stating that they were monolithic), the black granite statues, and one, which can hardly be other than the huge red granite colossus which now lies broken upon the ground, "the greatest of all in Egypt," though we know it never bore the inscription which he assigns to it: "Osymandyas the king of kings am I: if any one wisheth to know what kind of man I am and where I lie, let him beat one of my works!" Such an inscription, typical of those put into the mouths of Egyptian kings by the informants of the Greek writers, is perhaps possible under Senusert III, but never appeared on any Egyptian monument of the Ramesside period.

The pylon-walls of the Ramesseum served as a canvas on which the king's artists could depict, on a scale and with a detail never previously attempted, the heroic events of his war with the Hittites, the battle of Kadesh, and the siege of Dapur. A little rock-temple at Beit el-Wali is adorned with reliefs depicting a Nubian war, which seems to have taken place in the second year of the king's reign. In his first year he seems to have conducted a similar razzia against the Libyans of the Oases. The great war with the Hittites began in the fifth year (about 1295 B.C.), and lasted, on and off, till the conclusion of peace, more than fifteen years later (about 1279 B.C.).

This struggle, which left both combatants terribly weakened, was the turning-point of Egyptian history, which henceforth is a story of decline, which energetic monarchs like Rameses III and Shishak could do nothing to arrest. Rameses "the Great" had drained the strength of Egypt, and we see in the decadence of art and of general morale during the last century of the imperial period which followed his reign how exhausted the nation was, only three hundred years after the time of the heroes who expelled the Hyksos and founded the empire.

With the events of this period after his death (about 1234 B.C.) and the accession of his son Meneptah, the first of the weak and incapable monarchs of the decadence, we shall deal in the next chapter. But the main characteristics of the time may fitly be dealt with here.

10. Egypt under the Second Empire

Ramesside Egypt presents characteristic contrasts to the Egypt of the First Empire. The Atenist convulsion had torn the national mind to fragments, and when the fragments reunited they did not join precisely as they had been before. Egypt was as a man whose brain has temporarily given way: he regains his right mind, but he is not his old self. So Egypt was never again her old self. Externally XIXth-Dynasty Egypt may seem to resemble XVIIIth Dynasty Egypt closely enough, but if we look beneath the surface we see that in many respects the Egypt of Hatshepsut or Thothmes III was more like that of the Senuserts and Amenemhats than like that of the Ramessides. The XIIth Dynasty would have understood the XVIIIth: the XIXth, still more the XXth, would have seemed strange to it and, pre-eminently, foreign. The XVIIth-XVIIIth Dynasty was directly continuous with the XIIIth and preserved many of the traditions of the Middle Kingdom: to the people of Upper Egypt the Hyksos invasion had not been so catastrophic as the Atenist revolution proved to be. Although the language was changing with the lapse of time, the chanceries of the XVIIIth Dynasty retained the official phraseology of the XIIth. The cult of reality which was introduced by Akhenaten had one permanent result in the modernization of the written language. Official inscriptions now contained colloquial, almost slangy, expressions, which would have horrified the purists of the preceding dynasty. The ordinary colloquial mode of speech was reproduced in the monumental inscriptions. Laxity in phraseology was accompanied by laxity in inscription: under the XIXth Dynasty the sign-cutters first began to do poor and careless work on a large scale. The hieroglyphs, too, alter in appearance, becoming jejune and elongated: there is little possibility of mistaking an inscription of the XIXth Dynasty for one of the XVIIIth. In art, the naturalism of Akhenaten's time had its effect, and produced, among other results, the extraordinary battle-scenes with which the Rameses loved to cover whole temple-pylons, as at the Ramesseum. Rameses III's picture-record of the Defeat of the Northerners on the outer walls of Medinet Habu is in no way inferior in this regard to the Kadesh-reliefs of Rameses II. In these reliefs is well seen the style of sculpture in sunk relief (cavo rilievo) which now first makes its appearance on the grand scale, and is characteristic of the art of the Later Empire. A magnificent piece of naturalism in portraiture is the famous Turin statue of Rameses II, in which the monarch, then young, is represented in a loose dress of semi-state, such as no king had ever been depicted wearing since the archaic period. This, however, and the reliefs at Abydos, are too good to be regarded as typical Ramesside works of art. The degenerate results of the Atenist naturalism were usually allied to carelessness and bad work, which became usual in the lethargic later years of Rameses II, and may be considered characteristically Ramesside.

In other arts besides architecture and sculpture this long reign marked a decline. One sees a progressive degeneration of taste in the decoration of the tombs and in the workmanship of the small objects of art, the scarabs and jewellery. The reign of Rameses III seems to shew a momentary revival of art in the fine polychrome reliefs of faience which decorated the royal palace at Tell el-Yahudiya, and the design of the entrance-gate of Medinet Habu is certainly remarkable. But the inner courts of that temple shew heavy work, sausage-like columns and enormous hieroglyphs, deeply cut and hideous, which exhibit a terrible lack of taste. All the old style and dignity have gone.

Medinet Habu is by far the best work of the XXth Dynasty. Of the later kings we have practically no monuments of art but their tombs and those of their courtiers, and these are often decorated with a meretricious and vulgar taste that offends the eye. Growing poverty of idea accompanying poverty of purse is the chief characteristic of the later Ramesside period, after the collapse which followed the death of Rameses III.

The reinforcement of foreign blood and foreign ideas that empire had brought into Egypt did nothing to retard the decline of the nation: in fact, it hastened this process by introducing a confused hotchpotch of exotic ideas, as well as exotic blood, which, far from improving the national spirit, vitiated it and weakened it. The Delta was naturally far more overrun by foreign immigrants than the Upper country, and since Tanis, the de facto capital, was in the Delta, it was in the chief city of the kingdom and the residence of king and court that the foreign influences were most evident and did most harm. Semites and Iranians from the East and from Asia Minor, Mediterranean Greeks of Cyprus and the Aegean, Italians even, besides the half-barbarous Libyans from the West, crowded Tanis, Memphis, and the other cities of the Delta, and even Thebes had its foreign population. Some were slaves attached to the court of the king or the households of the great, some were warriors, others were merchants. In the reign of Rameses III we find many of the king's personal attendants foreigners: in the report of the trial of persons accused of conspiracy in the royal harem, among the judges are mentioned the cupbearers: Kedendenna, probably a Libyan or Northerner; Pirsun, also a foreigner; and Maharbaal, an obvious Phoenician; while among the accused was a Libyan named Inini. The warriors were mercenaries, chiefly Shardina, who were taken into the Egyptian service at the time of the Palestinian revolt, and since then had lived in the country, probably in camps in the Delta. Already in Meneptah's reign we find victory over the Libyans hailed partly because it allowed the mercenaries to lie down in the shade and do nothing, and in the Harris Papyrus Rameses III says proudly, detailing his good works: "I made the foot-soldiers and the chariotry to dwell (in their homes) in my time; the Shardina and the Kahak (Libyan mercenaries) stayed in their villages, lying full length on their backs; they feared nothing, for there was no enemy from Kush or from Syria. Their bows and their weapons reposed in their magazines, while they were satisfied and drunk with joy. Their wives were with them, their children at their side."

Despite this idyllic picture, the evils that would result from this mingling of unemployed and degenerating mercenaries with the people can be imagined.

With all these foreigners came their languages and their gods. New locutions, chiefly of Semitic origin, therefore became common in Egyptian mouths, and new gods, also mostly Semitic or at any rate Canaanitish, demanded worship from the votaries of Amen and of Ra. The Egyptian kings might erect temples to Amen or to the Aten in Canaan (Rameses III was the last to do so, as he was the last who had the power), to which the Syrians were bound to bow down, but the Syrian gods — Resheph, Baal, Kedeshet, Anaitis, and the rest — revenged themselves by filching from Amen and his peers much of their worship in Egypt.

The growing weakness and decadence shewed itself in the increasing insecurity of the country. A vizier revolted in the reign of Rameses III. The viziers had little but police duties to perform, and very badly they seem to have performed them, to judge from the tale of the tomb-robberies in the time of Rameses IX. The actual policing of Thebes was performed under their supervision by negroes of the tribe of the Matjoi, which seems to have been transplanted to Thebes and provided a sort of hereditary professional slave-police for the capital, rather like the Scythians at Athens. We know from the proces-verbaux of the trials of the tomb-robbers that in the judge's seat by the side of the vizier sat the High-Priest of Amen with another priest, besides two of the king's courtiers or cup-bearers, one of whom was his herald or sheriff, one military officer, one civil officer, and the mayor of the city. This was a sufficiently representative court; but though the vizier presides over the court, it is evident that the days of his absolute power and pre-eminence as the king's representative are gone. No priests had sat by his side in the time of the XVIIIth Dynasty, but now we may be sure that both he and the king's herald deferred in everything to the priests who had usurped seats on the bench, and that no decision would have been given, or if given would have been carried out, with which the High-Priest of Amen did not concur.

Of the growth of the priestly power, which under the XXth Dynasty reached its apogee, and of its decline, we shall speak later. Under the priest kings of the XXIst the powerlessness of Amen and of his ministers to rule the country was evident to all, and no doubt the deposition of the last priest-king and the reunion of the kingdom under the descendant of a Libyan mercenary of the Tanites was welcomed even at Thebes, especially since the Bubastites were politic enough to keep the worship of the "king of the gods" always in the forefront of the official religion. But he was no longer a real king of the gods of a whole kingdom, much less of an empire that had ceased to exist, and no longer commanded any special devotion except in his own city. Gradually in the popular religion of the rest of the country he became identified with Osiris, the god of the dead, whom he had eclipsed, and so the ancient deities came back to their own.

The dominance of the priest was accompanied by that of the scribe, and by the subservience of the soldier. Reverence for letters went hand in hand, as usual and ever unjustly, with contempt for the military profession. In this regard Ramesside Egypt reminds us not distantly of China. Priestly scribes, writing for the instruction of their pupils, deride the misery of the soldier who has always to be on guard on the desert frontier, or the wretched life of the mohar or royal messenger who is always restlessly wandering amid the dangers of foreign parts. This is often the tone of the pundit in an unmilitary nation, as the Egyptians really were and are, in spite of the deeds which they had once performed under the overmastery of the idea of revenge upon Asia. That impulse exhausted, the reaction was intense, and the scribes were now well in train to reduce the Egyptians to the condition of a nation guarded and ruled by foreigners, which they finally entered under the XXIInd Dynasty, and in which they have remained ever since.

In itself, however, the literary activity of the Ramesside period is very interesting. It was perhaps an activity of copyists rather than of authors, but to this copying we owe most of the monuments of ancient Egyptian literature that we possess. And it is a literature, for we have Egyptian love-poetry and novels as well as didactic and religious papyri. The love-songs are often very beautiful, and their imagery is strongly reminiscent of that of the "Song of Solomon," the Egyptian character of which is very striking. The novels and wonder-tales are equally Oriental, and the obvious parallel to them of the "Thousand Nights and a Night" is by no means far-fetched. The religious papyri are chiefly the work of the confraternity of Amen, and in them we see an organized attempt to exalt Amen at the expense of the other deities of the land. The henotheistic hymns in which the Theban deity is celebrated are often very fine in thought and diction: the example of Akhenaten's hymns to the Aten was by no means lost. And from the inscriptions which cover the walls of the royal tombs of this epoch we learn that the ancient chapters of the "Book of Coming Forth from the Day" into the night of the tomb (the "Book of the Dead," as we call it) were largely supplanted as guides to the next world by two compilations of the priests of Amen called "The Book of the Gates" (of the underworld) and "The Book of what is in the Underworld." But, under the Saites, when Amen's prestige had gone, the regular scriptures came once more into general vogue.

We possess, too, diaries and letters of officials of this period which are not without interest as throwing light upon the condition of the people, though their actual contents are usually jejune and dull. The spirit of the nation had become dulled: there was nothing of interest to record, and there were no interesting men to record it. What would we not give for diaries and letters of the reigns of Hatshepsut and Thothmes III? We have seen how interesting the letters of foreigners were in the time of Amenhetep III.

And as to the condition of the people on which these scanty letters throw a little light, all that can be said is that in spite of the changes in the persons and spirit of their rulers from age to age, the fellahin, though weakened and disorganized for a time by foreign admixture, remained the same in the Ramesside period that they had been under the XIIth and XVIIIth Dynasties, as they were to be under the Romans, and as they are now: working for their masters from year to year and season to season with and like their oxen, unchanging like their unchanging Nile.

CHAPTER VIII: THE HITTITE KINGDOM AND THE SECOND EGYPTIAN EMPIRE (1400-1100 B.C.)

I. The Folk and Land of Khatti

WITH the appearance of the Hittite king Shubbiluliuma as the conqueror and arbiter of Western Asia and successor to the heritage of Egypt we are finally brought into close contact with the world beyond the Taurus, the fourth region of the Nearer East. This world was as foreign to the Semites as was Egypt. Its natural conditions and its inhabitants were as strange to the peoples of Western Asia as were Egypt and the Nilotes, notwithstanding the fact that a certain amount of Mesopotamian culture had penetrated across the Taurus even in the earliest times, and, working gradually, had by the time of Shubbiluliuma given to the peoples of Asia Minor a slight veneer of the Eastern civilization above their own less-developed culture. But the Semite could never cross the Taurus in force, and even his influence soon became attenuated beyond it. The land was too high and rough for him, its air too keen. To the Egyptian the Kheta-land was probably a horror: the snow of Taurus alone would be enough to set a bar to any desire to make its acquaintance on his part. No Egyptian army ever attempted to cross it till Ibrahim Pasha marched to Konia and Kiutahia in 1832.

But to the hardy Anatolian the Semitic lands lay open as a prey. For the Mesopotamian he was a raider and spoiler who periodically descended upon the northern cities to slay and rob. No tic of common race or religion softened the antagonism between Semites and Anatolians; for the former the Northerners were outer barbarians, Goyyim, "the nations" who swarmed in the mountains which bounded the Semitic world on the north, and ruled the strange lands away to the dim northern sea. Generally they were called Khatti, a name which was used by themselves, the Biblical Heth, our "Hittites." For Asia Minor generally the usual Mesopotamian name was Mushki, and the Khatti were reckoned as Mushkaya. Of the fierce raids of the Khatti we hear early in Mesopotamian history. In later omen sagas the name of Sargon of Agade was associated with that of a king of Khatti. The first historical mention of them is that which records a calamitous invasion by the Khatti which took place at the end of the reign of Samsuditana, king of Babylon, about 1750 B.C. As we have seen, the invaders probably took Babylon, killed the king, and then retired, carrying with them the captured deities of Babylonia, and leaving the country and its capital desolate and open to the Kassites from the Zagros, who now founded the royal house of Karduniyash, which lasted for over four hundred years. This invasion was a mere raid from end to end of the great river-valley: when it was over the raiders returned at their leisure with their booty to their home beyond Taurus, where no avenger dared follow them before Tiglath-pileser I. Doubtless there had been other Hittite invasions of similar character before that which overthrew the First Dynasty of Babylon, and were to be others later; they served to stamp on the minds of the Asiatics the conception of the Khatti as a fierce and superhumanly energetic enemy.

The whole mountain complex of the Taurus and Anti-Taurus had been inhabited by the Anatolians from the beginning: the Semitic population stopped at the foothills, just as it does now; the boundary between Arabic and Turkish speech to-day is the ancient boundary between Semite and Hittite. But about the beginning of the second millennium B.C. a Hittite invasion or series of invasions which were not mere raids resulted, as we have seen, in the settlement in Northern Syria of a Hittite garrison, and many of the chief cities of the land were henceforth ruled by Hittite princes side by side with native dynasts and Aryan barons from Mitanni. The two foreign elements in Syria naturally soon came under the influence of the native culture, and it is probable that of the two the Anatolian element resisted it the best, since the Aryans probably had very little civilization, while the Anatolians had a very distinctive culture of their own. Carchemish has lately yielded good Hittite sculpture of the earlier period, resembling that of Oyuk. But eventually the Syrian Hittites succumbed, and though they retained much of their own culture, including their peculiar hieroglyphic system, yet their art became entirely babylonized or assyrized, as we see it in the later sculptures of the palaces of Sindjirli and Saktjegozu.

North of the Taurus, however, the Semitic influence could not pass. Only at Bor and Ivriz, just north of the passes, do we see a Semitic influence in sculpture; and these particular monuments are evidently of the latest of all Hittite productions.

In Anatolia the strong national consciousness of the Hittites prevented their culture from being deprived of its peculiar character by foreign influence, although it was surrounded on three sides by the more highly developed civilizations of Minoan Greece, Egypt, and Mesopotamia. Though at an early period the knowledge of the cuneiform writing on clay tablets had penetrated beyond the Taurus, and at the period of the empire of Khatti was used in the royal chancery at Boghaz Kyoi for the writing of letters and despatches and the keeping of archives, yet the national system of hieroglyphic inscription was always retained for sculpture on monuments, and even used by the semitized Hittites of Carchemish till a late period. The art which we see on the monuments of Boghaz Kyoi, Oyuk, and Yasili-Kaya, in the heart of Cappadocia, is purely national in feeling, and it is not often that there, in contrast to the Hittite sites south of the Taurus, we can descry traces of Babylonian or Egyptian influence in it.

The native art and writing of Asia Minor disappeared in time. But the national religion, which had given birth to both, survived them, and even to the latest days of paganism continued to mark out Asia Minor as a religious province distinct from Greece, from the Semitic world, and from Egypt. Characteristic was the universal worship of the Mother-goddess Ma, known to the Greeks and Romans as Cybele, and generally identified with Rhea or Demeter, at Ephesus with Artemis, elsewhere as the "Mother" simply, the Dindymene Mother or the Zinzimmene Mother, probably the original of the Mesopotamian Ishtar. Closely associated with her was the equivocal Attis or Agdistis, represented as male, but regarded sometimes as a eunuch, sometimes as either male or female. He was the sun, attending the mother-moon. Both were served by the eunuch priests, the Galli, who sometimes wandered throughout the country in troops, sometimes lived as the ministers of the deities on temple-lands of enormous extent, served by multitudes of serfs. The two chief of these temple-domains known to us are those of Komana in the valley of the Sarus amid the mountains of Taurus, and of Pessinus in Phrygia. In Roman times these lands became the property of the emperors.

By the side of Ma and Attis, whose worship was evidently the most ancient cult of Asia Minor, stood in later days Mithras the sun and Men the moon. These two deities would seem, however, not to be of Anatolian origin. Both are probably Aryan or Proto-Iranian gods introduced from the East. Men is identical with the Iranian Mao, Mithras with the Indian Mitra, and was worshipped, with the Aryan deities Indra and Varuna, by the Iranian royal family and nobles of the land of Mitanni, the nearest eastern neighbour of the Khatti kingdom, in the time of Shubbiluliuma and

Dushratta. Then, or before, the worship of Mitra probably passed into Asia Minor, and with it that of Indra and Varuna may well have come also.

The Iranian deities are not, however, mentioned in the list of Hittite gods in the Treaty of Rameses II with Khattusil, and it seems impossible to identify them among those on the sculptured rocks of the shrine of Yasili Kaya. Only the native Anatolian gods are seen at Yasili Kaya. We see a goddess, Cybele or Ma, standing upon a lion as she does on the coins of Greek and Roman times, and wearing upon her head a turreted head-dress almost identical with that which she is represented wearing in later days. Behind her is a youthful war-god armed with an axe and also mounted upon a lion, who accompanies her as the young god does the goddess on Cretan seals. He must be Attis. Behind him are two goddesses, also wearing the turreted head-dress, who stand above that extraordinary symbol, the Double Eagle, which, originating in the brain of some Hittite priest, was fancifully adopted by the Seljuk Turks of Anatolia as their symbol three thousand years later, and by them handed on to Byzantium, to become the cognizance of the modern states of Austria and Russia. Cybele, Attis, and the twin goddesses of the Double Eagle are approaching a venerable and bearded male god, who stands upon the shoulders of two spirits or worshippers of male form, bowing their heads beneath him. In one hand he holds a round-headed mace, in the other the curious symbol of divinity, which Cybele also holds, and above Attis has the body and legs of a man. Both this great god and Cybele are accompanied by crowned goats. Behind the god is a beardless duplicate of him, standing upon mountain-peaks, and beyond him yet another more remote deity, of more peaceful aspect. All wear the high cap and upturned shoes of the Anatolians, and all are evidently gods of the mountains: they or the animals that carry them are treading the topmost peaks. In another representation we see other gods, especially a male figure with two pointed wings.

Of these deities, it would seem very probable that the last is a form of Teshub, or, as the Egyptians called him, Sutekh, identifying him with the old deity of the Hyksos, whom the recorded traditions of the Delta and the Northern tendencies of the Ramesside kings had restored to a prominent position in the Egyptian pantheon in common with the old Egyptian god Set, with whom he had always been identified.

But though the winged god at Yasili Kaya is probably the same as this winged Teshub or Sutekh, his place there seems to be among the lesser deities. Judging, however, from the Egyptian evidence and that of the

Boghaz Kyoi tablets, Teshub was the paramount deity of the Hittite state. How his worship was combined with that of Ma and Attis we do not know. He was primarily a god of war, and was perhaps regarded as a wholly masculine form of Attis. Later on, when the Khatti state disappeared, the prestige of the royal war-god would naturally tend to diminish, and he would recede into the background of the national religion. But while warlike monarchs ruled, the worship of the war-god had naturally come to the front, and he had impressed himself on the minds of foreigners as the all-powerful deity of Khatti.

It is possible that the popular war-god was by no means very popular with the priests of Ma and Attis, and that his comparative insignificance at Yasili Kaya may thus be explained; unless, as is very possible, the winged god identified with Sutekh was but a form of Teshub, who in his highest manifestation is the bearded god standing upon the shoulders of his subjects, who solemnly receives Ma and Attis on their lions. This may be Teshub as Zeus, and the other Teshub as Ares.

Besides these chief gods crowds of other deities were worshipped by the Anatolians. They are mentioned in the famous treaty between Rameses II and the Hittite king Khattusil, which we shall discuss later, as the deities of various places, such as "the sun-god of Arnena," "the god of Khilpantiris," "the goddess of Khauka," "the god of Sarp," besides "the deities of the heavens, the earth, the Great Sea, the wind, and the storms." Important was Taskhil, "mistress of the mountains," who also presided over the taking of oaths and punished the oath-breaker. Among the djinns of the Anatolians we may place the two curious horned Cabiric figures that uphold a great crescent moon on the rocks of Yasili Kaya. These seem to be related to the animal-headed figures of the Aegeans.

Together with the gods in the sculptures appear the eunuch priests, bearing the magic lituus and carrying the curious emblem of the divinity that has already been described. On one relief at Yasili Kaya, Teshub himself (for it is, no doubt, he), wearing a great conical crown that is strongly reminiscent of the high feathers of the Egyptian Amen, places his arm affectionately round the shoulder of his priest, and both advance thus together, naturally giving rise to the mistaken impression which some observers have received that this group represents the king with his queen. But the true nature of the relief is evident enough. No king (unless this is the king in the capacity of priest) is represented at Yasili Kaya.

The native religion of the Anatolians seems non-Aryan. And other characteristics of this people — as, for instance, their matriarchal system — indicate a non-Aryan origin. Their personal appearance on the ancient monuments is neither Semitic nor Aryan. The men seem to have shaved the face regularly. We thus see their facial type plainly. It was peculiar, with high nose and retreating forehead and chin. The type is still common in Eastern Anatolia; it is the type of the modern Armenian, and is unlike any other in the Near East. Prof, V. Luschan calls it the "Armenoid" type. That it is Mongolian is not in the least evident. Their language also does not seem to have been Aryan, while the names of the kings of Mitanni were all Indo-European — Saushshatar, Shutarna, Artashumara, Artatama, Dushratta, Mattiuaza. In Khatti the kings all have native Anatolian names, which have no Aryan sound — Shubbiluliuma, Aranta, Mursil, Mutallu, Khattusil, Dudhalia, and Arnuanta; and the queens, as Pudukhipa and Muni-Dan, likewise. Mursil and Mutallu are typical names of Asia Minor: the former is well known in Greek times in the form Myrsilos, and the treacherous charioteer of Oinomaos of Elis, who delivered his master into the hands of Pelops the Anatolian, and was afterwards slain by him, was named Myrtilos. Motelis (Mutallu) was a Carian name, and the Carians spoke a non-Aryan tongue, like the Lycians, whose speech was probably akin to that of the prehistoric Greeks.

Probably the race was indigenous to Anatolia. The religion presents some apparent resemblances to that of the Minoan Greeks, who were certainly not Aryan speakers. But their facial type was not in the least like that of the prehistoric Greeks; it was much heavier and less prepossessing, and the modern people of Hittite type (we have no ancient Hittite skulls) are brachycephalic, while the Minoans were usually dolichocephalic like other Mediterraneans. We also see resemblances between the externals of Hittite religion and culture and those of the Etruscans in Italy. In this connexion the Greek legends of the Lydian origin of the Etruscans almost materalize into history. It is not impossible that in the course of the Great Migrations of the "Peoples of the Sea" in the fourteenth and fifteenth centuries B.C. tribes of Anatolians may have settled in Italy, though we can hardly conceive of the Hittites as a seagoing people. Also prehistoric Greek religion (at any rate in Crete) seems at times very Etruscan in character. How far the Anatolian, Aegean, and Etruscan cultures were related is one of the problems that now invite the attention of archaeologists, and it is a very interesting one. But we may doubt whether racially the upland Anatolians were akin, unless remotely, to the Mediterraneans.

The early history of the Western Anatolians, the Lycians, Karians, and Lydians living upon the shores of the Aegean, is unknown to us. Geographically always, and in the times of which we are speaking probably racially and linguistically also, they belonged to Greece. At the present time the Turks occupy the eastern shore of the Aegean in force, but the land they have taken, like the islands (still inhabited exclusively by Greeks), nearest to it, is geographically part of Greece, which, if we desired a new name for her, might well be called "Aegaea." Greece consists of the shores and islands of the Aegean. Her real eastern boundary is the sudden rise of land at the sources of the Aegean rivers of Asia Minor. The Anatolian highlands beyond are a different land, and we should expect to find there a civilization which, if related to that of the Aegean shores, would differ from it much to the same extent as the culture of the Hittites did differ from that of the Minoans. We should expect to find in these upland steppes and arid plains of Eastern Phrygia, Lycaonia, and Cappadocia a ruder and less developed culture, the civilization of a virile race of horse and sheep breeders, of warrior-farmers like the Anatolian Turks of to-day, and that is what we do seem to find. Such were the people of Khatti.

In later days, after the Indo-European Phrygians had invaded the land, the Halys marked the frontier between the races, between the Phrygians of the West and the "White Syrians" of the East. These "White Syrians" were the descendants of the earlier Khatti. In their day it is not probable that the western boundary of their race and dominion was fixed by the Halys: before the Phrygians came from Thrace it is most probable that the "White Syrians" extended westward to their natural boundary, the western edge of the central plateau, and the Hittite capital at Boghaz Kyoi, instead of being not far from the western frontier of the kingdom, was in reality set towards its north centre.

Of the beginnings of the kingdom of the Hittites we have no knowledge. Of their earliest history we know nothing as yet, but probably excavation, as yet hardly begun in upper Asia Minor, will tell us much. Surface explorations have shewn that neolithic sites occur all over Asia Minor, as in Armenia and Northern Syria. We know nothing of the development of the Bronze Age culture of the Hittites out of these beginnings, and nothing of its political history till the age of Shubbiluliuma. Probably there was no organized kingdom with a definite centre before the time of Shubbiluliuma; the early invaders of Mesopotamia need not have been the organized armies of an empire, but more probably were merely tribes temporarily confederated under a single head. Eventually, in the person of Khattusil I, king of Kussar, one of these leaders founded the great dynasty which was to combine the Hittites under one rule for two centuries. Shubbiluliuma, his son, the great conqueror, is the first whose records, inscribed in cuneiform on tablets, in the Babylonian manner, have been found at Boghaz Kyoi. Here, in an upland valley east of the Halys, are the remains of the capital city of the Hittites, Khatti, which perhaps bears the name of the people rather than the people that of the city, and was probably an artificial creation of Shubbiluliuma himself. This was the inmost lair of the Hittite spider.

The city lay upon the slope of hill overlooking the valley through which passes the modern route from Angora to Yuzgat. It commanded the pass from which the modern village of Boghaz Kyoi takes its name. The space occupied by it measured 2200 metres by 1100, and the circuit of the walls was about 5500 metres in length. Towers were placed along the walls at intervals, and a great citadel rose on the rock now known as Buyuk Kale. Smaller forts such as the Sary Kale and Yenidje Kale were placed on lesser rocky eminences. The walls are solid and formidable, being built of polygonal masonry. Subterranean corridors resembling the casemates of Tiryns occur. But though we have undoubted resemblances to Mycenaean fortification, the two styles are not quite the same. Several small posterns and three larger gates, one with a relief of a guardian-warrior on the doorpost, gave access and egress. In the acropolis of Buyuk Kale were found many of the archives discovered and published by Winckler. They had no doubt been stored there for safety.

On a great space in the northern part of the city are the remains of a great rectilineal edifice, with halls and passages and magazines, which perhaps resembles in plan the palaces of Achaian Greece. The latest explorers, however, consider it to have been a temple. Its walls, like those of other smaller buildings on the site, were built of brick upon a thick and solid foundation of stone. Remains of these other buildings, also of European rather than Oriental character, are clearly visible.

The contrast afforded by this national capital to the chief cities of Western Asia and of Egypt is great. Instead of a huge riverain metropolis seated in a plain basking in the warmth and light of the East, we have a fortress-city situated 3000 feet above the sea in a rugged land where snow lies throughout the winter, and the summer is as bright and invigorating as that of Europe. Khatti was a city built under European, not Asiatic, conditions; and, except in the matter of size, bore much the same relation to Thebes or Babylon that Sofia or Cetinje do to Constantinople or Cairo now.

Besides the palace and (probably) town at Oyuk not far off, there were other town centres in the Hittite territory, such as the ancient Iconium (which boasted herself older even than Damascus), the probably equally ancient ancestor of Caesarea Mazaca (the modern Kaisariyah at the foot of Argaeus), Tyana, or the holy places Komana and Fessinus, one at the eastern, the other at the western extremity of the land. But it is unlikely that, with the exception of Iconium, any of these were ever really great cities of the Mesopotamian or Egyptian type. Great cities are found only in fertile plains and by or near the banks of rivers. The Hittite towns must have been simple centres of the religious and marketing life of the peasant-farmers, and at the same time fortresses of refuge, into which not only men, but vast herds of horses, cattle, and flocks could crowd for safety in time of war. Of these "cities of refuge" Khatti itself was probably the greatest, and the circuit of its walls, as we have seen, is of enormous extent. Long after the fall of Shubbiluliuma's empire it remained a place of importance, and as Pteria it was well known to Herodotus as a city on the line of the "Royal Road" from the coast to Persia, the successor of a very ancient trade-route from west to east.

Outside Anatolia the chief Hittite city was Carchemish, and this, being no doubt of Syrian origin, was of the Asiatic riverain type. Hamath, Kadesh, and Aleppo also were merely Syrian towns conquered by the Hittites. Sindjirli was a small refuge-fortress, resembling Boghaz Kyoi (but very much smaller), and no doubt originally dating from the same period. Saktjegozu was a palace of later date, built upon a very ancient site.

Such were the chief centres of the Hittite kingdom, which we can imagine as a confederacy of tribes each with its centre round some shrine served by the strange eunuch priests, and all owing an allegiance to the "Great King" of Khatti, the sun (the incarnate sun-god, like the Incas), who ruled at Boghaz Kyoi with near him the central national shrine of Yasili Kaya, and no doubt the central controlling power of the priesthood, whose relations to the royal house we do not know.

From their own and the Egyptian monuments we know something of the personal appearance and costume of the kings, priests, and warriors of the Hittites, and also something of the gods whom they worshipped, and the writing which they used. Archaeological exploration is also beginning to tell us something of other matters, such as their burial customs and their ceramic art. At Carchemish we know that they buried their dead in cists beneath the floors of their houses, and both there and at Egri Kyoi in Asia Minor, we find a custom of partial cremation and burial in jars. Vases were buried with the dead. The earliest pottery at Carchemish is simple in character, and vases of a peculiar "champagne glass" form are found. Later on painted pottery appears, and painted ware has been found at Boghaz Kyoi and at Kara Oyuk in Cappadocia.

2. The Revolt of Palestine and Conquests of Shubbiluliuma

In the confusion which marked the end of the reign of Amenhetep III the North Syrian princes seem to have been uncertain whether their allegiance was due to Egypt or to Mitanni. The opportunity was opened to Shubbiluliuma, an energetic prince, to extend for the first time the central power of the "Great King" of Khatti from Cappadocia over the debated territory of Naharin. It might seem a dangerous policy to provoke the allied arms of both Mitanni and Egypt. But the king and his nation were young and vigorous, with an unassailable base and citadel in the highlands of Asia Minor from which to operate and to which retirement in case of check or defeat was easy. Mitanni, on the other hand, was an artificial state, without good natural frontiers, planted in the defenceless plain of Northern Mesopotamia, and surrounded by enemies. One of these, the young state of Assyria, was ready to take advantage of any disaster to Mitanni to push northward again the power of the Semites, which had been displaced southwards by the intruding Iranians who had founded the Mitannian kingdom; in Assyria Shubbiluliuma could expect an ally. Further, Mitanni was weakened by internal dissensions. The reigning king, Dushratta, was one of three brothers, sons of the king Shutarna. One of these brothers, named Artashumara, had succeeded Shutarna, but was apparently murdered. Dushratta, as we have seen from his letter to Amenhetep III, succeeded Artashumara and punished the murderers. From the Boghaz Kyoi documents we know that a third brother, named Artatama after his grandfather, the Artatama whose daughter Thothmes IV had possibly married, was throughout the reign of Dushratta the enemy of the latter, and had taken refuge in Naharin, beyond Dushratta's reach. Here he, with his son Shutarna or Shutatarra, and his grandson Itakama or Aitugama, seem to have lived as semi-independent dynasts, Itakama being prince of the town of Kinza; and here they intrigued against Dushratta with the Hittite king. Shubbiluliuma was not now concerned to attack Mitanni directly: the defeat which he had already suffered at the hands of Dushratta no doubt made him avoid this course, and with Naharin in his hands Mitanni, unsupported by Egypt, would be powerless. He accordingly stirred up a revolt of the Hittite and Amorite princes of the Lebanon, behind which he could occupy Naharin undisturbed.

The princes of the Lebanon had never been really loyal to Egypt, and had given much trouble to Thothmes III and Amenhetep II. Their disposition to disloyalty had always been checked by the loyalty of the settled cities of Naharin and Phoenicia, which had soon learnt to appreciate the benefits of the pax aegyptiaca, which secured them against the raids of both Hittite and Amorite. Now, however, the towns of Naharin were harried by the Hittite invasion of Shubbiluliuma, in alliance with Itakama. But Phoenicia, the base of Egyptian power in the North, was still safe, its egyptianized princes were faithful to Egypt, and had little love for the tribes of the Lebanon.

From them authentic intelligence of the proceedings of the Amorites could speedily be transmitted to Egypt. The Amorite chiefs therefore had at first to temporize. While in reality aiding the Hittites, they pretended to be defending Phoenicia for the king, and with a strange fatuity the Egyptians believed them. Then they threw off the mask as far as Phoenicia itself was concerned and set to work to subdue one city after another. But Egypt could still be deceived, and with consummate impudence messengers as well as letters were sent to Amenhetep in and to Akhenaten explaining away these inexplicable proceedings, and throwing discredit on the true despatches of the loyal princes, like Ribadda the chief of Byblos, who found themselves actually censured by the king for defending the king's land against his enemies. Abdashirta and his son Aziru, the leaders of the Amorites, conducted this campaign of mingled war and diplomacy with incredible craft and success.

Abdashirta, it is true, was checked at last, owing to the representations of Ribadda and the final conviction of the Egyptians that his protestations of loyalty were deceptive. Abdashirta had occupied the important strategical position of Simyra, which was garrisoned by mercenary warriors of the

Shekhlal, who are evidently the Shakalsha of later history and are probably to be identified with Pisidians of Sagalassos. When charged with this act of war Abdashirta pleaded that he had been asked to deliver Simyra from the Shekhlal, and that the Egyptians in the city were with him in the matter. Ribadda, however, never ceased to point out his treachery to the king, to Egyptian representatives in Phoenicia, and to Amanappa (Amenemapet?), who was apparently a travelling commissioner. In revenge Abdashirta tried to have him assassinated by a Shardina mercenary, whom he killed but not until after he had received nine wounds. Insistently he demands troops to restore the king's authority. Finally Amenhetep III seems to have been convinced, and sent an army under Amanappa, which retook Simyra, and apparently marched on into Naharin, where Egyptian authority was for a brief space restored. Shubbiluliuma, who had no intention of coming into direct conflict with Egypt (so strong still was the renown of the great Thothmes), retreated, abandoning Itakama, who on his next invasion fought against him. The Egyptian force soon retired, from Phoenicia as well as from Naharin, but Shubbiluliuma did not at once advance. The road was again open for an Egyptian army to march against him had he invaded Naharin. An Amorite revolt against Egypt was necessary, and there can be little doubt, after perusal of Ribadda's letters, that the speedy recrudescence of the revolt, under Abdashirta and Aziru, was brought about and supported by him. Meanwhile, till it should have gained head, he turned against Mitanni. In his account of his struggle with Dushratta, discovered at Boghaz Kyoi, he states that Dushratta had "risen against him," thus breaking the treaty which had been concluded between him, probably at his accession, and Artatama, Dushratta's grandfather, no doubt at the end of Artatama's reign. In consequence of this Shubbiluliuma now crossed the Euphrates and plundered the northern border of Mitanni. Dushratta, protesting, threatened that if he plundered the left bank of the Euphrates, which was his territory, he would plunder the right bank, whether it were his or not.

From this it would appear that both kings already laid claim to Naharin, which was rightfully Egyptian territory. Dushratta does not, however, seem to have carried out his threat They formally defied each other, but never actually came to blows. Shubbiluliuma had been made wary by his first defeat. He replied to a second defiance from Dushratta by an expedition against the land of Isuwa and by another against Alshe, probably the territory immediately north of Mitanni, and presumably then tributary to

Dushratta. The latter marched out to attack the Hittites, but Shubbiluliuma avoided battle, and returned to the Euphrates, which he crossed, and marched in force into Naharin, which Aziru's revolt had now again cut off from Egypt. The princes, who preferred Egyptian or Mitannian rule to that of the Hittites, resisted him; but Aleppo, Nii, Arakhti, and Katna were all conquered, and the people of Katna were carried off to Khatti. Of the capture of Katna we hear from a letter of its loyal prince Akizzi, who seems to have escaped. The land of Nukhashshi was conquered, and its king Sarrupsi fled, but his family was sent to Khatti. Kinza, the city of Itakama, his former ally, says Shubbiluliuma, he had not intended to attack, but Itakama, who no doubt resented his desertion in the previous Hittite invasion (in the year before?), and had probably made his submission to the Egyptian army of Amanappa, now attacked him with his father Shutatarra. The two were, however, defeated, and carried off to Khatti, whither the Hittite now retired with his booty. "On account of the disobedience of the king Dushratta have I plundered all these lands in one year, and brought them to Khatti," he says. "From the mountain Niblani, from the Euphrates have I made them my territory." He thus chooses to regard Naharin and Nukhashshi as Mitannian, not Egyptian, territory.

The death of Amenhetep III now probably occurred. Shubbiluliuma waited to see whether the new king of Egypt would be likely to attempt the recovery of Syria from the rebels, in which case the Hittites would probably have abandoned the latter and left Naharin to Egypt. Accordingly, when messengers from Egypt came to him with news of the accession of Amenhetep IV, Shubbiluliuma sent with an ill grace a somewhat surly letter of congratulation to the new king of Egypt, and refrained from any overt acts of hostility in Naharin. He awaited events. The Egyptian government took no measures to put down the revolt, in spite of the urgent advice of the King of Babylon. And though Dushratta badly needed the friendship of Egypt, and wrote to Amenhetep IV and his mother invoking it and reminding them of the political plans (against Shubbiluliuma) which he had concerted with Amenhetep III, Tii seems to have been unfriendly to him, and he complains of her irritation against him. Possibly in Egypt Dushratta was distrusted almost as much as Shubbiluliuma. Abdashirta was now attacking Byblos, and Ribadda writes to Egypt that he fears he will take it as he did Simyra. Dushratta now, with the idea of conciliating Egypt and gaining her assistance against his great enemy, marched to Phoenicia, and Ribadda reports that he had occupied Simyra, but was prevented from relieving Byblos from want of water, and so had retired again to his own land. This movement was really, in view of the threatening attitude of Shubbiluliuma on the flank of his line of march, a great proof of his desire for Egyptian friendship, but it was no doubt misrepresented to Egypt as an attempt at conquest of Egyptian territory. Either now, or shortly afterwards, Abdashirta was captured and killed, whether by one of the robber-bands or by Ribadda's men is not clear. His place was, however, at once taken by his sons, especially by the energetic Aziru, who had distinguished himself by assisting the Hittites to take the town of Katna, and by stirring up the land of Ube (Hobah) and its capital, Damascus, to revolt. He now attacked Simyra again. In Phoenicia the men of Arvad, the northern-most city, seem to have been the most anti-Egyptian in sentiment, as they had been in the days of Thothmes III. Probably this was caused by jealousy of the Southern cities, especially Byblos, which had always submitted peacefully to Egyptian supremacy. The Arvadites now appear in full alliance with the sons of Aziru, and Ribadda writes to Egypt to urge that their merchant-ships in the Delta ports should be seized. He could do little else. The Egyptian troops had been withdrawn, and the Amorites were in no mood to be awed by the appearance and reappearance of Egyptian commissioners such as Turbikha, the lieutenant in the North of the viceroy Yankhamu, or a certain Khai, whose loyalty, as well as energy, was suspected by Ribadda. Turbikha seems to have been as ill-informed as most of the Egyptian commissioners. he Syrian seaport town of Irkata, south of Arvad, still held out for the king, though pressed by the sons of Aziru. But Turbikha, instead of encouraging the men of Irkata, seems to have rated and abused them, and told them that the king "hated Irkata." The result was a letter of complaint from the town to the king. When the faithful adherents of Egypt were treated thus, it is no wonder that the revolt grew apace. Ullaza was soon taken by the sons of Aziru, and Simyra was besieged by them in alliance with the Arvadites. Ribadda's communications with Egypt were seriously interfered with, by the Phoenician pirate Yapa'addi of Dor, and the corn from Egypt on which he relied for subsistence for his garrisons was not sent. His letters grew more insistent and finally indignant in tone. Why, he asks, will the king not allow Yankhamu, the viceroy of Yarimuta (the Delta), to come to his assistance? he is a wise man and the king has no better servant than he. It would seem that jealousy of the powerful viceroy determined the king to retain him in Egypt even at the hazard of losing the empire, and Ribadda's praise of him probably did Yankhamu no good at the court, where the impression would be given that the viceroy had prompted Ribaddatoask for him. Also the sinister influence of the sons of Abdashirta at the court, where Aziru had a powerful friend in the Egyptian noble Dudu, would be actively exerted to prevent a decision so dangerous to their schemes as the dispatch of Yankhamu to Phoenicia. Constantly Ribadda asks for troops, especially for the redoubtable Sudanese, the men of Melukhkha and of Kuoh, whom in all probability the Semites feared far more than they did the Egyptians or the mercenaries from Asia Minor. He is ordered to "defend": how can he do so with no troops? His ancestors had never been abandoned in this way by the king's ancestors. Of old at the sight of an Egyptian the kings of Canaan fled, but now the sons of Abdashirta mock at the Egyptians! Finally his rage gets the better of him, and he roundly tells the pharaoh that he has lied in saying that he has sent troops. He was now hard pressed by Aziru, and all that the king cared about was that the despatch of tribute should go on as usual. The Egyptian commissioners seem to have had no orders but to see that tribute was sent, in spite of the impossibility of getting it. How can he obtain wood from Ugarit and Zalkhi with Aziru and the Arvadites in the way? All had gone wrong since Khai and Amanappa left Simyra with copper for Egypt. Finally Simyra fell, surrendered by the Egyptian commander Khaib: Biwari, another Egyptian officer, was killed.

The result was an alarming increase of the revolt. Zimrida, King of Sidon, gave up the Egyptian cause as hopeless, and allied himself with Aziru and the Arvadites against Byblos and the ancient rival of Sidon, Tyre, whose king, Abimilki, imitates Ribadda in writing despairing letters to Egypt. He is, however, more courtly in his phraseology than the energetic King of Byblos, and gives the impression of being a weaker man. He was honestly loyal to Egypt: in his fathers' time "the gods of his city had gone over to Egypt," and he obeys their behests. He tries to gain help by means of obsequious reports of his evil case. He is "a servant of tears," and is shut up in his island-city by Zimrida. But neither Ribadda's anger nor Abimilki's tears brought any assistance from Egypt. The time had indeed now gone by when it was possible to do anything to save the North, which was now entirely in the hands of Aziru, who had finally succeeded in taking Irkata as well as Simyra, and had killed the king who had so indignantly protested against the stupidity of Turbikha. Any soldiers that were left to Egypt by the pacifist fanaticism of Akhenaten were now all needed in the South, where the simmering anarchy caused by the wanderings of the Khabiri, Sa-Gaz, and other masterless men (Sutu or Beduins) blazed out into open revolt as a consequence of the Amorite rebellion. Here also Milkili and Labaya, two Canaanite chiefs, while in reality allied with the Khabiri, at the same time tried to delude the Egyptian court into believing them to be its loyal and energetic supporters. This they did, in spite of the protests of the Iranian princes of Megiddo, Biridiya and Yazdata, and of the insistent despatches of Abdkhiba, the native governor of Jerusalem, on one of which is written a note to the royal scribe who should translate it: "To the scribe of my lord the king, Abdkhiba thy servant: Bring these words plainly before my lord the king." And the gist of this letter is in the words: "The whole land of the king is going to ruin." Thus in the South Milkili and Labaya played the same "game of bluff" as Abdashirta and Aziru in the North, and Abdkhiba in the South had the same thankless task of combating the incredible apathy and ignorance of Akhenaten and his court as Ribadda had in the North. Perhaps he had more success in the end, as Jerusalem was nearer to Egypt than Byblos, and Yankhamu the viceroy of the Delta, to whose province Southern Palestine was attached, could hardly be deceived as to the truth of the protestations of Milkili and Labaya, and their allies Zimrida of Lachish (who was soon killed), and the Iranian immigrant, Shuyardata. Sudanese troops were sent to Jerusalem, but there they seem to have come into collision with the population, and caused such trouble that Abdkhiba complains bitterly of them. They had nearly killed him in his own house. Nothing went well for the Egyptians, and the whole country was terrorized by the Khabiri and the Sutu, who in the South seem to have attacked both the Egyptians and the Canaanites impartially. And here, too, the king demanded his tribute as if nothing was happening. Widya of Ashkelon has to send the tribute of Aten, as ordered. We can obtain no clearer idea of the obsession of the king's mind by his religious mania. Abdkhiba tries to arrest his attention by asking him to succour the territory of Jerusalem which bore his name: probably a temple of the Aten had been set up in Jerusalem, which may be the "Khinatuni" which has already been mentioned. But we hear nothing of the result of this clever appeal. Matters went from bad to worse. The Egyptian officials on the spot were utterly confused by the contradiction between the facts as they saw them and the foolish orders they received from home, and those specially sent from Egypt, ignorant of the local conditions, and not knowing whom to believe, committed mistake after mistake. Bikhuru, a general sent by Yankhamu to restore order, actually was so ignorant of his friends and foes that he sent a body of Arab auxiliaries against Byblos, who massacred Ribadda's garrison of Mediterranean mercenaries (Shardina), in Egyptian pay. The unhappy Ribadda may well have cursed the day when he refused to follow the counsels of his family and throw in his lot with the Amorites.

Finally, returning from some expedition without the walls, he found the gates of Byblos shut against him, and had to flee for refuge to Berut, where the king Ammunira received him.

The fall of Simyra and Byblos seems to have caused some commotion in Egypt. The loss of the gateway of Naharin and the expulsion of so prominent an Egyptian sympathizer as Ribadda from his city could hardly be ignored by the philosopher-king or explained away by the (probably well-paid) friends of Aziru at court. A wordy and pompous, weakly threatening, letter was sent by the king's orders to Aziru, bidding him restore Ribadda to his city, and demanding the reason of his friendship with Itakama, the Prince of Kadesh, who was now again an active ally of the Hittites. A bombastic threat that if he is an enemy he and all his house will be sacrificed (before Amen) by the king's own axe is followed by the tearful remonstrance, "Thou knowest that the king doth not wish to carry war through Canaan"; and the letter ends with a significant demand for the surrender of some Egyptian enemies of the king, Sharru, Tuya [Tui], Leia [Rei], Uishiari [Osirei, for Seti?], the son-in-law of Mania [Mena], Daasharti, Paluma, and Nimmakhe [Nebemhat?] with their sons and wives. We can hardly doubt that these were prominent Amonists who had taken refuge with Aziru from the king's fanatical wrath. So here again the religious obsession comes forth, and clouds the king's counsel.

Finally, after Aziru had killed Ribadda and the ruler of Berut, Ammunira, he was summoned to Egypt, and eventually he had to go. He went as a great vassal prince, slayer of the king's enemies, and defender of the empire against the Northern barbarians. The accusing voices of Akizzi of Katna, of Ribadda of Byblos, and of Abimilki of Tyre were now silent, and the Egyptian court was only too glad to compromise and accept the accomplished fact with as little loss of dignity as possible. Aziru probably acknowledged Egyptian suzerainty and returned to Syria as the ruler of a practically independent state of considerable extent. But he did not rule it long undisturbed. Shubbiluliuma's support had enabled Aziru to effect his first conquests after the death of Amenhetep III. Aziru had no doubt kept him quiet hitherto by protestations of friendship, if not by actual admission of supremacy. But his visit to Egypt and return to Syria, blessed by Egyptian recognition and no doubt anointed with the sacred oil as an Egyptian sub-king, must have been enough to provoke Shubbiluliuma to attack him at once. From the letters of the Hittite king lately discovered at Boghaz Kyoi we learn that he had regarded Aziru as his vassal, that he now considered that he had revolted from him, and that he defeated him and compelled him to swear allegiance to him and to obey Hittite orders. Thus the whole of Syria and Phoenicia was lost to Egypt. Bikhuru the general fell back on Jerusalem, and it cannot have been long before even that strong city also was abandoned to its Jebusite inhabitants, and all Palestine to the Khabiri, the wandering Hebrew tribes who three centuries afterwards founded, in the lands of which they had thus taken possession, settled and enduring kingdoms of their own.

Dushratta was thus isolated, and shortly afterwards was murdered by one of his sons. "When his son with his servants conspired and slew his father Dushratta and death found Dushratta, Teshub decided the right of Artatama and gave life to his son Artatama," says Shubbiluliuma in the preface to a treaty with Mattiuaza, son of Dushratta, found at Boghaz Kyoi, from which much of our information as to the Hittite wars is derived. Apparently Dushratta's exiled brother and rival Artatama and his son Shutatarra now seized the throne, driving out the son (Mattiuaza?) who had murdered Dushratta. He fled to Khatti. The result was a period of anarchy. "The land of Mitanni was entirely destroyed," says Shubbiluliuma, "and the Assyrians and the people of Alshe divided it between them." So Ashur-uballit seized the opportunity to occupy the portion of Dushratta's kingdom nearest to him. Saushshatar, the father of Artatama I, and the first Mitannian king of whom we have any knowledge, had carried off from Ashur a door of gold and silver and had set it up in his palace at Waraganni, his capital. Shutatarra gave it back to Ashur-uballit, no doubt under compulsion.

Shubbiluliuma now appeared upon the scene. "Till now had the Sun, Shubbiluliuma, the Great King, the noble King of Khatti, beloved of Teshub, refrained from crossing the Euphrates, and had taken neither taxes nor tribute from the land of Mitanni. But when the Great King saw the desolation of the land of Mitanni, he sent men of the palace, oxen, sheep, and horses, for the men of Khani (the Mitannians) there were in misery. Shutatarra and his nobles endeavoured to slay Mattiuaza, the son of the king; but he fled, and came to the Sun Shubbiluliuma, the Great King. The Great King spake: 'Teshub hath decided his right for him, since now I take Mattiuaza, the son of King Dushratta, by the hand, and set him upon his throne. In order that the land of Mitanni, the great land, may not disappear, hath the Great King Shubbiluliuma summoned it to life for the sake of his daughter. For Mattiuaza, the son of Dushratta, have I taken by the hand, and have given him my daughter to wife.'" The fruit was now quite ripe: by waiting Shubbiluliuma had attained all. "That the great land of Mitanni might not be destroyed utterly," and with a fine touch of contempt not for the sake of the rightful king, Dushratta's son, but for that of his daughter, to whom he now married him, the Hittite Bismarck entered Mitanni, drove out the Assyrians and the men of Alshe, ejected Artatama and Shutatarra, whom he had used and abandoned, and placed Mattiuaza on the throne of Dushratta as his son-in-law and vassal. The cautious yet calculating policy of years was finally crowned with the attainment of the position at which he had aimed from the first, and Shubbiluliuma now as an old man reigned undisputed lord over the whole of North-western Asia. Even the energetic Ashur-uballit had to give way before him. Assyria was not yet powerful enough to withstand the king of the Hittites in war, and her king had no desire to see the treasures of Ashur carried off to Asia Minor. By his politic evasion of direct conflict with Shubbiluliuma Ashur-uballit himself gave evidence of political sagacity not inferior to that of the Shubbiluliuma, and it may well be that from watching the career of the older Hittite monarch the Assyrian king learnt lessons which made him in after years, when he was himself an old man, the conqueror of Babylon and the dictator of Mesopotamia.

How long the revolt lasted till the final abandonment of Palestine after the subjection of Aziru by Shubbiluliuma we do not know. Before Aziru's capture of Simyra Ribadda speaks of the war as having lasted already five years, but we do not know whether he is referring only to the second revolt after the death of Amenhetep III or dates his five years from the beginning of the trouble, when Abdashirta took Simyra, probably a year or two before Amenhetep's death. Perhaps twelve or fifteen years (c. 1378-1365 B.C.) saw the whole tragedy played out from start to finish.

Of the Egyptian actors in the revolts we know nothing from Egyptian sources with the exception of Dudu, who is the Tutu buried at Tell el-Amarna. Yankhamu, the powerful viceroy of the Delta (Yarimuta) is unknown to the inscriptions. Perhaps Akhenaten or Horemheb destroyed all record of him.

Thus the conquests of Thothmes I and III were lost, by the ignorance and incapacity of the king, the folly and probably the venality of his courtiers, and the stupidity and possible treachery of some of his officers. The soldiers must have been utterly divided in opinion by the religious revolution, and without Amon to help them were, as they would have phrased it, as rudderless ships in the storm. Their world had been turned upside down, and it is little wonder that their brains and hands were paralysed.

Tutankhamen, the second successor of Akhenaten, seems, after the restoration of the ancient religion, to have attempted to recover Southern Palestine, In the tomb of Hui, viceroy of Kush, at Thebes, we have pictures of the bringing of tribute by the Asiatic chiefs, who say to the king: "Give us the breath which thou givest, O lord! Tell us thy victories, and there shall be no revolters in thy time, but the land shall be in peace." This is evidently a reference to the Canaanite revolt. That it was impossible in his reign to reconstitute in any way the old imperial officialdom of the Asiatic subject-lands seems to be shewn by the fact that this tribute of the North is presented by the two viceroys of the South and Kush, Hui and his brother Amenhetep, not by an officer detailed to deal with the affairs of the North.

Before his death Shubbiluliuma saw the coping-stone placed on the edifice he had raised, by the conclusion of a treaty with Egypt, probably under Horemheb, by which he must have been left in undisturbed possession of Naharin and Amurru, while Canaan and Phoenicia were left for Egypt to recover if she could.

3. Mursil and Seti I

At Shubbiluliuma's death his sceptre passed to his son Mursil, after the short intervening reign of an elder brother of the latter, named Aranda. The empire which Mursil inherited stretched from the Phrygian mountains, probably, and from the Black Sea to Carmel and Galilee in the south, and to the circumscribed northern frontier of Assyria and the mountains of Armenia in the east. We cannot doubt that Shubbiluliuma paid attention to the westward as well as to the southern and eastern expansion of his kingdom, and it may be he who is depicted on the rocks of Tmolos (Karabel) and Sipylos in Lydia, but from the references to unknown lands in his tablets we can at present learn nothing of possible campaigns as far as the Aegean: we may well do so later, however, when these tablets found at Boghaz Kyoi have been fully studied and published. Then we may gain important knowledge as to his relations with the now decaying and war-harried "Mycenaean" peoples of the Aegean basin. Over the contending Canaanites, Khabiri, and Beduins of Palestine south of Syria, left to their fate by Egypt for a time, neither he nor Mursil seem to have attempted to extend their rule.

They had no desire to come to close quarters with Egypt. The advent of a new dynasty had infused new energy into the counsels of Egypt, which was fast recovering from the stupor which the bouleversement under Akhenaten had laid upon her. Under Seti I she marched forth once more to reassert her Asiatic dominion. The "neutral territory" of Palestine which the Hittites had not attempted to occupy was retaken almost without a blow, Seti and his army entered Galilee, and for the first time the Egyptians and the Hittites met on the field. Shubbiluliuma had never crossed swords with Egypt.

The details of the campaigns of Seti I and Rameses II are neither so important nor so interesting as those of the campaigns of Thothmes III. We know much less of what happened, though the complete decipherment of the Boghaz Kyoi tablets may fill up the gaps in the Egyptian accounts. Seti undoubtedly modelled his action upon that of Thothmes. Like him, he started on his enterprise as soon as he had attained the supreme power, in the first year of his reign. Like him, also, his first campaign was directed towards the securing of Southern Palestine and Phoenicia, from which, as his base, he could attack the Orontes valley. As before, Phoenicia had to be subdued from the land side first, in order that her ships might be seized and utilized for the transport of troops directly to Northern Syria.

Advancing from the frontier-city of Tjaru, Seti pushed across the desert into Palestine, and the city of Pe-kanana, "the Canaan," was captured. It is probable that this was the capital city of Canaan, Jerusalem itself. Then the Jordan was crossed, and the king set up his boundary-stela at Tell esh-Shihab in the Hauran, marking his border over against the confines of the king of Karduniyash. Turning westward then, and still meeting with little resistance, apparently, he marched through the plain of Jezreel into Phoenicia, where also the princes seem to have made no opposition to the restoration of Egyptian supremacy.

Very possibly they welcomed the restoration. The connexion with highly civilized and luxurious Egypt could not but be more profitable to their commercial interests than subjection to the control of the Hittites. Further, Egyptian overlordship secured to the city-folk the control of the uplands, while Hittite predominance meant domination of the coast cities by the hill-folk of the Lebanon and the Orontes valley.

Probably it was the Phoenician feeling in favour of Egypt that lamed the arm of Mursil. At any rate, he made no attempt to prevent a seizure of Phoenicia. Had it been intended to exclude Egyptian dominion from Asia, Seti ought to have been met in the plain of Jezreel, where a Hittite victory would probably have shattered the projects of the Egyptian king. But apparently the king of Khatti regarded Southern Palestine, and Phoenicia also, as outside his regular dominion, and an Egyptian occupation of those countries as no infraction of Shubbiluliuma's treaty; he trusted also in the mountains of Lebanon and Hermon as his southern frontier, and his generalship was not sufficiently inspired to make him see the strategic importance of Phoenicia. He left considerations of strategy to the Egyptians, being content to let them (if they really intended to attack him afterwards) take what advantage they would, sure that in the end the hard bodies and sharp swords of his Anatolian soldiers would prevail against the weaker warriors of the South.

Countless prisoners of the Beduins and Khabiri were brought back to Egypt, where at the border, on the farther shore of the "Crocodile-river," Seti was met by a stately deputation of white-robed nobles and priests, who acclaimed him as victor over the Semites. Arrived in the Delta, Seti seems to have made his headquarters there for nearly two years without prosecuting his Northern campaign any further.

Probably he had no immediate intention of attacking the Hittites, but it may well be that in the third year Mursil shewed signs of invading Phoenicia, with the result that Seti put into operation the second phase of the Thothmosid strategy. Probably in his fourth year he advanced from Phoenicia (whether he went there by sea or land we do not know) over the mountains into the Orontes valley and attacked Kadesh, whether successfully or not is uncertain. In the field, however, a Hittite army was certainly overthrown, with considerable loss. It was the first time, as far as we know, that the Egyptians had come into actual conflict with the Hittites, and in the first bout victory declared for the Southerners. Whether the defenders of Kadesh were the redoubtable Anatolians, the real Hittites from beyond the Taurus, or not rather merely the local half-Semitic levies of the Orontes valley captained by Hittite and Mitannian chiefs, is, however, doubtful.

The result of the battle was that Mursil gave up all idea of ousting the Egyptians from Palestine and Phoenicia, while the Egyptian king was not anxious to try conclusions with him further. The prestige of Egypt had been restored and a Hittite army defeated in the open field: rich Phoenicia was once more Egyptian, and by its possession a complete check upon further southward extension of the Hittite power assured. Meanwhile the Hittites retained all the conquests of Shubbiluliuma practically unimpaired. A treaty between the two kings was concluded no doubt on much the same lines as the former one.

4. Rameses II and the Hittites

For the remainder of the reign of Seti, some fifteen years, the peace seems to have remained unbroken. But Rameses II deliberately broke it, with results in the long-run disastrous to his country. He was young, impetuous, and proud, and, to judge from his face as we see it in his mummy, not very intelligent. To count the cost of what he was about to do was probably beyond his mental capacity. He was aggressive from the first. Already in his fourth year (c. 1297-6 B.C.), he visited Phoenicia, which with Canaan had been partly occupied by the Egyptians since Seti's campaigns, without interference from the Hittites. In Phoenicia Rameses set up a boundary stela on the rocks at the entrance of the Nahr el-Kelb, "the Dog River," north of Beirut, Tyre, Sidon, and Beirut had evidently continued faithful to Egypt since their re-occupation by Seti, while Byblos, Simyra, and Arvad had never been recovered. Arvad had been anti-Egyptian in Akhenaten's time, and there is no doubt that the coast farther still to the north, the land of Alashiya and the town of Ugarit, were more or less part of the Hittite kingdom: Arvad and Ugarit sent contingents to aid Mursil in opposing Rameses.

The young king now definitely determined, in spite of the two former treaties, to attempt the recovery of the lost conquests of Thothmes III. His intention was obvious and well known, and Mursil summoned the ban and arriere-ban of his loosely confederated empire to oppose him. Besides the host of the Khatti themselves from the highlands of Anatolia and their close allies of Katawadana (Kataonia), he marshalled the Hittites of Carchemish on the Euphrates and of Kadesh on the Orontes, the men of Aleppo (Khilibu), of Nukhashshi and of Naharin, the Phoenicians of

Arvad, and the people of Ugarit and Kedi (the Gulf of Iskanderun), all former tributaries of Egypt, while from the western bounds of his empire came the Pedasa or Pisidians (Pedasians), the Ariunna, the Luka or Lycians, and even the Mysians (Masa) and Dardanians (Dardani): from Cilicia marched also the Kalakisha and the Mushant. Mursil collected his whole host to bar the only road by which the Egyptians could advance, the valley of the Orontes, with his frontier-fortress of Kadesh at his back. Rameses marched directly to meet him. He had with him the Shardina mercenaries who had been settled in Phoenicia or Egypt since the time of Amenhetep III, and no doubt the negro troops whom the Northerners so much feared; but the main body of his army seems to have been Egyptian, marshalled in a form which we have not previously met with in Egyptian history, as regular legions or divisions, each marching under the banner of a god. There were four of these, the legions of Amen, Ra, Ptah, and Sutekh (Set), the deities who were more especially venerated by the king's house. In all probability the Egyptian army was considerably less in number than that of the Hittites, but more mobile and better organized for battle. We know the events of the war from the relief sculptures of the Ramesseum, Karnak, and Luxor, as well as from two papyri.

Crossing the mountains from Phoenicia, the Egyptian army debouched into the valley of the Orontes, and marched downstream on Kadesh. The resulting struggle is interesting as the second pitched battle in history (the first was Megiddo) of which we have a detailed description, of course only from the Egyptian side, and that from the point of view of the king himself. There is little doubt, even when we make allowances for the royal vanity, that the chief part in the battle was actually borne by Rameses, whose youthful impetuosity and valour undoubtedly saved the Egyptian army from destruction. Mursil must have been an old man, and, though his tactics were well-thought-out and clever, was unable to supplement them by personal dash and vigour at the critical moment. We can restore the actual events of the fight with much accuracy, as Prof Breasted has pointed out. It is evident that, misled by the false report of spies specially sent out by Mursil, with orders to let themselves be captured and say that he was still in the vicinity of Aleppo, he pushed on with a small force ahead of his army to Kadesh, and was there cut off by the Hittites, who had been concealed to the north of the fortress, and now extended their left between the two portions of the Egyptian army, cutting the legion of Ra, which was marching up unprepared for battle, in two. Then Rameses' camp was surprised and taken while the king, unaware of what was happening in his rear, was attacking the right wing of the Hittites north of Kadesh. Swiftly turning about, Rameses retook the camp, and was compelled to fight his way with his chariots through the masses of opposing chariotry to join the legion of Ptah, which, with the vizier at its head and the survivors of the legion of Ra with it, was striving to effect his rescue. Of the prodigies of valour which he performed Rameses had much to tell, and no doubt he and his men did fight well. Finally the combined attack from north and south cut through the masses of the Hittite chariotry, which broke for the river, on the farther bank of which Mursil with the rest of his army awaited the decision of fortune, apparently unable to do much to succour his right wing. His good generalship had been brought to nought by the hard fighting and greater mobility of the Egyptians. In the rout many of the foremost leaders of the Hittites fell, slain by the sword or drowned in the river, before Mursil's eyes. Among them were Targamenasa and Payasa, his own kajens or charioteers; Kemaija and Tidur, chiefs of the "Tuhiru" or men of valour: Targatijasa and Agma, captains of the bowmen; Khilpsil, his scribe; Irbasunna, chief of the archers of Annasa; Garbatusa, Samartusa, Mejarima, Irbaur, Javajasa, chief of the land of Tanisa; and the Hittite king's own brother, Shubbijil or Sapajar. The flower of the Hittite host had perished.

The magnitude of the disaster probably determined Mursil to retreat northwards at once with the rest of his army, while the Egyptians were too exhausted to pursue. They also had suffered too heavily for any further operations to be attempted. We do not know that Rameses even attempted to take Kadesh or whether it surrendered without resistance. The Egyptian army certainly returned at once to Egypt with its prisoners, and we can well believe that Rameses' return was triumphal. The sculptors and scribes were put to work at once to immortalize this mighty battle, and we see the result of their labours in the temple-reliefs already mentioned and in the written poetical accounts which are associated with the name of the scribe Pentaur (Pentaueret) who copied them, though whether he was the original author of the poem (a veritable Ramessiad) that bears his name as copyist is doubtful.

At this juncture the aged Mursil, who, it is probable, was still reigning at the time of Rameses' invasion, and to whom we have ascribed the clever Hittite tactics at the battle of Kadesh, probably died, crushed by the disaster that had befallen his armies, and was succeeded by his son

Mutallu, to whom fell the task of restoring the prestige of Shubbiluliuma's empire.

Mutallu was the second son of Mursil. His elder brother, Halpashulubi, had apparently died before his father.

The new king determined on a vigorous offensive against Egypt. While Rameses was still pluming himself on the victory of Kadesh, the Hittite hosts were silently recruited, during a pause of one or two years, and then suddenly launched from the Orontes valley into Galilee. South Palestine was plunged once more into a ferment of war and revolt. The whole country went over to the Hittites, and probably only Phoenicia remained more or less faithful to Egypt. Rameses was compelled to reconquer all Palestine in the campaign of his eighth year (about 1292), beginning with Ashkelon, which was taken by storm, and ending with Dapur or Tabor, which was also captured after a siege. Ashkelon was defended by its revolted citizens only, but at Dapur a Hittite contingent fought with the Amorites. These exploits were commemorated at Karnak and the Ramesseum in the same style as the battle of Kadesh.

Mutallu's plan of campaign, momentarily successful, had failed, and he was now to see the war carried into Naharin, where no Egyptian had been seen for nearly a century. He does not seem to have made a very stout resistance against the northward advance which Rameses now undertook, to chastise his foe. Probably he was handicapped by revolt in other portions of his dominions: we hear of a general of the army and of a certain Sin-Teshub, son of Zida, who took up arms against him. The result was that Rameses took Katna and Tunip, and set up his statue in the latter city, while on the coast Arvad submitted, probably about the ninth or tenth year (1290). Egyptian supremacy appeared to be restored as it had been in the days of Amenhetep III, and Bentishina or Put-akhi, the king or paramount chief of the Amorites, the fourth successor of Aziru, was compelled to abandon his allegiance to Khatti, which had been maintained since the time of Aziru, and went over to Egypt. How long this renewed Egyptian supremacy in Naharin lasted we do not know. Mutallu never made peace, and Rameses had to be constantly fighting to maintain his conquests. Tunip revolted to the Hittites, and was attacked by Rameses, who seems to have been so suddenly surprised outside the city by a Hittite army that he had to fight without his armour — "his coat of mail was not upon him." This is related as an exploit at the Ramesseum, but that he retook Tunip is not stated, and the fight may in reality have been a severe defeat, glozed over by paeans concerning the king's personal bravery.

In any case, Mutallu eventually recovered control of both Naharin and Amurru, and removed the faithless Put-akhi from his kingdom, replacing him by a certain Shabili, and taking him as a prisoner to distant Khatti. There, so we are told in the Boghaz Kyoi tablets, Khattusil, the king's brother, begged his person from Mutallu, and kept him as a noble prisoner in the town or castle of Haggamissa, whence he emerged at the death of Mutallu, and was replaced on his throne by his protector Khattusil, now king of Khatti.

Mutallu died, after a reign of probably some fifteen years of incessant war, about 1280 B.C., and was succeeded by his younger brother, Khattusil, the third son of Mursil. Mutallu seems to have had sons, but possibly they were by wives of non-royal rank, so that none could succeed: one, named Urkhi-Teshub, is mentioned in the Boghaz Kyoi tablets as an emissary of his uncle Khattusil to the king of Egypt.

On his accession Khattusil was probably no longer young, and, weary of war, he seems to have proposed peace to Egypt. Reversing his brother's uncompromising policy, he also, as we have seen, restored the pro-Egyptian Bentishina or Put-akhi to his kingdom of Amurri, This was a stroke of policy likely to placate Rameses, who could at least set off the facts that the Hittites had proposed peace and had restored his man Put-akhi to rule over the Amorites against the unpalatable truth that fifteen years of war had been in vain, and that the territory actually held by the two empires was exactly what it had been in Seti's day, with not one rood, apparently, in favour of the original assailant, Egypt. The Hittites had simply been expelled from Palestine by the Egyptians, and the Egyptians from Northern Syria by the Hittites. No doubt both peoples were exhausted by the war: we can indeed, as we have seen, with some show of truth ascribe much of the decadence of Egypt during the rest of Rameses' reign, and that of the Hittite power under the successors of Khattusil, to the effects of this long and terrible struggle. The negotiations resulted in the conclusion of a formal treaty not only of peace but also of alliance between the two Great Powers, the Egyptian text of which has been preserved for us on the walls of Karnak and the Ramesseum, while parts of the cuneiform original draft seem to be preserved among the clay archives of Boghaz Kyoi. The actual negotiations seem to have taken place in Syria, and on the 21st day of the first month of the second season, in the 21st year of

Rameses (1279 B.C.?), the Egyptian delegates returned to Per-Rameses, where the king then was, with a Hittite envoy named Tartisibu and his assistant, who brought with them the text of the treaty, probably in Egyptian hieroglyphs and in cuneiform, engraved upon a silver tablet, which was solemnly presented to the king.

The text of the treaty is one of the most important diplomatic documents of antiquity. It is the only one of its kind that has been preserved, though we know that such treaties were common between Asiatic princes, such as the rulers of Babylon and Assyria, and that this was the third treaty that had been made between Khatti and Egypt. As a diplomatic document it is well ordered and logically arranged: and in its phraseology a curiously modern note is sometimes struck, especially in the extradition clauses, which attracted much attention before the discovery of the Tell el-Amarna letters and the correspondence of Khammurabi shewed us how very modern in some respects even these most ancient "ancients" were.

The high contracting parties are on a footing of perfect equality, according to the protocol: both are given the same epithet of p-tenil, "the valiant," and the one is styled "the Great Chief of Kheta" (p-sar-o n Kheta), while the other is "the Great Prince of Egypt" (p-hik-o n Kemet). The treaty begins with the statement that "at the beginning, for ever, the relations of the Great Prince of Egypt with the Great Chief of Kheta were that the God did not cause hostilities between them, by treaties." Mutallu, however, had fought with Rameses, but now that Mutallu had succumbed to his evil fate, and Khattusil was king, the latter had determined to be friends with Rameses and his sons' sons and with the descendants of Rameses for ever. "There shall be no hostilities between them, for ever. The great chief of Kheta shall not invade the land of Egypt, for ever, to take anything therefrom, and Rameses-Meriamen, the great prince of Egypt, shall not invade the land of Kheta, to take anything therefrom, for ever."

Then both kings declared their adhesion to the former treaties concluded in the times of Shubbiluliuma (Saplulu) and Mursil (called, by mistake, in the text "Mutallu"), but their provisions are not recapitulated. Two clauses then follow which specify the terms of a defensive alliance between Egypt and Khatti, directed against rebellious subjects of the one or the other as well as against foreign enemies. The Hittite king seems to have inserted here a clause to the effect that if on the occasion of a rebellion of one of his tributaries he has notified Egypt of his intention to proceed against him, and the subjects of the offending tributary have acknowledged him, the king of Khatti, as their lord, the king of Egypt shall make no claim upon the allegiance of this tributary or his vassals: "Usermara Setepenra, the great prince of Egypt, shall be for ever silent."

Follow the very important articles dealing with the extradition of political fugitives and of ordinary emigrants from one country to the other. There is no doubt that during the long war many "traitors" had taken refuge from the vengeance of their own monarch with his enemy, and we have seen that, a century before, Akhenaten had demanded from Aziru the bodies of certain persons, no doubt stubborn Amonists, who had fled from before his face to seek sanctuary in Amurri. The two kings being now friends, handed over their "rebellious slaves" to one another (but not, as we shall see, to be dealt with at pleasure), and each promised not to receive any "great men" of the other's land who might seek to take refuge with him. Similarly, if "unknown men" (that is to say, commoners) should come from Egypt to Kheta or from Kheta to Egypt, with the intent to settle and become foreign subjects, it was stipulated that they should be brought back at once to their own country. Evidently the legal principle that no man can change his country or his allegiance at his own will was fully recognized.

The next clauses of the treaty seem to be misplaced, no doubt by an oversight of the stone-cutter. The witness of the gods of Kheta and Egypt, which actually comes next, ought to be placed after the two clauses dealing with the amnesty of extradited persons, which should follow the other clauses dealing with extradition. The misplaced clauses provide that if any great men are handed over by one king to the other no punishment whatever shall be inflicted upon them: "let not one cause his wickedness to arise against him, let not his house be injured nor his wives nor his children, let him not be killed, let no injury be done to his ears, to his eyes, to his mouth, to his feet: let not one cause any wickedness to arise against him." These amnesty clauses no doubt refer to persons who had fled from one side to the other during the war, and not to future occurrences.

With these clauses the actual treaty was complete, and now came the witnessing by "the thousand deities, male and female," of Khatti and of Egypt. As the treaty is sent by the king of Khatti to Rameses for his final assent, these deities bear witness only to the words of Khattusil, not to Rameses' acceptance. The Hittite king invokes the whole of his pantheon, as well as "Amen, the Sun-god, Sutekh, the gods and the goddesses of the mountains and the rivers of the land of Egypt, of the heavens, the earth, the

Great Sea, the winds, and the storms." Follow the regular curses on the violator and blessings on the observer of the treaty, whose house, land, and servants will be blasted or preserved by the thousand gods of Khatti and Egypt according as he breaks or keeps it.

The final paragraph in the monumental inscription no doubt is not part of the treaty: it is a mere description, for the admiration of posterity, of the Hittite figures and seals on the silver plate: the seals of Sutekh, of the king Khattusil, and of his wife the queen Pudukhipa, and, most important of all, the seal of "the Sun-god of the land of Arnena," who here seems to take a more important position than Teshub.

The conclusion of the treaty was apparently received with great satisfaction by both sides. Pudukhipa the Hittite queen received a letter from the consort of Rameses, Nefertari (who is called "Naptera"), expressing her delight at the restoration of peace. Then Rameses was left to the congenial task of blazoning his victories over his new friends on the walls of the temples of Egypt, in order to persuade himself and his subjects into believing that he had been the conqueror, while Khattusil, as a sardonic comment on the vauntings of his "brother," quietly concluded a new treaty with Put-akhi which finally placed the Amorites under the heel of Khatti.

The peace lasted unbroken throughout the reigns of both kings. To the incessant wars of the two centuries since the invasion of Thothmes I succeeded a peace a slumber of exhaustion, over all Syria and Palestine, which lasted till the movement of the Northerners in the reign of Rameses III once more awakened the peoples to the realities of war and conflict.

Meanwhile, Phoenicia south of ever-rebellious Arvad continued to gather in wealth by exchange of commercial products and slaves under the congenial protection of Egypt, while the feuds of Canaanites and Khabiri seem to have been temporarily stilled. Egyptian residents no doubt sate in Gaza, Ashkelon, Jerusalem, or Megiddo, as in Tyre or Sidon, to watch and guide the local princes and chieftains. Peace being resolutely maintained between the two great protagonists, there was no opportunity for intrigue or revolt. To the north, the Amorites bore true allegiance to Khatti, while exporting to Egypt their cedar of Lebanon and the other wood which Egypt had always needed from their land. Egyptian emissaries cut down the valued timber in the territory of Khattusil, and no doubt paid for it much gold into the treasury of his vassal Put-akhi.

5. Assyria and Babylon in the Thirteenth Century B.C.

The mixed Iranian and Semitic populations of Naharin and Mitanni, however, apparently formed part of Khattusil's immediate dominions, and were not handed over to a sub-king like Amurri. The important Euphratean city of Carchemish, with a purely Hittite population, was the central fortress of this southern portion of Khattusil's realm, and the watch-tower from which the conquerors could observe the Assyrians and Babylonians. The Hittites did not attempt to conquer Assyria. the valour of the Assyrian soldiery was already well known, and would have made the enterprise too costly even had the Hittites been in the mood for further wars after their long struggle with Rameses, At the same time, the Assyrians feared the Hittites too much to provoke them to war, and contented themselves with insulting the weaker Babylonians on occasions when it could be done safely. This was not always the case. Kurigalzu "the Younger," who was placed upon the Babylonian throne by his grandfather the Assyrian king Ashuruballit, had developed into a monarch of firm character and, for a Babylonian, of unusually warlike propensities. He attacked the Elamites, captured their king Khurbatila with his own hands, sacked the capital, Susa, and brought back great spoil to Babylon. All through his long reign he seems to have been quietly disembarrassing himself of the Assyrian tutelage imposed by Ashuruballit, and the two elderly men who succeeded each other on the Assyrian throne, Belnirari and his son Arik-den-ilu, were not energetic enough to assert it. Adad-nirari, however, the son of Arik-den-iki, was young at his accession, while Kurigalzu was getting old. He accordingly arrogantly attempted to bring the Babylonian to book, with an unfortunate result: the Babylonians were victorious in the open field, and Kurigalzu imposed on the Assyrians his own views of the proper borders and relations between the two nations. Shortly afterwards he died, and Adad-nirari, smarting under defeat, seized the opportunity to attack his son and successor Nazimaruttash, but with what fortune we do not know: the old boundaries seem merely to have been reaffirmed afterwards.

Shalmaneser I, the son of Adad-nirari, was probably encouraged by the long-continued war between Rameses II and the Hittites to endeavour to extend his territory in a north-westerly direction. He appears to have ascended the Tigris to its source and then to have entered the Euphrates valley, which he descended in the direction of the later Samosata, taking tribute from the North Syrian lands of Musri and Arami. This expedition could hardly be regarded as otherwise than hostile to Khatti, though no conflict with the Hittites took place, and it may well have been planned in conjunction with Rameses as a diversion in favour of the Egyptians. When peace was concluded with Egypt, the Hittite distrust of Shalmaneser soon shewed itself Khattusil opened most friendly relations with Kadashman-turgu, the king of Babylon (the successor of Nazimaruttash), and when he died compelled the Babylonian officials to place his son Kadashman-buriash on the throne, by threat of war and conquest, in spite of the irritated protests of the Babylonian minister Itti-Marduk-balatu, who complained that Khatti did not write to the Babylonians in a brotherly manner but ordered them about as if they were vassals.

The death of Kadashman-turgu and accession of Kadashman-buriash must have taken place between the accession of Khattusil and the conclusion of the peace with Egypt, as we find Khattusil, in a letter to Kadashman-buriash to inform him of the treaty with Egypt, saying that he had formerly notified his father Kadashman-turgu when the king of Egypt had attacked Khatti (that is to say, on his accession, when he found the war going on). Khattusil cannot have been very long on the throne before the conclusion of peace, so that we can place the end of Kadashman-turgu's reign about 1280 B.C. This gives us the date of the Assyrian Shalmaneser I also.

Kadashman-buriash seems to have reigned but two or three years, and as, at the instigation of Khattusil, he made war upon Shalmaneser, there is every probability that he was defeated and slain by that monarch. Or perhaps treachery at home may have had something to do with his death. There was no doubt a pro-Assyrian party in Babylonia, which regarded the Northern kinsmen as much the same people as themselves, and desired the union of both countries under the rule of the Assyrian monarchs, who were pure Semitic Mesopotamians, and not foreigners like the Kassites. To this party the apparent dependence of Kadashman-buriash upon the dreaded Great King of Khatti gave a good pretext for action: if Babylonia was not to be absorbed like Mitanni or reduced to the position of a Hittite vassal like Amurri, the friend of Khatti must be deposed and the arms of Shalmaneser must be allowed to prevail. Assyrian domination was preferable to Hittite.

We do not know whether Is-ammi .... (the rest of his name is lost) and Shagarakti-Shuriash, the successors of Kadashman-buriash, were pro-Assyrian or not. Probably the first was, and a nominee of Shalmaneser; and the second not, since his son Kashtiliashu was strongly anti-Assyrian, and was attacked, defeated, and deposed by the energetic son of Shalmaneser, Tukulti-Ninib I, who assumed the Babylonian crown, and ruled for seven years in Babylon over both kingdoms (c. 1250-1243 B.C.).

The reign of Tukulti-Ninib marked the first advance of Assyria to a position of equality with Khatti. The inability of the Hittites to prevent the overthrow of their ally and the absorption of his kingdom by Assyria is proof of their decadence during the thirty years of peace that had elapsed since the conclusion of the war with Egypt. Probably Khattusil was now dead, and Dudhalia his son reigned in his stead.

6. The Decline of Khatti

During the whole of his reign Khattusil seems to have kept the peace resolutely, never allowing himself to be provoked into war by the restless aggressions of Assyria. Thirteen years after the signing of the Egyptian treaty, in the thirty-fourth year of Rameses II (about 1266 B.C.), the friendship of Egypt and Khatti was reaffirmed by the marriage to Rameses of a Hittite princess, daughter of Khattusil and Pudukhipa, who in Egypt received the name of Ueret-maait-neferu-Ra, "The Princess who seeth the beauties of Ra." Khattusil brought his daughter to Egypt himself in person, thus making a state visit to his brother-monarch, a thing probably unprecedented. Kings were not accustomed to visit one another's territory except with hostile intent. The Hittite emperor was accompanied in his progress to Egypt by a train of sub-kings and chiefs, among whom Put-akhi or his successors no doubt took the foremost place, with his brother-vassal the king of Kedi or Arzawa. They brought with them an immense amount of presents in gold and silver. They came in winter, much to the astonishment of the Egyptians, in spite of snow in the passes of Taurus and rain among the hills of Palestine, as the summer-heat of Egypt would have been felt unbearable by the Anatolians. And no doubt the snow and rain which seemed to the Egyptians to be so terrible an obstacle to marching in the winter-season in Asia were nothing to the Hittites.

The visitors were probably received, and the marriage celebrated, at Tanis (Per-Rameses): it is improbable that they journeyed to Thebes, where, indeed, the Court rarely was. At Abu Simbel we find a stela recording the marriage which ends with the words of Rameses speeding his departing guests and expressing the hope that they will not meet with snow and ice in the northern passes (Taurus) on the way back to far Anatolia. No doubt the Hittite king remained several months at Tanis, and his stay was probably a veritable prototype of "the Field of the Cloth of Gold."

We do not hear anything of a return-visit paid by Rameses to Khatti. Had he gone there he certainly would have been farther than any other Egyptian king: none before had ever attempted to pass the Taurus, even in war. Had he reached the Halys-land in peace as the guest of Khattusil he certainly would have given some ground for the later legends about Sesostris, who went to Colchis and Bactria. We do not know that he did not go. But if he did not, he did the next best thing, in sending one of his most valuable and venerated deities, Khonsu of Thebes, to the Hittite court just as Dushratta had sent Ishtar of Nineveh to Amenhetep III a century or more before. For there is little doubt that the famous story of "The Possessed Princess of Bekhten," though known to us only in a late and inaccurate copy made by priestly antiquarians in the time of the Ptolemies, refers to the reign of Rameses II, and that "Bekhten" (often supposed to be Bactria) is really nothing but "Kheta" misread in true Ptolemaic style. It is evident that the main facts of the tale are correct, and that it records a visit paid in the reign of Rameses II by the god Khonsu, son of Amen and Mut, to the court of the King of Khatti in order to cure his daughter Bintresh, sister of the Queen Ueret-maait-neferu-Ra. Previously Thutiemheb, an Egyptian wise man, had been sent by Rameses to attempt a cure, but had failed, for the Princess Bintresh appeared to be possessed of a devil. Accordingly it was determined to send her the wonder-working image of Khonsu Ari-sekheru, "the Plan-Maker," renowned as an expeller of evil spirits. The tale tells how Rameses asked leave of the great god Khonsu-em-Uaset-Neferhetep, the chief image of Khonsu at Thebes, for permission to send the Plan-Maker to Khatti, "Then said His Majesty before Khonsu-em-Uaset-Neferhetep, 'O good lord, if thou turnest thy face towards Khonsu the Plan-Maker, the great god, driving away evil spirits, he shall go to Bekhten.' The head was inclined deeply, deeply. Then said His Majesty: 'Send thy protection with him, that I may cause His Majesty to go to Bekhten, to save the daughter of the chief of Bekhten.' Khonsu-em-Uaset-Neferhetep inclined his head deeply, deeply." Then the Plan-Maker was taken to Khatti in great state, with ships (no doubt as far as Cilicia), chariots, and horses. Arrived in "Bekhten," he immediately effected the cure of Bintresh, and the tale recounts a marvellous dialogue between him and the expelled devil, who confesses himself his slave, and offers to go away to his own place, if the god will celebrate a feast with him and with the King of Bekhten. "Then this god bent down to his priest, saying, 'Let the King of Bekhten make a great offering before this devil.'" The king, who had been standing by during this remarkable interview, in great fear, did as he was bidden, and the devil finally departed. The king was now so convinced of the prowess of the god that he determined to keep him with him, and did so for three years and nine months, till one night he dreamt that he saw the god fly out of his shrine towards Egypt in the form of a golden hawk. "Then the King of Bekhten caused this god to proceed to Egypt, and gave to him very many gifts of every good thing, very many soldiers and horses. . . . Khonsu-the-Plan-Maker-in-Thebes arrived at his temple in peace in the year 33, the second month, the ninth day, of King Usermara Setepnera."

This date, and that of year 26 given for the departure of the god, should probably be emended to 43 and 36 respectively, as Ueret-maait-neferu-Ra is mentioned as queen, and the mission to cure her younger sister is very likely to have been sent out a year or two after her marriage, which took place in the year 34. The journey of Thutiemheb and the retention of the god are paralleled by the mission of a Babylonian physician and an exerciser to Khatti, which is mentioned in a letter from Khattusil to Kadashman-buriash in answer to an inquiry as to what had become of the two wise men, as they had never come back: the necromancer, Khattusil replied, was dead, but the physician would be returned at once. Khattusil seems to have been desirous of retaining the science of his wiser neighbours, whether exercised by human, daemonic, or divine agency, at his disposition as long as possible, when it was once in his power.

If it was Khattusil who sent back the image of Khonsu in the 43rd year of Rameses, we must credit him with a reign of at least twenty-two years. As he was the son of Mursil it is not probable that he reigned longer, and he must have been a very old man when he died, like his father and grandfather. We may therefore place the accession of his son Dudhalia about 1255 B.C. at latest.

Of Dudhalia, and his son Arnuanta, our only information is derived from the Boghaz Kyoi tablets. From them we see that Pudukhipa, the heiress of Katawadana, and powerful queen of Khattusil, still held supreme power during the early years of her son's reign: Rameses addresses a personal letter to her as queen, and when Dudhalia's name is first mentioned, she appears with him as co-regent. This is testimony to the important part played by the queen in the Hittite state, and no doubt more especially by the queen-mother, on the analogy of the relations between Cybele, the mother-goddess, and her son Atys. Similarly Arnuanta is mentioned in his records with his mother Tawashi. . . ., Dudhalia's wife, and his own wife Muni-Dan, "the Great Queen," who seems to have been at the same time his own sister. It is not impossible that this practice was now begun in imitation of the pharaonic usage, which originated in the desire to keep the royal blood pure, and soon resulted in destroying dynasty after dynasty.

The introduction of the practice seems to have synchronized with a decline in the royal house and state of Khatti. Arnuanta was probably the last powerful successor of Shubbiluliuma. After him we hear of no more Great Kings at Boghaz Kyoi.

We have seen that already in Khattusil's reign the central power at Boghaz Kyoi was unable to protect the eastern provinces of the empire from Assyrian attack, and was powerless to resent Shalmaneser's insolent march into Syria, so severely was it weakened by the struggle with Egypt. In Dudhalia's time these eastern provinces or dependent kingdoms were again ravaged by the Assyrians under Shalmaneser's son, Tukulti-Ninib, without a finger being stirred to help them, although the excuse of the absorbing war with Egypt was no longer available.

It must have been in the reign of Arnuanta that one of the southern Hittite kingdoms, probably that of Kadesh, came into collision once more with Egypt. After a reign of sixty-seven years Rameses II had died (about 1234 B.C.) and was succeeded by his eldest surviving son, Meneptah (Merenptah). Twelve of his sons had died before him, including his favourite, Kha-em-uaset, the high-priest of Ptah, who seems to have been a man of considerable energy and mental power. In the latter years of his father's reign he seems to have represented him in various ways, making progresses throughout Egypt to organize the repeated jubilees or Sed-festivals which Rameses celebrated at short intervals after his thirtieth year, and leaving the record of his presence in many temples. Had he lived, he would probably have been a worthy successor to his father. But he died, and the thirteenth brother, Merenptah, succeeded as an elderly man to a throne that was to prove uneasy.

7. Meneptah mid Israel: the Libyan Invasion of Egypt

The death of the old monarch of Egypt seems to have been regarded by the Palestinian tribes as a signal for revolt, and in his third year Meneptah was compelled to subdue afresh the now restricted Asiatic dominion of

Egypt. The main movers of the revolt seem to have been the Israelites, now mentioned for the first time in history under their corporate name of Israel (Isirail), and the cities of the Shephelah, specially Ashkelon and Gezer, soon to be occupied by the invading western tribes of the Philistines. Ashkelon and Gezer were taken, the latter after a formidable resistance, apparently, and the Israelites were severely chastised. In a triumphal inscription which Meneptah set up in his funerary temple in Western Thebes, built with the spoil of Amenhetep III's ruined fane, we read: "The kings are overthrown, saying 'Salaam!' Not one holds up his head among the Nine Bows. Wasted is Tehenu (Libya), Kheta is pacified, plundered is Canaan with every evil, Ashkelon is carried away, taken is Gezer, Yenoam is made as a thing that is not, Israel is wasted, he hath no seed, Khal (Palestine) has become as a (defenceless) widow before Egypt. All lands are united, and are pacified. Every one that is rebellious is bound by King Merenptah, given life like the Sun every day!" The king was so proud of the taking of Gezer that he added "Binder of Gezer" to his titles. The reference to Kheta, taken with other indications, probably points to a raid upon the Hittites of the Orontes valley, who had presumably afforded assistance to the Canaanites. With the kingdom of "Great Kheta" in Anatolia, however, Meneptah's relations were good, and he had already sent shiploads of corn, no doubt to Arnuanta, to succour "that Kheta-land" when it was devastated by a great famine, a severe blow to the disintegrating empire of Boghaz Kyoi.

The rising of the Canaanites had probably been planned owing to the growing weakness of Egypt in the Delta, which had for some time been threatened by a most formidable invasion of Libyans from the west, in alliance with certain tribes of the Mediterranean, which internal convulsions in Greece, Italy, and the Aegean, caused probably by invasion from Northern Europe, had now driven forth to lead a life of piracy. With these events, and with their probable causes, the second chapter has already dealt. Here it will suffice to say that not long before his death the generals of Rameses II had repulsed a first attack, apparently of Libyans alone, upon the Western Delta, and that two years after his repression of the Palestinian revolt, Meneptah had to face a renewed attack of the Libyans, this time in alliance with a confederation of seafaring tribes from Greece and the coast of Asia Minor, Akaiwasha (possibly Achaians from Greece), Tursha (Tyrsenians from Italy or Asia Minor?), Luka (Lycians), Shardina (Sardinians or else Sardians from Asia Minor), and Shakalsha

(Sagalassians from Asia Minor), "Northerners coming from all lands." The confederated tribes were defeated and more or less annihilated by the Egyptians at Piari in the Western Delta, and Egypt had peace from them, for a time.

8. The Successors of Meneptah and the Reign of Rameses III

The invasion had severely shaken the Egyptian state, already much weakened by the apathy of the last half of the reign of Rameses II. Meneptah died, an old man, after a short reign (about 1225 B.C.), and was buried at Thebes, where his body has recently been found. Then a period of thirty years of confusion in the state began, which had been unexampled for five centuries. Three kings reigned after him whose actual order of succession is by no means yet certainly determined — Amenmeses, Rameses-Siptah, and Seti-Meneptah, usually known as Seti II. The most recent view is that they succeeded in the order in which they are here named. Amenmeses seems to have been certainly a usurper; he reigned for a very short time, his tomb at Thebes was never completed and he was probably never buried in it; also he was never regarded as a legitimate king in later days. Nor was Siptah, who seems, however, to have reigned for some time, and to have been an active monarch. His energy was probably, however, not his own, as by his side stood an energetic man and woman, his chancellor Bai and his queen Tausret, the Thouoris of Manetho. Bai seems to have been the real ruler of the kingdom, in conjunction with the queen, who left a tradition of masterfulness behind her which was still current in Manetho's day.

Seti II was regarded as a legitimate king: possibly he was a cadet of the royal house who was viceroy of Ethiopia under Siptah, and used this prominent position as his stepping-stone to the throne. Since the time of Amenhetep III no serious wars had interfered with the peaceful development of Nubia: the few razzias under Rameses II were mere chastisements of isolated tribes. The gold-mines of the Etbai were steadily worked by the gangs of miserable slaves whom fate had sent there, and he who controlled Nubia now controlled most of the wealth of Egypt. Thus an energetic viceroy could interfere with effect in Egypt if the course of events gave him the opportunity. And the opportunity came to Seti as it had not come to any previous viceroy of Kush, who under the great kings of the last three centuries had had no chance of asserting himself. As king, however, Seti made no mark, and when he died anarchy resulted, the kingdom for a time falling into the power of a Syrian adventurer, whose name is not certainly known.

From this degradation it was, however, soon rescued by a soldier named Setnekht, a Northerner who was probably related to the royal house. He made himself king, expelled the Syrian, but reigned but a year, being succeeded by his son Rameses, who aspired to be a second Rameses the Great. Rameses III took as his titulary a careful adaptation of the titles of Rameses II, he gave his sons the same names as those of the sons of Rameses ii, and his whole reign was a sort of elaborate parody of that of his great predecessor, whom he imitated in every detail. This was a settled policy, designed to inspire the Egyptians anew with the spirit of the first half of the reign of Rameses II, when the young and victorious "Grand Monarque" was dazzling Egypt with the renewed glory of Thothmes III, and before the long-drawn-out struggle with the Hittites had exhausted the nation. The policy succeeded temporarily: for a short time Egypt was roused from her lethargy of over half a century, and was once more imposing and splendid till the artificial revival of Rameses in collapsed under his successors, and the empire fell into final decay. The fact that this breathing of life into the dying body was essayed and was for a time successful shews that Rameses III was no common man, and that had he chosen to strike out a new line of his own instead of imitating his predecessor, he would have left the mark of a great king of original genius like Thothmes III. But he chose his policy and followed it, with the result that his name is overshadowed by that of his probably much less capable but superficially more brilliant model.

In one important respect, however, Rameses III did not follow the example of his prototype; he embarked on no wars of aggression. He had the evils of this policy before his eyes in the exhaustion which he was trying to cure. In Egypt, as in other countries, strong government had too often, indeed usually, meant war and foreign conquests. Rameses III did successfully what Hatshepsut had tried to do in advance of her time; he combined strong government with peace, with the result that, at his death, after a reign of thirty-one years and forty days, he left an Egypt peaceful and wealthy, even wealthier perhaps than in the days of Amenhetep III, but unhappily without the stamina which she had possessed in the days of the magnificent emperor. We know how rich Rameses left Egypt in the record of his benefactions to his people and to the gods, which was copied on papyrus at the time of his death and buried with him as a testimony of his virtue to the gods of the underworld, and is now in the British Museum, where it is known as "the Great Harris Papyrus." The wealth of the country in grain, cattle, silver, and gold was largely shared between the king and the gods, and we can well imagine that so astute and careful a ruler as Rameses III knew well how to turn much of it into his own coffers. So that we can understand how in later days he was regarded as the legendary wealthy king, the Croesus of ancient Egypt, and is so commemorated by Herodotus in the figure of his "Rhampsinitos." On the walls of the treasure-chambers of the splendid funerary temple which he built at Medinet Habu, in Western Thebes, we see reliefs representing the magnificent specimens of the goldsmith's art, the heaps of gold rings, the bags of gold-dust and ingots of gold which Rhampsinitos presented to his own shrine. In his day indeed "the heaps of precious ingots gleamed" in hundred-gated Thebes. But all the gold of Nubia could not serve to arrest the progress of Egyptian decay more than a short time. The splendour of Rhampsinitos did not mean real strength.

9, The Great Libyan and Northern invasions of Egypt

However, under this king, the state was still strong enough to defend itself victoriously against external enemies. Rameses III had to defend Egypt against renewed attacks by the Libyans and Mediterranean tribes. Recovered from the blow dealt them by Meneptah thirty years before, and encouraged by the rumours that reached them of the internal dissensions of the Egyptian state, the barbarian tribes again combined to possess themselves of the fat lands of the Egyptian Delta. Twice did they make the attempt, and twice they were driven back into Libya. Between these two attacks from Libya, Rameses was threatened by a danger from the east even more serious than that from the west, and this also was warded off and victory gained for Egypt by the energetic king.

The first Libyan attack was defeated in the fifth year of the reign; the great victory over the European and West-Anatolian tribes who came down through Palestine in a regular Volkerwanderung nearly as far as the borders of Egypt, was gained in the eighth year (about 1196 B.C.). This war was the greatest national danger that the Egyptians had experienced since the invasion of the Hyksos. The catastrophe is concisely recorded thus in the inscription of Rameses III: "The Isles were restless, disturbed among themselves at one and the same time. No land stood before them, beginning from Kheta, Kedi (Cilicia), Carchemish, Arvad, and Alashiya.

They destroyed [them, and assembled in their] camp in one place in the midst of Amor (Amurru; Palestine). They desolated its people and its land like that which is not. They came with fire prepared before them, forward towards Egypt. Their main strength was [composed of] Pulesti, Tjakaray, Shakalsha, Daanau, and Uashasha. These lands were united, and they laid their hands upon the land as far as the Circle of the Earth. Their hearts were confident, full of their plans."

Khatti was already probably weakened by the great famine in Meneptah's reign, and so, at the end of the reign of Arnuanta or early in that of an unknown successor, ended Shubbiluliuma's empire, after two centuries of power. But Egypt was not yet to be overrun a second time by a foreign conqueror. Her king saw that a vigorous offensive was the best defence. Advancing by sea and land along the coast towards Palestine, he fell with ships and chariots upon the barbarian host, wearied by long journeying and incessant fighting, and inflicted upon it a complete defeat. The foreign fleet was annihilated, the warriors on land were killed, taken, or put to flight, and no doubt most of the women and children were carried into captivity. As the king says in his inscription, they were trapped like wild-fowl. Taken by surprise in the "harbour-mouths" where their ships had collected, they found their escape seawards barred by an undreamt-of Egyptian fleet which attacked them like "a full flame" as they lay anchored or drawn up upon the shore, while they were taken in rear from the land side, for the arrival of the Egyptian fleet upon the scene had accurately sychronized with the appearance of Rameses with his army. Then, when the seafarers had been disposed of, the army met and defeated the slower moving land horde, which had not yet reached the rendezvous. "Those who reached my frontier, their seed is not; their heart and their soul are perished for ever. As for those who had assembled before them on the sea, the full flame was in their front, before the harbour-mouths, and a wall of metal upon the shore surrounded them. They were dragged, capsized, and laid low upon the beach; slain and made heaps from stem to bow of their ships. And all their belongings were cast upon the waters."

The outer walls of the temple of Medinet Habu are sculptured with pictures of the great fight. We see the bird-beaked ships of the Aegeans, some capsized, others with their masts falling. From the crow's nest of one tumbles a feathered warrior of the Pulesti, transfixed by an Egyptian arrow. Among them drive the lion-headed galleys of Egypt, manned partly by Egyptians, partly by Shardina mercenaries, who fight with other Shardina who are allied with the Pulesti, like Varangians fighting with their Byzantine masters against their Norman brethren. The appearance of an Egyptian fleet must have been entirely unexpected by the would-be invaders. So far as we know, no former Egyptian ruler had attacked the Northern seafarers on their own element, and the fact that he foresaw the probable success of so unprecedented an attack and organized a war-fleet with which to accomplish it, redounds greatly to the credit of Rameses III as an organizer, as the accurate timing of his operations by land and sea does to his credit as a general.

Where the sea-fight actually took place is unknown. Latterly it has been supposed that it was fought far north on the Palestinian coast, even in one of the Phoenician harbours. It seems more probable, however, that the older view, according to which it took place close to the actual frontier of Egypt, is the correct one. Possibly the "harbour-mouths" referred to are the mouths of the Pelusiac Nile, a very probable rendezvous for the Northern ships, which had long been accustomed to the navigation of the Nile-mouths. The Egyptian galleys, also, do not look as if they were intended for work so far away from the Nile as Phoenicia: they seem river-craft rather than seagoing ships, being frailer and lower in the water than the long-ships of the Northerners.

Nor is it probable that the land battle took place any farther north than the southern Shephelah. The remnant of the Pulesti and the other tribes who escaped the sword of Rameses were not driven very far north, if, as is probable, it was now that they settled in the Shephelah and founded the new nation of the Philistines. Rameses himself advanced to the confines of the Egyptian dominion to restore his authority which the invasion had shaken, and found occasion to enter Amor or Amurri, which had been undisputed territory of Khatti for nearly a century. No doubt the anarchy caused by the Northern invasion or the destruction of the central Hittite power made it necessary for him to take some guarantee for the peaceableness of the Hittite dynasts on his frontier: he seems to have taken Kadesh and other places which were defended by Hittite soldiery. That he actually advanced to the Euphrates is improbable; though he places in his lists of conquered towns names of places in Naharin which are known to us from the time of the XVIIIth Dynasty, this is due probably to a very bad habit which began in his reign, that of copying the names of cities captured in the wars of Thothmes III and placing them to the credit of kings who never came within hundreds of miles of them.

Returned to Egypt, Rameses had a respite of about two years before the last of the three great Libyan attacks on Egypt was met and vanquished in the eleventh year of his reign. This time the Westerners came alone, without Northern allies. Probably the Tamahu, or Libyans living immediately on the Egyptian border, would not have been desirous of repeating their disastrous experience of six years before, had they not been driven forward by an invasion of the redoubtable Mashauasha or Maxyes from the modern Tunis, who pushed on forward, carrying the Tamahu with them against Egypt. The result was defeat in the Delta, and the enslavement of those who were not killed. According to the inscriptions, 2175 men were slain, while 1494 men and 558 women were captured. Kapul, the chief of the Mashauasha, was captured, and Mashashal, his son, was killed.

The remaining twenty years of the reign of Rameses III were entirely peaceful, and were troubled only at the end by the harem conspiracy, which has already been mentioned. He was succeeded by several of his sons in succession to one another, who all bore the same name as he.

To the last Ramessides of the XXth Dynasty, the last of the imperial pharaohs, we shall return later: we have now to turn our attention to the apparent effects of the great invasion from the West upon Assyria and Babylon.

10. Assyria and Babylonia (1250-1100 B.C.)

Although the Western invasion never actually reached Assyria, its repercussion nevertheless severely affected the young kingdom of Northern Mesopotamia, which at the same time, after a short period of great energy under Tukulti-Ninib, who had taken and ruled Babylon for seven years, was so vigorously attacked by the Babylonians, whose national spirit had been aroused by their subjection, that in its turn the Assyrian power was temporarily overthrown. The struggle against this fierce onslaught of the Babylonians had occupied all the force that Assyria had to dispose of, and she was utterly unable to prevent the western districts of her kingdom, which had been added to it by the warlike kings of fifty years before, from being overrun by hosts of Anatolians who had been forced out of Asia Minor by the Westerners.

The rule of Tukulti-Ninib was brought to an abrupt end by a revolt of "the nobles of Akkad and Karduniyash," who set Adad-shum-usur, son of Kashtiliashu, the king whom Tukulti-Ninib had carried off to Assyria, upon his father's throne; while "against Tukulti-Ninib, who had brought evil upon Babylon, Ashur-nasir-pal, his son, and the nobles of Assyria revolted, and from his throne they cast him, and they besieged him in a house in the city of Kar-Tukultininib, and they slew him with the sword." Thus perished the conqueror miserably at the hands of his own son, and Kashtiliashu was avenged.

In Assyria Ashur-nasir-pal I, the murderer of his father, was probably succeeded after a very brief reign by Tukulti-Ashur, in whose time, six years after it had been carried off, the image of Marduk was restored to Babylon. Probably this was effected by priestly influence rather than war, and we can well imagine that the weakness and troubles of the Assyrian royal house at this time were popularly ascribed to Tukulti-Ninib's sacrilege. For we know nothing more of Tukulti-Ashur, and very soon afterwards we find two kings seated side by side upon the Assyrian throne, Ashurnarara and Nabudani, and we possess a late Assyrian copy of a letter addressed to them by Adad-shum-usur of Babylon. They disappear in their turn, and next we hear from the later chronicles that Bel-kudur-usur of Assyria and Adad-shum-usur fell in battle with one another, after Adad-shum-usur had reigned thirty years (about 1243-1213 B.C.). Victory seems to have rested with the Babylonians.

To Bel-kudur-usur succeeded Ninib-apal-ekur, and to Adad-shum-usur his son Melishipak II, who was destined to illuminate the close of the long Kassite dynasty with a brief flash of military energy and glory. Following up the victory which his father had gained, though at the price of his life, Melishipak, with his son Marduk-apal-iddina, triumphantly invaded Assyria, and it is not at all certain that he did not so completely reverse the result of Tukulti-Ninib's time as actually to conquer and hold the whole country, handing it over to his son Marduk-apal-iddina to govern as King of Assyria. Our information is most scanty, but from various indications this seems probable. If so, the dominion of Khammurabi was restored, and Assyria was under Babylonian rule for some years, as Melishipak reigned fifteen years, and his son (Merodach-baladan 1) thirteen; if they had been expelled from Assyria it is hardly likely that they would have had untroubled reigns at home. Also, we hear nothing of any Assyrian king after Ninib-apal-ekur till Ashur-dan defeats Zamama-shum-iddina the ephemeral successor of Marduk-apal-iddina (about 1185 B.C.), and restores the Assyrian kingdom to its old limits and more, adding to it lands beyond the Zab which had previously been considered Babylonian. If

Ashur-dan was the son of Ninib-apal-ekur, he was probably a little child when, about 1210 B.C., the Babylonians conquered the country. If his father was killed then, he was probably in hiding or exile till, fifteen years later, as a young man, he was able to assert his right to his kingdom. The defeat of Zamama-shum-iddina probably marks the final victory of the young king, who took the trans-Zab lands as a lesson to Babylonia of the futility of conquest and success.

The failure of Melishipak's revenge sounded the death-knell of the long-enduring Kassite dynasty, which had ruled Babylonia for nearly six hundred years. Bel-nadin-shum, successor of Zamama-shum-iddina, was the last Kassite king, and he died or was murdered after a reign of only three years, about 1180 B.C. The new dynasty, "of Pashe," that now took up the reins of power in Babylonia, was probably of native Babylonian origin. Perhaps a really native dynasty was considered to augur a more lasting success of Marduk against his enemy Ashur; but we hear of no collision between the two nations till the time of the sixth king of the new dynasty, Nebuchadrezzar I (about 1125 B.C.).

Assyria needed time to recover from the disasters that had followed the murder of Tukulti-Ninib. These had not come singly. As has already been mentioned, the Babylonian attack was practically contemporary with the loss of the western conquests of Tukulti-Ninib to a horde of Anatolians from "Mushki" (Meshech), that is to say Asia Minor west of the Taurus. The lands of Alshe and Perikuzzi were lost, and later on Kummukh (Kommagene) was invaded and occupied by the "Mushkaya." Tiglath-pileser I, at the end of the twelfth century, speaks of their invasion as having taken place about fifty years before his time. This is evidently a very vague number, and we can hardly err in regarding the invasion as a direct result of the great migration of the Westerners which, in the first decade of the twelfth century, "overran all lands, beginning from Kheta," and was only stopped on the borders of Egypt by Rameses III. As the invaders are not called specifically "Khatti," but by the more general term of "Mushkaya," they were probably a horde of Hittites from Cappadocia and other Anatolians, who had been compelled to cross the Taurus in search of new land after their own had been desolated by the passing of the great wandering of Aegeans and Western Anatolians, displaced by the Achaians(?) and Phrygians. The date of their invasion may with great probability be placed between 1190 and 1180 B.C., before Assyria had yet freed herself from the Babylonian control imposed by Melishipak. As the king and court of Assyria were practically non-existent, the outlying provinces were without any form of control, and no doubt the derelict Alshe and Perikuzzi were an obvious and easy prey to the dispossessed and land-seeking Mushkaya.

Assyria was, however, not dead, though she needed nearly a century to recover from her disasters. Ashur-dan reigned peacefully till he reached a good old age, dying honoured by his descendants as the reconstructor of the state. The short reign of his son and successor, Mutakkil-nusku, was equally peaceful. But in that of his son, Ashur-rish-ishi, the old warlike spirit of Assyria began to reassert itself, expeditions were undertaken against the Northern tribes, and war broke out with Babylon. After several unimportant reigns, the dynasty of Pashe had given to Babylon an energetic king, Nabu-kudur-usur or Nebuchadrezzar I. He was successful as a warrior against Elam, but against Assyria he failed. The cause of the conflict was not now any attempt on the part of either combatant directly to invade and conquer the other. The fighting took place in North-western Mesopotamia, in the Euphrates valley somewhere about the mouth of the Khabur, where for centuries had run the march between the Hittite empire and that of Babylon. This certainly looks as if the Assyrian had been the aggressor: a Babylonian attack on Assyria would have been directed straight up the Tigris valley. Probably Ashur-rish-ishi, who was a warrior, and had campaigned against the Kuti and other mountain-tribes, had turned his arms eastward and had invaded Babylonian territory in Mesopotamia. Here he was met by a Babylonian army, which was defeated with the loss of forty chariots and its commander-in-chief Karastu: Nebuchadrezzar does not seem to have been present in person. The result was that most of the Upper Euphratean territory of Babylon was now transferred to Assyria (1125 B.C.).

It would seem that Nebuchadrezzar had specially directed his attention towards this outlying region of his empire, and had aspired to succeed to part of the inheritance of the Hittites, which was now being dispersed. Amurri had fallen to him, or to one of his predecessors (perhaps Melishipak), so that at this time Babylon exercised at least a nominal authority in the West which had hardly been known since the days of Khammurabi. Egypt, indolent and degenerate under the Ramessides of the XXth Dynasty, had neither wish nor intention to dispute it with her. But Assyria, under Ashur-rish-ishi, was ambitious, and under his successor, Tiglath-pileser I (reigning in 1107 B.C.), made her first essay as world-conqueror, a sort of rehearsal of the Sargonide conquests of the eighth century. Before Tiglath-pileser Babylon shrank within herself, and not only abandoned all her western possessions, but was twice the prey of the conqueror, who styled himself King of Sumer and Akkad. And in the north Assyria finally triumphed over the relic of Khatti when Tiglath-pileser, having in successive campaigns first expelled from their conquests the Anatolian tribes of Mushki who had been settled in the upper Euphrates valley and Kommagene (Kummukh) since the troubles at the beginning of the reign of Ashur-dan, secondly subdued Shubari, and thirdly raided Northern Syria (Naharin) west of the Euphrates, then conquered Musri, a Hittite land, and finally penetrated the Taurus to Kumani, which has been identified with Komana of Kataonia (Katawadana).

The Assyrians then entered Anatolia. The city of Khunusa (possibly Iconium) was taken and burned, its triple wall destroyed, and its site sown with salt. Finally the royal city of Kibshuna (Kybistra?) was besieged and surrounded and its walls destroyed. Then the Assyrian king returned to his own country, having subdued all lands from the Lower Zab to the "broad land of Kumani, the land of Khatti and the Upper Sea of the West" (the Black Sea).

Thus were even the remnants of Shubbiluliuma's empire destroyed. The Assyrian had not attempted to penetrate to Boghaz Kyoi: probably the imperial town had lain desolate since the catastrophe of the Western Invasion. The name of Khatti still survived even as late as the eighth century, when Carchemish was still the centre of a Hittite nation, but it was the name merely of a petty people; its glory had long departed.

11. The Decadence of the Egyptian Empire

Meanwhile in Egypt the empire of the Ramessides was tottering to its fall. The symptoms of decay in the body politic were too marked for even the energy of Rameses III to delay the catastrophe for long. And after his death the nation had no capable men left. Rameses IV was a miserable devotee, who spent his days praying to Amen, Osiris, and any god whom he thought would hear him, to grant him length of days like Rameses II, for had he not even in four years of reign given to Amen as much wealth and privileges as Rameses II had in his sixty-seven years of reign? We know from "The Great Harris Papyrus," the record of the gifts given by or confirmed to the temples by Rameses III at the end of his reign, that the estate of Amen then comprised over ten per cent of the cultivated land of

Egypt. We can imagine that during his six years' reign Rameses iv increased this proportion very largely, and that under his successors, who were wax in the hands of the priests, it increased more than ever till (and we are not surprised to see it) in the reign of Rameses IX the High-Priest of Amen is in wealth and power on an equality with the king himself, and in that of Rameses XI is regent of the kingdom, the pharaoh being a mere faineant.

The result was not long delayed. When the life of the eleven and last Rameses came to an end after a reign of nearly thirty years (about 1100 B.C.), Herihor the high-priest quietly assumed the crown, inscribing his priestly title before his name within the royal cartouche.

His authority was not recognized in the North. When the kings had abandoned Tanis and removed to Thebes, the city of their god and his priest, their mentor, a governor of the North, was appointed to represent the king at Tanis and was characteristically described by the Thebans as "him to whom Amen (not the king) has committed the charge of his North-land." In the reign of Rameses XII the governor of the North was a certain Nesibanebded, who, from his name ("He who belongs to Mendes"), was a Northerner, but was married to a princess of Thebes, named Tent-Amen. When, in the fifth year of the reign of Rameses XI (c. 1117 B.C.), Herihor sent an official named Unamon to Byblos to obtain wood for the building of the great festival barges of Amen, he gave him letters to Nesibanebded, the Regent of the North, and his wife Tentamen, in order that he might be given passage on a ship for Byblos, as a messenger of Amen. In Unamon's report Tentamen is always mentioned on an equality with her husband, owing, no doubt, to her royal birth, Unamon gives "them" the letter of Herihor, and they reply: "I will act according to the word of Amen-Ra, king of the gods, our lord." From Unamon's description, it appears that Nesibanebded was in close relations with certain great Phoenician merchants of Tanis," and himself owned ships, manned by Egyptians, upon the Great Sea. Probably he took a considerable part in the active commerce of the time. The shadowy pharaoh Rameses XI was thus from the beginning of his reign compelled to see the authority that rightfully belonged to him usurped not only in the South by the High-Priest of Amen, but also in the North by a wealthy lay satrap, the associate of the great merchants of Phoenicia.

It was then natural that when he died, Nesibanebded should have proclaimed himself king at Tanis, doubtless in right of his wife, simultaneously with the assumption of royal power in the South by Herihor. No struggle between the two took place. Both were old men, each could be of service to the other; the nation, which had not known civil war for centuries, was probably disinclined for it, and since the time of Rameses III the military forces of the crown in South and North had probably fallen into complete disorganization. The situation was accepted during the reign of Herihor, but when he died, after a reign of about seven years, his son, the high-priest Piankh, was unable to continue the royal dignity, and the whole land acknowledged the authority of the Tanite king Aakheperra Psibkhannu I. Piankh's son, Pinetjem I, married Maatkara Mutemhat, daughter of King Psibkhannu, and at the death of the latter (after a long reign of forty-one years according to Manetho) the royal authority over the whole land seems to have devolved upon the Theban, who became king. Then by a new arrangement, the High-Priesthood of Amen was separated from the kingship, and was held in succession by two of Pinetjem's sons, Masaharta and Menkheperra-Psibkhannu, the last of whom survived him, but did not succeed to the crown, which passed to a Tanite, probably a grandson of Psibkhannu I, named Amenemapet, Menkheperra remaining simply High-Priest. There is little doubt that these curious "rotativist" arrangements were due to a family compact devised at the death of Herihor in order to avoid the anomaly of two pharaohs reigning contemporaneously, a phenomenon to which neither princes nor people were yet used. The compact, if there was one, was, however, not kept by Menkheperra, who soon began to use regnal years, and finally adopted the royal cartouche. He became totally independent of the Tanite king, from whom he evidently feared attack, since he equipped a considerable fortress at el-Hebi in Middle Egypt to guard his northern frontier. His second son, Pinetjem II, who succeeded him, reigned contemporaneously with Neter-kheper-Ra Siamon of Tanis, the successor of Amenemapet. This pair was succeeded by two kings, Ded-khepru-Ra Psibkhannu in the South, and Hetj-hek-Ra Hor-Psibkhannu (Psusennes II) in the North, with whom the XXIst Dynasty came to an end (c. 945 B.C.), and with it the last trace of the rule of imperial Thebes. The reign of the Bubastite Sheshenk (Shishak) who founded the XXIInd Dynasty belongs to a new age and a later chapter.

Our knowledge of the insignificant kings of the XXIst Dynasty is derived but slightly from monumental records. After Herihor's time the priest-kings had neither the means nor the energy to build much, and had no glorious deeds to chronicle in everlasting stone. A stela at Karnak records how Men-kheper-ra Psibkhannu brought back from the Oasis a body of exiles who had been sent there: we have little else. The Northern kings built at Tanis and at Memphis; Siamon is specially notable as a builder. But their efforts could not effect much, and so little did they do or say that we know hardly anything about them, and can but guess at the length of their reigns with the help of Manetho. But we have considerable knowledge of the priest-kings through a somewhat peculiar source, the small dockets and inscriptions on the wrappings of the mummies of some of these kings, their relatives, and also of their great predecessors, which were found at Der el-Bahri in 1881. We have seen that tomb-robbing was by no means unknown in Egypt; and in the reign of Rameses X a royal commission was appointed to examine into the reported violation of royal tombs. Finally, so seriously endangered were the royal mummies (which had been mostly found intact in the time of Rameses X), that under the Theban priest-kings the practice began of actually moving them from their tombs and hiding them in deep pits or other places of shelter, such as the tomb of one of them. When things concentrated in one or two places only, better guard could be kept over them. As we know, the device was effectual, and preserved in the pit of Der el-Bahri and in the tomb of Amenhetep II the bodies of most of the great Theban kings, and of their successors the family of Herihor, who had themselves buried with them, in order to share their safety and at the same time avoid the expense of making elaborate royal tombs for themselves. Many of the ancient royal mummies had been found damaged, and were re-rolled in new bandages. When this was done, the name and year of the priest-king then reigning were inscribed upon the "restored" mummy. The date, too, of the removal from the original tomb was placed upon the corpse, and when, as was sometimes the case, there were several different removals from one tomb or pit to another, the date and name of the king under whom it was effected were regularly noted. This custom has told us all that we know as to the lengths of reigns and mutual relationships of the Priest-Kings.

Under the XXIst Dynasty the Egyptian empire no longer existed, except in Nubia. Rameses III had seemed to restore the dominion of Egypt in Asia after the defeat of the Northerners, but as a matter of fact Palestine was abandoned to the Philistines, who settled there, perhaps owning a shadowy Egyptian overlordship for a time. The Sinaitic peninsula was finally abandoned after the reign of Rameses VI. Then Egypt owned not a rood of land east of the Isthmus.

A curious sidelight on the decline of Egyptian power and prestige in Asia at the end of the XXth Dynasty is given by the Golenischeff Papyrus, which is a report of the envoy Unamon, who was sent in the fifth year of Rameses XI by the high-priest Herihor to Phoenicia, which has already been mentioned in connexion with the political arrangements at the beginning of the XXIst Dynasty. Still more interesting is its account of the state of Palestine. The coast-cities are absolutely independent of Egypt. Dor is in the possession of the Cretan (?) Tjakaray, ruled by a prince with the Semitic name Badiel. Zakarbaal, the prince of Byblos, openly contemns Egypt to Amen's ambassador though he came with recommendations from the sovereigns of Tanis and their Phoenician friends. "I am neither thy servant," he says, "nor the servant of him that sent thee." He adds that he had detained ambassadors of Rameses X fifteen years in his land, where they had died, and he will shew Unamon their graves if he likes. One of his retainers tells the envoy that the shadow of Zakarbaal is the shadow of Pharaoh his lord: i.e. that Zakarbaal is Unamon's lord and master. But the name of Amen still commands some veneration in Phoenicia, and Egyptian amour propre is solved by a grudging recognition of spiritual influence, if not precisely authority. The ambassador is saved by the prince of Byblos from the Tjakaray pirates of Dor, who had pursued him to Byblos on a charge of stealing silver from one of their captains, by allowing his ship to start from Byblos ahead of them: they might catch him if they could. This was not very complimentary to Egypt, but Unamon escaped them, only to be wrecked on the coast of Alashiya, where he was well received by Hatiba the queen. The papyrus here breaks off, and we do not know how the envoy of Amen returned to Egypt.

Even were the Report of Unamon a purely literary and imaginary work, a novel of adventure, it would have given us invaluable hints as to the relations between Egypt and her erstwhile subjects at the end of the Empire. But there is no reason to doubt that it is a real report of a real envoy, who went through various surprising adventures, and chronicled them in a picturesque style of writing. It is interesting enough, but it must have been bitter reading at Thebes.

Ten or fifteen years later, in the north of Egypt's lost dominion, the coming event of Assyrian empire was to cast its shadow before it when

Tiglath-pileser, conqueror of the Hittites, marched to the seacoast at Arvad. Here he embarked upon a ship of the Arvadites to see the wonders of the great deep and assert his sovereignty over it as over the land by the slaughter of one of its mightiest denizens, a great dolphin, as he had slain elephants and wild bulls in Mitanni. The men of Arvad had of old always been opponents of the Egyptian connexion, and since the time of Rameses II they had been independent of and more or less subject to the Hittites. Tiglath-pileser claimed their allegiance as the successor of Khatti in the hegemony of Western Asia. It might well have been expected that he would have extended his dominion southwards over Palestine, now torn by the wars between the Philistines and the Jews, but he did not. His wars with Elam and with Marduk-nadin-akhi of Babylon, second successor of Nebuchadrezzar I, occupied him fully for the rest of his short reign, and he never reappeared in Syria, which was left to its own devices. His momentary appearance as a great conqueror in Phoenicia had no doubt caused a certain commotion in Egypt, and we find the king of that country (probably Nesibanebded) sending gifts to please the Assyrian, among them a crocodile and a hippopotamus, which were taken to Nineveh to be shewn to the people as extraordinary trophies.

So the story of the Egyptian Empire ends.

CHAPTER IX: THE KINGDOMS OF SYRIA AND PALESTINE (1400-854 B.C.)

I. Philistines, Hebrews, and Aramaeans

THE advance of Tiglath-pileser I to the shores of the Mediterranean was not followed by any extension of Assyrian power in the West. He was almost immediately recalled to the East by the attack of the Babylonian king Marduk-nadin-akhi, who took the city of Ekallati, and removed to Babylon the statues of Adad and Sala, the gods of the city, which were not recovered till the time of Sennacherib. Tiglath-pileser took a swift revenge, defeated the Babylonian near the Lower Zab, and overran Babylonia, taking Babylon itself, besides Sippar, Opis, and other cities. This was a death-blow to the Babylonian ideas that had come to the front during the last few reigns: the vain dream of reducing Assyria to obedience to her old mistress was finally given up, and the Babylonians sank back apathetically into an anarchic condition under weak and undistinguished kings whose names are of no interest. The dynasties "of Pashe," "of the Sea-Land" (probably Chaldaeans), and "of Bazi" follow one another, and finally the throne is occupied by "the Elamite," some unnamed usurper from the East. These weak dynasties lasted for over a century: the various kings contended with each other and murdered each other, probably, undisturbed by the advent of a foreign conqueror. For Assyria, too, had fallen into a somewhat similar condition of weakness. The promise of Tiglath-pileser's reign was not fulfilled.

The great king had been a conqueror in peace no less than in war. He changed the capital back from Calah (Nimrud) to Assur (Kala'at Sherkat), and beautified the royal city in the numerous new palaces and temples. Foreign trees were planted to give arid Assyria some greenery and shade: herds of oxen and of deer, flocks of sheep and goats and troops of horses, were imported from the West to increase the wealth of the land. But his successors were far less intelligent than he, and his work was abandoned. Ashur-bel-kala I and Shamshi-Adad, his sons and successors, desired nothing better than to live at peace and in family alliance with Babylonia, and probably hardly stirred from their palaces. Then an eclipse falls over

Assyria, and, as in the case of Babylonia, we know nothing of her history for a full century or more.

The moment was auspicious for the rise of a new power in the land of Syria and Palestine. This middle-land had of old been the meeting-place and battlefield of Egypt, of Babylonia, and of the Hittites, and lately Assyria had stretched forth her hand towards it. Now Egypt, Babylon, Khatti, and Assyria seem all at one time to be paralysed. Assyria had done her work in destroying Khatti, only to be herself stricken with a palsy immediately afterwards. Egypt and Babylon were degraded: the kingdoms of drivellers. With Mesopotamia, Anatolia, and Egypt all powerless, the Middle-Land was free. And into this free land fortune had but recently injected three new racial elements, all of which made for freedom and independent development. These were the races of the Philistines and the Israelites in the South, and the Aramaeans in the North. The Israelites and Aramaeans, being Semites, were in time able to absorb the Canaanite and Amorite inhabitants of the land they subdued, but the Philistines were unable to do this. They were not Semites, but Aegean foreigners from Crete, uncircumcised strangers with whom it was impossible for the Semites to amalgamate. The final victory of Israel over the Philistines was as natural a result as the victory of Saladin over the Crusaders: the battle of Baal-perazim was but repeated at the Horns of Hattin. The Philistines were destroyed or absorbed by the Orient, as the Crusaders were later.

The Hebrew and Aramaean invasions preceded that of the Philistines. Probably the Aramaean conquest of Syria was rather a gradual infiltration than a definite conquest achieved at one period of time. The Aramaean tribes, who seem to have developed their nationality on the banks of the middle Euphrates, were originally more or less nomadic "Suti" or Beduin, who were always trying to possess themselves of the outlying lands of their settled neighbours, on the one hand the Babylonians and on the other the Syrians. Their great settlement in the land of Ubi or Hobah, of which the capital was the ancient Damascus (already an important place in the time of Thothmes III), probably took place during or shortly after the confusion caused by the Palestinian rebellion against Akhenaten and the destruction of Mitanni by the Hittites, when, also as we shall see, in all probability the Hebrew invasion of Palestine also took place. Damascus now became the centre of an Aramaean state, and gradually in course of time the Amorites and Hittites of the Orontes valley and Northern Syria were swamped and absorbed or driven out by the steady pressure of the Aramaeans. On the south the new-comers came into contact with the Hebrews: the boundary between Hebrews and Aramaeans being on the east of the Jordan the Yarmuk, while on the west it ran northwards up the Jordan valley to the mountains where the tribal territory of Asher marched with the seacoast of the Phoenicians.

Between Aramaeans and Hebrews there was probably no very great difference, and it is probable that on the frontiers the two races from the first coalesced, so that the northern tribes, such as Naphtali, could easily change from Israelites into Syrians. And in the heart of the Hebrew nation we might trace a distinct Aramaean strain in Abraham and his family (who came from Harran in Mesopotamia, which had been Aramaean long before Damascus), if we could assume that the Jahvist writer had misplaced these events in time, and had ascribed to the age of Chedorlaomer and Amraphel an episode which really belongs to the period of Joshua. For in the older period there had been no Aramaeans yet in Harran. But it seems more probable that the Abrahamic legend really relates to the time of the first migration of the ancestors of the Hebrews (the Hyksos?) from Northern Mesopotamia into Canaan, before they entered Egypt, and that his Aramaean connexions were ascribed to him because he came from Harran, where Aramaeans lived in the Jahvist's time. And it was natural to ascribe Aramaean connexions to the forefather of Israel, since it was easy to see that between Hebrew and Aramaean there was no very great gulf fixed, and it was no doubt traditionally known that both had entered Syria and Palestine from the desert at the same period and more or less in alliance. The genealogy of the children of Nahor (Gen. xxii. 20 ff.) preserves, as Prof. Meyer points out, an ancient tradition of the lands inhabited by the Aramaeans before they had occupied Southern Syria and Damascus, and, no doubt, before they had crossed the Euphrates valley to Harran. It is noticeable that the full-blooded descendants of Nahor are the true proto-Aramaeans, if we may so call them, of the desert (Us and Buz, etc.), while his bastards by a concubine are towns of the cultivated land, like Tahash, which is the Takhisa of the Egyptian inscriptions, whose chiefs, a century or more before it became Aramaean, were fastened to the bows of his ship by Amenhetep II and nailed upon the walls of Napata in far Ethiopia. The inclusion of Tahash, and omission of Damascus and Harran, shew that the list must have been made before 1300 B.C. There is no reason to suppose that in the reign of Amenhetep II (1450 B.C.) Takhisa was Aramaean any more than Damascus was. But in the time of Tiglath-pileser I (11 00 B.C.)

there were Aramaeans about Harran, and not very much later we find the kingdoms of Zobah and Damascus at war with David of Israel. These kingdoms must have taken some time to establish and consolidate, so that it is probable that Damascus and Harran both were taken by the Aramaeans in the course of the thirteenth century. Damascus very possibly became Aramaean after the devastating passage of the Northerners from Asia Minor (which shook the Hittite power to its foundations and nearly exterminated the Amorites) had left the ancient city open to occupation by the desert-tribes.

Neither Israelites, Aramaeans, nor Philistines seem to have made much impression on the Phoenicians, who were secure in their island-forts and on the decks of their ships. The Suti and the Khabiri had plagued them in the time of Akhenaten, and that these were the ancestors of the Hebrews seems very probable: but from the Biblical narrative we see that the Hebrews never acquired any Phoenician territory. The tribe of Asher on the Phoenician border became instead almost Phoenician itself, and had little sympathy with the less civilized tribes to the South. Across the Lebanon the Aramaeans could not easily penetrate. In the mountains the remnant of the Amorites and Hittites of the Orontes valley no doubt gathered and formed a protection to the coast-people, who went on with their trafficking undisturbed by the comings and goings of conquerors and conquered at their backs. The terrible progress of the Northerners spared them by land, as the invaders naturally marched by the Syrian Heerstrasse, the historic Orontes valley. But by sea they were vulnerable, and that they learned at the hands of the Philistines and Tjakaray. We see how these pirates plagued them in the eleventh century from Unamon's account of their behaviour at Byblos while he was there, and the tradition, preserved by Justin, that in 1209 B.C. Tyre was taken by the rex Ascaloniorum, no doubt refers to a Philistine attack not long after the establishment of the foreigners in the Shephelah. But no attack ever really affected the Phoenicians, who preserved their individuality intact from the days of Thothmes III to those of Alexander. Their merchants pursued unhindered and intrepidly their way to the utmost ends of the Mediterranean and beyond, and the trading-factories were now founded that soon developed into the great colonies of Gades, of Tharshish, of Utica and Carthage. This last, the greatest Phoenician colony, was founded not long after the time of Ahab and Ethbaal, towards the end of the ninth century; Utica and Gades were much older; Tharshish was a trading-centre as early as the time of Hiram I and Solomon.

2. The Hyksos, the Khabiri, and the Hebrews

The great racial movements of the Israelites and Aramaeans must have been concluded, and the conquerors settled in their new homes, at latest by the end of the thirteenth century. In the case of the Hebrews this is confirmed by the inscription of the Egyptian king Meneptah, who speaks of the people of "Isirail" in a sense that leaves no doubt that Israel was in his time (not before 1250 B.C.) a settled nation of Palestine, probably in Mount Ephraim. This fact renders it difficult to accept the current view that places the Exodus (the beginning of the Israelite migration from Egypt, that was followed by the years of the Wandering) in the reign of Meneptah.

The view that the Exodus took place in Meneptah's reign has always been open to the objection that not enough time was left by it for the period of the Judges. A late Hebrew tradition ascribed a length of four hundred and eighty years to this period. This tradition had to be ignored, and the period of the Judges reduced by one-half. Yet, in view of the total absence of any information from Egyptian or other contemporary sources concerning the Exodus, it was natural that the reign of Meneptah should have been generally chosen as that of the Pharaoh of the Exodus. Rameses II did very well for the Pharaoh of the Oppression, since he built largely in the Wadi Tumilat, the Land of Goshen (as, for example, at Pithom), and "Pithom and Raamses" were the store-cities which, according to the Hebrew account, had been built by their ancestors under the pitiless lash of the Egyptian taskmasters. Meneptah, too, was a very weak successor to his masterful father, and after his time Egypt fell into a period of decline. All this was regarded as the result of the blow inflicted upon Egypt by the Exodus.

But the continued study of the Tell el-Amarna tablets and the discovery of the "Israel-stele" have had the result of shaking the confidence even of conservative investigators in the Meneptah theory. The word "Isirail" in the stele cannot be anything else than Israel: it is certainly not Jezreel, as has been suggested, since a Hebrew z could never be reproduced by an Egyptian s, and it is not a place-name but a folk-name, being "determined" by the sign of "people," not that of "town." If we try to combine the fact that there were already Israelites in Palestine who were smitten by Meneptah with the theory that the Exodus took place in his reign, we are driven to suppose, with Prof. Petrie, that these Israelites of the stela either were a portion of the nation who had been left behind in Canaan or were the result of another Exodus previous to the main one, which happened after Meneptah's victory. In the lists of Thothmes III place-names have been noticed which appear to read Yeshap'il and Ya'keb'il, and are claimed as indicating settlements of Josephite and Jacobite tribes in Palestine at a time when, according to the current theory, the main body of the "Israelites" was still in Egypt. If these Joseph-el and Jacob-el tribes had come out of Egypt, the earlier Exodus must have taken place before the time of Thothmes III: i.e. the two Exoduses were separated by nearly four hundred years. This seems improbable. So that if we continue to place the Exodus in Meneptah's reign on the authority of the names Pithom and Raamses (of which the latter certainly cannot be earlier than the reign of Rameses II, since it is "Per-Rameses," the royal burgh at Tanis), we must assume that only part of the Hebrew nation had passed into Egypt, the rest having remained in its ancient seats in Palestine, where the Josephites and Jacobites were found by Thothmes III, and we must suppose that it was these stay-at-home Israelites that were defeated by Meneptah before the Exodus of their brethren under Moses and Aaron.

Against this view we have the fact that we have from Egyptian annals no trace, other than the doubtful one of these names of Joseph-el and Jacob-el, of the peculiar and independent nationality of the Israelites in Palestine before the defeat of the Isirailu by Meneptah. Till then, the name Israel does not occur. This being so, we should naturally suppose that the Israelite tribes had reached Palestine at a date not so very long before the time of Meneptah, and that at some unknown date (many years) before their arrival, they had come from Egypt, where they had sojourned for a long period of time. On this view it is not necessary to suppose a remnant left behind in Canaan, or an Exodus earlier than the main one, for this will be placed long before Meneptah's days. The only objection to this view, that the names Pithom and Raamses are but little earlier than the time of Meneptah, is easily disposed of. They may perfectly well be the interpretations of a scribe who knew their names as those of Egyptian cities which existed in his time in and near the Land of Goshen. The title Zaphnathpaaneakh, given to Joseph by "Pharaoh," is known to be no older than the tenth century B.C. at the earliest, and may be as late as the seventh, to which century the names Potiphar, Potipherah (Petephre, "He whom the Sun hath given"), and Asenath, which occur in the Joseph-story, also belong. These names were put into the sacred story by scribes who knew them as typical Egyptian names of their own day. And Pithom and Raamses may well be interpretations of the same character, but of earlier date.

In favour of this view can be adduced another ancient and contemporary authority besides the Israel-stele: the Tell el-Amarna letters. It seems very probable that the "Sa-Gaz" tribes of Suti and their congeners the Khabiri who devastated Canaan in Akhenaten's time are no other than the invading Hebrews and other desert-tribes allied with them. It was natural that so far-reaching a conclusion as this should have been treated with the utmost caution at first; but it has now been debated for some years, and many of those who at first doubted now admit the cogency of the identification, which is accepted by competent authorities.

In my own view, the probabilities are all in favour of the identification. We have invading nomad tribes called Khabiri (Habiri), coming out of the south-east, apparently, and overrunning Canaan at a period which can be very definitely dated about 1390-1360 B.C. The Tell el-Amarna letters shew us how their raids were feared by the Canaanites, and we see that after Akhenaten's withdrawal of Egyptian authority, they were left at the mercy of the Khabiri, who eventually dominated the whole country. The Biblical narrative tells us of invading nomad tribes called 'Ibrim, coming out of the south-east, and overrunning Canaan at a period about four hundred years before the time of Solomon. Eventually they settled down under the rule of their own "Judges," and gradually, displacing or absorbing the Canaanites whom he had not destroyed in the first rush of their assault, became the dominant people of Palestine. The parallel is surely very complete when, in the reign of Meneptah, rather more than a century after the invasion of the Khabiri, we find a people called Isirail established in Palestine who are never mentioned before.

If the Hebrews are identical with the Khabiri, we must place the Exodus before the reign of Amenhetep III; the question is, how long before? It is at least probable that the ancestors of the Israelites abode very many years in the wilderness before they, taking advantage of the weakness of Amenhetep III's later years, crossed the Jordan. "Forty" years means but many, probably very many. The influence of the desert in the moulding of the Israelite character is very evident, and the God of Israel is in his original aspect a god of the desert and the bare mountain, of the gebel rather than of the rif, the fertile Canaanite plain. Desert Edom was the blood-brother of Israel, though no love was lost between them, and the connexion with purely Arab Midian was close in legend and no doubt also in fact. Whether Sinai was the mount which we call Sinai, or whether the real Sinai is to be found east of the Gulf of Akaba, remains doubtful; but, whether the main portion of the Wanderings took place east or west of that gulf, the fact remains that the ancestors of the Hebrews did wander in the desert regions bordering on Canaan and must have so wandered for many years. Two centuries seem hardly too long for this period of nomadism, and thus we are naturally brought back to the moment which seems most appropriate for the departure of a Semitic tribe from Egypt, pursued by Pharaoh and his host, before the reign of Amenhetep III. This moment is the beginning of the XVIIIth Dynasty, and it surely does not seem so very improbable that Josephus may have been right, and that, as has already been noted above, the Biblical account of the Exodus is the Hebrew version of the Expulsion of the Hyksos? Aahmes was the Pharaoh who "knew not Joseph," who had been raised to favour under the Hyksos kings, whose names were not only Semitic, but in one case, that of Yapekhur or Yakephur (Yekebel?) seem to point to connexion with Jewish tradition. Abraham will on this view be the traditional tribal leader, who in the time of Khammurabi led the Hyksos-Hebrews down from Harran in Northern Mesopotamia, where they originated, through Syria, where he defeated the five kings, to Southern Canaan, where they remained for some generations before they entered Egypt, in the days of Joseph the son of Jacob (Yekeb).

There seems to be no inherent impossibility in this view of the origins of the nation of Israel, though in the present state of our knowledge we cannot regard it as anything more than a theory, which may justifiably be regarded as plausible. But we may definitely, if we accept the identification of the Khabiri as the Hebrews, say that in the Tell el-Amarna letters we have Joshua's conquest seen from the Egyptian and Canaanite point of view!

3. The Hebrew Conquest of Palestine

The reason for the invasion may well have been the traditional one. These tribes, that had been nomad for generations, cast longing eyes upon the "Promised Land" where their ancestors had lived before they went down into Egypt. The desert-tribes always desire the fat lands of the settled, and in this case there was an ancient claim of right.

From the Biblical account it would seem that after passing through Moab and sojourning for a time in the neighbourhood of Pisgah, the main body of the invaders crossed the Jordan near its mouth and first entered the territory of the Canaanite city of Jericho, encamping on the way at an ancient stone circle and holy place with the usual name of Gilgal. Jericho was taken "at the edge of the sword," and Ai followed, after an initial check. The hill-country was then entered, and the ark of the Lord was no doubt now set up at Bethel, and later at Shiloh, which became the religious centre of the Northern tribes.

The Biblical account goes on to describe a march of Joshua south-west from the hill-country into the Shephelah, in which the kings of Lachish and Gezer were defeated, and Lachish taken; after which Joshua marched to Hebron. This raid was followed by the war with the confederated kings of the North, under the leadership of Jabin of Hazor.

The whole facies of this account, with its raidings, destroyings, and burnings by the fierce invaders from the desert, reminds us forcibly of the evidence of the Tell el-Amarna tablets as to the doings of the Khabiri and the Suti all over Palestine from North to South. "So Joshua smote all the land, the hill country, and the South, and the lowland, and the slopes, and all their kings." Yet we cannot identify any persons mentioned in the Book of Joshua with any of the men who play a part in the contemporary record of the Tell el-Amarna letters, nor do Bii-idiya and Shuyardata, Abdkhiba and Labaya, appear in the Biblical narrative. Names, especially foreign names like those of the immigrant Iranian chiefs ("Shuyardata" and similar appellations), are easily altered and forgotten in traditional accounts.

In one thing the Tell el-Amarna letters and the Book of Joshua agree. The territory of Jerusalem forms a rock against which the waves of Eastern invasion beat in vain: neither Khabiri nor Hebrews can gain a footing therein. Joshua is obliged to avoid it in his march to Lachish and Hebron: and we do not know that Abdkhiba ever lost the city; Jerusalem, though it might be surprised by a coup-de-main, was not yet to be taken and held by desert-hordes.

Certainly the Biblical account of the invasion by way of Jericho, whether this was really the route of the northern (Israelitish) tribes only or not, bears all the marks of being a genuine tradition and no doubt states a historical fact. The war with Jabin may or may not really belong to this period, but that the tradition that Lachish, Ekron, and Gezer were taken at this time is trustworthy seems to be shewn by the non-mention in it of Philistines in the Shephelah. The inhabitants are all Canaanites.

But this flash of light upon the actual invasion, of the Northern tribes at least, is followed by darkness. We have the traditions of the wars against Sihon and Og, which may really belong to the period before the crossing of the Jordan, or may be an echo of later wars transferred to the Mosaic period. We have also the remarkable story of the treaty of the tribes of Simeon and Levi with the Canaanites of Shechem which established an Israelite clan (Dinah) in that city, of the quarrels that ensued, of the massacre of the Shechemites, and of the destruction and expulsion of Levi and Simeon that followed. They were driven southwards, and Judah, if it was originally settled in Mount Ephraim with them, followed to its new seat in the southern land. The first part of the story may well reflect an actual occurrence; the second looks very like another account, from a point of view less favourable to Israel, of the movement of Joshua to Judaea. We seem to be reading in both cases reconciliations of the fact that Judah, Simeon, and Levi lived south of Jerusalem with the view that the whole nation had crossed the Jordan at Gilgal. Yet, just as the story of Joshua's raid is not in the least improbable, neither is it unlikely that these three tribes, defeated by the Canaanites, were cut off from the main body of their people and driven southwards.

Although we know nothing of the details of the war, it is evident that the anarchy depicted in the Tell el-Amarna tablets gradually subsided, leaving the intruding tribes in possession of two enclaves of hill-territory — Mount Ephraim in the north and Judah in the south — with Jerusalem as a Canaanite barrier between them. Although for a time the Judahites occupied the Shephelah, they were afterwards expelled: in the plains the invaders could do nothing against the Canaanite chariots, and when, as probably happened, the princes seriously banded themselves together to repel the invaders from the rich lowlands, the immediate issue of the conflict was not doubtful. Also, it is not improbable that Shubbiluliuma intervened in support of the Canaanite chiefs, though he does not seem to have exerted any authority over them.

Of the wars of Seti I and Rameses II with the Hittites we hear nothing from Biblical sources, nor is this to be wondered at if the Hebrews were at this time strictly confined to the hill-country. The Egyptian reoccupation of Palestine was probably no more than a securing of the Heerstrasse from the Shephelah to the plain of Jezreel and thence to the valley of the Orontes: the establishment of Egyptian authority over tribes that would be regarded merely as marauding highlanders would hardly have seemed worth the trouble involved. Wholesome fear of the allied Egyptian and Hittite powers no doubt kept the hill-men quiet: it was not till the feeble and apathetic old age of Rameses set in, and his death was followed by the Libyan attacks on Egypt, that the war-flame again blazed up in Palestine. Then it was, no doubt, that the Canaanites combined to throw off the foreign yoke, and the Israelites descended from their hills to help them, with disastrous results to themselves: "Israel is desolated, his seed is not," says the inscription of Meneptah

Israel had become a people of sufficient importance to be specially mentioned by a pharaoh. We can imagine that the "men of valour" had been first overthrown in the plain, whither they had sallied forth to help the Canaanites, and that afterwards the Egyptians carried fire and sword through the hill-territory of Mount Ephraim: the whole people, women as well as men, is indicated by the ideographs used in the inscription as "desolated," and their "seed was not."

Recovery from this blow must have taken many years. The darkness remains unbroken till suddenly there is another flash of light which, like that which shews us the crossing of the Jordan, gives us a fleeting glimpse of Israel at a period midway between the war with Meneptah and the Philistine invasion, i.e. about 1200 B.C. This is the account (Judges V.) of the fight at Taanach in the magnificent Song of Deborah —

" Awake, awake, Deborah:
Awake, awake, utter a song;
Arise, Barak, and lead thy captivity captive, thou son of Abinoam!

The kings came and fought;
Then fought the kings of Canaan;
In Taanach by the waters of Megiddo:

The stars in their courses fought against Sisera,
The river Kishon swept them away,
That ancient river, the river Kishon.
O my soul, march on with strength!
Then did the horsehooves stamp
By reason of the prancings, the prancings of their strong ones.

The Song is undoubtedly contemporary with the event described in it, and records a crushing defeat inflicted upon the Canaanites at Taanach by some of the Israelitish tribes under a leader named Barak, of the tribe of Naphtali. In this fight the formidable chariotry of the Canaanites, against which the Israelites had as yet been able to make but little headway in the plain, was for the first time discomfited, and the Canaanite leader Sisera "lighted down from his chariot, and fled away on his feet." The Song directly mentions Ephraim, Benjamin, Machir (= Manasseh), Zebulun, Naphtali, and Issachar, as the allied tribes, and the brunt of the fighting fell upon Zebulun and Naphtali. Reuben was undecided how to act, "Gilead abode beyond Jordan," Dan and Asher remained supine in the seacoast territory which they then occupied, south of Phoenicia. From the fact that Jabin, king of Hazor in the Orontes valley, whose general Sisera is said to be in Judges iv., is not mentioned in the Song, it seems probable that Sisera and he had originally no connexion, and that the mention of him here is due to a confusion of the battle of Taanach with another fight at the period of the first invasion, in which a king Jabin of Hazor was defeated.

We then find that at the beginning of the twelfth century the Israelites of Mount Ephraim were able to try conclusions with and defeat the most powerful ruler of the Canaanites, and had before this conquered and occupied a seacoast territory, reaching probably from Akko to Dor. The seacoast tribes, Dan and Asher, were already engaged in trading in imitation of the Phoenicians, and were beginning to lose the fierce, warlike energy of the old Khabiri, which was still preserved by the tribes who followed the sword of the son of Abinoam and were inspired by the songs of Deborah.

4. Israel and the Philistines

Then must have come the catastrophe, of which we find no contemporary record preserved in the Book of Judges, the invasion of the Northerners, their settlement "in the midst of Amurru," their defeat by Rameses III, and the final occupation by the Philistines of the Canaanite seacoast and the Shephelah. Israel saved her nationality and name by retreat into the hill-country; the seacoast was given up, and Dan and Asher no longer dwelt by the havens of the sea. A new "oppressor" had entered the land, more formidable by far than the Amorites or Canaanites had ever been, even with all their chariots of iron. Since they had established themselves in the hill-country east of the Jordan, the Israelites had never acknowledged a Canaanite master, but they were compelled to submit to the Philistines, who, used to real mountains and real hill-fighting in their native land of

Crete, pursued them to the fastnesses which neither Canaanite nor Egyptian had tried to reach. The superiority of the European armature of the Philistines, with their bronze-plated corselet, large round buckler, great broadsword (possibly of iron), and huge spear "like a weaver's beam," over the feebler weapons of the Semites was so marked that no further reason for their complete subjugation of Palestine need be sought. The legend of Goliath preserves the popular impression among the Israelites of the gigantic stature and impregnable armour of their conquerors. No doubt the possession of iron weapons contributed materially to bring about the complete victory of the invaders.

The Israelites must have been driven into the hills at the first onset, before Rameses III checked the invasion on the borders of Egypt. The surge-back of the invasion into Palestine, and the following campaign of Rameses, probably began an epoch of sanguinary war which lasted till the invaders had finally established their new state in the cities of the enslaved Canaanites of the plain. Then must have followed perhaps half a century of peace, before, at the beginning of the eleventh century, the conquerors bent themselves to the task of completing their conquest by the subjugation of the hill-country between the Shephelah and Jordan.

It is possible that the Philistines had already tried to enter the hill-country, and the late remembrance of "Shamgar the son of Anath, who slew of the Philistines six hundred men with an ox-goad," probably refers to some repulse of the Philistines by the half-armed Hebrew fellahin. But no attempt had ever been made to establish Philistine settlements in the highlands. Gath was the farthest settlement inland, on the western slope. This was partly due to the dangerously hostile temper of the driven-in Hebrew population, but also because, as in their native country, the invaders preferred to constitute their cities in places not far from the sea, from which they could at once control the sea-ways and the vine-bearing hills and upland summer pastures of the interior.

Before dealing with the Philistine subjugation of Israel, we must glance at the constitution of the new foreign state in Canaan, which by 1100 B.C. had probably reached its complete development.

With the possible exceptions of Lydda and Ziklag, no new cities were founded: the conquerors lived in the ancient Canaanite settlements of the Shephelah, which had often figured in the Egyptian invasions for centuries back. The chief settlements were established in the five towns of Ashdod, Gaza, Ashkelon, Gath, and Ekron, which apparently retained their

Canaanite names under the new rule. Over each of these cities ruled a "tyrant" or seven, assisted by his nobles. The five sevens met in council to deliberate on the common affairs of the nation, probably at Ashdod, which seems to have held the hegemony. The tyrant of Ashdod probably commanded in chief when the whole war-force of the confederacy was called out.

The Pentapolis evidently comprised the whole strength of the Philistines, properly so called. The Tjakarai of Dor in the North and the Cherethites of Ziklag, far inland in the Negeb south of Philistia, both tribes of the same Cretan origin as the Philistines and allies in the great invasion, were not formally included in the confederacy, but no doubt their alliance could always be depended upon.

The chief Canaanite cities of the South, which may have been colonized but were not capitals of the serens, such as Rakkon and Joppa on the seacoast, Gezer, Jabneel, Lachish, Sharuhen, and Gerar inland, were probably organized after a time as subject-allies of the confederacy. It is uncertain whether the town of Lod (Lydda), afterwards and now so important, was an ancient Canaanite centre or was not rather a new Philistine foundation, perhaps a colony from one of the chief confederate cities: it is not mentioned in the older Egyptian inscriptions, as the other Canaanite towns are, and its name has a foreign, and even specifically Cretan, appearance: we may compare Lod with the Cretan place-name Lyttos, The Cherethite centre in the south, Ziklag, oddly drive so far inland into the Negeb, as if in vain search of more fertile territory, has a name which is quite un-Semitic, and was very probably given it by the Cherethites: the place was probably a new foundation.

As has already been said, of the civilization of the Philistines we have actual remains only in the great quantity of "Late Minoan" pottery found in the excavations of the Palestine Exploration Fund in the mound of Tell es-Safi, the site of Gath, and at 'Ain Shems (Bethshemesh) and certain peculiar buildings and tombs at Gezer and Tell es-Safi. Since the Philistines, though they came from Crete, were not originally, it would seem, Cretans (but rather Lycian conquerors who were expelled or had migrated from the island, where they had settled), and, further, were a people whose civilization had probably been impaired by long migrations and wars, it is probable that any buildings they would erect in Palestine would not shew much trace of the old Minoan architectural genius. Still, admixture with the Canaanites would revive in them something of culture and luxury, and we hear in the Books of Judges and Samuel of temples and palaces in their cities imposing enough to impress the Hebrews, and also of theatres in which crowds of the nobles and their retainers, besides the common people, could assemble under one roof to watch public spectacles. We are at once reminded of the "Theatral Areas" of the Cretan palaces of Knossos and Phaistos, and of the gladiatorial games that, we know, went on in them, by the Biblical account of the exhibition of the captured Samson in the theatre of Gaza —

"Now the house was full of men and women; and all the lords of the Philistines were there; and there were upon the roof about three thousand men and women, that beheld while Samson made sport."

We seem to see the lords and ladies of Knossos at the palace-sport, as they are depicted on the Knossian frescoes, with crowds of faces of the men and women of which the halls were full, and the court-ladies looking down from their balconies at the bull-leaping and the boxing! So must many an Israelite captive have been forced to make sport for the Philistines in their theatres, and the indelible memory of many such scenes is preserved for us in the picture of the final victory in death of the Hebrew sun-hero, Samson, whose oppressors were naturally imagined in the guise of the greatest oppressors the hill-men had ever known.

The Philistine state and culture were but the products of a foreign military garrison, and had only one guarantee of permanence: the continued racial purity and energy of the conquering tribes. When this began to fail, as it did within two centuries of the conquest, the end was at hand. Like the Ionians at Miletus and elsewhere, later on, the Philistines dwelt with the natives in the old native centres, merely adding a veneer of their own culture to that of the Canaanites. They took over the Canaanite gods and worshipped them. The Semitic Dagon at Ashdod was easily identified with some Aegean male deity, and Ashtoreth and Derketo at Ashkelon with the goddess who, as we see, ruled paramount in Cretan religion. So the conquerors soon became semitized: probably in a century they were already talking Canaanite. In the time of David we certainly hear nothing which causes us to suppose that Philistines and Israelites, though deadly enemies, did not speak almost the same Semitic tongue. Nothing but a few peculiar names of the Philistine aristocracy, a few Greek loan-words in Hebrew, and the "Minoan" traditions of Gaza and Ashkelon remained in later days to mark a distinction between Philistia and the rest of Palestine.

So the semitized Philistines of David's day were by no means the same men as the warriors of the Migration. They were unable to prevent the founding of the new independent kingdom of Israel, and even lost to David one of the limbs of their confederacy, the city-state of Gath and its dependencies. In the succeeding reign they had become Egyptian tributaries when Sheshank I restored the Egyptian dominion in Palestine.

The confusion into which the Philistine invasion had thrown the whole of Palestine, gave an opportunity to her eastern neighbours to attack her. The Bne Qedem, the "Sons of the East," gathered like the vultures out of the desert to seize an easy prey. Arab Midian, and Moab and Ammon, always ill-wishers of their sister Israel since she had conquered her way past them into the rich lands of Canaan, now came up against her to raid and destroy. An interesting legend brings an otherwise unknown king, Kushan "the doubly wicked," from the Euphrates-land to oppress Israel some time in the twelfth century: who he was, we know not. A tribal hero, Othniel, was said to have inflicted a disaster upon him. A more definite "oppression" is that of the Midianites, about 1100 B.C., which must have affected the Philistines as well as Israel, for the raids of the Midianites "destroyed the increase of the earth, till thou come unto Gaza." The Biblical narrator is very definite as to the loss and disaster inflicted on the Israelites by these raiders; to avoid the Midianites the people fled for refuge to caves in the hills, "and Israel was brought very low because of Midian."

It can hardly be imagined that this would have been the case but for the overwhelming disaster which the whole nation had recently suffered at the hands of the invading Philistines, which in the north had destroyed the budding promise of a civilized Israelitish State with a seaboard, havens, and ships, and in the south had reduced the Hebrews to the position of a mere hill-tribe. Arab razzias, as the Midianite invasions were, could not of themselves alone have brought Israel so low.

We have two legends of successful reprisals against the Midianite raiders, which have been combined into one. Gideon and Jerubbaal appear to have been two distinct local leaders, one of the Manassites of Ophrah, north of Shechem, the other of the Gadites in Gilead, on the other side of the Jordan. Gideon attacked the Midianite camp beneath Mount Gilboa, and slew the Arab princes Oreb and Zeeb. Jerubbaal led a long chase of a Midianite band, also under two princes, Zebah and Zalmunna, into the eastern desert, where he annihilated them. The description of the deaths of Zebah and Zalmunna, and of the spoil of golden earrings worn by the

Arabs (because they were Ishmaelites), and the necklaces of golden crescents that were about their camels' necks, gives a vivid impression of this victory of the Israelitish frontiersmen over the splendid nomads of the desert.

The Midianite raids were evidently directed roughly by way of the valley of the Jabbok, and thence through the Plain of Jezreel to the Shephelah, so that they may well have raided as far as Gaza in the days before the Philistine power was firmly established. That the northern rather than the southern route was taken shews that the Midianites wished to avoid touching the territories of Edom, Moab, and Ammon. Edom, the country between the Dead Sea and the Gulf of Akaba, was now developing into a strong State under a settled kingly rule, under a dynasty probably of Aramaean origin; and in the reign of the fourth king, Hadad I, had inflicted a severe defeat upon the Midianites in the territory of Moab. The Moabites may very well at this time have been dominated politically by the Edomite kingdom: Bela', son of Beor, the first, 'alluph or "duke" of Edom, is evidently duplicated in the Balak, "king of Moab," who summoned the prophet Bala'am "son of Beor" to curse the Israelites at the time of the invasion. Balak may be the Edomite King Bela' (whose name may also appear in that of Bala'am or Bile'am), if it may be supposed that in the list Hadad I is the first really historical king, and that Khusham and Jobab are two traditional names that cover a number of "dukes" between the period of the Hebrew invasion (c, 1370 B.C.) and the time of Hadad (c. 1150 B.C.). Balak and Bala'am are made contemporary with the Hebrew invasion, so that probably the presumed Aramaean conquest which gave Edom a king in Bela ben-Beor may have taken place about the same time, and was part of the same general unrest of the Suti or desert-tribes, Aramaean as well as Hebrew.

We hear of no direct Edomite attack on Judah at this time, though the eternal fighting between the Judahites and the Amalekite tribes on the borders of Edom and Judah never ceased, and now the border-unrest had without doubt been increased by the incursion of the Cherethites from the coast into the Negeb. The campaign of Saul against Agag was probably a retaliation for a long series of injuries suffered from Amalek during the period of confusion after the Philistine invasion.

Nor were Moab and Ammon loth to take part in the "oppression" of their weakened Hebrew kinsmen. A king of Moab named Eglon seems, with the help of the Ammonites, and perhaps in conjunction with Amalekite raids from the south, to have possessed himself of territory on the right bank of the Jordan, which he retained till his assassination by a popular hero who is named Ehud.

The Ammonites naturally attacked the territory of Gilead, and the story of Jephthah is to be referred to a border-war at this period.

So Israel was ringed about with foes, and now the Philistines determined to make their dominance unquestioned as far as the Jordan. A century had elapsed since the deluge of their advance had swept over Palestine. The anarchy which resulted had died down; the new state which they had founded had become organized as we have seen, and was ready to impose its rule on the recalcitrant hill tribes. An opportunity was probably afforded them by anarchy following the death of the would-be king Abimelech, son of Jerubbaal, the victor against Midian. Abimelech seems to have attempted to rule part of Israel definitely as a king, in imitation, no doubt, of Edomite royalty. The result was a fierce civil war centering in Shechem, Abimelech's own town, which had revolted from him. The burning of Shechem and the death of the tyrant Abimelech at Thebez shortly after seem to have made a very deep impression on men's minds at the time, and the relation of these events is one of the most definitely historical in the Book of Judges. They are probably to be placed not long after 1100 B.C.

The Philistine invasion, which resulted in the speedy subjugation of Israel, is dated at the end of the High-Priesthood of Eli, great-great-grandfather of Abiathar, the companion of David. Eli's grandson, Ichabod, was born immediately after the catastrophe. This would put the event, as Prof Eduard Meyer has shewn, about 1080 B.C.

The Philistine victory seems to have been attained at a single blow, in the battle of Eben-ha-ezer, which resulted in the complete annihilation of the Israelite army and the capture of the sacred ark of Yahweh, which had been brought solemnly forth to battle in charge of Hophni and Phinehas, sons of Eli, its priests. After the capture of the palladium of Israel and the ensuing destruction of the national sanctuary at Shiloh, probably little resistance was made: the conviction of the divine wrath would be so strong as to paralyse all further action. Yahweh had delivered His people into the hands of the Philistines. And so "the Philistines held rule over Israel." The conquered people was disarmed, and "there was no smith found throughout all the land of Israel: for the Philistines said, Lest the Hebrews make them swords or spears." All metal-working was, apparently, forbidden. Garrisons or posts were established in certain places to hold the land down.

The most important seem to have been placed at Beth-shean in the north (to command the passage from the Jordan to the Vale of Esdraelon), in Mount Ephraim, and at the pass of Michmash and Geba between Mount Ephraim and Jerusalem, and south of Jerusalem at Bethlehem. Philistine officials were appointed to gather the taxes laid upon the conquered, and kept watch upon them from the fixed posts.

Thus for over half a century, probably, the Philistines controlled all Palestine. The revolt against them, which resulted in the establishment of Saul's kingdom in Israel, was religious in its origin. Though on account of plagues in their cities, which, in accordance with the ideas of the time, they ascribed to the outraged Israelitish god, the Philistines had restored the Ark of Yahweh to its sanctuary, the Hebrew priests had never forgiven the insult which their deity had received at the hands of the "uncircumcised," and Samuel the prophet, a fierce monotheist, and hater of all who worshipped other gods but Yahweh, was the leading spirit of the revolt.

Saul was the creation of Samuel and, possibly, the priests, but seems by no means to have become their slave, as was expected of him. The ecclesiastical control was evidently exercised constantly and irritatingly. Samuel had no intention of setting up a really independent monarch. What he wanted was a leader in war, a man "head and shoulders above the people," who would do the work of getting rid of the Philistines and then obey him, Samuel, for the rest of his life. He thought he had found his man in Saul. The king, however, was a man of character, and was by no means inclined to follow the programme thus marked out for him. Quarrels arose between him and Samuel, who, with the thoroughness of the zealot, wished the enemies of Yahweh to be rooted out with all their possessions, while the king naturally desired the best of the booty and of the slaves captured in war for himself and his followers. The breach widened, and after the death of Samuel culminated in the massacre of the priests at Nob by Saul's retainer, Doeg the Edomite. The support of the outraged priests was naturally given at once to his young rival, David, who secured the throne with their help, but was able to keep, them subordinate to the royal power, which he firmly established in his stronghold at Jerusalem.

The revolt of Samuel and Saul probably began in the land of the Israelites beyond Jordan, in Gilead, which does not seem to have been subject to the Philistines, who possibly never crossed the Jordan. The current genealogy makes Saul a Benjamite of Gibeah, but Prof. Winckler has shown reason for the belief that he was really a Gileadite. His first warlike expedition was directed against Nahash, king of the Ammonites. Also it is more probable that the revolt began in the Trans-Jordan lands than in the country dominated by the Philistine garrisons. It is significant that we are told that while in the revolt the Israelites had no weapons owing to the prohibition by the Philistines of metal working in any form, Saul and Jonathan his son (that is to say, Saul and his men) possessed weapons. The Gileadites were properly armed.

The defeat of Nahash secured the allegiance of the people to the new leader, and Saul now crossed the river to attack the Philistines. A sudden attack overwhelmed the garrison at Geba, "and all Israel heard" the sound of Saul's trumpet. The great fight at Michmash followed, which was decided against the Philistines by the defection of their Hebrew auxiliaries to the insurgent side. The retreating soldiers were followed by the refugees, who had hidden themselves from the conquerors in the hill country of Mount Ephraim, "and they smote the Philistines that day from Michmash to Ajalon."

For a time the Philistines were expelled, and Saul now turned his arms against the Amalekites in the south.

The Hebrew victory was sullied, according to our ideas, by the savage sacrifice of the captured Amalekite king to Yahweh by Samuel with his own hands, and Saul, as ever, seems to us a more humane man than his fierce mentor. To the men of that day, however, Saul no doubt seemed a leader of somewhat weak character except in actual battle, and it must be remembered that even Egyptian kings were accustomed to sacrifice captured chiefs to Amen with their own hands. Samuel's action cannot be judged by modern standards of conduct.

The Philistines had been swept out of the hills by the victory at Michmash, but it was not long before they advanced to regain what they had lost. Continuous fighting followed, which lasted during the whole of Saul's (probably short) reign. The king was able to repulse every attack, and among the warriors who distinguished themselves in this fighting was David, son of Jesse of Bethlehem in Judah. "Then the princes of the Philistines went forth, and it came to pass, as often as they went forth, that David behaved himself more wisely than all the servants of Saul: so that his name was much set by." And he married Michal, the king's daughter.

The king's jealousy was eventually roused by the successes of David, whom he at the same time justly suspected of intriguing with Samuel, who had already marked him out as the destined successor of the recalcitrant and independent Saul. The royal enmity became so marked that the young warrior was compelled to fly the kingdom. He at first pursued the war against the Philistines on his own account, and, after his abandonment of the hill-fort (not "cave") of Adullam, he attacked a Philistine force which was besieging the town of Keilah, and defeated it, afterwards making the place his headquarters. Saul's pursuit was, however, so relentless that David was compelled to enter into relations with the Philistines, and became the vassal of Achish, king of Gath (then, apparently, the hegemon of Philistia), receiving from him the Cherethite town of Ziklag, far to the south beyond Saul's reach, as a fief. He and his men were now compelled to march against Saul, as the auxiliaries of Achish, on the great expedition which the Philistines launched against Israel by way of the plain of Jezreel, which had always remained in their hands. In spite, however, of the politic desire of Achish to use David and the prestige of Yahweh's oracle (the presence of which at Ziklag must have considerably weakened the allegiance to Saul of many in Israel) in order to further the designs of the Philistines, the Cretan chiefs refused to admit the Israelite rebel to their councils or to utilize his aid. They suspected his good faith, and Achish was compelled to send him back to Ziklag (which he found devastated by the Amalekites on his return). David thus took no part in the final struggle on Mount Gilboa, when Saul and Jonathan were both slain.

It is probable that Achish now re-established the Philistine hegemony over Israel, but in a modified form. Ishbaal (Ishbosheth), son of Saul, was set up as king of Israel, with his residence at Mahanaim, while the southern part of the country was given to David, who reigned as king at Hebron. The Philistine garrisons were not reinstated, but both kings no doubt remained tributary to the Philistines. David had no intention of remaining in this position for long, however. His submission to Achish had been nothing but a means of escape from Saul. He fully intended to drive out the conquerors, depose Ishbaal, and continue Saul's kingship over the whole land in his own person. The ephod and the priests were with him, and though Samuel was now dead, his choice of David as Saul's eventual successor held good, and was no doubt accepted by the majority of the people, Ishbaal was only maintained as king in Mahanaim by the sword of his general Abner, against whose skill was soon pitted the fierce military virtue of David's general, Joab, for the king of Hebron lost no time in attacking his northern rival. The Philistines probably saw no reason to support either party against the other, and were well content to let their turbulent vassals destroy one another.

The defeat and defection of Abner and subsequent murder of Ishbaal, which placed all Israel under the undisputed rule of David, was calculated to disturb their complacency, as putting too much power into the hands of the energetic king of Hebron. And it was followed by an unexpected event which moved them to immediate action against him. The important town of Jerusalem, which three centuries before had been the centre of the Egyptian power in Southern Palestine, had, at the time of the Hebrew invasion, though perhaps carried by a rush, never been retained by the conquering tribes, and had never been re-taken, probably on account of its strength. It had remained in the power of its Canaanite inhabitants. David now possessed himself of it by a coup-de-main, and transferred himself to it from Hebron. At Hebron he had been always under the eye of his overlords, but now he was again the free man, in possession of an impregnable fortress, an inexpugnable focus of renewed rebellion. The distrust of the Philistine lords was amply justified, and Achish, if he still lived, must bitterly have rued his old complaisance towards the clever Hebrew leader. It was at once determined to attack David, and a powerful Philistine army moved up into the hills directly against Jerusalem. The expedition failed disastrously, David won two brilliant victories, at Baal-perazim, where the images of the Philistine gods were captured, and in the valley of Rephaim, where the invaders were so thoroughly routed that David smote them from Geba as far as Gezer, where the broken army regained the plain.

The tables were now turned. David followed up his success by invading Philistia, directing his attack against Gath, the most important Philistine centre at the time, and the nearest to the Israelite hills. Fighting of the fiercest character seems to have taken place round Gath, for the Philistine warrior-oligarchy was now at bay, and fighting for life, Gath, however, fell, and then David seems to have marched directly against the Philistine "mother city," Ashdod, situated about twelve miles to the west, near the coast, Ashdod was taken, and then the Israelite king returned triumphantly to his capital. Gath and its immediate dependencies, which had originally been Israelite territory, but had been torn from Israel by the Philistines soon after their immigration, were annexed by David, and the new condition of things was significantly shown by the fact that hundreds of Philistine and Cherethite warriors now took service at Jerusalem as the bodyguard of the Israelite conqueror. Mercenary service was characteristic of the races associated with the Philistines (the Shardina, especially), as of their relatives the Carians in later days; and mercenaries only take service with powerful monarchs who can pay them well and maintain them in plenty; so that his guard of Pelethites and Cherethites is significant evidence of the growing dignity and importance of the king of Israel.

The land was now definitely freed, and the event was marked by the solemn entry of the Ark of Yahweh into the new capital.

5. The Kingdom of Israel

The plans of Samuel had triumphed, but his policy was not destined to be carried out in its entirety. No warrior-king would submit to be the puppet of the prophets and priests. Saul had not, and indirectly owed his death to them in consequence. David, more wily, was devoted to them until the consummation of his kingship, and then had become too great a king to be controlled by such men as Abiathar and Zadok. He then deliberately set to work to bind the priesthood to him in a subordinate position by filling up the priestly offices vacant after the massacre at Nob with his own nominees, chiefly his own sons. Thus he hoped to prevent the possibility of too much religious interference.

The organization of the kingdom was modelled generally upon those of the neighbouring realms, but was naturally far more military in character than the organizations of either Egypt or Babylonia. Military personages like the sons of Zeruiah, like Benaiah ben-Jehoiada the Hebrew commandant of the Philistine guard and executioner-in-chief, Ittai the Philistine of Gath, one of David's most trusted soldiers, and Uriah the Hittite mercenary from the North, were far more prominent in the actual administration of the kingdom as well as in the royal entourage, than the treasurers and other non-military officials. It would have appeared a very barbarous kingdom, its organization a very rude imitation of those of the great empires, to an Egyptian or a Babylonian. Learning was probably unknown. Scribes existed, but it is uncertain what script they used, as we do not know whether the Phoenician or Aramaic alphabet (which had probably already been devised) had yet spread to southern Palestine. For foreign correspondence cuneiform may still have been used (though Aramaic is quite possible), and David had a Babylonian scribe, Shavsha (Shamsha) by name, to conduct the diplomatic correspondence with neighbouring monarchs which followed the rise of himself and his kingdom in the world's estimation.

The soldiers were not content with the defeat of the Philistines and recovery of Gath, and a series of campaigns was soon inaugurated against all the ancient enemies of Israel round about, in turn. Moab, in spite of the hospitality which she had afforded to David's parents when he fled from the anger of Saul, was first attacked, overthrown, and two-thirds of her inhabitants slaughtered. The remaining third submitted to annexation. Ammon was obviously marked out as the next victim, and so the king Hanun, son of Nahash, formed an alliance with the Aramaean tribes to the north against Israel. Ambassadors sent by David were villainously entreated, and Joab thereupon attacked with his army, completely defeating the allies. Whether now or somewhat later, the king's town of Rabbath-Ammon was taken, and its people horribly massacred by David. Ammon then ceased to exist as an independent kingdom.

The defeat of the Aramaean allies of Hanun was news displeasing to Hadadezer, the chief Aramaean king, who ruled in Zobah (a territory the precise frontier of which is unknown to us, but may be placed south of Damascus), and whose empire extended far to the westward and even included the Aramaean tribes on the other side of the Euphrates. Summoning even these distant subjects, his general Shobach advanced against the presumptuous Israelite king, but was severely defeated at Helam (Aleppo?). The Syrians of Damascus came vainly to his aid, and the end of the war was the annexation of Damascus and its district to the kingdom of David.

The defeat of the Aramaeans and the conquest of Damascus brought David into immediate contact with the important kings of North-Syria. An old enemy of Hadadezer, Toi, king of Hamath, whose kingdom now probably marched with that of David, sent him a friendly embassy, and Hiram of Tyre, the chief Phoenician king, became his friend and ally.

Against the powerful North-Syrian princes David had no mind to carry on war; the forces at his command would not have sufficed in number to effect anything more than a mere raid had he advanced against them victoriously, while success against their vast hosts was improbable. He contented himself with the acquisition of Damascus: no further northward extension of the kingdom is indicated.

The borders of the land being extended thus far northwards, the turn of the south now came. Edom, which, as far as can be learnt from the Biblical narrative, had given Israel no provocation, but had always been disliked by the Israelites, was attacked and overthrown, and a general massacre of the male inhabitants was, as usual, carried out by Joab and Abishai, the savage sons of Zeruiah, The Edomite king, Hadad II, the eighth of his line, seems to have been killed in battle, and his son Hadad III, whose mother, Mehetabel, was an Egyptian, fled to Egypt, where he married a royal princess, and lived as a pensioner of Pharaoh till the death of David seemed to open for him a prospect of regaining his inheritance.

Edom was annexed as far as the sea at Ezion-gebei (Akaba). The Hebrew dominions were not rounded off by a final conquest of the whole of Philistia. Not even tribute seems to have been sent to Jerusalem, and it may well be that the southern Philistine chiefs had voluntarily placed themselves under the protection of the north-Egyptian pharaohs at Tanis, who seem to have been energetic princes (Siamon now reigned), and with whom at any rate the Israelite king would have no desire to try conclusions. That this is the correct explanation is shown by the fact that when Shishak had invaded Judah after the death of Solomon he recorded the names of all the captured cities, and among them those of the Philistine towns are not mentioned. From this it would seem that they were already re-subjected to Egyptian rule, and in Solomon's time we find that the Pharaoh of Egypt considers Gezer as his, to burn and destroy, without opposition from the Hebrews.

Thus in the course of a few years David had raised Israel to the position of an important kingdom, with considerable territory. For the rest of his life he lived the normal life of an Oriental monarch, troubled by the usual harim-jealousies and hatreds, disobediences, and rebellions of his children. The rebellion of Absalom was sufficiently serious to necessitate the king's flight from his capital. His last days were troubled by the attempt of Absalom's brother Adonijah to seize the crown in despite of his half-brother Solomon, the king's son by Bathshtoa, to whom it had been devised by the king under Bathsheba's influence. Solomon was immediately consecrated as king, and associated with his father on the throne, which he occupied without a struggle on the king's death.

Solomon's accession was marked by the proscription of the supporters of Adonijah, chief of whom had been Joab and Abiathar, the ancient friends of David. Despite his services, Joab fell by the hand of the king's executioner, Benaiah, the son of Jehoiada; and Abiathar, saved from death by his holy calling, was banished to his patrimony of Anathoth, the more courtly Zadok succeeding him in his office. It was said that David, who had no love for his old companion-in-arms, had on his deathbed charged Solomon to put Joab to death.

The new reign marked a new epoch in the history of the Jewish state. Solomon was no "Roi des Gueux" like Saul, no successful condottiere like David; he was a typical Oriental Sultan, magnificent (so far as his means would allow), wise (in the belief of the vulgar), and without doubt tyrannical. He had been born in the purple. The element of simplicity which remained in his father's character till the end was unknown to him and to the men of his generation, who had been born after the close of the old republican days. Israel had now become great, and her king, enriched by the tribute of all. the lands from the Euphrates to the River of Egypt, was a monarch by whose side the farmer-leader of the old confederation, Saul, was a mere rustic. Civilization had progressed considerably in Jerusalem during the latter days of David: Solomon was pre-eminently a civilized man, a man of marked aesthetic tastes: he loved the majesty and splendour which his wealth enabled him to show, especially in the building of the great Temple in Jerusalem. This was probably the first building of any architectural pretension erected in Israel, and its wonders, as the Israelites considered them, made an ineffaceable impression on the popular mind. Solomon merely aped the splendours of Egypt and Babylonia, but in Oriental tradition he has become a Sultan more magnificent than Sesostris or Sardanapalus, and the wielder of supernatural power, for he could command the Jann or Jinnis, the Powers of the Air, and they did his bidding. He was the wisest as well as the most mighty and magnificent of rulers.

Here we have a true portrait exaggerated. Solomon was no warrior like his father; he had had no experience of war and the camp in his youth, and had no desire to make acquaintance with them. If difficulties arose, he endeavoured to avoid them by diplomatic means, for he had inherited his father's diplomatic talent, and probably his diplomacy was managed with a finesse which, coupled with his patronage of the mysterious arts of civilization and his great ability in the amassing of wealth, gave him his deserved reputation for wisdom.

This "wisdom" was the keynote of his reign. Loving wealth, he bent his whole energies towards its acquisition by the means of peaceful commerce. His kingdom lay athwart the main lines of communication between Egypt and Mesopotamia, Arabia and Asia Minor, and, under wise governance, seemed destined to be wealthy and prosperous. As the heir of the kingdom of Damascus, he ruled up to the Euphrates and held the great trade-crossing at Tiphsah (Thapsacus). As the heir of Edom, he held Ezion-geber on the Red Sea, at the head of the Gulf of Akaba. And, though not he, but the Pharaoh of Egypt, was the sovereign of Philistia, yet Gaza is traditionally assigned to his kingdom; and it is by no means impossible that this important trade-centre was given him by the Egyptian monarch Hor-Psibkhannu, possibly with his daughter, the daughter of Pharaoh, king of Egypt, whom Solomon took to wife.

This marriage-alliance with Egypt secured peace on the south-western frontier, and the alliance with Hiram of Tyre, the most powerful Phoenician prince, at the same time secured Solomon's communications with the Phoenician cities and the Phoenician communications with Arabia. Under the protecting aegis of the king of Palestine the caravans passed continually from Egypt to Mesopotamia, from Phoenicia to Arabia, in peace; the old days of the robberies of the Suti and the "SA-GAZ" seemed forgotten. The king himself, we are told, equipped, with the aid of the Phoenician Hiram, a great naval expedition which sailed from Ezion-geber to the land of Ophir, and brought back the famous cargoes of the wealth of Ind which are described with so much detail in the Book of Kings. The resemblance of this expedition to those of the old Egyptian monarchs, notably Hatshepsut, to Punt has always been remarked, and it has often been assumed that Ophir was Punt, and that it is therefore to be sought on the African Somali coast. Among the products of Ophir, however, there are certain things mentioned, such as the apes and peacocks, for instance, which are certainly Indian; so that it is quite probable that Ophir is really the Konkan or Cochin coast, and that Solomon's Phoenician sailors reached India, unless, as is possible, they went only as far as Southern Arabia, where they received the Indian products brought by the local traders.

Relations with the civilized communities of Southern Arabia are indicated also by the legend of the coming of Balkis, the queen of Sheba, to Jerusalem in order to visit the wise and magnificent king.

A less commendable side to the "wisdom" of Solomon is exhibited in the story of his astute dealing with Hiram in the matter of the Galilaean towns which were handed over to Tyre in payment for cedar and gold.

The reign of Solomon early became the theme of popular romance, and but few really historical events of it are recorded at all. This presents us with a strong contrast to the clear sequence of events, the genuine history, of the reigns of Saul and David. But we can see that towards the end of his reign the power established by David had weakened. "Adversaries were raised up" against him in the shape of Hadad the Edomite and Rezon the Syrian. David's great conquests, Edom and Syria, revolted, and the Jewish power had become so enfeebled by the luxury and pacifist policy of the king that it was unable to retain these conquered lands. Hadad III of Edom, the young son of the second Hadad, who had been killed fighting against Joab's cruel invasion, had fled to Egypt, where, as was commonly the case of exiled Asiatic princes, he was maintained at the royal court in a manner befitting his rank, and given Pharaoh's wife's sister as his bride. Their son Genubath, who was born in Egypt, bore, apparently, an Egyptian name. We do not know the name of the king who patronized Hadad, but it was probably the last Tanite, Hor-Psibkhannu, or Sheshenk I.

The growing weakness of Solomon encouraged Hadad to make his way back from Egypt to his lost kingdom, and he seems to have re-established its independence, as did Rezon that of Syria, without much trouble. At the end of Solomon's reign the Israelite kingdom was reduced to its limits in the time of Saul. At his death it split again into its two natural divisions of Judah and Israel, and the kingdoms of David and Ishbaal were restored, with the difference that Jerusalem was now the capital of Judah, instead of Hebron.

6. The Kingdoms of Judah and Israel

Events had taken their course natural in an Eastern state. To the warrior who had carved out a kingdom for himself succeeded the magnificent son, powerful and wise but feeble in old age, to whom succeeded the prodigal tyrant who brought all things to ruin. David, Solomon, and Rehoboam are paralleled in Egypt by Thothmes III, Amenhetep III. and Akhenaten; in modern history they correspond to Henri IV, Louis XIV, and Louis XV. The folly of Rehoboam was the opportunity of an Israelite David, Jeroboam the son of Nebat, to seize the throne for himself. Probably he intended to seize the whole inheritance of David, but Judah and Benjamin remained faithful to their worthless sovereign, and Jeroboam had to content himself with the northern division of the kingdom. Religious discontent probably gave him a means of exciting disaffection. Solomon, a broad-minded man, interested in all things foreign, had been tolerant in religion, and had even, so men said, been himself prevailed upon by his foreign wives to sacrifice to deities other than his own. The peculiar temper of the Hebrew prophets, which did not tolerate that any reverence should be paid to other gods but Yahweh, or to Yahweh in iconic form, was excited by this cosmopolitanism, and even before the death of Solomon, a religious fanatic named Ahijah seems to have started in the North the revolt which the ambitious son of Nebat soon used for his own purposes. Ahijah's purpose was not effected, for no sooner was Jeroboam firmly established in power than he abandoned the aniconic cult of Yahweh and offered public sacrifices to the bull-images at Dan and Bethel. The Israelitish kingdom was henceforward by no means solely devoted even to the worship of Yahweh, whether aniconic or not, and a constant fight was waged for two centuries by the prophets against the idolatrous tendencies of the royal court and the majority of the population. This struggle produced that splendid prophetic literature of the Old Testament to which we owe so much, not simply as a source of historical information, but as a mighty religious force which has deeply modified the whole national character of the Christian peoples.

Judah and Benjamin remained on the whole more faithful to the God of their forefathers, probably owing to their possession of the national sanctuary that Solomon had built. It must also be remembered that Israel was now and remained far more civilized, as well as more populous and prosperous, than Judah, and so was more open to the corrupting influences of the non-Hebrew peoples with whom she was in constant contact. Judah, isolated in her hills, led a simpler life, in spite of her possession of Solomon's capital.

Jeroboam's easy inclination in religious matters was perhaps natural: both his mother and his wife were Egyptian. And this fact also makes it the more probable that his successful revolt was closely connected with the Egyptian invasion under Shishak (Sheshenk I, first king of the XXIInd Dynasty) in the fifth year of Rehoboam (about 925 B.C.), which resulted in the capture and sack of Jerusalem. We can well see that these two events were closely inter-related, and can assume that the revolt of Israel followed the fall of Jerusalem. We need not suppose that Jeroboam was merely the tool and nominee of Shishak, but it was natural that, being half-Egyptian himself, he should lean greatly upon Egyptian support, and, as a mark of his alliance, take, like Hadad of Edom and Solomon himself, an Egyptian princess as his wife.

7. Egypt and Palestine (1000-854 B.C.)

We have seen that the weakening of the Philistine power during the long war with Saul and David probably induced the Philistines to acknowledge Egyptian supremacy as a means of protection against the Hebrews. This was perhaps in the time of Siamon the Tanite (c. 995-977 B.C.), of the XXIst Dynasty, when Gaza probably became Egyptian once more. The Egyptian supremacy seems to have been real. It was not challenged by either David or Solomon, the latter of whom was friendly with Egypt, and married the daughter of the king, probably Hor-Psibkhannu (Psusennes II), the successor of Siamon. We have seen that Gaza may have been given by Psusennes to Solomon as the dowry of his daughter. He certainly gave Gezer to his daughter and her husband, after he had chastised it with fire and sword. Solomon re-fortified the city, which was one of the most important in Palestine, and had been one of the chief places of the Philistines. For these events we have only the evidence of the Biblical history: the Egyptian records, miserably jejune at this period, tell us nothing.

At the death of Psusennes II the Egyptian kingdom passed to another dynasty. A successful soldier, of Libyan descent, named Sheshonko or Sheshenk, succeeded him, and as a mark of the change of dynasty the capital was transferred from Tanis to Bubastis, no doubt Sheshenk's own town. He legitimatized his claim by marrying a Tanite princess, Karamat, daughter of Psusennes.

Sheshenk's first enterprise was the assertion of his authority in Upper Egypt, and the termination of the dual system of government which had obtained for over a century. The rule of the theocracy at Thebes was ended by the appointment of the king's own son Auput as High-Priest. Thebes appears to have submitted without demur, and was henceforward specially favoured by Sheshenk and his successors, who aspired to honour Amen not less than their great predecessors of two or three centuries before, and to revive his ancient glories so far as lay in their power. Sheshenk began to build an enormous hall at Karnak before that of Seti and Rameses, but the architects of his day were not as those of the great period: they had no experience in gigantic works, the columns they put up were too weak to carry any roof, the hall was never completed, and now only a single pillar of this badly planned work remains.

To honour Amen fitly records of successful war were also necessary as decorations of his temple. These were provided by Sheshenk's expedition into Palestine, the triumphal record of which was placed upon the walls of Karnak, and has given us a valuable confirmation of the historical truth of the Jewish chronicler's statement as to the capture of Jerusalem by "Shishak." Here again we see that the Egyptian did not strike till he could be fairly sure of victory. Solomon had been too powerful for any attack to be made upon him: but no sooner was he dead, and the tyranny, weakness, and unpopularity of Rehoboam made manifest, than the plans of the pharaoh who had taken Gaza were resumed by his Bubastite successor. Sheshenk had reigned about twelve years, probably, before the death of Solomon took place, and his Palestinian expedition was carried out five years later, when he must have been getting on in years. He died, perhaps, less than five years (c. 920 B.C.) after his triumphant return to Egypt. He had brought with him the golden shields of Solomon's temple and the rest of the treasure of Yahweh's service, which it had been the chief object of the expedition to secure for the enrichment of Amen, who was no longer so wealthy as he had been of old. No attempt was made to hold Palestine: the Jewish kingdom on her immediate border seemed to forbid all prospect of any future restoration of the empire that Egypt had held for six hundred years and more. Yet one more attempt at its restoration seems to have been made, if we are to identify the "Ethiopian" Zerah, who was defeated by Asa of Judah, the second successor of Rehoboam, with Osorkon I, the successor of Shishak. The defeat was final (c. 895 B.C.).

The remaining kings of the XXIInd Dynasty — Takeloti I, Osorkon II, Sheshenk II, Takeloti II, Sheshenk III (who reigned over fifty years), Pimai, and Sheshenk IV — were of no historical importance whatever. Osorkon II built a splendid "Festival-Hall" at Bubastis to commemorate his Sed-festival; and the land seems to have had peace. But in the same reign the shadow of the tribulation to come at the hands of the Assyrians first appeared, when the great battle of Karkar was fought (854 B.C.), in which Shalmaneser II contended with the Syrian Benhadad II of Damascus, Irkhuleni the Hittite king of Hamath, and Ahab of Israel. It has been supposed that Egypt sent a force to aid the allies, but this is improbable, as the "Musri" from which 1000 men came to help Ahab and his allies is more probably the North-Syrian land of this name than Egypt.

With the battle of Karkar the history of the kingdoms of Syria and Palestine merges into that of Assyria.

8. Archaeological Results in Palestine

The archaeological discoveries of the last few years in Palestine have hardly shed as much light as had been hoped upon the ancient culture of Palestine.

An important result for the historian is the fact that no difference can be traced in the town-strata between what is Canaanite and what is Hebrew. Their cultures were indistinguishable as, probably, in reality the peoples were also. The difference between them was exaggerated by the Judahite monotheists. All the Palestinians, from North Phoenicia to Judah, were Canaanites. We cannot therefore talk of pottery or what not from Palestinian sites as "pre-Israelite" and "Israelite," for we cannot distinguish them.

With the exception of the Philistine pottery at Tell es-Safi, most of the actual spoils of excavation are somewhat dull and uninteresting in comparison with the brilliant results of similar work in Egypt and Greece. But this is the fault of the Canaanites themselves. In comparison with the Cretans or the Egyptians they were a dull and uninteresting people: brilliant conceptions or mighty works in art or architecture were not to be expected from them. Still, one is surprised at the absence from the Palestinian excavations of anything of real importance in the history of man's handiworks. For the period 1200-700 B.C., positively the only outstanding object is the strange altar discovered by Sellin at Taanach. The Tell es-Safi pottery is not Palestinian but Aegean, and so cannot be credited to the Canaanites. So also with the "most artistic" objects from Gezer. In this lack of originality we can see a considerable resemblance to their cousins, the Phoenicians. The luxurious civilization of the period before the Egyptian conquest, of which we gain an idea only from Thothmes III's loot at Megiddo, was probably entirely imitative, though this cannot be said definitely, as the excavations have revealed not a trace of it. War no doubt destroyed it. The ceaseless war of Egyptian and Hittite and the Israelite invasion must have lowered the level of culture in Canaan enormously. The comparative peace after the treaty of Rameses II with the Hittites no doubt allowed civilization to raise its head once more: the Israelites were becoming traders and seafarers. Then the Philistine invasion threw all back again, and it was only by slow and painful degrees that in the time of Solomon art and handiwork (still imitative, however, and of Phoenician inspiration) once more began to take high place. The tradition of Solomon maintained itself at Samaria, we cannot doubt. But of this we have nothing, as yet. War, probably, has destroyed or spoiled everything of importance. Unless the Assyrian capture and sack in 722 B.C. destroyed all remains of this age, we may, however, hope that the excavation of Samaria, now in progress, may tell us something of the culture of Israel, which must have been affected strongly by that of Northern Syria. From the last excavations and archaeological discussions we are beginning to see a possibility that the Syrians had an art of their own, owing much to Anatolia and much to Babylonia-Assyria, but still with a certain originality which that of Phoenicia lacked. This Syrian art may towards the end of its day have exercised considerable effect upon the nascent art of Greece, and perhaps formed a bridge between the vase-painters of Ionia and the sculptors of Nineveh.

The actual results of the excavations on southern sites are what might have been expected: high-places, bethels and innumerable sacrificed children buried in pots beneath buildings. All small objects are crude and poor. Of great interest are the huge stone walls of the towns, going back to megalithic times, and testifying by their existence to the insecurity of the settled inhabitants from Beduin raids and the attacks of conquerors from Egypt or the North.

If the Palestinians as a whole lacked artistic originality and could build nothing but bare walls, if they lacked imagination as regards the works of their hands, if their sense of the beauty of form and line in material objects was blunt and poor, yet we know to what heights and depths of imagination and imagery the poets and prophets of Israel could attain, dowering the world with a poesy, a music and frenzy of words, that is one of the greatest possessions of our civilization for all time.

CHAPTER X: THE ASSYRIAN EMPIRE

I. Renewed Rise of Assyiria: the Reign of Ashur-nasir-pal

THE division of the Jewish kingdom, and the internecine war in Palestine that resulted therefrom, coincided with a renewed rise of the Assyrian power.

Between Ashur-erbi, in whose reign the Syrian cities of Pethor and Mutkinu, and with them probably the whole trans-Euphratean dominions of Tiglath-pileser I, were lost to the Aramaean invaders, and Ashur-nasir-pal, who recovered North Syria, nearly two centuries elapsed. For over a century after the reign of Ashur-erbi Assyrian history is a blank, till the name of an Assyrian king is once more mentioned; this is Tiglath-pileser III, a contemporary of Solomon and of Shishak. Of this third Tiglath-pileser we have no contemporary record: we know him only from an inscription of his grandson, Adad-nirari II.

The reign of Adad-nirari II marks a new era, not only in the history of Assyria, but in that of the world, for another reason. It so happens that from his time the list of the limmi or eponymous magistracies of the years was kept without omission till the close of the Assyrian empire. As has already been said, by means of this list we can fix without the possibility of error the exact dates of most of the chief events in the history of Assyria. With the limmi of 893 B.C. (the year in which the continuous record starts) accurately dated history begins.

Adad-nirari died in the year 890, leaving a kingdom heartened by successful conflict with Babylonia to his son Tukulti-Ninib II, a warrior who might have rivalled the exploits of Tiglath-pileser, had he not been carried off early by death (884), after a successful campaign on the northern border.

He was succeeded by his son Ashur-Nasir-Pal III. (884-860), in whose twenty-four years' reign the renewed military activity of Assyria suddenly burst forth from her borders with irresistible force in the direction of Syria, with the result that in a very short time the dominion of Tiglath-pileser I was restored, and the foundation of the empire of the Sargonides was laid.

The new conqueror was a man not only of military genius but of a ruthless and unsparing nature that beat down all opposition by the method of absolute annihilation. No human pity existed in the breast of Ashur-nasir-pal: the sufferings of defeated men whom he tortured were to him no more than those of crushed ants; nay, less, for he gloried in the tortures which he inflicted on the bodies of those who crossed his will. His usual procedure after the capture of a hostile city was to burn it, and then to mutilate all the grown men prisoners by cutting off their hands and ears and putting out their eyes; after which they were piled up in a great heap to perish in torture from sun, flies, their wounds, and suffocation; the children, both boys and girls, were all burnt alive at the stake; and the chief was carried off to Assyria to be flayed alive for the king's delectation.

To Ashur-nasir-pal and his son Shalmaneser II was due the military organization of the Assyrian state which soon made it mistress of Western Asia. We know little of the actual organization of the nation for war, except that there was a small standing army of royal troops, which was increased in war-time by the mobilization of all the men, who were all able-bodied warriors of a hardy farmer or yeoman class. It was in these sturdy Assyrian fellah infantry, who were largely armed with the bow, that the strength of Assyria lay. The power and effect of the infantry-soldier was greatly developed by the Assyrian kings, and it was to their bowmen, who could destroy the chariots and horsemen of an enemy at a distance, that they owed their victories, even as the English kings owed the discomfiture of the chivalry of France to the long-bows of the English yeomen. The power of the chariotry now began to wane, and the chariot became somewhat demode in war. Further, the Assyrians greatly developed siegecraft, and probably were the inventors of military engineering. To so well-devised a machine of war victory fell, if not always easily, at least surely and inevitably, till it fell to pieces, as will be seen, two centuries later. The chief commander under the king was called turtan, and under him was the rab-shakeh.

The campaign of Tukulti-Ninib in the North was carried to a successful conclusion: it was necessary first to restore Assyrian prestige among the turbulent mountain tribes and ensure their quiescence before proceeding to conquest in the West.

Ashur-nasir-pal shewed his thorough and comprehensive spirit from the first: beginning with the tribes of the Zagros, east of Assyria, he systematically marched through their valleys and mountains with fire and sword in a circular movement like the sweep of a scythe, round through Southern Armenia to Commagene and Cilicia. Then he was ready to cross the Euphrates, Bit-Khallupi, an Aramaean state on the riverbank, was conquered. Babylon, however, which had remained passive since her defeat by Adad-nirari II, now took alarm, for she always laid claim to the suzerainty of the lands of the Middle Euphrates, through which ran the caravan-routes of her merchants to Syria, and never willingly admitted Assyrian or other control over them. Nabu-pal-iddina, the king of Babylon, accordingly assisted the king of the land of Sukhi (the "Shuhites") to resist Ashur-nasir-pal, with no result but the ruin of the king of Sukhi. The fall of the Sukhi king was the signal for the collapse of the independent states of Naharin which had grown up since the time of Tiglath-pileser I. The Aramaean state of Bit-Adini on the left bank of the Euphrates was finally overthrown and destroyed. Carchemish, the capital of the southern Hittite kingdom that had come into existence at the break-up of the empire of Shubbiluliuma, and had probably attained to considerable power during the eclipse of Assyria, was taken, and its king, Sangara, submitted to the conqueror (876 B.C.). The river was then crossed, and Naharin lay at his feet. Apparently without meeting resistance Ashur-nasir-pal marched south through Northern Syria to the Orontes, which he crossed, entered the Lebanon, and descended to the sea, where he received the submission of the Phoenician cities. The chief Syrian king, at Damascus, was too paralysed by the swiftness of his advance to offer to dispute his passage.

Then Ashur-nasir-pal turned slowly back to the Euphrates, and completed his work by a movement the reverse of that with which he had commenced his series of campaigns. Starting from Commagene, his scythe swept round the upper valley of the Tigris into Armenia and so round again to the Zagros.

His military work effectually done, Ashur-nasir-pal turned to the peaceful development of his empire, to which he seems to have devoted the same relentless energy. Many fine temples and palaces were built by him. For the ruthless conqueror and enslaver was (whether from mere superstition or not) so far civilized as to build well and finely, and to employ sculptors to decorate his buildings who were unrivalled in Assyria for two centuries and whose work became the model for the artists of the neighbouring lands. The military nature of the empire was emphasized by the removal of the capital from the ancient Ashur, with which were associated traditions and memories not always military, and not always pleasing, perhaps, to Ashur-nasir-pal, to Calah, the ancient artificial creation of Shalmaneser I, which had been abandoned for many centuries.

Here the headquarters of the "supreme war-lord" were set up, and hence, from a barrack-like town, he ruled.

Ashur-nasir-pal left a renewed empire to his son Shalmaneser II (860-825 B.C.), who maintained the tradition of his father's rule to the day of his death, in a duller and less inspired, but perhaps somewhat more humane, manner. At any rate, we do not hear so much of his holocausts as we do of those of his father.

2. Reign of Shalmaneser II

The beginning of his reign had to be signalized, as was his father's, by war. During the peace of the latter years of Ashur-nasir-pal the tributary states on the Euphrates had not dared to raise their heads, and there is nothing to shew that they intended to do so at the death of the old king. But it was evidently considered necessary that they should be terror-struck, lest the idea of rebellion should occur to them. In his first year Shalmaneser marched against Bit-Adini, whose king, Akhuni, called to his aid the neighbouring princes beyond the Euphrates. This temerity was punished, after three years, by the total destruction of the little Aramaean kingdom. Its weak allies had already fallen away. The destruction of the tributary kingdoms now brought Shalmaneser face to face with the more powerful countries of the South, the two Aramaean states of Hamath and Damascus, and the kingdom of Israel. Hamath had submitted to Ashur-nasir-pal, but Damascus had not, nor had the conqueror made any attempt to subdue the southern Syrian kingdom. Israel had stood as yet without the sphere of Assyrian ambitions.

In the year 854 B.C., however, we find Ahab of Israel allied with Irkhuleni of Hamath and Benhadad II of Damascus against Assyria at the great battle of Karkar. It is improbable that Ahab was a very willing ally. Since the Aramaean rebel Rezon, son of Eliada, had revolted from Solomon, Damascus had been a thorn in the side of Israel. The division of the Israelite kingdom gave the rulers of Damascus an opportunity to make their new power seriously felt in the South. Judah, fearing annihilation at the hands of the more powerful northern kingdom, had sought the alliance of Damascus. Abijah, son of Rehoboam, concluded a treaty of amity with Tab-Rimmon, son of Rezon, and Asa, hard pressed by the Israelite usurper Baasha, appealed to this treaty in order to bring up Benhadad I, son of Tab-Rimmon, against Israel. Baasha was defeated, and Judah had peace for a time. But the attention of Benhadad was now directed towards the North, and the threatening rise of Assyria. Judah was unable to resist the dominance of Israel, under her energetic king 'Omri; and Jehoshaphat, son of Asa, became the vassal of 'Omri's son Ahab. The energy of 'Omri, his subjection of Moab, and consequent hold on Judah, by no means pleased the Damascenes, and Benhadad II (Hadadezer) attacked him, taking Ramoth-Gilead from him, and compelling him to grant the Syrian merchants privileges in his capital city of Samaria.

Following Assyrian example, Benhadad attacked Israel again after the accession of Ahab, and besieged Samaria, clearly stating a claim to overlordship, which Ahab evidently admitted. The Syrian king seems, however, to have presumed tyrannically on this admission, and Ahab, who had relations with other northern princes who would naturally be none too friendly to the powerful Benhadad (he had married Baalizebel or Jezebel, daughter of Ethbaal of Tyre), may have been able to summon help from the north, possibly from the North Syrian Hittites. In any case the Syrians, after a severe defeat at Aphek, were compelled to evacuate Israel. A treaty followed which granted Israel the same commercial rights in Damascus that had been given to the Syrians in Samaria. The overlordship of Benhadad seems to have been still admitted, for now Shalmaneser II was marching south, and we find Israelites as well as Hamathites arrayed against him beneath the banner of Benhadad. Had Ahab dared to refuse assistance, he would surely never have helped Benhadad to resist the greatest danger that the Syrian kingdom had yet faced.

Benhadad II (or Adad-'idri, as they called him) was the most redoubtable foe that the Assyrians themselves had yet faced. It is evident that the battle which took place at Karkar in the Orontes valley was indecisive. The Assyrians of course claimed a victory, and it is possible that they remained in possession of the field. But they retreated immediately afterwards to the Euphrates, leaving Benhadad in undisturbed possession of his realm. The losses of the Syrians had, however, no doubt been terrible, and Ahab, who regained his kingdom with his contingent, evidently thought the moment opportune for revolt against his exacting suzerain. He summoned his own subject-ally Jehoshaphat of Judah to his aid, and the two kings went up to retake Ramoth-Gilead, which had been Syrian since the time of 'Omri. But Ahab had miscalculated Benhadad's weakness, and in the battle that followed, of which we have so picturesque a description in the Book of Kings, he was killed, fighting valiantly to the last (852 B.C.). Jehoshaphat retreated safely with the defeated army, as the Syrians were too exhausted to pursue. When he regained his kingdom he took the opportunity to throw off his allegiance to Israel, refusing to allow Ahab's son Ahaziah to participate in the profits of the commercial route which he now opened to the Red Sea at Ezion-geber through the territory of Edom, which was subject to him. Moab at the same time revolted successfully from Israel under its King Mesha, who tells us on his stela of victory, the famous "Moabite Stone," which he set up at Dibon, how in the latter years of Ahab he destroyed the Israelite garrisons and freed his land, how he made the slaughtered Israelites a "gazing-stock" unto Moab, and how he dragged the sacred vessels of Yahweh before his god Chemosh. This inscription is one of the most important, and one of the very few contemporary, documents of Israelite history.

Benhadad was quite unable to interfere further with the southern kingdoms. He needed all his strength to meet the renewed attack of Assyria, which could not be long in coming. The king of Carchemish, no doubt stirred up by Benhadad, delayed it during the year 850, but after his defeat Shalmaneser marched to glut his vengeance on Damascus. He was again baulked by the fierce resistance of the Syrian king (849). The attack was continued in the next year without result; and in 846 Shalmaneser, furious at this unexpected resistance, called out the enormous army, for that time, of 120,000 men, for the war. How Benhadad resisted this armament successfully we do not know, but he did, and Shalmaneser now abandoned his direct attack. He waited for a more favourable opportunity, more than ever determined, with a doggedness worthy of his father's son, to make Damascus his tributary. Meanwhile he contented himself with consolidating his power in Northern Syria, and received the complete submission of the Phoenician cities (843).

Ahaziah of Israel had been succeeded after a reign of perhaps only a few months by Jehoram, an energetic monarch, whom Jehoshaphat of Judah saw fit to placate by renewing his subject-alliance to Israel, and affording assistance to Jehoram in the re-subjugation of revolted Moab. Probably an independent Moab under an energetic king like Mesha' seemed a greater danger to Judah than an almost nominal subjection to Israel. The attack of the two kings, aided by the contingent which Edom owed to Judah, against Mesha' failed. After initial successes, in which Mesha' was reduced to great straits, and sacrificed his eldest son to Chemosh in order to gain the help of the god, the expedition was compelled to evacuate the Moabite territory, and to return by the way it had come, through the waterless deserts round the southern end of the Dead Sea From the curious phrase in which this retreat is chronicled in the Book of Kings, it is evident that the Israelites ascribed their defeat directly to the intervention of their enemy's god, Chemosh, after the king's devotion of his first-born.

This disaster (about 850 B.C.) was followed by the death of Jehoshaphat and the revolt of Edom from Judah. Jehoram of Judah, the successor of Jeshoshaphat, was defeated in an attempt to subdue it, and narrowly escaped with his life. After a reign of a few years he was succeeded by his son Ahaziah. Now came the murder of Benhadad II by his successor Hazael (843), and Jehoram of Israel, baulked in the direction of Moab, eagerly seized the opportunity to effect the recovery of Ramoth-gilead, summoning to his aid his kinsman and vassal, Ahaziah of Judah, the great-grandson of Ahab and Jezebel. The attack on Syria seems to have been at first successful, and Ramoth-gilead was taken, though Jehoram was wounded in the fight. In order to heal his wounds, the king returned to Jezreel, leaving at Ramoth-gilead a garrison, among the officers of which was a certain Jehu, son of Nimshi. The steady idolatry of the house of 'Omri had always been a scandal to the monotheistic devotees of Yahweh, and Ahab and Jehoram spent the whole of their reigns in continuous religious conflict with the monotheists, led by the great prophets Elijah and Elisha, whose crusade was chiefly directed against the Baal-worship which Jezebel had introduced from Phoenicia. Now, when Jehoram was incapacitated by his wounds, Elisha planned a bold stroke against him. He had evidently marked out Jehu as a warrior fit to lead Israel, and sent one of his younger followers, whose name is not handed down in the chronicle, to Ramoth-gilead with orders to anoint Jehu king. The wily prophet counted upon the awakened ambition of Jehu to do the rest. Nor was he disappointed. The garrison of Ramoth-gilead accepted Jehu as king, and the would-be usurper struck swiftly. He set out from Ramoth-gilead and drove "furiously" to Jezreel, where followed the murders of Jehoram, of Ahaziah, who was with him, and that of the old queen Jezebel, which is so stirringly described in the Book of Kings. By a concession to poetic justice, the chronicler makes the murder of the two kings take place in the vineyard of Naboth, which Ahab had unrighteously taken.

A massacre of all the living members of the house of 'Omri followed, and even relatives of the murdered king of Judah were treacherously slain by the usurper. Then came the expected holocaust of the priests of the Phoenician Baal, which Jehu owed to the prophets of Yahweh who had made him king. Jehu, however, while zealous against Baal and his worshippers, was no orthodox votary of Yahweh: he continued the worship of the national Israelitish bull-idols at Dan and Bethel which Jeroboam had set up.

Now came the opportunity of Shalmaneser. Syria and Israel were both weakened by renewed war, and their new kings were neither of them yet firmly established on their thrones. Although Jehu had murdered Jehoram, the enemy of Hazael, it was not probable that he would voluntarily return to the position of Ahab twelve years before, and assist the Syrians, after the successful recovery of Ramoth-gilead. The neutrality, if not the active help, of Israel could therefore be counted on. Judah, now in the throes of a furious religious proscription of the royal house, which had been tainted by the blood of Jezebel and Ahab, and their Baal-worship, would naturally sympathize with Jehu's attitude.

Accordingly, in the year 842 Shalmaneser marched south. He met Hazael on the slopes of Hermon, defeated him and drove him back to Damascus. The whole of his territory was mercilessly ravaged even as far as the Hauran, but Damascus itself was too strong to be taken. Jehu more than fulfilled expectations as to his attitude, for he sent an embassy to Shalmaneser with rich gifts, which the Assyrian king construed, rightly or wrongly, as tribute. The tribute of Jehu was commemorated on an obelisk of black stone, set up in the royal palace at Calah, which is now in the British Museum. Shalmaneser sought compensation for the failure of his long war against Syria in further conquests in the direction of the Taurus. In a few years the Assyrian yoke was firmly settled on the necks of all the peoples from the Cilician plain to the Euphrates, while the Phoenician cities, and Hamath also, paid tribute to Nineveh rather than to Damascus. In so far the power of Damascus had been definitely curtailed. She obtained compensation in the subjection of Israel, which was abandoned to her without compunction.

More than by the conquest of Cilicia the failure of the Syrian war was overshadowed by Shalmaneser's great success against Babylonia, which he made tributary. The period of Aramaean migration had been of weakness and turmoil for Babylonia as for Assyria. The Chaldaean tribes from the southern shore of the Persian Gulf had also overrun Babylonia, and had given her a short-lived dynasty. An unnamed Elamite is also chronicled at this time as reigning over Babylonia. About 950 B.C. a native Babylonian dynasty began to reign, which soon found itself at war with Assyria. The kings Shamash-mudammik and Nabu-shum-ishkun were defeated in succession by Adad-nirari II, who, however, shewed no desire to conquer Babylonia, and made peace, which was cemented by a mutual marriage-alliance. Nabu-pal-iddina, the next Babylonian king, aided the people of Sukhi, as we have seen, against Ashur-nasir-pal, but otherwise preserved peaceful relations both with him and with Shalmaneser II. About 853, however, he was deposed, and his son and successor, Marduk-shum-iddina, being seriously threatened by a revolt under his brother Marduk-bel-usate, was ill-advised enough to call Shalmaneser to his aid. The Assyrian king, smarting from his first repulse at the hands of Benhadad, was by no means averse to this chance of reaping cheap laurels. He invaded Babylonia, defeated the rebels in two campaigns (852-851 B.C.), drove out the Chaldaeans, and during the rest of his reign the Babylonian king was his vassal. The easy submission of the Babylonians was due to the fact that their commercial relations with Phoenicia and Anatolia were in no way damaged, but rather fostered, by the Assyrian conquests. Of old Babylonia had always sought to control the whole course of the Euphrates as far as Northern Syria in the interest of these commercial relations, and Nebuchadrezzar I and Marduk-nadin-akhi had contended for this with some success against Assyria. The Assyrians, however, were not a commercial nation, and had no desire to divert any of the western trade to themselves. They only desired tribute and acknowledgment of their superior prowess, and were quite willing to leave commerce to the Babylonians. When the Babylonian merchants realized this, and saw that under the firm Assyrian rule of Northern Syria their trade was free from possible interference by the petty princes of that region, they naturally became opponents of all war with Assyria, and were perhaps even prepared to welcome Assyrian suzerainty over their own country, as this would guarantee their commerce the full protection of the Assyrian arms. Henceforward opposition to Assyrian control came only from ambitious princes and occasional popular patriotic movements: the merchants, the most important element in the body-politic, formed an unwavering pro-Assyrian party, which was ever ready to barter its self-respect for shekels.

Towards the end of his reign, Shalmaneser II ceased to lead his armies personally, and handed over the supreme command to his turtan or commander-in-chief, Ashur-dayan. At the same time a younger son, Shamshi-Adad, was put forward as the successor to the throne, to the prejudice of an elder brother, Ashurdaninpal. Probably Shamshi-Adad was the candidate of the army and the powerful turtan. At any rate, when Ashurdaninpal revolted and carried with him the greater part of the kingdom, including even Nineveh and Assur, the royal military headquarters of Calah remained faithful to Shalmaneser and Shamshi-Adad, together with probably the whole of the army. So popular was Ashurdaninpal that the whole military strength of the crown was unable to suppress the revolt finally till six years after the death of Shalmaneser and the accession of Shamshi-Adad (825 B.C.). It was not till 819 that the civil war ended. In the turmoil both Hamath and Babylonia had revolted. Babylonia was at once attacked (818), but it was not till six years later that Shamshi-Adad finally defeated the Babylonian king Marduk-balatsu-ikbi at Dur-Papsukal in northern Babylonia, entirely routing his army, which comprised as many Elamite and Chaldaean mercenaries as Babylonians, killing 5000 of them, taking 2000, and capturing a hundred chariots.

3. Adad-nirari III and his successors

Soon after this great fight Shamshi-Adad died (811), leaving his kingdom to his son Adad-nirari III, who, now that Babylonia was subdued, was at liberty to turn his attention to the North and West, which Shamshi-Adad had never had time to visit. The first years of Adad-nirari's reign were occupied in the chastisement of the Kurdish tribes, which had not been carried out since the time of Ashur-nasir-pal. Then he turned to Syria. Hamath submitted, and the Phoenician cities resumed their tribute. Then came the turn of Damascus, Benhadad III or Mari', as the Assyrians called him, the son of Hazael, was besieged in his capital and compelled to pay tribute (805 or 804 B.C.). Jehoahaz, the king of Israel, who with his people had had to submit to long years of Syrian tyranny, welcomed the Assyrian as a saviour, and eagerly sent him tribute. Probably Adad-nirari advanced south into Palestine, for he records that not only Bit-Khumri ("The House of 'Omri" or Israel), but also Edom and Palestine (Philistia), "as far as the great sea of the setting sun," submitted and paid tribute. Judah is not mentioned, and was probably regarded as a mere vassal of Israel, Edom had preserved her independence after the defeat of Amaziah, and so her submission is recorded separately.

In practice this submission meant a restoration of independence to the Palestinian kingdoms, or rather to Israel, which always treated Judah as a subject-ally. Joash of Judah, who alone survived the massacre of the House of David by Athaliah, and had been made king by the High-priest Jehoiada, had to submit to Hazael with his suzerain Jehu: an actual Syrian occupation of Jerusalem had only been avoided by heavy bribes. Amaziah, son of Joash, who succeeded after his father's murder, gained a success against Edom, and was so puffed up thereby that he challenged Jehoash of Israel, the son and successor of Jehoahaz, to combat. The contemptuous reply of Jehoash to this challenge, recorded in the Book of Kings, was justified in the result of the struggle. Amaziah was completely defeated, Jerusalem was taken, its walls broken down, and the golden vessels of the Temple carried off to Samaria (circa 793).

Flushed with this success, Jehoash turned his arms against Syria, and in three campaigns; against Benhadad III, son of Hazael, regained the whole of the original territory of Israel east of the Jordan. His son Jeroboam II (782-743) pursued the war with such vigour that he finally succeeded in taking Damascus and even Hamath. It is not improbable that these successes were gained by him in alliance with the Assyrian kings Shalmaneser III (782-773) and Ashur-dan III (773-764), who warred against Damascus, Arvad, and the Syrian principality of Hatarika or Hadrach, which now appears as a new centre of opposition to Assyria.

Although the resistance of Damascus, exhausted by war, was at last broken, Syria was only held by constantly repeated punitive expeditions. The Assyrians never attempted to organize their conquests in a homogeneous empire as the Egyptians always tried to do. They only raided for tribute, and kept the peace so that the commerce of Babylonia should not suffer so long as Babylonia remained submissive to them,

4. Assyria and Urartu (Van)

The task of controlling Syria was rendered the more difficult by the steady growth of a new power in the rear of Assyria, which compelled the kings to keep near home armies which might have been employed in the west. This new power was the Kingdom of Urartu or Ararat, so called by the Assyrians after the central district of the kingdom, in which stood the great mountain which still bears the name of Ararat. The people of Urartu called their kingdom Khaldia, after their chief god Khaldis. They seem to have been a warlike tribe which advanced either westward from the Hellespont, or southward from the Caucasus and by the shores of the Euxine into Armenia, taking the lands of other tribes or absorbing them, until it came into contact with the outposts of Assyria. The Mesopotamian culture had slowly penetrated up the courses of the two great rivers into the

Armenian uplands, and the Khaldian tribes had so far imbibed Babylonian civilization that their kings used the Assyrian script and language for official inscriptions. Later on the cuneiform script was adapted for writing the language of Urartu itself, Vannic as we call it from the fact that its chief monuments, and those first deciphered, were erected on the shores of Lake Van, where was situated Turushpa, the later capital of the kingdom. The decipherment of the Vannic inscriptions has revealed to us the whole history of the state of Khaldia.

The original capital of the land was named Arzashkun, and was situated in the valley of the Araxes. The first kings mentioned in the inscriptions are Lutipris and Sarduris I, who was a contemporary of Ashur-nasir-pal. In the accounts of the sweeping operations from end to end of the northern regions which marked the beginning and end of that great warrior's reign, no mention is made of Sarduris, but it is more than probable that he felt the weight of Ashur-nasir-pal's arm. Shalmaneser II is the first Assyrian king who states that he came into actual hostile contact with Urartu, whose king was then Arame. In 860, 857, and 845 Shalmaneser ravaged Arame's country and finally destroyed Arzashkun. Later, when Sarduris II had succeeded Arame, the Assyrian turtan Ashur-dayan attacked (in 833 and 829). Ten years later again the turtan of Shamshi-Adad led an expedition against Ishpuinis, the successor of Sarduris II. These successive attacks seem to have strengthened rather than weakened the hardy mountain-state, while the Assyrians gained no real advantage from them. In alliance, apparently, with Urartu, stood the Mannai, an Iranian folk of Median stock, and the Protomedes, to whom the name Madai properly belonged (it now first appears in history), in the country east of Lake Urmia. Against them, several expeditions were directed by Adad-nirari III, who is supposed to have reached the Caspian in one of them. Meanwhile Menuas, son of Sarduris II, had extended the dominion of Urartu to the western shores of Lake Urmia. Argistis I, his son, conquered the whole of Kurdistan and Armenia, as far west as Milid or Melitene (Malatiya). All the conquests of Ashur-nasir-pal were lost, in spite of the feverish efforts of Shalmaneser III to recover them. The proximity of the territory of Urartu to the centre of the Assyrian power now became directly dangerous to the empire. Soon the actual frontier was the mountain-range now known as the Judi Dagh, less than a hundred miles from Nineveh itself. But the kings of Urartu did not dare to try conclusions with Assyria in the plain of the Tigris. The humiliation of an actual invasion by the despised peoples of Na'iri was spared to the proud Ninevites. Their loss of prestige, however, was enormous, and to this we may ascribe the renewed restlessness of Syria in the reign of Ashur-dan III which the Assyrians, fearful of leaving the mountain-barrier unguarded, were unable to pacify. After the unsuccessful expeditions of 772 and 765 B.C. against Hatarika (Hadrach), the centre of the revolt, Ashur-dan and his successor dared not leave Assyria. The west was practically left to itself, and Jeroboam II of Israel seemed likely to be the heir of Assyria in the Aramaean countries.

5. Assyrian Decline and Revival of Babylonia

The discontent of Ashur-dan's subjects at their loss of territory and prestige was rapidly growing, till in 763, the year of his death, an event took place which brought matters to a head. The total eclipse of the sun in that year was regarded as a portent, a sign of celestial wrath. Assur, the home of Assyria's most ancient traditions, revolted and was joined by other cities. The king was probably murdered. For six years civil war raged, while pestilence devastated the land. But finally Ashur-dan's successor, Adad-nirari IV, to whom the army continued faithful, prevailed, and in 758 the revolt was quelled by the capture of the city of Gozan.

The civil war had resulted, however, in a further serious loss. During the struggle in Assyria, Babylonia revolted, and re-established its independence under a king named Nabu-shum-ishkun II, After the suppression of the Assyrian revolt Adad-nirari IV made no attempt to regain the authority of Assyria in Babylonia, which had been undisputed almost since the time of the battle of Dur-Papsukal fifty years before. Adad-nirari III had completed the work of Shamshi-Adad by a final expedition, which resulted in the deposition of Bau-akh-iddina, the last Babylonian king of his dynasty, who was carried off to Nineveh with the treasures of his palace. He had no successor, and for nearly fifty years Babylon was without a king, being treated as an integral part of Assyria. This interregnum is marked by the conclusion of the "Synchronous History" of Assyria and Babylon, a chronicle, composed in Assyria probably by order of the third Adad-nirari, of the relations of the two kingdoms down to what no doubt seemed to be the final extinction of Babylonian independence. This event was probably regarded with equanimity by the pro-Assyrian party of the merchants. But the sign in the heavens, the eclipse of 763, and the revolt of Assur, stirred the people to revolt, and Nabu-shum-ishkun restored the ancient kingdom. The

Assyrians accepted the accomplished fact, and when Nabu-shum-ishkun died (747), his son Nabunasir (Nabonassar) ascended the throne of an independent kingdom which had before it prospects of regaining the position it had held in the days of Nebuchadrezzar.

For the state of Assyria seemed to be fast going from bad to worse. After the death of Adad-nirari IV in 755, Ashur-nirari III made one fierce attempt to restore the authority of Assyria in the west, and then sank into apathy. For years he did nothing, till at last, in the year following the accession of Nabunasir in Babylonia, the army, which had hitherto remained faithful, was no longer able to brook the degeneracy of the descendants of Ashur-nasir-pal. The significant revolt of Calah, the imperial military centre, took place in 746, and in the next year the general Pulu ascended the throne, the way to which had probably been cleared by the assassination of Ashur-nirari.

6. Tiglath-pileser IV and the Revival of Assyria

The first act of the new king was significant. He named himself Tiglath-pileser, taking the name of Assyria's greatest warrior-king, who had extended the power of Nineveh to regions where it had never been felt before or since, and in whose days Assyria had for a short time attained a greatness which the empire of Ashur-nasir-pal and Shalmaneser II had never reached. The name of Tiglath-Pileser IV was an earnest to the Assyrians of renewed youth, renewed glory, and renewed empire; a promise of a speedy return to the brave days of old.

Nor was this implied promise belied. With the new blood royal the whole empire seemed suddenly rejuvenated, her military spirit revived as if by magic; while the kings of Urartu checked their advance, the Syrian revolters were cowed, Israel resumed her accustomed position as a suppliant, and the rising hopes of the separatist party in Babylonia were dashed to the ground.

The first concern of the new king was to bring the Babylonians to a sense of their dependence on Assyria. He did not attempt to dethrone Nabunasir or to bring him into subjection, but merely carried out a military promenade into the northern part of the revolted kingdom, at the same time chastising the predatory Aramaean tribes who had occupied the middle course of the Euphrates and were no doubt interfering with the course of commercial traffic. He thus at the same time impressed the Babylonians with a sense of his military power and of the commercial advantages which they would gain by friendship with him.

His first real task lay in the West, in the resuscitation of the Syrian empire of Ashur-nasir-pal. But first a sudden attack delivered across the Judi Dagh drove back the tribes who had approached too near the centre of the kingdom from the north-east. All danger of attack in his rear, either from Babylonia or from the direction of Media, being thus removed, in 743 Tiglath-pileser advanced to the Euphrates with the intention of invading Syria, The Syrian chiefs, alarmed at his advance, combined under the headship of Mati'ilu the chief of Arpad, a city north of Aleppo, to resist him, and at the same time summoned to their aid the King of Urartu, Sarduris III, successor of Argistis I, whose dominions included Kummukh (Commagene), and therefore reached the confines of Syria. Sarduris, equally alarmed, determined to strike quickly, and unexpectedly marched down the Euphrates gorges to attack the Assyrian advance in flank. Tiglath-pileser wheeled to meet the danger, and completely defeated Sarduris. Syria was now exposed to the Assyrian attack; about 741 Arpad was taken, and the whole west submitted.

A general alarm now filled all the lands of Syria and Palestine. The independence of the various states was at stake. Jeroboam II of Israel was lately dead (743), and his death was the signal for anarchy in the northern kingdom. His son Zachariah was murdered by Shall um, who was in his turn murdered by Menahem. This anarchy seems to have given an opportunity to the aged Azariah of Judah to create for a moment a Judaean hegemony over the northern state and its northern dependencies, Damascus and Hamath. For some unknown reason we hear little in the Book of Kings of Azariah (Uzziah) except that he finally became a leper. But in Chronicles we find legends of his activity as a warrior against the Philistines and the Arabs, and in this case the usually less trustworthy narrative of the Chronicler is borne out by the Assyrian evidence. For a dispassionate examination of this evidence shows us that it is hardly likely that the "Azriyau of Ya'udi," who now appears as the fomenter of resistance to Assyria in Southern Syria, is any other than the king of Judah. We have no warrant for supposing the existence of a Syrian state named "Judah," of which we have no other knowledge whatever, and when the king of this state bears the same name as that of a king of the historical Judah who actually reigned at this time, we have no option but to conclude that he is this king, and that "Azriyau of Ya'udi" is Azariah of Judah.

Azariah, as the overlord of the Israelitish dependencies conquered by Jeroboam II, would then naturally be regarded by the Assyrians as the instigator of the resistance which they now encountered in southern Syria. In 739 Tiglath-pileser was recalled from a campaign in the Armenian mountains by the threatening aspect of Azariah and his vassals or confederates, of whom Panammu of Samal was the most conspicuous. The Syrian campaigns of 739 and 738 were sufficient to overthrow the confederacy, and with it the dream of a resuscitation of the Solomonic empire. Kullani (Calno) fell, Hamath followed, Samal became directly subject to Assyria, and not only Rezin of Damascus, but also Hiram of Tyre and Menahem of Israel, paid tribute to the invader. Azariah now died, and was succeeded by Jotham (739).

No mention is made of tribute from Judah, probably because Tiglath-pileser was satisfied with the destruction of the confederacy, and was now anxious to return to Assyria to complete the final settlement with Urartu which had been begun in the previous year, but had had to be suspended in order to effect the chastisement of Azariah and his confederates.

Three campaigns carried the Assyrian arms through Media, to the foot of Demavend, and through Urartu to Lake Van, where, on the shore of the lake, lay Turushpa, the capital of Sarduris. Tiglath-pileser was unable to take the city, of which the citadel was an inexpugnable rock (the modern castle of Van), but he broke the power of Urartu for many a year.

During his absence the Palestinian princes raised their heads. They were not yet resigned, as Northern Syria was, to the futility of resistance. Pekahiah, the son of Menahem, had been murdered by Pekah, the son of Remaliah, who now joined with Rezin of Damascus, the Philistine chiefs, and the princes of Edom, to attack Jotham of Judah, the successor of Azariah. The motive of the attack was clearly the desire of revenge for the ephemeral supremacy of Azariah, which all the allies had resented bitterly. It was against the proper order of things that the little kingdom of Judah should control them. as owing to a peculiar combination of circumstances, she had been able for a moment to do. In the midst of the confusion Jotham died, and was succeeded by Ahaz, who sought his only means of immediate salvation in an appeal to Assyria, despite the opposition of the prophet Isaiah, who saw that the result would be the vassalage of Judah, This vassalage, however, Ahaz was ready to accept as the price of safety.

Tiglath-pileser at once answered the appeal, and in 734 he appeared in Syria, immediately after the destruction of Urartu. He did not, however,

336

attack the confederates in the rear. In order, probably, to make the Palestinians feel that distance afforded no safety from his arm, he marched down the sea-coast to the hitherto unvisited and unconquered land of Philistia, which had even in Solomon's days preserved its independence of Israel, and during the two centuries that had elapsed since, had never acknowledged the suzerainty either of Israel in the warlike days of 'Omri, or of Judah in those of the recently deceased Azariah. So far had the foreign blood of the Cretan immigrants infused a feeling of independence and military capacity into the Canaanites of the coast.

Hanun of Gaza, the paramount chief, was the object of the Assyrian march in 734. Resistance to Assyria was vain; he fled to Egypt. The statue of Tiglath-pileser was set up in his palace, and sacrifice was offered to Ashur in the temples of his gods, who, with the royal treasure, were carried off to Assyria, The enslavement of Israel was postponed for the moment by the murder of Pekah by Hoshea, who immediately made his submission to Tiglath-pileser, and was allowed to remain king with the loss of half his territory: all the land east of the Jordan, Galilee and Naphtali, with the towns of Hazor, Kadesh, Ijon, Yenuam, and others were directly annexed to Assyria, and the tribes of Reuben and Gad and the half-tribe of Manasseh carried away captive.

The turn of Rezin followed. Damascus was taken, its king killed, its territory annexed, and its people carried captive "to Kir" (732).

The Philistines could not reconcile themselves immediately to slavery. Mitinti, king of Ashkelon, tried to revolt when the Assyrians were besieging Damascus, and when the fall of that city, which, apparently, he had not expected, was announced he went mad with fear of the consequences of his rebellion, and his successor Rukipti hastened to make his submission to the conqueror. Metenna, the king of Tyre, followed suit directly after the death of Rezin, and was mulcted in an enormous tribute, proportionate, no doubt, to the wealth of his city. The neighbouring lands, Ammon, Moab, and Edom, now sent tribute to the all-powerful Assyrian, and even an Arabian queen Shamshi "of Aribi," was forcibly brought under the yoke. At the courts of the subject princes officials called kipi or "residents" were appointed, and the desert frontier of Egypt was placed under the surveillance of a certain Idibi'ilu, apparently a Beduin chief, who was called the "Kipii of Musri" (Egypt). Over the districts actually annexed to Assyria, which included Philistia and the whole of Palestine and Syria north of Galilee and east of the Jordan, with the exception of

Phoenicia, were appointed governors called skuparshaku, (military commandant) or bel pikhati (district-lord). Nearly half the population in each conquered state was carried into captivity, and their place taken by foreign captives from Armenia and elsewhere, colonists from Babylonia, and others. Thus the native population in each case was weakened beyond recovery, while the introduced foreigners, being hated by the natives as much as were their Assyrian masters, naturally made common cause with the latter and upheld Assyrian rule. Former kings of Assyria had carried away the conquered captive, but Tiglath-pileser was the first to regulate this practice as a reasoned policy.

The western world being now at his feet, Tiglath-pileser returned to Mesopotamia to put the coping-stone on his edifice of renewed empire by the annexation of Babylonia. The opportunity was favourable. Nabunasir had died in 734, and his son Nabunadinziri had been deposed by a certain Nabushumukin, who in his turn had been swept aside by a Chaldaean chief named Ukinzir, who invaded Babylonia and subjected it to him. We can imagine how the merchant-princes of Babylon cried out to Assyria for deliverance from this disturber of peace and commerce. In 731 the unwearied Tiglath-pileser entered Babylonia and drove Ukinzir back into his own country on the southern shore of the Persian Gulf. In 729 the war ended, and the Chaldaeans of Bit-Amukkani, Ukinzir's kingdom, and of Bit-Yakin, the Sea-Land, submitted. And now the crown of Tiglath-pileser's work was attained when in 728 he came to Babylon and "took the hands of Bel" as king of Sumer and Akkad, a title which he had claimed, in the right of his predecessors, on the occasion of his first invasion fifteen years before, but which was only now confirmed by the priests of Bel in Babylon itself. It was fitting that the conqueror should die, as he did, in the course of the next year (727).

7. Shalmaneser IV: Assyria and Egypt

His successor, Shalmaneser IV (727-722), was confronted on his accession by a new situation in Palestine. The advance of Tiglath-pileser to the frontier of Egypt had caused a great stirring of dry bones in the decaying realm of the pharaohs.

The Bubastite dynasty came to an inglorious end about 740 B.C., and the kingdom at once fell apart again into the two distinct regions of North and South, which the first Bubastite, Shishak, had been at such pains to reunite. The South, true to the cult of the Theban Amen, transferred its allegiance by a natural transition to the descendants of the Priest-Kings of the XXIst Dynasty, who now held sway at Napata in Nubia. Thither, to the southern sanctuary of Amen, established probably under Amenhetep III, the chief priestly families had retired on the accession of Shishak and the deposition of the last high-priest of the line of Herihor in favour of the Bubastite prince Auput. There, in far Nubia, the high-priests of Amen of the old line had continued to reign as kings independent of Egypt, and now the Napatan monarch Piankhi, son of Kashta, naturally resumed sway in the name of Amen over Thebes and Southern Egypt. He claimed, indeed, the sovereignty of the whole land by right of descent, not only distantly, through the blood of the Ramessides which had mingled with that of the high-priests, but also immediately, in right of his mother the Egyptian princess Shepenapet, daughter of Osorkon III, the last Bubastite king whose rule was acknowledged at Thebes. Sheshenk IV (c. 777-740 B.C.), the last king of the XXIInd Dynasty, was succeeded by a certain Petubaste, who is recorded by Manetho as the founder of the XXIIIrd Dynasty. In all probability he had been associated with Sheshenk IV for many years before the death of the latter long-lived king, and in his fifteenth year (c. 740 B.C.) he associated with himself a prince Auput. He was, however, actually succeeded (c. 735 B.C.), after a reign of twenty-four years, by Osorkon III, whom we cannot suppose to have been associated with him, unless, as is not impossible, he is identical with the prince called Auput in Petubaste's inscription, and changed his name on his accession. Osorkon III certainly reigned some twenty years, if not more. With him was associated for a short time a third Takeloti, who probably died before him. He submitted to Piankhi in 728, and probably went on reigning as sub-king. We do not know whether Kashta, his Ethiopian son-in-law, actually reigned contemporaneously with him for a short space. It is most probable that he had died about 730 B.C., and that Piankhi and Amenirtis his sister-wife, the children of Kashta and Shepenapet, were, as Amen-worshippers and Thebans in origin, welcomed by Thebes as her rightful monarch in despite of their grandfather at Bubastis.

The princes, priests, and people of the North were by no means ready to acknowledge the primacy of Thebes and the supremacy of Amen. The priests of Hershef of Herakleopolis, birthplace of the XXIInd Dynasty, of Bast of Bubastis, and of Ptah of Memphis, would especially be moved by jealousy of Amon to resist the kingship of his worshipper. So the whole of the kingdom north of Sitit split up into a dozen or sixteen small principalities, and the rulers of the more important of them who could lay claim to near connexion with royalty assumed the uraeus-diadem as kings, just as their forerunners of a thousand years before had done. These kings were Namilt (Nemart) of Ekhmunu (Hermopolis; Eshmunen), Pefnef-didi-Bast (or Pefza-didi-Bast, "Bast-giveth-his-breath") of Henensu or Hnes (Herakleopolis; Ahnasiya), Auput of Tent-remu, who ruled the Wadi Tumilat from the neighbourhood of Bubastis to the desert and the Red Sea, and Osorkon III, who maintained a circumscribed state in Bubastis itself It is evident, from the names they bear or from the cities they ruled, that these princes were all directly connected with the Bubastite family. Of the princes of less royal blood, who did not immediately assume the urreus, the most important were Pabasa of Khriaha (the Egyptian Babylon), Petisi of Athribis, Pimai of Busiris, Pathenef of Pasopdu, Tjedamenefankh of Mendes, and Akanesha of Sebennytos. Of these the last four were of Libyan descent, and the last of all bears a Libyan name. Eight other less important independent barons are mentioned at the time, of whom one, Tefnakht, chief of a small district on the western border of the desert, near Sais, soon made himself the most important of all. The undisputed rule of Piankhi (established about 730?) only extended as far north as Siut: north of that place Nemart or Namilt of Herakleopolis merely acknowledged Piankhi's overlordship, retaining his royal position and title. The chiefs farther north owed no allegiance to any suzerain till they were all compelled to submit to Tefnakht, who suddenly came forward as a claimant to general dominion. In a short time he conquered the whole Delta, and established himself at Memphis, where he prepared to invade the Upper Country and extend his authority if possible over the whole land. Namilt, alarmed by his energy, transferred his allegiance from Piankhi to the new power, Purema and Lamersekni, the Ethiopian commanders in Upper Egypt, anticipating an immediate attack, sent an urgent appeal to Piankhi at Napata for aid. An army was despatched, which, after great religious ceremonies at Thebes, advanced north, and defeated the confederates of Tefnakht (who does not seem to have been present himself) in a great battle at Per-pega, near Herakleopolis. The defeated chiefs dispersed, each to his own city, and even Namilt managed to double back southwards to Hermopolis, where he was at once besieged, while the towns of Pemje (Oxyrrhynchus), Tetehne (Tehnah), and Hetbennu were taken by storm. The escape of the chiefs and the prolonged resistance of Hermopolis did not please King Piankhi, who now repaired to the seat of war to take command in person. The record of his campaign is preserved on a great stela found at Jebel Barkal in 1862, and now in the Cairo Museum, which he dedicated on his victorious return to Napata.

The capture of Hermopolis was delayed by the politic generals, probably in collusion with the defenders, till the royal arrival, three days after which Namilt's queen appeared to plead with Piankhi for the safety of her lord and his city, which was granted her. Piankhi received Namilt's submission, and entered the town in state to make offering to the gods. There he found that Namilt's horses were starving, and this seems to have led to an explosion of the royal anger against the unlucky besieged, who was vehemently reproached for treating his horses so. The whole is naively chronicled in the inscription, no doubt by express command. Namilt suffered nothing more than the loss of his portable wealth, and retained his royal dignity still.

The fall of Hermopolis determined Pefnefdidibast of Herakleopolis to surrender at once, and Medum, Ithttaui, and the other towns south of Memphis followed the example of Herakleopolis. Memphis, however, resisted.

Apparently the priests of Ptah were devoted to Tefnakht, who was one of their number. To a summons to surrender and promise of lenient treatment from Piankhi defiance was returned. Tefnakht, however, thought it well to abandon the city himself, and rode northwards secretly under the pretext of raising the Delta nomes. Piankhi then attacked, and by a stratagem succeeded in taking the city. The river was high, and the shipping of the town lay high alongside the river-wall. Piankhi embarked his army on his own ships, moored them alongside those of the enemy, boarded them and passed over them on to the wall. "So Memphis was taken as by a flood of water; a multitude of people were slain therein, and brought as living captives to the place where His Majesty was. And afterwards, at dawn of the next day, His Majesty sent men into it, to protect the temples of the god." The king then entered, and was received humbly by the priests. Heliopolis was then visited with great religious ceremony. The submission of all the Delta kings followed, and was solemnly received at a great durbar held at Athribis. Tefnakht, closely pursued into the marshes of the West, finally sent in his submission, and was pardoned after taking an oath of allegiance before the gods in the presence of the chief priest Pediamennesettaui and the general Purema, Of all the Northern chiefs, only King Namilt was allowed to enter the royal chamber, because he was pure and ate no fish, as the Delta kings did. To the priestly Nubians fish, especially sea-fish, was an abomination.

The whole story is told with a curious naivete and obvious truth which differentiates it very much from other official inscriptions. The Nubian king is much more human than any of his predecessors since Thothmes III. His piety and at the same time his humanity, to beasts as well as men, were evidently characteristic of the man, and throughout there is evident a keen joy in fighting which had been unknown to Egypt for centuries.

His work done, Piankhi returned to Napata, leaving, in all probability, his son Shabaka as his regent and commander-in-chief in the North. The great expedition had taken place, probably, in the year 728 or 727 B.C. In the next year Shabaka came into hostile relations with the Assyrians. The energetic young Nubian regent, ignorant of Assyrian power and ferocity, no doubt thought himself and his black soldiers fully a match for all the legions of king or turtan, and was anxious to bid defiance to the new Hyksos. The accession of a new king in Assyria seemed to afford a possibility of successful action. In 726 Hoshea of Israel and the king of Tyre, relying, as we read in the Book of Kings, on the promised help of "Seve (So), king of Egypt," refused his yearly tribute. Now that the theory of the existence of a hitherto unknown land, bearing the same name as Egypt (Musri), in North Arabia, to whom this Seve, the Shabi or Sibi of the Assyrians, and the "Pir'u of Musri" also mentioned in the Assyrian inscriptions, were assigned, is generally discredited, we have returned to the original and perfectly natural identifications of Seve or Sibi with Shabaka (the Sebichos of the Greeks) and of "Pir'u of Musri" with Pharaoh of Egypt. Unless, therefore, the Biblical mention of Seve in connexion with Hoshea in 725 is not a misplacement from the year of Sargon's victory at Raphia in 720, when "Sibi, the commander-in-chief (turtan) of Pir'u king of Musri," is mentioned as defeated by the Assyrians (he is not mentioned in 725), we must suppose that Shabaka, who is certainly Sibi the turtan of 720, was already turtan five years earlier, when Seve, inaccurately described as king, is recorded in the Book of Kings as the fomenter of Hoshea's revolt. He would naturally be left in command in Lower Egypt by his father Piankhi after his return to Napata.

Shalmaneser IV struck quickly at the rebels. Tyre submitted almost immediately, but with Hoshea the duel was to the death. For over two years, from 724 to 722, Samaria was blockaded and finally closely besieged. The whole land was laid waste. No help came from Egypt. The murder of Shalmaneser and accession of Sargon in 722 happened shortly before the fall of the city. When the end came, Hoshea was blinded and his whole land and people annexed. The actual captivity of Israel, however, probably did not take place till two years later.

8. The Reign of Sargon (722-705)

Sargon, the new Assyrian king, was apparently not present at the fall of Samaria, and threatening events near home prevented him from taking immediate advantage of the great blow which his generals had struck at the rebellious Westerners. The preoccupation of Shalmaneser IV in the West had given an opportunity to the Aramaean and Chaldaean tribes, who were always persistently pressing into Mesopotamia, to make another bid for the control of the Southern kingdom. The nomad Aramaeans again blocked the Euphratean commercial highway, and Marduk-pal-iddina (Merodach-baladan) of Bit-Yakin, the Chaldaean chief who had escaped when Ukinzir and his city had been destroyed by Tiglath-pileser IV, again appeared on the scene, this time as a claimant to the kingship of Babylon, presumably in succession to Ukinzir. By himself, Marduk-pal-iddina would not have been more formidable to Assyria than Ukinzir had been, but he was backed by an unexpected and sinister ally. The kingdom of Elam, which had not meddled with Mesopotamian affairs for centuries, had gradually become alarmed by the growth of the Assyrian power, not only in Babylonia but also in Media, which lay across the Zagros and therefore in rear of Elam. So Khumbanigash, the Elamite king, determined to resist further Assyrian encroachment, in alliance with Marduk-pal-iddina. In 721 he entered Mesopotamia and laid siege to the fortress of Dur-ilu, on the Lower Tigris. Sargon advanced to its relief, but was defeated by the Elamites before its walls, and compelled to return to Assyria, contenting himself with harrying the Aramaean tribes. Marduk-pal-iddina was acknowledged by the Babylonians as their king.

This defeat had immediate results in the West. The Egyptian intrigues bore fruit in the revolt of Hamath and Damascus under a certain Ya'ubidi, who was joined by the kingless remnant of Israel at Samaria, and by Hanun of Gaza and the Philistines, with Shabaka in Egypt at their back. Sargon, abandoning all plans of recovering Babylonia, marched west in 720, defeated Ya'ubidi at Karkar, and finally met the Philistines and Egyptians, under the leadership of Hanun and Shabaka, at Raphia, on the Egyptian border. It was the first time that the Egyptians had come into hostile contact with the new Assyria, and the result was their complete defeat. The Ethiopians were unable to effect anything against the trained legions of Sargon, and Shabaka fled "like a shepherd whose sheep have been taken," while Hanun was captured. An actual invasion of Egypt was only staved off by the offering of gifts, which the Assyrian king chose to regard as the "tribute" of "Pir'u king of Musri," and rather insolently chronicled in the same category with the tribute of the Beduin queen Samsi and the gifts of the far away Ithamar, king of Saba, in Southern Arabia, which were brought to him while in Philistia. He then returned to Assyria, completing the punishment of Israel by carrying into captivity twenty-seven thousand two hundred and ninety of the flower of the nation, who, so we are told by the chronicler of the Book of Kings, were settled in the Assyrian territory of Gozan and in distant Media, while their place at Samaria was taken by "men from Babylon, and from Cuthah, and from Ava, and from Hamath, and from Sepharvaim," a mixed horde of Syrian and Babylonian prisoners, from whom, by admixture with the remnant of Israel, the later nation of the Samaritans was formed.

The crushing defeat of Egypt at Raphia and the final destruction of Israel left Sargon free to turn his attention away from the West, not, however, to Babylon but to the wild tribes on the always threatened and disturbed Northern frontier. He had no desire to renew the contest with Khumbanigash, and Marduk-pal-iddina continued to reign in Babylon under the aegis of the redoubtable Elamite. Campaigns in the Northern mountains promised Sargon cheaper and more certain laurels. An action in that direction was now necessary, since Urartu was once more raising its head, and its king, Rusas I, successor of Sarduris III, was preparing war and trouble for Assyria in alliance with a new power, "Mita king of Mushki" (Anatolia), whose name certainly represents that of the famous Midas-kings of Phrygia.

9. Mita of Mushki: the Midas-kings of Phrygia

We have heard nothing of Anatolia since the days of the Cappadocian campaign of Tiglath-pileser I and the final break-up of the Hittite power. In these dark centuries must be placed the irruption from Europe of the Indo-European tribes of the Eryges or Phrygians, who were of the same stock as the Thracians, and closely related in race and language to the Hellenic Greeks. These tribes seem to have overrun the peninsula in the tenth and ninth centuries (possibly penetrating as far east as Armenia, where they may have given a European language to the native people whom they ruled),and everywhere overlying and mingling with the old native(Hittite)population (except in Lycia and Caria, perhaps in Southern Cappadocia, and certainly in Cilicia). We find a trace of their presence on the historic hill of Troy, in the shape of a post-Mycenaean settlement with bucchero pottery of a barbaric type, and further excavation of the ancient sites of Asia Minor would doubtless reveal many traces of their first semi-barbarous culture overlying the older strata of the Hittite civilization. The black pottery of the seventh settlement at Hissarlik which is ascribed to them certainly gives the impression of a culture and art semi-barbarous, as was the contemporary culture of the first iron-using inhabitants of Greece, in comparison with that of the Greek islanders of the preceding age. But the description of the armour, chariots, and horses of Rhesos the Thracian in the Iliad shew that the Aegean culture had reached Thrace by the ninth or eighth century, and that the people from whom the Phrygians sprang were by no means barbarians. Of their later culture and art there remain monuments in the shape of the sculptured facades of tombs in the district of Kiutahia, which though much affected by Hellenic influence, yet retained certain national characteristics, especially in their geometrical ornamentation, an old inheritance from their forefathers; the same ornament which the Aryan Greeks brought with them from the North into Greece. The heraldically opposed figures of lions which appear upon them, and remind us so much of the famous gate at Mycenae, were presumably derived from Minoan art.

The old Anatolian culture must soon have affected that of the invaders, and we see that the Anatolian influence was especially prominent in religion. In Phrygian religion, as we know it later, we can see the two strands of religious ideas side by side, the Indo-European gods with their drunken wine-feasts that came from Thrace, and the adopted deities of the soil with their strange priesthoods and their un-Aryan rites. By the side of their own gods, such as Bagaios (the Persian bhaga, Slav, bogu) or Papas ("Father") or Osogo ("Thunderer"), who is the same as Greek Zeus, as Men the Moon-god (who keeps his true Aryan sex, while in Greece Selene is feminine from pre-Aryan (?) tradition), and as a young male deity named Sabazios or Atys (who is the Thracian Dionysos), we find the Anatolian Great Mother called by the Phrygian names Ma or Kybele, and her son-husband who was identified with and called by the name of Atys. The ancient worship of the Mother at Pessinos, with its great priesthood, remained, and secured the veneration of the new-comers.

We may conceive of the Phrygians as a people composed of an Aryan aristocracy ruling over and gradually mixing with the Anatolian peasants, whose language was supplanted by that of their rulers, just as the old idioms of Greece were supplanted by Aryan Greek, and in Ireland Irish was supplanted by English. The Phrygians always appear as a people of peasants, primarily devoted to agriculture, much resembling the modern Anatolian fellahin. The fostering of agriculture was the main duty of the kings and nobles, and in the mythology of Phrygia the heroes of the tilled field take rank above those of the field of war, and the bucolic pipe of Lityerses is of more account than the trumpet of Ares. For the Phrygian the ark of the covenant was an ancient wain, preserved at Ancyra, in which, it was said, Gordios, the first Phrygian king, had used to bring home his sheaves.

But as the wealth of the state increased, so the kings increased their pride, and finally a Midas (the kings were alternately named Gordios and Midas) went forth to conquer, and established an empire which reached the Halys and beyond, while the state of Lydia was tributary to it. So the poets tell us, and the Assyrian record of Mita of Mushki lends considerable probability to their tale. It may be that he was the wealthy conqueror himself, that very Midas at whose touch all things turned to gold. It may be that the poet's Midas is a compound of several of the kings of the eighth century; but it is more than probable that the historical "Mita of Mushki" is one of those who bore the name of Midas. He, or one of his predecessors, seems certainly to have pushed his dominion as far as the Taurus, where he came into communication with the kingdom of Urartu, and in alliance with it into conflict with Sargon of Assyria about the year 720.

For ten years Sargon was engaged in the task of combating the ceaseless revolts and attacks of the Northern tribes, urged on by Rusas and Midas in the background. Tiglath-pileser IV had sought to establish in the heart of the borderland between Armenia and Media a dependent state, largely composed of conquered and deported tribes from other parts of Western Asia, which was known by the name of the Mannai, the Median tribe to which, probably, the land really belonged. This tribe perhaps gave its princes to the new state (though imported Semites sometimes appear, as Ashur-li' and Itti, whose principalities were carved out of Median territory). Iranzu, the prince of Mannai, was loyal to Sargon, and so bore the brunt of the attack organized by Rusas. Year after year the war went on; Ullusunu, the grandson of Iranzu, went over to the enemy, and so did Ashur-li' and Itti. They were conquered, and the two rebellious Semites were deported to Syria. Ullusunu's submission was the signal for war between him and Rusas, who deposed him, and set up as king of Mannai the Median prince Daiukku, who was known to history long before the decipherment of the cuneiform inscriptions, for he is the "Deiokes" who is stated by Herodotus to have been the founder of the Median monarchy. There is little doubt that Herodotus' information was correct, but it was not till later that Deiokes established his power, for his first appearance as a ruler was unfortunate: he was deposed by Sargon and deported to Hamath (715). In the next year Sargon was able to crush Rusas himself; the important town of Musasir was destroyed; and Rusas in despair killed himself.

Meanwhile, farther west the intrigues of Midas had resulted in a general unrest among the Hittite princes of Melitene and Kommagene, and even Carchemish, undefended though it was by the huge mountains which were the protection of the more northern tribes, was foolish enough to revolt. Pisiris, the last king of Carchemish, paid for his temerity by the loss of his kingdom (717). After the destruction of Rusas, Sargon turned to deal with the mountain Hittites. Tarkhunazi of Milid and Mutallu of Gurgum, who had deposed and murdered his own father Tarkhulara, a faithful vassal of Assyria, were both subdued in succession (712-711). Midas himself was too wary to advance into actual contact with Sargon, and was too far off to be attacked by him. He contented himself with carrying on a frontier war in the passes of the Taurus with the Assyrian governor of Kue (Cilicia), who in 715 reported successes against him. No attempt was, however, made by Sargon to emulate the victories of Tiglath-pileser I, and invade Cappadocia. Babylon and Egypt both lay in his rear, always ready to cause trouble, and a disaster in the unknown land west of the Taurus would have been the signal for immediate revolt in Palestine and direct attack by Marduk-pal-iddina and his Elamite ally.

In 711 a revolt actually did break out in Palestine, which was directly attributable to Egyptian incitement. The disaster at Raphia in 720 had temporarily ruined the power of Shabaka and the prestige of the Ethiopians in Lower Egypt. Shabaka must have abandoned the Delta altogether, and retired to the South for several years, since in 711 we again find him in Lower Egypt, now no longer as turtati but as king; and in the intervening period of nine years between his defeat at Raphia and his appearance in 711 we must place the independent reigns of Tefnakht and his son Boknrenef, the Tnephachthos and Bocchoris of the Greeks (XXI Vth Dynasty). It is evident that after Raphia Shabaka had fled to Upper Egypt, and that Tefnakht immediately seized the opportunity to revive his old pretensions to the pharaonic dignity. It is improbable that his reign lasted more than two years, for about 718 he must have been succeeded by Boknrenef, who took the throne-name of Uahkara, which was pronounced by the Greeks as "Bokkhoris." This king, who reigned peacefully in Lower Egypt for about six years, was magnified considerably in the stories of Egypt which the Milesian traders who were now beginning to frequent the Nile-mouths brought back with them to Greece. He was reputed to be a prince of very great wisdom, and his father had been a great warrior. Certainly he shewed his wisdom when in 715 he pacified any suspicion of his intentions in the mind of Sargon by sending him presents, which were regarded as tribute, and again classed in the same category with the gifts of Samsi and Ithamar.

Some three years later his reign was brought to an end by a second Ethiopian invasion. Shabaka, who had now succeeded Piankhi as king (about 715?), in 712 overwhelmed the Lower Country, and, according to the Greek tradition, which may be perfectly correct, captured Bocchoris and burnt him alive. This imitation of the customs of the contemporary Assyrian conquerors is significant: the lenity of Piankhi had already begun to go out of fashion, and the iron was soon to bite into the souls of the Egyptians.

Shabaka's renewed rule, now as king, was marked by a renewal of the intrigues of ten years before against the Assyrians in Palestine. He was too energetic to remain passive like Bocchoris, too apprehensive (and probably too insecure in Lower Egypt) to invade Palestine. So, like Rusas and Midas, he sowed revolt. In 715 Ashdod revolted, under the leadership of a Greek adventurer, a "Yavani," from Cyprus or Ionia, but with little success. The Yavani escaped towards Egypt, but was captured by a Sinaitic chief, and sent in chains to Assyria. Judah seems to have taken part in the rebellion, Hezekiah the king, son of Ahaz, must have submitted promptly, and Sargon called himself "subjugator of the land of Judah, whose situation is far away."

Sargon did not attempt to attack Egypt: he was as unwilling to penetrate into the foreign and unknown Nile-land as into the equally foreign and unknown Asia Minor. And he now intended to subjugate Babylonia finally. Shutruk-nakhunte, the king of Elam, who had succeeded Khumbanigash in 717, made no move to support Marduk-pal-iddina, who was driven into Chaldaea, while Sargon, welcomed as a deliverer from Chaldaean oppression, "took the hands of Bel" as king in Babylon in 709 B.C. The complete defeat of the Chaldaeans in their own country followed, and Bit-Yakin was annexed and peopled with wretched Hittites from Kommagene, the captured Chaldaeans being probably sent to Samaria or Hamath. And the conqueror celebrated his triumph by a festal reception of gift-bearing ambassadors from Midas, now desirous of peace, and of tribute from seven kings of the island of Cyprus, who had apparently acknowledged Assyrian overlordship in 715 (when Tyre, probably after some unrecorded revolt, had formally submitted). They had set up in their island, probably in the Phoenician city of Kition, a stela with a figure of the Assyrian king as an emblem of their vassalage.

But for two final flares of revolt by Mutallu of Milid (in alliance with Argistis II of Urartu) and by Median tribes in the next year, all was now peace. Only Judah and the Phoenician cities still preserved a semi-independent position within the empire; elsewhere the local rulers had all been removed and their territories had been directly annexed to Assyria and were administered by Assyrian officials. The boundaries of the empire had been rounded off and fixed from Cilicia to the Persian Gulf. This was the work of Sargon, who had thus brilliantly belied the unfavourable augury of the defeat of Dur-ilu at the beginning of his reign.

In the midst of his wars Sargon had found time to be one of the greatest builders of temples and palaces that Assyria had known. He seems to have been of a more religious turn of mind than his immediate predecessors had been, and in his reign the whole pantheon of deities is often mentioned, whereas they seem to have been devoted almost solely to the worship of the soldier's god, Ashur, whose name occurs almost solitary in their inscriptions. Not content with the old royal palace of Calah, and the temples of Nineveh, he erected at a spot a short distance north of Nineveh, now known as Khorsabad, his great royal city of Dur-Sharrdkin ("Sargonsburgh"), which was excavated by Botta, whose many trophies are now in the Louvre at Paris. The palace of Khorsabad, with its endless sculptured corridors wreathed round a central ziggurat-temple, was of enormous extent, and occupied many years in building. In 707, on his return from Babylon, the king formally took possession of his new abode, and the images of the gods were solemnly inducted into their temples.

He lived at Khorsabad only for two years. In 705 he died, probably by the hand of an assassin, and was succeeded by his son Sin-akhi-irba ("Sin [the moon-god]-has-increased-the-brethren"), known to us as Sennacherib, and to the Greeks as Sanacharibos.

10. The Reign of Sennacherib (705-682)

The new king was a man in some ways of lower intellectual calibre than his father, and certainly much less far-seeing and politic. The carefully thought-out schemes by which Sargon had re-established the empire and had sought to organize it in one great whole were unknown to him: he was restless and erratic in his military movements and in his policy. His campaigns were often planned and his victories achieved in defiance of strategical considerations, and in his policy he allowed himself to be carried away by the violence of his character into most impolitic acts. Thus he succeeded in raising for Assyria a furious foe in Elam, and in estranging from the Assyrian connexion the whole population of Babylonia, where priests and merchants now combined with Chaldaeans and Aramaeans against the sacker of Babylon and the desecrator of their holiest shrines. He was a vainer man, too, than his father, and we hear of his deeds not merely as incidents of each year of his reign, but pompously chronicled and arranged in "campaigns," which were inscribed upon clay cylinders, to be kept in the royal library, a custom followed by his successors.

The looseness of the ties that bound the subject-provinces to Assyria, in spite of all that Sargon had achieved, were, as usual, shewn at the beginning of the new reign. The Median conquests of Sargon fell away at once, and no attempt was made to recover them. And in a year's time Marduk-pal-iddina was once more in the field to recover Babylon, this time aided by an Elamite army sent by Ishtar-Khundu, the successor of Shutruk-nakhunte. He was expelled, the Elamites were defeated, and Sennacherib placed a native Babylonian of the old royal house, named Bel-ibni, on the throne of Babylon as a tributary king, thus giving up the claim of Tiglath-pileser IV and Sargon to be kings of Babylon themselves (702). In the next year Sennacherib was called to the West, where a general defiance of Assyrian authority had broken out, no doubt inspired by Egyptian intrigues. Luli (Elulaios) of Sidon seems to have imposed his authority over all Phoenicia and had tried to subdue Cyprus, while

Hezekiah of Judah, with the connivance of Shabaka, had had the temerity to substitute in Philistia his overlordship for that of Sennacherib. In Ashkelon a revolution had deposed Sharruludari, son of Rukipti, and in Ekron the king Padi was similarly deposed and sent to Jerusalem in chains. Sennacherib struck Luli first, drove him across the sea to Cyprus, and put Ethbaal in his place as king of Sidon. Phoenicia submitted, and the kings of Ammon, Moab, and Edom, by no means inclined to view an increase of the power of Jerusalem with pleasure, at once put themselves at the feet of Sennacherib. Mitinti of Ashdod, too, who had reigned there after the expulsion of the "Yavani" in faithful dependence on Assyria, was eager to assert his loyalty. Leaving Hezekiah on one side for the moment, Sennacherib pushed on to Philistia, where he took Ashkelon, and sent the new king, Sidka, prisoner to Assyria. Beth-dagon and Joppa were then taken, and the Assyrians were nearing the border of Egypt. This time Shabaka was moved to give substantial help to the Palestinians. He assembled an army, composed of the ban of the Delta under the local knights (who still ruled there under the Ethiopian hegemony), stiffened by his own Ethiopian troops, "the army of the kings of Musur, and the soldiers, the archers, the chariots, and horsemen of Melukhkha (Nubia)." Shabaka himself does not seem to have been present. At Eltekeh, near Ekron, the battle was joined, and, as at Raphia, ended in the defeat of the Egyptians. "The sons of the kings of Musur" and some Ethiopian generals were captured, and the beaten army made the best of its way back across the desert to Egypt. Ekron then surrendered, and Padi, who seems to have been handed over by Hezekiah, probably in an attempt to conciliate the anger of Sennacherib, was reinstated as king. Lachish was then formally beseiged, and eventually taken. The siege was specially commemorated in reliefs on the walls of Sennacherib's palace at Nineveh, and seems therefore to have been regarded as a great feat of arms. Hezekiah was now shut up in Jerusalem, "like a caged bird," as Sennacherib says in his account of the campaign. The whole territory of Judaea was ravaged. "200,150 people," probably meaning the whole country's population, were "regarded as spoil," though we are not told that they were carried into captivity, as it is sometimes supposed. Jerusalem was then besieged, but Sennacherib, probably disinclined to remain any longer in the West, tied to the siege of an almost impregnable fortress, soon returned to Assyria, leaving the siege to be conducted by the turfan, the rab-saris, and the rab-shakeh. In the Book of Kings we read a vivid description of Hezekiah's attempts at negotiation with these officers, of their insolent taunts to the Jewish deputies who went to interview them, and especially of the famous speech of the rab-shakeh in Hebrew in order that all the besieged might hear, in spite of the frantic prayers of Hezekiah's deputies that he would speak Aramaic, and not "talk in the Jews' language in the ears of the people that are on the wall." "What confidence is this wherein thou trustest?" shouted the Assyrian. "Thou sayest, but they are but vain words, I have counsel and strength for the war! Now on whom dost thou trust, that thou rebellest against me? Now, behold thou trusteth upon this staff of this bruised reed, even upon Egypt, on which if a man lean it will go into his hand and pierce it: so is Pharaoh, king of Egypt, unto all that trust on him! . . . . Hath any of the gods of the nations delivered at all his land out of the hand of the king of Assyria? Where are the gods of Hamath and of Arpad? Where are the gods of Samaria, [Hena, and Ivah]? have they delivered Samaria out of mine hand? Who are they among all the gods of the countries, that have delivered their country out of mine hand, that Yahweh should deliver Jerusalem out of mine hand?" We might be inclined to regard this as a speech of the Thucydidean order and a picturesque concoction of the chronicler, but that it is alive with the spirit of the time, and is exactly what we know the rab-shakeh is likely to have said. Hezekiah's prayer, too, "of a truth, Lord, the kings of Assyria have destroyed the nations and their lands, and have cast their gods into the fire," is no invention of a chronicler living perhaps long after the Assyrian terror had passed away. The whole story of the siege in the Book of Kings is as contemporary with it as is Sennacherib's own account, and we cannot doubt the speech of Rab-shakeh is correctly reported: it must have burnt itself into the brains of all that heard it.

But, cheered by the support of the Prophet Isaiah, Hezekiah held out against capture and storm, until compelled by the defection of the Arab mercenaries who formed part of the defending force, he proffered a modified surrender, which the wearied Assyrians were ready to accept, and sent his tribute back with them to Assyria. The Philistine towns which he had occupied were handed over to Padi of Ekron. Hezekiah, convinced that Yahweh alone had delivered him, signalized the return of peace by an access of monotheistic fervour, and destroyed Nehushtan, the brazen serpent, which, according to legend, Moses had set up in the wilderness, and was, in all probability, actually a very ancient image that had been brought by the ancestors of the Israelites from Egypt. Hezekiah was sincerely religious, but very little of a politician, and almost immediately after the deliverance of Jerusalem he was foolish enough to receive ambassadors from Merodach-baladan (Marduk-pal-iddina) the Chaldean, who was again asserting his claim to the Babylonian throne. For this folly he was deservedly rebuked by Isaiah, who saw clearly that a friendship with Merodach-baladan would simply result in again bringing Sennacherib down on Jerusalem, which this time would certainly share the fate of Samaria.

Marduk-pal-iddina had taken the opportunity of Sennacherib's absence in the West to invade Babylonia; Sennacherib invaded at once in his turn, after he had come back from Jerusalem, and in 700 expelled the troublesome Chaldaean not only from Babylonia, but also from Bit-Yakin: he took ship thence, and escaped into the Elamite territory of Nagitu, the neighbourhood of the modern Bushire. Sennacherib now replaced Bel-ibni, the puppet-king of Babylon, by his own son, Ashur-nadin-shum.

The annals of the following years present a curious example of the royal vanity. In 699 Sennacherib deigned to conduct in person a series of raids on the hill-villages of Mount Nipur (the Judi Dagh), north-east of Nineveh. He was carried in his palanquin most of the way, but occasionally was compelled by the roughness of the hill-paths to dismount and go on foot, sometimes even leading the attack himself on foot. This was magnified by the court historians into a marvellous feat, and the whole razzia dignified as the royal "fifth campaign." But a very serious campaign in Cilicia, which took place in the next year, was not only not recorded as a royal campaign, since the king himself took no part in it, but was actually omitted from the later records of the king's reign. We know of it only from a recently discovered cylinder, which was dedicated in the eponymy of Ilu-ittia, 694 B.C., and buried as a foundation-deposit in the wall of one of the new gates of Nineveh which Sennacherib set up in that year. On this cylinder the records of recent important campaigns are given, although they were not conducted by the king in person: but on later cylinders of the reign such campaigns, however important they might be, were omitted and razzias like that of 699 appear in the official records, while the great Cilician campaign of 698 was forgotten. As it is, we are not told the names of the generals who conducted that campaign. Sennacherib merely says that he "sent his army."

The war of 698 is of special interest on account of the fact that certain traditions respecting it have been handed down from Babylonian sources by Greek historians, and the probability that it marked the first open collision between the Greeks of the new Hellenic world and the great Oriental empires. In 720 a single nameless Greek seems, as we have seen, to have temporarily made himself tyrant of Ashdod till his expulsion by Sargon; and in 709 Cypriote princes, among them no doubt Greeks, had submitted to the same king, who speaks of having drawn the Ionians "like fish from the sea," and given rest to Kue (Cilicia) and Tyre. This evidently refers to a capture of Greek pirates infesting the coast; no land-warfare between Greeks and Assyrians had taken place, so far as we know, till the year 698.

Sennacherib tells us that in that year Kirua, governor of Kue, revolted in alliance with "the people who dwelt in Ingira and Tarsus," and seized the great trade-route through the Cilician Gates from Syria to Anatolia, stopping all traffic. After a severe campaign, too dangerous for the king to accompany it in person, Kirua and his allies were finally defeated by the royal generals. The spoil of Tarsus was carried to Nineveh, and then Sennacherib made a triumphal progress to the scene of the victory and set up a memorial of alabaster to commemorate it in Illubru, the conquered city of Kirua.

Now Berossos described a great campaign of Sennacherib in Cilicia against Greeks, and of his description the two versions of Alexander Polyhistor and Abydenus, preserved by Eusebius, differ, the one in making the battle with the "Greeks" a land-fight, the other in making it a naval combat. Polyhistor says that when Sennacherib had received a report that the Greeks had made a hostile descent on Cilicia, he marched against them and defeated them, suffering himself great loss, however. The text of Eusebius goes on to say that to commemorate the victory, Sennacherib erected a statue or likeness of himself at the place where the battle was fought, and commanded that his victory should be described upon it in Chaldaean characters, to hand it down to posterity. Polyhistor adds that Sennacherib built the city of Tarsus in imitation of Babylon. The account of Abydenus makes Sennacherib defeat a fleet of "Greek ships" in a fight off the Cilician coast; he also says that Sennacherib founded an "Athenian" Temple with columns of bronze, on which he engraved his mighty deeds; and explains Polyhistor's remark about the similarity of Tarsus to Babylon, by saying that Sennacherib made the Cydnus traverse the centre of the city as the Euphrates traverses Babylon.

We only know of one expedition to Cilicia in the reign of Sennacherib, that of 698 against Kirua. Before the new cylinder was known, a single reference to war in Cilicia on another document was confused with the "fifth campaign"; Mount Nipur was supposed to be the Taurus, and the raids of 699, which actually took place in the Judi Dagh, not fifty miles from Nineveh, were transferred to Cilicia. We now see how matters really went, and also that the campaign against Kirua and the people of Ingira and Tarsus who seized the Cicilian caravan-route can be none other than the campaign against the Greeks in Cilicia described by Berossos. We can understand how, in spite of Sargon's reprisals, Ionian sea-rovers and would-be colonists had finally effected a landing on the Cilician coast and had probably mixed easily with the population of Tarsus and the Aleian plain, which according to later tradition was of much older Greek origin, and was descended from those who had followed the hero Mopsos hither after the Trojan war.

When the invaders and the revolted governor had been subdued by his generals, after a hard struggle, the king of Assyria came in state and inaugurated his triumphal stele amid the ruins of Illubru, as both he and Berossos state; and from the Babylonian historian we learn that he re-established the ancient city of Tarsus, after it had been taken from the new-comers, "on the model of Babylon" (Sennacherib would have said Nineveh), and with a temple, probably of Ashur, the columns of which were bronze, like the bronze columns which he was setting up about the same time at Nineveh.

For several years now the king was busy with the building of his walls and palaces at Nineveh, and led no warlike expeditions personally. In 695 his unnamed generals captured Til-garimmu (the Biblical Togarmah), the capital of the State of Tabal (Tubal), whose people were the Tibareni of the Greeks, in the mountains north of the modern Malatiya and Albistan. Tabal had appeared before in the history of the Assyrian empire; it was probably first subdued by Ashur-nasir-pal, and was chastised by Shalmaneser li (in 838 B.C.); in the time of Tiglath-pileser IV we find it a very submissive vassal; in 718 it had revolted under the influence of Mita of Mushki: of the cause of the war of 695 we have no knowledge.

In 694 Sennacherib's restless activity moved him to a remarkable adventure, which he calls his sixth campaign. He resolved to strike at Merodach-baladan in his retreat on the Elamite coast of the Persian Gulf, and in order to do this he had great ships on the Phoenician model built at

Til Barsip, on the upper Euphrates, and manned by Sidonian sailors: the flotilla thus prepared sailed down the river to the gulf with an army on board, which was safely ferried over to the Elamite coast after the favour of Ea, the god of the Ocean, had been propitiated by the offerings of a golden ship, a golden fish, and other objects, which were solemnly cast into the sea. The Elamite coast was ravaged, and hundreds of the fugitive Chaldaeans and their gods, with Elamite prisoners also, were brought back to Babylonia, where Sennacherib, who had not trusted himself to the uncertain favour of the sea-god Ea, awaited them. Whether Merodach-baladan had been killed we do not know; he never reappeared.

This expedition was a declaration of war against Elam, and Khallushu, its king (who had acceded in 699), furious at the ravaging of his coast, delivered an immediate counter-stroke by invading Babylonia and capturing Sippar, with the Assyrian king of Babylon, Ashur-nadin-shum, Sennacherib's son, Khallushu set a certain Nergal-ushezib on the throne of Babylon, and then returned to Elam, carrying Ashur-nadinshum in his train. Sennacherib was thus cut off from Assyria, but Nergal-ushezib was unable to make headway against his advance from the south, was defeated at Nippur, and carried off to Assyria (693). Sennacherib then attacked Elam, but the king Kudur-nakhkhunte, who had succeeded Khallushu in the meantime, retired before him into the mountains, and the Assyrians effected nothing, finally returning to Nineveh. Directly they left the country, the Babylonians made a certain Mushezib-marduk king (692). In the next year Sennacherib moved south against him, and the terrified Babylonian summoned Kudur-nakhkhunte's successor, Umman-minanu, to his aid, bribing him with the treasures of the temple of Marduk, which he took from their house and sent to Elam. Umman-minanu responded to the bribe, and the Elamite army met Sennacherib at Khaluli on the Tigris. A great battle ensued which is most picturesquely described by Sennacherib's historian. "Like a great swarm of locusts which spreads itself over the land, so marched they in warlike array against me, to bring me to battle. The dust of their feet rose before me like a heavy stormcloud, which covered the copper-coloured face of the wide heaven. By the town Khaluli, on the bank of the Tigris, their forces deployed: they set themselves in order against me, and clashed their weapons together. But I prayed to Ashur, Sin, Shamash, Bel, Nebo, Nergal, Ishtar of Nineveh, and Ishtar of Arbela, the gods in whom I trusted, for the defeat of the mighty foe; and they heard swiftly my prayer and came to my help." The rest of the inscription describes nothing but the personal prowess of the king himself in inflated language, which was no doubt pleasing to the royal ears: how much relation it may have borne to fact we cannot tell. The description is a paean of victory, but it is not impossible that the battle really resulted in an Assyrian defeat, for Sennacherib certainly had to retreat to Assyria, leaving the Elamites in possession of the field, and Mushezib-marduk in possession of Babylonia. But Khumbanudasha, the Elamite general, was killed, and Nabu-shum-ishkun, son of Merodach-baladan, an exile in Elam, was captured (according to the official account by the king's own hand). This, and the heavy losses of the Elamites, were probably the only Assyrian claims to victory.

For a year Sennacherib remained quiet, till the death of Umman-minanu in 689 gave him the opportunity of carrying out a scheme of revenge on Babylon which should be complete and lasting. Suddenly advancing, he took the city, sent Mushezib-marduk away captive in company with the image of the god Marduk itself, and then deliberately destroyed Babylon. The population was expelled, the city burnt, and the canal of Arakhtu turned over its ruins. The destruction of Babylon effected, Sennacherib returned in triumph to Nineveh.

Of the remaining eight years of his reign we have no information from his own annals, which now cease. This silence probably hides a great disaster in the West of which we gain only fragmentary hints from other sources. The defeat of Eltekeh (701) had soon been followed by the death of Shabaka, who was succeeded by his son Shabataka (Shabitoku) an unimportant ruler of whom we know little beyond the fact that he made some sort of treaty with Sennacherib of which the seal has been found in the ruins of Nineveh. In 689 or 688 he was succeeded by his uncle Taharka (Tirhakah), a younger brother of Shabaka. Probably the new king again endeavoured to stir up rebellion in the West, which had been absolutely quiet for over ten years. But Hezekiah, again wisely counselled by Isaiah, took no part in the rebellion. Sennacherib once more arrived in the West (687 or 686?), and took Libnah, which had revolted. Here he heard that Tirhakah was preparing to advance against him, so, to forestall him, he himself crossed the desert and laid siege to Pelusium, There, however, his army was smitten by pestilence, and he was forced to return with all speed to Assyria. Such is possibly the story of the campaign which is passed over in silence by the Assyrian historian, but is recorded by Herodotus and by the Jewish chroniclers. The Jewish account seems, however, to be confused, as it stands, with that of the earlier invasion of 701. In the story of the Second Book of Kings, Tirhakah is spoken of as king, which he was not till 689 at the earliest. And it is certain that Hezekiah, after the siege of 701 was raised, sent heavy gifts to Nineveh, which he would hardly have done if in that year Sennacherib's army had been decimated by plague and the king himself forced hurriedly to return to Assyria. The fact of the disaster seems vouched for by the Egyptian testimony quoted by Herodotus not much more than two centuries later, and by that of the Biblical record: it would naturally not be mentioned by the Assyrians.

We have no official Egyptian account of the disaster to Sennacherib. In the popular tradition preserved by Herodotus the name of the Egyptian king is given as "Sethos," but this is no argument against his indentity with Tirhakah; the true appellation of the monarch has disappeared in favour of that of the great Seti, probably on account of the legendary connection of Seti I. and his Palestinian wars with Pelusium, and from a confusion of the name of the Ethiopian king (recorded by Manetho) "Zet" (who is probably to be identified with Kashta, the grandfather of Taharka), with the better-known "Seti." An Ethiopian had ruled at the time: Zet (Kashta) was a well-known Ethiopian: "Zet" in the popular mouth would easily become confused with "Seti," whowas connected in tradition with Pelusium: hence Herodotus' "Sethos." It is impossible to reject the whole story to the actual period of Seti in face of the direct mention of Sennacherib (Sanacharibos), which makes obvious the identity of the disaster to his army in the Egyptian with the disaster to his army in the Jewish legend.

The only campaign recorded of Sennacherib in his later years is one against the Arabs, probably a mere razzia, which is mentioned by his son Esarhaddon. He no doubt busied himself with the rebuilding of Nineveh, which he had transformed during his reign into a mighty capital, worthy of the empire and intended by him to eclipse Babylon. In his inscriptions he tells us how his forefathers had never sought to beautify Nineveh, to straighten its streets, to plant plantations, or even to build a proper wall; and that he was the first to carry out a thorough scheme of reconstruction in the capital: "the people of Chaldaea, the Aramaeans, the Mannai, the men of Kue and Cilicia, the Phoenicians and Tyrians who had not submitted to my yoke, I carried away, and I set them to forced labour, and they made bricks." The great mound on which the royal palace buildings were set, now known as Kuyunjik, was enlarged by the diversion of the river Khusur, and a new and splendid palace built. The mound of

Kuyunjik, and that now known by the name of the prophet Jonah, whose reputed tomb stands upon it (Nebi Yunus), upon which was situated the imperial armoury, formed two great keeps, joined together by a wall, part of the west wall of the city, facing the Tigris. The huge walls were carried round an irregularly-shaped space enclosing more than double the real area of the city: within this space plantations and parks of great size were included, which were watered by means of elaborate aqueducts constructed from springs in the hills north of Nineveh. The walls were double, and each one bore a sonorous Sumerian name; the inner was Bad-imgalbi-galukurra-shushu (in Assyrian, duru sa namrirusu nakiri sahpu, "The Wall whose splendour overthrows the Enemy"), and the outer was Bad-garneru-khubukhkha, "the Wall that terrifies the Foe." Fifteen gates give access to the city, each bearing an ordinary name, such as the "gate of Ashur" or the "Quay-gate," and an Assyrian honorific title. The ruined walls of Sennacherib still remain as a range of high mounds surrounding the site of the ancient city, which was about three miles long and about a mile broad at the northern end, narrowing to little more than a thousand yards at the southern. Such a city, with such walls and palaces, was in truth a worthy rival to Babylon in size, and in splendour there is little doubt that Sennacherib's capital would entirely have eclipsed Babylon had the ancient city still existed. But in 694, when the huge walls of Nineveh were completed, Babylon was a ruin and a waste.

"And it came to pass, as he was worshipping in the house of Nisroch his god, that Adrammelech and Sharezer his sons smote him with the sword: and they escaped into the land of Armenia. And Esarhaddon his son reigned in his stead." So the Biblical tradition registers the death of Sennacherib, and the Assyrian record agrees indirectly. From a broken cylinder of Esarhaddon we learn that he was suddenly called away from his government to contest the succession to the throne, which had been seized by his enemies, and that he pursued them and defeated them in Khanigalbat (Melitene). Further, he calls himself "the avenger of the father who begat him." Four sons of Sennacherib are mentioned: Ashur-nadin-shum, king of Babylon, who was carried off to Elam; Ardi-Belit, who was certainly regarded as crown-prince as late as 694; Ashur-munik; and Ashur-akh-iddina ("Ashur-hath-given-a-brother"), the Biblical Esarhaddon. We may well identify Ardi-Belit and Ashur-munik with Adrammelech and Sharezer, whose names in the Biblical narrative are evidently mere appellations of Assyrian sound, conferred upon them by the chronicler in ignorance of their real names, Esarhaddon had probably displaced Ardi-Belit in his father's affections towards the end of his reign, as we have a document in which he is given rich gifts and his name is changed to Ashur-etil-ukin-apla ("Ashur-the-hero-hath-established-a-son"): it is probable that Sennacherib now intended him to be his successor. Esarhaddon was certainly away in a provincial government when the two elder sons, seizing the opportunity of his absence, murdered their father in order to secure the inheritance to themselves. It has been suggested, with great probability, that Esarhaddon, whose partiality for Babylon was marked during his reign, had been made governor of Babylonia, and was there when the news of his father's murder (at the end of 682) arrived. Six weeks later he had expelled the parricides from Nineveh, and then pursued them into Khanigalbat, whence, after their defeat, they fled into Armenia, no doubt to the court of Rusas II., the King of Urartu.

II. The Reign of Esarhaddon, 681-669.

The formal assumption of the kingship took place at the beginning of 681. The first act of the new reign, in contradistinction to all those that had gone before, was a peaceful one; an act of conciliation and reparation to the Babylonians for the destruction of their city. Esarhaddon had determined to rebuild Babylon, and in 680, "in the tenth year" after the destruction, the walls, towers, and gates were set up again, the Chaldaeans who had invaded the site were chased away, and the inhabitants were summoned back to their ancient abode. Three years later the rehabilitation of the city was complete. The Babylonians were thus conciliated, and when, about the same time, a son of Merodach-baladan attempted to raise a Chaldaean revolt, he met with no sympathy and was compelled to fly to Elam. The Elamites too, who seized the opportunity of Esarhaddon's absence in the West in 675 to invade Babylonia, and actually captured Sippar, also had to retreat before the general hostility; and soon after the "gods of Agade," which they had taken from Sippar, were peacefully returned by them to Esarhaddon. His abstinence from a campaign of revenge secured their friendship also. Thus we see a notable change from the wild, vain, and unthinking proceedings of Sennacherib. Esarhaddon was a prudent and wise statesman, and he deliberately set out to pursue a peaceful policy in his southern dominions with the object of securing a free hand in the great enterprise on which he had determined, the conquest of Egypt, while at the same time keeping one hand free to strike at the mountain-tribes of the North, who were now threatening to burst their barriers under the pressure of the nomad tribes of the Gimirrai. These, the "Gomer" of the Hebrews and "Kimmerians" of the Greeks, had come down from the northern steppes through the passes of the Caucasus, and, contemporaneously with the related tribe of the Treres, which had apparently come through Moesia and across the Hellespont, were now in full possession of the northern part of Asia Minor, and meditating a descent upon Mesopotamia. One body actually penetrated the mountains through the gorge of the Euphrates in 678, and was driven back by the Assyrians into Anatolia. Here for a time the Kimmerians and their allies the Treres ranged unchecked, as great a scourge to the civilized inhabitants as were the Huns to the Romans. The pre-occupation of the Kimmerians in the North-West did not, however, relieve Assyria from the fear of barbarian invasion. Other tribes, set in motion by them, were gathering in the North-East, threatening destruction to the kingdom of Urartu and grave danger to Assyria. A chieftain named Kastarit, lord of Kaskashshi, headed a combination of the Medes under king Mamitiarsu, of the Mannai, and of a horde of Scythians under their king Spaka, which came into collision with Assyria. So redoubtable was this foe considered that the king anxiously consulted the oracles and soothsayers concerning him, and we possess an interesting collection of their answers. The war lasted for several years, ending in 672 with the reassured inviolability of the northern frontier. Esarhaddon had apparently beaten the barbarians at least partly by fomenting divisions in their ranks. One of the chieftains of the Scythians, who had entered Mannai in rear of the Kimmerians, was brought by the gift of an Assyrian princess of the blood-royal to aid Assyria against Spaka and Kastarit. The name of this chieftain was Bartatua, and he appears in the history of Herodotus as the Scythian prince Protothyes, father of that Madyes who afterwards ravaged Syria to the borders of Egypt The result of Esarhaddon's war was probably to make Bartatua king of the Scythian horde in Armenia and Mannai in place of the defeated Spaka, and he was important enough for his name to be faithfully handed down in the chronicles which are the basis of the remarkably accurate Herodotean account of the early history of Media.

After the defeat of this barbarian confederation, the great enterprise of the conquest of Egypt could be entered upon without much danger of an attack from the rear. During the ten years that had elapsed since the beginning of the reign the Palestinians, doubtless stirred up by Egypt, had given trouble. The walls of Sidon were destroyed in 678, and an Assyrian fort called Kar-Esarhaddon was built close by to overawe the town. The king, Abdimilkuti, was beheaded, and the same fate befell a Cilician king, Sanduarri, who had made common cause with the Sidonians. All Phoenicia then submitted under the leadership of Baal, King of Tyre, between whom and Esarhaddon a solemn treaty was signed, which, however, was broken by the faithless Tyrian as soon as he thought he had an opportunity of throwing off the yoke. A few years later (in 673) the kings of Cyprus, nine Greeks and one Phoenician, tendered their homage, and this was probably a confirmation of a previous submission (not mentioned) after the fall of Sidon. The acknowledgment of Assyrian overlordship made to Sargon in 709 was thus repeated to his grandson. The Cypriotes, Greeks though most of them were, followed obediently in the wake of the Phoenicians, to preserve their island from the scourge of Assyrian invasion, which would have been quite possible in Phoenician ships. No doubt the tale of Sennacherib's exploit in the Persian Gulf was well known in Phoenicia, whence he had taken his shipwrights and sailors. From Palestine also came assurances of loyalty. King Manasseh of Judah, the son and successor of Hezekiah, whose title is given as "king of the city of Judah" only, thus shewing that his authority extended no farther than the walls of Jerusalem, brought his tribute to Esarhaddon in person, probably at Tyre, in the same season, 677-676. He was evidently regarded as a personage of quite minor importance, and to the insignificance of himself and his "kingdom" is due the fact of his long and undisturbed reign: Hezekiah must have died about 693, and fifty years later we find Manasseh still king of Judah.

This powerless monarch, content to vegetate interminably within the walls of Zion and feebly persecute the priests and prophets of Yahweh, whose courage and counsel had maintained his father in a position of no little dignity in the terrible days of Sennacherib, could be of no use to Tirhakah as an ally. And the princes of Edom, Moab, and Ammon were as powerless and as fast bound to Esarhaddon's chariot-wheels as was Manasseh. Sidon was destroyed. Tirhakah could do nothing but await the inevitable doom which was fast descending upon Egypt. The intrigues of the past sixty years had done nothing but rouse a determination in the mind of an Assyrian monarch who combined the policy of Sargon with the temerity of Sennacherib to destroy Egypt. We need not blame Esarhaddon for not having realized the impossibility of permanently annexing Egypt. The Assyrians were probably very imperfectly acquainted with the peculiarities of the Nilotes. They did not fully realize the enormous racial difference between the Egyptians and the fellow-Semites over whom they, the Assyrians, had domineered for centuries; they did not understand that they were about to conquer and hold down by the sword a people utterly alien from them, worshipping deities utterly different from theirs, a people, too, whose bitterest memory was that of an enslavement by Semites a thousand years before. Among the Asiatics the Assyrians could everywhere find friends as well as enemies, but every Egyptian was bound to be their fierce enemy, filled through every fibre of his being with loathing of them. Such a country and people could never be held down for long. Dead though Egyptian vigour had seemed to be for centuries, it could not but be roused by the domination of the new Hyksos, as in fact it was: the result of the Assyrian domination was the renascence under the Saites. Esarhaddon and Ashurbanipal missed, too, the one and only means by which they could have secured Egyptian loyalty: they never mounted the throne of the Pharaohs. Had they done this, had they assumed the insignia of Egyptian royalty, offered their fealty to Amen, entered the sacred Benben-chamber of Ra at Heliopolis, and come forth Sons of the Sun, it may be that the story of the end of the Assyrian empire might have been different from what it was. But an Assyrian king could no more do this than an ancient Pharaoh could have taken the hands of Bel at Babylon and become king of Sumer and Akkad had he conquered Karduniyash. The gulf fixed between the two races was too great: the mere idea of such a policy would have been rejected by Esarhaddon at once. And so the possibility of making Egypt an Assyrian province was lost. The reckless Cambyses had no such scruples, and the wise Persian Darius saw that the policy into which Cambyses had blundered, hardly knowing what he was doing, was the only one by which Egypt could be secured to his empire. And by becoming Pharaoh Darius paved the way for the Macedonian and Roman dynasties.

So Esarhaddon, knowing nothing of these things, and regarding the Egyptians merely as cowardly intriguers and worshippers of cats and dogs who submitted to the rule of black men, prepared for the step which was to go far to weaken his empire and bring about its fall. In 675 he had reconnoitred his desert route to the Egyptian frontier, but the war with Kastarit and Spaka summoned him back, and it was not till 670 that at last (after a revolt of Baal of Tyre, instigated by Tirhakah (Taharka), had been subdued) the Assyrians invaded Egypt. The blow which the world had expected for half a century had fallen. Tirhakah could only meet inevitable defeat: but he fought before he fled. During his undisturbed reign of nearly twenty years, secured him probably by the prestige which the retreat of Sennacherib from Pelusium had unjustly given him, he had done nothing but build little temples. To organize a defence efficient enough to repel the legions of Assyria was impossible. With careful policy Esarhaddon had been at pains to conciliate the Beduin shekhs of the desert, who supplied his army with water. So he crossed the wilderness safely, burst through the frontier defences, put Tirhakah and the ban of the Delta to flight, and reached Memphis. The ancient city resisted with fanatical fury, but it was stormed and given to the sword. The queen and the prince Utjanhor were captured, but Tirhakah fled to Thebes, whither Esarhaddon made no attempt to follow him, but received the submission of the princes of the Delta and of the valley immediately south of Memphis: a more extended military occupation was evidently impossible. Twenty kinglets were recognized and Assyrian garrisons placed in their cities to watch them, the henchmen of a "hard lord," the first really foreign conqueror that Egypt had known since the Hyksos. The Assyrian then returned to Assyria, setting up stelae at Samalla and at the mouth of the Nahr el-Kelb in Phoenicia, on which we see him standing in majesty, while Baal of Tyre and Tirhakah of Egypt, whose negroid features are malignantly caricatured, kneel in chains to lick the hem of his robe. With supreme irony, the Assyrian monument is placed immediately by the side of the ancient stele of Rameses II.

But Tirhakah had never been chained and was by no means inclined to lick the hem of Esarhaddon's robe. In the Upper Country he had summoned all to his aid, and no sooner had Esarhaddon left Egypt than he descended suddenly like a storm, took Memphis, and massacred the Assyrian garrisons. Furious, Esarhaddon started to return to Egypt, but was taken ill and died on the way (end of 669). He left a political testament by which he willed that his two sons Ashurbanipal and Shamash-shum-ukin should inherit the empire, the latter as king of Babylon under the general control of his elder brother the king of Assyria. The queen-dowager Nakia, widow of Sennacherib and mother of Esarhaddon, for whom she had acted as regent during his absences from Assyria, issued a proclamation to the nation enjoining fidelity to the new kings.

12. The Reign of Ashurbanipal (669-626)

Ashurbanipal immediately proceeded with the Egyptian war. In Syria he received the accession of contingents from the subject-states, including a small force sent by Manasseh of Judah. At Karbanit, within the Egyptian frontier, the armies met (668), and Tirhakah was again defeated. Memphis was occupied, apparently without a blow, and a Phoenician flotilla which had been collected for the purpose, and had entered the Nile, sailed upstream to Thebes. The city was abandoned by Tirhakah, and surrendered by Montemhat the governor. Tirhakah fled to Napata. No harm seems to have been done to Thebes, as Montemhat had surrendered voluntarily. He was made a petty king of the Thebaid, like the Delta-princes, whose names are given us in an interesting list of the governors and petty kings confirmed or appointed by Esarhaddon, and reinstated by Ashurbanipal.

Of these Delta-princes several were important enough to have lived in popular tradition, and in papyri of the Roman period we have the story of the Holy Boat of Amen and the Thirteen Asiatics and that of the Fight for the Armour of King Inaros, which together form the Petubastis-Saga, the central figure of both stories being the Petubaste of Tanis who is mentioned in Ashurbanipal's list. Pakrur of Pisapd appears prominently in the saga, and the names of Tjeho and Pimai also were preserved. The atmosphere of the time, with its petty warring kinglets, was well preserved in these stories, and the tale of the fights with the Thirteen Asiatics, who with the aid of "the Horus-priest of Buto" seized the holy boat of Amen and desired to possess the revenues of the god, but were finally routed with the aid of Min-neb-mai, "prince of Elephantine," is obviously reminiscent of the conquest of the country by the Assyrians in alliance with traitorous Egyptians, and the resistance to them of the Thebans and Ethiopians, the latter being personified in Min-neb-mai. The "Asiatics" are called Amu, "Shepherds," just as were the Hyksos: the Assyrians were the Hyksos of this later day.

Ashurbanipal's return to Assyria was the signal for Tirhakah's return from Napata. He had opened secret negotiations with the princes Niku of Sais, Sharruludari of Pelusium, and Pakruru of Pisapd, which, however, were discovered, and Niku and Sharruludari were sent in chains to Nineveh, while Tirhakah, bereft of his allies, was easily driven back to Nubia by the Assyrian generals (667). On the arrival of the two captives at Nineveh we can have little doubt that the traitorous Assyrian Sharruludari was at once flayed alive, but Niku the Egyptian was not only spared but treated in an unprecedented manner, which shewed that Ashurbanipal inherited the diplomacy of Esarhaddon, and knew when to conciliate. Niku was treated as a king, dressed in costly raiment, and a ring was placed on his finger as a token of investiture; then, impressed, as was hoped, by the majesty and clemency of Assyria, he was sent back to Egypt as viceroy, while his son (probably he who was afterwards Psammetichos 1) was given the Assyrian name of Nabu-shezibanni and made governor of Athribis.

The new policy worked well for a time, while the Ethiopians remained quiet. But in 663-662, the last year of Tirhakah and first of his successor Tanutamon, who was associated with him in that year, the young Ethiopian king (Tanutamon) invaded Egypt in force. We know the course of events from a triumphal stela set up by him at Napata on his return, in imitation of Piankhi. He met with no resistance in Upper Egypt, which looks as if Niku's viceroyalty had not extended very far south, certainly not so far as Thebes, which received Tanutamon with open arms. Memphis was taken with great slaughter of the Assyrian garrison, and the ban of the Delta, led by chiefs who could be but half-hearted in the cause of Assyria, was scattered. Niku was killed, and his son Psamatik (Psammetichos) fled to Assyria. Pakrur of Pisapd headed a deputation of the Delta dynasts which, at a durbar summoned by Tanutamon, tendered to him their submission. Probably Pakrur had taken refuge in Nubia after the failure of the plot of five years before, had accompanied Tanutamon southwards, and was placed by him in authority over the Delta.

Ashurbanipal's punitive expedition was led by the king in person, and was intended to teach the Egyptians a lesson. The Delta was easily recovered, and Tandamane (as the Assyrians pronounced the name of Tanutamon) was defeated in Middle Egypt, and fled with a swiftness which makes ridiculous the inflated language of his triumphal stela at Napata. Then Thebes, which had been spared seven years before, was given up to sack and destruction. It was utterly plundered, and Ashurbanipal returned to Nineveh laden with loot and prisoners carried away captive: among the trophies are specially mentioned two large pillars or obelisks, "made of shining zakkalu-stone." The city was probably set on fire, and remains of this destruction have recently been uncovered at Karnak, where the houses burnt probably by the Assyrian soldiery on this occasion can now be seen. A curious relic of the sack has also been discovered in the shape of an Assyrian helmet, found near the Ramesseum. Montemhat, the prince of Thebes, tells us in his funerary inscription how the whole city (as well as Upper Egypt generally) was wasted and the temples stripped of all their valuables, and how in the ensuing years he strove to do his best to restore at least the Theban temples to a little of their ancient splendour. But the city never recovered from the blow. Its temples remained the chief sanctuaries of Egypt, but the city itself was destroyed, its inhabitants had been carried off to Assyria and their place taken by unhappy Elamites; henceforward there was no Thebes which could be the civil as well as the religious capital of Egypt. The "Diospolis" of the Graeco-Roman period was but a knot of villages clustering round the ancient and magnificent temples, nothing more.

Psamatik was restored to the position of viceroy, and Egypt, stunned by the destruction of Thebes, lay quiet. Tanutamon made no further attempt to conquer Egypt, and Psamatik secretly prepared for the day when he should be able to cast off the Assyrian yoke and himself ascend the throne of the Pharaohs. The opportunity came some ten years later. For the time, however, Assyria seemed supreme. On his return to Assyria after the defeat of Tanutamon, Ashurbanipal paid Ba'al of Tyre for his treachery by besieging the city, which finally surrendered. The other Phoenician cities, and Sandasharmu of Cilicia, probably the successor of Sanduarri, submitted. The tribute of Mugallu, king of Tabal, now appeared, and was followed by a solemn embassy from Gugu (Gyges), king of Lydia, "a far country across the sea, of which," says Ashurbanipal in his inscription, "the kings my fathers had not heard." Assyrian prestige had reached its height, and had penetrated through the medium of the Greeks of Cyprus (the way through Anatolia was barred by the Kimmerians) to the shores of the Aegean.

Lydia had now taken the place of Phrygia as the chief Anatolian power. The Phrygian monarchy had broken up under the shock of collision with the Kimmerians, whose hordes, driven westward by Esarhaddon in 678, had carried destruction throughout the peninsula. The last Midas killed himself in despair (by drinking bull's blood, so the story went) at the ruin of his kingdom (about 675), and Gyges of Lydia succeeded to the chief place in Asia Minor and at the same time to the position of protagonist in the war with the Kimmerians, who were still ravaging the land, a horde of half-naked warriors riding wild steeds barebacked and swinging in their hands mighty swords with long and heavy leaf-shaped blades which could shear through many a well-made helm.

The embassy to Ashurbanipal was probably moved by some hope of active Assyrian assistance against these Gimirrai. Ashurbanipal gave none at the time, and later on was too busy with the struggle with Elam to be able to give any. Nevertheless Gyges regarded him as an ally against the barbarians, and on one occasion sent him two captive Kimmerian chiefs chained, as an appropriate present. The Lydian king was able to bring the war to a successful conclusion without Assyrian help, and this fact probably decided him later on that he could do without Assyrian friendship; hence his alliance with the revolted Psammetichos of Egypt.

The Elamite war was undoubtedly entered upon by Ashurbanipal with a light heart, after the oracles had assured him of victory. Apparently the war was provoked by an Elamite invasion of Babylonia, and Ashurbanipal seized the opportunity to make an end, as he thought, of Elam for ever, as his father had thought to make an end of Egypt. All seemed favourable for the enterprise: the empire seemed to be at the height of its power and prosperity; Egypt lay prostrate at the feet of Assyria; Lydia courted her friendship; Urartu was powerless; only Elam still defied her. Why, then, should not Elam also be destroyed, and a veritable pax assyriaca be ensured over the greater part of the Near East? The difficulties of the enterprise were underestimated; it was carried through to a successful conclusion in the end, but at terrible expense in men, which contributed even more than the strain of the retention of Egypt to bring about the collapse of the empire. Towards this event Assyria was fast moving; but it would have been a wise prophet who had dared to foretell it in the year 660, when she seemed to dominate the world.

Our information as to the course of events during the last half-century of Assyrian empire is somewhat defective owing to the absence of a list of limmi. The existing copies of the eponym-lists break off about this time, and no new list giving names after the year 666 has been found. We are therefore reduced to conjecture as to the precise dates of events fully described in the royal annals. The Elamite invasion of Babylonia seems to have taken place while Ashurbanipal was absent in Egypt, probably in 668, after his father's death. Peace was patched up, but Te-umman, the successor of Urtaki, the Elamite invader, was a person of even greater temerity than the latter, and again provoked war by making an unjustifiable demand for the surrender of all the male members of the Elamite royal house, who had fled to Assyria at the death of Urtaki. This may have taken place before the Egyptian expedition of 661. On his return from the West Ashurbanipal found that the bold Te-umman had invaded Assyrian territory in revenge for the rejection of his demand, and was advancing from Dur-Ilu up the Tigris valley directly upon the capital. Before the counter-advance of Ashurbanipal's army (the king himself did not lead it, though the official account pretends he did) he retired, and was finally manoeuvred out of the plain into the mountains, whither the Assyrian army immediately followed him, driving him steadily back to Susa, where, at Tulliz on the river Ula (Eulaeus), a battle was fought in which Te-umman was killed. Ashurbanipal made Khumbanigash, son of Urtaki, king of Elam as a vassal of Assyria, with diminished territory, of which much was given as a fief to Tammaritu, son of Khumbanigash. The Assyrians then evacuated the country (in 658?), and Ashurbanipal commemorated his triumph by representing himself on the walls of his palace-corridor as feasting with his wife with the head of Te-umman suspended from a tree near by.

The spirit of the Elamites was, however, by no means broken, and revived somewhat when an unlooked-for rebellion in Babylonia seemed to give a hope of the recovery of complete independence. In 652 Shamash-shum-ukin, brother of Ashurbanipal, and vassal-king of Babylonia, rebelled, with the object not merely of making himself independent of Assyria, but of conquering Assyria, deposing his brother, and becoming head of both nations himself, but with Babylon, instead of Nineveh, as the centre. Whether other causes beyond mere personal ambition caused Shumash-shum-ukin thus to break the relations which had existed for nineteen years between himself and his brother, it is difficult to say: but it is probable that his revolt was symptomatic of the tendency towards a renascence of Babylonia, now first apparent, which was to find its opportunity in the destruction of Assyria. The Babylonian king's preparations seem to have been of a very far-reaching kind, and he set on foot a general conspiracy among all the chief feudatories of the empire, extending from Elam to Judah and Phoenicia. The conspiracy seems to have been discovered first by the Assyrian officials who actually controlled local government in Babylonia (the king having been a mere figure-head), with the result that Shamash-shum-ukin was forced to shew his hand, probably before he was ready. The rebellion broke out in Southern Babylonia, Ur and Erech were captured, the Chaldaeans appeared under a grandson of Merodach-baladan, and Khumbanigash of Elam also invaded with an army. But the Elamite camp was a mere hotbed of intrigue and murder; Khumbanigash was killed by his son Tammaritu, and he was driven away by Indabigash, who withdrew his army from Babylonia. The whole revolt was too badly organized to succeed. Ashurbanipal, encouraged by a favourable oracle from the moon-god, marched southward, blockaded Sippar, Kutha, and Babylon, and drove the Chaldaeans into Elam. The three cities were all stormed, and Shamash-shum-ukin set fire to his palace and perished in the flames (648). Ashurbanipal then himself "took the hands of Bel" and ascended the Babylonian throne under the name of Kandalanu (the "Kineladanos" of Berossos) The Chaldaean army had been driven into Elam, and Ashurbanipal now demanded from Indabigash the surrender of its commander. This being refused, Ashurbanipal's army again entered Elam. Indabigash was murdered by his successor Khumbakhaldash III, who, however, was unable to stem the Assyrian advance. Susa was again captured (647) and this time was utterly destroyed; among its spoil is mentioned the statue of the goddess Nana of Erech, which had been carried away to Elam by Kudur-nankhundi 1635 years before, according to the computation of Ashurbanipal's scribes. It was now solemnly returned to its shrine. The grandson of Merodach-baladan avoided his inevitable surrender by Khumbakhaldash to Assyria by falling upon the sword of his shield-bearer. Finally Khumbakhaldash himself was captured, and led away captive. With his disappearance the kingdom of Elam, utterly destroyed, ceased to exist.

Ashurbanipal now turned to vengeance upon the Western friends of Shamash-shum-ukin. Chief among these had been the Arabs of the Hauran, the "dwellers in the tents of Kedar," and the Nabataeans, "The king of the land of Aribi," Yailu, who had been appointed by Esarhaddon, had made common cause with Shamash-shum-ukin, and now an Assyrian army was sent against him. Defeated, and probably killed, he was succeeded by a certain Uaite, who, in no way inclined to submit to Assyria, partly turned the tables by raising war and revolt from Edom to the gates of Damascus. There, however, he was defeated, and fled. Betrayed, probably, to the Assyrians, he was carried off to Nineveh, where Ashurbanipal treated him, and Adiya his wife, and his ally the king of Kedar, literally as dogs; chaining them in kennels like watchdogs before his palace-door. A body of the Arabs who had actually reached Babylonia in order to aid Shamash-shum-ukin were defeated, and their leader Abiyate made king of "Aribi" instead of Uaite. No sooner was he back on the steppe than he rebelled in his turn, but was eventually subdued; and the Assyrians captured from him so many camels that they were sold in the markets of Nineveh for a mere song — "a half-shekel to a shekel of silver apiece."

It is probable that after the defeat of Uaite, which probably took place about 646, occurred the captivity of Manasseh, king of Judah, which is recorded in the Book of Chronicles, though not in that of the Kings. The fact is not in the Assyrian annals either, but there can be little doubt that the account in Chronicles is a piece of genuine history, and that in his old age Manasseh was removed in chains to Babylon, no doubt to answer for a real or suspected participation in the schemes of Shamash-shum-ukin. Eventually he returned to Jerusalem, where he died (638).

About the year 645, also, must have occurred the chastisement of Tyre and Akko, for support which the Phoenicians, always restive under Assyrian rule, had given to the pretensions of Shamash-shum-ukin.

Not long after this the Kimmerians, who under their leader Tugdammi (the Dygdamis or Lygdamis of Strabo) had defeated and slain Gyges of Lydia (about 650), had in their turn been defeated and driven out of Western Asia Minor by his son Ardys, assisted by the Ionians, whose cities Tugdammi had sacked. They then attempted to break back eastwards over the Taurus by way of the Cilician Gates. Here they were met and defeated (about 64s) by the Assyrian army of Syria, returned from the war with Uaite; Tugdammi was killed, and the horde retreated northwards under his son Sandakhshatra. An embassy from Ardys, probably intended merely to compliment Ashurbanipal on this victory, was of course recorded by the Ninevite court-scribes as a servile offer to come under the Assyrian yoke.

After these victories, and the conclusion of amicable relations with Sarduris IV of Urartu, Ashurbanipal's active work came to an end. There is no doubt that he had not accompanied in person any campaigns since he went to Egypt in 661, yet about the year 642 (approximately) he celebrated a solemn triumph at Nineveh, to thank the gods for the victories which had marked his twenty years of rule. He rode to the temple of Ishtar in a chariot to the yoke of which were harnessed Khumbakhaldash, the ex-king of Elam; Pa'e, a claimant of the Elamite throne, who had given the Assyrians some trouble after the defeat of Khumbakhaldash; Tammaritu, son of Urtaki, who had once reigned over Elam; and Uaite the Arab.

There was one significant absentee from this company of insulted prisoners. Psamatik of Egypt was not there. The revolt of Shamash-shum-ukin had given him the opportunity of throwing off the weak Assyrian control, and he had taken it (about 651). Borrowing Ionian and Karian mercenaries from Gyges of Lydia (who was by no means inclined to be complaisant to an Assyria weakened by civil war and unable to help him against the Kimmerians), in order to stiffen his native soldiery, Psamatik must easily have mastered any Assyrian garrisons that may still have remained in Egypt. Then, unopposed by the Ethiopians, he assumed the Double Crown, and his rule as pharaoh was soon acknowledged as far south as Syene. Ashurbanipal made no attempt to reduce him. Probably he realized that constantly repeated wars of conquest in the Nile valley would soon use up his already terribly depleted army, and that without such continual conquests de novo it was impossible to keep a hold on the country. Egypt had remained quiet for as long as ten years, it was true, under the viceroyalty of Psamatik, but that was only because the Assyrian suzerainty was nowhere visible, and any Assyrian soldiers stationed there were no doubt regarded by the people as mercenaries in the pay of Psamatik. We may be sure that the Saite prince in no way flaunted his loyalty to Ashurbanipal before the eyes of his fellow-countrymen.

So Egypt started on a new course of independent development, under a new dynasty, whose founder had shewn abundant signs of political sagacity, and was very different from the tumultuous, ineffective, and unintelligent Ethiopians. The Assyrian decision to abandon the Nile valley was a wise one. But, naturally, the renunciation of the imperial projects of Esarhaddon was not considered a particularly appropriate theme for the court chroniclers: Egypt is simply ignored by them. If conciliatory ambassadors were expected from Psamatik with presents which might be construed as tribute, and enable the scribes to call him a vassal-king, none came; so Psamatik was not admitted to amity like Sarduris of Urartu. Neither did he figure bound to the imperial chariot-wheels in company with Uaite.

13. The Destruction of Nineveh

The Triumph of Ashurbanipal in 642 closes the history of his reign, so far as his own annals are concerned. All we know (and we do not know this from any contemporary Assyrian source) is that he died in 626, leaving an impoverished and tottering empire to ephemeral successors. The Scythians had probably broken through the Euphrates gorges and overrun Syria before he died, and the buffer-state of Urartu was no longer able to make any opposition to the attacks of the Medes and Mannai. In his younger days Ashurbanipal had chastised Khsheri (Akhsheri) the king of

Mannai, but, so far as we know, he had made no attempt thoroughly to terrorize the Kurdish tribes, as his forefathers would have done. No doubt his military power had become so weak owing to the losses in Elam that he was unable to contemplate a war of conquest in Kurdistan. Elam, which, in spite of its hostility to Assur, had for centuries acted as a buffer between the Mesopotamians and the restless young peoples of Iran, had been removed by Ashurbanipal's own act. Tardy friendship and perhaps alliance with Urartu strove to repair the error by the maintenance of a buffer in the north which should take the place of Mannai, long faithless to Assyria which had created it. But all was in vain, and at the close of Ashurbanipal's life the Medes under their king Uvakhshatra (Kyaxares) and the confederated tribes of the Umman-manda, as the mixed hordes of Scythians, Mannai, and Kimmerians in Armenia were called, were fast gathering behind the Judi Dagh, like vultures awaiting the last moments of their victim. That they attacked in 626, and that Ashurbanipal, the Sardanapallos of Greek legend, actually perished in the flames of his palace, is improbable. Ashurbanipal probably died of old age in his bed, like Louis XIV, amid disasters, doubtless, but not yet ruin. The Greek story of the death of Sardanapallos is probably a mixture of the historical suicide of Shamash-shum-ukin in 648 with the probable similar fate of Sin-shar-ishkun, the last king of Assyria, in 606. It was natural that Ashurbanipal should represent to the Greek mind both the glory and the tragic end of the Assyrian empire, and that the "sad stories of the deaths of kings" that came to Greece from far Mesopotamia should be told of the great Sardanapallos, for whom no death could be more fitting than suicide amid the ruins of his glory.

But a blow had been struck between 628 and 626 which brought Assyria to her knees. The barbarian Scyths, led by Madyes, son of that Bartatua or Protothyes, "king of Shkuz," whom Esarhaddon had feared so much, poured over the empire in resistless swarms, ravaging it even to the borders of Egypt, where King Psamatik was fain to buy them off with rich bribes. The terror which they inspired in Judah, where the pious Josiah was now reigning, is well reflected in the prophecies of Jeremiah: "they lay hold on bow and spear, they are cruel and have no mercy, their voice roareth like the sea and they ride upon horses." The village of Skythopolis in later times was the sole permanent relic of their invasion. But, as one pest kills another, Madyes in the course of his career of conquest is said to have disposed of the last of the older Kimmerian hordes that were still in the field. Herodotus relates how he was murdered by Kyaxares the Mede.

The great raid lost the whole west to Assyria. After the waters of the invasion had subsided, Josiah of Judah established an independent dominion. Then Babylon went, at the death of Ashurbanipal. As Kandalanu he reigned as king of Babylon peacefully till his death. And his ephemeral successors were recognized in Babylonia as kings of Babylon. But the national spirit of Babylonia which had been deliberately revived by Esarhaddon and Shamash-shum-ukin, had found a leader in a native Babylonian who, probably not long after the death of Ashurbanipal, established himself in Babylon itself as king, under the name of Nabu-pal-usur (Nabopolassar). The Assyrian monarchs were too weak to eject him: Sin-shum-lishir and Ashur-etil-ilani seem to have been miserable successors to the great Sargonide emperors. Assyrian power was soon confined to the home-land and parts of Babylonia. To this shrunken heritage succeeded Sin-shar-ishkun. He reigned powerless in Nineveh. The Median king Uvakhshatra (Kyaxares), who had succeeded in welding his own people and the wild hordes of the Umman-manda into an alliance inspired by a common hatred of the tyrant empire, was awaiting his opportunity to advance. The opportunity came after 608, when the unopposed advance of the Egyptian king Necho to the Euphrates shewed that Assyria had finally become impotent. Nabopolassar took the same event as the sign for the establishment of the complete independence of Babylonia, and concluded an alliance with Kyaxares, with the destruction of Assyria as their common object. Kyaxares then descended to the final scene. In 606, after a terrible siege, Nineveh was taken by storm, and the last king of Assyria perished in the holocaust of his palace, his courtiers, and his slaves.

The dramatic collapse of Assyria has furnished a theme for many a moralist from the time of Nahum the prophet, in whose lifetime Nineveh fell, to the present day. The tale of the destruction of the mistress of the world was speedily borne to the four quarters of Asia, and the astonishment which it created is evident in all the ancient references to it. We too, at the present day, feel something of this astonishment. Yet this portentous event, as it seemed to be, was the natural and inevitable result of the history of the Assyrian state. The very vigour and energy of the Assyrian kings and their people were the cause of their comparatively speedy downfall. The Assyrians had always been a manly nation: their kings and nobles were devoted to the chase and to war with a keenness which no other people of Near Asia had ever shewed; the people were hardy cultivators and farmers, splendid material for the creation of an incomparable army. This the military capacity of the kings created. So long as their conquests were not too far extended, did not demand too much blood from their subjects, and were not absolutely continuous, their empire was not weakened by the difficulty of controlling distant possessions, and could recuperate itself between its wars of conquest. But the terrible succession of war-lords inaugurated by Tiglath-pileser IV broke the back of the nation. Their insatiable lust of universal dominion pushed them ever forward, till they strained their power to breaking-point by the attempt to rule entirely alien and distant conquests such as Egypt, thus weakening their control over the mountain-regions immediately north of Assyria itself, that northern frontier which was ever the Achilles' heel of their empire. And the incessant demand for more men and more blood from their own people naturally meant speedy exhaustion even to the hardy Assyrians. The signs of exhaustion are already evident in the time of Sennacherib, who first recruited soldiers from the subject-peoples, to fill up the gaps in the army. This meant the admission of less valiant and less trustworthy elements into the fighting-line. The quality of the troops deteriorated swiftly towards the end, and when, after the slaughter of the Elamite war, Ashurbanipal was left with an army which must have contained but a kernel of genuine Assyrian warriors, he dared not pit them against the Ionian and Karian mercenaries of Psammetichos: so Egypt was abandoned. The confession that the Assyrian troops were no longer even the equals of the western warriors, whom under Sennacherib they had defeated in Cilicia (though even then with great difficulty), meant much. Towards the end of his reign, Ashurbanipal can have had but a shadow of the old Assyrian fighting-force. And in Assyria the degeneracy and disappearance of the army meant the degeneracy and disappearance of the nation. The army was the nation, and when Nineveh was destroyed, literally the Assyrian nation was destroyed also. Babylon and Thebes had been destroyed, but had soon risen again; their peoples continued to exist, and soon revived to resume their national life. But not merely Nineveh, Assyria never rose again, and the final blow killed her. No peace-organization of any proper kind existed to keep the empire together, as the successors of Tiglath-pileser IV were not intelligent enough to develop his system, which in the time of Sennacherib had probably degenerated into military force and nothing else.

At home nothing much in the way of organization other than military existed, probably, above the village communities.

The contrast to Egypt and Babylonia, whose age-long civil administrations kept these kingdoms together as indestructible units even when under foreign rule, is great.

That under more intelligent monarchs Assyria might have become a really great nation is evident from the fact that in the last years of her existence, when the army had become weakened and the king no longer went forth to war, her art and general culture took the opportunity to develop in a very remarkable way. The sculptures of the palace of Ashurbanipal at Nineveh mark great advance on older Assyrian art (as that of Ashurnasirpal's time), and in the representation of animals and the chase the king's sculptors shewed a power of observation, a love of truth, and a skilful hand previously unexampled in ancient art. The crudenesses of prehistoric Greek art, in spite of its naturalism, the inequalities and deadening conventions of Egyptian art, prevented the Minoan and Nilotic artists from ever producing anything so good as the smitten lioness or the wild horses of Ashurbanipal's reliefs. The heads of the chariot-horses, the beautiful Nisaean steeds from Media, were designed and carved by the unknown Ninevite sculptor with a mastery that even the horses of the frieze of the Parthenon can hardly excel. There is stiffness and conventionality in the human figures, there is laboured detail of clothes and accoutrements; but the animals are wonderful. The older carved ivories from Nimrud shew, too, what the Assyrian craftsman could do; and we need not seek for Phoenician origins or for Ionian inspiration for his work.

Of literature, as we understand it, the Assyrians had little notion, whereas the Egyptians had; and the fire of Hebrew poetry was unknown to them. What they possessed in the way of a literature was all taken at second hand from the Babylonians, who themselves possessed little that can be dignified by the name. But they had inherited or acquired something of the cultivated Babylonian antiquarian spirit, and Ashurbanipal, the savage torturer of his prisoners, was a zealous bibliophile, and collected the splendid library of Assyrian and Babylonian clay tablets which is now the greatest archaeological treasure possessed by the British nation.

With this artistic development and love of the antique went hand in hand a great increase both of luxury and of superstition. Sennacherib was the first Sargonid who no longer went forth to war himself, but stayed at home in his palace and took all the credit of the victories that his generals won.

Esarhaddon was more energetic in the field, but his Babylonian sympathies awoke in him a vein of religiosity that was unknown to Tiglath-pileser IV, and both he and his son Ashurbanipal were unusually superstitious for Assyrians, and always invoked the oracle of Ishtar of Arbela before undertaking any war. This religiosity shewed a loss of self-confidence and of the old simple belief in the impossibility of defeat, that was significant of degeneracy.

So Assyria and her kings went down to Sheol amid the curses of the nations. Only half a century after Thebes had been destroyed, "populous No-Amon, situate in the midst of the waters," Nineveh the destroyer had been dealt the same stroke of fate. Can we doubt that the Egyptian saw in this the vengeance of his outraged deities, and derived from it a renewed belief in their power and a renewed self-respect that was to go so far to restore Egypt to her old position of authority among the nations? Less than a century since Rabshakeh had jeered at Hezekiah in the hearing of the people on the wall, his successors had fled away "like the locusts" when the sun arose, "and their place was not known where they were." So the prophet Nahum blazed forth in splendid poetry the good news of the fall of the arch-enemy of Yahweh and of Judah: "Behold upon the mountains the feet of him that bringeth good tidings, that publisheth peace! O Judah, keep thy solemn feasts, perform, thy vows, for the wicked shall no more pass through thee; he is utterly cut off. . . . The Lord is good; a stronghold in the day of trouble; and he knoweth them that trust in him. . . . Woe to the bloody city. . . . Behold, I am against thee, saith the Lord of Hosts, and I will discover thy skirts upon thy face, and I will shew the nations thy nakedness and the kingdoms thy shame. And I will cast abominable filth upon thee, and make thee vile, and set thee as a gazing-stock. And it shall come to pass, that all they that look upon thee shall flee from thee, and say, Nineveh is laid waste; who will bemoan her? . . . Behold, thy people in the midst of thee are women, the gates of thy land shall be set wide open unto thine enemies: the fire shall devour thy walls, . . . Thy shepherds slumber, O King of Assyria; thy nobles shall dwell in the dust; thy people is scattered upon the mountains, and no man gathereth them. There is no healing of thy hurt; thy wound is grievous; all that bear the bruit of thee shall clap their hands over thee; for upon whom hath not thy wickedness passed continually?"

CHAPTER XI: THE RENOVATION OF EGYPT AND RENASCENCE OF GREECE

IT might seem that we could use the same term "Renascence" to designate the revivification of the Egyptian state under the rule of the Saites and the awakening to new life of civilization in Greece. But the two phenomena were very different from each other. One was a merely artificial revivification of an old Egypt long passed away, the other was a natural re-florescence of civilization in a shape very different from the Aegean culture of ancient days. The effect of the Egyptian renovation was but to intensify and emphasize the old age of Egypt, who had but painted her withered cheeks with artificial roses of youth; the Greek renascence was a true re-birth, the new Greece, ignorant of her forebears, was born anew as a young child. The archaistic movement which aimed at reproducing the ancient Egypt of the days before the Empire had begun in the time of Ethiopian domination. It set in, apparently, as a fashion of protest against the outworn and vulgarized culture and art of the Empire. The imperial tradition had not in the long run served Egypt, who had lost her empire and seen her own land overrun by conquerors. In the bitterness of subjection the Egyptians turned from the Empire towards the simple old days, as they seemed, of the Pyramid-Builders. Names and titles of that period reappeared, a kind of archaistic crusade sprang up, and eventually, when Tsamatik I restored the rule of the Pharaohs over the whole land, the archaistic mode was officially adopted by the state. It was as if a degenerate and worn-out England of the future, tired of the imperial pomp, were to go back for her inspiration to the Anglo-Saxon period, were to imitate that period in every way, in art, in costume, and in manners, to replace the dignitaries of the present day by "ealdormen," "jarls," and "thegns," and substitute for the Imperial Parliament an English comic-opera "Witenagemot." Such was the artifically rejuvenated state which Psamatik called into being on his attainment of complete independence of Assyria (650 B.C.). Babylonia also was seized at this time with the craze for archaism. The restored kingdom of Nabopolassar, of which we shall follow the fortunes in the next chapter, was marked, like the restored kingdom of Psamatik, by a revival of old days and old ways before the

Assyrian imperialism had existed. And Nabonidus, the last king of the last Babylonian dynasty, was, as we shall see, a learned archaeologist, an enthusiastic collector of ancient divine images, and energetic preserver of the most ancient temples.

And into the midst of this artificial juvenility of Egypt and Babylonia came the real youth of Greece and Persia. The Persian conquest of the Near East, and the final collision between Greece and Persia, belong to the next and last chapter of this book. With it our story ends. But before the Greeks came into conflict with the Persians they had established their new civilization on the coasts of the Levant and throughout the whole Mediterranean. It is the course of this expansion of renascent Greece that we have to trace as succinctly as possible. The internal affairs of Greece, and especially of the Hellenic mainland, call for our attention only in so far as they bear directly upon the general progress of Hellenic culture, especially towards the east and south, or affect directly the approach of the conflict with Persia. With the history of the Greek colonies of Magna Graecia and Sicily after their foundation we have no concern till Gelon of Syracuse defeats the Carthaginians and aspires to lead Greece against Persia.

The amalgamation of the Indo-European Greek-speakers from the north with the non-Aryan "Minoans" and "Aegeans" of the south had, as we have seen, already combined to form the Greek nation in the Homeric period. The new Aryan deities of the Hellenes either remained unchanged (like Hera, Hestia, Ares, and Apollo), or were identified with the older gods of the land (like Zeus himself), or were taken over unchanged (like Poseidon, Aphrodite, Artemis, Rhea, and Athene). In the Greek religion of the classical period we see a complete combination of the old and the new systems, though naturally those societies, as Athens, Crete, and Arcadia, which were either more strongly tinged with the ancient blood or were more conservative in spirit, clung more to the descendants of the old gods, while the more Aryan-Hellenic a Greek state was the more fervently it worshipped Apollo. The policy of the new-comers conquered entirely. In all probability the older people had had little feeling for civic freedom or desire to take direct part in the government of themselves. Of course, we know nothing directly on this point, but the definitely Aryan character of classical Greek institutions indicates a deficiency of political ideas among the pre-Aryan Greeks analogous to the similar deficiency among the peoples of Egypt and the Orient. When the Aryan Greeks came they were not, of course, savages, and brought some culture of their own. But the civilization of the older race conquered, and its presence brought about the sudden renascence of Greek culture. For a time, however, all was chaos, as we have seen, and a reflection of this period of confusion may be found in the fact that during several centuries communication between Greece and Egypt, which in the old days had been from the beginning of things so regular, ceased to be so. Though one or two Egyptian scarabs have been found with Geometric (Dipylon) objects in Greece, not a single pot or sherd of the Geometric style has yet been found in Egypt. There was but little communication. Phoenician traders and slavers there were who carried on a fitful commerce with the Orient among the warring tribes of Greece, but they only brought goods to barter for slaves; they took away nothing else, seemingly. But amid this confusion the soul of Greece was striving to awaken, and in the Homeric society of Ionia, whither first Cretan colonists, and then Minoans and minoized "Ionians" from the Peloponnese and Attica had carried the remains of Minoan culture, the new Greek civilization was arising. The dorized peoples of Greece proper were slow to gain civilization. We must not be too sure that recent discoveries have proved that the Spartans were originally as civilized as the Ionians, and only adopted their historic military semi-barbarism artificially. For in Crete the Dorians had could hardly be aught but a descendant of the ancient militarism of the most barbarous stream (the Illyrian) of the invading Aryans. Still it is evident that the Laconians did eventually take part in the renascence of culture, and they received their impetus, apparently, from Ionia. And from Ionia came the great movement of Greek expansion that altered the history of the world.

The first effects of the Greek renascence and expansion were felt by the Semitic traders who had for so long monopolized the trade of the Mediterranean. By the end of the seventh century the Ionians had not only driven the Phoenicians from Greek seas, but had cut the lines of Phoenician trade in half, dividing Carthage and the colonies of Spain and Sicily from the mother-country and permanently laming their commerce. For the Greek trader was also commonly a pirate, and probably had as little compunction in warring down Phoenician competitors as ever had Elizabethan adventurers in capturing the galleons of Spain. Hence a Phoenician-Carthaginian hatred for the men of Yavan or Ionia that profoundly influenced the counsels of Persian overlords when the day came for the subjugation of Ionia after the defeat of Croesus.

In the eleventh century, as we have seen, the Phoenician merchants were supreme in the Delta ports of Egypt, and in the whole Levant. Greek pirates such as the Tjakaray probably did not trade on any great scale: Greece was in confusion and decadence, fast falling into barbarism. The Sidonian traders took their opportunity and, taking the risk of pirates, penetrated into the Aegean and had what trade there was. They established factories here and there, one cannot doubt, and certain Semitic names, as well as the tradition of their presence, bear out the probability. Corinth, for instance, which so far as we know was not a place of importance in the Mycenaean age, and has few heroic traditions, but is definitely associated in legend with a goddess of Semitic appearance (Medeia) and a god with a Phoenician name (Melikertes), was probably a Phoenician foundation. It may well have been the Phoenician traders who first saw the importance of the geographical position of Corinth on the Isthmus and made it an emporium of commerce between the two seas. Besides the case of Corinth, we have probable Phoenician traces, either in legend or in place-names, at Thera and Kythera, where the purple-fishery had attracted them; at Samos and Adramyttion on the Asiatic coast, whose names are certainly Semitic; in Imbros and Samothrace, seats of the worship of the Kabeiroi, the Kebirim or "Great Ones"; and in Thasos and Thrace, where Phoenician miners delved for gold even as late as the seventh century.

By the eighth century, however, their general activity in the Aegean must already have come to an end. In the Iliad they are already in process of withdrawal, though they still retain their commercial monopoly. In the course of the next century, 750-650, they disappeared from Greece, and are described in the Odyssey as trading chiefly outside Greek waters. The founding of Utica and Carthage a century earlier, and the conquest of Phoenicia by the Assyrians just at this period, no doubt had much to do with this divagation of their maritime activity. And the Ionian traders, freed from Phoenician competition in their own waters, now passed beyond them into seas the monopoly of Tyre and Sidon since the destruction of the ancient Keftian power in Crete.

The stories of the first Ionian shipmen who ventured out of the Aegean are enshrined in the great poem of the Odyssey, of which the oldest parts are probably no older than the ninth century. The original poem no doubt described a voyage of an Odysseus in the Black Sea, like the legend of the Argonauts. And it was probably to the Black Sea that the earliest maritime efforts of the renascent Greeks were directed. Later, as they came more into possession of their own seas, and the western waters attracted their attention, the tales of the sea-wanderer Odysseus were transferred to the West, the traditions of an old heroic Minoan-Achaian kingdom in the western islands of Kephallenia, Ithaka, and Levkas (no doubt quite historical) were attached to the story, Odysseus became king of Ithaka, and his wanderings extended to Italy, Sicily, and the Pillars of Herakles. Generally connected with the story we also find voyages to Egypt and the Libyan coast. The verisimilitude of the Odyssean references to Egypt are remarkable, and we can almost fix to the eighth century the passage (xiv. 257 ff.) in which Odysseus, lying guilefully, invents a tale of how he raided the Delta with his companions and was taken prisoner by the Egyptians. The world of the Odyssey is that of the ninth and eighth centuries, when the Ionians had begun their oversea voyages, but before they had actually founded colonies, with the possible exception of those which are traditionally the oldest, such as those on the Propontis and that at Cumae in Italy.

The traditional dates for the first Ionian colonies in the Propontis and Euxine are perhaps not too early, but those of the Sicilian colonies must be and should be brought down somewhat. Our archaeological information hardly enables us to date the first Greek colonies in Sicily so early as the middle of the eighth century. One may feel grave doubt whether the traditional second founding of Cyzicus on the Propontis in 675 B.C. was not really the first and only one: but we have no grounds to go upon such as those (chiefly connected with the date of the Odyssey, and that of the "proto-Corinthian" pottery) that induce us to take off half a century from the traditional dates of the Western colonies. We have to take off as much or more in the case of other traditional Greek dates, such, for instance, as the Eusebian for the Lydian Ardys, and the Herodotean for Gyges.

By the end of the eighth century, however, the great Greek colonizing movement had begun, which for a time made the whole Mediterranean Greek, until Persian protection enabled the Phoenicians to recover some of their lost ground in the Levant. The changing political conditions of the Greek states, combined with, in Europe, the paucity and poverty of Greek land, and in Asia the obstacle of the foreign power of Lydia, drove thousands of colonists to seek homes in the barbarian lands which their merchant adventurers had already reached and reconnoitred. The ancient patriarchal kingship of the Iliad had largely disappeared, and in its place by the beginning of the seventh century aristocratic government had succeeded it in most of the Greek states. This development probably began earlier in rich and prosperous Ionia than on the comparatively poor mainland of Hellas, The wealthy Ionian city-nobles, deriving riches from their new over-sea commerce and their position as middlemen for the Lydians and other inlanders, shared the royal power among themselves, making each city an aristocratic republic. The political discontents and feuds to which this gave rise found its outlet in colonization, by which cadet and frondeur nobles could found with their followers cadet city-states. In most cases the going-forth was entirely friendly and peaceful, and special relations were always kept up between the daughter and the mother-city; and when the colony herself colonized, the oikist of the new foundation came from the original mother-city.

The population of Greece was perhaps, too, increasing beyond the power of Hellas to bear it. In Asia there was no means of pushing farther up the river-valleys into the interior; the compact masses of the native population and their organization under wealthy and powerful kings made this impossible. And Greece proper was no more fitted for a large population then than she is now.

So the Greeks, first the Ionians and then the Continentals, were carried for the first time out of their own lands to make a greater Greece on the shores of the Euxine and the Ionian and Tyrrhenian seas. In Sicily and the Italian Magna Graecia, living side by side with native populations less cultured but willing to learn from, and even to a certain extent to coalesce with, the newcomers, Greek states were able to develop to their full power, and, possessing wider territory and more fertile soil than the parent cities, to attain, in a very short time, wealth and prosperity far surpassing what had been possible in old Greece. The luxury of the Sybarites became a proverb; the power and arrogance of Gelon, the tyrant of Syracuse, led him to claim the leadership of Hellas against the Persian.

The winter cold and the savagery of the Scyths prevented the colonies on the northern shore of the Euxine from developing to the same extent, and the colonies on the southern coast were unable to expand for the very reasons that barred the landward progress of the Ionian cities. On the Mediterranean coast of Asia Minor no new colonies had been possible at all; though probably attempts were made, as we see from Assyrian records. Phoenicia and Assyria were too near. Cyprus already had an ancient Greek population which, however, sent out no new colonies of its own. In Cyprus, largely owing to Oriental influence, the constitutional changes of

Greece had awakened no echo: kings still ruled her cities and went forth to war in chariots in the fashion of heroic days till the end.

On the coast of Libya, inhospitable though it was, colonization was possible, and was carried out in spite of great difficulties and only in obedience to the repeated commands of the Delphic oracle, whose priests largely directed the course of many of the colonizing expeditions. The state of Cyrene, ruled by kings who alternately bore the names of Battos and Arkesilas, was prosperous, largely owing to its export of the useful silphion-plant, which brought great profit to the royal house. The proximity of Cyrene to Egypt soon brought her under the political influence of the Nile-kingdom, and from vassalage to Egypt she passed into vassalage to Persia, taking no part in the struggles and glories of true Greece, with which the Cyrenians probably had little sympathy.

The settlements in the Egyptian Delta were of a totally different order. They were not colonies at all, but purely trading-stations, exactly like the "Treaty-Ports" in China. Real Greek colonies on Egyptian territory would have been impossible: only trading establishments were possible, and the Milesian traders had succeeded in founding one, called simply the "Fort of the Milesians," in all probability as early as the beginning of the seventh century. This foundation, which was a death-blow to Phoenician trade-dominance in the Levant, was perhaps nearly as old as some of the earliest of the true colonies. At the time of its foundation, Egypt was powerless to resent the intrusion of the Ionian strangers. The Delta was ruled by the local kinglets of Herodotus' dodekarchy; the Ethiopian Pharaohs had little concern with the extreme north of their kingdom, and the shadow of Assyrian invasion paralysed the whole land. So the Milesians established their fort and mart in the forerunner of Naukratis.

When the Pharaonic kingdom was restored by Psamatik I, the Ionian fort remained untouched by the Egyptians. It was close to Sais, the new capital, and had, indeed, probably been placed there with the express permission and encouragement of the Saite princely family, who no doubt had found profit in trading the products of their estates to the Milesians. Psamatik as Pharaoh extended his full protection to the Greeks, and, wishing to avail himself of their proved prowess as warriors, as well as merchants, himself established a second trading fort on the opposite eastern edge of the Delta, to which the Greeks gave the name Daphnai: this was intended as a bulwark of defence against possible attack from Syria as well as a trading-place, and served as a base for possible warlike expeditions into Palestine.

The long siege which Psamatik laid to Ashdod was no doubt chiefly carried on by Greek soldiers from Daphnai; and its length perhaps testifies to that Greek want of skill in the attack of fortified places which we shall see exemplified in the Persian war. An Assyrian army would hardly have needed so long to reduce Ashdod. Again, it was no doubt not merely Gaza, but also Daphnai, and her formidable armour-clad garrison of Greeks that, as well as the gifts of Psamatik, stayed the flood of Scythian invasion in the early part of the king's reign.

Meanwhile the Fort of the Milesians developed into the unique factory state of Naukratis, autonomous, and governed by its own magistrates chosen by the different states which contributed to the common treasury and participated in the common city-hall, the Helleneion, just as now at Shanghai the European communities combine in club and municipality.

At Naukratis, indeed, the Greeks must have felt the tie of common Hellenism more strongly than anywhere else in the world. Ringed round by a population of stupid fellahin, fanatically devoted to their gods and to the priests who served them, and hating by immemorial tradition everything foreign and not of their world, the Greeks of Naukratis had nothing but the royal favour and that of some of the great men, beside their own strong right arms, to defend them against a possible catastrophe. And this favour depended on their help in war, and no doubt a goodly share of the trading-profits. Throughout the reigns of Psamatik I and II and Necho this favour continued, but Apries, as we shall see, overdid it, and Egyptian national sentiment compelled Amasis to confine the Greeks to Naukratis, abolishing the settlement at Daphnai.

But meanwhile the Greeks of Naukratis had been made free of Egypt by the kings. They were not confined to the "treaty-ports," but could go where they willed, apparently, and sent home marvellous tales of the strange land in which they and hundreds of other Greeks lived, bound together by the necessity of watchfulness and protection against the weird people that inhabited it. And in the same category with the Greeks came the Carians, Lydians, and other people of Asia Minor, who felt greater kinship with the Greeks than with the Semites or Egyptians. The Semites remained apart from both Greeks and Egyptians. In Egypt at this time the new opposition between young Europe and the old East first became apparent.

The colonial movement, carried on largely under the auspices of the most renowned common oracle of Greece, created Hellenedom. As Prof Bury has pointed out, by the wide diffusion of their race on the fringe of "barbarous" lands, the contrast between Greek and non-Greek was brought home to the Hellenes, and, by consequence, the community of Hellenedom also. The joint-enterprises of different states also made for Greek unity, and nowhere can we find a better example of this than at Naukratis. So the Greeks gradually came to think of themselves as one race opposed to all "barbarians," but more especially to the civilized barbarians of Egypt and the East. The inevitable conflict was approaching. But during the seventh century the opposition of Greek and Oriental had not yet become acute: the Greeks still lived on terms of friendship with the rulers of Egypt, and Greek soldiers of fortune even took service under Nebuchadrezzar in Babylonia.

The schooling of the Greeks towards unity was undertaken to some extent by the Delphic priests, who sought to reinforce by the monitions of the Pythia the unifying tendency that the consciousness of common Hellenism had brought about. There was, of course, no thought of political unity: that would have been totally opposed to the whole genius of the race, and only possible had it denied its own ideals and adopted the very thing that it abominated as most un-Greek, the imperial despotism of the Easterns. The Sacred War (about 590) shews the reverence in which the Delphic oracle was now regarded by the whole of Greece, and the pan-hellenic vengeance which fell on Krisa testified to the unity that the Greeks could feel when insult was offered to the gods by one of their own numbers. A century later the strength of pan-hellenic feeling was to be tested to the full, not by a single Greek town, but by the whole embattled force of the emperor of Asia, in whose armies conquered Assyria, Babylonia, and Egypt marched but: as subject tribes. Hellenic patriotism won through, despite the cowards: but political unity did not come after that tremendous trial, nor was it in the mind of the nation that it should. Athens was punished for her unification of the maritime Greeks: Sparta for her attempt at land-hegemony. The unity of the Greeks was strongest in diversity. And when the Macedonian "unified" them, they died.

Leagues, whether temporary or lasting, between the cities meant no subjection to any one of them till the days of Athens and the Confederation of Delos. Such leagues were usually partly religious, partly commercial, and were often very ancient. One of the oldest religious leagues was the Amphiktiony which was formed (originally at Anthela) to protect Delphi; and of the commercial-religious leagues the oldest known is that of Kalaureia. The states which formed this alliance combined to make common offerings to the sea-god on the island of Kalaureia, off the Argolic coast by Troezen, a very central position for the purpose, and, then as now, an admirable little port. The original members of the league seem to have been cities of the Argolic and Saronic Gulfs only; Prasiai, Nauplia, Hermione, Troezen, Epidauros, Megara, Aigina, and Athens. As the colonizing movement went on, commerce between the eastern and western Greeks became ever more and more vigorous, and the Kalaureate League developed. The port of Boeotian Orchomenos, Anthedon on the Euripus, was admitted to the league (Orchomenos, as overlord of Anthedon, offering), and now the states of the league combined with Eretria and with Miletos, the ally of Megara, friend of Athens, the pioneer of Ionian oversea commerce and colonization, to control a sea trade-route from east to west, from Miletos to the Cyclades, where Faros was an important member, to the Euripus and the Saronic Gulf, then by way of the Peloponnesian coast round to the Ionian Sea. A land route from Anthedon by Orchomenos to the Corinthian Gulf no doubt supplemented the all-sea route. Eretria became the central point and mainspring of this league.

Commercial jealousies soon resulted in the establishment of a rival commercial route, with its centre in the city of Chalkis, the chief foe of Eretria. Samos, the rival of Miletos, Naxos, the rival of Paros, and Corinth, the rival of Aigina, combined with Chalkis to exploit a route by the Isthmus of Corinth, across which ships could be hauled from the Eastern to the Western Sea. The favourable commercial position of Corinth soon assured the predominance of the Chalkidian alliance in the West; the Eretrian colony of Korkyra was taken, and thereafter only one or two colonies were established in Italy and Sicily by the cities of the rival league. In the East, however, the Eretrian League well maintained its position; Miletos and Megara dominated the Hellespontine region. About the middle of the seventh century, however, broke out a direct conflict between the two Euboean centres of the rival leagues, Eretria and Chalkis. This, the Lelantine War, ended disastrously for Eretria, and her defeat reacted upon her allies. Samos now came more to the front; Corinth increased rapidly in wealth and power, while Aigina and Megara declined, and Athens (since her synoikismos one of the largest states of Greece) sank into temporary obscurity. In Egypt the effect was to throw open the factories of the Milesians to their Samian rivals, and at Naukratis we find the Samians by the side of the Milesians and Aiginetans. Only the eastern members of the Chalkidic League were interested in the Levantine trade: Corinth traded solely with the West.

Meanwhile the class-divisions of the Greek cities, accentuated by the rule of the aristocratic and timocratic oligarchies, were becoming fused to some extent by the common subjection of all, both noble and simple, to the tyrants. Rulers like Periander, Thrasyboulos, and the Peisistratids formed a necessary transition to the democracy, which was finally established in Athens by Kleisthenes, and to which, well led, Athens owed her greatness and Persia largely her defeat. Sparta underwent none of these radical constitutional changes, but her constitution changed, nevertheless. Her two kings still ruled Lacedaemon, but, unless they were unusually forceful men like the first Kleomenes, they could do little in despite of the checking authority of the Ephors, whose institution was traditionally assigned to Lycurgus in the eighth century, but was probably of later date. Argos was ruled by kings whose power was less trammelled. However, only one of them, Pheidon, was a man of sufficient force to make his state respected for a time in Greece. But the tyrants who came in the sixth century had all to be men of energy and force, or they fell. And while the fact of their rule stirred up democratic feeling, their love of splendour and patronage of the arts of civilization and commercial instinct greatly forwarded the rise of the new culture of Greece.

We see from the Homeric poems that the old tradition of civilization had never died out in Ionia, whither the expelled Achaians and Ionians had carried it. And it was in Ionia that Greek civilization was reborn, under the influence of the Oriental "mixed culture" that held sway in the inland kingdoms of Asia Minor and had been borne from Syria to the Aegean by the Phoenician traders. From the Phoenicians the Greeks took over the invention of the alphabet, and from the Lydians, it was said, that of coined money (though we may well doubt whether this was not really an Ionian invention first devised for the Lydian kings). In Ionia and the isles the debased Late Mycenaean ceramic was transformed into a new style, characterized by a scheme of decoration very Oriental in feeling, which, when art began to raise its head again in Greece proper, was carried thither, and displaced the harsh geometric style of the mainland potters. From Corinth, which seems to have been the main focus of distribution, the new ware was carried to the Corinthian colonies in the West. At Syracuse the earliest Greek vases, which must be almost coeval with the period of colonization, shew an interesting style of transition from the geometric style to this "Proto-Corinthian," as we call it. The further development of this style, and an elimination of its Oriental elements, quickly followed, and the Rhodian style in the islands, the Laconian-Cyrenaic at Cyrene and Sparta, the Daphniote and Naukratite in Egypt and largely under Egyptian influence, carry on the history of Greek pottery to the sixth century and the beginnings of the classical style of Greek vase-painting in Attica. The recent excavations at Sparta have shewn that in ceramic art the Dorian of the seventh and sixth centuries was by no means so inartistic as he has commonly been supposed to have been, and a practical identity of the Early Laconian styles with the Cyrenaic seems well assured, though it is by no means certain yet that the Laconian pottery was not of Cyrenaic origin. In any case the style was ultimately of Ionian origin; the Spartans were indebted for their early ceramic art to the Ionians.

At the same time the arts of metal-working and sculpture were revived, the former with great splendour. Most interesting examples of small metal-work of the eighth and seventh centuries were discovered in the course of the British Museum excavations at Ephesus in 1904-5. The relation of some of this gold-work to that of the Mycenaean tombs at Enkomi in Cyprus is of great interest, and is a proof of the permanence of the Mycenaean art-tradition in Ionia. Some of the finest relics of early metal-work yet discovered, of Ionian origin and shewing the typical Ionian use of Oriental designs, has been found in Crete, in the votive offerings from the cave of Zeus on Mount Ida, now in the Candia Museum. Crete too has yielded monuments of the most archaic Greek sculpture to Italian excavators at Prinias, a shrine on the eastern slope of Ida. They shew work crude and clumsy enough. Sculpture was slow in development at first, and seems to have received its great impetus from the Ionian connexion with Egypt. Ionian sculptors are said, no doubt with truth, to have visited Egypt, and we see in the works of the earliest sculptors of Greece a strong reflection of the hardness and stiffness of the Egyptian work of the Psammeticid period. Even the curious conventional "archaic smile," which is so characteristic of the early Greek statues of the renascence, is directly traceable to Egypt, where it was equally characteristic of a certain type of Saite work. And everywhere in Greece splendid temples began to rise in honour of the gods, and the architecture of Hellas was born. In Ionia Oriental influences, often specifically Hittite-Assyrian in character, are seen, and the Ionian pillar-capital derived its immediate origin from the Hittites of Boghaz Kyoi. In Greece proper and in the West the sterner

Doric column, derived from a simple wooden original, was more popular. In it (except for the fact that the tapering of the shaft is in the reverse direction) we see a strong reminiscence of the old Minoan column of Knossos, which like it had no base, and was weighted above with a massive swelling capital and abacus. The Early Doric columns, as at Corinth and Paestum, have enormous capitals of this type, which later on grew more restrained in girth, and shew the new Greek sense of proportion in their relation to the size of the column. The revival of the clumsy, overweighted Minoan capital soon disappears, and finally in the fifth century the grand Doric pillars of the Parthenon mark the apogee of Greek architecture, as its reliefs mark the apogee of Greek sculpture, now entirely freed from archaic clumsiness and Oriental convention.

When the Parthenon was built Greece had defeated the Persian, and had attained full consciousness of her superiority to the barbarian in culture as in arms. But a century earlier her art had seemed to shew no superiority to that of the Orientals. At the end of the seventh century Ashurbanipal's sculptors at Nineveh were representing horses which the frieze of the Parthenon can hardly equal, and lions which no sculptor has ever surpassed in careful observation and truthful delineation. Ages before, Egypt had produced portrait sculpture which no Greek or modern can rival for fidelity and force. But yet already a century or more before Pheidias one can see in Greek art the one thing that was to make it the first true unified art in the world, the sense of proportion. Truth for an Assyrian or Egyptian could be exercised in the case of a horse or a lion, or (in a simple age) a human portrait. But if a god or a king was to be represented proportion was not considered, and even an ordinary human being could not, though his size might be correct, be shewn with fidelity to nature. Similarly in imperial Assyria, as in imperial Egypt (the renascent Egypt of the Saites had better taste), the houses of gods and kings, though their detail might be good, had to be enormous and entirely disproportionate in total size to the scale of its ornamentation. The Greek temple was small, but looked more splendid than any tower of Babel: it was built with a sense of proportion. The Greek sculptor and vase-painter gave to their deities a proportionately more majestic stature than to ordinary mankind: they did not represent them twice the size or in any unnatural guise or in accordance with any barbarous convention that made the semblance of truth impossible. Kings were ordinary mortals, and were so represented. This was the new spirit in art that the Greeks, already before the Persian wars, had brought into the world. And it was a new spirit not only in art but in civilization generally.

Knowing what we do of the psychological peculiarities of the different races of mankind, it is perhaps not an illegitimate speculation to wonder whence the Greeks inherited this sense of proportion in their whole mental outlook. The feeling of the Hellenes for art in general was surely inherited from their forebears on the Aegean, not the Indo-European, side. The feeling for naturalistic art, for truth of representation, may have come from the Aegeans, but the equally characteristic Aegean love of the crude and bizarre was not inherited: the sense of proportion inhibited it. In fact, we may ascribe this sense to the Aryan element in the Hellenic brain, to which must also be attributed the Greek political sense, the idea of the rights of the folk and of the individual in it. The Mediterranean possessed the artistic sense without the sense of proportion: the Aryan had little artistic sense but had the sense of proportion and justice, and with it the political sense. The result of the fusion of the two races we see in the true canon of taste and beauty in all things that had become the ideal of the Greeks, and was through them to become the ideal of mankind. The sense of clarity and proportion permeated the whole cultured mind of the nation. We see it already in the seventh and sixth centuries in the arts of speech and song which now asserted their power over men, when the great lyric poets, whose inspiration was first gained in the tense struggle between the aristocrats and the demos, shed lustre on the names of the demos-born princes who fostered and protected them at their courts. We see it in the work of the Aisymnetai and lawgivers such as Pittakos, Zaleukos, and Charondas, who now heralded the development of reasonable law in the West. In politics we see it in the Solonian reform of the constitution of Athens in the first decade of the sixth century, a reform which for the first time in the world's history proclaimed justice for the common people, and firmly planted the democratic ideal (with all the defects of its qualities) in the soil of Athens. Finally we see it as clear and logical thought in the realms of abstract speculation, where the Greeks were already conquering their eternal place of priority and pre-eminence. So far as we know, the human intelligence first reached in sixth-century Greece the height which, lost for a thousand years during the Dark Ages, it has now since the Renaissance again attained. The contrast between even the average Greek mind and that of the Oriental or Egyptian of the sixth century B.C. must have been enormous: the gulf between the Greek philosopher or poet and the most learned of Babylon or Egypt, almost impassable. The somnolent priestly antiquarians of the Nile-land could communicate nothing more tangible to the Greek inquirer than the fact of the passing of innumerable generations of "men and the sons of men." Yet this fact of antiquity impressed the Greek because he was intelligent: he realized his youth in the world; but a few generations back his ancestors had been heroes, perhaps demigods, in the mist of the dark age of barbarism from which his race had but lately emerged. So it may be that Thales and Pythagoras really visited the Nile-land, as did many others of their countrymen at the time, and tried to gain some wisdom from the Egyptian priests, but they must soon have found Egyptian religious and "philosophical" ideas utterly unreasonable and useless to them: their own thought, even when it is mystical enough (as in the case of what we know of the Pythagorean teaching), has little in it of the barbarous confusion characteristic of Egyptian religious ideas: it is well-ordered and logical, and in it we see the final triumph of the European soul in the new Greece. The Greek philosopher created the disciplined mind of Europe, which rules the world to-day. From religion too Oriental ideas were kept far apart, and Semitic religious fanaticism was never admitted to it, though the Greek found hardly repellent, rather amusing in fact, the drunken orgies of the Aryan wine-god from Thrace and his crew. In the fury of the wine-intoxication there was also certainly something divine and mysterious. Mysteries he did not refuse, but they must be reverently and sanely mystical, as probably were those of Eleusis in comparison with those of Egypt. So "the early Hellene asserted his spiritual independence of the East."

Meanwhile in Egypt the renovation of the kingdom produced no real renascence. The archaism of art and government-titles, which sought to go back to the models of the Old Kingdom, was but a fashion, and meant nothing. The results of the decadent Empire and of the Ethiopian rule remained. Though the kingdom was reunified politically, the old division between North and South which had been revived by the Theban Priest-Kings continued in a peculiar political arrangement which first appeared under the Ethiopians: Thebes was ruled by a princess of the royal house as High-Priestess of Amen, bearing the title "Praiser of the God." The great queen Amenartas bore it under the Ethiopians, and under the Saites the best-known priestess-queen of Thebes is Nitakrit (Nitokris) in the reign of Psamatik I; it was her name that was transferred in Greek tales to the courtesan Rhodopis. Archaism had no power to abolish this political inheritance from the Ethiopians. The renovation of the kingdom was real in that it brought to the nation a prosperity that had been unknown since the time of the XXth Dynasty: the evidence of royal and general wealth is undeniable, and is best seen in the works of the Saite kings in the temples, especially those of the Delta, which reach their culmination of splendour under Amasis, just before the catastrophe which finally destroyed Egyptian independence. And it was this very prosperity, which rested on no real defensive power, but merely on the spears of Greek and Carian mercenaries, that was Egypt's ruin, the bait that drew the conqueror to her.

None in the seventh century, while Assyria still stood, erect though swaying, a corpse in armour, could have foreseen a conquest of rich and magnificent Egypt by the barbarous mountaineers of Elam and Anshan, still less the eventual struggle between Persia and Greece. Yet Persia came to the conflict merely as the heir of Lydia, whose kings, free from the fear of Assyria though still obsequious to her, had turned their faces to the West and aspired to subdue the Ionian cities to their will. But for the invasion and long-continued raids of the Kimmerians, which afflicted Phrygians, Lydians, and Ionians alike, they might have succeeded. After the fear of the Kimmerians was removed, Miletus, then the first of all the states of Ionia, had to bear the brunt of long wars with Sadyattes and Alyattes of Lydia, which only came to an end after the great battle on the Halys in 585 B.C., in which Lydia and Media came face to face. Behind the Mede stood his heir, the Persian, but none saw him. Croesus of Lydia, proud of his wealth and power, first made war on the Ionians, but soon the overthrow of Astyages by Cyrus brought his schemes of conquest to an end, and hurriedly he sought Greek friendship and alliance. But events, and the Persian, marched too quickly for him. And meanwhile, the continental Greeks continued to the end oblivious to the danger to their budding civilization which might arise from the East. That the Orientals were not all weaklings who required defending by Greek mercenaries they might have learnt from the struggle of Miletus with Lydia; but they took no thought of their Eastern march which had been so well defended by their Ionian brethren, whom they despised as themselves half-Oriental. Sparta had no thought but to impose her domination on the Peloponnese, Corinth no thought but for her commerce and the preservation of her colonies in dependence upon her, Athens no thought for anything but her local politics and constitution-making. Still, the iron wars of Sparta gave Greece the warriors who defended Thermopylae and nerved the Greeks to resist Persia in the open field, while the revolutions and constitutions of Athens gave her the democratic spirit which stood fast for Hellenic freedom against alien subjection, and the splendid culture of the Peisistratid age, as we know it from the sculptures in the Acropolis Museum and from the tradition of its literary energy, gave her citizens the feeling that their city was indeed no mean one, and fully worthy to be a protagonist for Hellas. Corinth, swayed by baser ideals than either of the other two, came worst of the three chief continental states out of the trial.

So the Greeks stood, energetic indeed, and doughty in war, but divided in mind, incapable of unity against a common foe, and, except the Ionians, ignorant of his power, at the moment when Cyrus destroyed the kingdom of Croesus, Egypt, incapable of action, could only watch the death that was coming upon her. Babylon already lay dead, Assyria was dead and forgotten.

We turn now to the events in the East which led up to the final catastrophe of the old order, and the new era of the world's history which began upon the day of Salamis.

CHAPTER XII: BABYLON AND THE MEDES AND PERSIANS: FROM THE FALL OF NINEVEH TO THE DEFEAT OF XERXES (606-479 B.C.)

I. Babylon and Egypt

AFTER the fall of Nineveh, the Assyrian claims to empire in Syria and the West naturally fell to Babylon, while the Medes took the Ninevite territory and the lands north and east of Tigris. Southern Assyria and Northern Mesopotamia were occupied by Nabopolassar, who ruled unchallenged to the bend of the Euphrates. Beyond the river, however, Pharaoh Necho, easily destroying Josiah and his army in the historic field of Megiddo, had seized the whole of Syria and Palestine, and a conflict was inevitable if Babylon intended to make good her claims to the inheritance of Asshur. Two years after the fall of Nineveh the collision between Egypt and Babylon took place, at Carchemish, and the motley host of Necho, composed of all the strange African subjects of Egypt with a (probably untrustworthy) "stiffening" of Greek and Carian mercenaries, went down before the Babylonians, led by Nebuchadrezzar, Nabopolassar's energetic son. Routed and disorganized, Pharaoh's host hurried back to Egypt, abandoning all the conquests of five years before, pursued by Nebuchadrezzar, who halted only on the borders of Egypt, where the news of his father's death reached him. This decided him to stop his advance, and return to Babylon to secure his succession to the throne, which, however, was undisputed. The whole of Syria as far as the border of Egypt became Babylonian, and the rule of Nebuchadrezzar was accepted everywhere but in Judah, where Jehoiakim, the nominee of Necho, had been left undisturbed as king. He paid tribute at first, but then, carried away by the religious fanaticism which Josiah had called into being, king, priests, and people united in a mad defiance of Babylon, in spite of the vigorous warnings of the prophet Jeremiah. The first capture of Jerusalem by Nebuchadrezzar followed (596), and Jeconiah or Jehoiachin, the young son and successor of Jehoiakim, was carried into captivity, with a portion of the population.

The revolt was probably not inspired in any way by the Egyptians. Necho was busy with great plans of internal development, and especially with the carrying out of his project to unite the Nile with the Red Sea by a canal: he had no desire to interfere further in Asia, and left Jeconiah to his fate.

Nor was Psamatik II (593-589 B.C.), the successor of Necho, desirous of war with Babylon. He was too much interested in Nubia to think of Asia. During his short reign serious attempts were made to recover part of the old southern dominion from the power of the Napatan kings. The Greek and Carian mercenaries were, as usual, employed to stiffen the native troops, and we have a record of them and their officers engaged on the expedition in a Greek inscription cut on the leg of one of the great colossi of Rameses II at Abu Simbel. This tells the passer-by that "when King Psamatichos came to Elephantine, those who sailed with Psamatichos, son of Theokles, wrote this. Now they came above Kerkis as far as the river let them go up. And Potasimto led the foreigners, and Amasis the Egyptians. And Archon the son of Amoibichos, and Peleqos the son of nobody, wrote this (lit. us)." Signatures follow: "Elesibios the Teian. Telephos wrote me, the Ialysian. Pabis the Qolophonian ... with Psamatichos ... what time the king sent the army for the first time." It is not impossible that this expedition was that ascribed by Herodotus to Psammetichos I. The historian says that Psammetichos pursued into Nubia a body of 240,000 native troops (Asmakh) who, tired of their three years' service at Syene, had deserted and were flying to Ethiopia. The inscription is certainly of the time of Psamatik II, and it seems quite possible that Herodotus ascribed to the great Psamatik's reign an event that really took place in the time of his less-known successor.

Haa-Ab-Ra Uahabra (589-565 B.C.), the Hophra of the Hebrews and Apries of the Greeks, is said by Herodotus to have been the son of Psamatik II. He was a warlike prince, but was not gifted with over-much wisdom. Nebuchadrezzar had kept the peace inviolate since the battle of Carchemish, and had employed his energies solely in the erection of his magnificent temples and other works at Babylon. It is possible that Apries took this military inactivity to mean powerlessness; he determined to make another bid for empire in Asia.

The Phoenician cities do not seem formally to have acknowledged the overlordship of Nebuchadrezzar, and, it may be, were more disposed to admit Egyptian than Babylonian dominion, Apries therefore took Phoenicia as his starting-point. Sidon submitted to him without striking a blow; whether Tyre also submitted peacefully or (probably in traditional opposition to Sidon) risked a sea-fight, is uncertain. In any case Tyre joined with Sidon in stirring up the embers of revolt in Judah, and King Zedekiah, relying upon the energy of Apries, gave way to the insensate war party. The gloomy prophecies of Jeremiah, who had no belief in the real power of Egypt, were disregarded, and the tribute due to Babylon was refused.

Nebuchadrezzar at once moved westward and appeared in North Syria (587 B.C.). There he personally remained, with his headquarters at Riblah on the Orontes, while a portion of his army marched south to the final conquest of Judah. He remained at Riblah in order to be able to meet in person any possible Egyptian attack from Phoenicia while his army was engaged in the South. Apries, however, had no intention of risking an attack on the redoubtable Babylonian king in his own chosen position, and returned by sea to Egypt, whence he advanced through the Negeb to the relief of Jerusalem, now being besieged. On his approach the siege was temporarily raised while the Babylonians moved south to meet him. Whether he was actually defeated or simply retired before the threatening Babylonian advance we do not know. He returned to his own country; Jerusalem fell, and Zedekiah the king was taken to Riblah, where, in the presence of the overlord whom he had betrayed, his sons were slain before his eyes, which were then put out. The majority of the Jewish nation was carried into captivity, only a miserable remnant being left behind, which, after the murder of Gedaliah, the governor appointed by Nebuchadrezzar, emigrated, under the leadership of Johanan the captain and Jeremiah the prophet, to Egypt, where Apries established them in the "king's house at Tahpanhes," the fortress which dominated the foreign settlement of Daphnai.

Tyre was now besieged, and the siege was prosecuted In a desultory fashion for no less than thirteen years. Finally, in 573, a treaty was made by which Ithobaal the king acknowledged the supremacy of Nebuchadrezzar. Sidon had submitted long before, no doubt.

Apries had afforded no help to the beleaguered Tyrians Probably no troops, either Egyptian or mercenary, could have been got to follow him against the Babylonians. We hear of a military revolt of the mercenary troops at Syene, which was quelled by the governor Nesuhor, and at the end of his reign he sent an Egyptian army against the Greeks of Cyrene, the disastrous defeat of which brought his absolute power to an end.

A Libyan chief named Adikran had begged Egyptian help against the Cyrenaeans, who were dispossessing his people of their lands. The

Egyptian military class, hating and ignorantly despising the Greeks and other foreign soldiers who were so high in favour at court, clamoured to be allowed to help the Libyans. Their annihilation by the Cyrenaeans turned the fury of the anti-foreign party at home against the king, who was no doubt suspected of having sent his warriors to their death by the advice of his foreign friends. A nationalist rebellion broke out, and a capable Egyptian general named Aahmes (Amasis), who had risen from the ranks, was sent by the king against the rebels, probably with the idea that being an Egyptian, they would obey him. They hailed him, however, as king; for Apries had become so hated by the common people on account of his foreign predilections that they were prepared to go the length of dethroning him. This, however, was not to happen. Apries, who had now alienated the nobles by cruelly punishing one of their number who returned unsuccessful from an attempt to treat with Amasis, was deserted by all, and Amasis was made co-regent with him (569 B.C.). The king remained in seclusion at Sais, while Amasis took over the actual government of the country.

But the fiery Apries could not brook control for long. Three years later he fled suddenly from Sai's, and gathering round him a large force of Greek and Carian mercenary freebooters, prepared to attack Amasis. A battle ensued, of which we have two accounts, one contemporary, given by Amasis in an official inscription, the other by Herodotus a century later. Both agree that Apries was completely defeated and afterwards slain, but while Amasis states that he was slain by his own followers as he slept in the cabin of the boat in which he had fled, Herodotus tells us that he was handed over by Amasis to "the Egyptians," who strangled him. Very possibly the Herodotean account is near the truth: it is more probable that Apries was killed at any rate with the connivance of Amasis than that he was murdered by his own men.

It is evident that his conduct in allying himself with the marauding foreigners of the North had put Apries entirely beyond the pale. He was regarded as an utter renegade, and it was only owing to the respect due to one who had been pharaoh that he was, as Amasis and Herodotus both testify, buried in royal state.

It has often been supposed that about the time of the conflict between Amasis and Apries (in 567 B.C.), Egypt was invaded by Nebuchadrezzar, who is even supposed to have marched as far as the First Cataract, This supposition rests on a misunderstanding of an inscription, and there is no proof of any such invasion. Jeremiah's prophecy that the Babylonian king would set up his tent on the platform outside the "royal house" at Tahpanhes cannot be taken (on the principle that the prophecies were made after the event) as proof that Nebuchadrezzar ever did anything of the kind. Jeremiah's knowledge of the world and the times had rightly served him in his predictions as to the futility of the Jewish resistance to Babylon; and it was natural that, with the knowledge of the Assyrian conquest of Egypt a century before, he should have prophesied the sequel, a coming subjection of Egypt to Nebuchadrezzar. But in the absence of contemporary proof from Egyptian or Babylonian inscriptions we cannot assume that the expected invasion ever took place. It is unlikely, for Nebuchadrezzar was growing old, and may have been afflicted with madness before the end. At any rate, in 562 he died. His successors, Amil-Marduk (Evil-merodach), Nergal-shar-usur (Neriglissar),and Labashi-Marduk(Labassoarchos), were undistinguished and short-lived. With the last, a boy who was allowed to reign only a few months, the Chaldaean dynasty of Nabopolassar came to an end (B.C. 556). The priests of Babylon, to whom the wars of Nebuchadrezzar seem never to have been very palatable, now themselves selected a king after their own hearts, the pious and peaceful archaeologist and amateur of ancient records, Nabuna'id (Nabonidus), son of Nabu-balatsu-ikbi, who was probably a wealthy merchant.

All the kings of Nabopolassar's dynasty had been great builders, of palaces as well as temples, and Nebuchadrezzar had been the greatest of them. The temples E-sagila at Babylon and E-zida at Borsippa were rebuilt by him, but his greatest work was the building of the walls of Babylon. He was primarily a soldier, and military works appealed to him more than religious. The plan was due to Nabopolassar, who had begun the work. Imgur-Bel, the ancient wall of the inner town, was completed, and the huge outer wall, Nimitti-Bel, was constructed round the whole vast city. Then at one point a great citadel was formed by the construction between the two walls, and connecting them, of a mighty platform of brick, on which rose a seemingly impregnable fortress. In addition to this isolated covering walls and ditches were constructed outside the great outer wall. The king also constructed new streets and secular buildings within the city, which now reached its apogee of splendour, and was the greatest in the world.

Nabonidus carried on the tradition of temple building and repairing. His archaeological instincts led him to conduct researches into the history of the temples which he repaired, and in inscriptions he commemorates the discovery of a foundation-stone of Naram-Sin or of Shagarakti-buriash with as much ceremony as an Assyrian king would have commemorated the defeat of an enemy. His knowledge of the period at which the early kings had lived was not always correct, and the guesswork dates which he seems at times to have ascribed to them (the instance of Naram-Sin is certain) have much misled modern historians.

The chief temples rebuilt by him were the sun-temple, E-babbar, at Sippar; the temple of Anunitum, E-ulbar, also at Sippar; and E-khulkhul, the far-away shrine of Sin at Harran in Northern Mesopotamia, which had been ruined by the Scyths or Medes half a century before. The king was entirely absorbed in architecture and archaeology, and left the civil and military direction of the empire very largely to his son Belsharutsur (Belsharezer or Belshazzar), who in the Hebrew accounts appears as "king" of Babylon.

2. The Medes and Persians

The peace was kept unbroken with the Medes, who do not appear to have attempted to attack their old allies. North of Babylonia the Tigris formed the boundary between the two empires; north of Assyria the boundary probably ran near the modern Diarbekr to the Euphrates, the right bank of which, perhaps as far north as the district of Malatiya, was now in the possession of the independent king, the Syennesis, who ruled Cilicia. His frontier with the Medes probably ran across the plateau of the Uzun Yaila to the Halys, which from Argaeus to the Black Sea separated the empire of Astyages from that of Alyattes of Lydia, as of old it had separated the "White Syrians" or Hittites from the Phrygians.

This boundary had been won by the Medes after a severe struggle with the Lydians (591-585 B.C.). The kingdom of Gyges had been severely shaken by the ravages of the Kimmerians, and Ardys and Sadyattes, his successors, had spent their strength in ceaseless attacks on the Greek cities of the Aegean coast. Accordingly, when Kyaxares attacked him, Alyattes, the successor of Sadyattes, was unable to retain his dominion beyond the Halys, The famous battle of May 28, 585 B.C., which was interrupted by a total eclipse of the sun, was followed by a treaty which settled the Halys as the frontier of the two kingdoms, negotiated by the Syennesis of Cilicia and Nebuchadrezzar of Babylon, whose mediation had been sought by the belligerents. The kingdom of Urartu was finally extinguished, and absorbed into the Median dominions.

Kyaxares now died, an old man, and was succeeded by his son Astyages, the Ishtuwigu of the Babylonian inscriptions, who reigned till 550, when his kingdom was taken by Cyrus the Persian. How far we may trust the stories of his ferocity it is impossible to say, but at all events the oldest Greek authority, Aeschylos, gives him a good character, and evidently regarded him as a great and dignified monarch. Under him the rule which the Indo-Europeans of Iran, swarming westwards like their ancestors the Mitannians and Kassites a thousand years before, had imposed on Armenia and Anatolia was consolidated; and when Cyrus deposed him and a Persian ruling house succeeded the Median no disintegration of the new empire took place. The Persians were of the same race as the Iranian Medes, their languages were almost identical; the accession of Cyrus was but a revolution in the ruling dynasty which in no way affected the empire. For this reason it seems unlikely that Cyrus was, as has often been supposed, of non-Persian race, and that Darius Hystaspis was the first genuinely Persian king. Cyrus is called king of Anshan in Elam by the Babylonians, but it does not follow that he was a non-Aryan Elamite in race: probably the Achaemenid house was purely Persian in blood, though ruling over non-Aryan Elamites. Also, it is hardly probable that if Cyrus had not been a Persian, he would have been known, as he was, to the Greeks as specifically "the Persian," and the succession of his house have been regarded, as it was, as a substitution for a Median of a Persian dynasty.

The Persians were the southernmost of the Aryan tribes of Iran. How long before the time of Cyrus they had established themselves eastward of Elam we do not know, or whether they were identical with the people of "Parsua" who are mentioned at a much earlier period as living in the Zagros region; if they were, they must have moved considerably to the eastward in the intervening period. We have no knowledge of how far eastward the dominion of the old Elamite kingdom extended, or whether Elamite tribes were dispossessed by the Persians from the land in which they founded their national capital Pasargadae, corresponding to the Agbatana of the Medes. Evidently the exhaustion of Elam in the struggle with Ashurbanipal gave them the opportunity to extend their dominion westward, and so we now find their ancient capital Susa in the possession of the Persian prince Cyrus, who was soon to make it the capital of the Eastern world.

The founder of the Persian kingdom in Anshan seems to have been Chishpish, the Teispes of the Greeks, son of Hakhamanish or Achaimenes,

Teispes must have reigned during the last quarter of the seventh century. The Babylonian annals tell us that Cyrus was the son of Kambuzia (Cambyses l), son of Kurush (Cyrus l), son of Shishpish, all of whom are given the title of "great king, king of Anshan." Darius Hystaspis, in the great inscription of Behistun or Bisitun, tells us that "My father is Vishtaspa (Hystaspes); the father of Vishtaspa was Arshama (Arsames); the father of Arshama was Ariyaramna (Ariaramnes); the father of Ariyaramna was Chishpish (Teispes); the father of Chishpish was Hakhamanish (Achaimenes)." That is to say, both Cyrus and Darius were descended from a common ancestor, Teispes son of Achaimenes, and since Darius belonged to the same generation as Cambyses (II), son of the great Cyrus, the number of generations agrees in both lines. Then Darius goes on to say: "Eight of my race were kings before; I am the ninth. In two lines (duvitaparnam) have we been kings." Evidently this refers to the two lines of descent, that of Cyrus and that of Darius himself, in the Achaemenid family from Teispes. We cannot suppose, on the authority of the genealogical speech put into the mouth of Xerxes by Herodotus, that an earlier Cyrus, an earlier Cambyses, and an earlier Teispes reigned between Teispes (the father of Ariaramnes) and Achaimenes, and thus make nine generations of kings before Darius in one line, in face of the direct statement of Darius himself at Bisitun.

It is evident that Darius counts his father Hystaspes as a king, whether from filial reverence or, as is very probable, because Hystaspes really was to all intents and purposes king of a distant portion of the Persian kingdom, the lands of Parthia and Hyrcania (Parthva and Varkana), the modern Khorassan, which he still governed under the rule of his son. There is no need for us to suppose the existence of two Teispes, three Cyrus, and three Cambyses, any more than that of two Kyaxares.

The mention of Teispes as the first king of Anshan by the Babylonians shews that he was the first Persian to rule in Elam, and he obviously seized that country at the death of Ashurbanipal, if not before. Achaimenes probably ruled Persia proper only. Whether it was he or a later king who brought Parthia and Hyrcania under Persian dominion we do not know, but it is probable that Cyrus already disposed of the forces of the north-eastern lands as well as of Persia and Elam before he attacked Media.

We need not suppose that Astyages was engaged in any war with Babylonia when Cyrus attacked him. Of the details of the ensuing war we only know that the Median king defended himself energetically, but was eventually defeated and handed over to the conqueror owing to the treachery of the Median chief Harpagos (550 B.C.).

The deposition of Astyages was evidently received without much opposition by the Medes, and the great Median noble house of Harpagos actively supported the usurper, who made little distinction between Medes and Persians, welding them into a people of which the two component parts were not more distinct than are Scots and English, Bavarians and Prussians, at the present day. The Greeks could speak of a Persian king or say that their traitors "medized," and call their temporary conquerors Medes or Persians indiscriminately.

It has been supposed that about this time lived in Iran the great religious reformer Zoroaster, and that the impulse which drove the Persians under Cyrus, Cambyses, and Darius to the conquest of the world was in its essence a spiritual enthusiasm inspired by the teaching of Zoroaster. Certainly tradition places the life of Zoroaster in the sixth century B.C. According to one tradition he must have been born about 599 B.C., and commenced his teaching, when forty years old, in Khorassan. There, at Kishmar, in the district of Turshiz, not far south-west of Mashhad, he planted, to commemorate the conversion of King Vishtaspa (Gushtasp), the famous cypress tree which was said to have lived until 861 A.D., when the khalif el-Mutawakkil had it felled and taken to Samarra on the Tigris, to be used in the construction of his palace. Now Vishtaspa (Hystaspes), the father of Darius, was historically the ruler of Khorassan (and Darius seems to call him king), so that the tradition may well refer to him, and he may have been converted by Zoroaster, who, if the traditional date be accepted, was not seventy years old at the accession of the son of Hystaspes. The influence of Zoroaster may perhaps be traced in the enthusiasm of Darius for truth and in his hatred of lies; "the lie" which he so constantly denounces in the inscription of Bisitun may well be the old unreformed Magianism which again and again strove to raise its head against the Zoroastrian reform. In any case he was probably the first strongly Zoroastrian king. It may then be that the doctrine of the prophet of Khorassan did, if he really lived at this time, have something to do with the enthusiasm and energy that gave the Persians in the sixth century the empire of the Eastern world.

At any rate the Zoroastrian reform must be dated before the time of Darius and probably long after the old days when, as we have seen, the Mitannians venerated the old Aryan deities, Indra, Varuna, and the

Nasatya-twins (Agvins) as their chief gods. Under Darius we find the Zoroastrian Ahura-Mazda the chief Iranian deity, and in the A vesta Indra and the Agvins (Naonhaithya) have become daevas or evil demons. Herodotus's description of the religion of the Persians in his day is a description of Zoroastrianism: he specially notes the peculiar Zoroastrian custom of allowing the bodies of the dead to be torn by birds and dogs. The Magi whom he describes are Zoroastrian priests, but their peculiarly powerful status in Persia was an inheritance from pre-Zoroastrian days. No Aryan, even before the separation of Indians and Iranians, had been able to sacrifice to the gods without the presence of the magus, the Indian Brahman (Lat. flamen); the magus was the embodiment of all wisdom and the sole interpreter of the gods. It was natural that so powerful a priesthood should come into conflict with the powerful Achaemenian kings, who were little inclined to tolerate opposition to their will, and we shall see that in the reign of Cambyses the royal and priestly authorities did come into collision. It is difficult to see whether Cyrus and Cambyses or the Magi who conspired against Cambyses represent Zoroastrianism: if Cyrus really wished to burn Croesus alive he can have been no Zoroastrian, as such a defilement of the sacred fire of Agni would never have been devised by a Zoroastrian prince. On the other hand, Darius, who was certainly a Zoroastrian, was opposed to the Magi who had conspired against Cambyses, and these therefore appear as anti-Zoroastrians. With Darius, however, the pre-Zoroastrian religion certainly come to an end.

3. The Conquests of Cyrus

The deposition of Astyages seems to have moved Croesus of Lydia to cross the Halys. Before advancing, he consulted the oracles of Greece, and though we may doubt the perspicacity of the Pythia in guessing the boiling of tortoise and lamb together in a brazen vessel, we may accept the final verdict, that if Croesus crossed the Halys he would destroy a great kingdom, as probably the actual historical answer. So Croesus, interpreting the Delphic saying in the only manner that occurred to him, crossed the river and seized Cappadocia. Cyrus had, however, no intention of accepting a truncated inheritance; he advanced in his turn, in the autumn of 547 B.C., and the indecisive battle of Pteria took place, Croesus now saw the formidable character of his adversary, and retreated across the Halys to Sardis, proposing to use the winter in summoning aid not only from Sparta, but also from his old ally, Amasis of Egypt, and even from the distant

Nabonidus, whom he no doubt wished to stir into an attack on Persia from the rear. Though Sparta certainly, and Amasis probably, would have sent active succours, it is highly improbable that the timid Nabonidus would have moved in response to the Lydian solicitation. But no time was given even for Sparta to help, Cyrus, knowing the hardihood of his Persians, had no hesitation about marching in winter, and advanced. The Lydian cavalry would not face the Persian camels, Croesus was defeated and shut up in Sardis, which finally fell before the slow-moving Spartans could come to the rescue. That Croesus was removed to Persia as a prisoner, and afterwards lived as a great noble at the royal court, seems highly probable, since Cyrus had not even put his old enemy Astyages to death.

Now followed the subjugation of the Ionian Greeks, which was completed by the departure of the Phocaeans to Alalia, and of the Teians to Abdera, What the Lydians had never been able to do, the energy of the Persians, allied to the knowledge of the art of siege-warfare which they had inherited from the Assyrians, effected in three years. Against the great mounds heaped up by Cyrus' general, Harpagos, to dominate their walls, against the battering-rams and "tortoises," the Ionians could effect little. For the first time Greeks were in the inferior military position. In addition to numbers, the Asiatics now brought science into the field. The experience of half-a-century later shewed that in the open field the heavy-armed Greek warriors were more than a match for the Persians; but the first Greek experience of the new rulers of Asia was gained in siege-operations, and the result must have caused a great wave of depression to pass through all Ionia. It is no wonder that Bias of Priene advised a wholesale migration to Sardinia. The outlook must have seemed hopeless, and the pompous warning which the Spartan envoy Lakrinas had delivered to Cyrus at Sardis must have caused many a wry smile among the Ionians after Phocaea had fallen. The reply of Cyrus, Zoroastrian-sounding enough in its contempt for those who met together in the agora to cheat each other with lies and false oaths, shews the Persian's estimate of his new subjects. But the Persians did not yet know that all Greeks were not tunic-trailing nobles and chaffering hucksters. The Spartans went back as pompously as they had come, and placidly continued to rule the Peloponnese from their unwalled village under the shadow of Taygetus, while the Milesians confirmed the contempt of the Persians by their treacherous submission, in the interests of their trade. This made a united Ionian resistance impossible.

Harpagos completed his work by the conquest of Caria and Lycia, after a Lycian resistance which is rendered immortal by the holocaust of Xanthus.

Cyrus, meanwhile, had returned in triumph to Iran, and was now to complete his work by the overthrow of Babylon. This took place speedily. The enemy in the rear was not to be permitted further existence. Already in 546 we find that Southern Babylonia had been invaded from Elam, and a Persian governor installed at Erech. Then came a pause, due perhaps to complications elsewhere, and it was not till October, 539, that the blow finally fell. Then Gaubaruva (Gobryas), the Persian satrap of Assyria, crossed the Diyala (Gyndes), and completely defeated the Babylonians at Opis. Belshazzar, who commanded the Babylonians, was probably slain. Nabonidus, who was at Sippar, fled to Borsippa, and Sippar was taken. Two days later Gobryas entered Babylon without fighting. But the great citadel and royal palace of Nebuchadrezzar may still have held out even after the death of Nabonidus, which now occurred at Borsippa. The siege of the citadel continued throughout the winter. Finally, when its resistance was almost overcome, Cyrus himself appeared upon the scene, and entered Babylon in triumph, amid the jubilation of priests and people. Not long after, the citadel seems to have been stormed (March, 538) in the presence of the conqueror.

Thus the neo-Babylonian monarchy came to an end. Its miserable collapse was largely due to the rather absurd character of Nabonidus and his foolish quarrel with the priesthood, which had raised him to the throne. In pursuit of his archaeological hobby he had insisted on turning Babylon into a sort of central museum for the ancient images of the gods of all the other cities, collecting them there from all parts of the land. He was simply a collector of old gods, and in his enthusiasm for this occupation he recked nothing of the anger of the local priesthoods and the despair of the people at being deprived of their divine protectors. Also, he was deficient in respect for Marduk, and preferred Sippar to Babylon as his residence. The result was that the whole nation was disaffected, and on the walls of Nebuchadrezzar's palace the writing was clear to all, that his kingdom would be taken by the Medes and Persians.

Cyrus was hailed by the Babylonians as a deliverer. He posed as the protector of the gods, whose images he sent back to their shrines all over Babylonia. And henceforth, except during the reigns of Darius and Xerxes, the Babylonians were the obedient subjects of the Great King.

The whole Babylonian empire acknowledged Persian rule. Tyre and Sidon transferred their allegiance without difficulty to the new king of the world, and the Syennesis of Cilicia became his tributary. In Palestine the deported Jews of Babylon were allowed to essay the foundation of a new Jewish subject-community at Jerusalem, under the leadership of Sheshbassar (or Shenazzar) and Zerubbabel (537). Herein Cyrus again shewed the wise tolerance of the religions of the subject-races that became a characteristic of Persian policy, and contributed very greatly to the stability of the empire.

Amasis made no attempt to dispute the Babylonian inheritance with Cyrus. He was now an old man, and though a soldier in his youth, had never shewn any sign of warlike tendencies, although the weakness of Babylon under Nabonidus would have made it easy for him to have taken Palestine from her, at any rate before the conquest of Lydia made it advisable for him to support Babylon as much as possible against Cyrus. His only act of foreign aggression was the conquest of Cyprus, which was effected by the arms of his Greek mercenaries. Cyrene voluntarily became his tributary, and he interfered as suzerain in the affairs of the royal house, besides making a Cyrenaean lady, Ladike, his queen. This connexion, and the force of circumstances, gradually made him who had been placed upon the throne as a protest against Greek influence in Egypt as great a supporter of the Greeks as Apries himself. At the beginning of his reign he had compelled all the Greek settlements in the Delta to a synoikismos in one place, Naukratis, which was close to the royal capital, Sais, and so immediately under the royal eye. Daphnai was abandoned, and all the Greek colonists concentrated at Naukratis, which was a purely Greek city-state, with a constitution partly Dorian, partly Ionian. All the most popular deities of the Greeks had their temples within it, and a great temenos and hall of assembly, the Helleneion, was built by the offerings of the Greek states whose merchants frequented Naukratis. The city flourished exceedingly, and in it the trade connection between Greece and Egypt developed enormously. Besides traders, Greek artists and thinkers now came to Egypt, and were well received by the king, who had thrown off all restraint in his intercourse with the foreigners. The proximity of Naukratis to Sais enabled him to see the useful side of Greek civilization, and the coming of men of finer brain than the ordinary merchants and mercenaries enabled him to appreciate its higher side, which afforded such a contrast to the dull conservatism and fanaticism of his own people. Also political reasons moved him to court the Greeks in every way. They indeed were his sole hope in case of a Persian attack. Nabonidus was useless. Only from his Greek friends could any effective succour be expected. Polykrates, tyrant of Samos, was now the most powerful ruler in Greece, and with him Amasis concluded a friendship which only ended when the Samian seemed unable to resist any longer the pressure of Persia. To Hera of Samos he sent divine images, and to the Dorian Athena of Lindos in Rhodes two stone statues and a corslet of linen marvellously woven. The Greeks of the mainland were also courted, and specially the shrine of Delphi had been honoured by the politic Egyptian king, as by his ally Croesus. When in 548 the temple was burnt to the ground, and the Athenian Alkmaeonidae undertook its restoration, Amasis sent a thousand talents of the then valuable mineral alum to Greece for the work. But after the overthrow of Croesus the Ionians were too fearful, and the Continental Greeks too careless of the Persian danger, to be likely ever to give direct help to Egypt. Polykrates was a broken reed upon which to rely, and the Spartans, the only Greeks who seemed capable of meeting the Persians on equal terms, were too few and too unused to foreign war to attack Persia in Ionia, still less to bring active aid to Egypt. And as yet their slow minds would have been incapable of so revolutionary a conception, though they could, and did, attack the Ionian allies of Persia when it was too late. So Amasis fell back into apathy, dying, happily for himself, before the blow fell (526). His son Psamatik III was left to meet it.

But the expected stroke was not delivered by Cyrus. After the conquest of Babylon the great king seems to have waged war, according to Berossos against the Dahae of Parthia, according to Herodotus against the Massagetae, a Scythian tribe of the arid region beyond the Jaxartes, to which his dominions certainly now extended. Here he met his death, either in battle or from sickness, and his crown passed to his son Kambujiya (Cambyses), who had already reigned as subordinate king of Babylon (529 B.C.).

4. Cambyses in Egypt

Cambyses at once prepared to carry out the next act of the Achaemenid programme, the conquest of Egypt. The successive steps of the Persian progress to the dominion of the world seemed to be the inevitable blows of fate. Like Babylon, Egypt lay inert, as if fascinated, before the Persian approach, and unable to defend herself. The native Egyptians did nothing.

The only resistance was offered by the hireling Greek soldiers, themselves disheartened by the conquest of Ionia, and probably largely reduced in numbers since that event. Also, the fleets of their countrymen, both enslaved and free, were arrayed against Egypt in conjunction with those of Phoenicia. For Polykrates, seeing which way the wind was blowing, had placed his ships at the disposition of Persia, and though the Spartans decided to interfere in order to prevent this, their interference, as we have seen, came too late to help Egypt or hearten the Greeks in Egypt to strike stoutly in her defence. True, at the battle of Pelusium, when Psamatik III gave battle to the Persian, the mercenaries endeavoured to hearten themselves, it is said, by a bloody sacrifice of the children of Phanes the Halikarnassian, who had deserted from Egypt to Persia; but the scale was weighted against them, and their valour evaporated when battle was joined. The native Egyptians were massacred, and the remnant fled with the king into Memphis, where the strong fortress of the "White Wall" afforded shelter and promised some hope of successful resistance. The prospect of a new Asiatic conquest had driven both king and people mad with rage; a Persian herald, sent on a Mytilenian ship to demand surrender, was torn to pieces, together with his Greek crew. But mere fury was of little avail against the warriors of Persia, and the few remaining Greeks in the service of Egypt had probably already deserted; Memphis was taken, and, so we are told, vengeance taken by Cambyses for the murder of his herald. As a matter of course, the king of Egypt was deposed, and removed to Asia; Cambyses ascended the throne of the Pharaohs.

As at Babylon, so in Egypt. The Persian king became an Egyptian pharaoh. The Assyrian kings had taken the lands of Bel, and become kings of Babylon, but the gods of Babylon were their gods, and the idea of becoming Egyptian monarchs and bowing down before Amen and Ptah had probably never occurred to them. Such a means of conciliating the conquered would have been beyond their comprehension. To the Persian, however, who himself worshipped Ahuramazda, and concerned himself nothing as to the religion of others, Bel was every whit as foreign a deity as Amen; and when a Persian king had naturally become king of Babylon, as the Assyrians had before him, by taking the lands of Bel, there was no reason why his successor should not don the double crown, and make offerings to the deities of Egypt as king. It is to the Gallio-like indifference of the Persians as to the religions of their "slaves," rather than to deep and calculated statecraft, that we may attribute the first adoption of this policy, which was singularly successful in attaching both Babylon and Egypt (the latter for a time at least) to Persia.

The appearance of Cambyses on the throne of Horus "of the living" was stage-managed by a prominent Egyptian functionary named Uzahor-resenet, Admiral of the Fleet, and Lay Warden of the Temple of Neith at Sais, and so one of the most important men in the kingdom, and one most likely to be consulted by the new ruler on all questions relating to the religious side of the Egyptian state. He tells us on his statue (now in the Vatican Museum) how he was charged to compose the new king's religious or "Horus" name (which, by the way, he did very badly, devising a most uncouth and unusual appellation), and how he expounded to the ignorant monarch the mysteries of the temple of Neith. He also obtained the royal firman to remove from the precincts of the temple the foreigners who had taken up their abode there, and to restore to the priests of Neith the revenues which had been taken from her, as from the other deities, by Amasis for the support of the Greek mercenaries who had proved so useless in the day of trial.

Cambyses was, in his own mind, only on the threshold of his career of conquest. Cyrene submitted hastily to her new overlord in Egypt, and Cyrene seemed a handy stepping-stone to the conquest of distant Carthage. On the way thither also was the mysterious oasis of Ammon (the modern Siwah), where, a few centuries before, emigrants from Thebes had set up an oracular shrine of the Theban god. Cambyses had occupied Egypt as far as Aswan with his troops, and no doubt abode some time at Thebes. Thence, since the Phoenician sailors definitely refused to sail against their Carthaginian kinsmen, and it was impossible to force them to do so, he determined to send an army to the Oasis of Ammon. The expedition reached the oases of el-Khargah and ed-Dakhlah safely, but then, striking north-westward towards Siwah, was lost in the sands of the desert and never heard of again. The Persians recked little of deserts; they knew their own hard salt waste of the Kavir and the terrible Dasht-i-Lut, they thought little of the mere steppe between Mesopotamia and Syria; but they did not know the moving sand-dunes of the Sahra, which make it impossible (as Rohlfs found in 1874) to march north-westward from Dakhlah too far south of the regular route to Farafrah, The Persians must have missed this, the proper way to Siwah, and so perished miserably.

Meanwhile, Cambyses himself prepared to restore Nubia to Egypt and to overthrow the kingdom of Napata. Since Tanutamon had retired from

Egypt, the Napatan realm had been ruled by a succession of princes, whose names are known to us from their inscriptions at Gebel Barkal. Probably in the reign of Aspalut or Aspelta, the successor of Tanutamon, we hear of a heretical sect of "raw-meat-eaters" who took possession of the temples, and were exterminated by the king. Other kings, Piankh-aluro, Horsiotef, and Nastasenen or Nastesen, followed. Horsiotef seems to have held Syene, and it was in his time that the Asmakh, probably, emigrated to Ethiopia.

Nastasenen was probably the king against whom Cambyses marched. He seems to have been the viceroy of Meroe, the southern centre of the Nubian kingdom at the modern Bagarawiyah near Shendi, which later became the sole capital of the Ethiopian kings. On his stela at Gebel Barkal, Nastasenen says that he was called by Amen from Meroe to rule in Napata, and sent messengers north to Dongu-uer (Dongola) to announce his accession to "the royal crown of Horsiotef and the might of Piankh-aluro." The expedition of Cambyses, unsuccessful though it was, seems to have shaken the Nubian kingdom considerably. We need not suppose that Cambyses ever actually reached Napata, but it seems that about this time the Nubian capital was transferred to Meroe. It is probable that Nastasenen took the step of retiring to his own city of Meroe in alarm at the approach of the conqueror, although he says he routed "the man Kambasauden," and took all the flocks and herds which his soldiers had brought with them for their subsistence. It was easy, after the Persian retreat, for him to boast that he had beaten Cambyses, and it is probable that he did no more than capture the Persian convoys; this, however, necessitated the retirement of the invaders, and caused the terrible loss of life from starvation in the retreat through the barren region of the Second Cataract, which ruined Cambyses' army.

That the two disasters partially unhinged the mind of the Persian conqueror is probable enough. We have no valid reasons to dispute the Herodotean account of his fury, and of the outrages which he offered to the Egyptians and their gods, to doubt that he slew Apis, or even that he violated the mummy of Amasis. To put these stories down to a supposed "Egyptian-Greek" campaign of calumny against the virtuous Persian is, while apparently so critical, in reality quite uncritical procedure. These wild things are exactly what an infuriated Aryan, maddened by utterly unexpected failure, would do in such a land of "devils" (daevas) as "Mudraya" (Egypt) would now appear to him to be. To the sorceries of

Egypt and her demon-gods, creatures of Angromainyus, he would ascribe these catastrophes, and run amok among them. And we have the testimony of Uzahorresenet, writing in the reign of Darius, to the terrible "calamity" which came to pass in Egypt, when the divine offerings were discontinued, the temples desecrated, and the school of sacred scribes (no doubt necromancers in Persian eyes) was ruined. His rage was scarcely glutted, when more news of ill-omen reached Cambyses from Persia. This was the rebellion of the false Smerdis, with regard to which the account of Herodotus has been completed by the inscription of Darius at Bisitan.

5. The False Smerdis and the Reign of Darius

Bardiya (Smerdis), the brother of Cambyses, had been privily murdered by the latter before the expedition to Egypt. The long absence of Cambyses, and probably the rumours of his defeat in Nubia that had reached Persia, moved the Patizeithes or chief minister who had been left in charge at Pasargadae to bring forward his brother, a magus named Gaumata, as Bardiya, and to set him up as king. As the murder of the prince was not known, the false Bardiya was generally accepted by the Persians, and even by the Babylonians, as king. Gaumata was a Magian, and from the terms in which Darius speaks of his rebellion as connected ,with "the lie," which, after Cambyses had gone to Egypt, "multiplied in the land," it seems very possible that he was an anti-Zoroastrian, and represented the believers in the older Magian cult. To put down this revolt Cambyses now left Egypt, placing Aryandes there as satrap, and taking with him the strong Zoroastrian, Darius, son of Hystaspes, and the other chief leaders of his army. On the way, in Syria, either at Damascus or at Hamath, the king died suddenly (522 B.C.) It is uncertain whether he killed himself or died from the effects of an accident. The army, however, did not halt. Taking the body with them, the soldiers pressed on, led by Darius, eager to crush "the lie" and the impudent personator of the dead prince. The Magian retired from Persia into Media, which was probably more inclined towards the old religion, and the Persian nobles who were aware of his fraud prepared on the arrival of Darius and the army from Egypt to act against him. Gaumata was living in royal state at Sikayauvatish, a castle in the Median district of Nisaya. Thither Darius repaired, accompanied by six other nobles, Vifidafrana (Intaphernes) son of Vayaspara, Utana (Otanes) son of Cukhra, Gaubaruva (Gobryas) son of Marduniya, Vidarna (Hydarnes) son of Bagabigna, Bagabukhsha

(Megabyzos) son of Daduhya, and Ardumanish son of Vahauka. Having forced an entrance into the castle, they fell upon and murdered Gaumata. Then Darius, in virtue of his royal descent, was made king in succession to the childless Cambyses, his father Vishtaspa (Hystaspes), who was ruling Parthia and Hyrcania as satrap, being passed over, probably on account of age. He acknowledged his son as king and served him faithfully.

The new king was not, however, generally acknowledged by his subjects, and the first three years of his reign were taken up by the task of reducing to obedience the various provinces that revolted against him. The most formidable rebellion was that of Babylonia, under a certain Nadintu-Bel, who made himself king as Nebuchadrezzar III. After two defeats, Nadintu-Bel was shut up in Babylon, which underwent a long and wearisome siege before it was finally taken and the usurper slain. Meanwhile, Elam, Armenia, and Media had revolted, the latter under a certain Fravartish, who "said unto the people, I am Khshathrita, of the family of Kyaxares." This final attempt to restore the old Median kingdom was put down, and the Median cruelly executed. The revolt of Elam, under a Persian who gave himself out to be a native Elamite prince named Ummanish, had been easily overcome, and with it the Elamites disappeared from history. But now even Persia itself revolted under a second pseudo-Smerdis, named Vahyazdata, who resisted long until the fall of Babylon enabled Darius to bring his whole power to bear upon him. But then Babylon revolted again under a certain Arakha, and had to be subdued again. A Scythian or Saka, probably of the Caspian steppes, named Skunka, remained to be vanquished, and with him the last of the enemies of Darius near home disappeared. To commemorate his victories the king caused to be sculptured on a rock-cliff overhanging the main route from Mesopotamia into Persia, through the Zagros, a great tablet on which he represented himself with the conquered rebels bound before him; the accompanying inscription in Persian, Susian, and Babylonian describes his campaigns, and gives the glory to Auramazda. This is the tablet of Behistun or Bisitun, which was discovered by the late Sir Henry Rawlinson in 1837 and afterwards translated by him. To it we owe not only our first-hand knowledge of the early campaigns of Darius, but also our first real knowledge of the cuneiform inscriptions.

It now remained to Darius to consolidate his power on the confines of his empire. Oroites, the masterful satrap of Sardis, who had decoyed Polykrates from his island and slain him miserably, and had also murdered his fellow-satrap of Daskyleion (the Persian centre of government in Bithynia), was killed by a royal envoy. Then Aryandes, satrap of Egypt, who had arrogated to himself royal privileges, and seems to have revolted, had to submit on the approach of the king himself, and was executed, in spite of the fact that he had conquered Barka in Cyrene, and had carried the Persian arms as far west as the city of Euesperides (Benghazi). Darius came to Egypt in 517 B.C., and at once set himself to conciliate Egyptian sentiment by every means in his power. Uzahorresenet, who had inducted Cambyses into the kingdom, was entrusted by Darius with the task of winning over his countrymen, and seems to have been successful. Darius appears in the list of Egyptian pharaohs as Setetu-Ra ("Ra-hath-begotten-him") Ntariuash. As king of Egypt his reign was marked by peaceful energy, and the temple of Hibis in the Oasis of el-Khargah remains as an important monument of it. The Oasis seems to have interested the Persian monarch, probably from the resemblance of its natural conditions to those of the eastern parts of his own country, and a Persian method of irrigation by means of underground conduits beneath the beds of the desert-wadis, which collected water from the faults in the sandstone strata, was introduced at el-Khargah, no doubt by Persian engineers.

Darius now turned his attention to the West. In 516 Samos was taken by his generals in the interest of Syloson, brother of Polykrates, who was installed there as a tyrant without subjects, as the resistance of the Samians had provoked the Persians, against the wishes of Darius, to severe measures, and the island was "swept as with a net," and its inhabitants carried away to the mainland. Darius now himself came to Sardis, and determined to lead a great expedition against the Scythians of Europe, in revenge, so it was said, for the great Scythian invasion of Asia a century before. The whole force of the Ionian cities, under their tyrants, was convoked to the Bosphorus to meet the royal army, and among them were Histiaios of Miletos and Miltiades, the Athenian despot of the Chersonese. The Ionian fleet was sent on to the mouth of the Danube to build the great bridge which carried over the royal army, and guarded it while the king was engaged in his fruitless pursuit of the mocking Scythian, Idanthyrsos. According to Herodotus, the Ionians had the opportunity of breaking up the bridge, and leaving Darius to his fate in the Russian steppes, and Miltiades urged this course upon them. But he (according to the story) was overruled by the counsel of Histiaios, who pointed out to his assembled fellow-rulers that their rule in the cities depended on the Persian power alone, and that, were that destroyed, they would all be driven out, and democracies be installed in their place. This was true enough: the age of the tyrants was fast coming to an end in Greece itself, and only four years later the Peisistratids were to be expelled from Athens for the last time. So, naturally, their own interest prevailed with the Ionian rulers; the great opportunity was lost, and the way left open for a Persian conquest of Greece.

Darius returned in safety to Persia, while his lieutenant Megabazos subdued Thrace, and even received the unwilling allegiance of Amyntas, the king of Macedon.

About the same time (514), at the great Panathenaea, the deed of Harmodios and Aristogeiton proclaimed the fidelity of Athens to the democratic principles of Solon, and her hatred or the tyrant-system which played into the hands of Persia. And three years later Hippias was expelled by Kleomenes and the Spartans, acting in stupid obedience to the Delphic oracle, cleverly manipulated by the exiled Alkmaeonidae. The constitution of Kleisthenes followed (509), and Athens, despite the temporary episode of the aristocrat Isagoras (507), now became a free and democratic state.

The prestige of her resistance to Persia, which made her for all time the centre of "the glory that was Greece," was soon to follow. Anxious to conciliate Persia, she was first bidden to take back her tyrants and give earth and water to the Great King. She saw that there was no choice for her if she would not be ruled by tyrants again, and when a few years later the failure of the Persian attempt on Naxos had for the first time caused the Greeks to doubt the invincibility of the Asiatics, and the intrigue of Histiaios had stirred the Ionians to revolt, she threw in her lot with her brethren, and the burning of Sardis was her gage of battle thrown down to the ancient Eastern world (499). "Sire, remember the Athenians!" said daily the slave to Darius at Susa, and when first Cyprus and then Ionia were subdued, he ordered his satraps to destroy the insolent little city. The first expedition (in 492) by land and sea under Mardonius, proceeding by way of Thrace, was wrecked by the disaster off Mt Athos, when the fleet of the Persians was destroyed by a storm. Then, taking advantage of the factious attack of the Aeginetans upon Athens, the second expedition was launched, this time by way of the islands, under Datis and Artaphernes, and Hippias with them. Eretria was taken, and Athens seemed in instant jeopardy. Madly ran Pheidippides to Sparta, to invoke the immediate assistance of the titular head of Greece. But before the full moon allowed the pedantic Lacedaemonians to move without breaking their custom, the battle had been fought and won. Led by Miltiades, Kallimachos, and the other strategi, the Athenians and their solitary friends from little Plataeae had drawn up the line of their tribes on the sea-plain of Marathon, where Hippias had bidden the Persians land. And when battle was joined, the Persians were met not only with unexpected resistance, but with defeat. For the Athenians indeed "fought in a way worthy to be told. Of all the Greeks whom we know of they were the first to charge the foe at a run; they were the first to endure the sight of the Median dress and the men who wore it; for till then the very name of the Medes had been a terror to the Greeks." Panic took the Persians back to their ships, and the sailors shoved off with those who had got on board; those left behind were massacred Six thousand of the barbarians perished, and of the Athenians one hundred and ninety-two; and we have no reason to doubt the figures. After a half-hearted reconnoitring of the landing-place at Phaleron the defeated Persians set sail for Asia; and when the Spartans came, they could only inspect the bodies of the slain Medes, commend the Athenians, and march home again, as astonished, probably, as the Persians themselves.

The tremendous importance to the world's history, as we now know it, of the battle of Marathon must not lead us to a disproportionate estimate of its importance as it appeared to men at the time. To the Persians it was nothing; an "untoward event" of little importance that had happened to a small detached local force owing to the stupidity of its commanders. The failure of Miltiades at Paros shortly afterwards removed any doubts of the Persian power among the islanders who remained subject to the satrap of Sardis. That the news of Marathon in any way contributed to the Egyptian revolt four years later is not in the least likely. In Greece it merely caused the Dorian hatred of Athens to burn anew with the fuel of jealousy, and contributed largely to the "medizing" of Boeotia and Corinth ten years later. The Spartans, indeed, now began to regard the Athenians with respect, but its most important result was the effect it had on the Athenians themselves, the self-respect it gave them, and the confidence with which, when the grand struggle came, they unhesitatingly declared for resistance, and took the Greeks in spite of themselves to Salamis, Plataeae, and Mykale.

And in Themistokles, who succeeded Miltiades as the leader of Athens, the man appeared who knew how to use the new pride of his fellow-citizens in themselves for the purpose of defending Greece against Persia.

He saw that now the Ionian fleets were at the disposition of Persia, the Orientals were masters of the sea, and since Korkyra was far away and her help doubtful, and Aigina was the enemy of Athens, Hellas had no fleet with which to prevent the ferrying of a vast armada across the Aegean. On land, too, the Athenians must always take place very far behind Sparta, the acknowledged military leader of Greece. Had Athens a great fleet, however, she would take on the sea a place equal to that of Sparta on land, and do her part in the defence of Greece as the peer, not the humble follower, of Lacedaemon. And such a place alone was worthy of the city that had defied Darius to the death. So he utilized the necessities of the war with Aigina to persuade his fellow-citizens to the building of the great fleet that won Salamis for Greece, and thereby raised Athens to the splendid position which she held in the world throughout the next century, and which she will hold in the minds of men to the end of time. Themistokles might not, like Kimon, know how to twang the cithara and shine with the graces of society, but he did know how to turn a little city into a great one.

He was not, however, sufficiently powerful yet in the years that immediately followed Marathon, and had Darius himself led his hosts against Greece then, we may well doubt whether Athens and Themistokles could have saved Greece, and whether the civilization of Rome and Europe would have existed to-day. Furious at the insolent rejection of his demands for earth and water and at the small check, as it appeared to be, which the incapacity of his generals had brought upon the expedition sent to avenge the insult, Darius prepared to crush Greece, or rather Athens, for Sparta was unknown to him and he dreamt only of resistance from the Athenians. All Asia rang with his preparations. But, at the critical moment, Egypt, inspired by the oracle of Buto, revolted under Khabbash (486 B.C.). The rage of the Great King was thus diverted, and then, when preparing to crush ungrateful Egypt in person, he died (485).

Darius, the son of Hystaspes, is one of the greatest figures of antiquity. Like Cyrus, on whom he obviously modelled himself to a great extent, he was a new figure in the East which for a thousand years had groaned under the continual wickedness of the A.ssyrians. He was an intelligent and reasonable Great King. The like of Cyrus and Darius had hardly been seen since the days of the great Egyptian pharaohs of the XVIIIth Dynasty, and they, intelligent as they were, and far more humane than the Assyrians, fell far short of the Persians in virtue. The religion of Zoroaster seems to have really given the Persian monarchs high and noble ideas, and in them also we see, as well as his Berserker rage, the fundamental good-nature and "sweet reasonableness" of the Aryan, which was the chief virtue of the culture of the Greeks. This trait is more marked in Cyrus than in Darius, and Darius himself undoubtedly degenerated during his reign. Under Cambyses the Persian king had taken on many of the vices of the Semitic despots who ruled the world before him, and the generous warrior who so liberally rewarded Syloson, the great king who conferred benefits on conquered Egypt, was the same man who impaled Fravartish and would have enslaved Greece. Xerxes, his son, was as typical an Oriental despot of the weak kind as any of the weaker Egyptians or Assyrians before him. So the Aryan leader of his people, become an Eastern world-ruler, too soon became a degenerate Oriental. But, unlike his son, Darius had the old Persian virtue in his soul, and, despotic as he became, seems always to have set before himself the ideal of ruling as a beneficent leader of the people whom the grace of Ahuramazda had committed to his guidance. His only mistake was the expedition to Scythia, which nearly cost him his life and crown, and this was probably an instance of the characteristic recklessness of the Aryan. His expedition to Greece, had it been accomplished, would probably not have been a mistake. In the incapable hands of Xerxes, it was. The military genius of Darius we have seen in the fierce civil wars at the beginning of his reign; his political genius we see in his treatment of Egypt and in his great work, the organization of the empire in satrapies efficiently controlled by the king.

As an example of imperial organization, combining local autonomy and devolution of authority with an unquestioned central power, that of the Persian empire created by Darius stands unrivalled to this day. The organization of the Asiatic empire of Egypt by Thothmes III, remarkable as it was for its time, was loose and incohesive; the system of Egyptian residents at the courts of tributary kings and of the travelling commissioners who went round inspecting them was an extraordinary advance in the political development of the world, but it was constantly breaking down, and the regular appearance of the king with his army was necessary to hold the subject princes to their allegiance. A weak king at Thebes meant the collapse of the system; but a weak king at Susa meant nothing of the kind. The Assyrian system, such as it was, also needed a strong warrior-king to maintain it. For this was simply a crude method of forcible government by major-generals, and it was only fear that kept the nations subject; while the instinctive loyalty of the Assyrians to their king and Ashur their "lord" made revolts of distant military governors infrequent. But here also the king and his generals must always go forth to war to make their authority respected. This was not necessary in Persia. The Persian system developed out of the Assyrian; the Assyrian method was taken over by Cyrus, and the first satraps were the successors of the Assyrian military governors. But the greater distance from the centre of some of the governors made revolt more possible than in Assyrian days, and the conduct of Aryandes and Oroites brought about the reorganization of Darius.

The number of the satrapies was now fixed at twenty, including India (the Panjab, which had been subdued by Darius after the Scythian expedition, about 510 B.C.), or twenty-one including Thrace, which was lost by Xerxes. Persia itself, as the land of the royal house, was not included, and paid no taxes, but voluntary contributions. Media (Mada), Elam (Uvaja), Babylon (Babirus), and Assyria (Athura) formed separate governments. All Syria and Palestine was included in the Arabian satrapy. With Egypt (Mudraya) were associated the Phoenicians and Cypriotes, as well as the Cyrenaeans, and after the Ionian revolt for a short time Crete (?) and the Cyclades also. Yauna (Ionia) comprised the continental Greeks, the Carians, and Lycians, with its capital at Sardis. The northern centre of government in the Aegean region, Daskyleion, was the capital of the satrapy of Sparda, which comprised Phrygia and Mysia. Katpatuka (Cappadocia) and Armenia comprised the rest of Asia Minor to the borders of Athura (Assyria) and Media.

In each government by the side of the satrap, now a civil governor only, stood a general and a secretary, each independent of one another, but in direct communication with Susa. Each satrapy was absolutely independent as regards its internal affairs, but had to pay a fixed quota of tribute, usually in coined money now, to the royal treasury. For the purpose of the payment of this tribute, Darius imitated the Lydians and Greeks in coining money of a fixed standard, the gold "daric" which bore his name, one of the purest gold coins that ever was struck. This innovation in itself was a strong bond in the empire when all the Eastern world used the same gold coin with its device of the running Persian archer, bow in hand and kidaris on head. The royal authority was further safeguarded by travelling commissioners, the "eyes and ears" of the king; both office and name were probably borrowed by Darius from Egypt. Many of the subject nations still preserved their own native rulers, as Cilicia and the Phoenician and Ionian cities (the Persians naturally took the Ionian tyrants to be kings); Darius, following the policy of Cyrus, allowed the returned Jews at Jerusalem much political liberty under their own leaders, and permitted them to rebuild the Temple. In Egypt the problem was solved by the national acceptance of Darius, like Cambyses, as absolute Pharaoh, by priestly fiction "begotten of Ra." Like his predecessor, he was formally inducted as king, sacrificed to the gods, and especially honoured the Apis who had just died on his arrival in 517 B.C. But to Babylon he shewed no such grace; though he bore the title "King of Babylon," he never "took the hands of Bel," and "Babirus" was an ordinary province like Media or Parthia. But the Egyptians were too peculiar a people to be thus annihilated politically.

Such was the organization carried out by Darius, and it remained till the overthrow of Asia by Alexander, bringing peace and prosperity to the nations, notwithstanding the revolts of alien Egypt and the attacks of the freed Greeks.

The intention of Darius to enslave Greece must not, then, make us oblivious to his greatness as a king and ruler. Of the Greeks he knew hardly anything but their bad side; of the superiority of their culture to his he could naturally have little idea; he could only regard them as pestilent sea-pirates and incessant troublers of the coasts of Asia and enemies of his Phoenician and Egyptian subjects from time immemorial — a constant source of unrest on the borders of the empire.

6. Greece and Persia

The revolt of Khabbash was not subdued by Xerxes till 484; then a new Babylonian rising, under a certain Shemserib, delayed the preparations against Greece for another year, and it was not till 482 that the project could be taken up again at Susa. The delay of four years had stood Greece in good stead, and given Themistokles his chance.

The ostracism of Aristeides, too "just" a man for the stern necessities of the time, too upright to be of practical use when the Mede was knocking at the gate, left the field free to his great rival, the warrior-diplomat who saved Athens, Greece, and with her Rome and ourselves. Though, driven forth in his turn by his ungrateful fellow-citizens, Themistokles died the pensioner of Persia, he died so rather than in any way help to enslave Hellas: and when we praise our famous men, none is more worthy of our honour and praise than Themistokles, son of Neokles, the Athenian.

As archon in 482 he carried his proposals with regard to the navy, and laid the foundations of the maritime power of Athens. He also began the fortifications of the Peiraieus. The struggle was not long to be delayed. Next year Xerxes, full of the vain pomp of an Oriental emperor, came down (as the Greek phrase was) in state from Susa to Sardis, to be ready for the great campaign. In the spring of 480 his march to the Hellespont began. And now events began to move quickly. The imminence of the danger brought together all the Greeks who had not already, like the Thessalians and Boeotians, determined to submit to Persia without fighting.

A congress at the Isthmus put aside all local wars and disputes, and an embassy was sent to the distant colonists of Sicily to seek help from the wealthy and powerful Gelon, tyrant of Syracuse. But the arrogant colonial demanded as the price of his assistance the leadership of Greece either on land or sea. To this neither Sparta nor Athens would consent, and he bade the ambassadors go their ways. His arrogance was no doubt caused by the great defeat which, probably in the same year (481), he had inflicted on Hamilkar and his invading host of Carthaginians. It may well be that this Carthaginian attack on the Western Greeks was arranged in concert with Persia through the medium of the Phoenicians. It was of the highest moment to Persia that the wealthy and powerful Greeks of the West should be prevented from assisting the mother-country, and no means to this end more efficient could have been devised than an attack from Carthage. But the Carthaginian diversion was defeated too soon to enable this aim to be effected, and the powerful Gelon, made confident by his victory, would have proved a formidable ally to the Greeks had not his pride made him overstep the courtesy due to the ancient states of the motherland. Of the Western Hellenes, but a single trireme from Kroton took part in the battle of Salamis.

Meanwhile, Xerxes was pursuing his way to Thessaly. The numbers of his grand army were, of course, enormously exaggerated by the Greeks. So huge a force as they tell of could never have been maintained by any possible commissariat, and it is not probable that the whole force ever exceeded two, or at most three, hundred thousand men. Such a force is enormous enough for that time, and even now no modern general, equipped with all modern means of provisionment, would care to take it on one line of march from Asia Minor to Macedonia. A divided line of approach there became necessary, and by two routes the army debouched into Thessaly, where it was welcomed by the ruling Aleuadae.

The fleet coasted along the shore. In order to avoid the storms of Athos, which had destroyed the fleet of Mardonius twelve years before, it used the great canal which in the preceding year had been dug through the isthmus of Sane for this purpose. Finally, at Thermopylae the army, and at Artemision the fleet, came into contact with the Greeks. Thermopylae covered the name of Sparta and of Leonidas with an undying glory, Artemision first showed what the Athenians could do on the sea, though the command of the ships was given to the Spartan Eurybiadas: the Greeks were not used to Athenian command. But it was fated that Xerxes should reach his goal, Athens, and there lose the prize he had come so far to win. The Spartans at Thermopylae died, faithful to the traditions of their race, with a devotion which in modern days no nation but the Japanese can show. This little band could not stay the advancing hordes for more than three days, but that it did that was wonderful, and must severely have shaken the confidence of the Persians in their own prowess and have disquieted the unstable and ignorant king. And Demaratos, the exiled Spartan king who followed in his train, could only tell him that Sparta had eight thousand more warriors, every whit as good as these that had been slain. Xerxes marched on, trusting now only in his numbers. Delphi he left untouched, owing to a clever oracle which the Pythia had put forward to the effect that if Delphi were touched his cause would be lost. Thus indeed the god had defended his shrine. Phokis resisted; Boeotia submitted, as expected. Then Athens fell, and her citizens went on board their ships, to the protection of the wooden walls in which the Pythia had promised them salvation.

The Persian fleet now approached, and in spite of the selfishness of the Corinthian Adeimantos, who thought only of sailing away to defend Peloponnesos, the Greeks, thanks to the adroit stratagem of Themistokles, were compelled to remain and fight at Salamis, while Xerxes, from his golden throne on the slopes of Aigaleos, watched the fray in imperial state. Never had the world seen such a spectacle before, and it was indeed unparalleled, for here now and for the first time the ancient Oriental world met the new European world in deadly conflict, and, before the eyes of its omnipotent ruler, was defeated. All the nations of the Near East were assembled to do battle with their erstwhile sister, who had changed her character and was now no longer the most western nation of the East but the most eastern of the West, and had become the protagonist of the new civilization of Europe against the attack of the ancient civilizations of Asia and Africa. Phoenician, Cypriote, and Ionian ships formed the main body of the fleet, but Egyptian galleys were there also, manned by "the dwellers in the fens, skilful rowers of galleys." And on board fought not only Persians, Bactrians, and all the dwellers of Asia Minor, but also Egyptians and, if Aeschylus is not here using a poet's licence, even Babylonians. The fierce verse of Aeschylus, who himself fought in the battle, tells us how when day broke the whole of the Greek fleet advanced to the attack, raising the paean, while the trumpets blared defiance to the foe; and how ship met ship with the crash of brazen prows and the rending of timbers as figureheads were torn off and whole banks of oars were overridden and smashed, overturning and killing the rowers as they sat. The barbarian line was at once thrown into confusion; ship collided with ship; while the Greeks, still with order and method, smote remorselessly in all directions, striking and hacking at the wrecked and drowning barbarians as men do at tunnies, with fragments of oars and any weapon that came handy. The arrows of the Persian archers could do but little execution when their ships were foundering beneath them, and the rout became a mere massacre. Troops which had been placed (without any prospect of effecting anything, so far as we can see) on the island of Psyttaleia, were slain to a man by Greek marines landed there under Aristeides. The Persian allies now sought safety in flight, including Artemisia, the brave Carian queen, who was present in person with her ships. Those who could not escape were slain, "and the sea was filled with shrieks and cries, till with dark night the wailing ceased." Of the Persians a brother of Darius, Ariabignes, was slain, and Aeschylus tells us many another name of note, some genuine no doubt, others fictitious to suit the poet's rime. Long before the end, Xerxes, who had watched the disaster with growing horror, had risen frantically from his throne, and with a loud cry rent his robes and departed hastily from the scene.

He left Greece at once, pressing furiously homewards towards the Hellespont, lest his bridge should be broken down by the Ionians on hearing of his defeat; and his flight was urged on the faster by the politic ruse of Themistokles, who sent him a message saying that it was proposed to break down the bridge, but that he would hold back the Greeks as long as possible. And this he intended to do, for he wished to facilitate the departure of the Persians from Europe, and not to retard it. The frantic flight of Xerxes caused great miseries to the troops that accompanied him. Winter set in early, and the Strymon was crossed half-frozen, drowning many when the thin ice broke up as the morning sun grew powerful. He reached the Bosphorus to find the bridge broken down by storms, but crossed safely on shipboard, and returned to Sardis. Mardonius was left behind in Thessaly with an army which is said to have numbered 300,000 men; a figure which may safely be reduced by one-half or more. He had offered to carry out the conquest with the troops at his disposal. Early in the next year he advanced again to Athens, which was again abandoned. The insistence of Themistokles, and the threat of the Athenians to negotiate with Persia if they were not helped, compelled the Spartans to send out the largest army they had ever equipped, numbering in all about 50,000 men (of whom 5000 were Spartiates), to the Isthmus, although they had not yet finished celebrating the festival of the Hyakinthia. And for the Spartans to move before they had fulfilled their religious duties was unprecedented, and marked their appreciation of the need. The campaign of Plataeae followed, in which the Spartans, owing to the indecision of their leader, Pausanias, did not do very well till the actual shock of battle came. Then they acquitted themselves like Spartans, while the Athenians fought as well on land as they had at sea. The other Greeks did but little. The death of Mardonius and destruction of his army freed Greece; Artabazos with the remnant fled back to Asia, and after the final destruction of his fleet at Mykale, Xerxes, defeated and despondent, went up to Susa, the first king of the Persians who had been decisively worsted in war. Well might the Aeschylean chorus of Persians weep because Darius had not lived to lead the host to victory, "Darius, the master of the bow, beloved sovereign of Susa"! The flower of the Persian chivalry had perished in Greece, but it was perhaps for this very reason that no pretender arose among the nobles to challenge the rule of the defeated king. The disaster, even the defection of Ionia, in no way affected the equilibrium of the empire that Darius had organized so well. And, encouraged by the dissensions of Greece, Xerxes dreamed, thirteen years later, of his revenge. But the battles of the Eurymedon finally shattered this dream, and again it was Athens, now led by Kimon, which was the defender of Greece and of Europe.

On the At-Maidan of Constantinople, the ancient Hippodrome, still stands the stump of the brazen column of twisted serpents which Pausanias dedicated at Delphi in honour of his victory. On it we still read the names of the tribes of Hellenes who together defeated the invader. And among these are the names of the Mycenaeans and Tirynthians. So our history ends, as it began, with the name of Mycenae, and we see the last inhabitants of these ancient towns fighting to preserve intact that European civilization of which in the far-away heroic age their remote predecessors had helped to lay the foundation.

7, Conclusion

We have traced the story of the Near East from its beginnings till the climacteric year of Salamis and Plataeae. Greece, whose oldest culture was as old as Babylon and perhaps derived its ultimate origin from Northern Egypt, had gradually in the course of the ages become possessed by the spirit of the Aryan from the North and West. Then, after a terrible internal struggle, won through in a darkness which we cannot penetrate, the Eastern spirit left her, and she stood forth with a Western soul. The songs of Homer proclaimed her new spirit, and the war of Troy was but a rehearsal of the struggle of which Herodotus wrote The story and Aeschylus sang the victory.

The first phase of the conflict between the East and West thus came to an end, the first act of the drama that was to end with the conquest of Persia by Alexander. Then for a time the West imposed its ideals upon the East. But the Hellenistic East was an artificial creation. In its midst Judaism, thanks to the Maccabees, still kept pure the ancient traditions of the East. And when Jerusalem fell, and all the world seemed Roman, Christianity came, and, an Eastern religion, once more led the East back towards its old ideals. Then, after it had lasted a thousand years, Mohammed destroyed the work of Two-horned Alexander. The Crusades brought again into the Near East another artificial Western dominance, of the most extreme Western type, the incongruous remains of which are among the most interesting relics of past history in the world to-day. And now again, the Western world of railways and of finance is striving to impose its control over the dully resisting Easterns with what eventual result who can say?